Shakespeare Studies

Advisory Board

Shakespeare Studies

AN ANNUAL GATHERING OF
RESEARCH, CRITICISM, AND REVIEWS

IV

Edited by

J. LEEDS BARROLL

The Center for Shakespeare Studies
VANDERBILT UNIVERSITY
1968

WM. C. BROWN COMPANY PUBLISHERS
Dubuque, Iowa

Contents

Contributors

Gates Kennedy Agnew.
Assistant Professor of English, Indiana University.
Margaret Aston.
Folger Shakespeare Library.
Sylvan Barnet.
Professor of English, Tufts University.
J. Leeds Barroll, III.
Professor of English, Vanderbilt University.
Roy Battenhouse.
Professor of English, Indiana University.
Keith Brown.
Oslo, Norway.
Maurice Charney.
Professor of English, Rutgers University.
Thomas Clayton.
Associate Professor of English, the University of Minnesota.
Herbert R. Coursen, Jr.
Associate Professor of English, Bowdoin College.
John P. Cutts.
Professor of English, Wayne State University.
Clifford Davidson.
Assistant Professor of English, Western Michigan University.
Herbert S. Donow.
Assistant Professor of English, Southern Illinois University.
Marvin Felheim.
Professor of English, the University of Michigan.
A. L. French.
Senior Lecturer in English, La Trobe University, Melbourne.
Roland Mushat Frye.
Professor of English, the University of Pennsylvania.
Terence Hawkes.
Senior Lecturer in English, University College, Cardiff.
Allan Holaday.
Professor of English, the University of Illinois.
T. H. Howard-Hill.
University of Oxford.
Robert Guy Howarth.
Arderne Professor of English and Chairman of the Department of English, University of Cape Town, South Africa.
Stanley J. Kahrl.
Assistant Professor of English, University of Rochester.

James G. McManaway.

Consultant Emeritus in Literature and Bibliography, the Folger Shakespeare Library.

Joseph Margolis.

Professor of Philosophy, Temple University.

Leland Miles.

President, Alfred University.

Marco Mincoff.

Professor of English, the University of Sophia.

Robert L. Montgomery, Jr.

Professor of English, the University of California, Irvine.

Helen Morris.

Principal Lecturer and Head of the English Department, Homerton College, Cambridge.

Leonard Nathanson.

Associate Professor of English, Vanderbilt University.

A. D. Nuttall.

Lecturer in English, the University of Sussex.

Y. B. Olsson.

University of Newcastle on Tyne.

H. M. Richmond.

Professor of English, the University of California, Berkeley.

William Rosen.

Professor of English, the University of Connecticut.

Alice Lyle Scoufos.

Associate Professor of English, California State College, Fullerton.

Naseeb Shaheen.

Graduate Student, the University of California, Los Angeles.

Gunnar Sjögren.

Lund, Sweden.

Hallett Smith.

Professor of English and Chairman Division of Humanities and Social Sciences, California Institute of Technology.

John M. Steadman.

Senior Research Associate, the Henry E. Huntington Library.

F. W. Sternfeld.

Faculty of Music, the University of Oxford.

Robert K. Turner, Jr.

Professor of English, the University of Wisconsin, Milwaukee.

John W. Velz.

Folger Shakespeare Library.

Chauncey Wood.

Associate Professor of English, McMaster University.

Akihiro Yamada.

Associate Professor of English, Shinshu University, Agata, Matsumoto, Japan.

8

Announcement

A new annual series, *Shakespeare Studies Monographs*, appears concurrently with Volume IV of *Shakespeare Studies*. The Monograph Series will be concerned with bibliographical problems and with documents pertaining to the history of the drama from (approximately) 1480 to 1623. *Shakespeare Studies Monograph 1*, currently available, is *The "Shakespearean" Addition in the Booke of Sir Thomas Moore: Some Aids to Scholarly and Critical Shakespearean Studies* by Thomas Clayton. SSM 2, appearing early in 1970, will be *The Pavier Quartos and the First Folio* by William S. Kable.

Shakespeare Studies and the new Monograph Series are now published for the Center for Shakespeare Studies by the William C. Brown Company. All *business* correspondence including subscription-requests should therefore be directed to *Shakespeare Studies*, Wm. C. Brown Company Publishers, 135 South Locust Street, Dubuque, Iowa 52001.

All *editorial* correspondence concerning *Shakespeare Studies V* and SSM should be addressed to the Editor, Center for Shakespeare Studies, Box 1809, Station B, Vanderbilt University, Nashville, Tennessee, 37203. Manuscripts submitted for consideration should be accompanied with return postage but with *no* return envelopes.

Again, listed below are those abbreviations agreed upon for citation in Shakespearean journals and in the computer-generated concordances of Professor Marvin Spevack, and of Dr. Trevor Howard-Hill.

Ado	*Much Ado about Nothing*	MV	*Merchant of Venice*
Ant.	*Antony and Cleopatra*	Oth.	*Othello*
AWW	*All's Well that Ends Well*	Per.	*Pericles*
AYL	*As You Like It*	R2	*Richard II*
Cor.	*Coriolanus*	R3	*Richard III*
Cym.	*Cymbeline*	Rom.	*Romeo and Juliet*
Err.	*Comedy of Errors*	Shr.	*Taming of the Shrew*
Ham.	*Hamlet*	TGV	*Two Gentlemen of Verona*
1H4	*1 Henry IV*	Tim.	*Timon of Athens*
2H4	*2 Henry IV*	Tit.	*Titus Andronicus*
H5	*Henry V*	TN	*Twelfth Night*
1H6	*1 Henry VI*	TNK	*Two Noble Kinsmen*
2H6	*2 Henry VI*	Tmp.	*Tempest*
3H6	*3 Henry VI*	Tro.	*Troilus and Cressida*
H8	*Henry VIII*	Wiv.	*Merry Wives of Windsor*
JC	*Julius Caesar*	WT	*Winter's Tale*
Jn.	*King John*	LC	*Lover's Complaint*
LLL	*Love's Labour's Lost*	Luc.	*Rape of Lucrece*
Lr.	*King Lear*	PhT	*Phoenix and Turtle*
Mac.	*Macbeth*	PP	*Passionate Pilgrim*
MM	*Measure for Measure*	Son.	*Sonnets*
MND	*Midsummer Night's Dream*	Ven.	*Venus and Adonis*

Significant Articles, Monographs, and Reviews

January, 1968—December, 1968
By J. Leeds Barroll

When presenting our third annual gathering in this series last year, we observed that while the existence of at least two admirably thorough Shakespeare bibliographies makes further such compilation superfluous, a selected listing of certain material might have its own uses. The response from scholars has been such as to suggest the continuation of this series, and, for the benefit of new readers, it might therefore be well to reiterate some principles of selection.

A selected listing of significant material may have its uses if the term "significant" bears some relationship to whether an article or a monograph seems to enlarge the sum of factual knowledge concerning Shakespeare's life, immediate artistic milieux, or media. There is also "significance" in some efforts to explore the nature of the art-entities themselves with which Shakespeare challenges our comprehension. It is not simple, after all, to maintain the necessary distinction between two verbal structures, differentiating that verbal description which is "criticism" from the plays and poems which are themselves structured through words. When criticism, therefore, through consistent argumentation and an acute sense of the relativity of the verbal, succeeds so as to alter or at least to modify existing views on the nature of Shakespeare's art, those instances certainly warrant notice.

It is also extremely important to follow reviewings, for they are the complements, the Aristotelian end, as it were, to that beginning represented by the scholarship under scrutiny. And if we assume that scholarship is essentially a social act whereby knowledge is increased through the interchange of information and ideas, then investigation is meaningless when deprived of a reasoned and careful response. It seems important to note responses of this nature when they occur.

We also refer to "Ancillary Studies" in a third section, for although the reviewing-portion of *Shakespeare Studies* is properly the place for noting books, there are some, which though not directly pertinent, may contain material of possible relevance to matters Shakespearean, but which sometimes may not have too obvious a bearing upon the subject: in the latter case, the presumed relevance is indicated. In this section are also included certain books which will be subject to later review at length but which should be mentioned because of some particular characteristics which would make early allusion to them timely.

Significant work in all areas has doubtless been omitted: "to err" etc. Much of the correspondence received, however, has adverted to certain kinds of omission which derive from editorial principle rather than from neglect. It does not seem appropriate, for instance, to include in the listing articles and reviews appearing in previous volumes of *Shakespeare Studies* itself. This matter apart, however, and in the hope of avoiding serious omission, the Editor would be grateful for a continued reception of offprints and possible ancillary books published *since January 1, 1969*. It only remains for us to express gratitude to the community of Renaissance scholars as well as the publishers for their very generous response to our similar request last year: it is only human for this writer to wish that all such material could have been noted below.

F. G. A. M. Aarts, "Some Notes on Petrus Mountanus' *Spreeckonst* and the Pronunciation of English," *ES*, XLIX (1968), 229-234.

Aarts calls attention to certain comparison passages in the 1635 treatise of the Dutch phonetician Petrus Montanus (Pieter Berch), d. 1638. These passages throw possible light on some English pronunciations. See, for example, the discussion of the pronunciation of the initial g in *gnaw* and the comments on E. J. Dobson's evidence in such cases. Cf. also Maveety, below.

Michael J. B. Allen, "The Chase: The Development of a Renaissance Theme," *Comp. Lit.*, XX (1968), 301-312.

This well-documented article will be of interest to students of *Venus and Adonis* as well as to those who are concerned with Shakespeare's use of Actaeon in various imagery situations, although the primary emphasis is on Spenser and Ronsard. The author studies the patristic and iconological traditions underlying various versions of the Venus-Adonis story and of hunting motifs in general, especially when they may involve the figures of Diana or of Venus.

David M. Bergeron, "The Emblematic Nature of English Civic Pageantry," *Renaissance Drama*, N.S.,I (1968), 167-198.

This article is an interesting survey of the relationship between the formal emblem and the shows constructed by such pageant-writers as Munday and Middleton. The almost identical use of appropriate symbology in both emblem-books and masques, as in the "Truth-is-the-Daughter-of-Time" motif hints at how traditional imagery found its way into genres other than the poetic. Shakespeare's use of Rumour in *2H4*, one might observe, suggests how this aspect of Renaissance metaphor, of which emblems were one manifestation, may be relevant to any serious study of "imagery" in Shakespeare.

Kirsty Cochrane, "Orpheus Applied: Some Instances of his Importance in the Humanist View of Language," *RES*,XIX (1968), 1-13.

This is an important supplement to the work of D. P. Walker and Frances Yates on the role of the Orpheus figure in the Renaissance. Discussing this role as it applied to England specifically, the author traces several kinds of idealizations which tended to cluster around the Orpheus concept: Orpheus as Musician, Orpheus as Orator, Orpheus as Poet (as in Shakespeare's allusion: *TGV*, III.ii.78), Orpheus as organizer of society, Orpheus as Christ. Not the least interesting aspect of this article is the brief reference to Thomas Campion who seems to have shared with such a one as Mersenne a tendency to link effective music with the concept of persuasion for moral purposes. Orpheus with his lute, a figure which had expressed not only an artistic but an ethical aspiration, needed to be interpreted by musical humanists, in practical application, in terms of man's rational faculty: speech. This emphasis on the power of speech among musical thinkers which thus linked music with rhetoric, specifically, with persuasion, suggests an important dimension, one might think, of the role of song in drama. Ariel's (singing) role as Prospero's ethical spokesman may, for instance, be highly suggestive in the context of Cochrane's article.

Robert Egan, "A Muse of Fire: *Henry V* in the Light of *Tamburlaine*," *MLQ*, XXIX (1968), 15-28.

This article calls attention to the much-vexed problem of the genre of *Henry V* by linking the play with *Tamburlaine*, with Greene's *Alphonsus*, and Peele's *Battle of Alcazar*. "The over-victorious plot, the episodic structure, and the frequent use of a chorus" were a familiar framework of expectations and assumptions which Shakespeare used as a means of leading his audience into the play. It is unfortunate that this potentially seminal article adopts a dialectic which primarily takes its point of departure not from much of the better scholarship on *Henry V*, but from a criticism of certain highly subjective and evaluative remarks by Yeats and Stoll, thence proceeding to the thesis that "Henry wrestles success-fully with the dichotomy that destroyed *Tamburlaine*." Although this latter point may be true, demon-stration of the matter is often through the technique of drawing the concept of a Tamburlaine-like Henry from individual remarks throughout the play rather than from a consideration of the immediate contexts within which such remarks might have been made. For example: "In his first speech at Harfleur (III.i.1-34) he specifically repudiates the Christian for the conqueror, encouraging his men to abandon 'modest stillness and humility' and to replace the 'fair nature' of their humanity 'with hard-favored rage.'" This may well be the case, but demonstration would seem to require an attention to context which would perhaps be too lengthy for the confines of an article. Another difficulty may lie in the double thrust of the investigation itself. To demonstrate the existence of a genre through a study of form is one approach; to establish a genre through a demonstrated similarity of ethical emphasis shared by a number of works is another. The former is probably more convincing, and this line is what makes the article interesting.

Bridget Gellert, "A Note on 'Hamlet', II.ii.356-357," *N&Q*, XV (1968), 139-140.

The author suggests that Bright's *Treatise*, adduced by Dover Wilson as a source for Hamlet's reference to a southerly wind, may also allow us to read "hawk from a handsaw" simply as it stands. Emendation has attempted to place both objects in one category (the bird class or the tool class) as if for the sake of symmetry, but Gellert notes that Bright uses a hawk and a saw as examples of two different *kinds* of tool or instrument. A hawk was an example of what Bright classified as an obedient instrument which nevertheless has life and character of its own; a saw, with neither freedom nor life, was an instru-ment classifiable as a tool of the lowest grade. Thus, Hamlet's welcome to Rosencrantz and Guilden-stern—"when the wind is southerly I know a hawk from a handsaw"—becomes understandable as a comment on his suspicions about his two friends' relationship to the purposes of Claudius.

Jean Gagen, "Hector's Honor," *SQ*, XIX (1968), 129-137.

This study is an interesting discussion of the contradictions posed by the different evaluations and definitions of "honor"; a Cleland, for example, as opposed to LaPrimaudaye; the immediate problem of honor vs. the general challenge of Christian ethics. Suggesting modifications of Watson's and Siegel's views, Gagen's argument is ultimately supported by Doran's recent study (discussed in *Shakespeare Studies*, III [1967], 338) for he emphasizes the Renaissance concern for the outward form of honor, the reputation for virtue. And when applying this background to Hector's decision to retain Helen against his own former reasoning, Gagen is indeed thought-provoking in his suggestion that we see "Hector's dilemma as one which many Renaissance gentlemen had confronted and his decision one which Renaissance humanists themselves had often made without any sense of having shamefully abandoned their ideals." At the same time, however, it might have been useful for the author to con-sider whether an audience for *TC*—even if possibly composed of members of the Inns—might not have subscribed to a double standard in these matters. On the one hand there would be the code of ethics to which they as individuals might privately subscribe; on the other hand, there could have existed that possibly more difficult code of ethics which they, as audience, might have expected to see domi-nating and determining attitudes or events in a play. Television drama is a useful parallel as we observe the often homiletic characteristics of the figure whom the structure of the narrative expects us to support. If the parallel is not acceptable, we can, in any event, observe that Hector's concept of honor renders him armorless in the vicinity of Achilles just as his decision to retain Helen makes inevitable the continuation of the war and then the fall of Troy—of that which Hector was defending in the first place. In that case, an audience was being asked to associate Hector's honor with rather destructive consequences.

Rudolph E. Habenicht, ed., "Shakespeare: An Annotated World Bibliography for 1967," *SQ,* XIX (1968), 213-312.

The bibliography this year lists books separately from articles and essays. Sections VI ("Reviews of Books Previously Recorded"), VII ("Selected Reprints"), and VIII (the three-part index to Shakespeare's works, to topics, and to names) are an especially useful complement to this important annual listing.

J. R. Hale, "The True Shakespearean Blank," *SQ*, XIX (1968), 33-40.

"The word *blank* is never used in the sense of 'target' in the printed technical literature of the Elizabethan age, and only once, to my knowledge, in an unpublished work." The author reminds us that the term for the target in general was *mark.* The *butt* was the turf background against which *marks* were placed. The *prick* was a card which might be so placed, but it could be secured against any standing object or in the ground. Numerous quotations suggest that *blank*, in contradistinction to *OED*, meant "point-blank range." *OED*'s second example—"discharge at the blancke there of" does offer the author some complications, and it might have been worth investigating whether *at the blank* might have been a construction synonymous with "at point-blank range" depending on the idomatic senses of *at*. The more conservative conclusion suggested by the author's own unbiased presentation of evidence (especially from Smythe) might be that when *blank* occurs in any ballistics sense in Shakespeare, it most probably conveys Mod.E. "point-blank range" but may conceivably suggest "center of target," for it is significant that the two examples which show *blank* meaning "center of target" are from technical treatises.

Ejner J. Jensen, "The Style of the Boy Actors," *Comparative Drama,* II (1968), 100-114.

The author is concerned with a trend towards viewing the boy actors of the English Renaissance as primarily vehicles for satire and burlesque, especially in some recents studies of Marston's work. As a corrective, Jensen adduces contexts which indicate that their playwrights regarded the boys as serious artists fully able to compete with adults—a view presented, for instance, by Jonson on the subject of Pavy. The author also asserts what needs asserting: that an examination of the boys' acting-style may show that the plays of the children should be discussed in terms of principles that govern dramatic compositions. This is especially so if such an examination would begin with a view of the dramatic experience, work through demonstrable facts of theatre history, and in the dramatic texts themselves. In fact, he concludes, such investigation may show that any critical vocabulary employed in our writing about Shakespeare may be used with equal validity in the discussion of plays written for the private theatres. The article itself is usefully documented and it only remains to suggest some qualifications while agreeing with the thesis as a whole. Certainly the use of boys in adult companies in itself argues against the parodic contexts suggested by some commentators on acting in the private theatres. Desdemona was a boy, as was the Duchess of Malfi. Where proponents of the burlesque view may have a point, however, is in their adduction of those children's plays in which the boys were being required not only to impersonate adult females, but also, and more importantly, adult males. In such cases, some dimension of parody was theoretically possible. Aside from this consideration, it is worth remembering how hampered we sometimes may be by preconception. Children ranging between the ages of, say, ten and sixteen or more, simply cannot be classified as one group—biologically, emotionally, physiologically, or temperamentally. Such anthropological classics as *Coming of Age in Samoa* might also deter us from generalization, since we do not really know what "growing up" was, or meant between

14

1590 and 1620 in England. Given this ignorance, one might hesitate at any broad conclusions about what the little eyases ("young maturing hawks," as bird-handlers understand the term) were capable of. What might be suggested is that direction would have been much more important when a child was required to simulate adult male gestures and emotions for the scrutiny of an audience which may largely have been composed of adult males. All such questions, however, are raised anew by the bent of this article.

William S. Kable, "Compositor B, The Pavier Quartos, and Copy Spellings," *SB*, XXI (1968), 131-161.

D. F. McKenzie's study of the work of F's Compositor B in Q2 of *MV* (1619 "Pavier") suggested one important use to which the Pavier quartos could be put, especially since *MV* was printed before E (whose *do, go, heere* preferences were similar to B's) entered Jaggard's shop in 1622. But Kable suggests another theoretical use to which the Pavier reprints can be put, observing that once a *do, go,* or *heere* pattern has been utilized to assign a portion of the F text to Compositor B, the value of these identifying spellings is exhausted. Instead, one can move forward to discover a new group of words, through a study of the Pavier quartos, a group of words for which the compositor may not have an invariable habit (as with *do-go-heere*), but rather "a weak preference or indifference." For such words can be used not as identifying marks merely showing the presence of the compositor, but as a means of seeing through that compositor to the features of his copy. The author's rationale here is that "if the compositor has no set preferential spelling for a given word but varies his spellings in some relation to the variations in his copy, the forms of that word in his texts will directly reflect the forms which were in the copy." Again, "if the compositor does have some preferential spelling for a given word but is influenced by his copy to set another form from time to time, these occasional occurrences of the nonpreferential form(s) will again reveal copy spellings." The resultant hypotheses would therefore be useful for projections in cases where the copy is unknown, lost, or disputed.

Kable's article, on the whole, is the logical next step forward from Hinman's work, and there is so much material that space precludes anything but generalization here. 1) He establishes F's Compositor B as the man who set type for the entire set of Pavier quartos. 2) Having collated all the Pavier texts against their copy (Q1 of all plays but *Pericles* where Q3), and having compiled word-counts for over 500 individual words which were then analyzed in terms of orthographic groups in his University University of Virginia doctoral dissertation (1966), the author offers a sample report of B's preferences. 3) He discusses twenty-seven words where a preferential spelling by B can be established. 4) He presents a list of over a hundred words which, within the Pavier texts, demonstrably reflect the characteristics of copy, as opposed to B's preferential spellings. 5) He concludes with a brief glance at the last six pages of F *LLL* set by B. Kable examines thirty-one spellings which, at odds ranging from two-to-one to virtual certainty, according to the findings from work with the Paviers, should be reflections of spellings which stood in B's copy. Then, "controlling the experiment," as it were, he checks a non-Pavier, *LLL* Q1 (1598), which Greg argued was the copy for F. Twenty-nine of the thirty-one spellings posited by Kable's finding as copy-spellings do, in fact, occur.

There are many implications for textual study in this important article, not the least of which is that it points a way to method. Kable's mode of investigating B can be elaborated upon, for example, to determine what underlay texts for which the only known source is the First Folio, and which B himself set. One might also speculate that with Howard-Hill's study of Ralph Crane, some connection may therefore be verified or disproved between the scribe and Shakespeare's fair copies with consequent investigation of whether or not Greg's consignment of so many F-only texts to a source in Shakespeare's foul papers will bear scrutiny.

David Klein, "Time allotted for an Elizabethan Performance," *SQ*, XVIII (1967), 434-438.

This brief article is a most interesting re-examination of the problem posed by previous references to Elizabethan and Jacobean statements indicating that the performance of plays was meant to last for two hours. The most significant material is Klein's adduction of at least six statements between 1575 and 1610 which indicate the assumption of three-hour performances. Since several other statements also indicate performance-times of "too good hours and more" the implications for future research are obvious. We may add that the problem of assuming that Shakespeare's plays as they presently survive were either cut for performances or acted more quickly to suit two hours' traffic has always been that this theory casts some doubt on the provenance of long plays which first appear in F and are assumed to derive from the playhouse.

Richard Levin, "'Nuns' and 'Nunnery' in Elizabethan Drama," *N&Q*, XV (1968), 248-249.

The author presents a number of early seventeenth century contexts which support "nunnery" and "nun" as slang references to prostitution. This is useful since evidence to this effect has been rather more scarce than the many statements merely assuming that such evidence exists.

Richard Levin, "The Unity of Elizabethan Multiple-Plot Drama," *ELH*, XXXIV (1968), 425-446.

This is an interesting article, if only because there is not a great deal of significantly methodical writing on the subject of the multiple plot. "Although the campaign on behalf of the multiple plot has been won, that victory is still largely confined to isolated demonstrations (in articles, introductions to editions, and passages in books on other topics) of the integrity of some particular play." It should now be possible, the author argues, to draw upon this scattered material for a more general investigation focusing directly upon the basic problem involved in the defense of multiple-plot unity: "on the nature of the connections that can be established between plots." The author then proceeds to effect distinctions by using Aristotle's concept of four causes. One mode of connection between figures "from different plots" can be thought of as corresponding to Aristotelian *material* cause, for this mode of integration is "included" in the matter which the playwright has in hand, "prior to the action." This mode can create more complicated effects, yet remains static, unaffected by elaborations or even by "the temporal unfolding of the plots": in such a mode, donnés link persons in the play as friends, neighbors, or, more frequently, as blood relatives, and, in other instances, "geographically," as in Terentian situations, or as in cases which present a public gathering-place such as Bartholomew Fair. A second mode is taken to be equivalent to Aristotle's *efficient* cause—a situation in which a character or event "from one line of action directly affects the other." "It is significant that most of the older critics seem to have regarded this causal mode as the only means of integrating a multiple-plot play, for this helps to explain their hostile attitude." A brief example of the mode would be the marshalling of the factors of reciprocal interactions which follow the arrival of Lear and his daughters at Gloucester's castle whereby "plots" that seem unrelated at first, become "inextricably intangled." A third mode, corresponding to Aristotle's *formal* cause, "includes all the logical—or more accurately, analogical—relationships obtaining between the plots." This mode also figures much more prominently than these other modes in recent Elizabethan studies because it has been the primary focus of the whole revolution in defense of the multiple plot." All the relationships of the formal mode are "species of analogy, for they are based on the comparison of two or more persons, events, or ideas in one plot with an equivalent set in the other." This comparison must be significant in the sense that it may be reduced to "parallelism and contrast" or to "positive and negative analogy." A brief example would be the relationship of the "main plot" involving Lear and his daughters to the "subplot" involving Gloucester and his sons. The fourth and last mode of integration corresponds to Aristotle's *final* cause but the mode is "not coordinate with the other three, since it is the result of all of them together, and is in another sense their cause in so far as they are the product of conscious art." In the four-level hierarchy, it is "that for the sake of which'" the others exist. Thus, for instance, "the tragedy of Lear seems even more extraordinarily moving because our response to it is continually readjusted, and thereby heightened, in relation to the emotions evoked by Gloucester's fate, which is poignant enough in itself for any ordinary tragic effect, and yet is seen to be so much less serious and less internalized than Lear's."

It is surprising that Doran's chapters on the Fable in *Endeavors of Art* were not mentioned as one of the studies influential in making the concept of multiple plot "respectable," but a more pressing consideration has to do with definition. "Plot" itself, or "action" needs some explanation as a term within the author's critical framework, since this term, I take it, is the basic subject of the article. At the same time, it might have been useful for the author to have allowed us to consider with him what kinds of question his analyses may serve as answer to. The discussion of *material* and *efficient* causes answers questions about what make activities plausible to an audience. The discussion of *formal* cause is concerned with "a meaningful relation between plots" and the question of what is meaningful for a given play depends on a discovery of the *final* cause which, as the author defines it, represents a level which introduces the "major new variable": "the emotional quality of the individual plots"—serious or comic, and their "affective relationship." *Final* cause might then require the kinds of *a priori* formulations against which the author has warned us. The artistic intention of the dramatist is under inquiry at this level, then, but to describe the answer in terms of a "synthesis" is merely to adduce another word for "unity," a word dangerously suggestive of Hegel's triadic imperatives, and, if not that, then more mystical than analytical. "It might seem possible then to classify the kinds of affective unity in terms of the distinction between positive and negative vectors already noted in the formal mode, yet this is complicated by the need to take into account the mixture of these vectors in any formal relationship, and also the emotional distance separating the plots related in this way." Emotion is the constant.

This summary is necessarily brief, and does not take into account the many qualifications and examples which the author adduces in his discussion of each mode. If issue has been taken with certain points, these objections should nevertheless be understood as arising from a context of anticipating with pleasure further studies by the author.

Maxwell S. Luria, "Standing Water and Sloth in *The Tempest*," *ES*, XLIX (1968), 328-331.

This brief article traces the sixteenth-century allusions, some medieval *topoi*, and references in other scholarship, to the association existing between the concept of standing water and Sloth. Since many of the author's sixteenth-century English examples suggest the image of "standing water" as having merely pejorative contexts, and since the author himself finally describes "standing water" as "an image of moral obtuseness," the discussion does not quite establish the connection indicated by the title, but the work of the article suggests that the linkage might well be made.

Waldo F. McNeir, "The Role of Edmumd in *King Lear*," *SEL*, VIII (1968), 187-216.

Not only is this article a careful survey of the relative emphases in various studies of the character of Edmund since Bradley, but it is also a close examination of the characterization of the bastard, emphasizing especially the problems posed by Edmund's repentance. Surveying the various English Renaissance tracts describing the ideal process of repentance, the author indicates how Edmund's perception in these matters as he lies dying is, at best, flawed. This last problem is an especially interesting one for "repentance" has too often been taken to comprise a mere declaration of regret by a particular character, and criticism of Shakespearean and other characterizations in Renaissance drama may have suffered accordingly.

Stanley R. Maveety, "High Style, Strange Words, and the Answer to an Old Problem," *ELN*, V (1968), 159-163.

This is primarily a study of the odd-word usages of Francis Sabie, but in one instance, (p.163), the author demonstrates *hart / heart* as an example not "of relaxed Renaissance spelling" but as indicating the similarity of sound between *heart* and *hurt*. Word-play on these two concepts with the spellings *heart/hart* appears three times in Sabie's *The Fisherman's Tale.* Any such evidence which adds to the repertoire of pronunciations is of course quite welcome to students of the drama.

Norman Nathan, "Leontes' Provocation," *SQ,* XIX (1968), 19-24.

This suggestive article is concerned with the motivation which Shakespeare may or may not have furnished for the sudden jealousy of Leontes in *WT.* "The jealousy is sudden *and well* motivated," the author argues, and he alludes to the relativity of genre-requirements. An Othello, in a tragedy, is endowed with just as "sudden" overtly jealous behavior, but this may be accepted by an audience because the possibilities in the Moor's character have been previously presented. With Leontes, the technical problem derives from the requirements of tragicomedy which must work with speed to present us with a potentially tragic situation demanding, at the same time, a favorable resolution (my phraseology, not Nathan's). "The tragicomedy framework makes it desirable that little time be taken to prepare the audience for the turn of events" the author observes, and it would have been useful if this article had explored this matter more generally, outside of Shakespeare, if only to establish some norms for the genre. The value of the study, however, is its suggestion about the relative literal-mindedness of Leontes as this literal-mindedness is exposed in the first scene to the greater rhetorical fluency of both Polixenes and Hermione. In the queen's case, the verbal agility does breed ambiguities, for her use of "us" could refer to her singly as queen as well as to herself and her husband as a couple when she declares their love for Polixenes. At the same time, her employemnt of "friend" and "hostess" might, in the immediate context, be unfortunate, considering some seventeenth-century constructions of the term. On the whole, Nathan's observations require us to consider whether the problem of initial exposition in the final comedies and in other tragicomedies of the time was met by the presentation of material of a higher "density" of texture, and, if so, whether an audience had either learned to be alert to such matters or was composed of a society of requisite sophistication in the first place.

G. R. Proudfoot, "A Note on 'Titus and Vespasian,'" *N&Q,* XV (1968), 131.

By pointing out an allusion in *The Jew of Malta* to Titus' and Vespasian's conquest of the Jews, and by reminding us of the fact that an English version of this "Titus" story was available since 1558, this note contributes support to the theory that the play variously designated in Henslowe's diary as "tittus & vespacia," "titus & vespacia," "titus," and "tittus" was probably not Shakespeare's *Titus Andronicus.* (Receipts for the former play were noted on ten dates from 11 April, 1592 through 25 January, 1592/93.) It might be observed also that advocates of "titus" as *Titus Andronicus* too frequently ignore Henslowe's habit of abbreviating the names of those plays which he may have noted several times previously and from which he has gained good receipts. Thus, after "a knacke to knowe a knave" has been so entered three times between 10 (?) June and 22 June, 1592, it becomes "the cnacke" on 31 December, 1592, while three days later "titvs" appears for the first time after having been referred to as (e.g.) "titus & vespacia" seven times previously. Similarly, after (e.g.) "titus & ondronicus" has been so noted three times, it then becomes "andronicous" in the last two references on 5 June, 1594 and 12 June of the same year.

Ernest Schanzer, "Hercules and his Load," *RES,* XIX (1968), 51-53.

This note traces the supposed motto of the Globe to Steevens' quotation from the manuscripts of William Oldys (1696-1761) and speculates that Steevens, who also first alluded to a Hercules carrying a globe, may have derived this from Oldys too. This being the case, there is the possibility that the "Hercules and his load" carried away by the "little eyases" may have been a purely figurative allusion having nothing to do with the Globe itself. If so, then the discussion of the acting situation, one might imagine, would have little specific reference to Shakespeare's company, unless Oldys' information was itself accurate. An added problem is too often forgotten in this context, however. "Hercules and his load" derive from the 1623 Folio, not from the 1604-05 quarto. There is thus the possibility in theory that the whole passage about the children derives from events which might have occurred at any point during the seven years between Shakespeare's death and the publication of F, or, in any event, at any point between 1605 and 1623.

A. L. Soens, *"King Lear* III.iv.62-65: A Fencing Pun and Staging,' *ELN,* VI (1968), 19-24.

This article is interesting in its basic suggestion that Edgar as "poor Tom" is pretending to fence as he says "there could I have him now,—and there,—and there again, and there." Lear remarks: "What have his daughters brought him to this pass?" The author explores the various uses of "pass," especially as a fencing term, and notes too how Harsnet, a presumed source of *Lear,* constantly tends to employ fencing metaphor when discussing the exorcism of devils. Whether or not Lear is meant to be unintentionally punning, the article is quite useful in its allusion to modes of swordplay in the Renaissance and to the possibilities of the word "pass" when it is employed in many other Shakespearean contexts. See also the same author's "Two Rapier Points: Analysing Elizabethan Fighting Methods," *N&Q,* XV (1968), 127-128, which warns us that any judgment about the nature of Elizabethan fencing techniques, and thus of any Shakespearean fencing, must be drawn not from illustrations of the period, but from careful reading, unless there is indeed verbal support for the generally stylized pictorializations.

F. W. Sternfeld, "A Lost Poem by Queen Elizabeth I,' *TLS,* July 4 (1968), 705.

Under this rubric the author's letter to the editor notes that tunes for "Come live with me" and "Fortune my foe" are to be found in William Corkine's *Ayres* of 1610 and *Second Booke of Ayres* (1612). The letter also alludes to previous correspondence on the popular tunes of the day. Cf. also *TLS,* Sept. 12 (1968), 1032.

Franklin B. Williams, Jr., "Photo-Facsimiles of *STC* Books: A Cautionary Check List," *SB,* XXI (1968), 109-130.

This list of over 500 STC titles is limited to photo-facsimiles produced on some variety of printing press. The list does not include photographs and photostats, microfilm, or Xerox codices. There are obvious reasons for these omissions and they are detailed in the introduction which also surveys the state of the facsimile situation. Deliberately excluded are books printed abroad in Latin, single-sheet engraved maps and prints, indulgences, proclamations, bookplates, and several other kinds of items. A number of titles not listed in the original (1926) *STC* are included and each item has been personally inspected. A brief and interesting digression (p.114) disposes of a variant of the first edition of *Richard III* (STC 22314) which Greg mentions in his *Bibliography* (#142a) on the authority of Ashbee, Griggs, and Farmer.

S. P. Zitner, "Anon, Anon: or a Mirror for a Magistrate,' *SQ,* XIX (1968), 63-70.

This article seeks to bring the "Francis" sequence of *1H4* into the general structure of the play rather than to dismiss it, as many scholars have done, to the realm of nonsense. Appearing almost simultaneously with one by J. D. Shuchter in *Shakespeare Studies,* III (1967), 129-137, Zitner's essay serves to yoke Francis' inarticulateness with that of Hotspur to whom Hal next adverts in what would otherwise seem a *non sequitur.* "Having pierced Hotspur's mystery at a vital point, the Prince will now fully exorcise that wild valiance by clanking in its mail" as Hal suddenly desires to play Percy to Falstaff's Dame Mortimer. This element is not the primary emphasis of the article which itself has a broader argument, but it is the most convincing aspect of the general discussion.

Reviews

T. W. Baldwin, *On the Compositional Genetics of the Comedy of Errors* (The University of Illinois Press, 1965). See John P. Reddington in *SQ,* XIX (1968), 88-89.

Fredson Bowers, General Editor, *The Dramatic Works in the Beaumont and Fletcher Canon*, I (Cambridge University Press, 1966). See E. A. J. Honigmann in *JEGP*, LXVII (1968), 697-699.

Fredson Bowers, *On Editing Shakespeare* (The University Press of Virginia, 1966). See E. A. J. Honigmann in *Library*, XXIII (1968), 264-265.

O. J. Campbell and Edward G. Quinn, eds., *A Shakespeare Encyclopaedia* (Thomas Y. Crowell, 1966). See J. C. Maxwell in *RES*, XIX (1968), 70-73.

John Casey, *The Language of Criticism* (Methuen, 1966). See David Daiches in *RES*, XIX (1968), 339-344.

Mario A. Di Cesare, *Vida's Christiad and Vergilian Epic* (Columbia University Press, 1964). See I. D. McFarlane in *MLR*, LXIII (1968), 728-730.

Rosalie L. Colie, *Paradoxia Epidemica: The Renaissance Tradition of Paradox* (Princeton University Press, 1966). See U. Milo Kaufmann in *JEGP*, LXVII (1968), 308-311.

R. S. Crane, *The Idea of the Humanities* (The University of Chicago Press, 1967). See Lawrence Lipking in *PQ*, XLVII (1968), 455-471.

B. Danielsson and R. C. Alston, eds., *The Works of William Bullokar*, I (University of Leeds: School of English: Leeds Texts and Monographs, New Series I, 1966). See Hilda M. Hulme in *MLR*, LXIII (1968), 675.

Walter R. Davis, ed., The Works of Thomas Campion (Doubleday & Co., 1967). See Lloyd E. Berry in *JEGP*, LXVII (1968), 306-308, and Rhodes Dunlap in *PQ*, XLVII (1968), 601-605.

Giles E. Dawson and Laetitia Kennedy-Skipton, *Elizabethan Handwriting* (W. W. Norton & Co., 1966). See R. A. Foakes in *SQ*, XIX (1968), 184, and P. Davison in *MLR*, LXIII (1968), 169-170.

B. N. DeLuna, *Jonson's Romish Plot* (The Clarendon Press, 1967). See Peter Ure in *N&Q*, XV (1968), 274-276.

E. H. Fellowes, *English Madrigal Verse, 1588-1632*. Revised and Enlarged by F. W. Sternfeld and David Greer (The Clarendon Press, 1968). See *TLS*, June 6 (1968), 572.

Arthur Freeman, *Thomas Kyd: Facts and Problems* (The Clarendon Press, 1967). See E. D. Pendry in *RES*, XIX (1968), 430-431.

A. Bartlett Giamatti, *The Earthly Paradise and the Renaissance Epic.* (Princeton University Press, 1966). See G. R. Hibbard in *N&Q*, XV (1968), 115-116.

L. C. Hector, *The Handwriting of English Documents* (Edward Arnold, 1966). See P. Davison in *MLR*, LXIII (1968), 169-170.

Marvin T. Herrick, ed., *Italian Plays, 1500-1700, in The University of Illinois Library* (University of Illinois Press, 1966). See Christina Roaf in *MLR*, LXIII (1968), 490-492.

D. G. James, *The Dream of Prospero* (The Clarendon Press, 1967). See J. C. Maxwell in *N&Q*, XV (1968), 359-360.

George W. Keeton, *Shakespeare's Legal and Political Background* (Pitman, 1967), See A. F. Falconer in *RES*, XIX (1968), 313-315.

V. A. Kolve, *The Play called Corpus Christi* (Stanford University Press, 1966). See O. B. Hardison, Jr. in *MLQ*, XXIX (1968), 94-98.

J. W. Lever, ed., *Measure for Measure:* The New Arden Edition (Methuen, 1965). See J. J. Hogan in *RenQ*, XXI (1968), 228-230.

A Book of Masques: In Honour of Allardyce Nicoll (Cambridge University Press, 1967). See Stephen Orgel, *Essays in Criticism*, XVIII (1968), 310-321.

J. C. Maxwell, ed., *The Collected Papers of Sir Walter W. Greg* (The Clarendon Press, 1966). See Robert K. Turner, Jr. in *ELN*, V (1968), 234-237.

Irving Ribner, *The English History Play in the Age of Shakespeare:* Second Edition (Methuen, 1965). See R. L. Smallwood in *MLR*, LXIII (1968), 937.

Peter J. Seng, *The Vocal Songs in the Plays of Shakespeare* (Harvard University Press, 1967). See John Stevens in *ELN*, V (1968), 305-307.

Christopher Spencer, *Five Restoration Adaptations of Shakespeare* (The University of Illinois Press, 1965). See John Harold Wilson in *SQ*, XIX (1968), 181-182.

William B. Toole, *Shakespeare's Problem Plays* (Mouton, 1966). See Terence Hawkes in *MLR*, LXIII (1968), 677-679.

Rosemund Tuve, *Allegorical Imagery: Some Medieval Books and their Posterity* (Princeton University Press, 1966). See John M. Steadman in *MLQ*, XXIX (1968), 99-105.

Louise Vigne, *The Narcissus Theme in Western European Literature up to the*

Early 19th Century, tr. R. Dewsnap *et al.* (Gleerup, 1967). See R. M. Ogilvie in *RES,* XIX (1968), 215-217.

C. B. Watson, *Shakespeare and the Renaissance Concept of Honor* (Princeton University Press, 1960). See Charles Barber in *ES,* XLIX (1968), 66-68.

A. Williams, *The Drama of Medieval England* (The Michigan State University Press, 1961). See A. C. Cawley in *ES,* XLIX (1968), 245-247.

George Walton Williams, ed., *Romeo and Juliet* (Duke University Press, 1964). See Arthur Brown in *SQ,* XIX (1968), 178-179.

Emanuel Winternitz, *Musical Instruments and their Symbolism in Western Art* (Faber & Faber, 1968). See *TLS.* Aug. 22 (1968), 900.

Ancillary Studies

Charlton Hinman, ed. *The First Folio of Shakespeare: The Norton Facsimile.*
W. W. Norton & Co., Inc., 1968.

Although this important publication needs to be reviewed at greater length, it should be mentioned here. The method of reproduction especially deserves notes. The pages were reproduced by fine-screen (133-line) offset plates made from glossy photographs, no filters were used and no retouching has been effected. Reproduction is in half-tone offset at no reduction in the original size. The mode of selection is also important in that we now possess a hypothetically "ideal" copy, for many purposes bibliographically superior to any one copy of F itself since Hinman has compiled here a photographic facsimile which reproduces the latest state of every page. An appendix indicates which of the eighty Folger copies of F has been used for each page. Hinman's pagination can now be used too as a standard of reference superseding the sometimes-ambiguous signature-sequences of F, and his employment of the through line numbering advocated by McKerrow in his *Prolegomena* will establish another standard of reference, especially when the complementary lineation of the quartos relative to F's TLN is itself universally agreed upon. The high price of the 1968 edition need not deter interested scholars since the "Academic Edition" of the Norton Facsimile will appear in April. This will be priced at $15.00. It will bulk 2 inches as against the 2 15/16 inches of the more expensive edition, there will be no gold leaf on the upper edge of the page, and the end-papers will be plain. Paper itself will be low-acid rather than 100% rag. Binding will be in pyroxylin-impregnated cloth rather than leather. The book will be printed from the same plates and not reduced in size. The Norton Facsimile will be published by The Hamlyn Group in the U.K., appearing in the spring of 1969.

Marvin Spevack, ed. *A Complete and Systematic Concordance to the Works of Shakespeare.* Georg Olms Verlagsbuchhandlung, 1968.

This is another publication which will require more extended review but which should be mentioned in this space. Volume I (Comedies), Volume II (Histories and Non-Dramatic Works), and Volume III (Tragedies) are now available, III containing also *Pericles, The Two Noble Kinsmen,* and the *More* fragment. Volumes IV-VI, separately prefaced, will constitute a concordance to the complete works with cumulative statistical information, a context for each word, an index of all the words arranged according to frequency of occurrence, and a complete list of homographs. Volumes IV-VI, as described here, will be more understandable if we note that Volumes I-III constitute concordances to each individual play, the arrangement being as follows. *The Tempest*, for instance, occupies 81 pages of the first volume. We are first offered an alphabetical listing of all words occurring *only* in *The Tempest*. Each word is listed alone, without context. A figure indicates how many times the word appears in *The Tempest*. A second figure indicates the frequency of the word relative to all other words in the play. A third figure indicates how often the word appears in a verse line while a fourth figure indicates how often the word appears in a line of prose. Following this, act-scene-line references are given to indicate the locations of all occurrences. At the end of the listing of all words in *The Tempest* comes a listing of the same words, but divided now according to the character who has spoken the word. Thus we may note that Caliban utters the word "disease" once, in a line of verse, in II.ii.3. In the final three volumes the reader will find a complete alphabetical listing in the lines of context with which one associates such a concordance as Bartlett's. The line-references themselves must, of course, be based upon a particular text, and Spevack has chosen for his purpose the text of the forthcoming Houghton-Mifflin *Complete Works* being edited and lineated by G. Blakemore Evans *et al.* It is to be hoped that the forthcoming edition, with Spevack's concordance, will establish a uniform act-scene-line reference which will liberate scholars from the necessity of coping with the Globe-Bartlett combination which has already been deviated from in many instances. Finally, since Spevack's concordance has been generated by an IBM 7094 computer, scholars may wish to determine how this concordance differs from Howard-Hill's forthcoming concordance which is also computer-generated. Howard-Hill is concerned with an old-spelling concordance, invaluable to textual scholars who will wish to trace, say, the instances of a particular spelling often associated with a particular compositor or with a particular kind of pronunciation-possibility, and so forth. Howard-Hill's concordance will thus naturally use the Folio through line numbering which counts *every* typographical line (including stage-directions) after the head title of the play. Meanwhile, the contribution of Spevack's concordance is great, for while the bibliographer will require an old-spelling concordance, other scholars need to find words and their location in Shakespeare, and it is to Spevack's credit that he chose as the point of reference for his immense task a text under preparation by so conscientious an editor as Evans.

J. A. Lavin, "Additions to McKerrow's *Devices*," *Library*, XXIII (1968), 191-205

This article adds to instances of occurrence of particular McKerrow devices and also contributes six devices not recorded by McKerrow.

M. W. MacCallum, *Shakespeare's Roman Plays and their Background.*
Macmillan & Co. Ltd.; St. Martin's Press, 1967.

This well-known work has been out of print since 1949 and is now re-issued with a foreword by T. J. B. Spencer who devotes eight pages to a discussion of some of the scholarship on the "Roman" plays since MacCallum first published his work in 1910.

Edward W. Naylor, *Shakespeare and Music.* The Da Capo Press
& Benjamin Blom, Inc., 1965.

This is a republication of the revised 1931 edition printed by J. M. Dent & Sons Ltd. With the emergence of a number of recent studies on this general subject, scholars will welcome the renewed availability of Naylor's essay which might nevertheless be reconsidered in the light of Sternfeld's remarks in *Shakespeare Survey 15*.

W. Ebisch and L. L. Schücking, *A Shakespeare Bibliography: Supplement for the Years 1930-1935.* Benjamin Blom, Inc., 1964.

Although the limitations of the Ebisch-Schücking bibliography are well known, it is useful to have available a portion of the compilation from which the Gordon Ross Smith bibliography takes its point of departure.

F. P. Wilson, *The English Drama: 1485-1585*. Oxford History of
English Literature. The Clarendon Press, 1968.

F. P. Wilson did not live to finish the projected history of English drama which was to continue where
Volume II, Part 2, by E. K. Chambers, left off: at the accession of Henry VII. According to the publisher, Wilson had "effectively completed" the text presented here and also two later chapters "which
stand somewhat apart and are to be published separately." G. K. Hunter has acted as editor, and, in
addition, is responsible for The Chronological Table, the Bibliography, and the Index—no small tasks.
Since the work will obviously require review at a later date, it may suffice to indicate here that the
text devotes about a hundred of its 172 pages to the Tudor moralities and interludes, to masques,
pageants and entertainments, and to "sacred drama," while "comedy," "tragedy," and "The Theatre
before 1585" come down to us only in the remaining seventy-two pages.

The World of Richard III

by A. L. French

Richard III is the climax of the first tetralogy of Histories; historically it is the climax of both tetralogies. It has suffered from occupying this position because, on the whole, readers and even professional critics cannot be bothered with *Henry VI*, the understanding and appreciation of which involves, among other things, rather more than a nodding acquaintance with some complicated genealogies, together with an ability to respond to a kind of rhetoric which, compared with what we find in the mature Shakespeare, sounds primitive. *Richard III* has thus tended to get unhooked from its predecessors; but then if it is acted by itself, a great many references which are only meaningful in the light of *Henry VI* are baffling and have to be excised. Sir Laurence Olivier, in his film, did a dashing piece of surgery, with the help of Colley Cibber: Queen Margaret went altogether, and the Duchess of York was not much more than a shadow. But since so much of *Richard III* actually *turns* on what has happened before it opens, some of the film remained very obscure: for instance, the episode where Richard courts Lady Anne over the open coffin, not of her husband, but of Henry VI; or the point of Clarence's dream; or Richmond's claim that he has freed England from a long period of civil war. Moreover, if you remove or blur some of the distinctive kinds of interest that the play offers, you have to put something in their place; in practice this means making even more of Richard than Shakespeare does, but it also means turning him into a Punch or a Captain Hook—making him so outrageously and *obviously* wicked that he would not have taken in Edward IV's politically sensitive courtiers for five minutes (as Charles Lamb very acutely observed about George Cooke's performance of the part). So the play as a whole gets reduced to a *comédie noire*, or a hilarious melodrama, or something between the two.

Thus, I think we have to approach *Richard III* with a firm sense of what it is the climax *of*. If we do so, we shall find ourselves increasingly resisting the notion that the play is the climactic lesson taught by the Tudor Myth. According to that notion, Richard is (unconsciously, of course) the instrument of God's vengeance on the warring families of York and Lancaster; at the end Richmond arrives as a *deus ex machina*, destroys the few men who are still loyal to Richard, and brings the dreadful period of civil war to a final close. *Richard III* is read in this way by Tillyard, among others—as a simple piece of Tudor propaganda. But is it really as simple as all that? It is a highly-wrought piece, patently composed with enormous artistic care; and it seems unlikely to have been designed merely to enforce copy-book maxims about the Evils of Civil War and the Excellence of the Tudors.

Actually, as we ponder the play, we begin to wonder how far Richmond really is presented as an official Tudor hero. We see too little of him to be able to say anything definite, perhaps; but when he does at last appear, in Act V, his speech has a characteristic quality—it is simultaneously stiff and limp—which suggests, at the very least, that Shakespeare's imagination was not deeply engaged, whatever his "official self" may have thought or wanted to think.

It is Lord Stanley, Earl of Derby, who casts most light on the way we take Richmond, because it is Stanley alone who provides a bridge between the two reigns, and who actually gives England—symbolised by the crown—into Richmond's keeping. I propose, therefore, to begin by examining Stanley's role in the play. We first see him greeting Queen Elizabeth with the words: "God make your majesty joyful as you have been!" (I.iii.19).[1] The wavering rhythm reflects a wavering mind; he is not sure of his reception by Elizabeth (his wife and she are at loggerheads), so he begins with a feeble attempt at heartiness. After a conciliatory speech from the Queen, Stanley replies:

> I do beseech you, either not believe
> The envious slanders of her false accusers,
> Or if she be accused on true report,
> Bear with her weakness, which I think proceeds
> From wayward sickness, and no grounded malice.   (I.iii.25-29)

These lines have the unhappy air of explaining—and protesting—too much: his wife is not guilty, but then she may be; but if she is, she is only being perverse; but at the same time perhaps she is mentally unstable. Through the thick fog of excuses one can easily discern the main lines of the speaker's character: he is the eternal Trimmer, wanting to run with the hare and hunt with the hounds.

He does so with striking success until the very end. I pass over the episode where he pleads with Edward IV for his servant's life, because Stanley's function there is quite impersonal and merely serves to provoke Edward's moralising. More important is the episode where Catesby, sounded by Buckingham about Stanley's likely behaviour, says "He will do all in all as Hastings doth" (III.i.168)—a pointed and cynical comment on Stanley's lack of moral fiber. It is a true comment, yet intensely ironical in retrospect, for later on Stanley is most certainly not willing to follow Hastings to the block for the sake of the rightful king. Just before that Council scene, Stanley sends a messenger to Hastings with an account of a dream he has had:

> He dreamt the boar had razéd off his helm:
> Besides, he says there are two councils kept;
> And that may be determined at the one
> Which may make you and him to rue at th'other.
> Therefore he sends to know your lordship's pleasure—
> If you will presently take horse with him,
> And with all speed post with him toward the north,
> To shun the danger that his soul divines.   (III.ii.11-18)

Here we have a typical combination of timorous acuteness with timorous deference. The bathos in the fifth line is striking, the implication being—it backs up Catesby's comment—that he will do nothing without Hastings' approval. His perceptiveness contrasts amusingly with Hastings' stupidity:

> To fly the boar before the boar pursues
> Were to incense the boar to follow us
> And make pursuit where he did mean no chase. *(III.ii.28-30)*

Stanley, with the trimmer's quick instinct of self-preservation, has already guessed that the nobles are separating into factions, and he very much wants to be on the winning side. Hastings does not realize which way the wind is blowing even after Catesby has sounded him about his willingness to see Richard on the throne (39-40); all he can think about is his triumph over the Queen's kindred, a triumph which blinds him to the radical change in the political situation. Stanley enters at line 72, and in reply to Hastings' quip about the boar-spear, says:

> You may jest on, but, by the holy rood,
> I do not like these several councils, I. *(III.ii.75-76)*

His tone recalls that of the reported dream: the tone of a mind full of foreboding, but without the courage of its foreboding. The same discomfort, the same uneasy rhythm, pervades his words a few lines later:

> The lords at Pomfret, when they rode from London,
> Were jocund and supposed their states were sure,
> And they indeed had no cause to mistrust;
> But yet you see how soon the day o'ercast.
> This sudden stab of rancour I misdoubt:
> Pray God, I say, I prove a needless coward! *(III.ii.82-87)*

As yet he knows only that the "lords" have been imprisoned, not that they have been beheaded, a fact which Hastings delightedly brings out a moment later. To this news Stanley responds with the dark words,

> They [the lords], for their truth, might better wear their heads
> Than some that have accused them wear their hats. *(III.ii.91-92)*

Furness comments that the remark is meant as a sneer at both parties: "as far as truth and honour are concerned, the heads of the accused contain quite as much thereof as do the hats of the accusers: that is, none at all."[2] It is no accident that when Stanley is for once brave enough to show a little animus, Shakespeare makes him distribute it impartially and speak it obliquely.

By the time he reaches the council at the Tower, his spirits have improved; to Buckingham's question, "Is all things ready for the royal time?" (the coronation of Edward V), he replies, "It is, and wants but nomination" (specification of the day) (III.iv.4-5). But by the time forty-odd lines have elapsed, Stanley is aware—as no-one else is—that something is seriously amiss. Richard has drawn Buckingham aside, and after a whispered colloquy they go out together. At once Stanley makes a change of front, and haltingly explains that he is not quite ready after all:

> We have not yet set down this day of triumph.
> To-morrow, in my judgement, is too sudden;
> For I myself am not so well provided
> As else I would be, were the day prolonged.   *(III.iv.42-45)*

As Richard's absence lengthens, Hastings fills the time with a fatuous disquisition on the Protector's character—"by his face straight shall you know his heart" (which recalls the earlier, and doubly ironic, words of Buckingham at lines 10-12). Stanley replies to Hastings in a manner which suggests he now realizes that something is terribly wrong:

> What of his heart perceive you in his face
> By any livelihood he showed to-day?[3]

Hastings confidently replies,

> Marry, that with no man here he is offended;
> For, were he, he had shown it in his looks.   *(III.iv.54-57)*

Here the Quarto (but not modern editors) gives Stanley a reply which is wholly in character, "I pray God he be not, I say," which implies that apprehensiveness has become near-certainty. Any doubts he may have are immediately dispelled: Richard re-enters and arrests Hastings. Stanley says not a word, meekly obeying Richard's command, "The rest that love me, rise and follow me" (III.iv.78). Admittedly the Biship of Ely likewise follows Richard, but (as we learn at IV.iii.46) he loses little time in fleeing to Richmond.

Stanley next appears in IV.i where he comes to fetch Richard's wife to be crowned. In view of what has gone before, he certainly takes a remarkable tone with the three women—Anne, the Duchess of York and Queen Elizabeth:

> Let me but meet you, ladies, one hour hence,
> And I'll salute your grace of York as mother,
> And reverend looker-on, of two fair queens.   *(IV.i.29-31)*

Stanley feels no discomfort in his role as emissary of a usurping tyrant; so confident is he, indeed, that he genially hails the Duchess as mother (mother-in-law) of "two fair queens," though considering the circumstances he could scarcely have been more tactless. But then, when Elizabeth advises her son Dorset to escape to Richmond, Stanley says "Full of wise care is this your counsel, madam" (48), thus keeping a foot firmly in both camps. A moment later he brusquely urges Anne to hurry—"Come, madam, come; I in all haste was sent"; his only concern is for what may happen to him if Anne is late, just as a moment before his only worry had been that Dorset (or anybody else) might think badly of him. (It is noteworthy that IV.i, and Stanley's part in it, have no equivalents in Hall or Holinshed and are pure invention on Shakespeare's part.) Amusingly enough, the Stratford-upon-Avon production of "The Wars of the Roses" found Stanley's callous ego-centricity too much to stomach, and in this scene re-assigned his lines to Catesby!

Just after the coronation Stanley carefully reveals to Richard that Dorset has fled abroad (IV.ii.45-47), but is equally careful not to implicate anyone, least of all himself. To Richard's warnings at lines 84 and 89-90 he makes no reply, yet we notice that so far there is no question of his son's being held as a hostage for his good conduct (this happens towards the end of IV.iv, at 495-497). Richard merely says [my italics]:

> Stanley, look to your wife: if she convey
> Letters to Richmond, *you* shall answer it.

We next see Stanley in the role of a very circumspect bringer of bad news, towards the end of the fourth Act. What is striking here is that Stanley protests his fidelity to Richard on three several occasions within twenty lines. When Richard says "Thou wilt revolt and fly to him [Richmond], I fear," Stanley answers, "No, my good lord; therefore mistrust me not." Later he adds:

> Most mighty sovereign,
> You have no cause to hold my friendship doubtful:
> I never was nor never will be false.

Finally, referring to his son, he says "So deal with him as I prove true to you" (IV.iv.478-479; 492-494; 498). We need not go into the question whether the Elizabethans believed it was justifiable to commit perjury to save one's life from a usurper or tyrant. No doubt they did; but what strikes us about Stanley's behavior here is the quite needless emphasis Shakespeare gives to his protestations of fidelity—needless, that is, if we are really supposed to think of him as a determined opponent of Richard, who honourably and excusably lies to save his son and England. The triple emphasis suggests we are not meant to think of him as anything so blameless, and his past conduct is, we know, all of a piece with his present temporising. When Stanley talks with the priest in scene v of the same Act, we should be more inclined to credit his reason for not revolting against Richard (that his son is a hostage) if he had not already avoided committing himself when there was no danger in doing so. His question to the priest, "What men of name resort to him [Richmond]?" (IV.v.11) has the air of being an anxious attempt to find out which side has attracted more men of good birth.

Stanley's behaviour in the last act is of course conditioned by his son's being in imminent danger of execution; nevertheless, his accents are never those of a man who has really made up his mind. Consider, for example, what he says to Richmond on the night before Bosworth:

> I, by attorney, bless thee from thy mother,
> Who prays continually for Richmond's good:
> So much for that. The silent hours steal on,
> And flaky darkness breaks within the east.

In brief, for so the season bids us be,
Prepare thy battle early in the morning,
And put thy fortune to th'arbitrament
Of bloody strokes and mortal-staring war.
I, as I may—that which I would I cannot—
With best advantage will deceive the time,
And aid thee in this doubtful shock of arms:
But on thy side I may not be too forward,
Lest, being seen, thy brother, tender George,
Be executed in his father's sight.
Farewell: the leisure and the fearful time
Cuts off the ceremonious vows of love
And ample interchange of sweet discourse
Which so long sund'red friends should dwell upon.
God give us leisure for these rites of love!
Once more, adieu: be valiant, and speed well!   *(V.iii.83-102)*

The hesitant attempts to come to the point suggest Stanley is positively sweating with embarrassment. He is unable even to pretend confidence in Richmond's cause, as the halting rhythms of lines 91-96 show; his emphasis is on death, not victory (*"mortal-staring* war") and on uncertainty, not hope (*"doubtful* shock of arms"). He apologizes at some length—considering the circumstances—for not saying more, and ends by advising his stepson to be brave. Altogether it is a most unhappy performance. That the "unhappiness" in Act V was intended by Shakespeare is strongly suggested by a crucial omission he made from his chronicle sources. Holinshed relates that

> When King Richard was come to Bosworth he sent a purseuant
> to the lord Stanleie, commanding him to aduance forward with
> his companie, and to come to his presence, which thing if he
> refused to doo he sware by Christes passion, that he would
> strike off his sonnes head before he dined. The lord Stanleie
> answered the purseuant that if the king did so, *he had more*
> *sonnes aliue*; and, as to come to him, he was not then so deter-
> mined. . . .[4]

It is impossible to imagine the Stanley of Shakespeare's play returning so contemptuous and provocative an answer; by suppressing it, Shakespeare has emphasised Stanley's fence-sitting proclivities. And it was Stanley's intervention on Richmond's side, with "iii thousand tall men" as Hall puts it,[5] that decided the battle; in *Richard III* Stanley merely "denies" to come to the king's aid (V.iii.343).

All this adds up to a classic portrait of a time-server; the phrase "false, fleeting, perjured" applies more accurately to Stanley than to Clarence. If this seems unfair, consider Shakespeare's treatment of York in *Richard II*: York is presented as an honest and conscientious man (comic in his fussiness, indeed) who is genuinely

30

torn between his loyalty to the king and his sympathy with his wronged nephew Bolingbroke; whereas the only problem that distresses Stanley is the extreme difficulty of saving his own skin. And I cannot see that an actor, studying the part of Stanley, could possibly play it in a way fundamentally different from the one I have suggested.

Now Stanley not only provides some continuity between the two reigns, but also (as we saw) hands Richmond the crown and England—a point (V.v.7) at which stage-productions of *Richard III* tend to curl up in embarrassment. Stanley is, in fact, the only person left at the end of the play whom we have seen throughout and who has come through all vicissitudes; "j'ai survécu," he might say. We can hardly help feeling that something of his baseness rubs off onto the new regime, especially since the figure embodying that regime has, as presented, so little substance, and can hence offer so little resistance to someone who has been very much with us for five Acts. Whatever the official intention, the play itself would seem to have strong reservations about the New Order; despite Richmond's pious commonplaces it takes the most partisan efforts to find anything millenial at the end. It is possible to argue, as M. M. Reese does, that "the lifelessness of the character [of Richmond] shows how seriously Shakespeare took him,"[6] but this seems a desperate paradox. Perhaps an Elizabethan audience would have responded with naive approval to Richmond's prayer (V.iii.108 f.), but then what are we to make of the contrast between Richmond's and Richard's speeches to their respective armies? If Shakespeare's intention here was to withdraw our sympathy from Richard and transfer it to Richmond, why did he allow Richard to appeal to a simple bluff patriotism and even refer back to the days of Henry V? (and it was oddly tactless to remind the Elizabethan spectators that Henry VII, first of the Tudors, had been helped to the throne by French swords)—

> If we be conquered, let men conquer us,
> And not these bastard Bretons, whom our fathers
> Have in their own land beaten, bobbed, and thumped,
> And in record left them the heirs of shame....
> Fight, gentlemen of England! fight, bold yeomen!   *(V.iii.332 f.)*

If we go from this ringing rhetoric back to Richmond's flat admonitions, we can only conclude that, artistically speaking, Shakespeare was intent upon making Richmond as much of a cipher as possible. And there is no equivalent here to the scene in *Macbeth* (IV.iii) where the future monarch Malcolm acquires some dramatic and moral substance before the tyrant is killed and he takes over the government of Scotland. No doubt the Elizabethan audience, or at least the simpler souls among them, would have taken the future Henry VII as orthodoxy demanded; but Shakespeare, it seems, managed to satisfy his artistic (and perhaps political) conscience while at the same time offering nothing that was explicitly unorthodox or offensive, precisely as he does with that other sacrosanct English hero, Henry V.

Thus with regard to Richmond, *Richard III* by no means conforms to the Tudor morality-play pattern proposed by Tillyard and others. There are other respects too in which, if we take what Shakespeare offers, the play enlists feelings very wide of any conceivable Tudor mark. This is particularly true of Richard himself. For the awkward fact is that to some extent we sympathise with him rather than with any of the less obviously wicked characters.

Now commentators recognise this—they could hardly do otherwise—but they are puzzled to explain it or rather to explain it away (which is what they are logically committed to to). A. P. Rossiter, in one of the best detailed studies of the play, says:

> They [the Elizabethans] were . . . able to identify themselves with Richard while his author showed them the Superman; but all the while they anticipated the forthcoming destruction, and so were ready to step quietly out of his shoes into their own broad-toes ones, to make the best of two worlds which they were unable to choose between and lacked the philosophy to reconcile.[7]

This states the problem and a possible solution from the Elizabethan point of view, but it does not help a twentieth century reader to sort out his feelings. M. M. Reese sees the same problem but gives a different answer. Finding that "Richard . . . is too much of a monster—perhaps too much of a grotesque—to be taken altogether seriously," he nevertheless, and rather inconsistently, adds that "this will not diminish our pleasure in him as an entertainer," and concedes that "in the theatre it is difficult not to be on his side."[8] Unfortunately Reese does not divulge what he means by "to take seriously," "pleasure," or "on his side"—though the meanings are crucial to the problem he is discussing. Rossiter and Reese evidently see the difficulty—that the outrageously wicked Richard is the centre of energy and interest in the play—but neither has a satisfactory answer to the blunt but unavoidable question so raised: Do we in some sense *endorse* Richard's crimes? Nor does it really seem adequate to say, as L. C. Knights does of Marlowe's Barabas, that "through a half-complicity with him . . . we see how wicked the world is";[9] that "*half*-complicity" circles warily around the same problem. And it is not a problem peculiar to *Richard III*; it arises in any work of art in which the central figure is clearly presented as "bad"—in *Don Giovanni*, for instance, or *Boris Godunov*. But we cannot hope to solve the problem, or even pose it meaningfully, unless we take account of the sort of world that the work of art in question compels on us.

The world of *Richard III* is in fact highly distinctive. Negatively, we can define it by saying that it is the opposite of what we find in *Antony and Cleopatra*. Everyone notices the expansiveness of the latter: the action and imagery shift over vast areas of space; while the verse has a full swelling buoyancy. The world of *Richard III* is constricted ("tight" is Reese's excellent word[10]), sharply defined, without half lights or mystery. It is claustrophobic not only because it is small, but also because there is little implication of anything beyond it. It is no accident that prisons, both literal and figurative, bulk so large; phrases like "mewed up" or "franked up" are scattered throughout; the Tower of London and various castles and noble Houses figure prominently; while most of the scenes are clearly meant to take place indoors—*huis-clos*, we might say. It is a world where everyone is suspicious of everyone else, where faces are never the index of minds, where deception recedes in an infinite series, where the only truth is the chopper that chops off your head.

It will seem paradoxical to say that the play's atmosphere is the reverse of meta-physical when we remember the extraordinary number of references to God. God, indeed, is seldom off anyone's lips, least of all Richard's; and Richard is also fond of the Saints, particularly St. Paul. Yet we need only think of a play where religion is apprehended by the personae as a *mystery*—*Richard II*, for instance, or the explicitly pagan *King Lear*—to realise that the use made of "God" by the personae in *Richard III* is very different. Insofar as He is more than a convenient sanction for *Realpolitik*, He is apprehended in a sharply limited way, as a sort of tribal deity. It is unthinkable that anyone here should sound this kind of note:

> Not all the water in the rough rude sea
> Can wash the balm off from an anointed king;
> The breath of worldly men cannot depose
> The deputy elected by the Lord.   *(Richard II, III.ii.54-57)*

It is true that Richard III, trying to silence Queen Elizabeth and his mother, says:

> A flourish, trumpets! strike alarum, drums!
> Let not the heavens hear these tell-tale women
> Rail on the Lord's anointed: strike, I say!   *(IV.iv.149-151)*

But this is just another convenient formula which, even in the act of using it, Richard (we feel) has difficulty in taking seriously. "God" in *Richard III* is a highly jealous Old Testament figure whose main function is to bring curses to fruition. It is in this spirit that Queen Margaret invokes him:

> God I pray him,
> That none of you may live his natural age,
> But by some unlooked accident cut off!   *(I.iii.212-214)*

But since "God" is taken in vain so consistently, we cannot help feeling the strong-est dubiety when, in Act V, Richmond interlards his exhortations with pious ejaculations.

Again, when people in this play talk about the Succession, they usually do so in legalistic terms, like those Hastings uses:

> that I'll give my voice on Richard's side,
> To bar my master's heirs in true descent,
> God knows I will not do it, to the death.   *(III.ii.53-55)*

And the hypocritical arguments used by Buckingham in III.vii to win over the citizens all turn on the same principle of "true descent"; at no point is the divine aspect of kingship raised. When Queen Elizabeth upbraids Richard for breaking the promise he took before Edward IV, it is the contractual aspect of the oath she stresses:

> If thou didst fear to break an oath with Him [God],
> The unity the king my husband made
> Thou hadst not broken, nor my brothers died:
> If thou hadst feared to break an oath by Him,
> Th'imperial metal, circling now thy head,
> Had graced the tender temples of my child,
> And both the princes had been breathing here. . . .   *(IV.iv.379-385)*

When we turn back to the scene she refers to, where the nobles swore amity, we find King Edward taking what he imagines is a religious tone:

> Why, so: now have I done a good day's work.
> You peers, continue this united league:
> I every day expect an embassage
> From my Redeemer to redeem me hence;
> And more at peace my soul shall part to heaven,
> Since I have made my friends at peace on earth.   *(II.i.1-6)*

The lachrymose self-deception of Edward about what he has achieved on earth matches his startling assumption that he will go straight to heaven. His self-deception becomes even clearer if we come to *Richard III* from the *Henry VI* plays, for the pious reference to his Redeemer comes ill from a man who, we know, butchered Henry's son in cold blood. And we have gathered that since then he has lechered his way to exhaustion.

The frequent references to Charity and Conscience are similarly flat. Richard, in his wooing of Lady Anne, appeals twice to charity:

> Sweet saint, for charity, be not so curst,

and

> Lady, you know no rules of charity,
> Which renders good for bad, blessings for curses.   *(I.ii.49; 68-69)*

He attempts to silence Margaret with the same word, saying "Peace, peace! for shame, if not for charity,"[11] to which she replies:

> Urge neither charity nor shame to me:
> Uncharitably with me have you dealt,
> And shamefully by you my hopes are butchered.
> My charity is outrage, life my shame;
> And in that shame still live my sorrow's rage!   *(I.iii.273-278)*

Edward IV, on his death-bed, supposes himself to have done "deeds of charity" (II.i.50). The religious associations we attach to the word are, in all these cases,

34

heavily qualified by our knowledge of the speakers. The same is true of the references to "conscience" in III.vii; Buckingham may allege that Richard's refusal "argues conscience in your grace," and Richard may pretend that the whole proceeding is "against [his] conscience" (III.vii.174; 226), but we are by now well aware of the potentialities of "odd old ends stol'n forth of Holy Writ" (I.iii.337).

Only a couple of times does the play sound a deeper note—most obviously in Clarence's dream scene and with Richard towards the end of the piece. It is not for nothing that "Clarence's dream" should be one of the best-known speeches in *Richard III*; but both the play and the speech are denatured by the extraction. In its context it works potently to create eschatological terrors which show up the hollowness of the religious feelings presented elsewhere. It is immediately followed, we should note, by the murderers' uneasy discussion of Conscience, which in turn leads to the agonised debate between them and Clarence about law, justice and kinship. After Clarence has been killed, the second murderer utters the dismayed wish:

> How fain, like Pilate, would I wash my hands
> Of this most grievous murder! *(I.iv.272-273)*

From this moving note we pass straight to King Edward's self-indulgent religiosity, referred to above. The brooding sombreness of the Clarence scene[12] is taken up in V.iii, where Richard, also starting up from a bad dream, soliloquises about "coward conscience." But it is taken up with a considerable difference:

> What do I fear? myself? there's none else by.
> Richard loves Richard; that is, I am I.
> Is there a murderer here? No—yes, I am:
> Then fly. What, from myself? Great reason why—
> Lest I revenge. Myself upon myself?
> Alack, I love myself. For any good
> That I myself have done unto myself?
> O, no! Alas, I rather hate myself
> For hateful deeds committed by myself!
> I am a villain: yet I lie, I am not.
> Fool, of thyself speak well: fool, do not flatter. *(V.iii.182-192)*

At first sight this looks like a curious, and scarcely successful,[13] adaptation of the logic-chopping style employed in Richard's courting of Anne or Queen Elizabeth—

> Speak it again, and even with the word
> This hand, which, for thy love, did kill thy love,
> Shall, for thy love, kill a far truer love. *(I.ii.188-190)*

This elaborately witty style has established itself as pre-eminently Richard's—it is throughout the play his characteristic means of outwitting those whose minds are slower than his. Faced with a crisis of conscience, however, he can find no

35

other mode of self-expression: his mind is inadequate to its own moral dilemma. In any case the dilemma is, compared to Clarence's, superficial; Richard may say "My conscience hath a thousand several tongues" (V.iii.193), but "conscience" here involves mainly a feeling of uneasiness, not (as with Clarence) an awareness of damnation. Not long afterwards Richard, now himself again, confirms our impression of his inadequacy by contemptuously dismissing even such moral experience as did penetrate:

> Conscience is but a word that cowards use,
> Devised at first to keep the strong in awe:
> Our strong arms be our conscience, swords our law.   *(V.iii.309-311)*

The world of *Richard III,* then, is by and large the reverse of religious, in the sense in which I have used that term. So little eschatological is the atmosphere that, save at one or two points, there is no sense of a future, of a possible way out, of a means of paying moral debts and being free of guilt. The arrival of Richmond has more the air of a truce than of a victory. (This is not the case, or not intended to be, at the end of *Macbeth*: comparison points the contrast.)

The atmosphere which does emerge results partly from another feature of the play, mentioned above in passing. There is a continual atmosphere of suspicion, amounting at times to a sense of unreality. For one thing, people are always uttering dark threats against "some" whom they distrust —

> I was too hot to do somebody good,
> That is too cold in thinking of it now.   *(I.iii.311-312)*

or

> Well, Catesby, ere a fortnight make me older,
> I'll send some packing that yet not think on't.   *(III.ii.60-61)*[14]

For another, the lamenting women reinforce the sense of uncertainty by remembering the bloody past at great length, and thus making it a present fact: we are both caught in a rigid Ibsenesque determinism, and uncertain how it will manifest itself.

But the principal ingredient of the pervasive uncertainty is Richard's own histrionic talent, which several critics have noticed.[15] The diversity of the roles he assumes is truly astonishing. To Lady Anne he is the witty suitor, attractive in his very impudence, his inexhaustible fluency; to the Queen and her faction, the plain man wronged; to the murderers, the jovial employer; to Edward, in the reconciliation scene, first the humble and loving subject, then the outraged brother; to Buckingham and Stanley, at the end of the same scene, the moralising realist; to the young King, the genial but respectful uncle. Critics have made much of Richard's ruthlessness, but it needs to be said that his singular powers of dissimulation are coupled with an unusual sensitivity to people and atmospheres. He always finds just the right note to strike. Thus in the first scene of the play he exchanges bitter jokes with his brother Clarence, but with Hastings he adopts an earnest tone exactly suited to that naive soul — "'Tis very grievous to be thought upon." His awareness of other people has, in the best Hitlerian manner, an almost feminine subtlety. The list of roles he assumes is endless, but of course he finishes by deceiving even himself: his soliloquy in Act V shows that he is now unable to distinguish himself from the multiplicity of parts he has played. Indeed he can no longer distinguish a self at all, not at least until he returns to the daylight world in which he can "bustle."

Thus we have a situation in which on the one hand Richard is decidedly the play's centre of energy and interest, and on the other our complicity in his crimes is severely qualified by the very narrow limitations of his moral-dramatic being (as well as by our response to the sorrows of the lamenting women). So it is not a question of "identifying" ourselves with Richard up to a certain point in the action and thereafter dropping him and transferring our allegiance (like Stanley) to Richmond. It is a question of *how much* of ourselves we identify with Richard, and we are always conscious that he commands only a small part of our potential allegiance. Again there is a contrast with Macbeth, about whom we feel "There but for the grace of God. . . ." The quality of our response to Richard, together with the highly patterned writing and the stylised action, all mean that we take *Richard III* and its protagonist in a rather distanced way. It is Shakespeare's triumph that his "frame" is so exactly adequate to what it contains, that characters and themes never step out of the frame and by so doing wreck it.

There is perhaps one small exception: Tyrell, describing the death of the Princes in the Tower, indulges in some dubious sentimentalising:

> "Thus, thus," quoth Forrest, "girdling one another
> Within their alabaster innocent arms:
> Their lips were four red roses on a stalk,
> Which in their summer beauty kissed each other.
> A book of prayers on their pillow lay. . . ."   *(IV.iii.10-14)*

Just possibly some sort of irony is intended—the doomed heirs of York have lips like *red* (Lancaster-colour) roses; but one's main feeling is of discomfort, for the pathos is willed,[16] and the verse is all set to develop into one of those frigid games with words that disfigure so much of *Richard II*, where one sometimes feels Shakespeare has fallen victim to a kind of higher doodling. But what most often strikes us about *Richard III*, even outside the set speeches and well-known excerpts, is the perfection of the style within Shakespeare's self-imposed limitations. Take the following, for instance:

> Why, this it is, when men are ruled by women:
> 'Tis not the king that sends you to the Tower;
> My Lady Grey his wife, Clarence, 'tis she
> That tempers him to this extremity.
> Was it not she, and that good man of worship,
> Anthony Woodeville, her brother there,
> That made him send Lord Hastings to the Tower,

> From whence this present day he is delivered?
> We are not safe, Clarence, we are not safe. *(I.i.62-70)*

This is not memorable verse in the way that almost every line of greater Shakespeare plays is memorable; yet how delicately its rhythms hit off the particular persona that Richard is assuming at that moment; and—if we are looking for potentialities—how infinitely capable of development it is! Much of the writing in *Richard II*, on the other hand, represents a dead end, something that Shakespeare had to unlearn before he could go any further. Yet *Richard II* is a more popular play both with audiences and with examiners; partly, no doubt, because it is self-contained in a way that *Richard III* is not; and partly, too (one suspects) because its unevennesses and obscurities make it more "interesting" than the finished perfection of the earlier piece—though as a matter of fact *Richard II* does not make up for its messiness by any greater profundity, as I have tried to show elsewhere.[17]

Still, the phrase "finished perfection," in a Shakespearean context, suggests something more rich and penetrating than we find in *Richard III*, which is a triumph rather of the creative will than of the creative imagination—a triumph of that faculty which we find working so superbly in *Coriolanus*. In *Richard III* the distancing effect of the stylised, deliberate art means that the play is not a profoundly disturbing one; and our main criticism of it, when we think of it as the climax of the first tetralogy of Histories, must be that it is, perhaps, not disturbing *enough*. We could of course extract an extremely sombre vision of human life from the play, but it would be strictly a matter of *extracting*; as presented, its vision has little of the power to unsettle that we find in (say) *Measure for Measure*; and when we recall that there is in *Richard III* no Falstaff or his equivalent, we are inclined to comment that, as yet, Shakespeare's art lacks a whole dimension and that, though it is more complex than the "Tudor-moral" critics would have us believe, it is still relatively immature. But this need not prevent us from responding to the astonishing dexterity with which Shakespeare creates the play's distinctive world.[18]

Notes:

(1) I quote from the edition of *Richard III* in the New (Cambridge) series (2nd impression, London, 1961); where I question one of Dover Wilson's readings I say so. It is worth remarking that there are some odd things in this edition. The sd at IV.ii.115 should read not "goes" (which applies to Richard alone), but "exeunt all but Buckingham." At I.iii.41 the sd should not read "Enter Gloucester, Hastings, and Derby" but "Enter Gloucester, Hastings, and Dorset"; moreover, Dover Wilson's note alleges that the First Folio here reads "Enter Richmond," whereas in fact it reads "Enter Richard." There are impossible metrical knots at I.i.121, III.vii.29, IV.iv.95-96 and V.iii.151. All of these are repeated by the Signet Classics editor, who adds further metrical snarls of his own at II.i.114, IV.iii.19, V.iii.250 and V.iii.333 (Signet line-numbers).

(2) *Richard III*, Furness Variorum ed. (Philadelphia, 1908), p. 223.

(3) Dover Wilson inexplicably prints the feeble Quarto reading, "likelihood"—without comment. I follow F.1 and Peter Alexander's *The Tudor Shakespeare* (London, 1951).

(4)   Holinshed, 760/1, quoted in Dover Wilson, ed. cit., pp. 254-255 (my italics). Holinshed is here copying Hall: see Furness, ed. cit., p. 499.

(5)   Quoted in Furness, ed. cit., p. 498.

(6)   *The Cease of Majesty* (London, 1961), p. 212.

(7)   "The Structure of *Richard III*," *Durham University Journal*, XXXI (1938), 44-75; quotation from p.73. See also the title-essay in the same author's *Angel with Horns* (London, 1961).

(8)   *The Cease of Majesty*, pp. 217, 218.

(9)   *Further Explorations* (London, 1965), p. 93.

(10) *The Cease of Majesty*, p. 223.

(11) Both F.1 and Qq. assign this speech to Buckingham; Dover Wilson gives it to Richard. See Furness, ed. cit. p. 105, for a discussion. The ascription does not in any case affect my point.

(12) A. P. Rossiter notes (*Angel with Horns*, pp. 9-12) that Clarence's speech provides a *Leitmotif* which recurs in each of the play's "movements."

(13) Reese, for example (op. cit., p. 221), calls this "conscience" episode "uneasy" and "unconvincing."

(14) Cf. also the "some" at II.i.92, and the indefinite "those" and "them" at I.i.127-130 and I.iii.80-82.

(15) See for example *Angel with Horns*, pp. 16-19, and B. Spivack, *Shakespeare and the Allegory of Evil* (New York, 1958), pp. 386 ff.; and cf. the book mentioned in note 18, p. 89.

(16) In Heywood's *Edward IV* Tyrell also gets out of hand after the murder; but he is melodramatic, not sentimental (see *Edward IV*, Part II, III.v, ed. Field, Shakespeare Society [London, 1842]).

(17) See the present writer's "Who Deposed Richard the Second?" *Essays in Criticism*, XVII (1967), 411-433. Cf. also my two articles in *English Studies*, XLIX (1968), "Joan of Arc and *Henry VI*" and "*Henry VI* and the Ghost of Richard II."

(18) Since this article was first written I have read Dr. Wilbur Sanders's book *The Dramatist and the Received Idea* (Cambridge, 1968). It is gratifying to find some of my own ideas independently confirmed by so intelligent a critic.

Berowne and the Progress of Love's Labour's Lost

by Gates K. Agnew

I

Probably in the mid-1590's, possibly in revision of an earlier work, for an audience and occasion of which we have no record, Shakespeare wrote a play which still beggars description and flouts expectation.[1] It has not been popular with readers, lay or professional, and probably never will be. The reasons are not far to seek. It sacrifices the dramatist's familiar blank-verse conversations in favor of wit-combats and orations, which are cast in a profusion of metrical and stanzaic forms including lowly doggerel. It subordinates the customary progress of plotted events to a formal sequence of solo and ensemble set-pieces, which emphasize verbal rather than physical movement, thematic rather than narrative organization. Furthermore, this play exhibits a high proportion of characters who seem larger or smaller than real life, and it reflects in its language, with an immediacy unusual for Shakespeare, the colloquial and commonplace expressions of late Elizabethan culture.[2] Small wonder it is caviar to the general reader—whatever its real merits —and small wonder its merits should be subject to general skepticism in default of any clear appreciation of its novelty from generations of critics. Though it betrays affinities with most of the recently defined comic species, it cannot successfully be labeled and grasped as a festive comedy or "comicall satyre," or as a romantic or pastoral or five-act or happy or love-game comedy.[3] *Love's Labour's Lost* is a sort of theatrical *hapax legomenon,* a non-recurring dramatic structure of immense verbal ingenuity, built at a great expense of fanciful energy and characterized by its resistance to critical penetration from conventional perspectives. The general thesis of this paper is that *Love's Labour's Lost* achieves its special effect by flouting expectation, and that it is illuminating *because* it beggars conventional descriptions of comic drama. If this thesis is valid, we will have discovered an interesting new source-book for the study of Shakespeare's early development.[4]

That feature of *LLL* which more than any other sets it apart is Shakespeare's treatment of Berowne, the brilliant young scholar-courtier-lover of Navarre. His career determines the progress of the play hardly less than Gloucester's shapes the course of the early history play *Richard III.* Yet *LLL* is obviously an exercise in comedy rather than history, and Shakespearean comedy typically allows no such centrality to the male protagonist.[5] We are confronted, therefore, with a two-fold critical task. We must describe the peculiar assortment of traits which makes Berowne the most complex character created by Shakespeare before *Richard II,* and we must ask how the dramatist evaluates these traits and for what purpose he exploits them. Now it is one thing, and no easy task, to describe the consistency of mind and manner in Berowne; it is quite another to articulate what Shakespeare would have us make of this character as a major component of comedy. The question is how the ambivalent attractiveness of Berowne is sustained and given point within a particular dramatic context, and thus an analysis of his unconventional character necessarily leads to an examination of the "sophisticated" structure (to invoke Paul Goodman's terms)[6] which mediates between familiar expectations and the counter-conventional strategies of the dramatist. Berowne himself observes that *LLL* does not end in festive marriage "like an old play" (V.ii.864)[7]: I intend to argue that the play does not begin and does not proceed like "an old play" either, and that it does not because of Berowne's presence. This young man's mentality is the source of the play's deviation from conventional comic form, and it is therefore the appropriate starting point for our discussion; we will discuss subsequently the dramatic organization generated by Shakespeare's coming to terms with Berowne. We will find that *LLL* is organized as a vehicle for conveying Berowne and his admirers (i.e. the theater audience) from the ambivalent sphere of historical experience and psychological realism to the affirmative and symbolic realm of festive comedy.[8] Along the way we will also discover that the dramatic characteristics which have so often pre-empted the attention of readers — wittiness and verbal pyrotechnics, symmetrical patterning of character and event, and a persistent moralizing and intellectualizing strain — are integral to the dramatic vehicle which traces this unusual journey.

There are three characteristics or attributes which distinguish Berowne. Each of these three is more or less at odds with the conventional image of the youthful comic lover, and each therefore offers a point of reference for assessing Berowne's progress towards the realization of this traditional role over the course of the play. The first of these decisive characteristics is Berowne's loyalty and commitment to the company of young men who are variously called "vow-fellows" (II.i.38), "students" (II.i.64), "book-men" (II.i.227), "companions" (V.ii.93), and "gallants" (V.ii.126). This commitment or involvement has not always seemed clear because it is apparently at odds with Berowne's self-conscious iconoclasm and professed non-conformity during the opening scene, of which more later. Nevertheless, in his inauguration speech Navarre does address Berowne, Dumain, and Longaville indifferently as "fellow scholars" (I.i.17) whose oaths are already sworn to study together for three years. Even after his lengthy and accurate critique of the proposed academy, Berowne reiterates his obedience to this common pact, and again, at the very instant he prophesies the inevitability of its destruction because of the visitation of the French women, he subscribes his name "to the laws at large" (I.i.154). Later, when the young men mutually discover each other as "affection's men-at-arms" (IV.iii.287), Berowne is commissioned to justify their "sweet fellowship in shame" (IV.iii.49). He then joins them in the Masque of Muscovites and finally subjects himself with his fellows to the judgments of the women of France. The relish and enthusiasm with which he takes his place among the king's company vary markedly, from a low in the first scene to a high when he officiates at the metamorphosis of students into lovers in Act IV, Scene iii. But his own emphatic gesture of self-definition in subscribing to the oath despite every cavil, together

with his later actions and the unswerving testimony of the women and low characters: all establish Berowne's allegiance to the society of "brave conquerors" (I.i.8)
as a central attribute of his character. The significance of this loyalty as a deter-
minative factor in the frustration of the love-game is suggested obliquely by the
primacy which the Princess and Rosaline assign to solitude among the penances
prescribed for their lovers (V.ii.782-851).

Berowne's curious attachment to the company of Navarre is decisive and illuminating in that it symbolizes his identification with the desires and inclinations
of Navarre, Dumain, and Longaville. From one point of view, *LLL* is a play "about"
the worthiness of young courtiers in love, and Berowne is not distinguishable from
his companions in fitness as a lover. Yet in another sense, in sheer stature and
dramatic magnetism, Berowne is always more worthy than his fellows of our
interest and delight. His allegiance to the company of Navarre may be a telling
index of character, but it is his charismatic theatrical presence which initially
draws our attention and sets him apart from the other courtiers. Berowne alone
is a role player with a brilliant gift for disputation and a well-exercised self-consciousness. In any given situtation, his vow-fellows adhere inflexibly to a single
style, they are lacking in reflexive awareness, and they are virtually inseparable
in sentiment and temper. They are flat, plodding, stock figures; Berowne is a
vivacious, psychologically profound, three-dimensional portrait. They are always
viewed as at a distance or on the peripheries of the dramatist's attention; Berowne
lives in the main spotlight and invites, nay commands, the most intimate inspec-
tion.[9] As dramatic characters, Berowne and his three compatriots of Navarre
inhabit different levels of reality, and this divergence is not merely tolerated but
underscored and exploited by the dramatist. Yet whatever the dramatic force of
his individuality and iconoclasm, he may be quickly silenced by threat of excom-
munication from this company of faithful vow-men:

> *King.* Well, sit you out: go home, Berowne: adieu!
> *Ber.*   No, my good lord; I have sworn to stay with you.   *(I.i.110-111)*

What we find in Berowne is a marriage of an emancipated and subtle consciousness on one hand with the reflexes and promptings of a slavish votary on the other,
and this marriage is as provocative and interesting psychologically as it is paradoxical with reference to received convention regarding the comic lover.[10]

To describe Berowne in Rosaline's phrase as "another of these students" (II.i.64)
is thus to identify his motives and desires, but patently not his mannerisms or
dramatic personality, with those of the other young men. It is the second characterizing trait of Berowne that he shares with his fellows precisely the mentality
which is monumentally etched by Navarre in his opening summons to the heroic
quest, a mentality which nevertheless sanctions and supports his superiority to
Navarre, Dumain, and Longaville as a dramatic character:

> Let fame, that all hunt after in their lives,
> Live register'd upon our brazen tombs,

And then grace us in the disgrace of death;
When, spite of cormorant devouring Time,
Th' endeavour of this present breath may buy
That honour which shall bate his scythe's keen edge,
And make us heirs of all eternity.
Therefore, brave conquerors—for so you are,
That war against your own affections
And the huge army of the world's desires—
Our late edict shall strongly stand in force:
Navarre shall be the wonder of the world;
Our court shall be a little academe
Still and contemplative in living art.

(I.i.1-14)

We shall refer often to this speech because it is the central expression in *LLL* of that frame of mind which the dramatist pits against the affirmations of festive comedy. Suffice it here to observe that the young men of Navarre undertake a paradoxical venture which links a corporate, overtly moralistic self-assertion to an anxious preoccupation with death. As critics have pointed out, this academic retreat is a curious stratagem for acquiring the earthly renown Navarre seeks, particularly as it is undertaken to pursue a moral philosophy which declares war without nice distinctions on *all* desire—and that by young men who immediately prove themselves full of the most restless cravings and needs. This paradox and the rigidity of the king's moralizing are easily enough accounted for within the terms of comic tradition and Shakespearean practice: they suggest a conventional comic type, the *alazon* or boaster, in a variant form often used by Shakespeare, the kill-joy.[11]

The substance of the king's boasting, however, is not so readily explained with reference to customary comic tactics, much less those of romantic comedy. To be sure, the issues of fame and personal renown are not necessarily inappropriate to love comedy, for one of Shakespeare's favorite means of characterizing the young wooer, especially if he is to be pitted against an aggressively witty heroine, is to portray him emerging triumphant from heroic conquest at the outset of the play. But the protagonists in *LLL* seek fame to the exclusion of love by withdrawing from all feminine companionship. Their adversary is not a malevolent wrestler or a malicious brother but death itself, with time and "the huge army of the world's desires" thrown in for good measure. Indeed, their adversary is not death so much as the apprehension of death, and their enemy is (despite conventional expectation) not external but internal, and not a passive folly within (like Orsino's) but a force actively goading them to conquest: to become "the wonder of the world." In this figure of the young ruler reacting anxiously and aggressively to death with a rousing call to the hunt of fame, Shakespeare has chosen an ambivalent object of ridicule, and therein lies one secret of Berowne's peculiar charisma. The instant these young men cease seeming merely ridiculous—if such a moment is conceivable after the bathetic responses of Dumain and Longaville (I.i.24-32)—they will

43

come to seem pathetic or dangerous, or both. We value Berowne in large part because he arrives under the appearance of a traditional comic protagonist (in simplest terms, the festive *eiron*) to validate the audience's collective will to treat the academe *and* the mentality it reflects as the silliest stuff and nothing more. Yet Berowne is not what he seems. Having demonstrated in this first scene that he can subscribe to the king's vow while despising the academic project *per se*, he proceeds to reveal the domination of the king's mentality in the mounting of his own great enterprise. By degrees we come to realize that the soft hunt of love, which he champions from the first, is not a more "natural" alternative to the hard hunt of fame promulgated in the king's oration but merely an alternative expression of Navarre's main characterizing impulse, his self-assertion in reaction to the felt presence of oblivion in "the disgrace of death."[12] In other words, through Berowne the fame-seekers' mentality comes to pervade the wooing game and results directly in the delay of its consummation for reasons directly stated by the Princess:

> And out of question it is sometimes,
> Glory grows guilty of detested crimes,
> When for fame's sake, for praise, an outward part,
> We bend to that the workings of the heart.   *(IV.i.30-33)*

Closer examination discloses how intimately related are the motives and impulses underlying the double hunt—Navarre's hunt of fame and Berowne's hunt of love—in *LLL*, and how completely the ethos of the hunt shapes and controls the actions of the young men. The courtiers' pursuit of self-preserving or saving "merit" (conventional sixteenth-century theology is generally employed in *LLL* as psychological metaphor)[13] is diverted from the intellectual endeavor of stoicizing moral philosophy, evoked in Navarre's summons to the study of "living art," to the fashionable manipulation of platonizing amatory lore, as celebrated in Berowne's equivocating oration at the close of Act IV, Scene iii. "Th' endeavour of this present breath" which Navarre trusts to buy him a reprieve from oblivion is always a learned endeavour in *LLL*, whether its text be the Anglican Service of Baptism from the Book of Common Prayer or a little book of sonnets inspired by the success of Sidney's *Astrophel and Stella* published in 1591.[14] The love-game is no less a bookish fray than the projected war against affection and desire, to the extent that C. L. Barber would find the sole cause of the lovers' frustration in their habit of making love "by the book" (*Festive Comedy*, p. 93). The transformation of the pursuit of saving merit in *LLL* coincides with the identification of a new audience and object of the quest, not with any alteration in the questing spirit itself. The king's ambition, appropriately announced in imperatives, is that "Navarre shall be the wonder of the world" (I.i.12), and nothing less than the world will suffice to validate Navarre's heroic deeds. Berowne domesticates this ambition, substituting for the world a social coterie as milieu of his triumph, at first the young men themselves and later the coterie of the young women of France. Compared with Navarre's incredible aggrandizement of the world's esteem, Berowne's manipulation of audience is conceived in realistic and manageable terms and carried out with evident success for a time. After all, Berowne does win the theater audience's admiration as well as his fellows', and as all actors know, the esteem of an audience in a theater is an effective surrogate of the world's esteem.

Learning is, in other words, the weapon employed by the hunters after self-preserving fame and the common instrument of both aggression and defense, whether it manifests itself as the oratorical bombast with which Navarre seeks to outface death or the mocking jests which are Berowne's stock in trade. In both cases, demeaning others or putting them down turns out to be inseparable from the practice of enhancing a threatened self through verbal dexterity. Merit or worth is a relative matter to the young men (and to Berowne in particular). Learning appeals to the young men as to the pedant in the low plot as a means to be "singled from the barbarous" (V.i.76-77), and knowledge is thus defined negatively as the perception of "Things hid and barr'd . . . from common sense [i.e. from ordinary understanding]" (I.i.57).[15] Even Berowne's incisive ridiculing of the king's academy is but a whimsical strategy for preening his own feathers at his companions' expense, not an assertion of truth. He obstructs the progress of the oath in the first scene only so he can crow: "I have for barbarism spoke more / Than for that angel knowledge you can say" (I.i.12-13)—and this suggests another reason he can so facilely subscribe to the king's vow. In what Berowne calls "the kingly state of youth" (IV.iii.290), self-magnification takes the precedence of both fellowship and truth, and Berowne requires the society of others all the more urgently *because* of his instinct for self-assertion. Hence Berowne displays the mentality of Navarre, with its anxiety to escape obscurity through achieving fame and reputation, in the very act of debunking that "little academe, / Still and contemplative in living art" (I.i.13-14) which is the first-fruits of that mentality. Dull indeed is the member of the audience who is not thoroughly wedded to the fortunes of Berowne after the long first scene, but dullness appears a virtue (as Dull appears a virtuous character) when Berowne's most seductive trait, the liberal, critical spirit which is the enemy of all pretense, proves to be itself a sophisticated manifestation of the king's urge to be "the wonder of the world." Berowne, a member of the king's company, is a hunter after fame at the expense of the king's company (and potentially the women of France), and no less at the expense of any audience which accepts him as restorer of the comic equilibrium threatened in the opening scene by the solemn, ridiculous posturing of the other young men.

There is an incident in Act IV, Scene iii which illustrates the nature of Berowne's habitual self-assertion and foreshadows the impact it will have on the hunt of love in a manner technically characteristic of *LLL*. In this scene the unmasking of Berowne by Costard unites the four courtiers in eager anticipation of the assault on their maiden visitors. Just before Berowne's notorious idealizing justification of that assault, which brings IV.iii to its conclusion, Shakespeare inserts a wit-combat demonstrating that no mere proof of hypocrisy or apostasy can alter Berowne's habitual manipulation of his friends. The revelation that the courtiers are all in love but forms a new prelude to an old tune, Berowne now setting out to argue the vastly superior beauty of his dark-hued Rosaline. On this occasion, however, the vow-fellows return his verbal thrusts with interest, forcing Berowne into ignominious retreat ("I'll prove her fair, or talk till doomsday here" [IV.iii.271]), and they finally break off the interchange with a scurrilous jest which offers a startling and outrageous image of Berowne's perspective in the love-game. (As in Berowne's debunking of "angel knowledge" during the first scene, *their* purpose is more the exertion of power through words than the regarding of the truth in their own utterance; the rapprochement of the vow-men occurs under the aegis of the Berowne-spirit.) Longaville's comparison of Rosaline's complexion and the blackness of his shoe is lamely returned by Berowne, whose cheaply idealizing hyperbole earns from Dumain a conclusive and memorable retort:

> *Ber.* O! if the streets were paved with thine eyes,
>   Her feet were much too dainty for such tread.
> *Dum.* O vile! then, as she goes, what upward lies
>   The street should see as she walk'd overhead. *(IV.iii.275-278)*

Dumain's indecorous image is peculiarly disruptive to the ethos of romantic comedy in a way Shakespeare well understood—this is not a case of mere exuberant excess. Setting a young woman on a pedestal only to peak furtively beneath her skirts leaves quite a different impression from the most palpable bawdy of a Touchstone or a Falstaff and it is an impression well suited to the dramatist's purpose in *LLL*. Rosaline is exalted by Berowne in pursuit of self-exaltation, she is slandered by his fellows in their own self-defense, and both initiative and response tend to reduce her to the status of an object or counter to be manipulated. The young men are not passively ignorant of Rosaline; in the interest of the game they actively purge their conversation of real awareness of her as a distinct self. Surely it is because Berowne knows as little of Rosaline as the king knows of the world that he can be so ludicrously and surprisingly slow to plumb her disguise during the Masque of Muscovites.[16] He has no clue to her identity once she has obscured her dark countenance and exchanged with the Princess the tokens of praise conferred by their lovers. Berowne remains a stranger to her singular identity because "Th' endeavour of this present breath" is largely consumed in the protection and enhancement of his own singular identity.

Berowne's mocking wit is, of course, his third major defining characteristic. There is a darkness in this wit which corresponds to the blackness of Rosaline's beauty: in both cases unconventionality is a prime source of attraction and that attraction is felt to be ambivalent. Exuberance and facility of mind, in conjunction with an exceptionally active self-consciousness, are essential features of Berowne's public self, and they are manifested par excellence in the activity of wittiness. Before Costard appears at I.i.180, the first scene of *LLL* is mainly devoted to an exhibition of the wit which proceeds from this energy and mental dexterity, and at this juncture Berowne's word-games and the traits they express are apparently endowed with a normative value. He is sufficiently attuned to the desires of young men to revile asceticism and the pretensions it serves, and he does so with a vivacity and liberality of spirit which seem the very stuff of festive comedy

(I.i.36-93). This is the side of Berowne's wit, as we have suggested, which extorts admiration from the most unwilling audience and stirs the more enthusiastic to identify him as a dramatic portrait of Shakespeare himself—or better yet, of the man Shakespeare would like to have been.[17] The enchanting powers of Berowne's wit are celebrated very fully in Rosaline's early eulogistic portrait of her beloved:

> Berowne they call him; but a merrier man,
> Within the limit of becoming mirth,
> I never spent an hour's talk withal:
> His eye begets occasion for his wit;
> For every object that the one doth catch
> The other turns to a mirth-moving jest,
> Which his fair tongue, (conceit's expositor)
> Delivers in such apt and gracious words
> That aged ears play truant at his tales,
> And younger hearings are quite ravished;
> So sweet and voluble is his discourse.   *(II.i.66-76)*

In this passage, Rosaline refers at some length to the process of wittiness, and where she explicitly refers to the tongue (speech) as that which shows forth rational activity ("conceit's expositor"), the whole speech is based on the commonplace stoic assumption that speech is the index of the mind or "character": "Language most shewes a man: Speake, that I may see thee."[18] Rosaline's appraisal of the nature and purpose of Berowne's wit is therefore intimately related, indeed virtually equated with her appraisal of him.

There is another side to Berowne's word-play, however, and also another verbal portrait in which Rosaline delineates the character of her suitor. This one is uniformly condemnatory:

> Oft have I heard of you, my Lord Berowne,
> Before I saw you; and the world's large tongue
> Proclaims you for a man replete with mocks,
> Full of comparisons and wounding flouts,
> Which you on all estates will execute
> That lie within the mercy of your wit.   *(V.ii.831-836)*

In this estimate, Berowne is still given credit for a "fruitful brain," but the fruit is wormwood which must be weeded out. What had seemed vivacious, facile, and liberating in juxtaposition to Navarre's academe (and it is with reference to that context that we respond to Rosaline's initial praise of Berowne) appears self-defeating, equivocal, and even offensive within the realm of the love-game. I suggest that this appraisal begins to emerge as early as Act II, Scene i, when Berowne prowls about the stage challenging the women of France during the first confrontation of lords and ladies, fewer than forty lines after Rosaline's speech of praise (II.i.114-128, 180-193). Despite his admirable insouciance, Berowne's manner is intrusive, his words burdened with innuendo and tinged with polite scorn:

> *Ber.* Lady, I will commend you to mine own heart.
> *Ros.* Pray you do my commendations; I would be glad
>   to see it.
> *Ber.* I would you heard it groan.
> *Ros.* Is the fool sick?
> *Ber.* Sick at the heart.
> *Ros.* Alack! let it blood.
> *Ber.* Would that do it good?
> *Ros.* My physic says, ay.
> *Ber.* Will you prick't with your eye?   *(II.i.180-189)*

He is already something of a swaggerer on the make (and already meeting his match in Rosaline), and as such he plays the role of a male type which Shakespeare carefully prohibits from the forest of Arden or wood of Athens.

There are two formal evaluations by Rosaline of Berowne's wittiness, but there is only one character named Berowne, and if he is a complex character he is not schizophrenic. It is not Berowne's words and actions which alter or develop in the course of *LLL* but our angle of perception which the dramatist changes, together with (and through) Rosaline's. In fact Berowne's jesting is *never* unequivocal and non-exploitative though our awareness of this truth comes mainly in retrospect.

It is worth returning momentarily to the first scene to judge the ambivalence of Berowne's wittiness at the instant it shines to greatest advantage. We have suggested that he champions "barbarism" there explicitly to put down his fellows, but this deprecation of solemn learning also contributes to the advancement of Berowne's own version of fame's quest, the pursuit of "green geese":

> *King.* How well he's read, to reason against reading!
> *Dum.* Proceeded well, to stop all good proceeding!
> *Long.* He weeds the corn, and still lets grow the weeding.
> *Ber.*   The spring is near, when green geese are a-breeding.
> *Dum.* How follows that?
> *Ber.*   Fit in his place and time.
> *Dum.* In reason nothing.
> *Ber.*   Something then in rhyme.   *(I.i.94-99)*

Berowne's preference for wine, women, and song over the lugubrious conditions of the projected academe is gratifying as well as delightful because it validates our comic expectations. But his preference also foreshadows and facilitates the transition from the academe to the wooing game as vehicle of the hunt of fame, and it is this transition which Rosaline later describes as "gravity's revolt to wantonness" (V.ii.74). In place of the academic quest, Berowne would substitute a preoccupation with "green geese . . . a-breeding"—with special emphasis on the rhyme word "a-breeding"—and lest this reference to green geese remain equivocal, Shakespeare repeats it obtrusively during the episode in Act IV, Scene iii

48

where the shift from learning to loving is completed. Berowne's censure of Longaville's sonnet applies to all of the lovers' verses, including his own:

> This is the liver-vein, which makes flesh a deity,
> A green goose a goddess; pure, pure idolatry.
> God amend us, God amend! we are much out o' th' way.   *(IV.iii.72-74)*

The impulse which makes flesh a deity betrays the presence in the love-game of
the fame-seeker's mentality, and the wit-combat which follows on the subject of
Rosaline's beauty further explores the same theme as we have seen. Because
uncertain of their own value, the young men are skeptical of all value; whether
woman is flesh merely or deity itself is a matter to be determined by pure assertion.
So Berowne seeks and supposes he has found a green goose, a "wanton . . . that
will do the deed / Though Argus were her eunuch and her guard" (III.i.193-196).
The consequences are hardly less threatening to him (he fears she will cuckold
him[19]) than to the love-game.

The ambivalence of Berowne's wit may be traced to two sources, and Berowne's
judgment of Longaville's sonnet illustrates both of them. Berowne speaks in the
first person plural when passing his judgment: "we are much out o' th' way."
A moment later he explains he is sitting aloof "like a demi-god . . . in the sky" to
supervise ("o'er-eye") his fellows' wretched secrets (IV.iii.76-79). From on high
Berowne watches them betray the urges which make a mockery of their oaths,
yet he is no less guilty than they, and he is aware of that fact. Thus his scornful
deprecation of the others is also a gesture of self-contempt, and the whole interlude
constitutes an externalized dramatization of the conflict between consciousness
and desire which characterizes the soliloquy prefacing the unmasking process.
In that soliloquy as in the little symbolic drama which follows (IV.iii.21-208),
Berowne arraigns, cajoles, and then expediently capitulates to his own erotic
inclinations:

> The king he is hunting the deer; I am coursing myself:
> they have pitched a toil; I am toiling in a pitch,—
> pitch that defiles: defile! a foul word. Well, set thee
> down, sorrow! for so they say the fool said, and so say
> I, and I the fool: well proved, wit! By the Lord, this
> love is as mad as Ajax: it kills sheep, it kills me,
> I a sheep: well proved again o' my side! I will not love;
> if I do, hang me; i' faith, I will not. O but her eye,—
> by this light, but for her eye, I would not love her;
> yes, for her two eyes. Well, I do nothing in the world
> but lie, and lie in my throat. By heaven, I do love, and
> it hath taught me to rhyme, and to be melancholy; and
> here is part of my rhyme, and here my melancholy. Well,
> she hath one o' my sonnets already; the clown bore it,
> the fool sent it, and the lady hath it: sweet clown,

sweeter fool, sweetest lady! By the world, I would
not care a pin if the other three were in. Here comes
one with a paper: God give him grace to groan! *(IV.iii.1-20)*

Much in this remarkable passage deserves commentary: its reminiscences of
Shakespeare's Richard III and Sidney's Astrophel, the salacious play on "eye,"
the reveling of the rational consciousness in logic's humiliation by desire, the
predictability of the retreat to love melancholy, and the sincerity as well as ironic
resignation evident in the new commitment.[20] Its tone is of special interest since
it is never totally missing from Berowne's wittiness whether in his early posings
as the festive *eiron* or his later performance as the prostrate, peccant wooer. It is
a tone compounded of many simples: self-ridicule, frustration, as well as exuberance and pride in the ability to cope; moreover its mixedness becomes increasingly
evident as the play progresses, echoing the profound servitude to anxiety and
erotic necessity which is not obscured by Berowne's facade of independent volition and rational integrity.

The ambivalence of Berowne's wit, therefore, derives in part from the origins
of his carping spirit in a critical self-consciousness. He knows his fellows to the
extent that he knows himself, and he can convert that knowledge into power over
them. Another source of this ambivalent effect of Berowne's wit lies in the fact
that despite his apparent clairvoyance, he demonstrates little access to truths
not appropriable by this self-consciousness—which is itself compromised. Self-
consciousness and self-knowledge are not identical and they may be mutually
exclusive (especially in the simplified perspective of the drama): this recognition
is critical to a balanced response to *LLL*. The discrepancy between them is visible
in Berowne's incapacity to comprehend why the women of France cannot transform the wooing sport into a comedy during the fading moments of the play, and in
Berowne's inability to distinguish between objective truths of experience and the
useful truths he has created through witty use of language, as in his appeals to
plainness and simplicity of thought and deed during the final scene (V.ii.402-415;
743-766). In particular the prophetic pessimism Berowne exhibits at the conclusion of each major scene cannot logically be construed as the insight of genuine
wisdom. He anticipates the Masque of Muscovites, for example, with justifiable
foreboding—and only he among the young men does so:

> Sow'd cockle reap'd no corn;
> And justice always whirls in equal measure:
> Light wenches may prove plagues to men forsworn;
> If so, our copper buys no better treasure. *(IV.iii.380-383)*

Yet this prognostication proves to be hardly more than a resigned attempt to mute
the sting of anticipated disaster by celebrating the inexorability of that doom.
Certainly it is without measurable influence on his own conduct, and Berowne
finally stands totally dumbfounded at the unyielding determination of his mistress
to send him away. Again, his precocious prophecy that "Necessity will make us

all forsworn" (I.i.148) is powerless to relieve him from the toils of a youthful necessity which is indeed "not by might mastered"—not even the might of his acute self-conscious intellect—"but by special grace" (I.i.148-151). That grace—spite of pride—arrives with the women of France.

Berowne is, then, a member of the king's company, which means he is a votary to the cause of building life-preserving monuments to a self threatened by the disgrace of death. Initially these are monuments of verbal wit erected at the expense of his fellow votaries whom he "whips" for effect. Berowne is also a seeker after reputation who attempts to buy a reprieve from oblivion by making a name for himself in the soft hunt of erotic love. (The image of the commercial transaction, buying and selling, often reappears after Navarre's opening employment of it.)[21] He is, finally, a mocking wit whose double-edged tone betrays a sense of involvement in all the folly he despises; whose power of insight, falling short of the wisdom of self-knowledge, is impotent before the sway of necessity, whether erotic or purely psychic. On each of these three counts, the progress Berowne makes during *LLL* is negligible. His progress from audience to audience, from compatriots ripe for gulling to the visiting maidens seemingly ripe for putting down, effects a revelation but not a development of character—although there is certainly development in the response of the theater audience towards Berowne. That he loves Rosaline is true enough, and his final, self-compromising appeal to "Honest plain words" (V.ii.743ff) is pathetic rather than calculating in its inexorable drift from blank verse to rhyme, from humble sincerity to ostentation. He loves Rosaline, but his soliloquies indicate the vacillating manner in which he entertains that love. He is bold and frightened, contemptuous and self-pitying, frankly delighted and dismally resigned. His ambivalent "mounting mind" (to borrow the Princess' pun [IV.i.4]) is both attracted and threatened by the new form of obscurity which he perceives in the bland, undifferentiated, four-square mentality of the conventional romantic protagonist and also in the rigors of serving a Rosaline, to whom Berowne naturally ascribes the will-to-power which motivates his own actions.

II

In Thomas Mann's *Dr. Faustus*, the brilliant Adrian Leverkühn and his friend Serenus Zeitbloom Ph.D. understand the main protagonist of *LLL* in strikingly different terms.[22] In his oratorio based on Shakespeare's comedy, the young composer conceives of Berowne as a "grave" young man who is given to "embittered self-castigation" in soliloquies which are "half lyrically passionate and half burlesque" in tone and intention. To the academician, Berowne is the "sharp-tongued, merry" young man—and no more. From the foregoing analysis it seems proper to conclude that both Leverkühn and Zeitbloom are correct in what they perceive, and both mistaken in the exclusiveness of their judgments. I think we are justified in coming to a similar conclusion about the disagreement of critics over the more fundamental issue concerning the relative significance of character and characterization in *LLL*. John Dover Wilson, for example, claims the play is "deficient in characterization" and H. B. Charlton notes what he calls an "indifference to character"; however, T. M. Parrott argues that it is precisely "in the field of characterization" that *LLL* surpasses the other early comedies.[23] The fact is that there is evidence to support both sides of the argument again. We have observed how the very shallowness and sketchiness of the characterization accorded to Navarre, Longaville, and Dumain provide the dramatist with a necessary context and mechanism for the revelation of Berowne's grave, merry character; yet we have also seen that the four young men, despite discrepancies in development as dramatic characters (Berowne far outshining the others), share a complex mentality in common. In other words, the young men of this comedy "have the deeper parts for once"[24] and one of the results is an extremely sophisticated management of characterization, ranging across the spectrum from the stock type to the so-called three-dimensional, individualized personality. Our task now is to show what Shakespeare makes "for once" of his young heroes through an innovating re-deployment of the elements of the drama. The first step is a brief introduction to the curious structure of *LLL*, followed by a discussion of the roles played by the women of France, by the low-plot Worthies, and finally by the debate songs of Spring and Winter.

We have proposed that it is Shakespeare's intention in *LLL* to celebrate the Berowne-spirit and then subordinate it to the festive comic spirit — somehow without violating the integrity of either. The dramatist pours his energies almost impartially into two conflicting movements, towards clarification of a realistic impasse, yet also toward resolution of that impasse. These two movements are made to dwell together in dissonant harmony, and the dramatic structure which supports this process is as striking as it is unique among Shakespeare's plays, exhibiting two special features. It provides for an oblique revelation of dramatic truth, and it also provides for a progressive validation of that dramatic truth.[25] By "dramatic truth" I refer to that sense of meaning and value which is affirmed by the whole dramatic experience and which guides the audience's final appraisal of discrete elements of the drama. (The dramatic truth of comedy, and particularly early comedy, is by nature definite if not easily definable.) The constant recourse to oblique revelation in *LLL* accounts for the impression of "open-endedness" it seems to foster;[26] the progressive validation of this revelation explains how Shakespeare can dwell so heavily on ambivalence without finally resigning the tough coherence of comic form or the reassuring definitiveness of comic truth. As suggested earlier in this paper, the combination of these two features betrays an unusual relationship between the play and its audience. The presentation of Berowne seems calculated to charm and dazzle an audience into an enthusiastic and enduring identification with his values and desires. Only progressively and by indirection are we then brought to a twofold realization: that his brilliance is self-defeating and that he is no worthy lover being the very thing he scorns, a votary of Navarre's self-instituted hunt after fame. Lord Hamlet would have spied in *LLL* a comic-satiric version of his own "Mousetrap," with which Shakespeare sets out to catch the conscience of his audience and amend it.

One further comment on general structure will suffice. Because *LLL* does not begin or end like an old comedy, the most ordinary descriptive terminology often gives a misleading impression of its shape and substance, and quite obscures the inductive nature of its progress. Thinking of the play in terms of acts and scenes is a continuing source of erroneous assumptions because of the enormous variation in the length of scenes and in the number of scenes in each act. According to the New Arden text, the last of nine scenes in *LLL* constitutes more than one-third of the entire play, four times the length of either the second or third acts *in toto*, each of a single scene. The unmasking episode of Act IV, Scene iii represents not as one supposes the penultimate incident in the play but rather the play's arithmetic center, and those who buttress their case for extensive revisions in the low plot by pointing to the lateness of Holofernes' initial appearance neglect to mention that his introduction, though in Act IV, Scene ii, falls well within the first half of the play.[27] It is more correct to think of *LLL* as a play in nine scenes, weighted in length toward the odd-numbered (which focus on the courtly lovers), and dominated by a concluding scene which is half as long as the other eight together and which alone makes sense of those eight scenes in a rather unorthodox fashion. For until the last scene we cannot claim to know what will happen at the conclusion of *LLL*, and events of the first eight scenes certainly produce few certainties to support conventional expectations. A clown is punished for making love to his willing wench, and his judges transgress their own edict to make love to recalcitrant maidens. A visiting princess refuses to acknowledge her indebtedness to a young king, then gracefully proceeds to repay his debt-ridden love with charity. Flamboyant braggarts use words and people until a benevolent ? intervenes and letters and speeches come home to shed ridicule on them. A votary of fame disdains his fellows for being votaries of fame, a pedant arrogantly criticizes a pedantically fashionable poem, and a band of doubtfully worthy players prepares to entertain a doubtfully worthy audience of young men and their strangely defensive ladies. These are strands of a knot which only the last scene can untie, and the one predictable, familiar certainty we greet in that scene of *LLL* is the centrality finally accorded there to the women of France, to whom we now turn.

From their first appearance, the Princess and her ladies show themselves to be similar to the young lovers in the mode of their conduct but essentially unlike them in the mentality informing that conduct. The young women too are brought on stage with a peal of fame's trumpets, yet their entrance has little in common with Navarre's in the first scene. Indeed Shakespeare uses Boyet's opening exhortation to the Princess (II.i.1-12) as an occasion for her express repudiation of "the general world" and its opinion which Navarre so assiduously courts. This repudiation proceeds by isolating and debunking the motives of a self-flattering speaker, a tactic we have already learned to admire in Berowne:

> *Prin.* Good Lord Boyet, my beauty, though but mean,
> Needs not the painted flourish of your praise:
> Beauty is bought by judgment of the eye,

Not utter'd by base sale of chapmen's tongues.
I am less proud to hear you tell my worth
Than you much willing to be counted wise
In spending your wit in the praise of mine. *(II.i.13-19)*

This gracefully bantering reply—how controlled and self-assured in contrast to Navarre's rhetoric!—succinctly portrays the ethical character of the Princess in antithesis to the academe-builders' mentality. She not only understands but enjoys what Boyet is doing in flattering her, and her clarity of perception marks the difference between self-awareness and Berowne's self-consciousness. She enjoys Boyet because she is a proud woman, but she will neither allow her pride to be used, as shown in this incident, nor will she use others for the sake of her pride. The latter fact Shakespeare prominently establishes during the Princess' next appearance on stage when she explicitly brands as heretical the notion that beauty can be "saved by merit," in this instance the palpable merit of a purse bestowed on the Forester (IV.i.9-23).

The Princess' characterizing interchanges with Boyet and the Forester are surprisingly intricate and demand a closer attention than we can afford them. Yet is is clear and sufficient for our purposes that rather than exercises in self-aggrandizement or self-abnegation (or one through the other), they are premeditated[28] gestures of moral self-definition which evince neither self-righteousness nor disdain of worldly "endeavors." The Princess is skeptical of motives but she is also a worthy and beautiful creature, and she knows it. She manifestly appreciates ability to cope in the world, no sooner doffing the cap of humility than boldly enlisting Boyet's "worthiness" as a "fair-moving solicitor" for the diplomatic contest with Navarre. When she rebuffs the Forester it is only after she has patiently milked a compliment from him; yet in rebuffing him she also dramatizes the subordination of her own instinct for fame's praise. The Princess and by association her three companions are young women confident of their prerogatives, beautiful, and witty, and very humanly eager to be reminded of their place, their beauty, and their wit—all in all not unlike Berowne at his most attractive. But they are also possessed of a radical humility and self-knowledge which set them apart from the anxious young men. Shakespeare's complex task is to show how the women operate with these advantages within a mode of conduct established by the young men (the wit-combat) in order to offer their lovers, in thrall to the disgrace of death, a new *modus vivendi*.

Boyet's flattery and the Princess' two-fold response, parry and riposte, constitute a model for the interaction of lords and ladies later in Act II, Scene i and throughout the high plot of *LLL*. Masculine self-assertion is met with counter-assertion in such a way that the source of the original assertion is identified and ministered to while its object remains inviolate. The proud, omnicompetent courtier asserts himself in summoning the Princess to her duty; she parries and places his assertion but also grants lavish praise and dispatches him to exercise his competence. As a parting fillip she describes Boyet's expressed pride of service as "willing pride," and hardly has the king arrived a few lines later than the same motif is sounded in the parry and riposte of the wit-combat:

> King. Hear me, dear lady; I have sworn an oath.
> Prin. Our Lady help my lord! he'll be forsworn.
> King. Not for the world, fair madam, by my will.
> Prin. Why will shall break it; will, and nothing else.[29]   (II.i.97-100)

The pride of the young men, unlike that of their feminine visitors, is always "willing pride," and "will" does in fact account for the breaking of their oaths, whether we interpret it generally as ambition or more narrowly as sexual desire.[30] It must be emphasized that Shakespeare and the Princess are not just moralizing here at the expense of the young men: "will" itself is not simply evil but a morally ambivalent quantity, the efficient cause of both the aspiring academic vow (which is, of course, offensive to the young women) and its destruction. Nevertheless, the "will" that breaks Navarre's oath perpetuates a state of mind which leads to another recantation of vows, this time involving the women directly (V.ii.431-58), and transforms the love game into a hunt where the choice is between killing and maiming. Thus the Princess turns from the Forester in IV.i and addresses herself to the hunt with these words:

> Prin.   now mercy goes to kill,
> And shooting well is then accounted ill.
> Thus will I save my credit in the shoot:
> Not wounding, pity would not let me do't;
> That more for praise than purpose meant to kill.   (IV.i.24-29)

In the next scene Holofernes and Nathaniel will disagree over the sex of the quarry in the nobles' deer hunt (IV.ii.1-48), but both are right. The Princess tests herself in the role of the "suitor" (pronounced "shooter" at the Globe Theater[31]) in order that we, the audience, may have a fast point of reference for judging the impulses of the young men when two scenes later they become suitors in the hunt of love. She and her companions are the hunted and the hunters both, and their purpose in the hunt, which is something akin to the "marriage of true minds" Shakespeare celebrates in Sonnet 116, precludes a direct and explicit confrontation between the wooers and their judges. The exile of the lovers is the last and conclusive riposte delivered by the women, giving life by killing the courtiers' willful preoccupation with death, and the entrance of Marcade is Shakespeare's device for accomplishing this salutary disengagement.

The role of the women in the long final scene reveals the shift in audience perspective which Shakespeare effects in the course of *LLL*. The inauguration of Navarre's academic hunt had been without any prelude, without context or preparation. The audience is forced to provide *its own* standards of value and credibility. When, however, we arrive at the consummation of fame's hunt as translated into the romantic-sexual chase, we are carefully provided by the dramatist with a context and a well-developed frame of reference. Although in an important sense the first eight scenes of *LLL* form a preparation for the judgment denouement of the ninth scene, the lengthy prelude to the Masque of Muscovites has a crucial function, all the more so considering the degree of ambivalence fostered in those previous scenes. So it is of special significance that Shakespeare focuses narrowly on the four maidens of France at the beginning of Act V, Scene ii, as they verbally shadow-box together and then ready themselves for the onslaught of the Muscovites. Far from adhering to the men's point of view established earlier, Shakespeare now puts the women on stage alone for the first and only time in the play. Even Boyet, Berowne surrogate that he is, is absent from their discussion until sent in by the dramatist to herald the impending invasion. This prelude has three distinct movements, the last of which is the making of a compact to gull the young men by transferring identities (V.ii.79-156). The first is a "set of wit well play'd," a flurry of badinage at the expense of the wooers' love offerings. It is the range of tones which is arresting in this first interlude, from brittle insouciant mockery to the startling touch of pathos which a reference to Cupid produces. Rosaline tells us Cupid has been responsible for the death of Katherine's sister, and the brief history and moral which Katherine subsequently relates illustrate the proximity of solemnity and frivolity in their wit-play.[32]

> *Kath.* He made her melancholy, sad, and heavy;
> And so she died: had she been light, like you,
> Of such a merry, nimble, stirring spirit,
> She might ha' been a grandam ere she died;
> And so may you, for a light heart lives long.
>
> *Ros.* What's your dark meaning, mouse, of this light word?
>
> *Kath.* A light condition in a beauty dark. *(V.ii.14-20)*

After the Princess brings this movement to a formal close ("We are wise girls to mock our lovers so"), Rosaline briefly rejoices over Berowne's envisioned prostration before her, and we come to the central passage of this preparation for the Masque of Muscovites:

> *Prin.* None are so surely caught, when they are catch'd
> As wit turn'd fool: folly, in wisdom hatch'd,
> Hath wisdom's warrant and the help of school
> And wit's own grace to grace a learned fool.
>
> *Ros.* The blood of youth burns not with such excess
> As gravity's revolt to wantonness.
>
> *Mar.* Folly in fools bears not so strong a note
> As foolery in the wise, when wit doth dote;
> Since all the power thereof it doth apply
> To prove, by wit, worth in simplicity. *(V.ii.69-78)*

This is not witty interchange as in the section immediately preceding, not expository statement as in Boyet's subsequent description of Navarre's rehearsal, and not the conversational discussion of the Princess' response to Boyet's news. It is rather a single set speech formally organized in regular heroic couplets and divided among three speakers. It is a choric passage, and while its sententiousness perpetuates the veil of obliquity, that veil is increasingly transparent. For these lines gather up and summarize the ladies' response to the young men, and albeit in the form of tripping moral maxims, the lines touch the courtiers with shrewd, analytical penetration.[33] Rosaline's speech incisively describes the transition from Navarre's academe to Berowne's love-game. The latter is dangerous, she suggests, because it is causally related to the king's excessive "gravity." The Princess' "folly in wisdom hatch'd" comments on the subjection of learning to the impulses of both gravity and wantonness, and if the Princess' words glance back at the opening scene of *LLL*, and Rosaline's especially allude to the metamorphosis (in IV.iii) of the students into lovers, Maria's concluding observations both remind us of recent history and look ahead to the consequences of that history. When the mind "dotes" with its rational and "witty" faculties, it earns a special censure because it applies its special power "To prove, by wit, worth in simplicity." That line nicely catches what Berowne had set out to accomplish in Act IV, Scene iii where he in effect declared the values of the sexual chase to be none other than those of the marriage vow, that love (i.e. *his* passion) and charity cannot be severed.[34] But Maria's words are prospective as well as retrospective in function. If the doting mind attempts to prove that stupid or morally valueless things ("simplicity") are valuable (of "worth"), it may in return be obliged to prove its own plain, simple honesty, that is its "truth in simplicity" to read Maria's words from a different angle. Again, this is precisely Berowne's quandary and tactic in the middle of the last scene where he makes a show of abjuring "taffeta phrases, silken terms precise" (V.ii.406). His failure to move Rosaline seems directly related to a failure in both plainness and singleness of intention, in particular to the extreme artifice of his alleged recantation (it is a perfect exemplar of the "Shakespearean" sonnet form) and the gleaming mockery of the plain-style parody in the last couplet.[35]

> *Ber.* Henceforth my wooing mind shall be express'd
> In russet yeas and honest kersey noes:
> And, to begin: Wench,—so God help me, law!—
> My love to thee is sound, sans crack or flaw.
>
> *Ros.* Sans "sans," I pray you.   *(V.ii.12-16)*

The indifference displayed in critical literature toward the women's choric appraisal, accompanied by endless tributes to Berowne's sincerity, illustrates once more the efficacy of Shakespeare's "Mousetrap." It matters not that a mere four lines before this studied appeal to plainness, Dumain bluntly states the young men's strategy: "Let us confess, and turn it to a jest" (V.ii.390). The charismatic authority of Berowne is very strong right through the last scene, long after its foundations have crumbled. We do not argue with the ladies' choric assessment of their lovers because it does not *require* us to come to accounts, any more than Navarre had been arrested early in the play by the Princess' retort that will would shatter his ascetic vow. Even at the start of the last scene, the audience does not *hear* the ladies, in the same sense that Navarre did not hear the Princess in II.i. Nevertheless, the choric observations of the women contribute to a continuing process directed at a future conversion for young men and theater audience alike, and the women's authority awaits validation while Berowne's continues to flourish. Two events henceforth hurry this process of conversion to fruition (within the play proper for the theater audience, beyond it for the young men): the interlude of the unworthy Worthies, and Marcade's *coup de théâtre*.

It is the violent interruption of the wooing game by Death that finally invests the women of France with dramatic authority superior to Berowne's. The announcement of France's death is the water-shed of our emotions and sympathetic attachments, though it is the property of water-sheds to be well-established before their existence is noticed. In the renewed suits of the courtiers after Marcade's entrance, Shakespeare allows us the opportunity to re-orient our responses. Here, perhaps for the first time, we are compelled to mark and inwardly digest the discrepancy between the courtiers' response and our own response to an unequivocally significant event. The courtiers treat death as a threatening competitor; they fear it will "justle" their suit which "was first on foot...from what it purpos'd" (V.ii.737-38). Navarre and his conspirators do not hear the Princess' unanswerable reply to their redoubled protestations: "I understand you not: my griefs are double" (V.ii.742). Now the theater audience cannot avoid hearing her; now the "ear of grief" which Berowne sets out to "pierce" is our own as well as the women's. Yet as Berowne loses his status as a privileged speaker, a loss confirmed in his new appeal to "honest plain words,"[36] the audience also loses the safety and comfort of discipleship. Like Berowne we have had to lose ourselves, the self which has identified with Berowne, and discovery of another, profounder responsive self awaits comprehension of and a coming to terms with the self lost. This final revelation and reconciliation is the special function of the debate songs of Spring and Winter before which the audience and the women of France, no less than the young men of Navarre, are reduced to silence. *Love's Labour's Lost* unlike *A Midsummer Night's Dream* neither solicits nor anticipates our grateful applause.

A potential objection to this discussion of the young women deserves comment at this point. We have gleaned the characterizing mentality of the French maids mainly from the utterances of the Princess and have then attributed them to Rosaline, Maria, and Katherine by the same principle of association which operates in the men's company. Whatever the depth of their insights, however, whether established by profession or association, are not the followers of the Princess in certain respects no more ideal than their lovers? Mr. Harbage's indictment of manners and mores in *LLL* applies to all the main characters without regard to sex.[37] Is Rosaline's apparent shrewishness, for example, less compromising than Berowne's self-assertiveness? Do not the intramural word-games of the women compete all too well with the interplay of the courtiers for the prize in rudeness and petty bicker-ing? And if the young men seem often to straddle the line between bawdiness and outright obscenity, do not the lines most worthy of Samuel Johnson's famous cen-sure[38] emanate from the women's camp? Quite clearly, the women of France are not in some respects the conventional heroines of festive comedy, and it is because such questions as these derive from the perception of unconventionality that they deserve serious consideration and prove to be illuminating.

Three things may be said by way of response. First, Shakespeare is no more in-tent upon idealizing young women than young men in *Love's Labour's Lost*. The girls evoked by the text are vivacious to a fault, bright, and competitive, —very much like their young men. At the same time, nevertheless, they are disciplined by a self-knowledge, most fully expressed by the Princess, which the young men lack. The Princess enfranchises and enjoys the skipping, sometimes pungent, some-times frivolous word-play of her companions, but these "set [s] of wit" (V.ii.29) among the ladies are always, if not exclusively, a preparation for the larger *combat d'amour* in which the women will find themselves on the defense:

> *Prin.* Good wits will be jangling; but, gentles, agree:
> This civil war of wits were much better us'd
> On Navarre and his book-men, for here 'tis abused. *(II.i.225-227)*

So they exhibit both the sparkling complexity of Berowne and the powerful ideality of the Princess. They can be as silly and catty as school-girls,[39] and almost simul-taneously paragons of charitable dignity. Shakespeare's young women in this play celebrate self-consciously the bond of humanity which unites lover and beloved, and they do so despite the young men's repudiation of the bond and despite all the moralizing from their own lips which accompanies and follows that repudiation.

Second, because of Shakespeare's adherence to oblique revelation in this comedy, the contrasting rationales of the men and women are mainly portrayed in the manner of Lyly through symbolic symmetry of parallels and oppositions rather than through dramatic confrontations. Since the men are characterized through small-group interaction, the women are too. Since the young men wittily manipulate words to extort reactions from each other, the women do too. Indeed Shakespeare is at pains before the meetings of the last scene to demonstrate that the women use words no less fluently and a good deal more responsibly than the men. And since the young men are much obsessed with sexuality, it is Shake-speare's method to dramatize a balancing awareness in the women's camp. That is the function of the last interlude in Act IV, Scene i where Maria participates in the obscenity of Costard and Boyet (both alter egos of Berowne) and then puts it down. Maria knows what it means to "talk greasily" (IV.i.136). Indeed she is rather good at it herself — so much for realism. However, she also can perceive that the brand of sexual encounter she faces here is threatening to her humanity as well as her virginity. She departs the stage just as Boyet and Costard warm to the occasion, to join the Princess who had left before the subject was raised. The women under-stand, participate and take delight in the realm of sexuality. They are also chaste, as essentially pure as Miranda. Shakespeare will again have it both ways without seeming to be paradoxical.

Finally, there is the issue of Rosaline's shrewishness. It demands separate recognition because her private war with Berowne is always at or near the center of Shakespeare's dramatic focus. As in the case of Beatrice and Benedick, we may argue that Rosaline is a fitting adversary for Berowne in so far as she resembles him in the aggressive-defensive pursuit of self-esteem and "maistrie" in love. Yet it remains to be settled how the battle of the sexes, waged in a common arena with similar tactics, jibes with the alleged moral superiority of the women. Once more Shakespeare seems to insist on both elements of an apparent opposition without producing a paradox. Rosaline vindicates her own humanity by giving large rein to a very fundamental urge: to return aggression with interest, blow for blow. Berowne "asks for it" from the first moment he accosts Rosaline; he gets it and we love it. Nevertheless, the limits of shrewishness as a characterizing trait are carefully established in two ways. The limits are indicated most obviously by Rosaline's visible solicitude for the man she loves, especially during her last speech to him (V.ii.831-859). There she typically begins with triumphing (far more chaste than Berowne's at his fellows' expense in IV.iii.), and ends with something very much like a plea. Much earlier in the play, however, the dramatist had carefully insulated his women from the role of counter-aggressors as he explores their motives in the hunt of love. After the Princess' moralizing of the hunt in IV.i., Boyet pre-empts our doubts by raising the spectre of "curst wives" who hold "self-sovereignty / Only for praise sake, when they strive to be lords o'er their lords" (IV.i.36-38). The Princess, accused of making shrewishness a virtue, parries Boyet's quip and demonstrates her sophisticated self-awareness by laughingly embracing the role he proffers. She is, as Shakespeare's heroines typically are, her lord's lord in the wooing game. Like Rosaline she lords her power over her lover to the extent he forces her to, and then she gives it away to him as speedily as events will allow.

One way to test the substance of these observations on the women of Navarre and the peculiar *combat d'amour* of *LLL* is to see what sense they enable us to make of the little discussed low plot presented by Armado, Costard, Moth, Holofernes, Nathaniel, and Dull. We can do no more here than sketch the outlines of an interpretation, beginning with the most basic of propositions (that a low plot does in fact exist in the play), and progressing not far beyond a statement of its relationship with the high plot.

For the first half of *LLL*, until the young men of Navarre abandon themselves to the hunt of love in Act IV, Scene iii, the low characters perform for the theatre audience in the same role conferred on them by the courtiers. They are our "quick recreation" (I.i.160), our vivacious, lively entertainment. To be sure, Costard's liaison with Jaquenetta in the curious-knotted garden ironically undercuts the already absurd academe, and the preposterous utterances of Armado, Holofernes, and others are redolent with linguistic and topical satire. Irony and satire aside, however, these characters first and foremost lend *LLL* the aura of a "musical comedy without music," a collection of discrete, bravura performances whose only common trait is what one critic calls a "self-justifying aestheticism."[40] What "meaning" would be lost, for example, if the wit-combats of Armado and Moth, which constitute the bulk of Act I, Scene ii, were shifted to the fourth act, or excised entirely? The answer to this question depends on one's conception of the low plot in which Armado functions, and its relationship to the high plot.

The high plot as we have discussed it offers a precedent for affirming that there is an integrated low plot in *LLL* and not merely a random conglomeration of entertaining rustics and eccentrics. It is similar to the low plot of *A Midsummer Night's Dream* in tracing the cooperative making of an entertainment for the gentles, and it is organized like the main plot of *LLL* as a vehicle of progressive and indirect revelation. Following Costard's first-act appearance, three solemn pretenders are thus introduced at irregular intervals during the first half of the play together with their supporting cast. These three are Armado the braggert, Holofernes the pedant schoolmaster, and Nathaniel the fawning curate. The timing of their entrances seems at first glance of negligible significance. Yet it is after all no coincidence that Armado, the fashionable wooer of Jaquenetta, arrives immediately *after* the courtiers have forsworn the love-game and condemned Costard's sexual license.[41] It is no coincidence that the self-aggrandizing pedant Holofernes and his reverend parasite Nathaniel first appear in Act IV, Scene ii immediately *before* the courtiers seeming repudiation of academic aspirations in Act IV, Scene iii Just as Armado indicates the path Berowne will tread despite the king's monkish vow, so Holofernes and Nathaniel personify precisely the motives which the young men fail to rid themselves of when they declare themselves as lovers.

The accumulation of low characters is in retrospect by no means as random as it seems; neither are their utterances self-contained revue numbers only. The moral value of the characters and their words, for seven scenes latent in the shimmering delight of separable verbal celebrations, is appropriately revealed in the planning and execution of a *communal* ostentation in Act V, Scenes i and ii. The ostentatious low characters coalesce into a recognizable low plot in the act of preparing and staging that ironic Show of Worthies which is Shakespeare's climactic instrument for showing the plight of his lovers. In keeping with his oblique method, the focus of the revelation in the Show of the Worthies is upon the Worthies, although the more we know of them, the more we know of their audience, an impression cemented by the response of the courtiers as well as their initial responsibility for the pageant.

Shakespeare is quite explicit about the fact that the entertainment of these low characters has been commissioned by the courtiers who sit in its audience (V.i.104-112). In this it differs from Bottom's play in *Dream,* and the difference manifests itself in a wholly dissimilar relationship between actors and stage audience in the two plays. Navarre commissions an entertainment; Holofernes and Armado, though bitterly suspicious of each other, separate themselves from "the barbarous" to plan it (V.i.76 ff). The academic pedant Holofernes conceives the idea of the pageant of nine Worthies and then arrogates to himself responsibility for producing it, assigning to himself no fewer than three of the traditional nine roles!

Like Bottom's rude mechanicals, the players of *LLL* are judged less in accordance with the technical skill of their performance than the motives exhibited in distribution, preparation, and execution of their roles. Unlike Bottom's show, the pageant of *LLL* is composed of separable, individual performances which, in their discreteness, enable the dramatist to distinguish varying degrees of worthiness and unworthiness of the players, who in turn embody impulses visible in the adjudicating courtiers of Navarre.

After Costard performs, the Worthies are treated with increasing severity in Act V, Scene ii. Nathaniel as Alexander is quickly cowed by his audience and sent packing by Costard with a word of reproof and another of apology. What Nathaniel lacks in courage ("A conqueror, and afeard to speak!") he partially recoups in being "a marvelous good neighbor," and this insight is applicable to the courtiers (V.ii.557-580). They have been "shallow laughing hearers" in Rosaline's acute phrase (V.ii.850); they too have manipulated companionship in ministering to their own desires. Yet like Nathaniel they have in part victimized themselves; albeit in a somewhat different league, they are like him "very good bowler[s]." Unlike Nathaniel, Holofernes is treated quite unmercifully as Judas Maccabaeus, and for his persistence in his role he earns indentification with Judas Iscariot.[42] Learned labor devoted wholly to self-enhancement makes him both a traitor and a fool, in short a "Jude-as" (V.ii.620). Yet even the darkness in which he stumbles away is not unrelieved, for his misfortunes have at least prompted him to articulate the human values in which he has been egregiously deficient: "This is not generous, not gentle, not humble" (V.ii.621).

Armado's pretensions are stripped away with his sartorial finery in another kind of purgatorial experience (V.ii.624-704). Affronted and challenged to combat by Costard, Armado for the first time in the whole play stops acting the role of a Worthy in order, we later find, to play "honest Troyan" with Jaquenetta. Beneath his flaming doublet of taffeta and silk, and his verbal facade of taffeta phrases and silken terms, he reveals "the naked truth" (V.ii.699): he wears next his heart not the garments of heroic encounter but "a dishclout of Jaquenetta." And he accepts this naked truth with evident relief once the shock of recognition is past: "For my own part, I breathe free breath." We find that it is easier for the fantastic braggart soldier to adopt a counter-role (the honest soldier) than for the more realistically conceived courtiers to lose and find themselves. Nevertheless, Armado foreshadows the direction of the young men's "reformation," retaining his title to be called one of the most significant of the courtiers' alter egos among the characters of the low plot.

The character who shares this dramatic eminence with Armado is his rival Costard. This clownish malaprop is not easily categorized, for like other characters in the play he takes on characteristics of the environment he is thrust into. With the courtiers in the first scene, he displays something of the calculating self-consciousness generally associated with the licensed fool; elsewhere he seems to be close kin of Bottom, particularly in the Show of the Worthies. In this entertainment Costard is the first and only actor who can distinguish between the estimable role he plays and the humble nature of his own abilities (V.ii.541-556). Of his performance he concludes with foolish wisdom, "'Tis not so much worth; but I hope I was perfect. . . ." Awareness of this distinction enables him to assimilate criticism rather than being destroyed by it ("I made a little fault in 'Great'"), and consequently he fulfills his role and provokes Berowne's frank admiration: "My hat to a half-penny, Pompey proves the best Worthy" (V.ii.556). Costard, at once both "the best Worthy" and an incarnation of male sexuality, is certainly not easily labeled. But his function in the play is clear: he is "born to do [Berowne] shame" (IV.iii.202). It is in this capacity that he remains on stage after his own success in the Show of Worthies, a living, self-debunking standard prepared to cry shame upon Nathaniel and Armado, two other fantastic reflections of the Berowne-spirit. Since Costard's debunking always has a benevolent aftertaste, his silence during the baiting of Holofernes is telling.

Like its stock participants a well-worn piece of theatrical machinery refurbished for the occasion, the Show of the Worthies dramatizes objectively in a "public" symbolic pageant those insights regarding the courtiers which have been expressed by the women in the privacy of their own circle. This pageant is, in Berowne's words, "A right description of our sport." (V.ii.517), and the courtiers' acerbic merriment flourishes *despite recognition* that their "mocks come home by [them]" or boomerang (V.ii.625: the speaker is Dumain). Berowne and his fellows weigh the proportions of treachery and foolishness in the pretensions of the curate and the schoolmaster, and Costard uncovers the erotic desires hitherto masked beneath Armado's fashionable amatory lore and linguistic bombast. Shakespeare validates these judgments by involving the Princess' man Boyet among the ranks of the heckling courtiers of Navarre. If the contumely lavished upon the Worthies is itself "not generous, not gentle, not humble," it is also not misdirected, and the intensity and clairvoyance of the courtiers further argues a special intimacy in the relationship between them and the actors. Berowne had calculatingly wished for "one show worse than the king's and his company" (V.ii.509), but the dramatist gives us the *same* show in the form of a psychic allegory where embattled Worthies project the disconcerting conflicts which have long been at work amidst the constrained merriment of the love-game. The excitement with which the young men incite Costard and Armado to violent blows ("More Ates, more Ates! stir them on! stir them on!" [V.ii.678-79]) has little in common with the discriminating response of Theseus and his court. It is the fervor of a "civil war of wits" in earnest, and the psychic energy unleashed by the performance threatens to rend irretrievably the decorum of the love-game. The explosive moment passes when Armado abjectly refuses to fight (comedy can make even cowardice a virtue), but the impasse of the young men against themselves is mercifully resolved only by the dramatist's *deus ex machina*, the entrance of Marcade clad in black. Having insisted that the Show of Worthies be performed (though not responsible for actors and contents), the Princess initially berates her interrupting messenger, then anticipates both his mission and its meaning. The king her father, she exclaims is "Dead, for my life!" (V.ii.710).

III

It has been said, and often reiterated with but slight variation, that *LLL* traces the "victory of nature and experience over pedantry, rigid discipline, and the affectations of art,"[43] in other words that this play generally adheres to the shape and satisfies the conventional expectations of festive comedy as C. L. Barber understands the term. In these pages, I have argued rather that Shakespeare's "Pleasant Conceited Comedie" represents the progressive triumph of the festive muse over the realistic condition of handsome but anxious youthfulness in reaction to the fear of loss of identity or death, a condition which reveals itself in various misappropriations of learning. As in *Richard II*, Shakespeare's point of departure is a state approximating observed experience, namely the realistic and psychologically complex character of Berowne, and the tension between this state and the affirmative realm of comedy is witnessed in an expanding tone of *serio-ludere* which comprehends in close proximity extremes of insouciant play and calculating equivocation, both hard bawdy and pithy moralizing, and both mockery and pathos. Having established a vivid and subtle male mentality in the opening scene of *LLL*, Shakespeare then manipulates every force and form at his command — the ladies of France, the characters and conflicts of the low-plot, Marcade's *deus ex machina*, indeed the whole "mousetrap" structure of the play itself — to redeem and refashion that mentality in a comic mold. The young men must be recreated as young lovers, and the process turns out to be "too long for a play" (V.ii.868). This very fact is evidence of the dramatist's scrupulousness in respecting the integrity of the youthful assertion of self. It also suggests how he can admire and celebrate the brilliantly ambivalent virtues of a character simultaneously in need of genuine "reformation" (V.ii.859). For Shakespeare's final strategy is to take Berowne at his word, viewing him as denizen of "the kingly state of youth" (IV.iii. 290) and therefore as the product and victim of lack of years and inexperience. Like the young lover of sixteenth-century literary convention, Berowne in the final analysis is "more to be pittied than blamed"[44] because he is young and not *capable*[45] of self-control despite the fact that self-control is the very essence of what he claims for himself as a role-player and self-conscious man. Shakespeare claims for his young men the benevolent obscurity of this conventional role through repeated references to their youthfulness during the concluding assignment of penances.[46] But not until this point, when the young men are actually seeking judgment ("Studies my lady? Mistress look on me" [V.ii.827]) does the dramatist insist on youthfulness as a mitigating circumstance and thereby claim for passing time the power to shape and influence conduct at the deepest levels of volition.

To put the case in another way, while *LLL* seems to reflect no less than other Shakespearean comedies the process of romantic comedy isolated and analyzed by Northrop Frye (the movement from an "unnatural" to a "natural" state of affairs across or through a realm of the "physically natural"),[47] it derives its unique effect from a re-definition of these terms. I have argued that the "unnatural" condition of *LLL* is characterized not by an external bar to the nuptial consummation but an internal conflict which obscures the providence tangibly evident in the earthly paradise of youthfulness, especially young love. The saving power of the "physically natural" is expressed in those processes which the young men of Navarre seek in their anxious folly to control: sexuality, the passing of time, and death. The Costard-impulse of ungarnished sexuality (present in Berowne's earliest inclination toward "green-geese") destroys the life-denying academe; the symbolic year-long exile commits the young men to the atonement and reconciliation which can be wrought in and through the fullness of time; but most striking of all, the apparition of death which goads the young men into the hunt of fame, the hunt pursued first through academic moral learning and then in the fashionable and bookish wooing sport, reappears with benevolent irony as the gracious means of their deliverance. The death of France providentially makes available to the women of France in the ritual forms and assumptions of bereavement, a rationale for exiling their frustrated lovers without ostracism or alienation. Death clarifies experience where words fail, though itself death is an ambivalent good. It sends to earthly oblivion a king, yet emancipates that royal father from a "decrepit, sick, and bed-rid" condition of bondage. It forms the efficient cause of a melancholy estrangement of lovers, yet also the material cause of their hoped-for marriage of true minds. Berowne and his companions foreshadow Claudio's discovery about death in *Measure for Measure*: "To sue to live, I find I seek to die; / And, seeking death, find life" (III.i.42-43, Craig ed.)

The final debate of Spring and Winter brings our study of *LLL* to a summary conclusion. It inundates and obscures rhetorical tactics and the thrust and parry of wit-combats in an extraordinary outpouring of lyric poetry, which celebrates the prospective triumph of the "natural" festive affirmation over the realistic complexities portrayed in the young man of Navarre. The universalization of the dramatic impasse, in process since the entrance of Marcade, reaches a traditional culmination in the pastoral songs of *Ver* and *Hiems*. These lyrics, in their particular sequence, recapitulate the experience of the dramatic past (*Ver*) and lay the foundation for a hopeful and gratifying future (*Hiems*). The result is an ironic variant of traditional pastoral melancholy.[48]

Spring sings of the youthful year, a sensuous, rustic, golden age of the world where nature bestows every delight—yet fails not to remind men of human fears which no terrestrial bliss can eradicate or exorcise. Indeed it is precisely the beauty of spring which makes this fear graphically evident and emotionally binding. The season of "merry larks" and of "daisies pied and violets blue" is the time of "well-accomplished youth," "well-fitted in arts, glorious in arms," "sweet and voluble [in] discourse" (II.i.45,56,76). But it is also the time of the cuckoo, of "sharp wit match'd with too blunt a will" (II.i.49), of "green geese . . . a-breeding" (I.i.97) and "four woodcocks in a dish" (IV.iii.80), of "tricks . . . quillets" (IV.iii.285) and "maggot ostentation" (V.ii.409). The pregnant affirmation of the Spring but serves to throw into relief the presence of that which disrupts the most intimate human society, and what the commonplace cuckoo-cuckold motif lacks in immediacy and solemnity, it makes up in perverse ubiquity. *Ver's* first note is joy, but its last is fear; its free riches but serve to raise the spectre of poverty and suspicion. In like manner, though Navarre is the "sole inheritor / Of all perfections" (II.i.5-6), he attempts to barter the prodigal graces of youth for an epitaph on a brazen tomb. The consequence is "a king transformed to a gnat" (IV.iii.164), thence to a "slave-born Muscovite," and ultimately to a "hermit" (V.ii.806).

The Winter song resolves one paradox by offering another. It sings of more than the "snow in May's new-fangled shows" (I.i.106) which Berowne scorns, of more than any merely capricious or moralistic blighting of spring's pride and vitality. Rather it celebrates the death of the old regime which prepares the life of the new, the dissipation of the rank growth which assures future fertility. This is a comic view of winter in which "the sour cup of prosperity" (I.i.296) is drained and exchanged for the crab-filled bowl of fellowship-in-adversity. The enemy is now, at last, wholly externalized, and despite his strength that is comfort indeed. His blasts cannot obscure the merry note of the owl, an earnest of victory in the midst of trials and a witness that death's icy oblivion but makes sweeter tangible, present joys. Foul ways and blowing wind enhance and exalt the homely community of mankind, where not youthful blood but firewood burns to create the society of the hearth, and thoughts dwell on survival rather than the "surmounting" of an Armado (V.ii.660).

If so haunting a poetic dialogue and so unusual a dramatic resolution can be "compil'd" by "two learned men" (V.ii.876; i.e. Holofernes and Nathaniel), perhaps the academic criticism of LLL is to be thought capable and worthy of Rosaline's reformation. One sign of this reformation will be, I suggest, a willingness to move from criticizing Berowne's discrete pronouncements with Holofernes to imagining a whole theatrical performance which is *both* "quick recreation" and a symbolic drama about worthiness in love. Because its text resembles an orchestral score laden with tones which must be sounded to be comprehended, LLL challenges the critic to a new respect for the theatrical image and a more sensitive awareness of the complex interaction between the image and the response of the theatrical audience. As a dramatic *poem, LLL* is something of an absurdity, like Berowne's love poetry. But as drama which employs poetry (particularly as the *terminus ad quem* of its action), it has a startling and engrossing power, not unlike Holofernes' play for its auditors. Not by chance has dramatic performance been the primary stimulus of interest in LLL during this century, as evidenced, for example, by John Dover Wilson's graphic account of Tyrone Guthrie's 1936 production.[49] On the stage, the complexities and paradoxes in which the literary critic prosaically muddles are cast in a new light.

If Shakespeare's mature works are characterized by a complex simplicity, LLL more nearly approaches certain types of modern drama in its simple complexity. It is not Shakespeare's last attempt to transport his audience from a realm of realistically portrayed impulses to the golden world of festivity; those other essays are usually called "problem comedies." LLL succeeds in ways that they do not because it concentrates more narrowly on the problem of manipulating the audience's evaluative perspective. For the critic, then, as well as the student of the dramatist's development, the theatrical imagination seems to be a blessed key for opening an enormously rich, uplocked treasure. *LLL* is not a work which flatters audiences, and they may not wish every hour to survey it. But that does not make it any less the captain jewel of Shakespeare's works before *A Midsummer Night's Dream.*

Notes:

(1) E. K. Chambers assigns *LLL* to 1594-95 in *William Shakespeare: A Study of Facts and Problems* (Oxford, 1930) I, 270. Arguments for an earlier date are canvassed by Alfred Harbage, "*Love's Labour's Lost* and the Early Shakespeare," *PQ*, XLI (1962), 18-36. These are neither new nor convincing, but they show our total ignorance in regard to occasion of composition and the play's intended audience (if other than the public theater as many have supposed). The earliest surviving text, the First Quarto of 1598, refers to a performance before the queen "this last Christmas." The problem of revision between original composition and this first known performance is discussed by Richard David, editor of the New Arden *LLL* (Cambridge, Mass., 1951), xx-xxxii. He concludes the play was written in late 1593 and revised in 1597, but both dates rest on shaky evidence, as does the fact of a major revision itself.

(2) For years this contemporaneity in word and idiom was mistaken for obscurity, particularly by scholars seeking special insights from alleged topical allusions. Harbage *(op. cit.*, 23) lists the main studies in this vein. More recently it has become fashionable to deny that we are intended to concern ourselves with the signification of words in *LLL*. Apparently on the assumption that words unfamiliar to the modern reader were no less unfamiliar to Shakespeare's audience, A. C. Hamilton states in *The Early Shakespeare* (San Marino, Calif., 1967) that "the diction and melody of words is all that we do remember" (p. 130). This is a half-truth which has the unfortunate effect of perpetuating the old obscurantism. Like Ben Jonson's drama, *LLL* employs material which is unfamiliar yet obviously intended to be intelligible. Northrop Frye may have "not the faintest idea" what Shakespeare and Holofernes mean by the phrase "colourable colours" (IV.ii.148-49); nevertheless it is a variant of an Elizabethan commonplace and knowable. (Cf. Frye's "Shakespeare's Experimental Comedy," in *Stratford Papers on Shakespeare, 1961*, ed. B. W. Jackson [Toronto, 1962], 4; and Richard David's note in the New Arden edition.) Even the most exotic digressions of the low characters, like Moth's l'envoy in III.i, seem relevant enough and not particularly obscure unless one begins with an assumption of topical significance (see Stanley Greenfield, "Moth's l'Envoy and the Courtiers in *LLL*," *RES*, V [n.s. 1954], 167-68). Linguistic puzzles obviously remain, but they are minor compared with the burden of unfamiliarity borne by the vast majority of readers. That burden is sharply diminished with good direction and acting in the theater; *LLL* was not and is not for savants alone.

(3) See respectively C. L. Barber, *Shakespeare's Festive Comedy* (Princeton, 1959); O. J. Campbell, *Shakespeare's Satire* (London, 1943); H. B. Charlton, *Shakespearian Comedy* (New York, 1938), and E. C. Pettet, *Shakespeare and the Romance Tradition* (London, 1949); Richard J. Cody, "The Pastoral Element in Shakespeare's Early Comedies," unpubl. diss. (University of Minnesota, 1961); T. W. Baldwin, *William Shakspere's Five-Act Structure* (Urbana, 1947); J. D. Wilson, *Shakespeare's Happy Comedies* (London, 1962); Donald L. Stevenson, *The Love-Game Comedy* (New York, 1946). Several recent publications cover familiar ground regarding *LLL*: Peter G. Phialas, *Shakespeare's Romantic Comedies* (Chapel Hill, 1966); Ernest William Talbert. *Elizabethan Drama and Shakespeare's Early Plays* (Chapel Hill, 1963); Blaze Odell Bonazza. *Shakespeare's Early Comedies: A Structural Analysis* (The Hague, 1966); and A. C. Hamilton. *The Early Shakespeare*, the last the most impressive of the group. The reader should compare my understanding of *LLL* with E. M. W. Tillyard's discussion of the "male crudities" of the "adolescents" in *Shakespeare's Early Comedies* (New York, 1965). Other than Tillyard, only James L. Calderwood ("*LLL*: A Wantoning with Words," *SEL*, V [1965], 317-332) seems to give serious attention to the offensiveness

of the young men. The earliest study to attempt a comprehensive reading taking into account the death motif is Bobbyann Roesen's *"Love's Labour's Lost," SQ,* IV (1953), 411-26. Barber's *Festive Comedy* is the seminal work for virtually every discussion of *LLL* since 1959, including my own.

(4) The potential significance of *LLL* is suggested by the fact that it is Shakespeare's first play for which no major dramatic source is known or expected. See Geoffrey Bullough, *Narrative and Dramatic Sources of Shakespeare* (New York, 1957), I, 426. Experiment and innovation is not inhibited by the exigencies of the traditional comic plot, whether farce or romance; on the contrary, despite obvious debts to his predecessors in the drama (especially Lyly) Shakespeare is forced back to a unique degree on his own resources.

(5) Bertrand Evans to *Shakespeare's Comedies* (Oxford, 1960) reformulates the conventional view concerning the role of women in the comedies: "The heroines . . . either hold from the outset, or very shortly gain, the highest vantage point in their worlds" (p. 15). With this highest vantage point generally goes the dramatist's focus, and the consequent tendency toward insipidity in the young men of romantic comedy is common knowledge. The theoretical basis of this feminine ascendancy, which is thus a matter of both character traits and manipulation of the dramatic focus, is suggested in Suzanne Langer's essay on "The Comic Rhythm" in *Feeling and Form* (New York, 1953), 326-50. Actually, *LLL* is not the only Shakespearean comedy in which the heroine's superior awareness is *pitted against* a dramatic focus on the young men; that situation is especially noticeable in *TGV.* The singularity of *LLL* which I argue is far more emphatic in regard to the high comedies which follow it, and it is those, beginning with *MND,* which have shaped our comic expectations.

(6) *The Structure of Literature* (Chicago, 1954), p. 117.

(7) With a single exception (see n. 32), all quotations are from Richard David's New Arden edition of *LLL* (Cambridge, Mass., 1951). Quotations from other plays refer to Hardin Craig (ed.), *The Complete Works of Shakespeare* (Chicago, 1961).

(8) By festive comedy I refer specifically to "the holiday sequence of release and clarification" which dramatizes "a heightened awareness of the relation between man and 'nature'" as well as a "mockery of what is unnatural" and "another, complementary mockery of what is merely natural." "Nature" in this context is understood as a beneficent creation, namely that nature which is celebrated on holidays, and "individual" character is preceded by the festive role. See C. L. Barber, "The Saturnalian Pattern in Shakespeare's Comedy" in R. W. Corrigan (ed.), *Comedy: Meaning and Form* (San Francisco, 1965), 364-367; also Barber's *Shakespeare's Festive Comedy, passim.*

(9) Berowne is the only young lover, man or woman, to be left alone on stage to address the audience. This direct recourse to the theater audience, developed in two monologues (III.i.170-202 and IV.iii.1-20) and many briefer asides, reaches its peak in IV.iii and then is virtually cut off in the last scene.

(10) In 1879, Halliwell-Phillips claimed that "modern psychological critics" have vindicated the title of *LLL* to a place "amongst the very best productions of the great dramatist" (H. H. Furness, ed., *The Variorum Shakespeare,* IV [Philadelphia, 1904], 363). Whether or not *LLL* is a comedy of character, the fact is that Berowne is psychologically complex; he is both the pretender or intruder which Barber associates with comedy of character (*Festive Comedy,* p. 90) *and* the celebrant of festive comedy. Even Longaville and Dumain are described by their ladies in psychologically complex portraits (II.i.40-51, 56-63). This complexity is similarly evident in the resemblances between Berowne and the "gray iniquity" Falstaff in their praise of folly (Barber, p. 94), and an examination of Berowne's ancestors must include the comic vice Neither-Lover-Nor-Loved in John Heywood's *Play of Love* ed. John S. Farmer (London, 1905). Neither-Lover-Nor-

68

Loved mockingly courts a lady who, like those in *LLL*, "has wit to set wise men to school" and make good the proverb "Mockum moccabitur" (pp. 153, 156). Like Berowne, Neither-Lover-Nor-Loved in his prized autonomy views Lover-Loved as a "Woodcock" (cf. *LLL*, IV.iii.80), with the added complication that Berowne is *both* Neither-Lover-Nor-Loved and Lover-Loved in a single consciousness: thus there are "*four* woodcocks in a dish!" But the immediate sources of Berowne's character seem to be found in *Richard III* and in the character of Richard himself who provides Bernard Spivack with a major object of analysis in his book on the dramatic Vice, *Shakespeare and the Allegory of Evil* (New York, 1958). As Richard supervises the downfall of the gulls Hastings and Clarence, so Berowne at the beginning of Act IV. Scene iii "Like a demi-god" sits "in the sky, / And wretched fools' secrets heedfully o'er-eye" (IV.iii.77-78). He then steps forth like the Vice "to whip hypocrisy" (IV.iii.149). His call to arms at the end of the scene, "Advance your standards" (IV.iii.364), appears only twice elsewhere in Shakespeare, both times in *R3* (V.iii.264,348). The courtiers' primary amatory argument (e.g., in Berowne's speech "Your beauty, ladies, / Hath much deform'd us. . . ." [V,ii.746-747] or in the King's, "The virtue of your eye must break my oath" [V.ii.348]) is the same Richard uses against Lady Anne (I.ii.150 ff.); and Richard like Berowne is fond of asserting his plain simplicity (I.iii.51-53,142; III.iv.22-30); and both are skilled in employing scripture for strategic effect (R3, I.iii.334-338; *LLL*, I.i.148-159; IV.iii.157-160, etc.).

(11) See Wylie Sypher, "The Meanings of Comedy" in Corrigan (ed.), *Comedy*, 40-60.

(12) Borrowing Reinhold Niebuhr's analysis of the psychological roots of folly and sin, Navarre may be said to "fall into sin by trying to evade or to conquer death or [his] own insignificance, of which death is the ultimate symbol." Following Kierkegaard, however, Niebuhr realizes that anxiety is not only the precondition of folly and sin but the source of all human creativity; Berowne's verbal brilliance is a case in point. See *Reinhold Niebuhr: His Religious, Social, and Political Ideas*, ed. C. W. Kegley and R. W. Bretall (New York, 1956), p. 6, and Niebuhr's *The Nature and Destiny of Man* (New York, 1964), pp. 182-84. The relationship between fame, death, and individuality is asserted in secular terms by Oliver Elton, *Modern Studies* (London, 1905) in an essay entitled "Literary Studies"; "The desire for glory is but one form of our passion for our own identity . . . it is rooted in our stubborn wish to stamp ourselves, before we go, upon something, and so to prolong our real essence after our individual existence" (p. 38).

(13) The extensive use of theological and biblical language in *LLL* is partially traced by Richmond Noble, *Shakespeare's Biblical Knowledge and Use of the Book of Common Prayer* (London, 1935), pp. 142 ff.

(14) The historical distinction between the soft hunt of love and the hard hunt of fame is discussed in D. C. Allen, "On *Venus and Adonis*" in *Elizabethan and Jacobean Studies Presented to F. P. Wilson* (Oxford, 1959), 100-111. The phrase "Still and contemplative in living art" (I.i.14) is usually understood as a reference to the *ars vivendi* of Stoic philosophy; see J. S. Reid, "Shakespeare's 'Living Art'," *PQ*, I (1922), 226-227. Navarre's oration is a pastiche of learning, including sonorous phrases from the Anglican Service of Baptism (Richmond Noble, *op. cit.*, 142) which Berowne parodies: "Too much to know is to know nought but fame; / And every godfather can give a name" (I.i.92-93). Making a name for himself is an apt description of Navarre's intentions as evinced in his baptismal oration. Berowne's amatory learning is discussed in n.34.

(15) David ed., I.i.57n.

(16) Barber frankly wonders why the courtiers, especially Berowne, are so "unbelievably slow . . . to see the game" (*Festive Comedy*, p. 94).

(17) T. M. Parrott, *Shakespearean Comedy*, p. 125.

(18) Ben Jonson, *Discoveries*, lines 2031-32 in *Ben Jonson*, ed. Herford and Simpson (Oxford, 1947), VIII, 625.

(19) cf. III.i.192-96 and the final spring song, V.ii.884-901.

(20) The eye pun (cf. II.i.185-190; IV.i.116-117; IV.iii.9-11; IV.iii.275-278; III.i.193-194; V.ii.348-349) reflects and expresses the extreme views of young love in *LLL*; the eye is on one hand the source of ideal wisdom in Neoplatonic tradition; on the other it refers to the female gential organs. The pun is self-defining (see passages above), but see also Eric Partridge, *Shakespeare's Bawdy* (New York, 1960), pp. 109, 159. Thus Wilson is partially right in affirming that "the secret of the play" lies in the repeated references to women's eyes (*LLL*, ed. J. D. Wilson [Cambridge, 1962], p. xlv). It is interesting to compare Berowne's prose soliloquy (IV.iii.1-20) and Sidney's *Astrophel and Stella* Sonnet 47. Like Berowne, Astrophel is a courtier with heroic aspirations, a sensualist, a manipulator of Neoplatonism (Sonnet 25), and a Machiavel (Sonnet 69), as well as role-player who has less self-knowledge and self-control than self-consciousness.

(21) For example, the practice of flattery is described in the commercial metaphor by Berowne (IV.iii.236-238) and with different implications by the Princess (II.i.13-19 and IV.i.9-23). Navarre sets out to "buy the honor" (I.i.5-6) that will make him an heir of eternity, but by the last scene he exasperatedly asks the women of France, "what buys your company?" (V.ii.224). Rosaline's punning answer is "Your absence only" (225); cf. V.ii.256-261.

(22) *Dr. Faustus* (New York, 1948), p.216, Mann's academic narrator Zeitblom and Cyrus Hoy believe Leverkühn goes "deeper than the occasion warrants" ("*LLL* and the Nature of Comedy," *SQ*, XIII [1962], 35 and n. 4). As Hoy sees it, the phrase "gravity's revolt to wantonness," which Leverkühn insists on taking seriously, is more relevant to *Measure for Measure*.

(23) Wilson, *Shakespeare's Happy Comedies*, p. 71; Charlton, *Shakespearian Comedy*, p. 101; Parrott, *Shakespearean Comedy*, p. 123.

(24) Muriel C. Bradbrook, *The Growth and Structure of Elizabethan Comedy* (London, 1961), p. 90. See n. 6 above.

(25) As Evans asserts, it is "*the* way" of Shakespeare to keep his audience more informed than his participants in the drama (*Shakespearean Comedy*, pp. vii-viii). The oblique and progressive structure of *LLL* defines dramatic truth retrospectively and is therefore atypical. Again L. L. Schucking, *Character Problems in Shakespeare's Plays* (Gloucester, Mass., 1959) emphasizes "how careful the dramatist is to throw the brightest possible light upon his principal figures, especially when they are, or seem to be, in danger of appearing in a false light" (p. 59). Certainly there is such a danger in *LLL*, but the bright light is withheld until Marcade's entrance, and even there it operates, as it were, by reflection.

(26) Harbage, "*LLL* and the Early Shakespeare," 29-30.

(27) Scene lengths are respectively (David ed.) 298, 175, 258, 202, 148, 165, 383, 150, and 920. The mid-point is ca. IV.iii.104.

(28) The premeditation is Shakespeare's, of course, but the Princess shares her creator's transcendent knowledge of all happenings, and her role as moral spokesman is characterized by a reflective, even studious cast.

(29) I accept Professor Wilson's reading of II.i.100 in the Cambridge edition, which follows Capell.

(30) In *Rape of Lucrece* (line 487), Tarquin speaks of "My will that marks thee for my earth's delight." Beyond appetitive impulse, "will" also denotes sexual lust in these lines; elsewhere it may also refer to the sexual organ itself, especially in connection with the word "edge" as in the description of Longaville which illustrates a whole range of denotations: "a sharp wit match'd with too blunt a will;/ Whose edge hath power to cut, whose will still wills/ It should none spare that come within his power" (II.i.49-51). See Eric Partridge, *Shakespeare's Bawdy*, p. 221, and Alan Brien, "Down with Bowdlers," *New Statesman*, August 5, 1966, pp. 158-59.

(31) David ed., IV.i.107n.

(32) M. M. Mahood finds in the course of *LLL* at least ten meanings of "light" in *Shakespeare's Word-play* (London, 1957), p. 53. Nevertheless, Caroline Spurgeon identifies war and conflict as the dominant imagery of the play in *Shakespeare's Imagery* (New York, 1935), pp. 213, 271-272.

(33) This choric passage also refers to characters of the low plot (who themselves mirror traits in the noble lovers). The distinction drawn between wise foolishness and foolishness cuts across class lines.

(34) Muriel Bradbrook summarizes the conventional view in describing the oration as a "great speech in praise of the art of living" in *Shakespeare and Elizabethan Poetry* (London, 1961), pp. 215-16. Barber, on the other hand, is aware of Berowne's equivocation, adding that Berowne in alluding to the New Testament (*Romans* xiii, 8; *Matthew* x, 39) "merely leaps up to ring these big bells lightly" (p. 92). The attempted identification of "love" and "charity" is based on a piece of conventional Neoplatonic lore which is monotonously repeated in the Petrarchan sonnet tradition, but the operative concept in Berowne's speech comes from Ovid by way of Jean de Meun: "To win the Rosebud make it seem / That love platonic is your dream. / For rest assured, beyond all doubt. / That were your purpose once found out. / Your chance were lost." See F. S. Ellis trans. *The Romance of the Rose*, II (London, 1932), 14. Realizing how dangerous is the idealizing argument in the hands of the young lover, Bembo explicitly limits the practice of Neoplatonic love to the "Courtier not young" in Castiglione's *The Courtier*, trans. Thomas Hoby (1561) in *Three Renaissance Classics*, ed. Burton A. Milligan (New York, 1953), p. 606. The paradox represented by a young Platonic lover was evident to Shakespeare's predecessor Sir Philip Sidney, who mischievously refers to himself as a courtier of "not old yeares" in *The Defense of Poesie* (Albert Feuillerat ed. *The Prose Works of Sir Philip Sidney*, III [Cambridge, 1962], 3). In his sonnet sequence *Astrophel and Stella*, Sidney explicitly invokes Plato, "The wisest scholler of the wight most wise," to explain the "Strange flames of *Love*" which virtue raises (Sonnet 25), and by an equation of love and virtue attempts to silence the inner debate between reason and desire which begins in Sonnet 4: "Vertue alas, now let me take some rest. . . ." (cf. Sonnets 5, 10, 14, 18, 21). Yet despite its tactical value, the Neoplatonizing argument that love and charity are united cannot prevent the recurrence of sensual desires of Astrophel (cf. Sonnets 52, 71, 72 *et seq.*), and Berowne's oration concludes with sexual punning worthy of Falstaff: "Advance your standards, and upon them lords! / Pell-mell, down with them!" (IV.iii.364-365); cf. Falstaff's "pike bent bravely" (*2 Henry IV*, II.iv.55). Byron's acerbic comment is relevant to the tactical equivocations of Berowne, the young lover: "O Plato! Plato! you have paved the way, / With your confounded fantasies, to more immoral conduct . . . than all the long array / Of poets and romancers:—You're a bore, / A charlatan . . . no better than a go-between" (*Don Juan*, I:cxvi).

(35) Kenneth Muir alone seems to have discovered that this passage, V.ii.402-415, forms a conventional anti-Petrarchan sonnet. See "Shakespeare and Rhetoric," *Shakespeare Jahrbuch*, XC (1954), 50.

(36) See V.ii.743-766. Logic here is still pressed into the service of equivocation: Berowne admits everything and nothing, employing the same arguments the women have already rejected (cf. V.ii.347-350).

(37) Harbage, "*LLL* and the Early Shakespeare," 29: the "manners projected are atrocious and the characters uniformly barbarous."

(38) *Samuel Johnson on Shakespeare*, ed. W. K. Wimsatt (New York, 1960), p. 79.

(39) See, for example, V.ii.1-58; there (as in II.i.215-227) the girlish spirits of the women are disciplined and directed by the Princess after twenty-nine lines ("Well bandied both; a set of wit well play'd"); after forty-six lines ("A pox of that jest! and I beshrew all shrows! / But, Katherine, what was sent to you. . . ."); and after fifty-eight lines ("We are wise girls to mock our lovers so").

(40) Charlton, *Shakespearian Comedy*, 270; Cody, "The Pastoral Element in Shakespearean Comedy," 264.

(41) In I.ii, Armado engages in three formal combats with Moth (or French "mot" for "word": Furness, *Variorum*, p. 5 n. 13) who is an externalized critical self-consciousness of sorts. These three debates (beginning on lines 1, 35, and 61) are on subjects not irrelevant to the high plot: melancholy, three years' study, and love. Each interchange concludes with a scornful aside by Moth after Armado attempts to manipulate experience through words.

(42) As Holofernes arrogates three of nine roles to himself for the Show of Worthies, Moth's ironic aside makes other comment unnecessary: "Thrice-worthy gentleman!" (V.i.138). Contrast the response of Bottom's fellows to his ingenuous desire to play every role (*MND*. I.ii and IV.ii). Dull describes his treatment by the curate and pedant in IV.i.: it is "collusion" and "pollution" (43-46). The sexual innuendo in Holofernes' relationship to his students suggests the element of coersion in another way: "if their daughters be capable, I will put it to them" (IV.i.78-79).

(43) Madeleine Doran, *Endeavors of Art* (Madison, 1954), p. 63.

(44) Castiglione, *The Courtier, op. cit.*, 604. As Berowne says, "This love . . . kills me" (IV.iii.6-7), i.e. it reduces to obscurity the anxious selfhood which is not generous, not gentle, not humble.

(45) Berowne's admiration of the power to cope in feminine society is manifested in his delicious jealousy of Boyet, expressed at length in V.ii.315-334 and 459-481.

(46) See V.ii.814, 818, 826; also V.ii is prefaced by an account of boyish spirits in the courtiers' rehearsal (89-118). In Hector's words, the courtiers have "glozed, but superficially; not much / Unlike young men, whom Aristotle thought / Unfit to hear moral philosophy" (*Troilus and Cressida*, II.ii.165-167) —but their youth, here reiterated, is insulation against the judgment Holofernes identity; cf. V.ii.269-272, 600-615.

(47) Northrop Frye, "The Structure and Spirit of Comedy" in *Stratford Papers on Shakespeare*, 1964, ed. B. W. Jackson (Toronto, 1965), p. 7. Shakespeare's use of the color green in *LLL* suggests the play's deviation from the comedies of "the green world." When Armado claims his mistress' complexion is the conventional ideal of red and white, Moth contrasts these superficial colors with the underlying "green wit" of famous women: "Most maculate thoughts, master, are masked under such colors" (I.ii.79-102). Such "maculate" green thoughts serve to expose idealizing pretensions in *LLL* (as in the case of Armado himself); sexuality is an emancipating manifestation of the "physically natural."

(48) Cf. Bertrand H. Bronson, "Daisies Pied and Icicles," *MLN.*LXII (1948), p. 35.

(49) Wilson, *Shakespeare's Happy Comedies* pp. 62ff. See also Granville-Barker's seminal discussion of "style" in productions of *LLL* (*Prefaces to Shakespeare, I.* [London, 1927]). The theatrical as distinguished from the literary quality of *LLL* is indicated by the walk-on of Armado and Moth courting Jaquenetta, described by Costard as it is acted in dumbshow. Their appearance exhibits the thematic rather than narrative logic of the action; the dumbshow wooing furthers no narrative process but brings the conversation of Boyet, Maria, and Costard (on sexual matters) to bear upon Armado and the wooing in general. Richard David summarizes a common response to the passage: "What are they doing in this scene?" (IV.i.143-144n.).

72

The Dimensions of Time in Richard II

by Robert L. Montgomery, Jr.

The major force and interest of a play may sometimes rest in what we call its theme, in the concepts it seems to arrive at or to urge, and Shakespeare's *Richard II* (along with the group of chronicle plays to which it is related), has more often than not been submitted to this general kind of interpretation. For Miss Campbell it is "one of a cycle of plays teaching the lessons of political crime and political punishment," and individually it "comes to be also a play dealing with the problem of the deposition of a king." These issues are of course present in the play and were urgent concerns of Shakespeare's time. One might even concede that they provided its main interest to the audience of the 1590's and that when Miss Campbell writes, "Shakespeare thus offered the follies of *Richard II* only as a background for the presentation of the problem . . . ," she is doing no more than judging the play in its essential quality.[1]

Yet Richard as a character appears to most of us to be far more interesting than he would be if Miss Campbell's set of priorities were accurate, and those who have followed Richard Altick in examining patterns of imagery—they are especially abundant in *Richard II*—have at least been able to suggest that Shakespeare constructed something more searching and subtle than a dramatized comment upon history.[2] At the same time one wonders if there has not been too strong a tendency even on the part of those who have been responsive to the details of Shakespeare's imagery to arrive at abstractions and to view the play too emphatically as a mode of the conceptual. Such seems to me to be the difficulty in a recent piece by Ricardo J. Quinones which devotes some attention to *Richard II.*[3] He correctly emphasizes the importance of time in the play, providing useful and specific definitions (e.g. "Time is an agent of reality that leads the organism . . . to destruction"), but his achievement is essentially that of classifying a set of concepts.

Yet if *Richard II* has concepts of time in or behind it, its action and atmosphere are informed by senses of time which are both persistent and changing. Time is not, then, just an idea which the characters and the audience are meant to realize or the repository of a standard which the action should illustrate. It is a felt presence and an almost palpable condition, an element working energetically at the dramatic level, which is at least as important as the conceptual if we wish to grasp the nature of the play. *Richard II* does not work towards illuminating an idea of time; rather ideas of time help illuminate the situations of its characters.[4]

To put it another way *Richard II* is in part shaped by time, by the repeated use of the word and all that attaches to it. "Time" occurs thirty-three times, not so much as in *Hamlet* or *Macbeth* or even in the separate parts of *Henry IV*, but thirty-three occurrences is a good deal, and we must add some compounds or other forms of the word as well as related terms such as "minutes," "days," "years," and references to age, haste, slowness, and tempo. All these together have the general function of building and maintaining an atmosphere, a series of contexts, in which Richard and the others live and move. Time or a sense of time is evident in the most trival as well as the most crucial statements, from Richard's initial and largely formal greeting to "time-honoured" Lancaster to his final soliloquy ("I have wasted Time and now doth Time waste me"); from the shrill emphasis it provides in the quarrel between Aumerle and Fitzwater to Bolingbroke's solemnly weighted sentence on Bushy, Greene, and Wiltshire, which will end their "sinful hours" or his final remark about Richard's "untimely bier." Such references can be multiplied, and ignoring for the moment whatever poetic or figurative burden they may support, one is bound to notice that Shakespeare's repetition establishes time as a natural, fundamental part of the lives and language of the characters, almost as natural and fundamental as their very existence in the play.

Probably the simplest and most obvious way in which Shakespeare uses "time" is to indicate mere duration, either long or short, and through it to suggest emotional values which are more or less constant throughout the work. The play's opening line is positive: "Old John of Gaunt, time-honoured Lancaster."[5] Moments later Bolingbroke addresses Richard with corresponding fulsomeness: "Many years of happy days befall/My gracious sovereign," a greeting echoed by Mowbray: "Each day still better other's happiness . . . ." Such lines establish the conditions for later rather obvious ironies, since Gaunt's age soon becomes bitter to him, and Richard's days are short and tormented. The mood of felicity is countered in Act I, scene ii, when the Duchess of Gloucester, lamenting her husband's murder, intones that his "summer leaves" are "all faded," but the most important exploitation of this sense of time comes in Act I, scene iii, the occasion on which Mowbray and Bolingbroke confront each other in trial by combat only to have Richard interrupt and sentence them both to exile.

As the ceremony gets underway, Bolingbroke remarks that "Mowbray and myself are like two men / That vow a long and weary pilgrimage" (48-49). Here length of time first suggests hardship and endurance, and clustered around a general and increasing awareness of time are ceremonies of farewell which in turn anticipate what comes next, the sudden and painful sentences of banishment Richard imposes. It has been customary for critics to describe this scene largely as one of stiff formality designed to give point to Richard's capricious will, but if we stop at this, we miss the emotions Shakespeare generates by repeated emphasis on time and the act of saying farewell. Bolingbroke, for example, feels his youth and strength, but feels them in the environment of death:

> Not sick, although I have to do with death,
> But lusty, young, and cheerly drawing breath.   *(I.iii.65-66)*

In saying goodbye to his father he refers to the old man's youthful spirit and expresses through the occasion a hope for continuity and vigor, a hope which is almost at once frustrated by Richard's sentence of exile. Once the sentence is pronounced, Shakespeare lets the scene dwell not on the irrationality of Richard's behavior (indeed we have little sense at this point that it is irrational) but on the intense personal reactions of his victims.

Time now becomes much more closely linked to grief and leave-taking than to ceremonial formality. The very manner in which Richard delivers judgment allies length of time with pain and decay by evoking their opposites. He tells Bolingbroke that his banishment will last "Til twice five summers have enriched our fields" (140), and then dedicates more ponderously evocative language to Mowbray's "heavier doom":

> The sly slow hours shall not determinate
> The dateless limit of thy dear exile.
> The hopeless word of "never to return"
> Breathe I against thee, upon pain of life. *(I.iii.150-154)*

Bolingbroke pointedly notices "How long a time lies in one little word" (213).

Thus time expresses a destiny of suffering and alienation for at least two of the characters on the verge of parting from country, relatives, and peers. For Mowbray the occasion is tantamount to death:

> The language I have learned these forty years,
> My native English, now I must forgo.
> And now my tongue's use is to me no more
> Than an unstringed viol or a harp,
> Or like a cunning instrument cased up,
> Or, being open, put into his hands
> That knows no touch to tune the harmony. *(I.iii.159-165)*

The deeper associations of these lines strengthen the patriotic feelings later to be exploited by Gaunt's deathbed prophecy. Also for Mowbray exile is loss of status, of reason for being, and most profoundly a loss of control over the rhythm of his life. The penalty Richard exacts from him is, in his own mind, oblivion. And although Bolingbroke's sentence is less drastic and is reduced from ten to six years by Richard out of seeming regard for Gaunt's "grieved heart," neither Gaunt nor Bolingbroke is consoled. Even though Gaunt tries to pretend to his son that six years will pass quickly, to Richard he speaks differently and bitterly:

> I thank my liege that in regard of me
> He shortens four years of my son's exile,
> But little vantage shall I reap thereby. *(I.iii.216-218)*

Bolingbroke has just paid tribute to the power of the "breath of kings" over the lives of others, but Gaunt, noting that his "light" will soon be "extinct with age and endless night," adds that he has not a "minute" that the king can give:

> Shorten my days thou canst with sullen sorrow,

> And pluck nights from me, but not lend a morrow;
> Thou canst help time to furrow me with age,
> But stop no wrinkle in his pilgrimage;
> Thy word is current with him for my death,
> But dead, thy kingdom cannot buy my breath.   *(I.iii.227-232)*

These lines are part of Gaunt's lament over his son's exile; they also reflect a sharp sense of human impotence under the pressure of necessity. Although later in the scene Gaunt tries to cheer Bolingbroke by arguing that "six winters" are "quickly gone," that the pace and impact of time are simply a matter of subjective attitude ("Thy grief," he says, "is but thy absence for a time"), the result of the old duke's participation in this scene is to translate the "grief" imposed by time into a conviction that men are powerless in the grip of forces beyond them.

Richard is time's instrument. All but Richard are caught in the mood of helplessness. He manipulates and they are moved; the scene is shot through with expressions of their private feelings. Of those on stage Richard is least aware of the effects of time; Gaunt and Mowbray are most sensitive to it, shifting from an awareness of time as the passage of years to its more suggestive range as joy and grief, and finally as the threat of total obliteration of the self.

The suggestive and referential scope of "time" is more extensive elsewhere, touching on the natural cycle of life in man and in his world and involving eventually his moral and active response to his world.[6] The assumption throughout *Richard II* is that ideally man's life has a fitting, natural duration and a natural rhythm, one which Gaunt refers to doubly in Act II, scene i, when he repeats the truism that "the tongues of dying men / Inforce deep harmony" and then, turning to an image of speed, asserts that Richard's "rash fierce blaze of riot cannot last":

> For violent fires soon burn out themselves;
> Small showers last long, but sudden storms are short;
> He tires betimes that spurs too fast betimes..."   *(II.i.33-36)*

These aphorisms flow into Gaunt's prophecy and the agricultural and commercial imagery which dominates it. Two points preoccupy him: Richard has misused his power to violate time-honored tradition ("O, had thy grandsire with a prophet's eye / Seen how his son's son should destroy his sons"), and he himself has lived too long. He addresses Richard bitterly:

> Join with the present sickness that I have,
> And thy unkindness be like crooked age,
> To crop at once a too long withered flower.   *(II.i.103-105)*

Shakespeare has Gaunt contradict himself in this scene. Although he initially argues that Richard may heed the advice of a dying man, he ignores York's advice to be mild and succeeds only in infuriating the king. If Shakespeare is using Gaunt as his instrument to drive home the lessons of faulty kingship, he nevertheless seems aware also of the claims of human emotion. Gaunt's feeling that he is old beyond

76

his proper time, beyond usefulness or propriety, is poignant and strong. His sarcastic puns on his name and age when Richard first approaches his sickbed also remind us that his bitterness is personal as well as patriotic. His brother has been murdered and his son exiled. Gaunt's persistent dwelling on his age as a way of expressing these concerns is yet another example of Shakespeare's attention to the subjective dimension of time, but it suggests more than just painful helplessness and something other than time as malevolent mortality. It suggests also that a condition of each man's life is to have a time, to be fitted through it to a larger rhythm—or to be unfitted. Shakespeare's imagery of tempo adds a further value here. At the beginning of the scene York doubts that Richard will listen to sober advice and characterizes him in drastic terms:

> Where doth the world thrust forth a vanity—
> So it be new, there's no respect how vile—
> That is not quickly buzzed into his ears?
> Then all too late comes counsel to be heard
> Where will doth mutiny with wit's regard.   (II.i.24-28)

Seasonal time, expressed in terms of speed, lateness, uneven tempo, has moral implications. Both York and Gaunt comment didactically and critically on Richard's disastrous, unmeasured wilfulness and when Richard appears at Gaunt's bedside, the two antagonists pun on Gaunt's name and age, by implication underscoring Richard's raw, unseasoned youth.

I have dealt so far with two basic senses in which "time" is used: as a concept for expressing joy or grief and as a reference to seasonal time to suggest the relationships between the rhythm or tempo of human life and the larger cycles of nature. These concepts function in the play not so much as commonplace truths about the nature of life (which for Shakespeare's time they are) but as instruments for measuring the emotional weather and as a means, in the first two acts, of discriminating between Richard and those arrayed in one way or another against him. If natural time is stressed by Gaunt as a value with which Richard is out of step, it is also the pace of vital existence, the music of living so to speak, and all the characters except Richard see themselves and him as missing the natural harmony. They are depressed, apprehensive, hollowly confident, each in his own way conscious of being moved or manipulated by time moving too slowly or too swiftly. Time is either short or endless according to the mood or circumstances of the speaker; it is never, in the more emotional moments of these early scenes, just right.

Or, to put it somewhat differently, for Mowbray, Gaunt, York, and to a lesser degree Bolingbroke, the proportion and fit measure of life is unsuited to their wishes as creatures existing in time. This subjective tonality is, I believe, the essential note struck in the first two acts. Only in the middle of Act II do time and events begin to move against Richard, and then he, in his turn, becomes the victim of time. The emphasis of the play shifts from his harmful effects on others to his own declining destiny, and this movement is reflected in Shakespeare's development of Richard's increasing awareness of time.

In the earlier scenes of the play when he is able to wield power without interference, Richard uses time like a whip, but casually and carelessly, without the alertness of his victims to its weight and sting. On his lips "time" is initially a perfunctory compliment to Gaunt. When he sentences Bolingbroke to exile (Act I, scene iii), he orders him as we have noticed not to return "till twice five summers have enriched our fields," and a knowing audience will perhaps catch the irony when they recall that Richard is about to enrich his treasury at Bolingbroke's expense. Then, having sentenced Mowbray by emphasizing the "dateless limits of they dear exile," he offers callous words to Gaunt who is lamenting that he will not see his son again: "Why, uncle, thou hast many years to live," a remark totally inadequate to the emotion of the moment. Later in Act I, scene iv, he tells Aumerle almost with relish that he has no intention of letting Bolingbroke return from exile:

> He is our cousin's cousin, but 'tis doubt
> When time shall call him home from banishment.   *(I.iv.20-21)*

For "time" in the second line, we can easily substitute "Richard." And the scene ends by revealing the ugliest side of his character in his reaction to the news that Gaunt is mortally ill.

> Now put it, God, in the physician's mind
> To help him to his grave immediately.   *(I.iv.59-60)*

And then:

> Come, gentlemen, let's all go visit him.
> Pray God we may make haste and come too late!   *(I.iv.63-64)*

Richard's distorted and tasteless wit marks the first direct demonstration of his misuse of time, the first overt sign that he is devious and unscrupulous as a ruler. Time is here an index of the quality of his actions. When he learns that Gaunt is dead Richard's response is businesslike:

> The ripest fruit first falls, and so doth he;
> His time is spent, our pilgrimage must be.
> So much for that. . . .   *(II.i.154-155)*

The expression reminds us that the concept of time as the natural cycle is still in force, but Richard takes it almost literally and has no ear for York's warning with its wider understanding of time's meaning:

> Take Hereford's rights away, and take from Time
> His charters and his customary rights,
> Let not tomorrow then ensue today.   *(II.i.195-197)*

Shakespeare makes a sharp contrast between Richard's malicious wit and York's pious, sober counsel. "Be not thyself," York continues, "for how art thou a king / But by fair sequence and succession?" (198-199). Sequence, the order of succession in time and secured by time, establishes propriety in the world, dictating to Richard and to England the terms for what they ought to be. But York's advice and sense of values go unheeded, and the scene ends shortly with Richard's mind bent only on the speed with which he must get to Ireland. "The time is short," he says.

His time is indeed short. Tomorrow, if we take it to mean the survival of Richard's power, does not ensue today. Act II, scene iii records Bolingbroke's return to England and the beginning of his ascendancy. He expects his "infant fortune" to "come to years," an expectation that Shakespeare has already anticipated in the previous scene where the Queen anxiously complains that "Some unborn sorrow ripe in Fortune's womb / Is coming towards me" (II. ii. 10-11),[7] and when she mentions that Richard's "designs crave haste," Greene informs her of the defection of the Percys, and York comments, "Now comes the sick hour that his surfeit made" (II. ii. 84). The natural ripening of events and men's fortunes foreshadows the birth of Richard's downfall just as it engenders Bolingbroke's success. In scene iii York reminds Bolingbroke that he is premature: "Thou art a banish'd man, and here art come, / Before the expiration of thy time" (109-110), but although York is literally and legally correct, his words have no more force than his warnings to Richard.

The continual references to time in Act II help to articulate the antagonists' exchange of fortunes and suggest a way of moralizing their actions which culminates in the open allegory of the scene in the Duke of York's garden (Act III, scene iv). Most readers will recall the formal manner in which the gardener compares the garden to the realm and exposes Richard as a bad gardener through his failure to prune and trim and weed. I need only add that one important point in the allegory involves the notion that gardening and government must be carried on seasonably, with timeliness. In moralizing his figure the gardener comments first on Richard's condition:

> He that hath suffered this disordered spring
> Hath now himself met with the fall of leaf.   *(III.iv.48-49)*

Then he particularizes Richard's failure:

>   O, what pity is it
> That he had not so trimm'd and dress'd his land
> As we this garden! We at time of year
> Do wound the bark. . . .
> Had he done so, himself had borne the crown,
> Which waste of idle hours hath quite thrown down.   *(III.iv.55-58, 65-66)*

It is interesting that this emphatic estimate of Richard's stewardship comes well before the play is over. The gardener's words echo Gaunt's earlier indictment and anticipate exactly Richard's own retrospective judgment of his errors in his final soliloquy, which would suggest that what remains in the play is not only an object lesson, but a dramatization in terms of character, in terms of Richard's sensibility. What we are drawn into is more than a moral conclusion to the meaning of Richard's misrule; we are led to watch the unfolding of his fitful and painful realization of those deficiencies in his character which have already been outlined for us and for the other characters. The imagery of time supplies the context in which Richard comes to know himself as well as that in which others (including the audience) have come to know him.

In the first two acts Richard speaks with relative brevity, in the last three much more at length, philosophizing and elaborating. He is all too obviously defeated politically, his power of action and decision have collapsed, and his deposition is a foregone conclusion. Hence those portions of the second half of the play which are devoted to Richard examine a personal and inward reversal of fortune for which the outward events are in a sense preparation.

His inward condition begins to come into focus in Act III, scene ii, as we witness the histrionic gestures of his return home from Ireland. The language of time measures his state of mind; it also measures his state. Salisbury gives him the news already available to the audience: he has returned too late and his allies have left him:

> One day too late, I fear me, noble lord,
> Hath clouded all thy happy days on earth.
> O, call back yesterday, bid time return,
> And thou shalt have twelve thousand fighting men!
> To-day, to-day, unhappy day too late,
> O'erthrows thy joys, friends, fortune and thy state.... *(III.ii.67-72)*

The wish is, of course, vain and rhetorical, and what the lines convey, besides regret, is Richard's new subservience to time and to the necessity of events in time. There is a strong and conscious echo here of the manner in which time, at an earlier stage in the play, translated the feelings of others overtaken by time and Richard.

Richard's response is to blame time: "Time hath set a blot upon my pride" (81). His sense of victimization grows. Scroope almost at once brings him fresh "tidings of calamity," and Bolingbroke's power increases "like an unseasonable stormy day." Three of his closest advisers, Wiltshire, Bushy, and Greene, are dead, as he now learns, and in his familiar lament on the tribulations of kingship he shows himself conscious at last of the full extent of his impotence.

> Our lands, our lives, and all, are Bolingbroke's,
> And nothing can we call our own but death. *(III.ii.151-152)*

As we know, Richard does more than bemoan his own ill fortune; in an excess of despondency he generalizes rather wildly, and his vision of a king as subject to the whim of death "scoffing at his state and grinning at his pomp" is more revealing of Richard's temperament under pressure than a universal truth urged by the play. What is interesting here is that Richard sees himself, and all kings, as moved and manipulated by death in just the fashion that Mowbray and Bolingbroke felt themselves the victims of time and Richard. Of course, he goes too far. Gaunt and York had understood time as establishing custom, tradition, order, and legitimacy. Richard, having previously confused these values with his own person as king, now leaps to the other extreme:

<blockquote>
throw away respect,
Tradition, form, and ceremonious duty;
For you have mistook me all this while.   *(III.ii.172-174)*
</blockquote>

He understands only one of the dimensions of time; it is only mortality and an enemy, a reading close to the "envious and calumniating time" Ulysses emphasizes in *Troilus and Cressida*. From a false confidence in his power—"Is not the king's name twenty thousand names?"—Richard now gives way to an equally false acceptance of human impotence, and, by implication, to an abdication of responsiblity. By the end of Act III, scene ii, Richard thinks only in terms of comfort and despair and accepts the latter with a sickly zest.

The terminology of time is not, of course, the only means Shakespeare employs to dwell on Richard's self-absorbed melancholy. But it is noticeable that "time" makes a consistent appearance in the language used to convey his shifting, inconstant state of mind. And his sense of time and his own place in it permits Shakespeare the ironic parallelism which puts Richard in the place formerly reserved for his victims. In part the play is an exploration of the geography of suffering, less thorough than *Lear*, obviously, but still imposing.

Act IV, scene i, continues the exposure of Richard's grief. Here he extravagantly abdicates his very being. He will give up the crown, he says, "but not my griefs; still am I king of those" (193). Verbally he divests himself of everything else, status, property, dignity, and all their outward emblems. Ironically, he wishes "King Henry" . . . "many happy years of sunshine days" (221), and when Northumberland demands that he read a list of the accusations against him, he compares himself (for the second time) to Christ. Then:

<blockquote>
I have no name, no title;
No, not that name was given me at the font,
But 'tis usurped. Alack the heavy day,
That I have worn so many winters out,
And know not now what name to call myself![8]   *(IV.i.255-259)*
</blockquote>

Richard's nothingness is something he sees reached in time and inevitably bound up with it. He calls for a mirror and holding it before his face speaks in two tenses:

<blockquote>
Was this face the face
That every day under his household roof
Did keep ten thousand me? *Was* this the face
That like the sun *did* make beholders wink?
</blockquote>

And
<blockquote>
Is this the face which fac'd so many follies,
That *was* outfac'd by Bolingbroke?
A brittle glory shineth in this face;
As brittle as the glory *is* the face . . . .[9]   *(IV.i.281-287)*
</blockquote>

He then smashes the mirror. This speech and its concluding gesture are frequently cited as evidence of Richard's neurotic, self-dramatizing vanity. The judgment is overdrawn. For one thing, the glass is not used to demonstrate Richard's vanity, but the reverse: it is a crystal mirror, and Richard calls it a "flattering glass" (steel mirrors, by contrast, were supposed to reflect a true image). It is more appropriate to read the incident as a moment of partial self-recognition, as Richard's new discovery, following his resignation of pomp, ceremony, place, and title, that he has deceived himself and been deceived by others. And the shift from past to present tense is surely a bit of deliberate emphasis on Shakespeare's part. Richard has moved from what he was to what he is.

A more thorough awareness is still to come, and this Shakespeare locates in Act V, scene v, just before Richard's murder. His long, rather formal soliloquy marks the destination of his journey from self-willed tyrant to self-pitying victim to a state approaching repentance and resolution, at least to the extent that he is finally able to express his fault in broader terms than before. According to Peter Ure, Richard's fifth act soliloquy gives no sign that he possesses the power to create a new self, having symbolically destroyed the old in smashing the mirror.[10] But what is central to Shakespeare's characterization is Richard's sense of himself, not what he is unable to do, but what he is able to see, and in this final moment of his life, although still capable of angry feeling, he offers quite a different appraisal of his career than we have seen him do before. If his state of mind falls short of complete resolution, it is at least fluid and developing away from self-serving despair. It is instructive to examine the change.

The first section of the soliloquy would seem to express a radical nihilism. Beginning with his effort to "compare / This prison where I live unto the world," ranging through the observation that struggling ambition is futile, while "thoughts tending to content flatter themselves," Richard decides that he plays many people in one person and re-enacts in thought his kingship and his nothingness. As he has for some time, he still dwells on the idea of contentment:

> But whate'er I be
> Nor I, nor any man that but man is,
> With nothing shall be pleas'd, till he be eas'd
> With being nothing. *(V.v.38-41)*

Yet there is more here. Richard recognizes that he is *but a man* and is not yet nothing. Perhaps his mood is more settled than has been acknowledged.

The next part of the soliloquy is a meditation on time. Richard dwells on the lack of proportion, of measured rhythm, in his reign as it is set against his "true time," the time he ought to have kept.

> Music do I hear?
> Ha, ha! keep time—how sour sweet music is
> When time is broke and no proportion kept!
> So is it in the music of men's lives.
> And here have I the daintiness of ear
> To check time broke in a disordered string;

82

But for the concord of my state and time,
Had not an ear to hear my true time broke:
I wasted time, and now doth time waste me;
For now hath time made me his numb'ring clock;
My thoughts are minutes, and with sighs they jar
Their watches on unto mine eyes, the outward watch,
Whereto my finger, like a dial's point,
Is pointing still, in cleansing them from tears.
Now sir, the sound that tells what hour it is
Are clamorous groans which strike upon my heart,
Which is the bell—so sighs, and tears, and groans,
Show minutes, times, and hours. But my time
Runs posting in Bolingbroke's proud joy,
While I stand fooling here, his Jack of the clock. *(V.v.41-60)*

Loosely summarized these lines indicate that Richard knows he has violated natural and political order. He now has an ear to understand his failure—"And here have I the daintiness of ear / To check time broke in a disordered string"—and he accepts the responsibility.[11] Then he reiterates his painful sense of being at the mercy of forces beyond him. But the difference between this and his previous expressions of helplessness is that now he knows it is his own fault: "I wasted time and now doth time waste me." His suffering is no less acute, but it is now more manly. His time now is measured only by sighs, tears, and groans, and these define and fill up his existence. Moreover, his time, his power, place, and identity, are now Bolingbroke's and he must endure the maddening indignity of knowing that another has supplanted and surpassed him.

If this final soliloquy marks the final point at which Richard's introspection arrives, it also sums up a good deal of what has gone on in the play. Richard here grasps what first Gaunt and then York and then the gardener have said about the causes and consequences of his misrule (both Gaunt and the gardener have used the word "waste" in judging him), and his downfall has come to pass more or less as they predicted. But it is interesting to note that he does not view his career in quite the same terms as Gaunt and York. They invoked the concept of providential time, of a divinely established order as a standard for condemning his behavior. Richard referred to this standard only when he was suffering from an illusory and proud sense of his role, when in the midst of adversity he felt urged to accuse others of sacrilege (Act III, scene iii). But here at the end of his life, although he has not ceased to feel victimized and humiliated, he blesses whoever has "given" him the music which prompts this meditation upon harmony: "For 'tis a sign of love."

Despite its complexity, the imagery of time in this soliloquy moves through all the dimensions Shakespeare has established for it: it is expressive of subjective feeling; it invokes the broad theme of natural rhythm; and it provides the terms for Richard's assessment of himself as well as for our assessment of him. And it expresses finally, for Richard and for the audience, a way of distinguishing timeliness as a principle for human action from opportunism, a principle evident in Richard's failure to achieve it. Fittingly the play concludes with the imagery of rhythm as Bolingbroke commands his followers:

> March sadly after; grace my mournings here
> In weeping after this untimely bier. *(V.vi.52-53)*

Notes:

(1) Lily B. Campbell, *Shakespeare's "Histories": Mirrors of Elizabethan Policy* (San Marino, Cal., 1947), pp. 169, 211. Sen Gupta in *Shakespeare's Historical Plays* (Oxford, 1964) offers a healthy corrective. See pp. 18, 115, 116.

(2) Richard D. Altick, "Symphonic Imagery in *Richard II*," PMLA, LXII (1947), 339-365. Altick discusses a wide range of images and notes (p. 340) that the text is "one vast arabesque of language." He does not include the imagery of time in the "leitmotifs" he selects for comment.

(3) Ricardo J. Quinones, "Views of Time in Shakespeare," *JHI*, XXVI (1965), 327-352. Quinones postulates three general concepts of time: augmentative, contracted, and extended. Augmentative is a frame for judging actions and character and is prominent in the sonnets and history plays. Contracted time is psychological, a sense of the too great brevity of life, and Quinones finds it prominent in the love tragedies. Extended time, which he sees as the dominant perspective of the later romances, is essentially a concept of eternity. I agree with Quinones' view (p. 328) that "drama is made from the attempts of characters to deny, control, escape or understand the real, relentless, and unrecalling activities of Time," but in his discussion of *Richard II* he limits attention to Richard himself and essentially understands Shakespeare's use of time in the play, perhaps too exclusively, as a commentary on Richard's failure.

(4) A convenient general thematic summary of *Richard II* is in R. J. Dorius, "A Little More than a Little," *SQ*, XI (1960), 13-26. The following statement (p. 13) summarizes his approach: "Themes of negligence, excess, and waste are developed in *Richard II* primarily through several strands of imagery—those of time, the garden and sickness, and the farm and death."

(5) My text is the Arden Shakespeare edition, ed. Peter Ure (Cambridge, Mass., 1956).

(6) See Samuel C. Chew, *The Pilgrimage of Life: An Exploration into the Renaissance Mind* (New Haven, 1962), pp. 9-34, for an account of these and other representations of time common in the Renaissance.

(7) In this context Ricardo Quinones, pp. 333-334, has noticed that though Richard and his queen both occasionally employ language of birth and gestation (to express painful apprehension), they are a barren pair. He sees this language as Shakespeare's commentary on the barrenness of Richard's moral actions, as well as an expression of Shakespeare's understanding of the necessity for royal continuity to combat the inevitable effects of time. These extensions of meaning are plausible. It is also true that this kind of time-related imagery has a more immediate and subjective focus. For example, Richard in a moment of dejection says, "Let's choose executors and talk of wills. / And yet not so—for what can we bequeath / Save our deposed bodies to the ground?" (III. ii. 148-150).

(8) Critics have frequently seen Richard and Bolingbroke as parallel characters, the one up and the other down and vice versa, but if we consider Richard at this point in the play, morbidly sensitive to his lack of power and his nothingness, the balancing character is Mowbray, earlier Richard's victim, and one whose sense of loss went far deeper and received more feeling, more extended expression than Bolingbroke's. Cf. I. iii. 154-177: in this speech Mowbray is the real harbinger of Richard's woe.

(9) Italics added.

(10) *King Richard II*, Arden edition, p. lxxxiii.

(11) Harold Toliver remarks on the soliloquy: "His final invention of a kingdom and his final concept of time are thus extravagant, ineffectual, and personal . . . ," *JEGP*, LXIV (1965), 242. Richard is, certainly, powerless to reverse events, but his "concept" of time is effectual insofar as it expresses his recognition of the truth.

Shakespeare's Caskets:
Unity in the Merchant of Venice

by Herbert S. Donow

The apparent lack of unity between the several plots of *The Merchant of Venice* has attracted a good deal of critical attention over the years. Although undoubtedly there are problems of inconsistent emphasis and tone, much of the difficulty has been created by the tendency of certain critics to exaggerate the inconsistencies. The so-called "casket plot" and the elopement of Jessica and Lorenzo have been traditionally singled out as being dissonant elements in the play. It is my view, however, that these two lines of action, far from being incidental or irrelevant, are vitally important to the scheme of the play.

One obstacle to our perception of the play's structural unity has been our proclivity to reduce the play to three or four distinct plots. Although this technique may be instructive for those interested in the sources of the play, it quite obscures the fact that the play, existing as an entity, may be grossly misunderstood under that kind of analysis. Sir Arthur Quiller-Couch, one of the play's editors and critics, makes this sort of mistake when he observes that the play contains several "motives which mingle well enough in a medieval tale [i.e. *Il Pecorone*] but do not consort at all as themes for a drama."[1] Following the same line of reasoning. Harley Granville-Barker concludes that the "bond plot" and the "casket plot" are unrelated, involving wholly different themes. "The two stories do not naturally march together"; and then he adds that they differ in "their very nature."[2] More recently W. H. Auden has drawn a similar conclusion, writing that the "romantic fairy story world of Belmont is incompatible with the historical reality of money-making Venice . . . ."[3] Bernard Grebanier seems also to view the casket scenes as being essentially unrelated to the main action of the play, acknowledging only that the scenes "serve . . . the valuable dramatic function of enabling Shakespeare to move back and forth between Venice and Belmont, so that we sense time elapsing as the day of reckoning approaches."[4]

The most important assumption that this kind of criticism makes is that the focus of the play is on the collection of the bond, and that *The Merchant of Venice* is a play *about* a Venetian merchant. There can be no argument that the "pound of flesh" story is the most sensational part of the play and that it is, to modern sensibilities, the very crux of the play. However, if we make a specific examination of the action, we find that the main events center on the courtship of Portia and, secondarily, on Jessica's elopement. The eight scenes set in Belmont, involving 1,154 lines of the play's 2,580, are concerned either with the winning of Portia or the dalliance between Jessica and Lorenzo. Of the 1,426 lines set in Venice, over half are concerned with either the relationship between Bassanio and Portia (e.g.

the plans for Bassanio's voyage or the business with the rings) or Jessica's home life and clandestine flight with Lorenzo. Included in the latter category are Launcelot Gobbo's scene (II.ii) and the masquers' scene (II.viii).[5]

If we may measure a character's importance in terms of his frequency of appearance and of the number of lines he speaks, Portia and Bassanio are unquestionably the principal characters. They appear on stage, either together or singly, during 1,846 lines of the play, with Portia being present for 1,281 lines and Bassanio for 1,351. Of the two Portia seems the more prominent, for while Bassanio appears in several scenes in which he plays only a minor role, Portia never does.

Even if we reject the quantitative approach as a way to determine a character's importance, there is still the point that the play begins and ends as a story about the wooing of a romantic heroine. The action is generated by Bassanio's desire to win Portia, and it ends when the two lovers have removed all obstacles to their complete and lasting union. The "bond plot" with the mutual hatred between Shylock and Antonio and the issues of usury and anti-Semitism are not, for all their interest to us, vital to the structure of the play. They are important as themes, and without them the play would have little to excite a modern audience, but the primary dramatic situation is not significantly altered by the presence of these extraneous elements.

If the focus of the main plot is upon Portia, her courtship and her marriage to Bassanio, the elopement of Jessica is a parallel and related plot. There are a number of tangible similarities between the two young women which, when recognized, substantially challenge the view that the play is deficient in unity. The manner in which the two heroines eventually exchange places, with Jessica becoming the temporary mistress of Belmont and Portia journeying to Venice for her triumphant confrontation with Shylock, emphasizes the inter-relationship between the two plots and their heroines.

Most apparent of the links between these two characters is that both are the objects of active courtship and both are restrained by parental authority from following their own desires. Our first intimation that this is a major source of tension comes at the end of the first scene when Bassanio regales Antonio with a panegyric to Portia's beauty and virtue. The imagery of the speech, however, contains more than mere superlatives. Bassanio tells Antonio that Portia's virtue and beauty are known to all the world, and that she is "nothing undervalu'd / to Cato's daughter, Brutus' Portia" (I.i.165-166).[6] This allusion to the Roman Portia, a woman renowned for prudence and integrity and for her superiority to her sex,[7] creates our initial image of the Belmont Portia. Too many critics stop at this view of Portia, seeing her, as John Russell Brown does, as being rich, beautiful, and possessed "of wondrous virtues."[8] But Portia is not as tame as all that. For only a few lines after he compares her to "Brutus' Portia," Bassanio makes a qualification of this impression of great virtue by alluding to Medea. He refers to Portia's hair, a "golden fleece," and to her home, "her seat of Belmont Colchos' strond," and her many suitors, the many "Jasons . . . in quest of her" (ll. 169-171). If Cato's daughter is the epitome of restraint, rationality and virtue, Aietes' daughter is another matter.

Disloyal to her father for the sake of her consuming passion for Jason, Medea may well epitomize all that is irrational and dangerous in woman. And yet here in one woman, Shakespeare brings together these two extremes.

The paradox is resolved shortly after Bassanio's speech, however, when Portia and Nerissa take the stage, and we discover that Portia is chafing restlessly at her bit. She complains to Nerissa of how "the will of a living daughter" is "curb'd by the will of a dead father" (I.ii.24-25). Later she expresses this impatience to Morocco when she explains that the choice of a husband is not hers to make, for her father has, she tells him, "scanted me, / and hedg'd me by his wit" (II.i.17-18). Incipiently rebellious, Portia, like Medea, could prove unworthy of her father's trust by revealing his secret,[9] but her more rational nature prevails and she remains the dutiful daughter. Similarly "hedg'd" by Shylock's will, Jessica proves not to be so prudent.

Contrasted with the harmony of Belmont and the benevolent wisdom of its late Lord are the jarring open conflicts that beset Shylock's household. Where Portia's reckless impulses are held in check by her filial devotion, Jessica is drawn to repudiate her fealty to her father: "Alack, what heinous sin is it in me / To be ashamed to be my father's child! / But though I am a daughter to his blood / I am not to his manners . . ." (II.iii.16-19). This renunciation ought not to be viewed as a remonstrance against Shylock's public image and his unpopular occupation, since he has not yet risen to infamy, but simply as an abhorrence of him as a father.

Jessica's distaste for her father's manners is largely prompted by his meanness, a trait remarked upon by Launcelot Gobbo in his complaint about the drabness and austerity of his master's household. The house is little more than a prison. Unlike the house in Belmont, which gives one the impression of having airy portals, Shylock's house is characterized by locked doors and shuttered windows. When he takes his leave of her on his way to Bassanio's feast, Shylock repeatedly enjoins Jessica to keep the house firmly shut. He gives her his keys warning her to "Look to my house" (II.v.16). Moments later when he learns that there will be a masque given in the streets that night, he urges her even more strongly to "Lock up my doors," against the sounds of gaiety and music; "Clamber not you up to the casements then / . . . But stop my house's ears, I mean my casements . . ." (ll. 29-34). And yet once again before he leaves, he reminds her to "shut doors after you" (l. 52). Thus Jessica must bear a tedious life without love or freedom, without music, which Shylock excoriates, and without even benevolent guidance. Shylock, his Jewishness notwithstanding, is a stony-hearted Puritan of the most dismal sort.[10]

Both Jessica and Portia, subject as they are to the wills of their respective fathers, complain of feelings of ennui. However, as Nerissa points out to her mistress, "they are as sick that surfeit with too much as they that starve with nothing" (I.ii.5-6). The causes of Portia's apparent melancholia come from the abundance of goodness and love that her father has lavished upon her, while in contrast Jessica must live her life in a house which she calls "a hell" devoid of joy and love. Only Launcelot's merry wit occasionally relieves her life of its "tediousness" (II.iii.1-3).

Another important contrast between the two young women is the rank that each holds in her father's household. In the sense that each home is a microcosm reflecting its creator's values, the world of the Lord of Belmont is ordered around Portia. She is the focal point. His temporal wealth and power, as well as his wise judgment and goodness, create the environment in which we find Portia, the symbol of "belovedness." The failure of Morocco and Aragon in their attempts to win her stems from the fact that they offer inferior forms of love, as their selection of the gold and silver caskets is meant to denote.

If Portia is the greatest treasure of Belmont and, therefore, most highly loved, Jessica is not so happily blessed. Shylock has so disordered his household that the scale of values which we find there is warped and corrupted. Jessica is esteemed only to the extent that she is entrusted, reluctantly, with the guardianship of Shylock's ducats. His lust for "barren metal" supplants his love for fellow man and for his daughter. Shylock's world (and, by extension, the Venetian world) is an inverted one in which inanimate commodity is valued above all things, and the human soul least of all.

The world of Shylock is antithetical to that of the Lord of Belmont. Having sacrificed his humanity for his desire for goods, Shylock is beneath even the most natural form of love, that of a father for a daughter. He values Jessica as a possession. Hence, he is unable to distinguish his missing daughter from his missing ducats. "My daughter! O my ducats! O my daughter!/ Fled with a Christian! O my Christian ducats!" (II.viii.15-16). Note that it is not his newly Christianized daughter that provokes his lament; it is his now Christian ducats.

In view of the absence of love in her world, Jessica's escape is understandable. Preceded by Launcelot's departure, her flight can be explained, and at least partially justified, in legalistic terms. Although Launcelot is aware of the moral problem that is raised by leaving the master to whom he has been indentured, he establishes a *prima facie* argument that his master has failed to fulfill the terms of the contract; that is, from Launcelot's point of view, Shylock is starving him and depriving him of the right to wear livery. Disregarding Launcelot's clownish exaggerations, we would have to agree that Shylock forfeits his claim to Launcelot's services *if* he fails to meet the terms of the contract. It is appropriate that old Gobbo should reappear to "arrange" for a new indenture for his son, thereby giving the whole business the stamp of legitimacy. Jessica's elopement can be vindicated on these same grounds. If we have any doubt that Shylock was guilty in Launcelot's case, we can have none in Jessica's, for the love and care that are a daughter's right were certainly withheld from her. Her rash adventure, imprudent and ill-advised as it may be, can be defended. Shylock loses his claim, first to his servant, then to his daughter and finally to the "pound of flesh," because at each step he fails to see that servants, daughters and debtors have rights which must be acknowledged. By denying his obligations to them, he eventually forfeits his right to demand fulfillment under the contract.[11]

Although the abundance of moral literature of this time enjoins apprentices and children from rebellion[12] and the weight of orthodoxy is against any form of disobedience, there are too many happy exceptions in Shakespeare's comedy, as well as in the romantic literature upon whose tradition he depended, for us to take

Jessica's rebellion too seriously. Quiller-Couch is more Victorian than Elizabethan when he says that Jessica is "bad, and disloyal, unfilial, a thief; frivolous, greedy, without any more conscience than a cat. . . ."[13]

With these parallels and contrasts between Portia and Jessica, the Lord of Belmont and Shylock, and Belmont and Venice, we can see that one of the principal themes of the play concerns the relationship between father and daughter and the mutual obligations that are incurred by that relationship. In the process of looking from Portia to Jessica, we see that there exists between father and daughter a "bond" or contract that must be fulfilled if the relationship is to flourish. Portia's father has tendered her his love and protection, even though he is no longer there to bestow them directly; Portia in turn dutifully accedes to his wishes, thus demonstrating her own excellent virtue and presenting a reflection of her father's greatness.

All this is absent with Shylock and Jessica. There is no love, nor does Shylock offer genuine protection beyond the spurious guardianship that locks and walls can provide. Jessica, in the process of repudiating her kinship to her father, is guilty of no breach of faith, in a technical sense, but her failure as a daughter, prompted by Shylock's more profound failure as a father, is an instance of her imperfection. Portia's superior character will ultimately serve as a model from which Jessica, in emulation, will profit.

The similarities between Jessica and Portia are also useful in explaining the connection of the casket and elopement episodes and their relevance to the play as a whole. The Lord of Belmont, recognizing the materialism of the world (symbolized by Venice) and the tendency of most men to pursue vain things, creates a Utopian existence in which the values of the real world are inverted, that is, returned to their proper order. The analogy between Belmont and More's Utopia is apt when we recall that in both places gold is debased and the most common metals, lead in one instance and iron in the other, are exalted. The Lord of Belmont uses this expedient to place his daughter and his world beyond the reach of men with any but the highest standard of values.

The gold and silver caskets are chosen by Morocco and Aragon, respectively, because of their outward appearances. Morocco's choice, the gold casket, is based principally on his conviction that the casket with the greatest intrinsic value would logically be the appropriate place in which to find a paragon of feminine virtue. He says that only gold would be suitable as a "setting" for such a "rich gem" (II.vii. 54-55). His allusion to Portia as a "rich gem" is significant as an indication of his attitude toward her; she, like the gold, represents to him mere object wealth, sterile in its uselessness.[14]

Aragon is not as naive in judging the value of the metals. The gold casket is "what many men desire"; therefore, he rejects it on the ground that he "will not jump with common spirits" (II.ix.32). He recognizes that the "fool multitude" chooses "by show,/ Not learning more than the fond eye doth teach,/ Which pries not to th'interior . . . ." Ironically, Aragon's eye proves as "fond" as those of the "fool multitude," for he is inclined to pursue chimerical honor, ultimately no less vain and superficial. The verse which he discovers in the silver casket remarks upon the values which prompted him to seek Portia there: "Some there be that shadows kiss, / Such have but a shadow's bliss" (ll.66-67).

Bassanio's success demonstrates that he sees the world as Portia's father had, and he, therefore, avoided its pitfalls by refusing to be cajoled by appearances or by spurious values. His own wit proves equal to old Belmont's when he perceives that casket "which rather threatenest than dost promise aught" is the one which is least likely to deceive.

Portia's caskets are not only a focal point for some of the play's important themes, but they also provide a means for developing a connection between Portia and Jessica, for both heroines are associated with their fathers' "caskets," objects which prove to be metaphoric expressions of two opposed scales of values. The Belmont caskets serve as barriers between Portia and the "worldly chusers";[15] providing guardianship as they do, they are surrogates of her father. On the other hand, Jessica is protected by neither father nor casket; quite the contrary, she is elected to guard her father's "casket." Left by Shylock to keep an eye on his treasure, Jessica decides to abscond with the treasure and her lover, Lorenzo. Before leaving the house, she throws to Lorenzo a casket filled with gold, which, she declares, may be useful (II.vi.33). Shakespeare's use of the word, "casket," in this context is hardly accidental. In view of all the contrasts and parallels between Portia and Jessica, between the Lord of Belmont and Shylock and their respective households, this reference to a casket belonging to Shylock, only a few lines before the other caskets are shown to Morocco, is crucial.

Both the golden casket of Belmont and Shylock's gold-filled casket symbolize the corruption of human values. But where the one was designed to curb youthful passion and to effect a wise union, the other becomes the means by which the fires of passion are fed and a rash elopement rendered successful. The debasement of gold in the Lord of Belmont's casket signifies his wise rejection of worldly values, while the gold that fills Shylock's casket is an expression of his total and irrevocable commitment to materialism. These golden caskets, like as they are and yet different, draw our eyes to the contrasts between Belmont and Venice. Just as with the caskets, the similarities are superficial, at least at first. We see this nowhere better than when Jessica, about to flee, stops to "gild" herself "with some moe ducats," reminding us of Portia, described by Bassanio and Morocco in images of gold.

Although these contrasts of which I have been speaking are climaxed with Jessica's elopement and Bassanio's victory, the implications of the contrasts remain to be worked out. The two young women, freed now by marriage, leave their respective homes and, in effect, change places with each other. Jessica with Lorenzo comes to Belmont and replaces Portia, temporarily, as mistress of the island, while Portia, forced to separate from Bassanio, goes off to Venice. Jessica and Lorenzo, with Shylock no longer a threat to their happiness, openly enjoy each other's company in Belmont. Portia, however, must confront Shylock and until she does, she is constrained from openly consorting with her husband.

For the time Jessica serves in Portia's place, she rules in the blissful surroundings of Belmont, figuratively, a daughter of the saintly Lord. Force is given to this symbolic twist when Launcelot declares to Jessica that her hope for salvation rests in the hope that she is "not the Jew's daughter." For the moment, at least, as she lives what was meant to be Portia's life, the remark is true. At the same time, Portia is wresting from Shylock a daughter's portion, which she will bring back for Jessica when she returns to Belmont to claim her own portion.

The differences between the two women are sharply defined by means of this exchange of places. Portia, by Jessica's own account, is without peer. Bassanio will find in her "the joys of heaven here on earth" (III.v.70). Belmont will prove to this matchless pair an earthly paradise, and a place of redemption for all who come to its shores. However, despite this testimony, Portia's perfection is not made dramatically clear until she leaves Belmont, faces her great test in Venice, and returns.

Portia's development during the play involves an upward movement from the point where she must struggle against the weakness of youth and flesh and conquer her inclination to egoism (all characterized by the image of Medea) to the point where she demonstrates her ability to reject passion for higher forms of love.

If Portia seems to move upward toward some beatific ideal, Jessica, throughout the play, displays mortal weaknesses which render her incapable of enjoying the spirit of Belmont—and, therefore, the spirit of her newly adopted religion—until the final moments of the play when she falls under the redemptive influence of Portia. During Portia's absence, Belmont becomes a "bower of bliss" for Jessica and Lorenzo. Although I would be reluctant to press the analogy, since prurience does not seem to be a factor in the lovers' relationship, there is the distinct sense that their dalliance does not lead to consummation. Furthermore, all their verbal lovemaking during this period abounds with allusions to pagan love affairs parallel to their own, including that of Jason and Medea. Although all of these pagan lovers eventually came to grief, neither Jessica nor Lorenzo reflects upon this more serious implication of clandestine love.

A change is wrought in the lovers, however, when Stephano announces that Portia is approaching. Their love talk turns from the profane to more timeless things as they begin to contemplate "the floor of heaven." They discourse upon angels, heavenly harmonies, and the limitations of the human body, which Lorenzo now calls "a muddy vesture of decay." The passionate temper of their spirits is quieted by the music and by the knowledge of Portia's imminent arrival. Lorenzo's speech on the effect of music upon "a wild and wanton herd" characterizes the remarkable transformation that has occurred in him and his wife.

While these two are preparing for their benefactress' return, Portia, now within sight of her home, comments to Nerissa upon the light shining in the distance. "How far that little candle throws his beams! / So shines a good deed in a naughty world." Nerissa replies that the candle was not visible when the moon shone, and Portia aptly points out: "So doth the greater glory dim the less,—/ A substitute shines as brightly as a king . . . ." The relevance of the imagery to Portia and Jessica is obvious. For all Jessica's faults up to now, she has that light of virtue, visible now for the first time.

With Portia's homecoming, Belmont assumes the unmistakable character of an earthly paradise, and thoughts of Venice are, once and for all, put out of mind. The moral issues have been settled and the equilibrium of nature and the universe has been restored. And to remind us that this perfected world is a place for men and women to live in, Gratiano points out that there are yet two hours to dawn, and untried beds awaiting.

Notes:

(1) *The Merchant of Venice*, ed. Sir Arthur Quiller-Couch and John Dover Wilson (Cambridge, 1926), p.xi.

(2) "*The Merchant of Venice*" in *Prefaces to Shakespeare* (Princeton, 1946), I, 336, 338.

(3) "Brothers and Others," in *The Dyer's Hand* (New York, 1962), p. 221.

(4) *The Truth about Shylock* (New York, 1962), p. 243.

(5) To be more specific on this matter of quantifying would involve the pointless pursuit of dividing speeches; for example, one would have to attribute parts of Tubal's speeches (III,i) alternately to the elopement episode or to the bond.

(6) References are to the Arden edition of *The Merchant of Venice*, ed. John Russell Brown (Cambridge, Mass., 1955).

(7) In *Julius Caesar* Shakespeare has Portia tell Brutus, "Think you I am no stronger than my sex, / Being so father'd and so husbanded?" (II.i.296-297).

(8) Arden *MV*, p. xlviii.

(9) Some question on this point could be raised, and has been, to the effect that Portia and Nerissa conspire to tell Bassanio by means of their little song in which the words in rhyming position in the first stanza all rhyme with lead (III.ii.63-65). See note in Arden *MV*. p. 80.

(10) For a full exposition on this point see Paul N. Siegel, "Shylock the Puritan," *Columbia University Forum* (V.iv.14-19).

(11) Benjamin Nelson in *The Idea of Usury* (Princeton, 1949) quotes Martin Luther on the rights of a debtor: to wit, that while "everyone who receives a loan must return it," if "the law does not come to the creditor's aid, and does not restore his loan, he should bear it with even spirit as the law allows no one to suffer injury . . ." (p. 51).

(12) Louis B. Wright, *Middle Class Culture in Elizabethan England* (Ithaca, N.Y., 1958) has a number of chapters touching on this very subject.

(13) Quiller-Couch, op. cit., p. xx.

(14) Thomas Fujimura in "Mode and Structure in *The Merchant of Venice*," *PMLA*, LXXXI (1966), 508, points out other parallels between Morocco and Shylock indicating that their common attitude about gold is not incidental.

(15) Stephen Gosson, *The School of Abuse* (1579), ed. Edward Arber (Westminster, 1895), p. 40.

The Merchant of Venice

by Marvin Felheim

I

Certainly *The Merchant of Venice* is one of the most challenging of Shakespeare's plays. At first glance, the great court scene with Portia's justly famous speech on mercy and the lovely concluding act, so full of good will and magnificent poetry, seem to give the play its core of meaning: Christian charity and human love will and should triumph; three joyous couples and the merchant of Venice himself are at Belmont to celebrate victory and weddings.

But, on reflection, there are many disturbing elements to upset this all-too-easy view. For one thing, the play opens with inexplicable sadness; for another, the three principal characters—Antonio, Portia and Shylock—are shown more in seriousness than in joy; finally, their seriousness is tinged with a most unsettling kind of melancholy. In the very opening line, Antonio tells us: "In sooth, I know not why I am so sad" (I.i.1). He then rejects the suggestions of Salerio and Solanio who offer conventional explanations: worry over his "merchandise," love, and "because you are not merry" (a "humourous" explanation). True, Antonio seems to emerge from his melancholy with the appearance of his friend and relative, Bassanio. But we must note that Bassanio confronts him not merely with the face of friendship and kinship but with serious financial problems. So, his change of mood is prompted in large part by the need for his services as financier as much as (more than?) his position as friend and kinsman. Throughout the play, moreover, we never see Antonio in what might be called a merry mood, for almost immediately troubles, in the form of loss of his argosies and the resultant law suit, beset him. And the final moments of triumph are not really his: the saving of his life in Act IV is subordinated, dramatically, to Portia's success as a disguised Doctor of Laws, to the sentencing of Shylock, and to the exchanging of the rings; indeed, at the very moment when his life has been saved, Antonio must turn his attention to thanking Balthazar (Portia) and to persuading Bassanio "to let him have the ring." Then, in Act V, Antonio is by no means either the central figure or the most joyous. Portia apologizes for her seeming lack of courtesy and hospitality—

> Sir, you are very welcome to our house.
> It must appear in other ways than words,
> Therefore I scant this breathing courtesy—[1]   *(V.i.139-141)*

only to become embroiled at once in the question of the rings; again, Antonio must pledge himself for Bassanio, only this time he binds his "soul" rather than his flesh to assure Portia that her husband "Will never more break faith advisedly" (V.i.253).

Lastly, in the distribution of favors, Portia discloses that she has "better news in store" for him than he expects and she gives him a "letter,"

> There you shall find three of your argosies
> Are richly come to harbour suddenly,   *(V.i.276-277)*

but she adds, enigmatically,

> You shall not know by what strange accident
> I chanced on this letter,   *(V.i.278-279)*

a curious, somewhat callous attitude which belies the very assertion of friendliness and hospitality she had made earlier. Antonio's reply, less than half a line, is "I am dumb"; he even has difficulty in squeezing these three simple words in between Portia's disclosures and Bassanio's and Gratiano's amazement at their wives' virtuosity. To cap his pleasure, Antonio is finally permitted three more lines:

> Sweet lady, you have given me life and living;
> For here I read for certain that my ships
> Are safely come to road.   *(V.i.286-288)*

Thus the role of the merchant of Venice is concluded. One feels that perhaps Salerio was correct in his original diagnosis: that Antonio's sadness was because his "mind is tossing on the ocean." At any event, in this comedy labelled *The Merchant of Venice* one must agree that the merchant himself has rough sailing, that he opens the play a man wearied and sad, that he endures great tribulations and a serious trial in which his life is nearly taken, that his survival is merely a part of more exciting goings-on and that his eventual triumph is simply the inexplicable return of his ships. Indeed, he seems doomed, as he states initially:

> But how I caught it [sadness], found it, or came by it,
> What stuff 'tis made of, whereof it is born,
> I am to learn.   *(I.i.3-5)*

This notion appears to have had its origin in his (typically Shakespearean) philosophy:

> I hold the world but as the world, Gratiano,
> A stage where every man must play a part,
> And mine a sad one.   *(I.i.77-79)*

Thus isolated, the merchant appears a pathetic figure. I have not questioned here his goodness, his willingness to help others and his mercy to Shylock; presumably these qualities could provide him with a kind of quiet glow. But there is no indication that his initial unexplained sadness is ever mitigated or that the similarly unexplained return of his merchandise at the conclusion will do much to make him happy, for as he predicted

> . . . such a want-wit sadness makes of me
> That I have much ado to know myself.   *(I.i.6-7)*

Antonio is not alone in proclaiming his sadness, however. Portia's first speech picks up the theme: "By my troth, Nerissa, my little body is aweary of this great world" (I.ii.1). As in the case of Antonio, her statement suggests a kind of cosmic condition. And like Salerio and Solanio, Nerissa offers an explanation: that Portia has an "abundance" of "good fortunes," that she is simply too rich, surfeited and bored. But the Lady of Belmont rejects her maid's "good sentences." Her sadness has another cause: her father's will which has effectively "curbed" her choice of a husband. It is a mark of Shakespeare's subtle art that he puts these speeches of Portia and Nerissa in prose, just where one would expect poetry, whereas the opening speeches on "A Street. Venice" are in poetry. The purpose is not only to contrast the different types of melancholy in scenes one and two, but to establish, as well, the contrary nature of this play and to suggest that both a mingling of poetry with the business world of Venice and a prose basis for the beauty of Belmont are necessary conditions.

Finally, sadness is also typical of Shylock. The elopement of his daughter with a Christian, the loss of money and the punishments he suffers in court are calamitous episodes in his pathetic life. Clearly, then, a strain of melancholy pervades this comedy and conditions the over-all tone of the play. In this connection I feel that the concluding act, too, despite its apparent joyousness, has overtones of despair, even bitterness. As the last act begins, Jessica and Lorenzo are discussing love and nature: "The moon shines bright. In such a night as this" lovers have enjoyed . . . what? Well, Troilus "mounted the Troyan walls,/And sigh'd his soul toward the Grecian tents"; Thisby did "fearfully o'ertrip the dew,/And saw the lion's shadow . . .,/And ran dismayed away"; Dido stood "Upon the wild sea-banks, and waft her love/To come again to Carthage"; and Medea "gathered the enchanted herbs/That did renew old Aeson." Hardly a happy couple among the four. These lines, full of melancholy accounts of tragic loves and lovers, have been much praised, but most critics have failed to note that neither the subject matter nor the love affairs referred to give us a felicitious picture of love; on the contrary, the content of the lines is at odds with the situation itself (although Jessica and Lorenzo include themselves in the list of lovers) and casts a disturbing, howbeit lovely, tone over the moonlit scene. This mood, after an interlude on the nature of music, gives way to the workings-out of the ring plot. And so the act which began with reminiscences about unhappy loves and lovers concludes with the cynical resolution of the ring story.

II

Counter to all this sadness there is mirth, and there are joyous characters. Bassanio, Salerio and Solanio are consistently optimistic and cheerful, Bassanio particularly so in the face of odds. The course of the love affair between Jessica and Lorenzo runs smoothly, without a hitch. Portia, herself, has periods of intense happiness (in Bassanio's success in choosing the correct casket), of witty triumph (over the unsuccessful suitors) and of joyful satisfaction (both in court and in the final confrontation at Belmont). This beautifully maintained balance is characteristic of *The Merchant of Venice;* indeed, in this play, contrast is the primary dramaturgical method.

The setting provides the most obvious contrast: the Rialto and Belmont, the world of Venice, of usury, of the court, and the world of candlelight and music that is Belmont. We note that certain characteristics of the former place, the Rialto, are present in the latter; there are commercial and material aspects to Belmont, too; the dead, but legal, hand of a wealthy father lies heavily upon this rich world, the prize gem of which is Portia herself, the lady of the "sunny locks" which "Hang on her temples like a golden fleece" (I.i.170). Her riches, her beauty and her virtue are, in truth, like the rocks which shipwreck so many Venetian argosies. Even at the moment of Bassanio's triumph over the riddle of the caskets, the speeches of the lovers are replete with commercial terms; he says:

> Fair lady, by your leave;
> I came by *note,* to *give* and to *receive,*   *(III.ii.139-140)*

but he cannot be sure of his success

> Until *confirm'd, sign'd, ratified* by you.   *(III.ii.148)*

She replies, in part,

> That only to *stand high* in your *account*
> I might in virtues, beauties, *livings,* friends
> *Exceed account.* But the full *sum* of me
> Is *sum* of *something....*   *(III.ii.156-159)*

By introducing into Belmont these symbolic elements from the commercial world of Venice, Shakespeare fuses two aspects of life; they are not separate, the Rialto and Belmont, however much they may be geographically distinct. Bassanio is the "arrow ... adventuring" from one world into the other; in return, Portia brings wisdom, judgment, and poetry to Venice. The significant linkage of the two in marriage indicates the extent to which the two must be joined in order to exist; each is dependent upon the other and insofar as this is true this comedy presents us with the ultimate in realism: the acknowledgement that these worlds not only coexist but *must* coexist; this is the human condition, pictured without unnecessary sentimentality, with the romantic elements occupying their proper place, coordinated with the other elements, neither isolated nor superior but equal. The result is what can be called Shakespeare's comic vision, as steady a view of life as is possible, a world of sorrows and joys but essentially human, where even wedded love must wait upon more pressing obligations, where disguise, deception and cynicism can live side by side with sweeter qualities, where contrast and combination are the essential reality.

The delicate balancing of these contrasting elements is Shakespeare's great dramatic skill. And this device pervades the play. For example, there are the human contrasts between parents and children, specifically fathers and children, and between masters and servants. In the later category fit, for instance, Portia and her servants, Nerissa and Balthasar; when Portia disguises herself as a lawyer, to preach the gospel of charity, it seems significant that Shakespeare gives her the name of her servant, Balthazar. Shylock, on the other hand, speaks slightingly of the way Venetians treat some of their servants, those who are "purchas'd slaves," which

> ... like your asses and your dogs and mules,
> You use in abject and in slavish parts. *(IV.i.91-92)*

He sets up, as he always does, an absolute of behavior, an Old Testament absolute, against which the action plays. He carries the argument to an extreme: masters become owners, servants slaves. Our sympathies, as usual, are engaged by his characteristic manner. And we realize that he has made a telling point: that he also wants what is his, what he has bought and paid for. But his example also has the effect of setting up the opposite, the ideal, the world beyond Venice (an aspect, perhaps, of Belmont) where there are neither owners nor slaves. What inevitably happens when Shylock talks is that we are confronted with an ideal situation—where there would be no discrimination, no hatred or fear, no cruelty or inhumanity. But such a condition is always predicated in terms of opposites and in almost strictly legal terms, a world, on the one hand, where there is legal usury or, on the other, none at all. Reality—the world of legal usury which must be tempered by human charity—is the world Shylock rejects (or which rejects Shylock).

Not content with this relatively simple contrast which is presented to us in terms of a legal argument, Shakespeare complicates and expands it by the introduction of a specific comic application: Launcelot Gobbo, servant extraordinaire. And what is Launcelot's problem? He would leave the service of the Jew for that of Bassanio; to this end he engages in a mock controversy, between his conscience, which urges him to stay, and the "fiend" at his "elbow" who tempts him to go. The irony here is compounded by the fact that throughout the play the Jew, Shylock, is presented as the devil but, at this juncture, in a comic subplot, the devil is on the other, the Christian, side: "To be rul'd by my conscience, I should stay with the Jew my master, who—God bless the mark!—is a kind of devil; and, to run away from the Jew, I should be ruled by the fiend, who—saving your reverence!—is the devil himself." (The services of the learned Bellario himself would be needed to untangle this problem and this rhetoric!)

Then, let us note the way in which Shakespeare works out this situation. Launcelot and his father make their suit to Bassanio to accept Launcelot into his service; Launcelot's reasons are simple enough: he is, so he says, "famish'd" in the Jew's employ, and he is attracted to Bassanio "who indeed gives rare new liveries" (another contrast between Shylock's thrifty and Bassanio's spendthrift ways). But Bassanio has anticipated this request (why, one wonders) and tells them:

> Shylock thy master spoke with me this day,
> And hath preferr'd thee, if it be preferment

To leave a rich Jew's service to become
The follower of so poor a gentleman. *(II.ii.132-135)*

Yet this "poor" gentleman, we remember, has just borrowed three thousand ducats, has already acquired one servant, Leonardo, and "a follower or two," one of whom he orders to "give" Launcelot "a livery," and is well on his way to acquiring a fortune in Belmont. Then, there are further complications. Shylock warns Launcelot that, in Bassanio's service,

Thou shalt not gormandize
As thou hast done with me. *(II.v.3-4)*

(Whose version of life at Shylock's shall we accept? The comic Launcelot's? The villain Shylock's? Or, to add another note, Jessica's "Our house is hell"?) Anyhow, when we next see Launcelot, he has become well-established in Bassanio's service; indeed, there has been one positive result of his transfer for, according to Lorenzo, he has got "the Moor" (evidently another servant at Belmont) with child, a situation which allows Launcelot a few unfortunate puns on "Moor" and "more" but seems not to concern him otherwise. And so, one could moralize about the progress of Launcelot Gobbo as he has moved from Jew to Christian, from strict behavior (the result of hunger?) to loose morality (and one might add from being genuinely funny to being a boring punster), from being a person who could be a true help to Jessica (he robbed her father's house of its "tediousness" and carried letters between her and Lorenzo) to a Launcelot with whom, at Belmont, Jessica is "out."

All these contrasts, whether of physical settings or of human characteristics, have a common basis in the central moral contrast of the play. This contrast is variously embodied, but is nowhere more clear than in the confrontation of Shylock and Portia, specifically in the way in which each suggests one aspect of the Bible, Shylock appropriately the Old Testament and Portia aptly the New. For Shylock the world exists in terms of absolutes, in terms of justice, in terms of Old Testament morality. This approach is most interestingly summarized in his story of Jacob and Laban's sheep: ". . . thrift is blessing, if men steal it not" (I.iii.85). Or, as he tells Jessica, "Fast bind, fast find"—(II.v.53). For Shylock there can be no compromise: "all the eanlings which were streak'd and pied / Should fall as Jacob's hire"; this is the rule. Human beings are subservient to law, to an absolute code. So he sets up his frame of reference. What makes Antonio evil in Shylock's eyes is that "He was wont to lend money for a Christian courtesy"; Antonio was a man who behaved contrary to the customs of the Rialto (could this possibly be the cause of his sadness? his capacity to see the human condition and yet to act independently in terms of friendship and courtesy? is his a cosmic sadness?). And what should be done about him? Shylock, the Jew, the avenging arm of Jehovah, would act: "revenge," both in terms of Old Testament standards and in light of Christian behavior; "The villainy you teach me I will execute." Such a philosophy knows no compromise: "I say my daughter is my flesh and my blood" asserts Shylock (Jessica has already added the human corollary: "Though I am a daughter to his blood I am not to his manners"): further, rather than adjust to the world he insists "I would my daughter were dead at my foot, and the jewels in her ear; would she were hears'd at my foot, and the ducats in her coffin." This explains, too, his concern for his money, which, like his daughter, like Jacob's sheep, is his and his alone. He exists only on this level. "I crave the law," he cries: "I am a Jew," he states. Could anything be more clear?

As usual, Shakespeare does not stop here. For one thing, he has the advantage of writing at a time when the Jew's place in society was enigmatical, so, in the social sense alone, the role of a Jew cannot be seen simply from a one-dimensional point of view. The Jew, in the Renaissance world, was hedged about with restrictions and superstitions, so that neither his role nor his place in society were clear-cut; Shakespeare has all the advantage of this complex situation. Further, Shylock is, in a dramatic sense, a type character; he is the Old Vice, he is the "humour" character. He evidences this role, for example, in a typically Shakespearean way, in his attitude toward music and gaiety. For, when he learns that there are to be "masques" he warns Jessica against "the drum / And the vile squealing of the wry-neck'd fife," and orders her

> Let not the sound of shallow fopp'ry enter
> My sober house. *(II.v.34-35)*

His dislike for music marks him as a "villain," had not Salerio and Solanio already used the term to abuse him. But it remains for his new son-in-law, Lorenzo, to put the situation into proper philosophical and poetic terms. As he tells Jessica,

> The man that hath no music in himself,
> Nor is mov'd with concord of sweet sounds,
> Is fit for treasons, stratagems, and spoils. *(V.i.83-85)*

How like Shakespeare to give us both the theory and the reality.

Opposing Shylock is Portia. She stands for Christian charity and mercy—with some human variations (she can, for example, be most caustic about her suitors). Shakespeare shows us her essential character in two significant scenes, one when Bassanio chooses the lead casket and the other in the court in Venice. Like other comic heroines, particularly Rosalind and Viola, Portia is no demure, passive lady. Forced by the provisions of her father's will to wait for her true lover, she knows in advance whom she wants. In answer to Nerissa's inquiry—"Do you remember, lady, in your father's time, a Venetian, a scholar and a soldier?"—she blurts out, "Yes, yes, it was Bassanio," before her maidenly reserve prompts her to add "as I think, so was he call'd." And when Bassanio arrives, decked though he may be in borrowed garments, she begs him to "tarry" awhile.

> I could teach you
> How to choose right *(III.ii.10-11)*

she proposes, then withdraws her offer (it would be perjury) only to proclaim:

> One half of me is yours, the other half yours. (III.ii.16)

Then, she orders:

> Let music sound while he doth make his choice (III.ii.43)

(for Morocco and Arragon there had been only a "Flourish of Cornets"). And when, at last, Bassanio makes the right choice,

> And here choose I. Joy be the consequence! (III.ii.107)

her speech rises to the proper pitch, for she is

> Happy in this, she is not yet so old
> But she may learn; happier than this,
> She is not bred so dull but she can learn;
> Happiest of all is that her gentle spirit
> Commits itself to yours to be directed,
> As from her lord, her governor, her king. (III.ii.161-166)

Shakespeare preserves the human equilibrium by having her conclude this speech with the giving of the "ring," thereby setting up the somewhat lewd but earthly antithesis to all this lofty eloquence.

But it is in the courtroom that Portia reaches the apex; here, she truly embodies the spirit of Christian charity; for, as she makes clear,

> . . . earthly power doth then show likest God's
> When mercy seasons justice. (IV.i.191-192)

Ironically, it is not she ("He shall have merely justice," she decides) but the Duke and Antonio who practice what she has preached. But, here again, Shakespeare shows his great wisdom, his sense of decorum and reality, which allows the head of the state, the Duke, to be the God-like dispenser of mercy; Portia, having served as the agent of justice, reverts to the clever, somewhat niggling young heroine, concerned about her "ring." It is certainly notable, too, that Shakespeare chooses to present the voice of mercy in disguise. True enough, he had convention (the boy actor) and his source (Ser Giovanni's *Il Pecorone*) as a basis for so doing. But the fact that the words urging divine mercy are uttered in Venice under the cloak of a disguise is still significant. Is Shakespeare saying that mercy cannot come into the real world except it be protected by disguise? One remembers, as well, that Jessica and Lorenzo, two of the symbols of love in this play, cannot live and love in Venice, but must also resort to disguise in order to escape the realities of the city. Apparently only in Belmont can love and mercy exist without false faces, like the candle's beams ("So shines a good deed in a naughty world"), but here, too, we recollect, is the lead casket which contains a golden treasure and here, too, are the "rings," symbols of physical love. So the total picture is inevitably complex. And the motto for all might well be the lines spoken by Bassanio as he gazes at the caskets:

The world is still deceiv'd with ornament.
In law, what plea so tainted and corrupt
But, being season'd with a gracious voice,
Obscures the show of evil? In religion,
What damned error but some sober brow
Will bless it, and approve it with a text,
Hiding the grossness with fair ornament?   *(III.ii.74-80)*

There is another device which serves Shakespeare as a variation to his either/or presentation of comedy, a trinitarian concept. Superimposed upon the basic contrasts or duality, there are innumerable threesomes. There are three young women, two Christians and a Jew; consequently, three pairs of lovers. Antonio and Bassanio have three friends, the pair, Solanio and Salerio, and Gratiano. There are three Jews, Tubal and Chus, in addition to Shylock. Portia has three suitors, the Princes of Morocco and Arragon, who fail, and Bassanio, who succeeds. Further, the whole play is based on three plots: bond, casket, rings. The bond is for three thousand ducats for three months. There are three caskets, of gold, silver and lead. Later, Bassanio has three reasons for giving away Portia's ring ("to whom . . . for whom . . . for what . . ."), which arguments Portia parries with three of her own. In addition, in the last act, Portia has three letters which bring knowledge and rewards. But this concept of trinity is most noticeable in the phrasing. Antonio, speaking of his sadness, knows not "how I caught it, found it, or came by it." Solanio and Salerio, as has been pointed out, offer in turn three "causes." Portia, "thrice-fair lady" is, to Bassinio, a trinity: rich, fair, virtuous. Just so, Jessica, according to Lorenzo, is "wise, fair, and true." Shylock hates Antonio for three reasons, because he is a Christian, because "he lends out money gratis" and because "he hates our sacred nation." Morocco has a scimitar which slew "a Persian prince That won three fields," whereas Arragon enunciates the "three things" he and other suitors are "enjoined by oath to observe." In a climactic scene Portia "commits" herself to Bassanio, "her lord, her governor, her king." Bassanio later offers a "forfeit of my hands, my head, my heart" if Shylock will accept his offer to save Antonio. Even Launcelot refers to himself as "your boy that was, your son that is, your child that shall be." This constant use of triads lends both a consistency and a rhythm to the play. As a result of the playing of triads against a basic pattern of one-for-one contrast a rich and varied counterpoint emerges.

III

The use of food imagery in *The Merchant of Venice* is one of the most significant features of the play. Even in the sub-plot of the clown food plays an important role. Launcelot claims to leave Shylock's service because of hunger (it was a common enough trick for Elizabethan fools to pretend hunger; "anxiety about food and drink" is one of the principal characteristics of the clown as his role has been analyzed by Olive M. Busby who states that "this characteristic persists throughout the clown's history").[2] Shylock, as has been pointed out, warns him that he will not "gormandize" at Bassanio's; later, Shylock refers to Launcelot as "huge feeder." Jessica, on the other hand, tells Launcelot that for her at least he "didst rob" her home "of some *taste* of tediousness." At Belmont, however, Launcelot has a falling out with Jessica because of his suggestion that "this making of Christians will raise the price of hogs." In addition, one remembers that Old Gobbo has brought with him "a present" for Shylock, "a dish of doves," which he eventually gives to Bassanio instead. So far in this subplot, this imagery is used as one would expect; it unifies as it gives depth and it adds to the dramatic effectiveness of the scenes.

But another, and more provocative, use of food imagery is central to the meaning of this comedy. As I count them, there are twenty-three occasions in the play when someone is either invited to dinner or refers to the preparation of the meal. No one of these references is used in a figurative sense; all are literal references to a specific event. Yet no one of these meals is ever shown on stage, nor do we ever see any character in the act of eating. These references, however, serve a number of purposes. First of all, they indicate the continued existence of the everyday world at the elbow of the stage one. Further, food, as well as the preparing and eating of it, becomes one of the important links between the Rialto and Belmont inasmuch as supper is an activity worth mentioning in both places. In general, an invitation to sup, such as the Duke extends to Balthazar (Portia), is regarded as an act of courtesy and appreciation. On some occasions, too, eating offers an opportunity for the transacting of business.

Food also has ritual importance. In answer to Bassanio's invitation to dine, Shylock replies "I will not eat with you, drink with you, nor pray with you." Thus, in three (a magic number?) senses, he maintains his absolute obedience to his own religious code. Later he breaks this resolution, somewhat reluctantly as he is "right loath" to leave his "sober house" in the care of Jessica on a night of revelry. It is significant that he feels no friendliness in the invitation: "I am not bid for love." Nor has his decision to go been any less evilly prompted:

> . . . I'll go in hate, to feed upon
> The prodigal Christian.
>
> *(II.v.14-15)*

Such a supper party cannot result in anything good; nor does it. For, as an immediate consequence of his absence, Jessica elopes "in the lovely *garnish* of a boy" (is the implication that Lorenzo will feed better than Shylock?) and "furnish'd with . . . gold and jewels." So Shylock is made to suffer for the breach of his dietary laws, even though he later maintains, in a state of some emotion, it is true, that a Jew is "fed with the same food . . . as a Christian is."

Shakespeare's use of food here is both realistic and subtle. On the one hand, he effectively singles out that aspect of Jewish life—the observance of the dietary laws—which Christians have always found remarkable about the Jew. On the other hand, Shylock's refusal, at first, to break the law, then his willingness to do so are serious decisions. And they are connected, I believe, with the central meaning of the play in a profound way. To begin with, Shylock breaks the law not because he has to, but because of possible financial gain or revenge; in this sense, he is as much a sinner against Jewish law as Portia later tells him he is against Venetian and Christian laws. Further, Shylock's quest for the "pound of flesh" is a related theme. Granted, he is not a cannibal who intends to eat Antonio's flesh. But, on the other hand, why does he make this curious stipulation anyhow? Is Shakespeare here referring to the medieval superstition that Jews performed ritual murders? Or, more subtly, isn't he suggesting that, as a matter of fact, Shylock is here violating one of the essential creeds of Judaism. The Old Testament is full of restrictions about the taking of life, and, indeed about all kinds of blood-letting. Certainly the Noahide Laws strictly enjoin any such practice, for they clearly proclaim (Bishops' Bible):

> But fleshe in the lyfe thereof (which is) the blood thereof, that
> ye not eate. (*Genesis, ix.4*)
> Who so sheddeth mans blood, by man shall his blood be shed,
> for in the image of God made he man. (*Genesis, ix.6*)

Portia echoes these commandments as she warns Shylock:

> . . . if thou dost shed
> One drop of Christian blood. . . .   *(IV.i.304-305)*

Further, her stand as judge ultimately rigidifies into an absolute as uncompromising as that which Shylock had previously insisted upon. Although he had sworn "An oath, an oath, I have an oath in heaven" (IV.i.223), justice for Shylock is quite simply that which he had demanded: "I stand here for law" (IV.i.142). Hence, one sees in the trial scene that Shakespeare rewards Shylock with the same immediate retribution which overtook him when he broke the dietary law. In both cases, Shylock reaps a whirlwind of disaster.

The reason for suggesting that Shylock's fate is here a kind of Jewish judgment springs not alone from a reading of the text of the play but from certain corroborating evidence as well. The Noahide Laws, pre-Mosiac, are, as indicated, to be found in *Genesis*. So are many other details of *The Merchant of Venice*. For instance, Shylock defends usury by reference to the story of Jacob and Laban's sheep, which comes from Chapter xxx of *Genesis*. As J. L. Cardozo has pointed out,[3] the names Shylock, Jessica, Tubal and Chus, occur only in *Genesis*, Chapters x and xi. Finally, the episode in which Launcelot encounters, deceives, then craves the blessing of his "sand-blind" father contains the same elements as does the Isaac-Jacob story in *Genesis*, Chapter xxvii.[4] James T. Bratcher has summarized[5] all the articles which point up the many *Genesis-Merchant of Venice* parallels; in addition, he adds some observations of his own to show the relationships between the Lorenzo-Jessica subplot and details from Chapter xxxiv of *Genesis*. His conclusions, like those of Ginsburg[6] and Noble[7], are that Shakespeare used *The Bishops' Bible* of 1568. All of these factors imply a great awareness and subtle use of the first book of the Old Testament. (That Shakespeare may have used an earlier play which also incorporated these themes is a remote possibility, but is not relevant to this discussion.) My point is that the food image, pursued down devious alleys

104

it is true, exposes for us all the magnificent subtlety of this play and, indeed, clears up at least one problem. For I see Shylock not merely as one sinned against but also as a sinner, for whom punishment is immediate, overwhelming. Yet for the audience, seeing no real harm in the happy marriage of Jessica and Lorenzo and equally pleased at Antonio's survival, there is no tragedy here; instead, Shylock, by becoming a Christian, will automatically become eligible for all the blessings available to a member of Venetian society. In effect, just as *The Merchant of Venice* is, in one sense, a realistic play about changing economic conditions in Venice (the medieval church's strictures against usury which had been satisfactory for an agrarian society were ultimately giving way because of the needs of an emerging mercantile society for speculative capital), it is also, in another sense, an account of the slow absorption of many Jews into Christian society, a phenomenon which took place in western Europe in medieval and Renaissance times.

As one would expect in a comedy where food plays such a dominant role, there is a reference in the final scene. In this instance we find food used as an image to suggest a deepened emotional content in the poetry. Among the rich rewards which Portia brings back to Belmont from the trial is "a special deed of gift" for Lorenzo and Jessica in which Shylock had agreed to leave them "all he dies possess'd of." To thank Portia and Nerissa, Lorenzo uses a memorable image:

> Fair ladies, you drop manna in the way
> Of starved people.   *(V.i.294-295)*

Providentially, there is no moralist present to remind this "starved" pair of the ducats which they squandered in Genoa.

IV

A few final words remain to be said about the over-all plotting, for in this regard, too, *The Merchant of Venice* is an unusual play. For a comedy, the themes of this work are extraordinarily serious and profound; they plumb the depths of human behavior and human character. The enigmatic nature of Shylock, himself, to say nothing of, for example, Jessica or Gratiano, who frequently seems simply a loud-mouthed oaf, has troubled many readers. The play's wonderful poetry, some of it among the best Shakespeare ever wrote, sets it apart from other early and middle comedies such as *The Taming of the Shrew* or *Much Ado about Nothing*. Yet after all its superiorities have been enumerated, *The Merchant of Venice* remains in some ways a crude effort. The over-all machinery consists of three obvious, somewhat vulgar plots: the bond plot, the casket plot, the ring plot. All have been much handled and Shakespeare manipulates them rather mechanically.

The bond plot, resulting from Antonio's willingness to help Bassanio but his inability to meet the practical need other than through Shylock, is established first. It can be said to begin in Act I, scene i, and yields precedence only to the theme of sadness. The bond plot is resolved in the court scene, Act IV, scene i, except that one of its by-products (the "deed of gift" for Lorenzo and Jessica) carries over into the final act of the play. This plot concerns mostly Antonio and Shylock; the latter disappears from the action, unwell, at the conclusion of the courtroom scene; Antonio "hangs" around through Act V, not completely cured of his melancholia, a figure of Venice, somewhat out of place in the festive world of Belmont.

The casket plot begins, interestingly, in Act I, scene ii. Although Bassanio has, in scene i, approached Antonio with a request for three thousand ducats to enable him "to hold a rival place" among Portia's suitors, he does not mention that his success will hinge upon a "lott'ry," as Nerissa calls it. So not until we meet Portia and Nerissa in scene ii is the casket plot fully set forth. From that point on, until Act III, scene ii, when Bassanio chooses correctly, the scenes developing this story, all set in Belmont, more or less alternate with those connected with the bond plot. In a technical sense, the casket plot could be considered the main plot since it is the one which terminates or is resolved in what is traditionally the climactic act, III. The casket plot has a number of interesting overtones. For one thing, the whole situation vis-à-vis the caskets is based upon the will of Portia's dead father. Certainly she chafes a bit under its restraints: "so is the will of a living daughter curb'd by the will of a dead father," she remarks; one may even conjecture that her sadness is the result of this confinement although Nerissa, probably more correctly, attributes her "sickness" to "surfeit." One wonders, incidentally, why Portia suffers when it would seem reasonable to suggest that her legal acumen should enable her to get around the provisions; at any event, she doesn't suffer long; moreover, she balances whatever unpleasantness does exist with a degree of levity and a certain amount of vituperative cynicism at the expense of the suitors themselves. One particular requirement of the will carries a certain threat with it—that is, the requirement that the suitor if he "choose wrong" must agree

> Never to speak to lady afterward
> In way of marriage. *(II.ii.41-42)*

The casket plot builds mechanically to its conclusion, from the scene when Portia reviews the demerits of the present group of aspirants, through the two unsuccessful attempts of Morocco (II.vii.) and Arragon (II.ix.) to the third trial, the success of Bassanio. To heighten the mechanistic aspects of this plot, Shakespeare uses at least one external device, sound effects. For Morocco and Arragon, there is a "Flourish of Cornets"; for Bassanio, there is music, the lovely song, "Where is fancy bred?" Bassanio's character and chances are presumably enhanced by this tribute. At one point, too, during the interview with the Prince of Arragon, the "three things... enjoin'd by oath" upon all suitors are enumerated (as a possible parallel with the details of the bond?):

> First, never to unfold to any one
> Which casket 'twas I chose; next, if I fail
> Of the right casket, never in my life
> To woo a maid in way of marriage;
> Lastly,

106

> If I do fail in fortune of my choice,
> Immediately to leave you and be gone. *(II.ix.10-16)*

These requirements do, indeed, smack of the harsh commercial world of the Rialto; they certainly establish a kind of absolute mood over Belmont and its "golden fleece."

The ring plot takes up exactly where the casket one ends, for with Bassanio's success (III.ii.), Portia not only cedes to him herself and her fortune, but "I give them with this ring," and then she adds three (again magic?) restrictions

> Which when you part from, lose, or give away
> Let it presage the ruin of your love. *(III.ii.174-175)*

The working out of this story is accomplished in two subsequent actions: the first at court and immediately afterwards on "a street" in Venice, and the second at Belmont. The situation is not actually resolved until the final lines of the play itself. If the bond plot sets up the central contrast of the play (justice versus mercy) and if the casket plot establishes the quality of love necessary for a happy marriage, the ring plot certainly undermines some of the ideals of the play. It allows bawdyness, even on the part of Portia; it reduces the marriages and victory at court to a series of double entendres on the nature of chastity in marriage; it puts an extremely realistic, even cynical, conclusion onto a play in which many kinds of problems and many kinds of people have been exposed to searching poetic analysis.

The mechanistic aspect of this plotting suggests that *The Merchant of Venice* might best be analyzed in light of the Bergsonian theory of comedy: the notion of men as puppets, manipulated by a higher power. This idea stresses that comedy results from our perception of the limitations placed upon mankind. Such an awareness seems to underlie Nerissa's couplet:

> The ancient saying is no heresy:
> Hanging and Wiving goes by destiny. *(II.ix.82-83)*

This concept may also be found in the conclusion of *The Merry Wives of Windsor* where we find Ford's couplet:

> In love, the heavens themselves do guide the state;
> Money buys lands, and wives are sold by fate. *(V.v.219-220)*

In *The Merchant of Venice* sacred things, such as marriage and justice, are turned into subjects for or causes of merriment, and human beings are seen as the victims of destiny. The mixture here is what, finally, seems to me significant. For the parts all add up to a complex comic vision in which the unifying theme (and method, too, as I've tried to demonstrate) is realism. Hence Shakespeare's willingness to see all the facets of life and to present them with honesty and understanding. The main thrust of the comic elements in these early plays seems to me to be substantially realistic;[8] even the romantic qualities, as I see them, are a part of this larger concept.

Notes:

(1)   All citations are taken from William Shakespeare, *Comedies*, ed. Peter Alexander (London, 1951).

(2)   Olive M. Busby, *Studies in the Development of the Fool in the Elizabethan Drama* (London, 1923), p.63.

(3)   In *The Contemporary Jew in the Elizabethan Drama* (Amsterdam, 1925).

(4)   *Cf.* Dorothy C. Hockey, "The Patch Is Kind Enough," *Shakespeare Quarterly*, X (1959), 448-450.

(5)   *Cf.* his essay, "The Lorenzo-Jessica Subplot and *Genesis* XXXIV," in *Shakespeare 1964* (Fort Worth, Texas, 1965), pp. 33-42.

(6)   "Shakespeare's Use of the Bible," *The Athenaeum*, No. 2896 (April 28, 1883), pp. 541-542.

(7)   *Shakespeare's Biblical Knowledge* (New York, 1935).

(8)   Cf. my article, "Comic Realism in *Much Ado about Nothing*," *Philologica Pragensia*, VII (1964), 213-225.

Antonio and the Allegory of Salvation

by Allan Holaday

Having noted that Portia really does not need Shylock's mercy, since before the trial begins she has found the means to free Antonio, Professor Tillyard goes on to explain that "while the other persons on the stage can only think of Antonio's fate, she is thinking of Shylock's, she is imploring Shylock to recognise his own peril and to mind the salvation of his own soul."[1] Her effort fails, however, because "Shylock, obsessed with his hate, is deaf to the tones of her entreaty and has not the remotest idea that she pleads essentially for him and his welfare, that she is fulfilling the command of Christ to love your enemy."[2] But we who see the play, continues Tillyard, "should recognise the other issue [i.e., Shylock's salvation] and watch Portia in her struggle to break down Shylock's obtuseness, ready to take her words both in the way she means them and in the way the Venetians (the Duke perhaps excepted) do in fact take them. The audience are thus in a wonderfully happy position: ironically superior to most persons in the play by possessing additional knowledge and thrilled by the excitement of having two parallel meanings to apprehend."[3]

Even though Portia's parallel meanings, once they are pointed out, become quite apparent, I suspect that a very small proportion of any present-day audience does, unaided, recognize her concern for Shylock's soul and thus share the insights that Tillyard describes. Indeed, I assume that Shakespeare's own audiences would, in this respect, have fared little better than their successors except that some among them could recognize, as we usually cannot, a subtle clue to the play's ironies in the analogy that develops between Antonio's trial and the Parliament in Heaven.[4] For many viewers, realization that the merchant's ordeal revives, once again, the problem of the Parliament—that Portia and Shylock equate for the moment with Justice and Mercy—would, I think, have clarified the implications behind cryptic overtones heard in much of the play. In the expectation that it may perform like service for us, I turn now for a closer look at this central allegory and its relevant connotations.

The Reconciliation of the Virtues or, as it now is usually called, the Parliament in Heaven, takes this latter name from the law-court trial of mankind through which it depicts God's response to original sin. In late Renaissance versions of the allegory, mankind and the Four Daughters of God (i.e., the Heavenly Virtues) play central roles. Arraigned before God by Justice and Truth, man escapes immediate death, the specified consequence of disobedience, by the intervention of Mercy and Peace. But Justice, exemplifying the retributive spirit ascribed by commentators to the Decalogue, concedes no basis for debate; since, as she insists, the law requires death for disobedience, the transgressor, admittedly guilty, must die. Mercy, thereupon, interposes the issue of intent; man, she argues, was tricked into sin by the real villain, Satan; innocent of evil purpose, he deserves mercy. She then moves the attendant angels to sympathy for man by stressing the inequality of his combat with Satan and by describing his contrition and his desire to do penance. But her opponent's demand for letter-of-the-law justice deadlocks the issue until God provides a solution: If a perfect man, himself uninvolved in Adam's guilt, will die in mankind's stead, justice will be requited and the way opened for human salvation. The angels, momentarily hopeful, soon recognize the appalling difficulty of finding someone capable of such love; then Christ offers Himself, exciting new rejoicing in expectation of the Incarnation and Atonement.

To assert that part of Shakespeare's audience did recognize the informing allegory in Antonio's trial implies for the age a general knowledge of the Parliament, an implication supported by abundant evidence. Its frequent adumbration in sermons, commentaries, and in religious iconography, together with the Church's stress on a legalistic scheme of salvation, made it familiar to all ranks and determined for the most part its connotations. Indeed, it was sufficiently commonplace in the early seventeenth century to assure that almost any reference to strife between Mercy and Justice would bring its general outline to mind or, at the least, suggest its central theme, human salvation.[5] Thus, by utilizing the allegory to inform his climactic scene, Shakespeare could exploit a rich body of associations.

In detailing God's plan for humanity, the Parliament implies that individual man must share the responsibility for his fate. The Atonement makes salvation possible by exempting the race from that automatic condemnation demanded by Justice and thus grants each member an opportunity individually to recapitulate Adam's "trials" and thereby to improve his chance for heaven. Thus, the Parliament establishes the absolute necessity among men for Christian love, true justice, and the wisdom to conquer temptation. And though it indicates man's responsibility for his decisions, it asserts that each deed must be judged in its context; that such considerations as the individual's intention, his personal limitations, and the difficulties that he encounters, as well as the final outcome to which he contributes, really determine the goodness or badness of his act. In the course of the play, the dramatist, as we shall note, exploits all these connotations.

We ought, by the way, also to note that Shakespeare employs two kinds of "parallel meanings": those illustrated by Portia's plea to Shylock, in which she consciously creates the ambiguity; and others of which the speaker is, himself, totally unaware, even though, through them, he advances a developing under-theme. This second, more numerous variety provokes our curiosity at the very start of the play, indirectly hinting at Antonio's difficulty and heightening our sense of ironic advantage over most characters in the drama. Though elusive and seemingly disparate, these over-tones harmonize, finally, to confirm the salvation motif implied by the Parliament. They can even promote our recognition that, in their unnecessary fear for Antonio's life, his friends failed to sense the threat to his soul; or that, though Antonio did not require Shylock's mercy to escape the knife, he did need that mercy to awaken his understanding of Christian love. Thus, if we recognize their import in advance, we greatly improve our chance to understand Antonio's character.

Part of our difficulty in comprehending the merchant derives from his virtues; in contrast to the flagrant evil of Shylock, Antonio's conspicuous goodness, particularly evident in his love for Bassanio, encourages an assumption that he embodies perfection. Not only does he assure his friend that

> My purse, my person, my extremest means,
> Lie all unlocked to your occasions; *(I.i.138-139)*

in the showdown, he makes his promise good. But what one dare not overlook in one's admiration for these virtues is his cruelty to the Jew. Too enormous to dismiss as irrelevant, this brutality sharply distinguishes him from other of the Christians; though some chide, none approaches the contemptuous animosity of Antonio, who fails completely to understand that arrogance of this sort is the direct enemy of Christian charity; that love like Christ's and Portia's encompasses Shylock as well as Bassanio.

Antonio's excessive pride recently interested Professor Thomas Fujimura. Recalling the merchant's "strange over-confidence" and the "blindness of hybris" with which he agreed to the contract, Fujimura described Antonio's much discussed malaise as a "product of his spiritual condition, of his lack of charity and his ignorance of self."[6] In corroboration of Fujimura's interpretation, I find in the mistaken assumptions expressed by Antonio's Venetian friends several overtones which suggest that his "illness" does, indeed, derive from spiritual, rather than physical disorder. Salarino and Salanio, by supposing that Antonio's melancholy derives from concern about his ships, that is, about his material welfare, foreshadow the mistaken fears, evident later at the trial, that Antonio is in physical jeopardy. As Salanio insists,

> Believe me, sir, had I such venture forth,
> The better part of my affection would
> Be with my hopes abroad. *(I.i.15-17)*

He would, he continues, be forever plucking grass to test the wind and studying maps to find safe harbors. And Salarino adds that blowing on his broth or watching an hourglass would excite in him an ague of anxiety over imagined gales and sand bars. And then, with unknowing irony, he adds:

> Should I go to church
> And see the holy edifice of stone,
> And not bethink me straight of dangerous rocks,
> Which touching but my gentle vessel's side
> Would scatter all her spices on the stream,
> Enrobe the roaring waters with my silks—
> And, in a word, but even now worth this,
> And now worth nothing? *(I.i.15-36)*

The point, of course, is that the church should remind him of his need to attend, not to material, but to spiritual concerns. In language fraught with religious con-

111

notations, he unwittingly contributes to the play's subtle insistence that most men invert the proper order of things, giving pre-eminence to the material over the spiritual. And thereby he has begun to suggest what is really wrong with Antonio. The near parody in his concern for the wound in his vessel's side that would scatter her spices on the stream reveals Salarino's light-hearted indifference to things spiritual.

Other overtones continue to suggest this universal tendency to overvalue the world. Thus, a moment after Salarino's remark, Gratiano, who also shares the misconception about Antonio, echoes with unconscious irony Christ's "For what is a man profited, if he shall gain the whole world, and lose his own soul?"

> You look not well, Signior Antonio.
> You have too much respect upon the world.
> They lose it that do buy it with much care.
> Believe me, you are marvelously changed. *(I.i.73-76)*

Antonio's reply,

> I hold the world but as the world, Gratiano —
> A stage where every man must play a part,
> And mine a sad one, *(I.i.78-80)*

confirms what we readily sense: that his particular difficulty does not derive from the shallow materialism of the others. Unable to explain his trouble, he accepts it as his destined role. But he has, of course, prudently attended to economic matters:

> Believe me, no. I thank my fortune for it,
> My ventures are not in one bottom trusted,
> Nor to one place, nor is my whole estate
> Upon the fortune of this present year.
> Therefore my merchandise makes me not sad. *(I.i.41-45)*

The apparent safety of his merchandise, to be mocked later by rumors of its loss, again reminds us that material certainty is a paradoxical concept; that man's sole hope for permanence lies in things spiritual.

From similar passages we discover one reason why the Venetians misunderstand Antonio; like him, they fail to distinguish the spirit—the true reality—from its physical manifestation; that is, they confuse label with substance, accepting the name in place of the thing. Antonio's "The Hebrew will turn Christian. He grows kind" (I.iii.179) is thus exactly to the point, since, because of his spiritual blind spot, Christian Antonio rivals the Jew in his lack of charity. And Shylock's "kindness," which reminds Antonio of Christian behavior, is, as the audience knows, vicious hypocrisy. Exquisite irony of the same sort informs Launcelot's comment to Jessica: "Most beautiful pagan, most sweet Jew! If a Christian did not play the knave and get thee, I am much deceived" (II.iii.10-11), and also Gratiano's "Now, by my hood, a Gentile, and no Jew" (II.vi.51). And Antonio's "punishment" of Shylock, by insisting that the Jew submit to baptism, continues the ironic series. Here Portia's wisdom,

112

apparent in her efforts really to convert Shylock through Christian charity, contrasts with Antonio's stupidity in forcing upon the embittered Jew an empty label, making him a "technical" Christian. Then, finally, in Launcelot's response to the news of Jessica's having turned Christian, Shakespeare offers a devastating assessment of Antonio's way of converting people: "Truly, the more to blame he. We were Christians enow before, e'en as many as could well live, one by another. This making of Christians will raise the price of hogs. If we grow all to be pork eaters, we shall not shortly have a rasher on the coals for money" (III.v.23-28).

Having provoked our curiosity about Antonio's difficulty, Shakespeare in the casket episodes confirms earlier hints that he suffers from pride. As Fujimura notes, Morocco and Aragon serve as surrogates for Shylock and Antonio.[7] But we should also recognize that as surrogates, their chief function is to illustrate human temptation. Like Satan's testing of Adam in Eden and Christ in the wilderness, these episodes in Belmont exemplify those universal human trials through which men must pass to salvation. Thus, by depicting Antonio's counterpart, Aragon, in a symbolic quest for heaven, Shakespeare can shed light on Antonio; through Aragon's conspicuous error, the dramatist can guide his audience to an understanding of Antonio's similar but less obvious mistake.

But lest we miss the import of the caskets, Shakespeare, through a minor character, tells us what is going on; by Launcelot Gobbo's obvious enactment of a morality-play temptation scene, the dramatist reminds his audience that the caskets represent a subtler version of this same human experience. And because an Elizabethan audience's knowledge of current doctrine on temptation probably exceeded ours, we need to examine these scenes against a background provided by appropriate commentaries, particularly those of John Udall and Lancelot Andrewes.

In the first episode, Morocco, responding to external appearance, "Not learning more than the fond eye doth teach,/Which pries not into the interior," takes gold; deluded by sensory appeals, he, of course, repeats Shylock's error. Aragon avoids that mistake; but, failing to recognize his human limitation, he blunders into another trap: "Who chooseth me shall get as much as he deserves." Without the humility to understand, as Portia does,

> That in the course of justice none of us
> Should see salvation,   *(IV.i.199-200)*

or that prompts Hamlet's "Use every man after his desert and who shall 'scape whipping?" Aragon, like Antonio, falls victim to pride. We of the audience, aware that no one deserves heaven, that the chance for salvation comes by grace of Christ, understand that Antonio's pride, like Aragon's, will limit his ability to recognize his true good. As John Udall noted, "Two things [are] required to resist Sathan . . . wisedome to discerne him, and power to resist him."[8]

Thus, both Shylock and Antonio, deluded by Satan's tricks, choose unwisely. And both failures result, again in Udall's phase, from "our natural blindness" which inclines us to heed Satan, who can "make vertue to seeme vglie, and vice beautifull vnto man."[9] But the opportunity to choose, as Lancelot Andrewes explains, is a blessing, not a trap; it represents that second chance provided us by Christ's love. After the Atonement, temptations no longer are "signes and pledges of Gods wrath, but fauours"; "there is," Andrewes notes, "no place priuiledged from temptations"; but, because of Christ's Atonement and example, we enjoy a great advantage over Adam; "now when we are tempted, they haue not the force they had before."[10]

Udall further explains that the word *tempt* "is vsed in the Scriptures both in the Hebrew and Greeke tongue in more general signification, to trye."[11] And Andrewes adds that "The diuell indeede tempteth vs, but God (as our English translation hath it) trieth vs."[12] What they wish us to understand is that, though still on trial, we now enjoy a vastly improved chance for success. Now Satan's wiles no longer possess "the force they had before" because, through His submission to the three temptations, Christ demonstrated for human instruction not only that man can overcome, but showed him how to do so; His three temptations encompass all those that man must face and, of course, correspond to those that Satan originally employed against Adam. As Andrewes explains: "So may Christ and *Adam* be compared in these three temptations . . . . And vnder these three heads come all temptations."[13]

According to a usual interpretation, the three tests illustrate despair, pride, and overmuch love of the world. Thus, in *Christ's Victory and Triumph*, Giles Fletcher, following an elaborate depiction of the Parliament, describes Satan first offering Christ the stone and "Closely tempting him to despaire of Gods providence, and provide for himself"; then, on the pinnacle, urging him "To Presumption"; and finally, atop the mountain, "To Vaine-Glorie."[14] Similarly, Andrewes explains that "first, hee would haue brought him to murmur against God: secondly to presume: & thirdly to commit Idolatrie."[15] In other words, the episode of the stone- or stones-into-bread illustrates the temptation to despair or distrust in God's protective providence; that of the pinnacle, to submit to unwarranted presumption or pride; and that of the mountain top, to the lure of wealth and power, that is, of gold.

Background for the casket scenes also includes comment on a troublesome variation in the order of the trials as described by Matthew and Luke. Both list as first in the series the stone- or stones-into-bread; Matthew follows with the pinnacle temptation, then that of the mountain. Luke reverses the order of the final two. The accepted explanation held that, though Matthew's version was historically accurate, Luke's rearrangement made Christ's temptations exactly correspond to Adam's and thereby increased the instructive force of his account. Thus, because he wishes to stress the identicalness, not only of Christ's and Adam's trials, but also of those which men must continually face, Shakespeare, contrary to usual practice, follows Luke's order as he illustrates in these episodes all three temptations.[16]

Before Morocco arrives, several suitors, dreading failure, have despaired of God's providence and withdrawn. Next Shylock's counterpart, Morocco, who perceives only what "the fond eye doth teach," succumbs to the temptation of the mountain top, that is, to the lure of gold. And finally, Antonio's surrogate, Aragon, supposing that he deserves Portia, fails the test of the pinnacle, that is, of pride. But Bassanio avoids all these snares. Remembering that "He who seeks to save his life shall lose

114

it, but he who seeks to lose his life shall save it," Bassanio recognizes in the threatening motto of the leaden casket—"Who chooseth me must give and hazard all he hath"—a guide to the earthly choice by which one wins heaven.

Thus the casket episodes illustrate the failures of Shylock and Antonio, each of whom, through his particular blindness, has missed salvation. As Shylock's frustrations relate to his obsession for gold, so Antonio's lesser isolation, the source of his malaise, derives from pride, evident in his arrogant contempt for the Jew.

But in the final act, Shakespeare reconciles such failures with the concept of ultimate success implied by the Parliament; he accepts earthly imperfection as appropriate to its sphere and necessary to the scheme. In the opening scene Lorenzo, aware of that basic distinction between heaven and earth, illustrates man's position; though beneath "the floor of heaven," he and Jessica are yet bathed in moonlight; despite the limitations of earth, they bask in celestial light. But as Lorenzo tells his wife, men cannot, even in Belmont, hear the music of heaven:

> Such harmony is in immortal souls,
> But whilst this muddy vesture of decay
> Doth grossly close it in, we cannot hear it.　　　(V.i.63-65)

His comment prepares us for Portia's remark as she and Nerissa, homeward bound from Venice, approach her house.

> That light we see is burning in my hall
> How far that little candle throws his beams!
> So shines a good deed in a naughty world.　　　(V.i.89-91)

To Nerissa's observation that "When the moon shone, we did not see the candle," Portia replies: "So doth the greater glory dim the less." Tillyard suggests that in her metaphor of the candle, Portia alludes to Bassanio's effort to save his friend; but I accept a more usual interpretation—that she here recalls her own rescue of Antonio. For, as she points out, the candle is hers; its light originates in Belmont. And its beam has indeed shone a long way; as a consequence of her "good deed," Antonio got not only his life, but an improved chance for happiness; his rescue made happiness possible for Portia and Bassanio; and Shylock's defeat assured the good fortune of Lorenzo and Jessica.

Nerissa's comment—"It is your music, madam, of the house"—brings Portia's reply:

> Nothing is good, I see, without respect.
> Methinks it sounds much sweeter than by day.　　　(V.i.99-100)

She is observing, of course, that circumstances—the "setting" of an act—determine its degree of goodness. The light from Belmont—Portia's "good deed"—though inferior to that from the moon, still shines with heaven-like brilliance in this night on earth. Though Shylock lost a chance to begin his salvation and though Antonio has still to discover himself—that is, though in "perfection" the earthly trial, despite the efforts of Portia, fell short of its celestial original—much was accomplished.

And in the order that obtains throughout creation, all things aid all other things, the "imperfection" of one contributing to the ultimate "perfection" of all. Says Portia:

> The crow doth sing as sweetly as the lark
> When neither is attended, and I think
> The nightingale if she should sing by day
> When every goose is cackling, would be thought
> No better a musician than the wren.
> How many things by season seasoned are
> To their right praise and true perfection!
> . . . . .
> This night methinks is but the daylight sick,
> It looks a little paler. 'Tis a day
> Such as the day is when the sun is hid.   (V.i.102-108; 124-126)

Then, through the episode of the rings, Portia illustrates what she has just observed: that nothing is good "without respect," that sometimes one discovers the perfection of an act only through its context, including, of course, its final outcome and the intention behind it. Utilizing her husband's surrender of his ring, she fashions another illustration of this lesson from the Parliament, revealing to the group at Belmont that though she heard Bassanio's offer to sacrifice her for his friend, she now understands the virtue of his deed.

In the desperate moments of the trial, Bassanio had declared to Antonio:

> But life itself, my wife, and all the world
> Are not with me esteemed above thy life.
> I would lose all, aye, sacrifice them all
> Here to this devil, to deliver you . . . .

An audience understands, of course, the ironic edge on Portia's immediate comment:

> Your wife would give you little thanks for that
> If she were by to hear you make the offer.   (IV.i.282-287)

But later, with the trial safely concluded, she prepares to demonstrate that Bassanio was right; having saved Antonio's life, she requests from her husband the symbolic reward of his wife, that is, the ring. And though little time has passed, she reveals her new perspective on Bassanio's offer; to his protestations that the ring has for him and his wife great personal significance, she answers:

> An if your wife be not a madwoman,
> And know how well I have deserved the ring,
> She would not hold out enemy forever
> For giving it to me.   (IV.i.445-448)

Soon thereafter, at Belmont, she will demonstrate the accuracy of her prediction.

The audience, of course, recognizes with Portia and Nerissa that the young men

116

are but technically oath breakers; though maneuvered into seeming disloyalty, they intended no evil. Their wives, as spirits of literal justice, temporarily reject all talk of extenuating circumstances, deliberately refusing to consider their husbands' apparent defections as part of the effort that saved Antonio's life. When Bassanio tries to establish such a context for their act, Portia remains for the moment unrelenting:

> Sweet Portia,
> If you did know to whom I gave the ring,
> If you did know for whom I gave the ring,
> And would conceive for what I gave the ring,
> And how unwillingly I left the ring,
> When naught would be accepted but the ring,
> You would abate the strength of your displeasure.   *(V.i.192-198)*

But the men have, after all, offered Mercy's defense of Adam, establishing their lack of evil purpose and revealing the inequality of the contest in which they had no real chance of winning; furthermore, they have proved contrite and eager to do penance and have, in addition, contributed to a happy conclusion. Thus, since Portia—as the audience has known all along—is really not Justice but Mercy, forgiveness is inevitable.

I conclude, therefore, that Shakespeare intended the metaphor of the Parliament, embedded in the play's center, to epitomize the drama. Recognition of its message would indeed equip his audience to comprehend not only Portia's startling interest in Shylock's soul, but also the dramatist's concern with Antonio's salvation. Because it makes clear that the play is really about salvation, the Parliament establishes for the drama a unity of theme that can harmonize such seemingly disparate episodes as the trial and the business of the caskets and the rings.

Notes:

(1) *Essays, Literary and Educational* (London, 1962), p. 32.

(2) *Ibid.*

(3) *Ibid.*

(4) See my "Shakespeare, Richard Edwards, and the Virtues Reconciled," *JEGP*, LXVI (1967), 200 ff. Among critics who have noted Shakespeare's use of the allegory in the trial scene are Miss Hope Traver in *The Four Daughters of God* (Philadelphia, 1907), S.C. Chew in *The Virtues Reconciled* (Toronto, 1947), pp. 47 ff., and Nevill Coghill in *Essays and Studies, 1950* (London, 1950), pp. 17 ff.

(5) For accounts of literary and iconographic exploitation of the allegory during the Middle Ages and Renaissance, see Hope Traver, *The Four Daughters of God* and S.C. Chew, *The Virtues Reconciled*. Numerous examples of the commentators' stress on the conflict of Mercy and Justice over the fate of man survive; for a representative list of these, see C.A. Patrides, "Milton and the Protestant Theory of the Atonement," *PMLA*, LXXIV (1959), 10 f.

(6) "Mode and Structure in *The Merchant of Venice*," *PMLA*, LXXXI (1966), 509 f.

(7) *Ibid.*, p. 501.

(8) *The Combate betweene Christ, and the Deuill* (London, 1589), sig. B8.

(9) *Ibid.*, sig. B8^{r-v}.

(10) *The Wonderfvll Combat for Gods Glorie and Mans Saluation betweene Christ and Satan* (London, 1592), sigs. B1^v, B4^v.

(11) *The Combate betweene Christ, and the Deuill*, sig. B5^v.

(12) *The Wonderfvll Combate*, sig. C2.

(13) *Ibid.*, sig. C6^{r-v}.

(14) *Christ's Victory and Triumph*, Part II, gloss to stanzas 20, 31, and 38.

(15) *The Wonderfvll Combate*, sig. C6.

(16) John Lightfoot, in *The Works* (London, 1684), I, 498 f., notes that "the order in which *Matthew* had laid the temptation is the proper method and order in which they were done and acted"; but "The order laid down by *Luke* is so point-blank correspondent to the order of those first temptations, that we may well conceive that the reason of his ranking these in this method, is, that the Reader might compare and consider the one from the other." As Elizabeth Pope notes *(Paradise Regained: The Tradition and the Poem* [Baltimore, 1944], p. 8), "it seems to have been customary, almost obligatory, to use the Matthew order in every work which left the decision in the hands of the author..." And she adds that "*Paradise Regained* is the only exception to the rule that I have so far encountered."

118

"Strange Events": Improbability in As You Like It

by Sylvan Barnet

It must have been as apparent to their first audiences as it is to us that Shakespeare's comedies are filled with improbabilities. Criticism has duly noted them, but it has tended to regard them tolerantly, as unimportant bits that only slightly mar the whole. We are probably most at ease when we do not look at the improbabilities, when we can say with Dr. Johnson that Shakespeare's "persons act and speak by the influence of those general passions and principles by which all minds are agitated, and the whole system of life is continued in motion"; "his real power is not shewn in the splendour of particular passages, but by the progress of his fable, and the tenour of his dialogue"; he "exhibited only what he saw before him"; "his drama is the mirrour of life." Still, Johnson was no slower than other critics to see the improbabilities, especially those near the ends of the comedies: he attributed them to the dramatist's desire to finish the job now that the end was in view. "In many of his plays," Johnson says, "the latter part is evidently neglected. When he found himself near the end of his work, and, in view of his reward, he shortened the labour to snatch the profit."[1] Although some such explanation is psychologically plausible, it is of course artistically discreditable.

The present century, reacting against earlier critics' emphasis on the importance of plausible characters, fairly early came up with a counter theory: Levin Schücking and E. E. Stoll, for instance, suggested that Shakespeare was chiefly concerned with theatrically effective scenes, and was not overmuch concerned with plausible continuity of character from scene to scene. Here are three critics, talking of episodes in *As You Like It,* who invoke this principle with only minor variations. Michael Jamieson, writing of Celia's and Oliver's swift tumble into mutual love, says that it is "a speed . . . theatrically necessary."[2] John Palmer, writing of Oliver, says: "Shakespeare takes the bad brother for his plot but never takes him seriously as a person and throws him into Celia's arms at the end of the story with . . . nonchalance."[3] Kittredge, writing of Oliver's conversion, says: "Sudden conversion of the villain is often an imperative *coup de théâtre.* . . . We sometimes forget that we are just as conventional as the Elizabethans, though with a different set of conventions, and that to Shakespeare, the practical playwright, the conventions of his age were rules of the game."[4] C. L. Barber amplifies the importance of plot convention, saying that "it is not the credibility of the event that is decisive, but what can be expressed through it. Thus the shipwreck [in *Twelfth Night*] is made the occasion for Viola to exhibit an undaunted, aristocratic mastery of adversity. . . . What matters is not the event, but what the language says as gesture, the aristocratic, free-and-easy way she settles what she will do and what the captain will do to help her."[5] But one can ask Jamieson *why* the improbable speed is "theatrically necessary," and one can point out that it is really no swifter than the speed with which Rosalind and Orlando fall in love; all four experience love at first sight. If exigencies of concluding the play explain the speediness of the love between Celia and Oliver, how can we then explain the speediness of the love between Rosalind and Orlando, which occurs in the first act? One can reply to Palmer that it is no service to Shakespeare to suggest that he did not take seriously a character who plays a fairly large role; furthermore, the "non-chalance" with which Shakespeare seems to treat Oliver appears in the treatment of other characters too, for example, in the uncertain motivation of Jaques' melancholy and in Frederick's conversion. And Kittredge's explanation minimizes Shakespeare's artistry by suggesting that an episode is acceptable simply because other plays of the period have similar episodes. Finally, Barber's statement that "it is not the credibility of the event that is decisive" minimizes what is highly visible and cannot be minimized. I do not think that the patent improbabilities in the plays are transparent conventions, comparable to, say, the invisible fourth wall that allows us to see the deeds going on in a room on the stage. Rather, I will argue, these improbabilities are an essential part of the meaning—at least of *As You Like It.*

It is probably true that most of us cannot quite escape from a view of literature that in one respect may be called Aristotelian: we expect to see in literature (as distinct from history) deeds growing out of motives, and motives growing out of the conjunction of personality and circumstances: In such-and-such circumstances, such-and-such a man will probably act in such-and-such a way. We can recognize the necessity of conventions, but it will not quite do to suggest that improbable actions are acceptable merely because similar actions occur in other plays. We want to know what is achieved through the improbability—what is achieved through those fairies, those forests, those coincidental encounters, those shipwrecks. This paper will argue that Shakespeare goes out of his way to heighten the improbabilities in *As You Like It,* presumably for a purpose, and that it is therefore an error to dismiss them or to suggest that they are to be accepted unthinkingly as conventions.

As You Like It, for all of its gentle satire on pastoral life and literature, is nevertheless set in a world where, despite Touchstone's dial, there is "no clock i' th' forest." That is, this pastoral world is utterly different from the shepherd world that King Henry VI calls to mind when, like any of us trying to get through the working-day world, he enumerates a shepherd's chores:

> So many hours must I tend my flock;
> So many hours must I take my rest;
> So many hours must I contemplate;
> So many hours must I sport myself;
> So many days my ewes have been with young;
> So many weeks ere the poor fools will ean;
> So many years ere I shall shear the fleece.   *(III Henry VI, II.v.31-37)*

While it would be a mistake to say that nothing happens (as someone has remarked, dialogue is what characters *do* to one another), it is true to say that the characters in Arden are in a sort of suspended animation, waiting for the reformation of Oliver and of Frederick, and largely free from the need to make choices and to take effective action. Orlando, for example, defeats a wrestler and (on Adam's advice) runs away, but once in Arden he does very little until near the end, when he saves Oliver. Chance—or Providence—brings him to the good Duke and to Rosalind, and once there he gets what little direction he needs from Rosalind, who herself does very little, for she is in "a holiday mood," until near the end when she presides over the denouement. It should be noted that although at the end she is the mistress of ceremonies, in fact she has contrived almost nothing when compared, say, to Portia or to Helena or to Prospero or to the Duke in *Measure for Measure*. She does not arrange any of the meetings; at the end of the fifth act she runs things only because at the end of the first act she decided to adopt a man's attire. Even the decision to leave the court was forced upon her by her uncle, and the decision to adopt a disguise is a modification of Celia's idea. The characters, that is, live in a wonderful Eden-like world, and Shakespeare on three occasions calls attention to the improbability. Of her chance encounter with Orlando, Celia says, "O wonderful, wonderful, and most wonderful, and yet again wonderful, and after that out of all whooping" (III.ii.190). Commenting on Oliver's report of "Ganymede's" swoon, Orlando says he has heard of "greater wonders," referring to the amazing swiftness with which Celia and Oliver fall in love. And near the end of the play, Hymen says:

> Whiles a wedlock hymn we sing,
> Feed yourselves with questioning,
> That reason wonder may diminish
> How thus we met, and these things finish. *(V.iv. 137-40)*

But reason will not be able to diminish the wonder by explaining "how thus we met," because there is no explanation, other than, perhaps, guidance by Him

> that doth the ravens feed,
> Yea, providently caters for the sparrow. *(II.iii. 43-44)*

Orlando had sought out neither the good Duke nor Rosalind, but he encountered both. The echo of *Luke,* xii. 24 and of *Psalms,* cxlvii. 9, evoked by the reference to the raven, and of *Luke,* xii. 6, evoked by the reference to the sparrow, is underscored by the explicit reference to Providence, and in the final scene Hymen twice speaks of heaven, suggesting that there is "mirth in heaven / When earthly things made even / Atone together." Jaques gives us a comic version of the wonder evoked by miracle when, looking at the paired lovers, he says, "There is, sure, another flood toward, and these are couples coming to the ark" (V.iv.35-36). This sense of wonder, with a concomitant hint of Providence, is of course found elsewhere, not only in the romances, where it has often been noticed, but also in the earlier comedies, for example in *The Merchant of Venice,* where Portia's revelations, like "manna," leave the characters "amazed," and where the audience itself cannot but wonder how Portia has news that Antonio's ships are safe. In *As You Like It*, Hymen himself is part of the wonder that concludes the play; he is never explained in the play, and those productions that make him recognizably one of the Duke's men, or a Corin whose Falstaffian girth reveals his identity beneath his sheet, do an injustice to this element in the play. Rosalind, I have said, really does very little, but one of the things she does do is mysteriously produce Hymen.

In keeping with the strangeness of this world, Shakespeare in several places *lessens* the motivation he found in Lodge's *Rosalynde*. It is customary in critical discussions of Shakespeare's use of his sources, to point out how he increases the probability of his actions, as though he were writing *pièces bien faites*, or as though he felt compelled to heed Aristotle's comments on probability. Yet in fact he often lessens the probability. For example, Lodge's Sir John of Bourdeaux bequeathed Rosader (the youngest son, who thus corresponds to Orlando) "six-teene ploughlands," which was two more than he bequeathed to Saladyne, the oldest son. Saladyne has a long internal debate, weighing his father's moral exhortations against his own envious impulses, concluding with the decision to "raign . . . sole Lord over al thy Fathers possessions."[6] Shakespeare might have followed Lodge in having the eldest son envious of his young brother's ample possessions, but instead Shakespeare makes Oliver's conspiracy against Orlando *less* intelligible by giving Orlando only a "poor thousand crowns," a "poor allottery" that does not seem to interest Oliver. Near the end of the first scene, after we have witnessed the quarrel between the brothers but have been given no explanation for Oliver's treatment of Orlando, Oliver confesses he can offer no explanation, "for my soul, yet I know not why, hates nothing more than he." He indeed goes on to pay tribute to Orlando's virtues, and then suggests that because of them "I am altogether misprized," but this explanation appears as an afterthought, and although Adam later says that Orlando's virtues "are sanctified and holy traitors" because they arouse envy, it is clear that Oliver's motivation is thereby only the more mysterious. As Adam says of this wonder, "O, what a world is this, when what is comely / Envenoms him that bears it" (II.iii.13-14). The fact may be plain, but the motive remains mysterious.

Before proceeding to mention some other important instances where Shakespeare lessens the motivation he found in Lodge's *Rosalynde*, and heightens the implausibility of the action, it may be worth mentioning that Lodge's style itself — a sort of saner euphuism — is well-suited to the presentation of the moral debates that lend plausibility to subsequent deeds. It balances the arguments, giving the characters an internal complexity and allowing the reader to perceive clearly the forces that impel them to one course of action or another. The characters do not, of course, regularly act rationally, but we get a sense of persons subjected to various pressures and responding to these pressures according to their personalities. Indeed, *Rosalynde*, like Lyly's narratives, has a good deal of argument, but where in Lyly the elaborate structure of the speeches commonly obscures any advance in thought and diffuses any sense of personality, in Lodge the euphuistic manner is sufficiently restrained so that a sense of internal debate is conveyed. Here, for example, is the beginning of "Saladynes Meditation With Himself" on the conflicting impulses of avarice and filial duty:

> *Saladyne,* how art thou disquieted in thy thoughts, & perplexed with a world of restlesse passions, having thy minde troubled with the tenour of thy Fathers testament, and thy heart fiered with the hope of present preferment? by the one, thou art counsaild to content thee with thy fortunes; by the other. perswaded to aspire to higher wealth. Riches (*Saladyne*) is a great royalty, & there is no sweeter phisick than store. *Avicen* like a foole forgot in his Aphorismes to say, that golde was the most precious restorative, and that treasure was the most excellent medecine of the minde. Oh *Saladyne,* what, were thy Fathers precepts breathed into the winde? hast thou so soone forgotten his principles? did he not warne thee from coveting without honor, and climing without vertue? did hee not forbid thee to aime at any action that should not be honourable? and what will bee more prejudiciall to thy credit, than the carelesse ruine of thy brothers welfare? (p. 165)

That Saladyne comes to the wrong conclusion and decides to steal his brother's property is irrelevant; the point is that the monologue suggests a reasoning man. This emphasis on reasoning, again appropriately set forth in a balanced style, appears not only in the monologue but also in the intervening narrative links. For example, Lodge does not merely tell us that the usurper decided to hold a tournament, but that the usurper had a purpose in holding the tournament: "Thus continued the pad hidden in the strawe, till it chaunced that *Torismond* King of *France* had appoynted for his pleasure a day of Wrastling and of Tournament to busie his Commons heads, least being idle their thoughts should runne upon more serious matters, and call to remembrance their old banished King" (p. 168). Moreover, Torismond knows his audience, and calculates his action so that it will have the maximum effect. (In the following passage I add italics to clarify the point, and I omit Lodge's italics from the proper nouns.)

> *To* feede their eyes, *and to* make the beholders pleased with the sight of most rare and glistring objects, he had appoynted his owne daughter Alinda to be there, & the faire Rosalynd daughter unto Gerismond, with all the beautifull damosels that were famous for their features in all France. *Thus* in that place did Love and Warre triumph in a simpathie: *for such* as were Martiall, might use their Launce to bee renowmed for the excellence of their Chevalrie; *and such* as were amorous, might glut themselves with gazing on the beauties of most heavenly creatures. (p. 169)

This is a fair sample of the sort of thinking that is revealed throughout the story; it insistently announces itself and conveys a sense of a reasoning and in some degree reasonable world.

Although in a play there cannot be narrative links precisely like these, unless the dramatist uses a chorus, this sort of information can be conveyed through dialogue, soliloquies, and asides if the dramatist cares about it. But Shakespeare does not bother to tell us why a wrestling match is being held; "Tomorrow, sir, I wrestle for my credit," Charles tells Oliver. That is as much motive as we get, and while it tells us something about Charles, it tells us nothing at all about Frederick's reason for holding a tournament.

The reasons for Frederick's banishment of Rosalind are similarly less detailed and less plausible than those for Torismond's banishment of Rosalynde. Le Beau has earlier warned Orlando (and us) that Frederick is unpredictable:

> Yet such is now the Duke's condition
> That he misconsters all that you have done.
> The Duke is humorous. (I. ii. 254-56)

In the following scene he enters, "his eyes full of anger," and orders Rosalind to "get you from our court." When she asks how she has offended, he calls her a traitor, and when he is pressed for a more detailed explanation he answers, "Thou art thy father's daughter, there's enough." Rosalind points out that she was her father's daughter when Frederick first usurped the throne, and to Celia's interruption Frederick answers that he allowed Rosalind to remain for Celia's sake. But now, for some unstated reason, Rosalind is to be banished. When Celia protests further, Frederick at last offers something that can be called an explanation: Rosalind's very excellence is Celia's enemy because it diminishes Celia's excellence. This indeed is a reason, but it is a bad one, and we can only echo Le Beau's earlier conclusion: "The Duke is humorous." But that is a conclusion, not an explanation. In contrast, Torismond fears that "some one of the Peeres will ayme at her love, ende [i.e. consummate] the marriage, and then in his wifes right attempt the kingdome. To prevent therefore had I wist in all these actions, she tarries not about the Court, but shall (as an exile) either wander to her father, or els seeke other fortunes" (p. 176). This is a tyrant's logic, but it is logic; it allows us to follow Torismond's thought-processes, whereas Frederick's remain mysterious.

Celia's decision to flee with Rosalind marks a departure from Lodge, whose Alinda is banished by her father Torismond. Here we may at first glance feel that Shakespeare's action is more plausible: rather than have a father unnaturally banish his daughter, Shakespeare has the daughter leave the court in order to remain with her devoted friend. And yet again Shakespeare's action is more mysterious, more wonderful, for devotion of such magnitude is inexplicable. This is not to say that it is unreal, only that it cannot be explained in terms of cause and effect. On the other hand, Lodge provides an adequate explanation for Torismond's apparently impossible conduct. Torismond in a long speech attempts to argue with Alinda ("in liking *Rosalynd* thou hatchest up a bird to pecke out thine owne eyes"), then abandons his attempt to "alleadge policie" and curtly rebukes her, and finally, when Alinda threatens suicide, banishes her. Lodge patiently explains why Torismond banishes his own daughter:

> When *Torismond* heard his daughter so resolute, his heart was so hardned against her, that he set downe a definitive and peremptorie sentence that they should both be banished: which presentlie was done. The Tyrant rather choosing to hazard the losse of his only child, than any waies to put in question the state of his kingdome: so suspicious and feareful is the conscience of an usurper.   (p. 178)

If for a moment we wonder why Torismond should harden his heart, Lodge quickly explains the psychology of a tyrant: such a man will prefer his kingdom to his kin, "so suspicious and fearful is the conscience of an usurper."

In yet another crucial episode Lodge's usurper behaves more plausibly than Shakespeare's. Torismond banishes Saladyne in order to gain possession of all the lands of Sir John of Bourdeaux, Saladyne having enlarged his own holdings by annexing Rosader's. Torismond first imprisons Saladyne on account of "the wrongs hee proffred to his brother" (p. 198), and then banishes him, explaining "I spare thy life for thy fathers sake" (p. 199). Frederick, however, learning that Celia and Rosalind have fled the court, perhaps with Orlando, says (II.ii.17-19) that if indeed Orlando is missing he will send Oliver to find him. Five scenes intervene before this subject is returned to, when in III.i Frederick orders Oliver to find Orlando and confiscates Oliver's property. In this scene nothing is said of the likelihood that Orlando is with the two girls, and nothing at all is said of the girls; without reference to the earlier brief discussion of this likelihood it is unclear why Frederick is concerned about Orlando. Again we get a sense that the Duke is "humorous," unpredictable, rather than a coherent perverse character.

But of course in *As You Like It* the most unpredictable happenings (from the point of view of psychology, not of literary conventions) are the instantaneous love affairs and the conversions of the villains. Lodge's Rosader falls quickly, but Rosalynde is less precipitous. There is not space here to give in detail the process that Lodge sets forth at length, but a few short quotations will suggest his attempt to explain what happens to Rosalynde when she sees Rosader. She is "touched" by the "beautie and valour of *Rosader* . . . but she accounted love a toye, and fancie a momentarie passion, . . . and therefore feared not to dallie in the flame . . ." (p. 172). She sends Rosader a jewel and in return he sends her a poem. "*Rosalynd* returning home from the triumph, after she waxed solitarie, love presented her with the *Idea* of *Rosaders* perfection, and taking her at discovert, strooke her so deepe, as she felt her selfe grow passing passionate. . . . Sucking in thus the hony of love, by imprinting in her thoughtes his rare qualities, she began to surfit with the contemplation of his vertuous conditions . . ." (p. 174). There follows a long internal monologue, "Rosalynds Passion," full of doubts and self-rebukes, but

125

concluding with the assertion that if she loves, it must be Rosader or no one. Shakespeare assumes that beautiful young people fall in love for no apparent reason. This assumption is especially evident in the love exchanged between Celia and the reformed Oliver. In Lodge, Saladyne, repentant and reunited with Rosader, saves Alinda from "certaine Rascalls that lived by prowling in the Forrest." When Alinda recovers her composure, she looks upon her rescuer and begins "to measure everie part of him with favour, and in her selfe to commend his personage and his vertue, holding him for a resolute man, that durst assaile such a troupe of unbridled villaines" (p. 222). Her love for him, that is, is partly rooted in her gratitude for his actions; his love, too, is a little less than instantaneous: "*Saladyne* hearing this Shepheardesse speake so wisely began more narrowly to prie into her perfection, and to survey all her liniaments with a curious insight; so long dallying in the flame of her beautie that to his cost he found her to be most excellent . . ." (p. 222). Shakespeare, on the other hand, goes out of his way to insist upon the suddenness and the improbability of the love between Celia and Oliver. There is no rescue from brigands, nor any other stated reason for it. (Perhaps it should be mentioned that Shakespeare's Arden, however green or golden, could have harbored brigands as well as a lioness and snake.) Rosalind is our source for what happened between Celia and Oliver:

> There was never anything so sudden but the fight of two rams
> and Caesar's thrasonical brag of "I came, saw, and overcame";
> for your brother and my sister no sooner met but they looked;
> no sooner looked but they loved; no sooner loved but they
> sighed; no sooner sighed but they asked one another the rea-
> son; no sooner knew the reason but they sought the remedy: and
> in these degrees have they made a pair of stairs to marriage,
> which they will climb incontinent, or else be incontinent before
> marriage. . . .
>
> *(V.ii. 29-38)*

This insistence on the suddenness and improbability of the experience suggests not that Shakespeare is winding things up quickly because (in Johnson's words) he is "in view of his reward," or that (in Paul V. Kreider's words[7]) Shakespeare is mocking his "patently inadequate plot," but that suddenness and improbability are part of the meaning of the play. It will not do to take Johnson's or Kreider's positions, or those of the critics mentioned earlier in this paper. Here is one more version, by John Wain, concentrating on the surprising conversions of Oliver and Frederick:

> The plot of *As You Like It*, like that of *Twelfth Night*, contains
> absurdities which, under the influence of the warmth and gaiety
> of the play, we swallow light-heartedly enough. The double con-
> version of the two villainous characters, Duke Frederick and
> Orlando's brother Oliver, is sketched in with a perfunctoriness
> that saves the play, perhaps, from ridicule; if Shakespeare had

> not shown us so plainly that he did not care whether we be-
> lieved in the story or not, if he had made it even a shade more
> credible, we might have tried to believe in it. And this could
> only have led to disappointment. We must take the action as a
> mere charade, and let Shakespeare guide our serious interest
> into areas where it has something to feed on.[8]

Wain's terms are a little uncertain; one does not quite know what to make out of
the shift from not *believing* in the plot to *feeding* on other "areas," but apparently
the point is that the plot is of no interest or consequence. Now, just as no one believes that the dialogue of a play is a transcript of real talk, or that the *dramatis
personae* are real people, so no one believes that the plot is an exact reproduction
of a chain of historical events. But plot, like dialogue and character, presumably
has some sort of intimate connection with reality. One might say that plot, dialogue,
and character are symbolic, standing for realities. In *As You Like It,* presumably
the sudden alterations in Rosalind, Orlando, Celia, and Oliver suggest changes in
personality of a sort suggested, say, in Ovid's *Metamorphoses.* In those legends,
suffering humanity—usually consumed by guilt or fear—is unable to continue its
existence, the metamorphosis representing the sort of change that in life is
accomplished by suicide, by retreat into a psychotic state, or by religious conversion. Tolstoi's conversion, preceded by enormous anxieties, contradictory actions
and suicidal impulses, is a familiar example from life of the sort of thing that much
of Ovid implies. And this brings us back to the matter of the conversion of Oliver,
for he not only falls in love with Celia but first loses the hatred for Orlando that
animated him when in the first act he said, "for my soul, yet I know not why, hates
nothing more than he." In Lodge, Saladyne repents while in Torismond's prison.
There is nothing strange here. Whatever our modern doubts about the value of
imprisonment, a stubborn part of our mind sees such a change as reasonable. A
man who is subjected to punishment, we think, is likely to avoid repeating the
sort of behavior that got him punished. Saladyne, in prison, "began to fall into
consideration . . . with himselfe" (p. 198), and by the end of a "complaint" he has
realized that he behaved badly. He vows to do penance, and to seek Rosader. But,
again, Shakespeare omits such motivation, heightening the abruptness of Oliver's
conversion, making it (like love at first sight) a matter of minutes. Certainly it is
understandable; Orlando nobly has saved Oliver's life, but Oliver in the first act
had clearly perceived Orlando's nobility and had hated him for it. Now, in an instant, Oliver is a new man. Asked by Celia if he is the man "that did so oft contrive
to kill" Orlando, Oliver replies:

> 'Twas I. But 'tis not I. I do not shame
> To tell you what I was, since my conversion
> So sweetly tastes, being the thing I am.   *(IV.iii. 136-39)*

Oliver explicitly speaks of his "conversion," and the experience he describes has
obvious affinities with religious conversion, which utterly transforms one's per-

sonality, as, for example, on the road to Damascus Paul's personality was transformed. And as Paul, who persecuted Christ, finally yielded utterly to him, so Oliver, who persecuted Orlando, yields to him "all the revenue that was old Sir Rowland's" (V.ii.10-11). I want to dwell a moment more on two other Biblical analogues. First, we might note that Orlando suspends the *lex talionis*, and requites evil with good. His action is not the mechanical counteraction evoked by Oliver's actions, but an act of overflowing love. Second, early in the play Orlando had introduced a reference to the parable of the prodigal son, quite rightly denying that he is a prodigal. But the parable in fact deals with *two* brothers, and Oliver in the earlier part of the play has the meanness of the second brother, who in the parable stands apart from the festivities that celebrate the return of the prodigal. In the last two acts we see that this cold brother is converted and drawn into the festivities; his transformation is confirmed by his experience of falling in love, an experience which similarly involves a surrender of the old self and provides a new perception of all experiences. And Oliver is awarded Celia; though he has labored in the vineyard only very briefly, his reward is full.

Shakespeare, it should be mentioned, did not need to convert Oliver merely to end the play; Oliver could have remained wicked, to be dealt with in an unwritten sixth act, as Don John in *Much Ado* is to be dealt with. Nor is Oliver's conversion necessary merely to provide Celia with a husband; one of Duke Senior's "loving lords" might have served. Similarly, Frederick might have been captured and pushed offstage. But Shakespeare gives us a different plot, and it is likely that his plot is meaningful rather than slipshod or perfunctory.

Frederick's conversion at the hands of "an old religious man" is only the last of a series of implausible happenings that suggests the existence of a benevolent Providence. *As You Like It* is not devoid of oblique references to Providence, some of which have already been glanced at. But it is in the strange happenings, rather than in the oblique references in the dialogue, that one perceives most clearly that (to quote from *Cymbeline*)

> The fingers of the pow'rs above do tune
> The harmony of this peace.

Or, to quote from *The Tempest:*

> This is as strange a maze as e'er men trod,
> And there is in this business more than nature
> Was ever conduct of.

Like Oliver's conversion, Frederick's is apparently triggered by a sudden experience, and it has "an element of marvel," to use words that William James in Lecture IX of *The Varieties of Religious Experience* used of conversion. But as James pointed out, conversion is often preceded by a hidden complex psychic state. James writes:

> A mental system may be undermined or weakened...just as a
> building is, and yet for a time keep upright by dead habit. But a

128

new perception, a sudden emotional shock, or an occasion which lays bare the organic alteration, will make the whole fabric fall together; and then the centre of gravity sinks into an attitude more stable, for the new ideas that reach the centre in the re-arrangement seem now to be locked there, and the new structure remains permanent.

Early in the play, by means of references to Frederick's unpredictability and to Oliver's confession that his hatred was inexplicable, Shakespeare indicates that the villains' personalities were unstable, and therefore that they were open to sudden re-information, or reformation. One might add here that the melancholy Jaques —whose melancholy is inexplicable, for it is not the scholar's or the musician's or the courtier's or the soldier's or the lawyer's, and it does not really seem to be the traveler's either—is a similar figure, puzzling because his principle of behavior is unclear. (There have, of course, been various studies of his melancholy, but the scholarship adduced to prove it is due to one or another cause is not substantiated in the play.) That he will seek out Frederick, because "Out of these convertites / There is much matter to be heard and learned," is not at all strange; earlier he was faintly associated with the humorous duke by virtue of being said to be "compact of jars." Jaques' discords, like Frederick's discordant actions, betoken a personality that has not become integrated, and at the conclusion of the play, after the report of Frederick's conversion, Jaques' intention to visit Frederick reminds us of this sort of anxious personality and it reminds us also of its great potentiality for change. In Jaques' statement that he hopes to learn "much matter" from the convertite, we may hear, very faintly, a voice like that of the jailer who asked Paul and Silas, "What must I do to be saved?" Zera Fink says[9] Jaques "has lost any real faith in life," but the implication of the play is, I think, that his dissatisfaction with things as they are prepares him for the possibility of conversion of the sort experienced by Frederick and Oliver, by the lovers.

These remarks do not, I hope, resemble those on the girlhood of Shakespeare's heroines, the child-bearing of Lady Macbeth, or the heavenly or hellish destinations of the figures in the tragedies. The point is not that the characters have a life before the first act or after the fifth, but that in the play as we have it they engage in strange behavior because strange behavior is what Shakespeare is talking about, not because he is employing meaningless conventions or winding things up quickly. In the romances the working of grace is more prominent, but even as early as *The Comedy of Errors*, when Luciana's words cause Antipholus of Syracuse to say, "Would you create me new?" (III.ii. 39) we find in Shakespeare suggestions of powers that mysteriously transform nature into something higher. Such inexplicable and wonderful transformations are entirely in harmony with another thread that runs through comedy, on which Puck remarked:

> those things do best please me
> That befall prepost'rously.[10]   *(III.ii. 120-21)*

In comedy we find things absurd to reason. As the etymology indicates, the preposterous is that in which the natural order is broken, the first coming last, and the conversions we have been speaking of involve the unnatural, the implausible. But it should be noted, too, that although in the last act of *As You Like It* some of the chief characters return to the court from which they had been exiled, what we saw at first is not what we now see last. The court society at the end is not identical with the court society of the first act, where a capricious usurper ruled, and where ribs were cracked. As Northrop Frye says, "The action of a Shakespearean comedy, then, is not simply cyclical but dialectical as well: the renewing power of the final action lifts us into a higher world, and separates that world from the world of the comic action itself."[11] There is at the end a return to the court, but the court now will house the rightful duke and a Rosalind and an Orlando transformed by love. Moreover, two former court-figures, Frederick and Oliver, who have undergone the greatest transformations, will not be there; though Duke Senior is the ruler of no mean city, these two feel the claim of a higher city, and Jaques also indicates an awareness of it. That is, Shakespeare's pastoral world in *As You Like It* is not only a place where innocence is achieved through retreat, abstinence, and self-sufficiency, as is common in pastoral literature; it is also a place where innocence is achieved through conversion, and, for Frederick and Oliver, through some degree of self-mortification.

Early in the play Jaques describes as a "strange eventful history" man's unhappy progress through seven rather uneventful ages; in the last act, when conflicts have been wondrously reconciled through patently unreasonable (but not therefore perfunctory or meaningless) transformations, Hymen justly speaks of "strange events." Had Shakespeare wished to write a more plausible play, he needed only to have followed his source more closely. But he apparently took pains to make his play implausible, and we ought not to let our awareness of conventions, or our tolerance for occasional perfunctoriness, mislead us into thinking that the plot of *As You Like It* is negligible, or that the play is about anything less strange than "strange events."

Notes:

(1) *Johnson on Shakespeare*, ed. Walter Raleigh (London, 1952), pp. 12-21.

(2) *Shakespeare: As You Like It* (London, 1965), p. 61.

(3) *Comic Characters of Shakespeare* (London, 1946), p. 32.

(4) Ed. of *AYL* (Boston, 1939), pp. x-xi.

(5) *Shakespeare's Festive Comedy* (Princeton, 1959), pp. 241-242.

(6) In *Narrative and Dramatic Sources of Shakespeare*, ed. Geoffrey Bullough (New York, 1957-), II, 166. All subsequent references to Lodge's *Rosalynde* are to this edition, with the page number in parentheses after the quotation.

(7) "Genial Literary Satire in the Forest of Arden," *SAB*, X (1935), 227.

(8) *The Living World of Shakespeare* (London, 1964), pp. 85-86. Compare Helen Gardner, "As You Like It," in *More Talk about Shakespeare*, ed. John Garrett (London, 1969). Gardner says on p. 19

that Shakespeare "handles very cursorily the repentance of the wicked brother," and on p. 20 that "the plot is handled in the most perfunctory way."

(9) Jaques and the Malcontent Traveler," *PQ*, XIV (1935), 250. Somewhat like Fink, James Smith takes a melancholy view of Jaques in "*As You Like It*," *Scrutiny*, IX (1940-41), 9-32.

(10) On re-reading the major critical discussions I find that in her essay on *AYL* Miss Helen Gardner quoted Puck's lines. Although the gist of my essay is very different from hers, I am doubtless indebted to Miss Gardner here. My essay is, hopefully, a footnote to hers, modifying her view that the plot is of minor importance.

(11) *A Natural Perspective* (New York, 1965), p. 133.

Theological and Non-theological Structures in Tragedy[1]

by Roland Mushat Frye

I. The Patterns of Difference

"Christian tragedy" as a critical concept has been widely discussed over the past ten or twenty years. The discussions have often been interesting and at times even brilliant, as literary and theological critics have analyzed the nature of tragedy and of Christianity and the relations between the two. Yet, despite all that has been said on this subject, I must confess that the meaning of the phrase "Christian tragedy" has never been clear enough for me, at least, to feel that I could treat it with precision. One could scarcely find two more complex words than "Christian" and "tragedy," and though we may be fairly sure what each refers to by itself, putting them together into a single phrase creates great ambiguity. Is Christian tragedy possible? Do Christian tragedies actually exist? Are the terms mutually contradictory? These are but a few of the questions which have been raised, and which have been debated at length. My own uncertainty on these issues is rather like that of Fitzgerald's Omar Khayyám

> Myself when young did eagerly frequent
> Doctor and Saint, and heard great argument
> About it and about; but evermore
> Came out by the same door wherein I went.   *(Rubáiyát, XXVII)*

Instead of engaging in a broad and theoretical discussion of Christian tragedy, what I wish to analyze here is the use of theological doctrine in building the structure of tragic drama. This approach has the advantage of being limited, specific, and circumscribed. It involves the accessible relations of theological doctrines to the construction of a tragic play. Some plays clearly are not subject to critical dissection along the lines of theological doctrine, and most of us think that Shakespeare's plays fall into this class of drama. On the other hand, there are plays in which the structural lines of the drama correspond with the structural lines of theological doctrine. A critical analysis or dissection of such plays along the lines of theological doctrine will at the same time reveal the dramatic construction of the play—or vice versa. Such plays may be said to have theological structures, or to be dramatically structured upon theological doctrines.

Christopher Marlowe's *Doctor Faustus* is one such tragedy, and John Milton's *Samson Agonistes* is another. A knowledge of certain Christian doctrines is necessary to a literary and dramatic appreciation of these two works. This is not to say, of course, that a knowledge of Christian doctrine is all we need, for obviously we need much more than theology, however relevant, in order to understand and appreciate even the most pervasively Christian works of art; it is merely to say that when these plays are not read with relevant Christian doctrines at least in the back of our minds, we are confused as to what takes place in them.

Whatever we may think of Marlowe's putative "atheism," it is clear that he has built his *Doctor Faustus* on the theme of the fall of a great man from felicity to misery in the precise sense of a fall from the possibility of grace to the certainty of damnation. Faustus consciously chooses to commit the originating sin of usurping upon deity; he makes a frightening contract with the devil; he is repeatedly counselled by both good and evil angels; he degenerates from a great and useful scholar to the status, at the very best, of a parlor magician; he literally commits adultery with the powers of darkness; and he is carried away to hell at the end of the play. The dramatic structure of the play is vertebrally theological.

The structure of *Samson Agonistes* is equally theological. The three central acts of Milton's tragedy carry Samson successfully through the archetypal temptations which the New Testament refers to as the world, the flesh, and the devil, or the lust of the eyes, the lust of the flesh, and the pride of life (*James*, iii.15; I *John*, ii.16). These three sins have traditionally been interpreted as summarizing the temptations to which the faithful man is subjected, and Milton uses them to dramatize the stages of Samson's development. Thus in Act II Manoa offers Samson an easy way out of his troubles. Manoa does this with good will, to be sure, but what he suggests amounts to an accommodation with the evils of the world, a willingness to live with and accept the worldly power of the Philistines whose dominance Samson was commissioned by God to oppose and overthrow. The next temptation, in Act III, is presented by Dalila, and it is the temptation to accept the comforts and pleasures of the flesh as an alternative to persistence in a divine mission. The final temptation is presented by the Philistine giant Harapha, and it is the most deadly of all. This—which amounts to the temptation of the devil—is that Samson abandon his faith in God, along with his faith that God has in fact any personal concern for him. It is only by struggling through the *agon* of these challenges, and emerging triumphant over each of them in succession, that Samson is re-established on a plane of greatness and prepared for the catastrophic victory of Act V. As a literary work, *Samson Agonistes* operates on a tightly wrought plot line, in which dramatic action is so integrally related to theological doctrine that the tragedy itself cannot be fully understood and appreciated apart from its inherent theological structure.[2]

Doctor Johnson did not recognize this progression through the archetypal or summarizing sins, and so concluded that though the tragedy had a competently executed beginning and ending, it lacked a middle. One could not ask for a clearer instance of the failure of aesthetic appreciation which is produced by a failure to see that certain literary constructions actually represent an organic projection of theological doctrine. This kind of theological structuring seems to most of us to be signally absent from Shakespeare's tragedies. Having experimented sympathetically with many possible theological structures for Shakespeare's tragedies, I for one have had to conclude that none of these allows us to approach the plays with a maximal understanding and appreciation. In my book *Shakespeare and Christian*

133

Doctrine I tried to treat these questions against a background of historical theology, and suggested the extent and the limits of Shakespeare's employment of theological material in his plays. Shakespeare often referred to Christian doctrine, and whenever he did we should surely attempt to understand what is said; not to do so would be to deny ourselves the fullest understanding and appreciation of his plays. We should recognize, on the other hand, that these references were subservient to the dramatic needs of a particular situation within an overall structure which was non-theological. Shakespeare's theological references, in short, were supportive and reinforcing rather than structural: they do not mark the vertebrae upon which he built his dramatic structures.[3]

Though there is no unanimity among Shakespearian scholars, there appears to be very widespread agreement upon these general principles. Taking these principles as a premise, then, what I propose to do here is to consider how the basic difference between the theologically structured tragedies of Marlowe and Milton and the non-theological structures of Shakespeare is represented in specific ways within particular plays. It would of course be possible to compare elements from all of Shakespeare's tragedies with *Doctor Faustus* and *Samson Agonistes*, but time does not permit, and so we shall focus primarily upon a comparison between Marlowe's Faustus and Shakespeare's Macbeth, and between Milton's Samson and the Antony of *Antony and Cleopatra*.[4]

II. Macbeth and Doctor Faustus

The story of Macbeth is in a number of ways parallel to that of Doctor Faustus. Both plays deal with initially great and useful men who succumb to different forms of demonic temptation, and both treat the degeneration of their tragic heroes as a consequence of the initial dedication to evil. Both men suffer from terrible fears and anguish of conscience and both are referred to by others as damned. In *Macbeth*, indeed, Shakespeare would appear to have adapted the dramatic patterns of degeneration which Marlowe established in *Faustus* in much the same way that he had adapted Kyd's revenge patterns in *Hamlet*. Furthermore, I think it is fair to say that in none of his tragedies did Shakespeare make more significant uses of theological material than he did in *Macbeth*.

There are nonetheless radical differences in development between the two tragedies. Marlowe's development is inherently, insistently, and essentially theological in a way that Shakespeare's is not. These differences may be seen even so early in the two plays as the initial temptations. The Evil Angel, upon first appearing to Faustus, urges him to "be thou on earth as Jove is in the sky" (*Faustus*, 104), while the enticement of the witches to Macbeth is that he shall be king of Scotland (*Mac.*, I.iii.50). Though Faustus expresses a desire for earthly dominion, his primary focus is at once more exalted and more specifically theological than is Macbeth's. It is more exalted in that he wants to be more than man—"Here, Faustus," he says to himself, "try thy brains to gain a deity" (*Faustus*, 91)—whereas Macbeth's ambition is bounded within "the swelling act of the imperial theme" (*Mac.*, I.iii.128f.). Faustus' fall is also specifically theological, for Marlowe has presented Faustus' sin in the very language which was used to describe original sin. The temptation which the serpent brought to Adam and Eve in *Genesis* was that they should be "as gods" and in *Paradise Lost* (V.77f.) Milton explicitly states that Eve's fall was to the enticement to "be henceforth among the Gods, Thyself a Goddess." Faustus, then, explicitly re-enacts the fall of man. Macbeth may be said to do the same thing only in the sense that every sin of every man is a product of original or originating sin. In other words, the specific doctrine of original sin is unmistakably introduced in specific theological language in connection with Faustus, but not with Macbeth.

What applies to the initial temptation also applies to the manner in which it is accepted. In *Faustus*, the fatal contract with Lucifer is given maximum exposure: Faustus debates it repeatedly in theological terms, and signs it not once but twice, early and late in the play, whereas we never see such a signing on the part of Macbeth, and Macbeth's almost casual comment in a line and a half is the only direct reference we have to his giving his soul to "the common Enemy of man." The bargain with Satan plays a part in *Macbeth,* as it does in *Faustus,* but the part is considerably muted, for Shakespeare's encompassing framework is not heaven and hell, but the life of man within the kingdom of Scotland.

It is quite obvious that the powers of darkness play an insistent and overt role in *Faustus*, whereas in *Macbeth* the demonic is cast in comparatively more ambiguous form. The Weird Sisters are instruments of darkness, and there are several invocations of the demonic, but the Weird Sisters—though clearly wicked—are not clearly devils. Macbeth is never accompanied by Mephistophilis or Lucifer, as is Faustus, and instead has the influence of Lady Macbeth who may have become a witch but retains humanity, whereas the closest we come to Satan himself is the poor attendant Seton whose name may have been a homophone for Satan.

Now it can surely be contended that Macbeth in Act IV, scene i, is playing the part of a conjurer, calling up spirits from hell, but a careful comparison of this scene with the conjuring scene in *Doctor Faustus* will again show a far greater theological explicitness in Marlowe's construction. According to Mephistophilis:

> the shortest cut for conjuring
> Is stoutly to abjure the Trinity
> And pray devoutly to the prince of hell.   *(Faustus, 287ff.)*

And this is precisely what Faustus in fact does, as he substitutes Belzebub, Demogorgon, and Mephistophilis for Father, Son, and Holy Spirit. When Macbeth commands the Weird Sisters, on the other hand, he does so with a minimum of theological reference. Theological discussions and debates are prominently featured in *Doctor Faustus*. Faustus questions Mephistophilis at some length about hell, and they discuss the worth of heaven and of the created world as well, while Mephistophilis even plays straight-man to Faustus as the two spell out a patently Satanic inversion of the questions and answers of the catechisms which were used to instruct Elizabethan children in the Christian faith. In each instance, these conversations serve to build an atmosphere in which the theological vertebrae of the play will stand out clearly. There are somewhat similar passages in *Macbeth*, but not developed on the same scale. Banquo's warning that "the instruments of dark- nes tell us truths" extends for less than five lines (*Mac*, I.iii.122ff.), and Macbeth's remarks on "th' equivocation of the fiend" and on "these juggling fiends" (*Mac.*, V.v.43 and V.viii.19ff.) run in total but a line or two more. Memorably expressed and dramatically significant though these passages surely are, they are given a more restricted role in *Macbeth* than are similar passages in *Doctor Faustus*. Marlowe writes like the trained theologian he was, and he gives us in dramatic form what amounts to an abbreviated pneumatology, to use the technical theological term which applies to the treatment of spirits and devils. Shakespeare makes no attempt to provide anything of the kind.

The same distinction applies to the treatment of human sin. In *Macbeth*, we have the famous "hell's gate" scene, in which the drunken porter pretends to be the gatekeeper of hell and "had thought to have let in some of all professions, that go the primrose way to th' everlasting bonfire." In fact, however, he does not do so, but only admits three sinners whose evils in various ways parallel those of Macbeth himself—"a farmer, that hang'd himself on th' expectation of plenty," "an equivocator, that could swear in both the scales against either scale," and the thieving tailor (*Mac.*,II.iii.1-22). The porter's opening speech thus reinforces the central themes of Macbeth's deceptive hopes for the future, of his skillful hypocrisy, and of his stealing the robes of majesty. This topical treatment of sin is intensely relevant as a commentary on the major action of the play even while it provokes laughter as an escape valve for emotional tension. As a theological treatment of sin, however, it is severely restricted when compared with what Marlowe provides in *Doctor Faus- tus*. Instead of three specific crimes recounted by a drunken porter, Marlowe gives us a parade of all of the seven deadly sins, presided over by Lucifer himself. "O, this feeds my soul," says Faustus, for at this point (a bit more than halfway through the play) he can take delight in evil by and for itself; he no longer requires to see it disguised, as he had when he first conjured up a devil, and then commanded it:

> I charge thee to return and change thy shape;
> Thou art too ugly to attend on me.
> Go, and return an old Franciscan friar;
> That holy shape becomes a devil best.   *(Faustus, 781 and 260ff.)*

The delight which Faustus takes in the parade of the seven deadly sins shows once more the full theological structuring of Marlowe's play, expressed in tra- ditional theological forms.

What is true of the two treatments of the demonic and of sin is even more con- spicuously true of treatments of the divine and of salvation. Again and again Mar- lowe reminds us that God is present and accessible to his protagonist; again and again Faustus reminds himself—and is reminded by others—of the judgment and mercy of God. Macbeth, on the other hand, mentions God only when he bemoans the fact that when the sleeping grooms said "God bless us," he could not say "amen." After this point he never once refers to God. And the name of Christ is never men-

136

tioned at all in *Macbeth*, though Faustus cannot wrench his mind free of the name of the Christ whom he had repudiated.

> Ah, Christ, my Savior!
> Seek to save distressed Faustus' soul, *(Faustus, 695f.)*

he cries out in near despair, or again he declares, this time clearly in a state of presumption:

> Tush, Christ did call the thief upon the cross;
> Then rest thee, Faustus, quiet in conceit. *(Faustus, 1147f.)*

Even in his last hour Faustus sees

> where Christ's blood streams in the firmament—
> One drop would save my soul—half a drop! oh, my Christ! *(Faustus, 1433f.)*

By these and other references Marlowe repeatedly directs our attention to God's judgment and the life to come. We are never allowed to forget for long that the everlasting destiny of the soul is at stake in Faustus' transactions: the good and evil angels appear to Faustus directly on four separate occasions and appeal to him to persist in evil or to repent, as the case may be. Even after the hardening of his heart precludes the direct sight of the good angel, an old man assures him that the good angel still hovers over his head "with a vial full of precious grace" *(Faustus,* 1292) for the salvation of his soul if he will only call for mercy. The play is permeated with references of all kinds to heaven and hell, and references abound to the grace of God and to repentance. The doctrine of repentance, with its full theological freight of meaning, recurs again and again in *Doctor Faustus*: "God will pity me," Faustus declares, "if I repent" *(Faustus,* 627), and he repeatedly debates as to whether he will repent and cast himself upon the mercy of God.

In *Macbeth*, on the other hand, the only full repentance referred to is that of Cawdor who "set forth a deep repentance" *(Mac.,*I.iv.6f.) before his execution early in the first act. Macbeth never specifically considers repentance; his only use of the word at all is when he hypocritically declares "yet I do repent me of my fury that I did kill" Duncan's drunken grooms, *(Mac.,*II.iii.106f.) and here the word conveys regret rather than repentance in the full theological sense which plays so prominent a part in *Doctor Faustus*.

It is not that Macbeth lacks a conscience, while Faustus has one. Macbeth suffers pains of conscience which are no less real than those of Faustus, and which are more powerfully expressed. I know of no literary work which makes an evil conscience so terrifying as does *Macbeth*. The external progression from murder to murder is paralleled by the internal progression from scorpions of the mind and sleepless nights and shattering fears to a state of mind so numbered in evil that life has lost all color, all beauty, all sense, all attraction. Whether Shakespeare could have created this horrifying portrait of psychological retribution apart from a knowledge of Christian theology is an interesting question, but it is a question which would lead us away from our primary critical concerns here. What is important for our purposes is the fact that in the drama itself Macbeth's conscience is made to speak without theological comment. "We'd jump the life to come," Macbeth says in an early soliloquy, and thereafter his conscience tortures him, but not in direct reference to God or to heaven or to any specifically theological order and frame of reference.[5] The emphasis of his conscience and of his fears, and of his entire story is underscored by the metrical beat of the verse when he declares that

> . . . *here*
> But *here,* upon this bank and shoal of time,
> We'd jump the life to come. — But in these cases,
> We still have judgment *here*; that we but teach
> Bloody instructions, which, being taught, return
> To plague th' inventor: this even-handed Justice
> Commends th' ingredience of our poison'd chalice
> To our own lips. *(Mac., I.vii. 5.ff. Italics mine)*

The basic structure of *Macbeth* keeps our attention rooted and grounded in the stage world of Scotland, and in the characters and events "here, but here, upon this bank and shoal of time."

Even when Macbeth confesses that he has given away his eternal jewel, his emphasis does not long linger upon the "eternal." What seems to concern him most is that he has "put rancours in the vessel" of his peace so as to make the seed of Banquo kings. Even as he mentions eternity, then, Macbeth's attention is focused upon the temporal world and specifically upon his place in that world (*Mac.*,III.i. 66ff.). Faustus laments "being deprived of the joys of heaven" in a way that Macbeth does not, and nowhere do we find in the Scottish king anything even remotely approaching the German scholar's poignant recognition that he

> must remain in hell forever, hell, ah hell,
> forever! Sweet friends, what shall become of
> Faustus, being in hell forever? *(Faustus, 320 and 1381ff.)*

Faustus' attention towards the end of the play is temporarily diverted from hell only by the demon who appears in the guise of Helen "to glut the longing of my heart's desire" (*Faustus,*1320). In comparison with the pains of hell, life seems very precious to Faustus at the end, and he begs for more time: "*O lente; lente currite noctis equi*" (*Faustus,*1428). Macbeth, on the other hand, neither fears the future life — indeed he does not even mention it — nor does he want a longer span of the present life. "I have liv'd long enough," he says and still later he declares that "I 'gin to be aweary of the sun." Life finally seems to him only a meaningless succession of tomorrows creeping along "to the last syllable of recorded time" (*Mac.,* V.iii.22;V.v.49 and 19ff.).

The final dispositions which the two dramatists make of their tragic heroes consistently maintain the same difference which we have observed throughout. Marlowe's ending is a theologically-oriented conclusion to a theologically-structured drama, and Shakespeare's ending keeps its focus upon the secular order. Whereas

Faustus is carried away to hell by a party of devils, Macbeth's head is impaled upon a pike, just as the heads of traitors were impaled in Shakespeare's London.

The emphasis in Macbeth remains an emphasis on "recorded time," on this world and on the kingdom of Scotland. If we would find doctrinal structures in *Macbeth*, then, it must be primarily in the doctrines of ethics, rather than the doctrines of theology in the broadest sense. Furthermore, even if some critics wish to postulate a dogmatic group of Elizabethan Christians, and to ask their opinion of the afterlife of a character like Macbeth, and even if they were to reply that Macbeth was as surely damned as was Faustus, the fact remains that Shakespeare, unlike Marlowe, did not spell out that answer in his play. And there is the even more important fact that he may scarcely be said even to have raised the question.

III. *Antony* and *Cleopatra* and *Samson Agonistes*

When we come to *Samson Agonistes*, we have another tragedy which is structured upon theological doctrines. Without a recognition of the three archetypal sins of the world, the flesh, and the devil, as developed in the New Testament and in subsequent Christian theology, the second, third, and fourth acts of Milton's tragedy seem merely episodic and quite unrelated to the first and fifth acts. Here doctrine is completely transmuted into dramatic structure, and there is nothing of Shakespeare's work which may be said to parallel *Samson Agonistes* even to the extent that *Macbeth* parallels *Doctor Faustus*. There is certainly no Shakespearean play in which the protagonist must meet and overcome a complete set of archetypal temptations taken directly from Scripture and theology.

It may thus appear unrewarding to compare Milton's Samson with Shakespeare's Antony. It is particularly true of Antony that he is no saint and it may be objected that he is therefore not fairly comparable to a hero of the faith. Yet Samson was no "saint" either, in the stereotyped sense, and was indeed just as fleshly a type as Antony. In fact, the two heroes have much in common. Both are marked by physical prowess and physical stamina, both are great fighters and great lovers, and neither is terribly intelligent. They are quite similar in their uxoriousness, in their "effeminacy" or subjection to woman; both are reduced to ignominy and shame before enemies to whom they had once been superior, or at the very least equal; both appeared to be invincible before their downfalls, and both downfalls are attributed to the influence of a woman.

In addition to such similarities in the tragic plot situations, there are similarities in themes treated within the two plays. Both protagonists are concerned with problems of personal identity. Samson is tormented by "restless thoughts" of "what once I was, and what am now" (*SA*, 19ff.), whereas Antony bitterly resents Caesar's "harping on what I am, Not what he knew I was" (*Ant.*, III.xiii.141ff.). Early in the play Antony declares that

> These strong Egyptian fetters I must break,
> Or lose myself in dotage,   *(Ant., I.ii. 113f.)*

while the chorus comments on how Samson, drawn away by Dalila's charms, was

> enslav'd
> With dotage, and his sense deprav'd
> To folly and shameful deeds which ruin ends.   *(SA, 1040ff.)*

That choral comment sounds much like Enobarbus on Antony. The imagery becomes even more reminiscent of *Antony and Cleopatra* when the chorus goes on to ask

> What pilot so expert but needs must wreck
> Embark'd with such a steers-mate at the helm?   *(SA, 1044f.)*

This steering imagery is apt for Dalila's control over Samson, though it does not grow directly out of the story as it does when Antony uses it to appeal to Cleopatra after their flight from Actium:

> Egypt, thou knew'st too well,
> My heart was to thy rudder tied by the strings,
> And thou shouldst tow me after.   *(Ant., III.xi. 56ff.)*

Both men are publicly reviled, and for the same reasons. Antony commands the messenger from Rome to "Speak to me home, mince not the general tongue" *(Ant., I.ii.102)*, and Enobarbus in a typical mood of protest tells Cleopatra of the popular reaction to Antony:

> He is already
> Traduc'd for levity, and 'tis said in Rome
> That Photinus, an eunuch, and your maids
> Manage this war.   *(Ant., III.vii. 12ff.)*

Samson's situation is similar, and he acknowledges how much he is traduced when he cries out,

> Am I not sung and proverb'd for a fool
> In every street...?   *(SA, 203f.)*

Both protagonists are thus confused by the loss of a public image of themselves to which they had become accustomed, and both are disturbed by the new and degrading reputation they have achieved by subservience to a woman.

In the end, however, both come to terms with themselves and with their situations, and both reassert their own sense of integrity in an unmistakable fashion. Antony's last speech contains a reminder of his former greatness, when he was "the greatest prince o' the world, the noblest," followed by an assertion of his continuing nobility:

> and do now not basely die,
> Not cowardly put off my helmet to
> My countryman: a Roman, by a Roman
> Valiantly vanquish'd.   *(Ant., IV.xv. 54ff.)*

Samson's last speech is a similar assertion of his rediscovered integrity, as he is led away to the Philistine holiday:

> Happ'n what may, of me expect to hear
> Nothing dishonorable, impure, unworthy
> Our God, our Law, my Nation, or myself.   *(SA, 1423ff.)*

There thus appears to be a considerable similarity between the basic situations and the treatment of themes which we find in *Antony and Cleopatra* and in *Samson Agonistes*. For our purposes, this is a fortunate coincidence which provides us with many specific instances of the difference in operation between theological and non-theological structures of tragedy.

In *Samson Agonistes*, as in *Doctor Faustus*, the ultimate transactions are between man and God, and even though the deity never appears on the stage, every significant action of the human protagonist is considered in terms of the divine reaction. On the other hand, in *Antony and Cleopatra* as in *Macbeth*, the transactions of the protagonist are primarily with other characters, and are not consistently gauged by the divine reaction. This is not to say that references to God or the gods are not introduced into the Shakespearian tragedies, for they are. Neither is it to say that the transactions in *Doctor Faustus* are not largely, and those in *Samson Agonistes* entirely, between human characters. The difference is that in the tragedies of Shakespeare the human interactions are not consistently and primarily focused against the divine judgment, whereas in the other two tragedies the interactions are consistently projected within such a focus.

Consider, for example, the fact that Samson and Antony both admit to having violated certain standards in their relations with Dalila and with Cleopatra. Antony confesses that "I have not kept my square"—a rather vague confession which may refer to a prudential standard of behavior, or which may refer to a high ethical standard, but which on either count is as devoid of theological coloring as a statement could possibly be. With Samson, the situation is diametrically different: he too confesses that he has "not kept" something, but his reference is totally theological: "But I God's counsel have not kept" (*Ant.*,II.iii.6, and *SA*,496f.).

What the protagonists say of themselves is paralleled in what others say of them. When Scarus comments upon what Antony violated in his flight from the sea battle at Actium, the reference is again without a trace of theological awareness:

> I never saw an action of such shame;
> Experience, manhood, honour, ne'er before
> Did violate so itself.   *(Ant., III.x. 22ff.)*

When Manoa speaks of Samson's subjection to Dalila he declares that Samson did "violate the sacred trust of silence," as Samson is judged in explicitly theological terms (*SA*,428). Now Samson's submission to Dalila is sufficiently like Antony's to Cleopatra that the kind of prudential and ethical judgment which is made of Antony could have been applied to Samson, and conversely the kind of theological judgment which is made of Samson could have been applied to Antony. Not the same theological judgment, to be sure, for the cases differ too markedly for that, but when Antony gave up "his potent regiment to a trull" and threw the civilized world into chaos, it would have been an appropriate theological judgment to say that he had violated the laws of God as well as the honor of man. Similarly, Samson's weak submission to Dalila could with equal propriety be said to have violated experience, manhood and honor, as well as his Nazaritic vows. But the focus is not blurred: Samson's trespass is judged primarily in theological terms, and Antony's in terms which are primarily those of human prudence and ethics.

It is true that in the fifth act Agrippa says of the dead Antony's "taints" that "you gods will give us some faults to make us men" (*Ant.*,V.i.32f.), but however true and appropriate we may think these words to be, we can scarcely regard them as having more than a casual place in the play: *Antony and Cleopatra* is not structured on the relationship between the gods and our faults, or our virtues either, for that matter. The gods are introduced rhetorically, but not structurally, into the judgments and actions of the play. So it is with the account of Hercules' desertion of Antony, which merely reinforces the established course of the action without playing any causative part in it. When music is heard under the earth in token that "the god Hercules, whom Antony lov'd, now leaves him" (*Ant.*,IV..iii.15f.), we may be saddened, and we may be interested, but we accept the news as little more than an episode. Apart from this reference to the demigod, no theological significance has been attached to Hercules in the play. He does not directly figure in the action elsewhere, and is referred to only in an oath and as Antony's ancestor. His defection is not nearly so important as that of Enobarbus. All that it does is to support our already established understanding that Antony's cause is on the decline.

Such references to the gods are so casual and isolated as to be merely rhetorical or reinforcing adjuncts to the major themes and events of the tragedy. Antony himself does not mention the gods with sufficient frequency and force to establish them as significant factors in his own consciousness, much less in the play as a whole, but we should give some notice to one comment he makes shortly before his attempted suicide:

> Since Cleopatra died,
> I have liv'd in such dishonour that the gods
> Detest my baseness. *(Ant., IV.xiv.55ff.)*

Now that comment seems quite appropriate to the Olympian gods and to a system which exalted human honor and dignity, just as it would be inappropriate to the Judeo-Christian God who shows considerable predilection for the dishonored and the base. It is thus a mark of theological decorum that the Roman Antony should speak in these classical terms, but how structurally important to the tragedy is it that Antony feels the gods detest his baseness? I suggest that it is of relatively little structural importance when compared with the very weighty considerations of his supposed loss of Cleopatra and his own fear of "the inevitable prosecution of disgrace and horror" (*Ant.*,IV.xiv.65f.). Antony rarely indulges in theology at all, and even when he speaks appropriately of classical religion, the words are more significant as rhetoric than as implementing beliefs.

142

When Samson speaks of the divine disapproval, on the other hand, we know that his sense of that disapproval is one of the most important factors in his existence, a factor which serves both to punish and to sustain him. To his father he says:

> Appoint not heavenly disposition, Father,
> Nothing of all these evils hath befall'n me
> But justly....
>
> (SA,373ff.)

Of the painful visit from Dalila he comments that

> God sent her to debase me,
> And aggravate my folly.
>
> (SA, 999f.)

In an even more striking speech, he says of the abuse heaped upon him by the giant Harapha that

> all these indignities, for such they are
> From thine, these evils I deserve and more,
> Acknowledge them from God inflicted on me
> Justly, yet despair not of his final pardon
> Whose ear is ever open; and his eye
> Gracious to re-admit the suppliant.
>
> (SA, 1168ff.)

Throughout *Samson Agonistes* we are never left in doubt as to the crucial importance of Samson's relations with God and of God's displeasure with Samson. When comparable considerations are introduced into *Antony and Cleopatra*, we are left with the feeling that they may be appropriate but that they are not significant for the play's development. In *Antony and Cleopatra*, Caesar's displeasure is far more important to the dramatic structure than is the displeasure of the gods—and Octavius Caesar may scarcely be treated as a surrogate for God in any meaningful theological sense.

Caesar looms very large in this play. In addition to the intermittent conflict which Antony wages with himself to determine which side of his nature will be predominant, the most persistent conflict in the tragedy is that between Antony and Caesar. Upon receiving word of Antony's death, Caesar comments that

> I must perforce
> Have shown to thee such a declining day,
> Or look on thine: we could not stall together
> In the whole world.
>
> (Ant., V.i.37ff.)

This posing of an irreconcilable opposition is not infrequent in Shakespeare, and we may recall Coriolanus' reference to a time "when two authorities are up" and Hamlet's to the "fell incensed points of mighty opposites" (*Cor.*,III.i.109 and *Ham.*, V.ii.61). In such situations there must be a battle to the death, without compromise and without quarter. Such was the conflict between Antony and Caesar, and the development of this conflict is one of the major features of the plot of *Antony and Cleopatra*.

In *Samson Agonistes* there is parallel confict, but it is not between two men: it is rather between two gods, to determine which is the true god and which the false. "All the contest is now," as Samson says, "'Twixt God and Dagon," and Manoa states the necessity for final resolution in words which are a formal parallel to those of Caesar:

> for God,
> Nothing more certain, will not long defer
> To vindicate the glory of his name
> Against all competition, nor will long
> Endure it, doubtful whether God be Lord,
> Or Dagon. *(SA, 461 f., 473ff.)*

The parallel, as I suggest, is a formal one between two specimens of the tragic genre, but despite the formal identity it involves totally different implications. Both plays develop a tragic "competition," but whereas Caesar calls Antony "my competitor In top of all design," when Milton introduces the word "competition" into his tragedy it is in reference to the conflicts between the true God and the false (*Ant.*, V.i.42f and *SA*,476).

This formal parallel with subjective difference is most marked in the challenges to personal combat which are featured in the two plays. Samson repeatedly challenges the Philistine giant Harapha to a mortal combat which will decide "whose god is strongest, thine or mine,"

> By combat to decide whose god is God,
> Thine or whom I with Israel's sons adore. *(SA, 1155, 1176f.)*

Harapha's reply is equally theological:

> Presume not on thy god, whate'er he be,
> Thee he regards not, owns not, hath cut off
> Quite from his people.... *(SA, 1156ff.)*

Here the assault involves doubt of God, and a denial of his personal concern for Samson—both representing crucial temptations which Samson must overcome. Along with the struggle between the Hebrew and the Philistine conceptions of God, there is also the struggle within Samson himself to recover a confident certainty of God's concern for him as an individual. The conflict between Samson and Harapha unites in itself both of these larger struggles, so that it tells us something (though in a limited way) about the nature of Samson and of Harapha, but even more importantly it is designed to tell us something about the nature of God.

The exchange of challenge and reply in *Samson Agonistes* may tell us less about the human qualities of two men there than does the comparable situation in *Antony and Cleopatra*, but Shakespeare makes no pretense whatsoever to tell us anything about God, or even about ideas concerning God. His contest is purely human and without major theological overtones. Antony sarcastically suggests that Caesar may be a commander who is no warrior, and declares

144

> I dare him therefore
> To lay his gay comparisons apart
> And answer me declin'd, sword against sword,
> Ourselves alone.   *(Ant., III.xiii.25ff.)*

The point is structurally important, for it shows in the words of Enobarbus that Caesar has "subdued" Antony's judgment as well as his fleet (*Ant.*,III.xiii.36f.). Caesar's reply to the challenge is both caustic and devastating:

> let the old ruffian know,
> I have many other ways to die; meantime
> Laugh at his challenge.   *(Ant., IV.i.4ff.)*

The turning point has been passed, and the end foreshadowed, in Caesar's absolute confidence in his worldly resources, even as he refuses the challenge. The same formal point of tragic structure is seen in Harapha's evasion of Samson's challenge, in that it shows the turning point where Samson has successfully dealt with the final temptation and foreshadows the end by displaying Harapha's lack of confidence in his Philistine god as compared to Samson's absolute confidence in Jehovah.

The end comes for the two tragic heroes in ways which are at once similar and different. Both are "self-kill'd," but for Samson this form of death came, as the chorus says,

> Not willingly, but tangl'd in the fold
> Of dire necessity, whose law in death conjoin'd
> Thee with thy slaughter'd foes in number more
> Than all thy life had slain before.   *(SA,1665 ff.)*

It was theologically important that Samson not be represented as willfully commiting suicide, but there was of course no such restriction in connection with Antony who eagerly embraced death:

> I will be
> A bridegroom in my death, and run into't
> As to a lover's bed.   *(Ant., IV.xiv.99.ff.)*

The two deaths are appropriate within the dramatic frameworks which the two poets constructed for telling their ancient stories. Antony retained his honor, his dignity, his virtue, as these are understood in his play:

> Peace!
> Not Caesar's valour hath o'erthrown Antony,
> But Antony's hath triumph'd on itself.   *(Ant., IX.xv.13ff.)*

There could have been no other appropriate ending for the defeated Antony. Samson's death is equally fitting,

> With God not parted from him, as was fear'd,
> But favoring and assisting to the end.   *(SA, 1719f.)*

Each play also closes upon the reassertion of order, and the order which is restored in each maintains dramatic decorum. In *Samson Agonistes* it is the divine order, now made unmistakably clear to man:

> All is best, though we oft doubt,
> What th' unsearchable dispose
> Of highest wisdom brings about,
> And ever best found in the close. *(SA,1745ff.)*

The tone here is permeated with religious conviction, as well as expressed with classical restraint. In the last lines of the play, Milton declares of God that

> His servants he with new acquist
> Of true experience from this great event
> With peace and consolation hath dismist,
> And calm of mind, all passion spent. *(SA,1755ff.)*

An Aristotelian catharsis is clearly invoked in these lines, but it is a catharsis inspired by and infused with Judeo-Christian faith. Milton closes on the peace which passeth all understanding, the peace which the world as such neither knows nor can give.

The peace with which *Antony and Cleopatra* closes is a very worldly peace indeed, as imposed by Octavius Caesar. Even before Caesar calls in the last words of the play for "high order in this great solemnity," he has already made it clear that his victory will introduce a new order. "The last of many battles we mean to fight," he says early in Act IV, and shortly thereafter he declares,

> The time of universal peace is near:
> Prove this a prosperous day, the three-nook'd world
> Shall bear the olive freely. *(Ant., V.ii.364; IV.i.11f.; IV.iv.5ff.)*

As with all of Shakespeare's tragedies, the end comes with order restored after chaos and peace after strife. The general pattern is the same wherever Shakespeare uses it, but here the tragedy closes on what is historically the *pax Augusta* or the *pax Romana*.

IV. Pax Augusta and Pax Dei

Let us now attempt to draw together this analysis of the differences between theological and non-theological structures in tragedy. The basic issue is as to how fully developments of plot and character represent dramatic adaptations of theological doctrine. In the analysis of this issue, certain questions repeatedly arise. For example, does a play's inception, its development through crucial or pivotal incidents, and its ending accord in some meaningful way with the structures of theological doctrine? Are the conflict and "competition" of the play related to the divine order with sufficient consistency and force to make divine references a major influence, or are such references more accurately described as rhetorical and supportive? Is the divine presence in rejection and acceptance, judgment and

146

mercy sufficiently strong in the play to shape or even to affect the major actions of the plot and of the characters? Are the internal struggles of the characters directly and meaningfully related to God? Is guilt directly and primarily associated with a character's relations to God through his relations with others, or is that guilt primarily concerned with his relations to society and to himself? Is conscience kept within a framework which is primarily social and personal, or is that primary framework meaningfully and consistently embraced in the larger order of divine will? And finally, is the re-establishment of order at the end of the play fundamentally theological or secular—is it, in short, the *pax dei* or the *pax Augusta*?

In considering these and related issues we have examined four great plays in minute detail. The cumulative effect of this examination has been to illustrate in specific instances the essentially secular rather than theological nature of Shakespeare's tragic construction in *Macbeth* and *Antony and Cleopatra*, as distinguished from the essentially theological structuring of *Doctor Faustus* and of *Samson Agonistes*. A brief recapitulation of a few of the differences may be in order now.

When Faustus makes his pact "to gain a deity," the central doctrine of original sin is specifically introduced as the inception of the dramatic action in Marlowe's tragedy; Macbeth, on the other hand, has committed his crimes only to secure the kingdom of Scotland. Satan and his agents are overtly presented by Marlowe; the powers of darkness are more ambiguously presented in *Macbeth*. Repentance and salvation are again and again urged upon Faustus; such references do not appear in *Macbeth*. Macbeth's evil conscience is terrifying, but he does not fear retribution in a future life as does Faustus. Indeed, Shakespeare may scarcely be said even to have raised the dramatic question of eternal salvation or damnation. Faustus is carried to hell, whereas Macbeth's head is impaled on a spike, the two final dispositions epitomizing the consistent differences between the theological and secular structures of these tragedies.

Antony and Samson have much in common. Each is tormented by questions about his personal identity, and both have been traduced as fools destroyed by women. In the end, each reasserts a sense of his own integrity. Samson's actions, however, are consistently gauged against the divine reaction; the second, third, and fourth acts of *Samson Agonistes* deal specifically with the archetypical New Testament sins of the world, the flesh, and the devil. Antony's transactions are primarily with other characters, with little or no reference to the gods. Antony says, "I have not kept my square." Samson's plaint is, "But I God's counsel have not kept." Divine disapproval is most important in Samson's life. Caesar's displeasure is far more important to the dramatic structure of *Antony and Cleopatra*. There is a formal parallel in the two plays in the conflict between Caesar and Antony, on the one hand, and between God and Dagon, on the other. The purpose of Samson's repeated challenges to Harapha is to prove whose god is God. The struggle between Antony and Caesar is developed without major theological comment. Caesar evades Antony's challenge because he is certain of his power; Harapha evades Samson's because he is uncertain of Dagon. The deaths of the two protagonists are appropriate in their dramatic contexts. In each play, order is restored. Milton makes divine order the theme of his ending, and invokes the peace that passes all earthly understanding, the *pax dei*. Shakespeare closes *Antony and Cleopatra* with the *pax Romana*.

That difference between the endings is symptomatic of the overall difference in dramatic orientation. Anyone who is even casually acquainted with St. Augustine and with Christian theology knows that there is a vast difference between the *pax dei* and the *pax Romana*. This is not to say that the peace of the earthly city is evil and certainly not that it is undesirable. It may be morally good, and as peace it is surely desirable. There is, after all, the strongest authority for the view that we should "render to Caesar the things that are Caesar's, and to God the things that are God's" (*Mark,*xxii.13-17; *Matt.,*xxii.15-22; *Luke,*xx.20-26). The distinction is not only well established, but for our purposes it is critically useful.

Of Shakespeare's personal religious convictions, we know virtually nothing. It is of course true that all the solid evidence we have shows him to have been a conforming member of the Church of England, but we do not know whether this was a matter of deep conviction or of mere convenience. We may never know more than we do now, and fortunately it is not necessary that we should. What is fundamentally important is the existence of his plays, and it seems abundantly clear from these that, whatever may have been Shakespeare's personal faith or lack of faith, he understood the drama and the profession of the dramatist as belonging among those things that are Caesar's, and that he structured his plays in accordance with this understanding.

Notes:

(1) This paper, in substantially its present form, was read before the Twelfth International Shakespeare Conference at Stratford-upon-Avon in September, 1966.

(2) F. Michael Krouse's Milton's *Samson and the Christain Tradition* (Princeton, 1949) offers a valuable analysis of these theological-literary relations, though his analysis sometimes seems lacking in clarity and consistency, and the aptness of his conclusions is sometimes disappointing.

(3) I can scarcely overemphasize the need to take Shakespeare's theological references and allusions seriously, and nothing which is said in this paper should be construed otherwise. In the interest of balance and proportion we should assign theology the importance Shakespeare often gave it, but without allowing it to usurp upon the integrity of his drama. What I intend in this paper is a critical analysis working out from the historical-scholarly treatment of these same relationships in *Shakespeare and Christian Doctrine* (Princeton, 1963).

(4) The references to *Doctor Faustus* are to C. F. Tucker Brooke's edition of *The Works of Christopher Marlowe* (Oxford, 1953); the Milton references are to Merritt Y. Hughes' *John Milton: Complete Poems and Major Prose* (New York, 1957); the Shakespeare references are to the New Arden editions by Kenneth Muir and M. R. Ridley, respectively, of *Macbeth* (Cambridge, Mass., 1957) and of *Antony and Cleopatra* (Cambridge, Mass., 1956).

(5) There was no necessity for Shakespeare to avoid references to God in the serious contexts which are our only concern here. The *Acte to Restraine Abuses of Players* (May 27, 1606) did not preclude the kind of theological references which are relevant to my argument; it only sought to restrain those who "jestingly or prophanely speake or use" the divine names. See E. K. Chambers, *The Elizabethan Stage* (Oxford, 1951), IV, 338-39, and I, 303.

"If I Were Brutus Now...":
Role-playing in Julius Caesar

by John W. Velz

As he portrayed the fall of Julius Caesar, Shakespeare had the theater much on his mind. As the play opens, spectators on their way to Caesar's public triumph are bitterly reminded that they once were spectators at the triumphs of Pompey, and Caesar's attendance at the Lupercalian ceremonies in I.ii is accompanied by sennets and a pageant. Caesar's refusal of the crown is wryly described by Casca as an event staged for an audience:

> If the tag-rag people did not clap him and hiss him,
> according as he pleas'd and displeas'd them, as they use
> to do the players in the theatre, I am no true man.[1]

Brutus encourages the conspirators with a theatrical simile:

> Let not our looks put on our purposes,
> But bear it as our Roman actors do,
> With untir'd spirits and formal constancy.   *(II.i.225-227)*

Cassius thinks of the assassination itself as a spectacle on a stage:

> How many ages hence
> Shall this our lofty scene be acted over,
> In states unborn, and accents yet unknown!   *(III.i.111-113)*

Brutus and Cassius plan to march the successful conspirators in a kind of triumph through the streets:

> Bru. Then walk we forth, even to the market-place,
> And waving our red weapons o'er our heads,
> Let's all cry, "Peace, freedom, and liberty!"
> . . . . . .
> Cas. Brutus shall lead, and we will grace his heels
> With the most boldest and best hearts of Rome.[2]

The two orations of Act III manipulate an audience which is actually on the stage.

Shakespeare often alludes to the implications and techniques of his profession, but there are three reasons why this theatrical orientation is fully appropriate in *Julius Caesar*. The play portrays what Shakespeare and his audience regarded as one of the great dramatic events in world history; if all the world is a stage, the greatest of players were on it when Caesar died. Second, the thrasonical Caesar whom Shakespeare elects to present is a self-dramatizer, and appropriately evokes an atmosphere of tableau, posture, and pageant. Third, Brutus yearns to ritualize Caesar's death, to "carve him as a dish fit for the gods" (II.i.173);[3] the contrived formalism of theater is a fit background for the sacrifice Brutus would make of his victim.[4]

One theatrical element—assumption of roles—dominates *Julius Caesar*. Role-playing contributes to plot and theme, and it provides a major force for unity in the play.

Numerous characters in *Julius Caesar* adopt, or consider adopting, roles which other characters have played. The title of this article is drawn from one of the hypothetical transfers; Cassius contemplates in soliloquy his preliminary success in luring Brutus toward the conspiracy and muses that

> If I were Brutus now, and he were Cassius,
> He should not humour me. *(I.ii.311-312)*

As he works on the crowd in Act III, Antony, in mock self-deprecation, also imagines himself a Brutus:

> I am no orator, as Brutus is,
> . . . . .
>   But were I Brutus,
> And Brutus Antony, there were an Antony
> Would ruffle up your spirits. *(III.ii.219-230)*

Portia supposes herself an alter-Brutus. Protesting to her husband by "that great vow / Which did incorporate and make us one" (II.i.272-273), she demands to be made a party to the conspiracy. Because she is fused in marriage with Brutus, she believes that she shares his nature and can adopt his role.[5] That she cannot play the part adequately is underlined by her pathetic nervous crisis in II.iv just before the assassination. At Philippi in V.iv, Lucilius actually does adopt the name and role of Brutus, enabling the real Brutus to escape encirclement:

> And I am Brutus, Marcus Brutus, I!
> Brutus, my country's friend; know me for Brutus![6]

But in a sense this instance of "becoming" Brutus is as hypothetical as the musings of Cassius and Antony, because moments later Lucilius makes it plain that Brutus is *sui generis.* When common soldiers take him a captive to Antony, he contrasts his lot with Brutus':

> I dare assure thee that no enemy
> Shall ever take alive the noble Brutus.
> . . . . .
> When you do find him, or alive or dead,
> He will be found like Brutus, like himself. *(V.iv.21-25)*

It is not only Brutus whose abilities, ideals, or lot are echoed in the imitation of others. Three Roman heroes who do not appear on the stage are nevertheless

150

present in the behavior or attitudes of characters conscious of following heroic precedent. As he prepares to take the field at Philippi, Cassius remembers Pharsalus, calling Messala to witness

> that against my will
> (As Pompey was) am I compell'd to set
> Upon one battle all our liberties.   *(V.i.74-76)*

He recalls that Pompey was pushed into a disastrous battle by the bad advice of his own allies—an analogy to the strategy conference in which he himself has yielded to Brutus (IV.iii.195-224), and a sinister portent for the action yet to come. Portia identifies herself proudly not only as the wife of Brutus, but also as the daughter of Marcus Porcius Cato; a woman "so father'd, and so husbanded" (II.i.297) can keep secrets and play a Stoic's role, she insists. As she reveals that to play this role she has wounded herself, Portia becomes a miniature of her Stoic father, whose famous self-immolation at Utica Brutus alludes to at V.i.102-103. Like Portia, Young Cato sees himself in their father's heroic role:

> I am the son of Marcus Cato, ho!
> A foe to tyrants, and my country's friend.
> I am the son of Marcus Cato, ho!   *(V.iv.4-6)*

Dying, as his father died, in the struggle against tyranny, he may "be honour'd, being Cato's son" (V.iv.11). The third hero who is vicariously present in the play is Lucius Junius Brutus. Aware of the reverence in which Marcus Brutus holds his idealistic ancestor, Cassius shrewdly reminds him that

> There was a Brutus once that would have brook'd
> Th' eternal devil to keep his state in Rome
> As easily as a king.   *(I.ii.157-159)*

Cassius' technique is masterful. He has built toward this climactic appeal with vague contrasts between the decadent present and the noble past (148-156), and he follows it with the device of fastening an exhortation to Marcus Brutus on the very statue of his ancestor (I.iii.145-46). The implied analogy serves its purpose; Brutus later thinks of the ancient republicanism of his family as he fills the gap in the allusive instigation Cinna has thrown in at his window:

> Thus must I piece it out:
> Shall Rome stand under one man's awe? What, Rome?
> My ancestors did from the streets of Rome
> The Tarquin drive, when he was call'd a king.   *(II.i.51-54)*

And it is at this point that Brutus makes his moral commitment:

> Am I entreated
> To speak, and strike? O Rome, I make thee promise,
> If the redress will follow, thou receivest
> Thy full petition at the hand of Brutus.[7]   *(II.i.55-58)*

151

Pompey, Marcus Cato, and Lucius Junius Brutus are, then, a triumvirate of republicans whose struggle against tyranny in the noble past is consciously re-enacted by Cassius, Portia, Young Cato, and Brutus. Balanced against these idealists who model themselves on a bygone heroism are those characters in the play who are firmly committed to the decadent present which Cassius complained of and who successively assume the role of the tyrant, Caesar. The name and the spirit of Caesar dominate the last half of the play from the moment when Antony foresees "Caesar's spirit, ranging for revenge" (III.i.270). Antony himself is that imperious spirit for the moment, as he orders Octavius' servant to keep his master out of Rome and then proceeds to defeat the conspirators with his oration.[8] It is Octavius, however, who will emerge as Caesar, both in spirit and in name. At the beginning of Act V he points out that Antony's prediction of the conspirators' military strategy was erroneous and he insists on rearranging Antony's own battle plan:

> Ant. Octavius, lead your battle softly on
>   Upon the left hand of the even field.
> Oct. Upon the right hand I. Keep thou the left.
> Ant. Why do you cross me in this exigent?
> Oct. I do not cross you; but I will do so.[9]

Antony gives another order, restraining Octavius from an immediate charge on the enemy, but as he gives it he calls Octavius "Caesar."[10] Octavius himself asserts his inheritance of Caesar's name and is avenging power when he interrupts the flyting which preoccupies Antony, Brutus, and Cassius:

> Look,
> I draw a sword against conspirators.
> When think you that the sword goes up again?
> Never, till Caesar's three and thirty wounds
> Be well aveng'd; or till another Caesar
> Have added slaughter to the sword of traitors.   *(V.i.50-55)*

Addressed to "Caesar," Brutus' reply (56) tacitly validates Octavius' assertion that he is "another Caesar," and neither Brutus' patronizing "Young man" (60) nor Cassius' taunting "A peevish school-boy" (61) can seriously diminish this claim. At the end of the play Antony looks back to the conspiracy, but practical Octavius looks ahead to the spoils of victory; the future and the role of Caesar will be his.[11]

The assumption of Caesar's role first by Antony and then by Octavius points to one reason why Shakespeare included so much role-playing in *Julius Caesar*; it is the means of underscoring a major concern of the action, the process by which a new Caesar emerges from the wreckage of the conspiracy. That Caesarism is a foregone conclusion is clear in III.ii. The First Plebeian, swayed by Brutus' oration, spontaneously demands a Caesarean triumph for his new idol: "Bring him with triumph home unto his house."[12] Immediately the thought of Brutus as a new Caesar grips the crowd:

> 3. *Pleb.*   Let him be Caesar.
>
> 4. *Pleb.*   Caesar's better parts
> Shall be crown'd in Brutus.   *(III.ii.52-53)*

It is bitter irony that Brutus, the character in the cast who least desires to be a Caesar, should be the first to be offered the role. When Antony's appeal to their emotions begins to reverse the impact of Brutus' sober speech, the Plebeians again assume that there will be a successor to Caesar:

> 2. *Pleb.*   If thou consider rightly of the matter,
> Caesar has had great wrong.
>
> 3. *Pleb.*   Has he, masters?
> I fear there will a worse come in his place.   *(III.ii.111-113)*

And the oration sweeps to a climax in which the idea of Caesarism is inherent: "Here was a Caesar! when comes such another?" (III.ii.254). The crowd shouts "Never, never!" but Antony has caught their earlier mood, and he knows that the role of Caesar will be transferred to the man who can play it best.

Role-playing is, then, crucial to the plot of *Julius Caesar*; it is common in both of the two opposed sets of characters, and the roles each faction elects to play convey thematic or philosophical values. The republicans see themselves in roles from the heroic past, while the monarchists look to a prototype who appears onstage and who belongs fully to the Rome of the present. The outcome of the action is implicit in this subtle difference.

The dominance of Caesarism is also suggested by the fact that numerous other characters, especially republicans, adopt Caesar's characteristic trick of speech. Seventeen times in the three scenes in which he appears, Caesar refers to himself as "Caesar." Some critics have been harsh with him for this idiosyncrasy, regarding it as an indication of his fatuousness. But Shakespeare could have found the impersonal style in Caesar's *Commentaries*,[13] and he may have thought it a mark of the Roman (perhaps of the noble Roman) to see oneself from the outside, to talk of oneself as of an object. Certainly the last of Caesar's impersonal references to himself comes at the moment of his death, when the time for pretense is past: "Then fall Caesar!" Whether Caesar's mode of speech is pompous or noble, it echoes throughout the play as others unconsciously imitate it, giving us the sense that they are playing Caesar's role. Cassius calls himself by his name twelve times; Brutus speaks of "Brutus" eleven times. Antony (4), Casca, Portia, Metellus, Octavius ("Caesar"), Pindarus, Titinius, and Lucilius all echo the Caesarean mode of speech.[14] When instances occur in the last half of the play, it is as though we were hearing the voice of Caesar, even from his enemies, after he himself is gone.

In a different sense, Caesar's voice echoes in III.iii, as Cinna the Poet unconsciously reenacts the events of II.ii and III.i. His death is a pathetic microcosm of the assassination. Like Caesar, Cinna goes to his death despite a portentous dream. Like Caesar, he speaks of his unwillingness to leave his home:

> *Caes.*   The cause is in my will: I will not come.   *(II.ii.71)*

Cin.   I have no will to wander forth of doors.   *(III.iii.3)*

Yet each man is drawn "forth" despite premonitions of disaster.[15] Cinna, on his way to Caesar's funeral "as a friend" (III.iii.22), surely expects no attack from the Plebeians who love Caesar; his violent death, like Caesar's, comes at the hands of men he considers friends.[16] And as the Plebeians repeat "Tear him to pieces! . . . Tear him . . . tear him . . . Tear him . . . tear him!" (III.iii.28-35) we are reminded of the imagery of dismemberment Brutus has applied to Caesar's assassination:

> O, that we then could come by Caesar's spirit,
> And not dismember Caesar! But, alas,
> Caesar must bleed for it.[17]   *(II.i.169-171)*

Unconscious adoption of the role of Caesar, whether ironic (as in the reflection of his style by others) or pathetic (as in the echoes of his words and attitudes by Cinna), does more than suggest the continuing presence of Caesar after his death. As echoes of his words or style reverberate through the play, they provide a continuity to the unconscious ear which tends toward unity. Roles which are played not once but again and again by successive "actors" have an effect as much structural as thematic. A crucial repetition of this sort underscores the assassination as the moral center of the play and draws events in the first, third, fourth, and fifth acts toward that moral center and toward one another.

Four characters in *Julius Caesar* offer their deaths to others.[18] Caesar begins the sequence at the Lupercal. As Casca cynically tells it,

> he pluck'd me ope his doublet, and offer'd them his
> throat to cut. And I had been a man of any occupation,
> if I would not have taken him at a word, I would I
> might go to hell among the rogues.   *(I.ii.261-265)*

Though Casca's reaction to this flamboyant gesture is facetious, it has a more profound meaning as an ironic adumbration of the assassination—it is Casca who first rears his hand against Caesar in III.i. As Caesar offers his throat to the populace he also foreshadows his own readiness to die at the last moment of his life: "*Et tu, Brute?*---Then fall Caesar!" (III.i.77). Antony recreates the assassination for the Plebeians in his oration, giving special emphasis to Caesar's willingness to die:

> . . . when the noble Caesar saw him [Brutus] stab,
> Ingratitude, more strong than traitors' arms,
> Quite vanquish'd him: then burst his mighty heart;
> And in his mantle muffling up his face,
> > . . . great Caesar fell.   *(III.ii.186-191)*

When he offers to let the conspirators kill him over Caesar's body in III.i, Antony plays the same role that Caesar has played at the Lupercal. Though the stakes are higher and the emotion more intense, Antony does not expect to be taken at his word any more than Caesar did; he can afford this melodramatic offer, since before his entrance he has been told of Brutus' solemn promise:

154

> ... so please him come unto this place,
> He shall be satisfied; and, by my honour,
> Depart untouch'd. *(III.i.140-142)*

As he elaborates his paradoxical appeal, Antony proposes his death as an analogue to Caesar's. He is to die at "Caesar's death's hour" (154) beside his corpse (162), at the same bloody hands (158) which wield "those your swords, made rich / With the most noble blood of all this world" (155-156). Antony's speech becomes an exaggeration of Caesar's loss of will to live; Shakespeare here makes Antony repeatedly "beg" (164) his death of the conspirators: "there is no hour so fit" (153), he is "apt to die" (160), he beseeches the assassins to fulfill their pleasure (157-159), he can imagine no more pleasing death (161). Yet, no matter how sincerely he feels his loss, how closely he identifies himself with his dead friend, Antony shows the ability to take advantage of this emotional moment, a trait which will enable him to assume the role of a pragmatic tyrant, at least temporarily.

The third offer of death is Brutus'; he tells the Plebeians that

> as I slew my best lover for the good of Rome, I have the
> same dagger for myself, when it shall please my country
> to need my death. *(III.ii.46-48)*

Adrien Bonjour suggests that Brutus' offer is as shallow as Caesar's in I.ii, manifesting his realistic awareness of how to mold a crowd with theatrics.[19] Remembering Brutus' desire to make Caesar's death a sacrifice (II.i.166-174), we may take him more literally here. He offers himself as he has offered Caesar—an immolation "for the good of Rome." Like Antony before him, Brutus offers to die by the same weapon that killed Caesar.

Cassius continues the pattern in IV.iii, when he offers Brutus his dagger and urges him to stab him to the heart.[20] The offer is as hyperbolic as the theatrical gestures of Caesar and Antony which it echoes, but Cassius is not insincere here, any more than Brutus was in III.ii. The bitterness of broken friendship is in his words as he remembers that Brutus has stabbed a friend before:

> Strike, as thou didst at Caesar; for I know,
> When thou didst hate him worst, thou lov'dst him better
> Than ever thou lov'dst Cassius. *(IV.iii.104-106)*

As Cassius offers himself to the blow,

> there is my dagger,
> And here my naked breast, *(IV.iii.99-100)*

Shakespeare provides an emphatic piece of stage business which must remind the audience of earlier occasions at which bared breasts are mentioned or seen. Caesar, of course, has opened his doublet to the crown in I.ii; Cassius himself has appeared onstage in I.iii with his bosom audaciously exposed to the thunderstorm.[21] Most emphatic of all, at an intense moment in his oration, Antony has pulled the mantle off Caesar's body to reveal him "marr'd, as you see, with traitors" (III.ii.199).

When, one after another, they offer to die on the swords or knives of others, Antony, Brutus, and Cassius do more than unconsciously recreate the role which Caesar originated at the Lupercal. Each of them at the moment of his offer is fully conscious of his own relationship to the assassination: each of them speaks of Caesar's death when he offers his own. And the behavior of these three imitators of Caesar looks forward to Philippi as well as back to the central event of the play, for Brutus and Cassius both will die in a sense offering their deaths to Caesar. When Cassius dies on the words:

> Caesar, thou art reveng'd,
> Even with the sword that kill'd thee,   *(V.iii.45-46)*

he echoes the proposals of Brutus and Antony that they should be victims of the same weapons that killed Caesar. And Brutus' attitude at his death mirrors both the willingness of Caesar to die and the four willing offers of death which have punctuated the play:

> Caesar, now be still;
> I kill'd not thee with half so good a will.   *(V.v.50-51)*

The effect of the repeated pattern of offers is, therefore, dual: to lead us radially to the central assassination, and to heighten the poetic justice with which Brutus and Cassius die by the sword in the fifth act.[22]

Role-playing is recurrent and striking behavior among the characters in *Julius Caesar*. The roles men deliberately choose to play delineate the opposed forces in the action and sketch the theme of Caesarism triumphant over political idealism. At the same time, there are other roles which men play without awareness that these are parts which others have played before them. This unconscious role-playing is one means by which Shakespeare draws *Julius Caesar* into structural coherence.[23]

Notes:

(1)   I.ii.225-258. All quotations from *JC* in this article are from T. S. Dorsch's Arden Edition (1955).

(2)   III.i.108-121. There is an echo, perhaps, in Cassius' language of Marullus' hypothetical description of Caesar in triumph:

> What tributaries follow him to Rome,
> To grace in captive bonds his chariot wheels?   *(I.i.33-34)*

(3)   For an analysis of this side of Brutus' character, see Brents Stirling, "'Or Else This Were a Savage Spectacle'," *PMLA*, LXVI (1951), 765-774.

(4)   The play alludes to many formal ceremonies, ranging from "the order of the course" and the ceremonies of the Lupercal (I.ii.11, 25) to the "respect and rites of burial" which are due Brutus at the end of the play (V.v.77). Antony requests permission to perform a rite for Caesar, to "speak in the order of his funeral" (III.i.229-230); put in these terms the request has a predictable appeal for Brutus. (Brutus himself insists that "Caesar shall / Have all true rites and lawful ceremonies"— III.i.240-241.) Caesar performs the ceremony of classical hospitality when he offers wine to his

"friends" at the end of II.ii, and a formal loving cup ratifies the restored friendship of Brutus and Cassius after the quarrel (IV.iii.157-161). Stirling argues effectively that Brutus' ingenuous attempt to make murder a sacrifice is undercut totally by Antony's oration and by his characterization of the conspirators as hounds (III.i.204; V.i.41, 43). But ceremony pervades the world of the play; if Brutus is a ritualist he is in harmony with his culture.

(5)   Maurice Charney considers that "it is significant how often Portia uses Brutus' words — it strengthens the bond between them and attests to Portia's dependence on her husband." (*Shakespeare's Roman Plays: The Function of Imagery in the Drama*, [Cambridge, Mass., 1961], p. 61.).

(6)   V.iv.7-8. This speech is unassigned in the Folio, and some scholars have believed that it is Brutus who insists on his identity here (most recently Mildred E. Hartsock in "The Complexity of *Julius Caesar*," *PMLA*, LXXXI [1966], 60). But Plutarch makes it virtually certain that Lucilius is the speaker here. In "Marcus Brutus" he recounts the exploits of Brutus' lieutenants in the second battle, "who valliantlie ranne into any daunger, to save Brutus life. Amongest them there was one of Brutus frendes called Lucilius, who seeing a troupe of barbarous men making no reckoning of all men else they met in their way, but going all together right against Brutus, he determined to stay them with the hazard of his life, and being left behinde, told them that he was Brutus . . ." (Geoffrey Bullough, ed., *Narrative and Dramatic Sources of Shakespeare* [N. Y., 1964], V, 128-129.) The marginalium on this passage reads "The fidelitie of Lucilius unto Brutus."

(7)   The Second Plebeian also sees Brutus in a traditional family role; after Brutus justifies tyrannicide in his oration, this man shouts enthusiastically, "Give him a statue with his ancestors" (III.ii.51). Caius Ligarius, too, thinks of Brutus as "deriv'd from honourable loins" (II.i.322).

(8)   Norman Sanders disagrees; he argues that "Antony in his oration . . . [like Brutus in his] never attempts to attract the power of Rome to himself. Rather, what he does achieve by verbal means is what the conspirators did physically in the case of Caesar: that is, to deprive someone else of power" ("The Shift of Power in 'Julius Caesar'," *REL*, V [1964], 32). But in IV.i Antony is firmly in command: he orders Lepidus about and labels him "a slight unmeritable man" (12); it is he who provides Octavius with intelligence of the movements of Brutus and Cassius and who calls for a council of war.

(9)   V.i.16-20. It has often been observed that Shakespeare modified his source in this episode; in Plutarch it is Brutus who insists on having the right wing and Cassius who yields to him. Maurice Charney suggests that "Shakespeare seems to be deliberately developing Octavius" (op. cit., p. 76n) and he points out that Octavius' "I will do so" echoes Caesar's imperious insistence on his will at II.ii.71: "The cause is in my will: I will not come" (p. 76).

(10)   V.i.24. The first reference to Octavius in the play prefigures this climactic admission that Octavius is a reincarnation of Caesar; Antony asks the servant at III.i.276 "You serve Octavius Caesar, do you not?" reminding us of Octavius' family relationship to Julius Caesar. But three times in Acts III and IV he is "young Octavius" and six more he is simply "Octavius."

(11)   Sanders (op. cit., p. 34n) suggests that the roles of Julius Caesar and Octavius might effectively be doubled to underline the shift of power to this new Caesar.

(12)   III.ii.50. This citizen obviously is fond of processions; a moment later he repeats the suggestion: "We'll bring him to his house with shouts and clamours" (54).

(13)   Norman N. Holland believes he did (*The Shakespearean Imagination*, [New York, 1964], p. 138). Without discussing the question of style, T. W. Baldwin finds the evidence for Shakespeare's having studied the *Commentaries* in school inconclusive. See *William Shakespeare's Small Latine & Lesse Greeke* (Urbana, Ill., 1944), II, 569-572.

(14)   It is perhaps significant that characters often use third person for first at moments of profound seriousness or emotional intensity, when pose is unlikely: Portia pleading to be more than a harlot

to Brutus, Titinius killing himself out of friendship for Cassius, Pindarus sadly leaving Cassius' dead body, Casca committing himself to the conspiracy. This third-person pattern is supported by more than twenty passages where characters use the name of the person addressed where we would expect a second-person pronoun: e.g., "it sufficeth / That Brutus leads me on"; "I should not then ask Casca what had chanc'd." From a different perspective, R. A. Foakes has discussed the prevalence and the importance of personal names in *JC*; see "An Approach to *Julius Caesar*," *SQ*, V (1954), 259-270.

(15) The word "forth" echoes and re-echoes somberly: see II.ii.8, 10, 28, 38, 48, 50, and III.iii.3, 4.

(16) Compare Caesar at II.ii.126-127:

> Good friends, go in, and taste some wine with me;
> And we, like friends, will straightway go together.

(17) Most of these echoes of Caesar's death in Cinna's are discussed by Norman H. Holland, who draws conclusions different from mine. See "The 'Cinna' and 'Cynicke' Episodes in *Julius Caesar*," *SQ*, XI (1960), 439-444.

(18) The fact is noted briefly by Adrien Bonjour in *The Structure of Julius Caesar* (Liverpool, 1958), p. 30, n. 33.

(19) *Ibid.*, p. 20.

(20) Twice before Cassius has impulsively volunteered his own death. When Casca tells him that Caesar is to be crowned on the Ides of March, Cassius replies:

> I know where I will wear this dagger then;
> Cassius from bondage will deliver Cassius.   *(I.iii.89-90)*

When he wrongly believes that the conspiracy has been discovered, he threatens to kill himself:

> If this be known,
> Cassius or Caesar never shall turn back,
> For I will slay myself.   *(III.i.20-22)*

Brutus keeps him from the rash act; the scene is an ironic prefiguration of Cassius' impulsive and mistaken suicide at Philippi.

(21) Shakespeare concentrates the image in I.iii; Cassius emphasizes that he is "unbraced" (48), bare-bosomed (49), and that he presents himself directly to the lightning (51-52) which itself "seem'd to open / The breast of heaven" (50-51). Cassius, who offers to have his heart taken out of his bosom (IV.iii.102-103), may recall to us Cinna the Poet, whose name has been plucked out of his heart (III.iii.33-34); and Cassius' request of Brutus during the quarrel foreshadows his request of Pindarus at the end of his life:

> with this good sword,
> That ran through Caesar's bowels, search this bosom.   *(V.iii.41-42)*

(22) The fact that Caesar, Brutus, and Cassius all are killed with swords is doubtless responsible for a number of references to stabbing scattered through the play. Casca facetiously puts the case that "if Caesar had stabb'd their mothers" the Plebeians would have forgiven him (I.ii.271-272). In two passages already quoted (I.iii.89-90; IV.iii.99-100) Cassius speaks of daggers turned against himself. Portia reveals that she has wounded herself with a knife; Titinius kills himself onstage with Cassius' sword; and Messala, carrying the news of Cassius' death to Brutus, chooses an apt metaphor:

> . . . I go to meet
> The noble Brutus, thrusting this report

Into his ears. I may say thrusting it;
For piercing steel and darts envenomed
Shall be as welcome to the ears of Brutus
As tidings of this sight. *(V.iii.73-78)*

(23) I wish to express my gratitude to the Folger Shakespeare Library for the Fellowship under which this article was written in the spring of 1968.

Hamlet's Place on the Map

by Keith Brown

The purpose of this study can be simply defined: it is an attempt to relate Shakespeare's handling of the Hamlet story to that particular continuum formed in most Elizabethan minds by the blurring-together of the concepts of geography, cosmography and cosmology. It will be evident from this description that we shall not, therefore, be especially concerned here with what is often called, perhaps a little tendentiously, "Hamlet's Danish Background" (i.e., with attempts to make cross-links between what we see and hear in that play and the real sixteenth-century Danish court). But it will be evident, too, that a line of argument is nonetheless implied which must plainly impinge upon such territory at least at some point: and that point is in fact a convenient one at which to begin.

I

Those who feel urged to explore what even Professor Dover Wilson acknowledges to be the usually high degree of local color in *Hamlet*[1] always come eventually to geographical considerations; and in this connection are then naturally apt to ask one or both of two things: (i) why did Shakespeare or one of his predecessors transfer to Elsinore a tale orginally set in Jutland? (ii) is the story of Fortinbras's expedition really meant to make any sort of practical sense?

The answer to the first of these questions is of course obvious—and indeed by now familiar— enough; the second has been equally confidently answered, but still to my mind warrants a moment's further reflections, nevertheless. As far as Elsinore itself is concerned, the essential point is patently just that the guns of its fortress-palace commanded the narrowest part of the narrow Sound of Denmark. With the opposite coast also in their hands, (for it is often forgotten that at that time Denmark still included much of what is now southern Sweden) the Kings of Denmark could thus open or close the gates of the Baltic at will, and had indeed long since taken advantage of that fact to levy steadily rising admission and exit fees on all passing shipping: the famous Sound Dues of Elsinore. As often pointed out, this was an institution of painful interest to all the western maritime states during a period of rapidly expanding Baltic trade, and made the name of Elsinore not only well known but symbolic; it was the place where the King of Denmark mainfested not only his authority within his own domains, but also his ability to impose his will upon a wide range of surrounding states.[2] Obviously anyone aware of this would be almost bound to feel that Elsinore offered a much apter setting for the tragedy of a Prince of Denmark than the obscurity of Jutland.

Nonetheless a skeptic might well still inquire, of course, whether this power and symbolism *would* really have been appreciated outside Denmark—for example in London—by more than a relatively limited number of diplomats, merchants, and seamen? (After all, what London audience would today respond very powerfully to the name of that vital artery, the Malacca Straits?) Various commentators dispose of this doubt in various ways; but what surely must have fixed the meaning of Elsinore most firmly in the minds of Shakespeare's fellow citizens was simply their patriotic interest and pride—clearly enough reflected in Hakluyt—in the opening-up of the North-East Passage: an achievement of little real commercial value which nonetheless, as a recent editor of Giles Fletcher remarks,[3] offered a certain psychological compensation for their failure to keep up with the mid-century feats of the Spaniards and Portuguese in the New World. One of the attractions of undertaking this hazardous Northern route was that it offered a way of reaching the supposedly rich markets of Russia that would outwit the Danes by avoiding Elsinore (a purpose neatly frustrated, in a further demonstration of Danish power, by the successful imposition of dues on this route too.)[4]

But then there is the rather different "problem" of Fortinbras's expedition. What, if anything, is to be made in realistic terms of a line of march which apparently suggests that Norway, Denmark and Poland are contiguous states? Or what, again, are we to make of an apparently shrewd and politic ruler like Claudius permitting a fiery young prince with a grievance to take an army with cannon—even under due regards of safety and allowance—right past his court? One excellent answer, of course, is that we are meant to make nothing of such things: Shakespeare himself, it may be said, plainly had a mind above such tediously literal-minded trifling. But even if he did, how could anyone aware of the facts altogether shut out of his mind the recognition that a real-life Fortinbras would also have passed by Elsinore in just the same way? For Elsinore was the regular crossing-place from the Scandinavian peninsula for anyone en route to mainland Europe: the Dover of the Sound, quite as much as the Gibraltar of the Baltic. It was precisely to keep an eye on this natural crossroads that the Danish kings maintained their presence there; not within any ordinary castle, but within fortifications internationally renowned for their strength.[5] Thus, (given the contiguity of Norway-Denmark-Poland) Hamlet's meeting with Fortinbras's troops, and the latter's reappearance in the last scene, in fact make perfectly good practical sense whether Shakespeare really intended it or not; and anyone who had interested himself even vaguely in the excitement over northern exploration would certainly have had at least some dim awareness of this (just as he would also have acquired at least some sort of notion of whereabouts Norway was, too, since so much of the North-East Passage route lay along its coasts). And in this connection it seems fair to point out that elsewhere in his works Shakespeare does himself in fact show traces of having been touched by this general excitement; which indeed it is difficult to see how he could wholly have escaped anyway.[6]

But what then of the great Contiguity Question? No normal Elizabethan Londoner is really very likely to have known, after all, that "for brief periods in the eleventh century" the fiefs of the Kings of Norway, Denmark and Poland actually *were* contiguous.[7] On the other hand, what he would have known, even at the lowest estimate, was that Norway-Denmark was now a dual monarchy: a fact which even in itself, of course, naturally suggests the idea of contiguous kingdoms. Moreover, our Londoner would presumably have had at least *some* sort of vague inkling that the Kings of Denmark had also always held extensive northern German principalities, about whose eastern frontiers he would doubtless have been very vague. Clearly, no more than this is really needed to give a convincing "feel" to Fortinbras's expedition: especially for anyone attentive enough to notice that the latter's men are in fact granted leave to pass, not through *Denmark,* but through the King of Denmark's "dominions."

Nonetheless, it ought to be pointed out that better information would by no means have destroyed this effect of plansibility. For one thing, although commentators seem rather mystifyingly inclined to shirk saying so, Norway and Denmark *were* virtually contiguous states in Shakespeare's day;[8] and were moreover firmly credited with a clear common frontier in the extremely widely-used Ortelius atlas (further discussed below.) And many maps further (wrongly) suggest, what at least one popular little reference-work firmly states: namely, that Denmark adjoins *Pomerania;* a duchy containing *places . . . belonging unto Polande . . . called the Palatynes of Pomerania.*[9]—Suppose Fortinbras's private army to be bound towards one of these "places," therefore, and an explanation is then provided, not only of their route,[10] but also of their curious success in annexing part of the territory of one of the strongest states in Europe, that would surely have satisfied even the most literal-minded Elizabethan! Meanwhile the more literary-minded, of course, could always reflect that Shakespeare's "Polacks" were in any case just an up-to-date re-labelling of the Slavs of the source-texts: a race in manifest land contact with the Danes in many parts of Saxo's *History.* Either way, it is at least clear enough that nothing can be proved from the line of Fortinbras's route-march that would embarrass those who choose, unfashionably, to see real knowledge of a real Denmark behind the imaginative shaping of Shakespeare's play.

II

But something else has surely become clear over the past few pages, too: namely, that there is another and rather different way to bring geographical considerations to the study of *Hamlet,* which our discussion of these minor aspects of the "Danish Background" theorist's case has already been obliquely illustrating. For although a good deal has been written about Elsinore as a real "place on the map," so to speak, there nonetheless seems to have been relatively little curiosity about the maps at which Shakespeare himself might actually have looked. This is true both of discussions of *Hamlet* in particular, and—though to a lesser extent—of general discussions of "Shakespeare's library," and it seems equally unsatisfactory on both counts.

For it is worth remembering that Shakespeare's lifetime spans what might well be called the Heroic Age of modern cartography. In 1570, Abraham Ortelius had published an enormously popular compilation which may be loosely described as the first modern atlas; twenty-five years later, the career of his friend Mercator was crowned—posthumously—by the publication of his own great *Atlas*. Rivals and plagiarists of Mercator and the other major cartographers abounded: the very volume of publication is itself an indication of the level of public interest. Already in 1570, in his preface to the first English edition of Euclid, the celebrated Dr. John Dee could write of people making use of maps "to beautify their Hall, Parlers, chambers, Galeries, Studies, or Libraries with," and the taste was one which grew steadily for the next half century. "What greater pleasure can there now be," inquires *The Anatomy of Melancholy*, "than to view those elaborate Maps of Ortelius, Mercator, Hondius, &c. To peruse those books of Cities, put out by Braunus and Hogenbergius?"[11] When another future devotee of Euclid, the young Thomas Hobbes, took delight to lie "gaping on Mappes" in "booke-binders'" shops during his Oxford student days, not long after the publication of *Hamlet*, he was reflecting a general contemporary interest as well as his own boyish romanticism. It is naturally an interest which Shakespeare also reflects. His casual reference in *Twelfth Night*—a play not too distant in date from *Hamlet* (and containing the reference to Barents' voyages noted above)—to "the new map with the augmentation of the Indies" (III.ii.85) confirms both that he did himself share something of the contemporary map-consciousness and that he took it for granted that his audience did so as well.

Such interest was well justified. Not only were the voyages of exploration steadily extending the areas which could be reliably shown on the map, but through the joint efforts of map-makers and mathematicians—not least in England— the science of cartography was itself simultaneously taking enormous strides forward. One result of this was the introduction to England of the art of globe- making, interest in which is reflected both in Donne's correspondence and in his poetry. Presumably it may also have had some effect on the choice of a name for the Globe theatre, too.

This latter speculation is worth looking at a little more closely, in fact, for it illustrates very well a curious cross-link in the history of ideas between Elizabethan cartography and the Elizabethan theatre. The title of the Ortelius atlas referred to above was *Theatrum Orbis Terrarum.* To quote Mr. R. A. Skelton:

> In the title which he chose for his atlas, Ortelius combined two figurative elements, each of which already enjoyed an independ- ent life of its own. The Romans and (after them) the mediaeval schoolmen, who visualised the habitable world as a circular disc, referred to it as *orbis terrae* or *orbis terrarum*, and this use was taken over by Renaissance geographers . . . . . . The word *theatrum* (or its vernacular equivalent) had also acquired currency in its transferred sense of a scene where action takes place.[12]

In short, for Ortelius "all the *round* world's a stage"—and "round," not only as a modern globe is round, but as round also as the old disc of the *Mappa Mundi* (with which it has been shown that an English educated audience could still be expected to be fairly familiar even as late as the 1630s.)[13] It is thought that Ortelius had fetched this conceit from Cicero (*In Verrem*, XIV, 35), but it seems to have been the diffusion of his own atlas throughout the countries of Europe which brought the notion into common currency in most languages and literatures.[14] If only perhaps by proxy, therefore, the *Theatrum Orbis Terrarum*, a standard work of reference in England as elsewhere,[15] was thus plainly among the god-parents at the christening of the Globe Playhouse; and the implications of this fact obviously work both ways. If a cartographer could help put into currency the notion of a theatre as a kind of "double" of a terrestrial globe, it would be reason-able enough for his contemporaries (not least when themselves men of the theatre) to incline, in turn, to "see" maps much more as a kind of potential *stage for action* than we would normally do today. Indeed, this is precisely the idea implicit in one early map-publisher's boast that "geography [it is clear from the context that he really means cartography] brings before the eye the scenes of the excellent deeds performed by great men of past ages."[16] And any such natural tendency to think in this way would be still further reinforced, both by the little action-drawings with which maps were often decorated, and also by the more-or-less standard pattern of titlepages for atlases of the period, depicting a design strongly suggestive of the classical proscenium of the Palladian theatre.

However, with this preamble let us turn again to *Hamlet*. When Shakespeare began to prepare the play as we know it now, an apparently theatre-minded Danish princess with a like-minded husband[17] was obviously on the verge of becoming Queen of England.[18] Even if this does not explain Shakespeare's com-pany's choice of the old play of *Hamlet* for refurbishing, it is hardly a fact that can have slipped his mind entirely, once he began to think about his new project; and we know from *Macbeth* that he did allow such considerations to have some shaping effect on his work. This in itself would be quite sufficient to explain his becoming alert to information about Denmark—as it seems to be common ground that *someone* who handled the play-texts we now possess must have been; and, once alerted, his curiosity could be readily enough supplied. There would have been his colleagues' reminiscences of that country; there was Saxo's History;[19] and, as we have seen, he might well also have turned for information to some more modern account of the country, such as those convenient written descrip-tions of the areas depicted, with which all atlases of his day accompanied their plates. At all events, it would have at least been odd if no bell had ever rung in his mind when he did catch sight of Denmark's easily recognisable outlines, on the wall maps which he was bound to be seeing from time to time anyway.

Which specific maps may actually have been available for Shakespeare's inspec-tion on the walls of his friends' and patrons' parlors, chambers, galeries, etc., however, it would be fruitless to inquire; for the possibilities are too various.[20] But when it comes to atlases, on the other hand, the field narrows drastically: Ortelius' *Theatrum*, though getting a shade old-fashioned, was still the recognised

standard work, and Mercator's much superior *Atlas* had yet to take over the dominant position.[21] Meanwhile a deservedly respected though unsuccessful (i.e. less
widely distributed) competitor of Ortelius and Mercator had been Gerard de Jode,
whose *Speculum Orbis Terrarum* (1578) was republished by his son, in a somewhat refurbished form, as *Speculum Orbis Terrae* (1593).—Cartography too, as
the *Speculum's* titlepage emphasises, could also claim to hold, as 'twere, the
mirror up to nature.

If Shakespeare did look at any of the relevant maps in these atlases—especially
if he did so after browsing through Saxo—he would surely have been struck by
two things: firstly, by Elsinore's then central position *in Denmark* (and the curious
symmetricality of that kingdom); and secondly by Denmark's (and Elsinore's) central, not to say pivotal, position in *"the northern world" as a whole,* as Elizabethans generally conceived it. In both respects the maps afford a kind of emblem
on the play.

The symmetry of Denmark was of course an old idea. Saxo, in his prefatory
account of the Danes' kingdom (which Ortelius, with due acknowledgement,
copies) describes the island of Zealand—on which Elsinore stands—as being

> . . . by far the most delightful of all the provinces of our country
> [and] held to occupy the heart of Denmark, being divided by
> equal distances from the extreme frontier.

Denmark, in short, is being figured here as a kind of broken circle, or perhaps
rather a kind of "bulls-eye" of broken rings of land-water-land. The west coast of
Jutland forms the perimeter on one side, and the frontier of the old Danish provinces in what is now southwest Sweden roughly continues the same arc on the
east. The Mercator map of Denmark (reproduced here) illustrates this "circular"
conception with curious—if largely fortuitous—fidelity, even using the island of
Bornholm to carry on the line of the outer ring over the Baltic. On the other hand,
the comparable Ortelius map visually makes much less of the notion of a circular
Denmark—although compensating for this by reproducing the relevant part of
Saxo's description in its accompanying text. Instead, this particular map emphasises much more the aspect of *symmetry,* by transforming Denmark's "Swedish"
provinces into something not far removed from a mirror-image of Jutland: but
again Zealand remains clearly the "heart" of the country.

Alternatively, of course, Shakespeare could have turned rather to Ortelius's map
of the Northern Regions (—which is certainly the likeliest map for anyone curious
about the Northern voyages to have looked at). Had he done so, once again everything would have conspired to bring his attention eventually down on to that round
island bearing only two names: *Elsenor,* and *Coppenhagen.* Certainly the map
would have made clear enough to him just why the imposition of the Sound Dues
at Elsinore affected all the trading nations of northern Europe. And it would have
shown him too, as he oriented the wars described by Saxo on the map before him,
that the still-remembered Danish incursions into England[22] had been only one
manifestation of a kind of explosion of conquering energy which had in fact radi-

ated outwards in every direction (and he might have noted that this would be a particularly apt note to touch in a play likely to be seen by Anne of Denmark). The accompanying text would have told him, moreover, that even in his own day influence extended outwards from that castle on the Sound, not only through its effect on trade routes and in memories of old Viking raids, but also in terms of a direct political authority still reaching even into the semi-mythical fringes of the northern world: up Norway to the Mare Congelatum, with that mysterious land marked *"Pigmei hic habitant"* not far away across its icy waters; out past Shetland and the Orkneys, the Faeroes and Iceland, to a scarcely less mysterious Greenland.

The "Northern Regions" of Ortelius, in short, are nothing more or less than the Theatre of the Danes, enclosed by the land ocean of Russia to the east, and the Atlantic to the west. Few if any of the other parts depicted, from Normandy[23] to the Baltic littoral, had escaped some impulse of Danish power at one time or another; and even at the most conservative estimate Shakespeare would unquestionably have known enough to have got some impression of this, had he turned to Ortelius's map with his mind running on Denmark. Had he turned instead to the equivalent plate in De Jode's *Speculum,* the impression would have been very

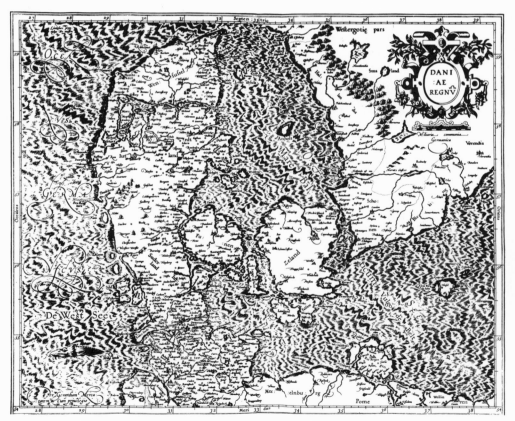

Figure 1: *Daniae Regnum* from Gerard Mercator, *Historia Mundi* (Düsseldorf, 1595).

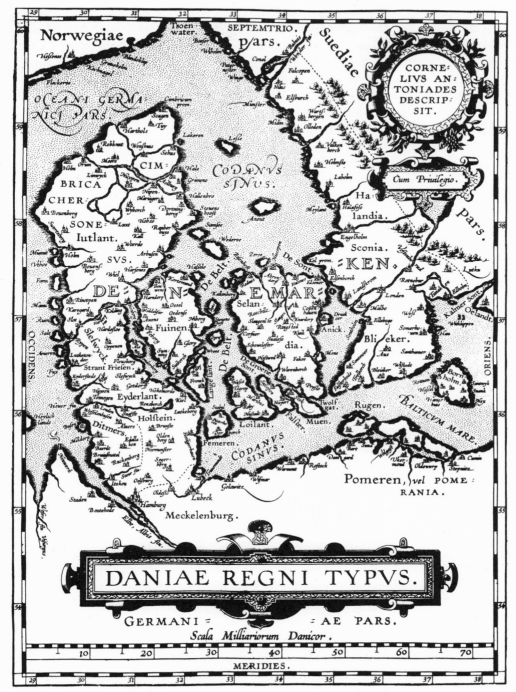

Figure 2: *Daniae Regni Typus* from Abraham Ortelius,
Theatrum Orbis Terrarum (Antwerp, 1595).

The maps appearing in this article have been reproduced through the courtesy
of the Syndics of the University Library, Cambridge.

little different. The De Jode map narrows its focus a little, not reaching so far as to Normandy or Greenland; but to "compensate" for this, Denmark takes on a more *physically* central position. The same may also be said of the various maps of Europe as a whole, at least for anyone looking at them conscious—as we today, of course, are not—of the Northern Regions as a natural subdivision of the map. Ortelius's own map of Europe, for example, sharpens-up one's sense of Denmark's being somehow the focal point of a very wide region by—*inter alia*—balancing the Baltic against the North Sea, widening the former and well-nigh closing off the latter. It also has the white "ocean" of Asia beginning on a line which is almost the exact mirror-image of the configuration of his Norwegian-Scottish-Irish coast—thus making Denmark the rough centre of an enormous boundary arc, apparently tidily laid out out by Providence.

Suppose, then for a moment that Shakespeare did in fact look at Mercator's and/or Ortelius's maps of Denmark and then perhaps turned on to some map of the larger area: supposition made the more plausible by the corresponding hints that he did take the trouble to look up the *pictures* of Elsinore in Braun & Hogenberg's *Civitates Orbis Terrarum*.[24] If he had done so, the information he had picked up by reading and hearsay could thus have begun to dispose itself in a tidy visual pattern on the maps before him; while the latters' own configurations, as he absorbed them, would have begun to suggest a matching pattern—equally tidy, and with connotations of its own. I have attempted to describe above how the sixteenth-century draughtsman's instinct to "compose" his maps in aesthetically satisfying ways (which perhaps reflects in part a subconscious feeling that the Creator himself would have behaved in the same way) tended to encourage him to utilise the bulls-eye of Denmark as the visual hinge or focus for what would appear to be a vast geographical disposition of Providence, embracing the whole of the Northern Regions; and if the reader grants even this much, then he grants sufficient for my purposes here. But it is worth taking at least some account, too, of the further possibility of this notion actually presenting itself to Shakespeare in the form of an analogy, between the Northern Regions, with Elsinore at their heart, and the old Jerusalem-centered *Mappa Mundi*—a map in which mere physical position acquires intensity of meaning "by the superimposing of spiritual senses over the physical."[25] The *Mappa Mundi* centres on Jerusalem, not only because *Ezekiel* (V.5.) tells us that God had *set it in the midst of the countries and nations round about her*, [*cf.* the Mercator phrase about the shipping of all nations being drawn to Elsinore "as to a center"] but also because the Holy Land:

> represents the natural hub of Christian experience, which spreads out from this centre to the fringe of circumambient waters, where Pagans live, close to Leviathan (both whale and Devil) together with . . . semi-homines . . . and others whose distance from full humanity could be measured by their geographical distance from that area where humanity had been most fully realised.[26]

168

I do not wish to make too much of this parallel, or to say that it "must" have occurred to Shakespeare; but it is at least a pleasingly complete one. The significantly-placed central land, the circumambient waters, the peripheral pagans and semi-homines (and the Leviathans!)—all this characterises the Northern Regions very aptly.

Still, let us return to the real point at issue. The dangers of the self-indulgent game of "liking-to-picture-Shakespeare-doing-X" are of course notorious: it tends to begin by making intuition and analogy-spinning into a cheap substitute for real evidence, and to end by decoying one further and further away from the actual plays. But the image of Shakespeare browsing like Marlowe through the pages of (let us say) the *Theatrum,* until a pattern of this kind emerges before him, is perhaps in a different category; for to contemplate this (surely obvious) possibility can serve as an effective practical way of bringing into focus an aspect of *Hamlet* which most critics would apparently acknowledge, but to which they are prevented from doing justice by their failure in this instance to make the right links with the relevant historical context.

The "aspect" of *Hamlet* here referred to is, of course, that claustrophobic quality so regularly detected in the play. R. A. Foakes surely put the general view well enough for example, in the 1956 *Shakespeare Survey:*

> For all its spaciousness of diction the Court of Elsinore is closed
> and secretive. Only rarely does the action move into the open
> air; and in these scenes there is no sense of unoppressed space.[27]

Professor Foakes is here stressing *Hamlet's* "spaciousness" of *diction* merely to counterbalance what he considers to be a previous general over-emphasis on the motifs of disease and corruption (and, he might have added, of tethered or hunted animals) in the imagery: it is of the play's essence he feels, that both elements are always co-present and in mutual tension. In this he is surely correct; but what he does not seem to have noticed is that a matching *geographical* spaciousness similarly counterbalances that kindred "sense of oppressed [physical] space" of which he then goes on to write. Critics generally, indeed, very seldom seem to spell out explicitly the extent to which this oppressiveness is in fact presented by means of contrasts with the very wide horizons around the Court of Elsinore, and that "constant going and coming" which caught Granville-Barker's eye. Nor do they often seem very plainly to link the close relationship between King and country, which the play insists on, with the at once contrasting-yet-identical relationship between the Court *and the surrounding world as a whole.* Yet surely the link is there. The Court of Elsinore, a corrupted center breeding disorder, "occupies the heart" of Denmark in every sense of the word, but it lies also at the centre of a wide ring of *other* lands, real countries, to the north, east, south, and west; and of this also the play is careful to make us aware. Something more is involved here than just a mechanical "Marlovian" use of geographical reference for vaguely impressive effect. In each case, we learn just enough about the country in question to give it a certain imaginative reality for us (e.g., the "little eyases" passage, and the impression of Laertes' life in Paris): and to each country, in one way or another, influence from the Court of Elsinore extends, always malign.

"Elsinore's a prison," say critics and directors, almost unanimously. "Denmark's a prison," says Hamlet. "Then is the world one," says Rosencrantz, cheerfully ignorant of approaching death. It is, and it is not. When—to take only the most obvious examples—we see Hamlet seeking to escape from the Court to Wittenberg and denied leave, or the happy Laertes parting from his trammelled sister, then the outer world plainly represents at least the *hope* of freedom: freedom from the prison of Denmark, and, *a fortiori,* Elsinore. The most striking instance of this is perhaps Hamlet's sea voyage: it makes a curious counter-part to the strange case of the false Danish dogs. For the latters' mutinous turbulence, though apparently beyond control by Royal Switzers, is nevertheless suppressed effortlessly—almost, one might feel, magically—as soon as it impinges on the immediate circle of the Court: even though infection from that very Court was the ultimate cause of the mutiny. Whereas Hamlet himself, on the other hand, sets out *from* Elsinore under escort, the prisoner, in various senses, at once of Claudius, his situation, and himself; yet is no sooner at sea than he (i) simultaneously foils Claudius's plot against him and disposes of his escort of childhood friends, and (ii) becomes involved in the swift violent activity of the fight with the pirates— through which his freedom of action is still further ensured. Unless one counts Claudius's despatch of Ambassadors to Norway, this is the only set of major actions by a major character to achieve immediately successful effects without subsequently rebounding upon their author: and it all happens outside Denmark. Up to a point, therefore, the outer world indeed seems to represent freedom.

But of course that point is soon reached. Laertes goes off happily enough to the liberty of life in Paris, but—in what from other points of view appears to be a curiously unnecessary scene—a spy is soon despatched after him; and anyway it will not be long before he is sucked back into the miasma of Elsinore, to join his family in death. Wittenberg is no better a refuge than Paris: a tentacle reaches out there from the Court and pulls in Rosencrantz and Guildenstern. Hamlet finds a kind of freedom on the way to England (as a prisoner of pirates!) but had he actually arrived there he would have found death. And England itself is stressed, again with what from other points of view seems to be a rather gratuitous emphasis, to be a cowed, defeated kingdom, as submissive as Norway. Lastly there is Poland: a country over which the previous King of Denmark has been victorious— and which, by the present Danish ruler's pleasure, a future Danish monarch is to defeat again. (Claudius himself, in keeping with this general impression of military energy, has even found time to serve against the French.) The catalogue could be extended, but the implication is surely already clear enough: the influence of the Court of Elsinore reaches out over the whole geographical world of the play, precisely as the effects of Claudius's crime—and Hamlet's own constant philosophical questionings—similarly reach both up to the heavens and down beyond the grave.

The wide ring of the horizon seems, indeed, to "respond" to the wide arch of the

170

heavens in *Hamlet* to an extent which it now perhaps requires an act of historical imagination fully to grasp;[28] although there are plenty of things in the play that should jog our attention towards it. (For example: Claudius's light-hearted but unconsciously ironic boast that even the heavens will react to his cannons' earthly thunder.) At a time when Heaven and Purgatory/Hell were imaginatively conceived of so very definitely *as places,* when Lapland witches sold the winds of heaven to any passer-by, when pygmies could still dwell in a nameless territory only some hundreds of miles north of John O'Groats—and when, indeed, the fires of Hell and the cries of the damned still poured out of a volcano (Mt. Hecla) on the King of Denmark's own domains—cosmographic thinking was still very much a fluid combination of geography and cosmology.[29] The things dreamt of in heaven and earth were not very sharply differentiated by their presumed location; and Hamlet's image of death as "an undiscovered country" was in fact an analogy so precise as to be scarcely a metaphor at all (especially—it is perhaps unfair to add!—if one happened to have been thinking in terms of the Northern Regions, now being probed at a terrible cost, whose own undiscovered countries could be expected to be all dead winter lands of ice and snow).[30]

This "bifocalism" of Elizabethan cosmography in fact conditions the whole patterning of *Hamlet.* Today, of course, the notion of dying as *departing* (as in "passing" bells) is a dead metaphor which one only takes literally at the risk of raising a snigger. But allow it its proper force in *Hamlet,* and the play's steady stream of deaths and ghostly manifestations falls well enough into place as one more dimension of its "constant comings and goings." The fact that this was a way of thinking more natural to the Elizabethans than to us explains, for example, both Horatio's valedictory *"and flights of angels sing thee to thy rest"* and the slight discomfort that is sometimes nowadays felt with this particular line.[31] It jars on us today, to be presented with this sudden image of the death-ridden court as a sort of transit camp, with Hamlet, as it were, unhappily called away by air at the very moment when Fortinbras and the ambassadors are arriving by sea. But it does so only because we have allowed our minds to slide over similar bracketings of ideas earlier in the play. If we had taken more seriously Hamlet's constant yet shifting vision of death *as a journey*—to Heaven, to Hell, to an unknown country, or (most terribly of all) merely "through the guts of a beggar"— we would be in more need of Horatio's phrase to stabilize for us (emotionally if not intellectually) our vision of that journey upon which the Prince himself is now setting out; and we would the more readily recognise in it, too, the completion of a pattern.

Is there, after all, really no similarity between Hamlet (in, perhaps significantly, another speech which has given trouble to critics) debating whether a sword in Claudius's back is more likely to send him *down* to Hell or *up* to Heaven: and King Claudius, stopping his nephew departing one way (to Wittenberg) only to send him himself another way (to England)? Or—better perhaps—between the return of father and son alike to plague Claudius for his crime, irrespective of whether he personally despatches them to the next world or to the far side of the North

Sea? Whatever may be thought of these particular analogies, certainly one does not have to look further than the great *To be, or not to be* soliloquy to see how in general the next world holds out very much the same *sort* of illusory hope of disengagement as retreat to Paris or Wittenberg. The sour little debates over the dead Ophelia's heavenly status only serve to underline this (just as the royal interference with the Church's proper funeral rites on this occasion, since it is twice emphasised, might conceivably be seen as one more royal attempt to command the heavens as well as the earth).

Thus it is surely no accident that *Hamlet*, a play whose very first scene includes a speech setting the action firmly in a Christian context,[32] is also the only one of the major tragedies that seems to be paying any real attention to conventional Christian cosmology. Plainly, Hamlet's own searing vision of mankind—and not least himself—as the ambiguous mid-point between matter and pure spirit, is well and aptly reinforced by this further invocation of the old semi-medieval picture of man as standing also on the mid-plane (in an almost absurdly literal topographical sense) between Heaven and Hell. But for Hamlet himself, of course, this general dilemma of the universal human situation has one very special aspect.

For if we all exist, alas, on a mid-plane between Heaven and Hell, spirit and matter, then in the world of the play, Hamlet, the doubly rightful heir of an usurped crown, stands right at the mid-point *of* that plane. Time and again the play invokes, in various forms, the notion that monarchy is the hub of the wheel of society— or, when it fails, the centre of a kind of whirlpool which will pull all around it down into the gulf (III.iii.16);[33] so that it is clear that Hamlet's fumbling attempts to redress his private family honour are somehow also a drama about a mystical *crisis*, at the very centre of human life[34]—and of life seen, not as in *Lear*, in terms of the stripped-down individual, but as inseparable from a socio-religious context.

It is a crisis which cannot be simply defined: if it could, *Hamlet* would be no more than a brilliant specimen of a minor art-form, a straight-forward allegory. Instead, its many facets cut puzzlingly across each other. The King is of the same ambiguous mortal nature as his subjects, and has himself the same uncertain spiritual destiny; yet Heaven apparently chooses to invest him with a spiritual responsibility for them quite equal to his practical importance in the state. And the implications of these twin responsibilities work against each other, in complicated ways which many critics have explored, without ever exhausting the ultimate paradox. It is plain, for instance, that from one point of view the play represents a convulsion by which the world rids itself of an infection lodged at its very heart: yet the result is only that Fortinbras comes to the throne after proving his wholesome virtues by destroying far more men than Claudius, in a pointless war which is itself the expression of a diseased condition of society. Worse still, this disease—"th'imposthume of much wealth and peace"—is presumably *itself* the fruit of good government by a wholesome king.

Plainly such paradoxes, with their further unmistakable yet obscure implications of the intermeshing of a divine with a human order, do indeed engage with "the very centre" of human life, socially conceived, at least as life appeared to the

172

sixteenth century. But to set such paradoxes at the very heart of an action, and then to locate that action itself squarely at the geopolitical heart of what was widely understood as a distinct region of the globe—being careful, too, sufficiently to sketch in the ring of the surrounding horizons in the play itself—is indeed to produce a drama whose reverberations can only properly be defined by proud analogy with the splendour of the *Mappa Mundi's* conception of the whole world disposed symmetrically about a (literally) central Christian story.[35]

III

However, when one reaches Jerusalem it is clearly time to stop and take stock a little. In the first place, it needs to be stressed that to invoke the *Mappa Mundi* in this way is not to seek to emulate one fashionable kind of bad criticism by proclaiming the discovery that Hamlet, like Eeyore, "is Christ."[36] That discovery has of course been made, of Hamlet as of many other classic victim-heroes; but it is ultimately uninteresting because—like the discovery of Hamlet's Oedipus and Orestes complexes— it tells us nothing *particular*: Christ, for that matter, potentially lives equally in all of us, as the Church indeed teaches.

Secondly, it should perhaps be made plain, too, that it is not claimed that there is anything unusual about the basic conception of *Hamlet* that has been elaborated here. What *is* claimed, is just that it is possible to show how, out of the implications of certain usually unnoticed historical and cartographic facts, an unaccustomed yet natural and easy chain of reasoning leads to what is in essentials an already familiar and well-attested view of this play. The value of this exercise primarily lies in the demonstration that a still further dimension—a further ring of coherent significance, not perhaps previously brought wholly into focus— in fact confirms by enriching this already existing view. Indeed it also clarifies it; as a closer look at one fairly standard formulation will show. Here, for instance, is Mr. H. V. Dyson making a point in passing, in his 1950 British Academy Shakespeare lecture:

> The world of Hamlet the prince is only a part of that presented
> to us when we watch the play. There is a world of historical
> and geographical reference that offers a fit setting for the tragic
> events and the tragic speculation. Centred in Denmark our
> minds move to Wittenburg and Paris, England and Norway and
> Poland, and by remoter allusion, Bethlehem [*to which might
> be added Rome, Troy, and even Vienna, incidentally.*] Airs
> from Heaven and blasts from Hell fan us. . . . The ghost rouses
> the echo of a cock-crow that has sounded from the beginning
> of our era.[37]

Obviously there is no very scandalous misrepresentation in this; yet surely the key to the characterization of Shakespeare's Prince is precisely that in his case the familiar distinction which Mr. Dyson is here taking for granted for once does not really hold. It is true, certainly, that there is no question of the division

Figure 3: *Septentrionalium Regionum Descriptio* from Abraham Ortelius,
Theatrum Orbis Terrarum (Antwerp, 1595).

between the interior mental world of someone like Laertes, for instance, and the
wider world against which that particular personal tragedy is played out; yet
half the fascination of Hamlet himself (as well as the explanation of his famous
"delay") lies, surely, in the fact that for him this world of wider reference essentially *is* his own mental world too. Indeed Shakespeare seems to be at some pains
to exhibit the "open," kaleidoscopic quality of his hero's mind in virtue of which
this becomes true; and what Hamlet makes his boast, that he *could be bounded
in a nutshell and count myself king of infinite space,* is manifestly part of his problem, even kingdoms of that sort, of course, being apt to give their monarchs all
too little chance to pursue their private affairs in single-minded peace. Moreover,
what is in any case particularly remarkable about *Hamlet* as a *play* is the way in
which this natural character-versus-context has been for once taken up *and
absorbed into something larger,* becoming just one permutation of a much more
wide-reaching theme: a constant exploration of the contrast-yet-relatedness of
one cluster of concepts, involving ideas and images of universality/freedom/
independence/spaciousness, to another involving particularity/centrality/depend-
ence/boundedness: all in various senses, literal, metaphorical and metaphysical,
and all interpenetrating and commenting on each other.

Consider, for example, that single brief speech of Hamlet's just alluded to. Even
within so small a compass, the conceptual jolts in its rapid transitions, first from

174

the notion of fantastic imprisonment (*in a nutshell*) to that of extreme freedom (*king of infinite* [mental] *space*), and then to the idea of the *destruction* of such freedom by "bad dreams" somehow mysteriously outside that "infinity" although equally within the mind, afford a kind of handy laboratory demonstration of the reaction working on a larger scale throughout the whole play. And the play's geographical dimension does not just afford "a fit setting" for this reaction: it is intrinsic to it.

Finally, it seems necessary here to stabilize those apparent shifts of ground, which will have been noticed in this article, between approaching the works of sixteenth-century cartographers as potential (or even probable) Shakespearean *source-texts,* and simply treating the contemporary map of northern Europe as a useful aid to the study of *Hamlet.* Here we must distinguish a little. In the first place, it is obvious that, although Shakespeare plainly did not expect his first audiences to follow his drama map in hand, it may well still help a modern reader to study the atlases at which Shakespeare might have looked, simply because it brings him closer to the mental picture of the world which any reasonably intelligent Londoner around 1600 could have picked up by "osmosis" even without setting eyes on a map. Consciously or not, Shakespeare must be assuming that his audience will possess that kind of mental background; and the main way in which it changes the normal vague modern impression of the play's general wide-rangingness, is by transforming it into wide-rangingness about a recognisable geopolitical centre for an accepted division of the globe. And after the successes of Herr Hochhuth, it would be particularly absurd to feel that one must *disallow this* as a factor in what one might term the conceptual mechanism of the play— or in one's response to it, merely because some post-Romantic theory told us that Shakespeare was not supposed to write that kind of drama.

Secondly, though, any Elizabethan who *did* happen to be particularly clear-headed about geography could *also* have had the pleasure of appreciating, of course, that this element of general geographical consciousness in *Hamlet* did appear in fact to be worked out with a good deal of quiet tidiness. He might have picked up the reference to Normandy, for instance, noted the neatness of the strategy of Forninbras's movements, and some of the other things mentioned above—and indeed ended, as I have done, by wondering quite how far this "tidiness" really goes. And it does seem clear that it at least goes further than even a good audience could reasonably be meant to grasp from a performance: which is as much as to say that it appears—as I have already argued—to be implying something about the whole genesis of Shakespeare's conception of the Hamlet story.

Why, for instance, is there no mention in *Hamlet* of the Swedes? After all, they are mentioned in both source-texts, they had been subject to the Danish crown for some time during the later Middle Ages, and were in Shakespeare's day quite as much Denmark's "natural" enemy as France has usually been England's, but had still not yet got the upper hand. Thus, they would have fitted very well into the picture which the play gives us of Denmark as a dominant military centre; and the impression which we also receive of a relatively realistic, contemporary Denmark makes their omission even odder still, when so many other countries are brought in. Is this a bogus problem? Perhaps so, but it is worth noting that it can be solved, nevertheless, by taking seriously what has been said above the play's seemingly deliberate establishment of the wide ring of the horizon around Elsinore; for before Denmark lost her provinces east of Zealand, Sweden was essentially a *northern* rather than, as today, an eastern neighbor to her. (This is not special pleading: Sweden and Norway are in fact listed together as Denmark's northern neighbors in the text of later editions of Mercator's *Atlas*). Shakespeare, even if wishing effectively to "place" Denmark at the centre of a wide ring of surrounding lands, would of course have had no occasion to use two separate countries to indicate the same point of the compass.

And then there is the matter of the Roman allusions in *Hamlet*. The usual response of commentators to these, apart from noting their more obvious reverberations, seems to be just to invoke the theory that Shakespeare was working on *Hamlet* fairly soon after writing *Julius Caesar*. But that, of course, does not really say very much: after all, he does not seem always to echo one play in the next in quite this way. On the other hand, it *is* reasonable to assume, for a great many cultural reasons, that the Elizabethans must almost certainly have tended to look at their maps with the kind of freshness of eye nowadays characteristic rather of an intelligent schoolboy than of the normal adult: an eye, that is to say, particularly alert to balance, pattern, symmetry, and representational silhouettes such as the "boot" of Italy. And if one looks at the map of Europe in this frame of mind, one of the first things to catch one's attention is of course the way that Denmark "balances" Italy, astride the long axis of the continent. (Certainly this is a fact which had caught Archbishop Abbot's eye, at all events, since he begins his remarks on that country with the observation that "As *Italia* lieth on the south of Germany, so *Denmark* lieth on the north").[38] Even in itself, this truism carries a natural suggestion of an analogy that would have seemed far more immediately striking to any sixteenth-century Englishman than it does to us, whose image of Denmark is perhaps rather of an admirably sensible butter-producing Welfare State. When the King of Denmark was still to all appearances the most powerful Protestant monarch in Europe, when all the northern sea-roads led to Elsinore, when the Danes still figured along with the Romans in Englishmen's consciousness as one of the five conquerors of Britain, when it was beginning to dawn on men's minds that the old northern world, of which Denmark had been in every way the centre, in many ways offered a curious duplicate to the classical world they had so long supposed to be unique (i.e. possessing an analogous pantheon, etc.), and when the extent of the Danish empire at its high point was fairly generally understood, it was only natural enough that antique Roman thoughts should intrude on a playwright working with some consciousness of the real sixteenth-century Denmark in his mind. Such thoughts, indeed, intruded themselves even on Mercator's consciousness, for he quotes a piece of verse comparing Canute the Great with the conquerors of Classical antiquity on the first page of his text to the map of Denmark here reproduced;

(although no one seems to have drawn the conclusion that he must therefore previously have written a play about Julius Caesar).

That Shakespeare *was* thinking of Denmark at least to some extent in geographic—and hence directional—terms, is perhaps suggested also by some of Hamlet's own remarks. Speaking of Danish drunkenness—i.e., at a point when it is quite beyond question that it *is* the actual Denmark which we are meant to have in mind—Hamlet describes this vice as damaging his country's reputation both "east and west." Obviously this is a phrase that would come naturally enough to anyone thinking not only of the real Denmark as he wrote, but also of where it was: the word *easterling,* for instance, in Elizabethan times primarily meant an inhabitant of the Baltic littoral, and it may be noted that in *King John* the Duke of Austria refers to England as "that utmost corner of the west" (II.i.29).

Similarly, Shakespeare is also sometimes allowed to be thinking of "where Denmark was" when Hamlet says he knows a hawk from a handsaw "when the wind is southerly," *i.e.,* when people arrive from Wittenberg. Is it merely a coincidence, then, that when Hamlet admits mockingly to being mad "north north west," he is naming the only direction which does *not* suggest another country, and from which Claudius cannot fetch spies, since it points out through the ring of surrounding lands and away up the North Sea to the open ocean?[39] This is not to suggest that the commonly accepted reading of this passage in terms of falconry is wrong: after all, that reading already coexists successfully, in the minds of the editors of both the *Cambridge* and *Arden* editions, with quite different secondary meanings for both "hawk" and "handsaw," as well as with an echo of Timothy Bright. But the probability that Shakespeare ever got as far as Chapter XXXIX of *A Treatise of Melancholy*—with the views of which not everyone agreed anyway—does not seem conspicuously stronger than the reasons for thinking that he is likely to have seen a map of northern Europe; and in any case, what brought this particular melancholy-hawking-compass-bearing collocation of ideas into his mind? The image does, after all, come at the end of a passage in which Hamlet greets *new arrivals* at Elsinore—which, even on the most modest estimate, would not seem to reduce the possibility that it has something to do with a conscious orientation of the action of the play in the poet's mind.

"Something to do with a conscious orientation": perhaps, in the circumstances, the phrase should be defined. Needless to say, I am not suggesting that Shakespeare solemnly plotted this particular remark of Hamlet's with the help of a pocket compass. I do suggest that it might be thought to reflect a general sense of orientation in Shakespeare's mind while he wrote the play—a sense good enough for him to be able to achieve this (seeming) kind of almost inadvertent precision in a small detail quite casually, without particular conscious reflection; a sense, that is to say, good enough to suggest that a study of at least one map of Denmark and the Northern Regions should perhaps be included among his source-material for this play. And, once one *does* allow that possibility, on this or any other grounds, then of course it becomes necessary tentatively to speculate a little further, about even those larger parallels between map and play which could *not* be claimed to have left some explicit mark on isolatable passages in the text. For when all is said and done, the fact remains that, for whatever reason—or none at all—the map does afford a kind of pleasing "emblem" of a major aspect of the play. And, like any other emblem, it is one which it can be instructive to contemplate.[40]

Notes:

(1) The New Shakespeare : *Hamlet*, ed. J. Dover Wilson. Introduction, p. lv, n.1. [Prof. Dover Wilson's precise words are that "there are indications that at some period the *Hamlet* plan was handled by a dramatist who knew more about Denmark than Shakespeare appears to have done." But there do not seem to be any very compelling reasons for thus denying Shakespeare credit for a knowledge of Denmark evinced in what all editors seem to take as being, in every important respect, Shakespeare's own play. After all, we know some of his colleagues had performed in that country, so he did not have far to go for information about it.]

Among explorers of *Hamlet's* possible Danish background it is perhaps sufficient to mention here only three names. In *The Guns Of Elsinore* (London, 1964), Martin Holmes provides a useful compilation and expansion of virtually all the more interesting points made by previous investigators in this field. Since then a Swedish scholar, Gunnar Sjögren, has also published a number of interesting articles and papers. (The latest, which appears in this issue of *Shakespeare Studies*, provides references to all the others and affords in passing a convenient resume of their main contents.) And in Poland an interesting edition of *Hamlet* (with parallel English text) was published in 1963 by Witold Chwalewik, under the auspices of the Polish Academy. Though not, of course, primarily concerned with the question of Danish background, the notes to this edition score at least some palpable hits on this and other topics, and well repay study.

(2) As Mercator puts it: "At this place all the ships that are bound toward the East, *are compelled to come as to one common Center* . . . and sometime 300 ships do arrive there together in one day out of divers parts of Europe". (My italics) [This and subsequent quotations from Mercator are in the language of an early English translation: *Historia Mundi or Mercator's Atlas . . . Englished by W.S.* (London, 1635).]

(3) Giles Fletcher, *Of The Rus Commonwealth*, ed. Albert J. Schmidt, (Ithaca, N.Y., 1966), Introduction, p. xiii.

(4) See Charles E. Hill, *The Danish Sound Dues And The Command Of The Baltic* (Durham, N.C., 1926), pp. 71-73.

(5) The later editions of Mercator's *Atlas* specially mention the strength of its walls, for instance. Many other illustrations of its repute could be supplied.

(6) As has often been remarked, there seems to be a quite specific reference to the northern voyages of Barents in *TN* (III.ii.25-28). These particular voyages attracted so much attention in England that in 1631 "the world" was described by an English writer as still speaking of "the Dutch-mens hard Winter in nova Zembla." (Quoted in R. R. Cawley's *The Voyagers and Elizabethan Drama* [London, 1938], p. 241. The whole of Bk. III of this invaluable study, however, can really be cited as documentation of what has been said about Northern discoveries above).

(7) Chwalewik, p. 154. [Needless to say, Prof. Chwalewik himself does not credit Shakespeare's audience with this knowledge either; although he does point out that such historical allusions as they *would* have been likely to recognise could also well be taken to suggest a period "roughly corresponding to the reign of Canute the Great."]

(8) A narrow corridor of land did in fact intermittently give Sweden a western outlet to the sea; but this corridor was quite frequently in the King of Denmark's hands, and agreements normally assured Danish-Norwegian transit rights even when it was not. Most maps likely to have been

178

available in England either failed to show it or were very ambiguous, although the Ortelius map referred to above perhaps abolishes it most firmly of all.

(9) *Abraham Ortelius His Epitome of the Theater of the Worlde* (London, 1603), p. 49. (This is the English translation of a popular work of which there were many earlier editions in Latin, French, and other languages.) For what it is worth, it may be noted that the same work also accounts (p. 94) for the sledded Polacks: "Under the crowne of Polonia are contayned *Lituania, Samogitia* [. . . etc.] *Lituania* is very much pestered with fennes bogges and forests, and in the summer tyme they can neither go into it or issue foorthe, by reason of the waters, but in the winter, when all is frozen up, they passe over the yce withe sleddes drawne by horses." But indeed Cawley is right in saying that peoples in that region were in any case so regularly associated with sleds that "it is hard to understand how the German critics could have given themselves so much trouble over the line" *(The Elizabethan Voyages*, p. 247, n. 78).

(10) Of course there are still further possible "explanations" of Fortinbras's line of march: Gunnar Sjögren, for instance, has set out a model demonstration of the fact that at least some—though clearly not all—Elizabethans actually thought Danzig to be a part of Denmark ("A contribution to the geography of *Hamlet*," *Shakespeare Jahrbuch*, Band 100/101.) Or then again, it would be quite easy to mis-read the *Carta Marina* of Olaus Magnus in the way discussed below. It is surely neither necessary nor possible to choose between all these alternatives (beyond noting, perhaps, that Sjögren's theory is the only one which would seem to depend upon Shakespeare never look-ing at all attentively at a map, or at some such work as Abbot's little book). What they *all* prove, is simply that there is not necessarily any (sea-coast-of-) bohemian casualness about geography in the Fortinbras sub-plot. And anyone who supposes that the famous sea coast reference in WT nonetheless automatically disposes of the idea of ever taking other Shakespearean geographical references literally, should in any case read the New Arden note to WT. III.iii.2.

(11) *The Anatomy of Melancholy*, pt. 2, sect. 2, number 4.

(12) R. A. Skelton, Bibliographical Note to facsimile edition of *Theatrum Orbis Terrarum* (Amsterdam, 1964), p. viii.
   Though the point affects my own argument only peripherally, it is perhaps worth noting how great a simplification this is likely to be of the full intellectual context in which Ortelius arrived at his choice of title. See, for example, Ch. VI ("The Memory Theatre of Giulio Camillo") in Frances Yates' *The Art of Memory* (London, 1966).

(13) G. K. Hunter, "Elizabethans and Foreigners," *Shakespeare Survey*, 17 (1964), 39, n.1.

(14) Skelton, *loc. cit.*

(15) It has been proved, for instance, that Marlowe used it. See M. E. Seaton, "Marlowe's Map," *Essays and Studies*, X (1924), 13-35. [Reprinted in *Marlowe: A Collection of Critical Essays*, ed. Clifford Leech (Englewood Cliffs, N. J., 1964).]

(16) From the (Latin) Address to the Student of Geography, on A. Lafreri's re-issue of the *Carta Marina* of Olaus Magnus (1572).

(17) English royal players had been sent for to perform at her arrival and wedding celebrations in Scotland; and again, as it appears, for the celebrations at the christening of her eldest son (when they were well rewarded). At other times, too, James stoutly backed up English actors who had run up against civic disapproval in Scotland. See "English Players in Scotland" in E. K. Chambers *The Elizabethan Stage* (Vol. II).

(18) Far too much is sometimes made by modern commentators of the possibility that Essex might have followed Elizabeth on the throne. What Essex himself thought about his contemporaries' expectations on that subject is clearly enough shown by the fact that when he made his move against Elizabeth he tried to make it with James's backing, and under colour of securing James's

unequivocal right of inheritance to the English crown. James's claims were widely enough recognised in practice, even by Elizabeth herself, but of course had never been *formally* ratified. When James finally came into his inheritance he was at pains to let it be known that he regarded Essex as "my martyr."

(19) Saxo was quite surprisingly well known to the Elizabethans and Jacobeans, relatively speaking at least (no doubt in part because of the light the later sections of his work intermittently throw on early English history). For evidence of this, see the various references to him noted in passing in M. E. Seaton's *Literary Relations of England and Scandinavia in the Seventeenth Century* (Oxford, 1935): a list which makes no pretensions to completeness, and which even my own reading has shown to be easy to extend.

Shakespeare's own evident interest in English history is therefore a factor which should surely be taken into account in the Saxo-versus-Belleforest controversy. A general reading of Saxo affords a most striking image of Denmark as the centre of a Scandinavian military energy striking outwards in all directions, especially eastwards along the Baltic and westwards into the British isles. This seems to me to be also very much the effect given by the play, and it is something which comes through much less clearly in Belleforest, or indeed even in Saxo's own Amleth tale, narrowly defined.

Certainly Shakespeare could have learned something of this from many other sources than Saxo, but it is at least one point in the latter's "favour" when he and Belleforest are singled out as rivals for the distinction of being Shakespeare's source.

(20) Although it would be pleasant to suppose that on somebody's parlor wall Shakespeare had in fact seen Olaus Magnus's splendidly exciting (and decorative) map of the Northern Regions. This features a battle on sea ice (though only between Russians and Swedes), people travelling over Baltic ice on large horse-drawn sleds, ice all the way along the Baltic coast, and prominently-drawn cannon guarding the Sound.

Moreover, because of the similarity of the Latin forms of their names, the map could also appear, to a hasty or ill-informed eye, to place the Duchy of Great Poland squarely where Macklenburg should really be (i.e., squarely up against the frontiers of the King of Denmark's own German duchies); thus disposing once more of any mystery about the latter part of Fortinbras's expedition. The commoner "latinisation" of *Mecklenburg* would appear to have been *Megapolis*, but on this map it appears as:

MAGNOPOL

IA

DUCATUS

(At this time Great and Lesser Poland were recognised subdivisions of that kingdom).

(21) As shown by the fact that a second edition of Mercator's *Atlas* did not appear until 1602. (And it may be noted that anyone wishing to argue that Shakespeare may nevertheless have seen the Mercator volume, will at least have to ask themselves why he did not then borrow more heavily from the full list of Danish noble surnames which it provides.)

(22) There has long been a tendency for the English to picture themselves subconsciously as somehow belonging to a nation and state virtually created *ex nihilo* in 1066. It is a frame of mind which makes "Anglo-Saxon England" seem about as remote from post-Conquest England as the Iron Age tribes of pre-Roman Britain (and the hold which this notion has had is well enough shown by the vogue among present-day historians for stressing the essential *continuity* of Anglo-Saxon and Norman England: no one labours a point of this kind if he supposes himself to be preaching to the converted.) The Elizabethans, however, do not seem to have had quite this feeling about 1066; and perhaps because they did not therefore feel so unnaturally cut off from their Anglo-Saxon forebears, memories of those forebears' struggles with the Danish invaders were still surprisingly alive in their minds. This is true not only of educated persons with a taste for history but also of

180

ordinary country folk: consider, for instance, the superstitions associated with the Danewort, a crimson flower believed to grow with particular profusion at the still-remembered sites of battles between Dane and Englishman.

(23) What a graceful touch, it might be thought, to make that perfect French cavalier M. Lamord a Norman.

(24) See Martin Holmes, *The Guns of Elsinore* (London, 1964), pp. 47-48.

(25) G. K. Hunter, "Elizabethans and Foreigners," *Shakespeare Survey*, 17 (1964), 37.

(26) *Ibid.*

(27) R. A. Foakes, "*Hamlet* and the Court of Elsinore," *Shakespeare Survey*, 9 (1956), 38.

(28) The Preface to the courteous Reader, in *Historia Mundi or Mercator's Atlas Englished by W.S.* refers to "the neare affinitie which this noble Science [i.e. geography] hath with Astronomie, which mounting above the earth doth contemplate the Heavens." Of course that is still true enough; but no one nowadays is likely to proffer this as a *justification* for studying geography, which is what is intended here.

(29) The quotations illustrating these three terms in the *NED* are very instructive on this point.

(30) "Unfair" or not, one finds a similar collocation of ideas in Donne's "I saw him go / O'er the white Alps alone".

(31) See, for example, Dover Wilson's comment in *The Essential Shakespeare* (London, 1948), p. 107.

(32) Marcellus's "Bird of Dawning" speech. But of course the opening scene "places" the action in other ways, too; and of these the Roman echoes, linking the action of the drama with the death of another great leader in another centre of terrestrial power, are particularly worth noting in the present context. They will be discussed more fully below.

(33) There is the same concatenation of ideas in *Richard III* (III.vii. around line 128.) Even so, it may be worth noting that the Maelstrom, half way up the Norwegian coast, is a conspicuous feature of some maps of the Northern Regions.

(34) In this context it is hard not to remember, too, the multiple ironies inherent in Polonius's promise to the royal murderer that he *will find / Where truth is hid, though it were hid indeed / Within the centre.*

(35) Whether or not they "can only be defined" in this way, they should certainly also be related to Elizabethan chorography. It is worth quoting Prof. E. G. R. Taylor on this point: "The contrast in view-point and emphasis between the chorographical description of the sixteenth century, and the corresponding regional description, analysis and synthesis of the twentieth [is something which] a study of Robert Dallington's books . . . shows very exactly . . . . . . *The two major headings under which observations were to be grouped by the traveller were (a) the Country and (b) the Government. The Country was to be examined first in respect of its Situation, and then of its Parts. The Situation was in turn to be looked at from a double aspect, first its Cosmography, i.e., World Aspect, and second its . . . Regional Aspect. Under "Cosmographical situation" were grouped Clime, Degree, and the Planet ruling the disposition of the Air" (Late Tudor and Early Stuart Geography 1583-1650* [London, 1934], p. 39. My italics. The detailed citation from Dallington draws on his *A Survey of the great Duke's State of Tuscany in the year of our Lord 1596*, printed 1605.)

The further metaphysical overtones inevitably aroused by a reference to Cosmography at this period, I have noted earlier.

(36) C. J. L. Culpepper's famous study of the sacramental meaning of *Winnie-the-Pooh* has been reprinted in *The Pooh Perplex*, ed. F. C. Crews (New York, 1965).

(37) *Proceedings of the British Academy*, Vol. XXXVI, 88.

(38) Abbot, *A briefe Description of the whole World*, (London, 1598) Art. De Danis.

(39) *Cf.* Francke's note to II.ii.360 (quoted in Furness): *Perhaps the meaning is: Great powerful tempests in the moral world, apparitions from the mysterious Hereafter, can make me mad, can crush my reason; but such people as you are, I have yet wit enough to avoid.*

(40) *BIBLIOGRAPHICAL NOTE.* In addition to the works referred to in the footnotes, a reader interested in testing or extending the thesis presented in this paper may wish to consult N.E. Nørlund, *Danmarks Kortlaegning Første bind* (København, 1942), and B. Bramsen, *Gamle Danmarkskort: en Historisk Oversigt med Bibliografiske Noter for Perioden 1570-1770* (København, 1952).

In Search of Yorick's Skull:
Notes on the Background of Hamlet

by Yngve B. Olsson

Ironically, a student of Shakespeare's *Hamlet* finds himself in a situation which is the exact opposite of Hamlet's with Yorick's skull in his hand: there is the infinite jest, and the most excellent fancy, there are the gibes and the gambols, but where is the skull?

An answer that points to the available texts, from the First Quarto (Q1) of 1603 onwards, would meet with the obvious objection that the texts do not represent the real basis of the play: before them lie the years back to 1589 with the reference to a play *Hamlet* in Thomas Nashe's prefatory epistle to his friend Robert Greene's pastoral *Menaphon*.[1] The first time Shakespeare's name has been found linked with *Hamlet* is in Gabriel Harvey's marginal note in his copy of Thomas Speght's edition of Chaucer, which he is supposed to have written some time between 1598 and February 1601.[2] So it is not clear what connection, if any, Shakespeare had with the play in the previous ten years or so. He may have been the original author.[3] He may have been the adaptor of an earlier play which is now lost.[4] There is no further information to be extracted from the other early references to *Hamlet* as listed by E. K. Chambers, among which the most interesting is the entry in Philip Henslowe's diary under the 9th of June, 1594.[5]

The fact that we have to deal with a first version of *Hamlet* of uncertain authorship and unknown form makes it unprofitable to discuss the relationship between it and the extant texts which bear Shakespeare's name. What they do have in common is the story, but even with this known quantity difficulties arise, since we want to know (a) the sources used by the author of the original play, whether he was Shakespeare or not, and (b) in case he was not Shakespeare, what other sources than the original play may have contributed to the *Hamlet* that we know. In other words, it is impossible to decide to what extent Shakespeare has made direct acquaintance with the sources of the Hamlet story. Besides, the Hamlet story was available in more than one version. If there are details in one that do not occur in another but which are to be found in the play, that may be an indication of a relevant source. But if two (or more) versions of the story agree with each other and with the play, this does not exclude the possibility that the dramatist saw them both (or all), in which case it is impossible to say which particular one first drew his attention to a certain significant detail. Finally, since we have to do with a work of art by a genius, we must allow a wide scope for what may have been created or re-created by the dramatist's imagination. Nevertheless it may be of some interest to study the ramifications of the Hamlet story, which are wider than is generally known, and to consider the extent to which they may have penetrated into the

Hamlet play. We shall mainly be concerned with the oldest accounts (before Belleforest) in order to provide material for a discussion whether one or more of these may have contributed to the play besides, or perhaps even instead of, Belleforest. Even if the present study should not lead to a conclusive result, the facts presented and the spotlights thrown may not be entirely without value.

In the first place, it is remarkable that an English dramatist should choose a Danish theme at a time when Scandinavia was largely *terra incognita*.[6] The simple reason may be that the story of Prince Hamlet was a good story and well suited for the playwright's purposes. *Beowulf* is an obvious parallel. But even so, what gave him the incitement, unless the material came into his hands by mere chance? The fact that the name of *Hamlet/Hamnet/Hamlin*, etc., was common in England is no proof that the Danish story was generally known.[7] *Hamlet* is not the same word as the Scandinavian name *Ambale/Amlodi*, etc., which was latinized *Amlethus* (Saxo) or *Ambletus*.[8] Both the etymology and the form are different—note especially the absence of the initial *H* in Scandinavian, even if it was natural for the English, once the story was adopted, to replace the foreign name with the familiar. Neither is there in Scandinavian any equivalent of the double form *Hamlet/Hamnet* referring to the same person, as was the case, for instance, of Shakespeare's own son (1585-1596).[9]

There may, however, be some connection between the evidence available of a *Hamlet* play in England in the late 16th century and what we know about Anglo-Danish relations at that time. The first two dates when there is any mention of the play are, as we have seen, the years 1589 and 1594. In 1589 James VI of Scotland, who was believed to be the successor to the English throne, was married to Princess Anne of Denmark. In 1594 the royal couple celebrated the baptism of their first-born son, Henry Frederick.

E. K. Chambers, pointing out the hard climate for plays in Scotland between the royal weddings of 1503 and 1589, gives an account of the negotiations between King James of Scotland and Queen Elizabeth of England "for to have her Majesties players for to repayer into Scotland to his grace."[10] There is no absolute certainty, however, that any English players actually went (Chambers), but neither is there any definite proof to the contrary. If a prospective visit to Scotland was cancelled, there was good reason for it. The new Queen's crossing was delayed for months by unfavourable winds, which made it impossible for her to get any further than Norway, and in the end King James had to go to Scandinavia himself to meet her, where the wedding ceremony took place in Oslo. But it is natural that King James's request should have caused some interest in England's theatrical world and that arrangements should have been made for a suitable repertoire to be presented at the Scottish court. Besides, hopes and speculations must have centered on the arrival of Anne of Denmark, a "sensuous and spectacle-loving lady" (Chambers). This is all the more likely as English musicians, jesters, and players have been to the Danish court in 1585 and 1586-87 and so had brought home first-hand knowledge. Among them there were future members of Shakespeare's own company: William Kempe, George Bryan, and Thomas Pope.[11]

184

In 1594, "probably for the baptism of Henry Frederick on 30 August," there were certainly English actors in Scotland, even if the *True Accompt of the Baptism* does not explicitly state that they took part in the plays given at the festivities.[12] Their leader was probably Laurence Fletcher, who was to figure as the first name—just before William Shakespeare's—on the list of actors in King James's letters patent of 1603 which made the Chamberlain's Men into the King's Men.

In Nashe (1589) and Henslowe (1594) we may have reflections of these two Court events (1589 and 1594). It is true that they only refer to *Hamlet* as familiar and *Hamlet* as acted in London, but the fact that this happens when it does may be more than a coincidence. It would not have been unlikely for an English company of actors to prepare for the Royal Wedding by causing to be written and performing a play with a Danish theme as a compliment to the Queen: the very fact that Nashe referred to it shows that *Hamlet*, though indifferent to him, was considerable enough to warrant an allusion. And it is not impossible that the play was revived during the preparations for the Baptism, when there was a chance of going to Scotland after a cancellation of the journey of 1589.

The connection between *Hamlet* and the Scottish royal family is more safely established when we reach the first two printed versions, Q1 and Q2. In the sub-title of Q1 there is a reference to the performers of *Hamlet* as *his Highnesse seruants*, which, since "his Highnesse" must refer to King James, presumably indicates publication "after 19 May 1603 when the former Lord Chamberlain's men received their patent as servants of the King."[13] On Queen Elizabeth's death (24 March 1603), King James had started from Edinburgh (5 April), been met by the London crowds (7 May) outside the City, which was suffering from the plague, proceeded to the Tower (11 May) without passing through the City, and a few days later (14 May) taken up residence at Greenwich.[14] On 19 May he signed the Patent for the King's Men. The King did not return to London till 25 July (St. James's Day), and then only for his coronation at Westminister, whereupon he withdrew to Hampton Court.[15] The projected "Triumphant Passage" through the City could not take place because of the increasing number of plague-deaths, the situation grew steadily worse, with a peak about 1 September, and the hopes of a royal entry into the City in October when Parliament opened came to nothing; it was not until 15 March 1604 that the triumphal procession could safely take place.[16] It passed from the Tower to Westminister, and in it could be seen "the nine leading actors in the King's company as members of the royal household, each of them having received four and a half yards of red cloth to wear on the occasion. The actors named were the same nine share-holders mentioned in the patent of May 17 *(sic)*, 1603."[17] In other words, one of them was William Shakespeare.

Consequently Q1, printed after 19 May but before the end of 1603, came into being in one of the bad plague years. From the publisher's point of view the situation must at first have seemed most promising for good sales: the company who owned the play were now the King's Men, the play itself, already popular, had the added attraction of dealing with the home country of the new Queen, and the coronation would as usual draw big crowds of visitors to London. It must have been important to get the book out in time, whatever manuscript was available. But then the plague increased in severity, which cannot have been without influence on conditions in the printer's office. All who could left the City, and there cannot have been many skilled labourers about who could satisfactorily decipher a manuscript or distinguish between blank verse and prose. The plague may even have had the effect that J. Roberts' printing-office closed down, whose name had been entered in the Stationers' Register under 26 July 1602 for "A booke called the Revenge of Hamlett Prince Denmarke." Could this possibly be confirmed by what happened to the series of annual almanacks printed "for the assignes of James Roberts"? Pollard & Redgrave list five (No.434, 465, 483, 525, and 532) of which copies exist for the years 1602 and 1604, but not for 1603, and another two which, with no copies extant for 1603, were printed in 1604 (No.452 and 501).[18] A full investigation into the influence of the 1603 plague on printing conditions would be necessary to carry this point beyond the sphere of probability and conjecture. Roberts' name does not occur on the title-page of Q1, but appears in Q2. As booksellers/publishers figure in Q1 "N.L. and John Trundell," in Q2 "N.L.," N.L. stands for Nicholas Ling, whose device decorates the title-pages of both Q1 and Q2. If there had been anything irregular in Ling's association with Q1, which was not printed by the copyright-holder, it is not very likely that his name would still be found in Q2.

During the plague, in which about 30,000 people died in London of a total population of not more than 250,000, the theatres had been closed for about a year—March/April/May 1603 to April 1604—and the players toured the provinces.[19] After their return to London there was plenty of time to settle down and put right what had happened in the previous months of uncertainty and confusion before, at the end of 1604 and the beginning of 1605, Q2 was brought out. Not only could Q2 rightly claim to be "enlarged to almost as much againe as it was"; it also carried as its hall-mark, instead of the more commonplace headpiece in Q1, the Royal Coat of Arms. The reference to earlier performances "in the Vniversities of Cambridge and Oxford" which was to be found in Q1 was excluded, although it must have been a sign of recognition: Hamlet could no longer be ridiculed as it had been by Nashe in 1589 when in his preface he presented it to the "gentlemen students of both universities" as an example of bad Seneca;[20] it was not only worth a marginal note as pleasing to "the wiser sort";[21] it now bore the seal of its triumph and was presented in all its glory with the full pompous speeches, the poetry and philosophy, and the exciting story from Denmark's blood-stained past.

It may be objected that Hamlet would have been a sordid play to perform on state occasions and very bad propaganda for Queen Anne's home country. But, it must be remembered, Hamlet shows the end of the strifes and miseries of an old dynasty. Fortinbras brings in fresh blood, uniting Denmark and Norway in new strength and with new hopes for the future of the twin monarchy, which was later to be reunited by Queen Anne's own great-great-grandfather, Christian I, with whom the House of Oldenburg received the Danish crown in 1448 and the Norwegian crown in 1449. If national sensitivity happened to be greater than the appreciation of a fascinating play, it could always have found comfort in the fact that it was Fortinbras who must have been the more immediate ancestor of the contemporary royal family in Denmark.

For, it may have to be stressed, to Shakespeare's contemporaries *Hamlet* was not legend but history. Firstly, we have become accustomed to the First Folio's rough division of Shakespeare's plays into comedies, histories and tragedies, perhaps without realizing that to the editors of F 1 "histories" seems to have meant only plays dealing with *English* history. Secondly, we may be influenced by modern critical historiography. Nobody would deny that among the "tragedies" such plays as *Julius Caesar* and *Antony and Cleopatra* could claim to be classified as "histories" as much as any of the plays about English kings. If pressed on this point, an Elizabethan may even have admitted, without the reservations of the modern historian, that all the other main characters of the "tragedies" were historical figures, representing the histories of Mediterranean states ancient and modern *(Coriolanus, Titus, Romeo and Juliet, Timon, Othello),* Britain and Scotland *(Cymbeline, Lear, Macbeth),* and Denmark *(Hamlet).* In the last case he would have had the full support of A. Huitfeldt, the foremost contemporary historian in Denmark (see below, p. 188).

The two names usually mentioned in connection with the "historical" sources of *Hamlet* are Saxo and Belleforest.[22] Saxo's Danish Chronicle, written about 1200, was printed for the first time in Paris (1514) in an edition by Christiernus Petri, Canon of Lund: *Danorum Regum heroumque Historię stilo elegantia Saxone Grammatico natione Sialandico necnon Roskildensis ecclesię pręposito....* Its second and third editions came out in Basle (1534) and Frankfurt (1576), after which there is a gap till the first Danish-printed edition in Latin appears in 1644. Belleforest's adaptation and dilution of Saxo was published in French from 1576 onwards,[23] but did not appear in English translation till 1608, so if any author of *Hamlet* used this source, he must either have known French sufficiently well to read it in the original language or had access to a translation in manuscript or in an earlier version now lost. We do not know if any of these conditions were met — conditions which do not apply to the four other Shakespearean works linked with Belleforest, which all had English versions[24] — and since the translation of 1608, as is generally known, has been clearly influenced by Shakespeare's play, it would be well to explore very carefully the question of whether or not any adequate alternative sources could have been used.

And there seem indeed to have been other sources which might have been used for the play, whoever first wrote it. In the sixteenth century "the wiser sort" had at their disposal a work compiled by the German Achilles Pirmin Gasser (Gassarus) (1505-1577).[25] It was published in several editions from 1533 onwards — among the seven copies in the British Museum there are four editions, the first of which was printed in Antwerp under the title of *Historiarum et chronicorum mundi epitome, velut index usque ad 1533. Accessit brevis catalogus omnium cum imperatorum tum pontificum Rom. usque ad Carolum V. & Clementem VII.* As the title indicates, the book lists the main events up to the compiler's own times from the beginning of the world. The first and last entries run (the year of the world on the left and the year before, or after, Christ on the right):

Adam and Heua primi homines finguntur.   5199

. . . .

Henricus octauus Anglicae rex, repudiata
priore uxor, alteram ducit.   1533

On the first pages of the Antwerp edition, full as they are of biblical, mythological and classical material, it is only the following Danish kings who have been considered worth mentioning: anno mundi 4609: Dan, the first Danish king, with his sons and successors Humblus and Lotherus; under 4714: Gotherus (whom the Venice editions call Gothermus); under 380 B.C.: Rhoe; under 4898: Hotterus, and under *4891: Horuuendillus decimus nonus Danie rex*. From the five eras (ætates) up to the birth of Christ only four more Danish kings, Vuermundus, Hugletus, Fridleuus and Frotho III, are mentioned out of a total of 30.[26] So here, among the most distinguished Danish kings, it is possible to find Horwendillus, Hamlet's father. Later editions of Gasser were revised and enlarged, and in the edition of 1538 ("nunc denuo quam accuratissime tum emendata, tum ab ipsomet autore diligentissime ædita") the year of the Horwendillus entry has been changed and, what is more, been expanded. It now runs in full:

4951   Antiochus Theos Syriæ tertius rex,
              hic ab uxore, ob alteram inductā,
              ueneno necatur.
              Horuuendillus rex nonus decimus
              Danię, à fratre Fengone occiditur.

The celebrated Gabriel Harvey's copy of this edition, autographed and dated 1576, is in the British Museum, with copious marginal notes. The Horwendillus entry is one of those which have been underlined and, besides, the name "Horuuendillus" has been marked with a cross. In the space between this and the previous entry he has written "veneno extinctus" opposite "ueneno necatur" as a special memento.

If a person perusing Gasser was a dramatist looking for Danish copy, this would certainly be the first place to stop: here was fratricide, and echoes from the previous line of death by poisoning. Even if it is impossible to know if the author of *Hamlet* started to read up his material systematically and began with Gasser, it is interesting to note that here we have a historical source, read in England, in which Hamlet's father is described as *King* of Denmark, killed by his brother, and in which the previous line, though with a different reference, talks about *death by poisoning*. Both these details occur in Shakespeare's *Hamlet*.

There is some ambiguity in Saxo about the status of Hamlet's father. Although the text talks about Horwendillus and Fengo as holding Jutland, under King Roricus, Horwendillus is referred to as a king both in the series of kings and in a marginal note.[27] There was still the same uncertainty in 1603, when Arrild Huitfeldt published his *Danmarckis Rigis Krønnicke/ fran Kong Dan den første/ oc indtil Kong Knud den 6. som indeholder det fornemste/ hues Saxo haffuer skreffuet /redigerit til visse Aar oc Tid* (Copenhagen), i.e. "A Chronicle of the Danish Realm, from King

188

Dan I to King Canute VI, containing the substance of what Saxo wrote, revised with definite chronology." Under Rørick, or Roricus (p.11), he refers to one Horwendillus as a man who married the King's daughter Gerutha, but adds that "others" count him among the Danish kings. So if the English dramatist made Hamlet's father king, there was a Danish "historical" tradition to support him. Fengo, too is occasionally given royal status, and so is Hamlet, once. (See below, pp. 202, 208, and 211. Cf., for Belleforest, p.211).

In 1603 Huitfeldt is still dealing with Horwendillus as a historical character, and here as in several other places it is Gassarus who is quoted as his authority on the chronology.[28] The little book from 1533 was still in use.

In his prefatory epistle Huitfeldt expresses himself in appreciative terms about Saxo's style and diction, which, he says, used to be highly praised by Erasmus and other learned men, who marvelled at the oratory of a Dane in the days when language and learning were on the decrease and barbarism on its way back (fol. aij[r] — aij[v]). Huitfeldt's opinion of Saxo had not been shared by everybody. About 1350 Saxo's Chronicle was epitomized in a version which was circulated in several manuscripts. There is a modern edition by M. Cl. Gertz.[29] What the unknown epitomist objected to in Saxo and what he thought were the reasons why Saxo was no longer so widely read was partly his lack of concentration, partly his too great demands on the reader's knowledge of Latin.[30] Therefore he sets out to give a summary in plain words of the remarkable events described ("ideo hoc opusculum, excerptum de illo, ponit planis verbis notabiliora gesta ibi descripta").[31]

Compendium Saxonis became popular: there were not a few copies in circulation, and there was a translation into Low German.[32] To give an idea of the degree of summarizing it may be mentioned that the *Compendium* reduced the Horwendillus/Hamlet story to about half of its original length. It is difficult to tell what was the European circulation of the manuscript *Compendium Saxonis* or to what extent it may have become the basis of an oral tradition. We are on firmer ground when dealing with the next link in the chain, a text which gives not only a simplified and concise version of Saxo but which was also written with a certain critical sense, namely an impressive work in Latin by Albert Krantz (Albertus Krantzius) (about 1445-1517), *Chronica Regnorum Aquilonarium Daniae Svetiae Norvagiae.*

The most comprehensive study of Krantz and his histories has been made by V. A. Nordman: *Die Wandalia des Albert Krantz* (Helsinki, 1934), which also contains a biographical chapter, and *Die Chronica Regnorum Aquilonarium des Albert Krantz* (Helsinki, 1936).[33] Nordman gives a characterization of Krantz as a historian and an assessment of his reliability and importance in this field, but is not concerned with the literary implications of the Hamlet story. The only reference to Krantz I have found in the discussion of *Hamlet's* sources is in Evans's study of *Der bestrafte Brudermord* ("Fratricide Punished"), the German play printed in 1781 which has reminiscences both of the extant Shakespeare texts of *Hamlet* and of what may have preceded them (see above, note 7). Briefly mentioning Krantz, he points out that the only episode of the Hamlet story completely missing in Krantz is the uncle's attempt to use a girl in order to ascertain whether Hamlet is insane or not.[34] The only part of Krantz's story that he is really interested in for his own purpose (i.e. a comparison with the German play) is a detail connected with Hamlet's companions on his (first) journey to England, for which he gives the parallel place in Hans Sachs.[35]

Hans Sachs's German version of the Hamlet story, though dated 23 June 1558, seems to be too distant to be immediately relevant, but it is interesting on three scores:

(a) as is shown by its title, "Historia / Fongo ein Fürst in Itlandt Erwürget sein Bruder Horwendillem" (F., a Prince in Jutland, murders his brother H.), it focuses the attention on the murder story and not on Hamlet—like Gasser;

(b) it shows the free play a re-teller of a story could give his imagination when he felt the need for some concrete detail to give life to the bare facts of his source: for example, Sachs makes Fengo/Fongo stab Horwendillus in the back when they are out hunting; if Sachs, poet and dramatist, took liberties with his material, why not Shakespeare—with the difficulties this implies in stating more definitely what sources he may have used;

(c) in his very first line Hans Sachs gives as his source "Albertus Krantz" (noted by Evans, p.9), which may be a further indication that Albert Krantz deserves more attention.[36]

Albert Krantz, who was born in Hamburg, was famous not only as a historian, but also as a member of the University of Rostock, where he was Professor, Dean and Rector, as a theologian and churchman active in Hamburg, and as a widely travelled diplomat in the service of the Lübeck Hansa, who among other things took part in negotiations in Antwerp (1491 and 1497) with the English king, Henry VII.[37] His diplomatic skill was also used by the Danish king, John ("Hans" to the Scandinavians) (*1455; 1481-1513).[38] Like so many other practical politicians he found the study of history useful in his diplomatic work, and so wrote not only his Scandinavian history, which according to Nordman is his first, but also *Wandalia* about home, Baltic and, to a certain extent, Slavonic affairs, *Saxonia* about Germany, and *Metropolis* about the diocese of Hamburg-Bremen.[39] None of these works were printed before his death. The manuscript of *Chronica Regnorum Aquilonarium* was found by chance in 1543 at a library in Cologne by Henrich Eppendorff, who took it with him and published it, not, though, in the original Latin, but in a German translation, so that it could be read by everybody. This *Dennmärckische, Schwedische und Norwaegische Chronica* came out in Strasburg in 1545 and was dedicated to the king of what was then the greatest power in Scandinavia, Christian III of Denmark (*1503; 1536-1559), who was to be grandfather of Queen Anne of Scotland and England.[40] Nordman's description of the title-page (*Die Chronica*, p.10) and subsequent comments (*Ibid.*, p.13) show that he only knew the German translation entitled *Dennmärckische Chronick*, which is likely to have been of the same content as the similarly entitled copy in the British Museum and consequently only to have comprised the Danish and not the Swedish and Norwegian sections of the Latin original. The title-page of the full translation is reproduced here from the copy in the Gothenburg University Library.

190

Dennmärckische/
Swedische/vnd
Norwägische Chronica.

Durch den hochberhümpten Albertum Kran=
tzium von Hamburg/von anfang aller Mitt
nächtischen Länderen Künigen / iren
herrlichen Thatten/ vnd zůfälligen
Kryegßhandlungen/vffs fleissigst/
bitz vff die jarzal Christi
M. D. iiij.
beschriben.

Newlich durch Henrich von Ep=
pendorff verteütscht.

⚓ Getruckt mit Keyßerlicher Maiestät
Freyheyt vff Fünff jar.
Anno M. D. xlv.

¶ Zů Straßburg bey Hans Schotten.

CHRONICA
REGNORVM
AQVILONARIVM.

DANIAE
SVETIAE
NORVAGIAE

PER

ALBERTVM KRANTZIVM
HAMBVRGEN.
descripta.

ANNO
1562.

But the original Latin manuscript was too important not to be printed as well. Its first edition, from the press of the same Strasburg printer and still dedicated to the Danish King, has on the title-page the year 1546, but the colophon on p.756 (after a note to state that the author stopped at 1502, and the errata) contains the year 1548, which consequently is the date of publication.[41] On the next page (p.757) there starts an index, which in its very first column has the reference "Ambleti ficta insania & paternae necis ultio" (Hamlet's feigned madness & revenge for his father's death)—the theme of Shakespeare's play in a nutshell.

It was not long before the Strasburg edition of 1546/8 was out of print. Nordman mentions a reprint of 1561 regretting that there is no indication of the place of publication;[42] the British Museum has a copy with the same bibliographical short-coming, but dated 1562. Nordman must be certain of his date, 1561, since in a foot-note in *Die Chronica* (p. 15), he states that Johannes Moller in *Cimbria literata*, (Copenhagen, 1744), III, 389 and in *Isagoge ad Historiam Chersonesi Cimbricae* (Hamburg, 1691), p.35, "bezeichnet auf Grund einiger alten Bücherkatalogen 1562 als Erscheinungsjahr dieser Edition." The existence of a copy in the British Museum dated 1562 proves that Moller's "old book catalogues" cannot have been wrong.[43] After the reprint of 1561/2 there followed the two Frankfurt editions of 1575 and 1583, well produced but less spaciously printed and without the decorative initials.[44] All in all, the sixteenth-century publication list for the Latin editions of Saxo and Krantz looks like this:

1514	Paris	Saxo
1534	Basle	Saxo
1546/8	Strasburg	Krantz
1561/2	Strasburg (?)	Krantz
1575	Frankfurt	Krantz
1576	Frankfurt	Saxo
1583	Frankfurt	Krantz

Even with both histories available Krantz's work cannot be said to have been the less popular, and there is no reason why they should not both have found their way to England in an age when Latin was a more international medium than French.[45] It must have been an added attraction for an English reader to find that the general tendency in Krantz was to glorify the vitality of the Germanic world—including France, England and the two Sicilies—at the cost of the Roman and Romanic world.[46] In fact, his Norwegian section has a chapter inserted in which Krantz wanted to add to the glory of the Norwegian kingdom by giving a catalogue of the English kings from William the Conqueror of Northern descent and up to Henry VII.[47] This must definitely have had an English appeal.

In this connection it may be worth remembering a contemporary piece of evidence of how well the international book-trade operated; the eloquent and enthusiastic description of the great biennial book fair at Frankfurt written by Henri Estienne le Grand (Henricus Stephanus) (1528-1598), Huguenot scholar and writer, printer and

Text continued on page 200.

pulchrum cenferi debet. Hæc dicens, in campū defcendit, & pugnam
iniens fuperatur. Alium uictor dari popofcit. Cunctantibus Danis, il
le in fuorum caſtra lætus inuehitur. Sufficere poterat forte, Patriæ li=
bertatem meruiſſe: at infolentia uiri, maius aliquid molita, Danis coe=
pit infultare, quòd neminem arbitraretur in pugnam exiturum, for=
tiſſimo eorum pugile proſtrato. Mouit exprobratio uirum in exerci=
tu Danico præcipuum Vbbonem. Non finam, inquit, dedecus hoc
inurigenti noſtræ, ut nemo aufit in duellum prodire. Sed tuum erit O
Rex, præmia uincenti decernere, quo alacrius in pugnam prodierit.
Vidiſti, inquit Rex, armillas iam ante præmio decretas. Quid erit,
ait ille, fi te rei pœniteat, tuaquè dona in alium conferas? Quo certior
fis, inquit Rex, en præmia tua. & proiecit, ut manu caperet. Cun=
què nauium intercapedinem, uis iacientis minimè fuperaret, exce=
pit unda donum proiectum. Tum Vbbo. Etiam nunc alacrior pug=
nam ineo: quando tua Rex perfpecta liberalitate, ipfe non mercenna=
tius pugil, fed fpontaneus confpicior: & hoc dicens, defilit in campū.
Circumfunditur turba fpectatrix. Ibi Vuandalus prius uictor, occu=
buit cum conforte. Credo procurante fortuna: ne alter alterius exitio,
gloriam, uoluptatemḉ perciperet.

Vbbo pu=
gil. (margin)

℃ Fengo fratrem Horuuendillum perimit, ob Iutiæ præfectu
ram unicè adminiſtrandam. Ambletus timore patrui
infaniam ſtimulat, qua commoditate, paternę necis
ultionem ingenio mirabili adfequitur.
Caput. xix.

A TEMPESTATE uiri primarij Horuuendillus ac
Fengo fratres, Iutiæ præfecti, patris loco furrogati funt. Horuuendil=
lus autem præcipua uir audacia, tantum gloriæ bellicis laudibus con=
quifiuit, ut Regis germanam coniugio mereretur. Inuidens fraternis
profectibus Fengo, cùm uirtute æquare non poſſet germanum, confi
lia uertit ad fraudem: & intercepto fratre, peremit illum, uxore eius fi=
bi deuincta. Filium illa habuit prioris mariti fanguine Ambletū, ado=
lefcentem ingenio acrem, fed nulla re magis tutum, quàm infania fimu
lata. Nam patruus illum è uita fuſtuliſſet, fi non contemptum, illi fimu
latus furor ingeneraſſet. Obferuabat adolefcentem patruus oculis cu
riofis, & multis per occafionem ingeſtis tentamentis, experiri uoluit,
fi faperet. Sed ingenium acre omnem delufit obferuantiam. Erat inter
proximos Præfecto, qui operam pertentandi polliceretur per abfenti
am Fengonis. Nam fi quid ineſſet prudentiæ, tum apud matrem ab=
fente patrono quereretur adolefcens. Itaḉ recondidit fe obferuator in
triclinio, quo uteretur matris Ambleti fecretiſſimo. Nam fi quid inter

matrem

Fengo Rex (margin)

Fratricidiū. (margin)

Fengo murders his brother Horwendillus in order to become sole
governor of Jutland. Hamlet, from fear of his uncle,
simulates insanity, which gives him an opportunity
to avenge his father's death by an ingenious trick.

Chapter xix.

Fengo King.

Lords Horwendillus and Fengo, who were brothers, were at that
time elected Governors of Jutland to succeed their father. Horwendillus, who was a man of the greatest bravery, won so much
glory by his military exploits that he was given the King's sister in
matrimony. Envy of his brother's success and inability to match him
in excellent qualities turned Fengo's mind to deceitful plans: he took

Fratricide.

his brother by surprise, killed him, won the love of his wife [*or,
and killed him, after he had won the love of his wife — see text pp. 206-
207*]. By her former husband she had a son, Hamlet by name, a
young man of sharp intelligence, and indeed it was his feigned insanity more than anything that gave him safety. For his uncle would
have taken his life, if his feigned madness had not filled Fengo with
contempt. However, the uncle kept a close watch on the young man,
and frequently, when an opportunity offered to put him to the test,
tried to find out if he was really insane. But Hamlet was clever
enough to baffle all surveillance. In the entourage of the Governor
there was a man who undertook to arrange a conclusive test in
Fengo's absence, on the grounds that if the young man had a trace
of sense in him, he would complain to his mother while the master
was away. Therefore, in order to make his observations he hid in
the room Hamlet's mother used as her private chamber. For if mother
and son were going to have a conversation, it was bound to be there.
He crept under the bed and pulled down the counterpane in order
to conceal himself while he was listening inquisitively; and his
suspicion was justified. As soon as Hamlet had entered his mother's

.matrem ac filium colloquiñ futurum esset, ibi haberetur. Stratum lecti
superinduxit delitescenti sibi, curiosius exquirenti:nec illum fefellit su
spicio . Siquidèm ingressus ad matrem Ambletus, durius obiurgat,
20 quòd cruētis fraterni occisoris manibus se pateretur amplecti. Illa stul
titiam , pueritiamqʒ obiectat nato . Tùm ille expansis brachijs , quasi **Irisantę Ā**
uolaturus,lectum conscendit, Galli cantum imitatur: & inter agendū **bleti felix**
exerto gladio,latus defodit latentis,quem pedibus sub lectulo depren **exitus.**
dit.Ilico defectum in frusta igni applicuit, coctumquè suibus proijcit
25 quo potuit secretius . Inde regressus ad matrem , docet , quid sibi uelit
stulticiæ simulatio:quòd aliàs se tutum sub Tyranno non putaret. Re
uersus Fengo,amicū oculis requirit,auditurus, quid eo absente com⸗
perisset. Vbi non aderat,rogat ubinam sit? Ambletus omnes preueni
ens,Sues,inquit,illum exederunt. Videbatur insanię plenum respon
30 sum,& erat uerum . Ablegauit priuignum , data opera,ut perimeret:
nam id famulis ut curarent iniunxit . Ille autem miro ingenio sub per⸗
sona insanientis, prudentissimis illusit , uertitqʒ fraudem in Autores.
Longam huius fabulam Saxo texuit,de Anglorum Regis filia, quam **Saxonis f**
meruit uxorem : eaqʒ repudiata, Scotorum Reginam, forma & pru⸗ **bulæ.**
35 dentia præstantem,miris ambagibus meruerit:eaqʒ traducta, redierit
in patriam. Sed rebus serijs, anilibus nenijs similes narrationes insere
re,consilium non fuit.Reuersus in Patriam Ambletus,hoc peregit,ut **Vltio:**
Regia, cum Rege & optimatibus, per occasionem conuiuij con
cremata, ultionem sumeret paternæ necis. Populoqʒ per
/10 summam prudentiam facti sui reddens rationem,
persuasit, ut non solùm in eo conquiesce⸗
rent,sed uictorem meritis lau⸗
dibus attollerent.

¶ Ambleti cum Vuicleto bellum,atquè illius in
conflictu casus.   Caput.xx.

W ICLETVS inde successit Danię sceptris,Rorico de **Vuicletu**
45 medio facto.Is Ambleti matrē uiduam, iam Regijs opi⸗ **Rex.**
bus exuerat,filiumqʒ Ambletum in concilio Procerum
semper accusabat:quòd is Letrarū Rege cōtempto(locus is erat, quē **Letræ loc**
qui teneret,summū apud Danos Imperium gerebat)Iutiæ Regnum
occupasset. Sed Ambletus uincēs in bono malū,obsequijs & muneri⸗
50 bus Regem placare,suma animi moderatione conatus est:peruincere
aūt non potuit indignati Regis animū: quòd nomini , & rerū gestarū
glorię nō tàm inuideret,quàm suo capiti timeret:qʒ se contempto, Da
norū proceres Ambletum Regem haberent . Ita querelæ in conuitia,
& illa in rixam exierunt:inde ex contentione in apertum bellum est
peruen⸗

chamber, he reproached her severely for letting herself be taken into a fratricide's gory embrace. She, on her part, upbraided her son for his foolishness and puerility. Then Hamlet stretched out his arms as if he was going to fly, jumped on to the bed, and imitated the crowing of a cock; during his play-acting he lunged out with his sword and pierced the side of the eavesdropper, whom he detected under the bed by his feet. Without delay he cut up the body, boiled the pieces, and threw them to the pigs as secretly as he could. After that he went back to his mother and told her the real reason for his simulated foolishness: he considered it the only way of being safe under the Tyrant. On his return Fengo looked round for his friend in order to learn what he had found out during his absence. When he did not appear, Fengo asked where he was. Hamlet forestalled them all by saying, "The pigs have eaten him." This answer seemed to be completely mad, and yet it was true. Now Fengo sent off his nephew on an errand with the intention of taking his life: this was what he ordered his attendants to do. But through the extraordinary ingenuity he concealed under cover of insanity, Hamlet outwitted the Governor's clever servants and turned the trickery against its authors. Saxo has spun a long yarn about Hamlet concerning the King of England's daughter whom he won as his wife, how after deserting her he won the Queen of Scotland, of outstanding beauty and intelligence, after many adventures, and how he married her and returned to his country. But it is not our purpose to include such old wives' tales in serious matter. What Hamlet did achieve after his return home was this: he burnt down the royal palace with the King and members of the aristocracy during a banquet and thus took revenge for his father's death. And by rendering an account to the people of what he had done, in a most judicious way, he convinced them so that he not only put their minds to rest but also made them extol him as victor with well-deserved praise.

Happy ending of Hamlet's insanity.

Saxo's yarns.

Revenge.

Hamlet's war with Wicletus and death in combat.

Chapter xx.

After these events Wicletus succeeded to the Danish throne after Roricus had died. He had already robbed Hamlet's widowed mother of her royal fortune, and was always accusing her son Hamlet in the Privy Council of having shown contempt of the King in Leire (this was the place whose ruler had sovereign power over the Danes) and appropriated the Realm of Jutland. But Hamlet, striving to conquer evil with good, tried in a most conciliatory spirit to placate the King by obeisance and gifts. However, he was unable to allay the indignation of the King, for Wicletus did not so much envy him for

Wicletus King.

The place called Leire.

55 peruentum, collatiscp uiribus, rurſus Ambletus Regem conuertit in
fugam. Sed ille Scaniae praefectum exautorauit: quòd non ſatis con-
ſtanter ſe geſſiſſet. Reparatiscp uiribus, rurſus Ambleto bellū denun-
ciat. Iam quietis erat Ambletus, poſt longum militie laborem cupidiſ-
ſimus. Quid faceret? Vrgebat ab alterius parte ignominia recuſati diſ-
60 criminis, & poterat inferre nolenti: ab altera uerò commouerat deſy-
deratae quietis magna expectatio. Sed peruicit in uiro militari, bellici
ſplendoris reſpectus. Itacp bellum denuncianti, ſe refert occurſurum.
Vxorius iam erat, tanta illi uiciſſitudine amoris connexus, ut magis illius uiduitatem, quàm ſui diſcriminis periculum penſitaret. Illa mulie-
65 briter in maritum conuerſa, Ego inquit, mi coniunx, quem per maria
ſecuta ſum, etiam pugnantem non deſeram: idem mihi qui tibi uite fu-
turus eſt exitus. Credidit ille, & hoc animo in prelia mouit. Non abe-
rat longè, coniunx magnificè pollicita, cùm praelium ageretur. Sed
Ambletus tum conſertis uiribus, Ambletus cecidit. Egregia coniunx, oblita pro-
cadit. miſſi, foeminea fide in amplexus uictoris uolitabat. Hic Ambleti exi-
70 tus fuit: qui ſi parem nature ac fortune indulgentiam fuiſſet expertus,
aequaſſet fulgore Superos, Herculea uirtutibus opera tranſcendiſſet.
Vuicletum, tranquillam, ac diutinam Regni procuratione emenſum,
tandem morbus abſumpſit.

⊂ Vuermundus Vuicleti filius patri ſuccedit. Vſſo Vuer-
mundi filius, pro patre caeco, uno congreſſu binos
Duello ſternit; decp illius & corporis, & ar-
morum robore.   Caput. XXI.

Vuermun- VERMVNDVS illi filius heres extitit, ſceptricp poſt
dus Rex. patrem moderator. Hic prolixis tranquillitatis ocijs, feliciſſima temporum quiete decurſis, diutinam domeſtice pacis conſtantiam, incon-
cuſſa Rex ſecuritate tractabat. Sed hanc temporum ſuorum felicitatē
diu coniunx fuſcauerat. Adeò nihil eſt ab omni parte beatum. Iam in
Vſſo gigas. ſenium uergens, filium accepit Vſſonem, corporis mole cito grandeſ-
centem, ſed tam hebete ſenſu, tamcp lingua pigritante, ut diu plumbe-
us ſtipes haberetur: ſed in eo homine tam inſignis facta eſt rerum, mo-
rumcp conuerſio, quanta unquàm in ullo mortalium potuit eſſe maxi-
ma: ut ex ignauiſſimo fortiſſimus, ex ſtolido prudentiſſimus, ex mu-
to diſertiſſimus euaderet. Dum adhuc adoleſcentiam ageret, ſub im-
prudentiae titulo, ſplendidiſſimi uiri Frouuini, quem Iutiae praefece-
rat, filiam uxorem illi deſpondit: ut optimi ſoceri praeſidio, & floren-
tiſſimorum iuuenum, filiorum eius opera, tutius regnaret. Illatum eſt
Iutiae bellum ab Rege Suetie: quo in prelio ex prouocatione pugnans
Frouuinus, cadit. Toto perinde agmine uictor laetus in ſua redit. Poſt
ea infeſto

his fame and the glory he had won as fear for his own life and that the Danish nobility would turn away from him and have Hamlet for their King. Therefore grievance turned into quarrelling, and quarrelling into abuse; from contention there arose open war, and after joining battle Hamlet put the King to flight. But the King deposed the Governor of Scania for not showing enough constancy on the battlefield, gathered new forces, and again declared war on Hamlet. But now, after the long labours of war, Hamlet was very eager for peace. What was he to do? If he did not take up the gauntlet, there threatened ignominy for refusing a decisive battle—and, after all, the King was able to force a fight upon him even if he should refuse; on the other hand he was inspired with great longing for the peace he desired. However, he was a warrior, and consideration of military splendour prevailed. Therefore his answer to the King's challenge was that he would meet him on the battlefield. Hamlet was now deeply attached to his wife and so much in love with her (and she with him) that he cared more for *her* widowhood than the mortal danger connected with a decisive battle. She, on her part, turned to her husband, in the manner wives do, and said, "My dear husband! I have come with you across the sea, and I am not going to desert you in your battle. My life will have the same end as yours." He believed her, and in that spirit went off to the wars. She was not far away, this wife of magnificent promises, when the battle was joined. But in this combat Hamlet was killed. Forgetful of her promise, his excellent wife kept faith in women's fashion and hastened into the arms of the victor. This was the end of Hamlet, a man who, if nature and fortune had been as lavish in their gifts, would have equalled the gods in splendour and through his virtues excelled the labours of Hercules. Wicletus, who lived through a long and peaceful reign, was finally carried off by an illness.

Hamlet killed in battle.

bookman. His *Francofordiense Emporium, sive Francofordienses Nundinae* was published in 1574 and should consequently well reflect conditions at the time when the Frankfurt editions of Saxo and Krantz came out. In this volume (of which there is a copy in the British Museum) once gratefully dedicated to the magistrates of Frankfurt, Estienne relates how "those celebrated universities of Vienna, of Wittenberg, of Leipzig, of Heidelberg, of Strasburg, and, among other nations, those of Louvain, of Padua, of Oxford, of Cambridge—these academies, I say, and many others which it would take too long to enumerate, send to the Fair not only their philosophers, but also poets, representatives of oratory, of history, of the mathematical sciences, some even skilled in all these branches at once."[48]

If, for reasons indicated above (p.187), we leave Belleforest out of account, it would not be surprising if it was through Krantz that the writer of *Hamlet* made his first acquaintance with the Horwendillus/Hamlet story. Krantz's history was more modern than Saxo's and perhaps easier to obtain. Even if both were within easy reach, it would only have been human not to tackle the more ambitious text first: Krantz was less detailed, and his Latin was simple enough compared with Saxo's. What is more, Krantz gives an explicit reference to Saxo, so anybody who wanted another and a fuller version just had to take it and follow it up.

The relevant section of Krantz's chronicle does not amount to more than about 650 words, that is to say between an eighth and a ninth of the corresponding text in Saxo, which runs to about 5,500 words. It is rendered here with a parallel translation into English. The facsimile text is from the first Latin edition of 1546/8. The copy it has been taken from is the one in Gothenburg University Library, to which thanks are due for permission to reproduce the text. The numbering of the lines has been added for easier reference to the text of the article, and is followed in the translation as closely as possible. (See text and translation above, pp. 194-199.)[49]

As regards the text itself, the Frankfurt editions differ slightly from the Strasburg printing in spelling and punctuation. They both have *coniux* for *coniunx* (l. 68), in spite of *coniunx* in ll. 64 and 57. There are no chapter headings, and the marginalia have been changed. They are only three, and run as follows.

Against 1. 2:	Fengo fratris à se cæsi coniugem & regnum inuadit.	Fengo kills his brother and takes his wife and his kingdom.
Against 1.18:	Insaniæ prudens simulatio.	A well-advised simulation of madness.
Against 1.56:	Ambleti de rege victoria, deinde mors.	Hamlet's victory over the King and subsequent death.

The two Frankfurt editions are almost identical, the only differences being in some points of spelling (not punctuation), in the division of lines, and in the size of the printed surface on the page.[50]

Krantz's dependence upon Saxo is common knowledge;[51] a full list of the places that go back to him, including the Horwendillus/Hamlet story, is given by Nordman.[52] This does not mean slavish copying; the only passage lifted straight from Saxo (apart from the trivial collocation "Reuersus Fengo" in ll. 26-27) consists of

200

the contrasting epitaphs of Hamlet and Vuicletus ("Hic . . . absumpsit." in ll. 70-74).[53] Such loans were by no means uncommon in an age with different views on originality from our own.[54] But it is difficult to improve on Saxo's grandiloquent conclusion, which thus may have met the English dramatist's eye for the first time in Krantz's *Chronica*. This is the passage that gives the mould for the Hamlet character as we know him: the man on whom nature had lavished her gifts and to whose fate overtones cling of great things that might have been. The direct reference, if it is a reference, is used by Hamlet about himself, but with an original touch of irony: "My father's brother; but no more like my father /Than I to Hercules" (I.ii.153).[55] The general feeling of Hamlet's superiority is there all the time, so much so that the play could be said to be built round the theme of *seem, be*,[56] and *would-have-been*. Hamlet is the "expectancy and rose of the fair state" (III.i.152). When he is dead, Fortinbras, a man of action and of few words, even finds time in the long string of orders for practical arrangements to give him the epitaph: "For he was likely, had he been put on,/To have prov'd most royal" (V.ii.389-390). And it is left to the spectator's imagination what would have been if Claudius and not Polonius had hidden behind the arras in the Queen's closet.

It is interesting to note that in the corresponding place Belleforest declares that as regards Hamlet, "if his fortune had been equall with his inward and naturall giftes, *I know not which of the auncient Grecians and Romans* had been able to have compared with him for vertue and excellencie."[57] He does mention the name "Hercule" later on, but only after having enlarged upon the reasons for Hamlet's undoing: that he had the fault of not being a man who was "seigneur, et dompteur de ses affections" and restrained "the unbridled desires of his concupiscence" but gave way to "the desires and inticements of his flesh," which caused him to "become a foole, and (as it were) incensed, dote on the presence of women" ("fol et insencé à la poursuite des femmes").[58] "De telle faute," Belleforest continues, "a esté chargé le grand Hercule des Hebrieux Sanson" ("This is the fault that Samson has been accused of, the great Hercules of the Hebrews"—or, in the somewhat obscure translation of 1608, "This fault was in the great Hercules, Sampson").[59] Belleforest thus mentions the name Hercules in connection with the fatal blemish in Hamlet's character—which completely changes the emphasis (from a man of virtue to excel the labours of Hercules to an infatuated fool like the great Hercules of the Hebrews), and, besides, uses it metaphorically and not in a direct reference. Therefore, even if the name occurs in both Saxo, Krantz, and Belleforest, it would seem that the sense in which it is used in Shakespeare's *Hamlet* agrees more with the two Latin texts than with Belleforest.

Krantz shows his independence of Saxo not only by a drastic compression of the material, but also by his critical attitude, reflected in ll. 33-37 (with the scathing marginal note "Saxonis fabulæ").[60] These lines refer (a) to Hamlet's first visit to England (the visit Shakespeare was later to make him start in the company of Rosencrantz and Guildenstern), which lasted for a whole year and during which he married the King of England's daughter,[61] and (b) to his second visit to England, his journey to Scotland and his bigamy with the Scottish Queen, all of which took place after his revenge.[62] Modern research has shown how sound Krantz's judgement was: Jørgen Olrik declares that story (a) has its origins in an Oriental tale, and that story (b) is a separate romance deriving from Saxo's own times and strongly influenced by the chivalrous literature of Western Europe.[63] There is nothing about Hamlet's vagaries in Britain in Shakespeare's play. This does not mean that Saxo has been dropped as a source at the end of the Third Book, where the revenge is described, but also that the episode of Hamlet's first marriage, *before* the revenge, has been omitted. It would of course not have been beyond the playwright's dramatic sense to achieve that concentration by himself, but here is Krantz's book which makes it perfectly clear what is fable and what is not. It may have given the direction of the dramatist's thoughts from the very start, before Hamlet's relationship to the women had yet taken shape in his mind, or it may at least have given him authorization for simplifying his plot. It is also worth mentioning that there is no indication in Krantz of the length of Hamlet's first stay in England (cf. ll. 33-37). Saxo, on the other hand, makes him spend a whole year there (Liber Tertius VI:22: "Apud quem annum emensus, impetrata profectionis licentia, patriam repetit"). If the English dramatist had read Krantz, he would not feel that it mattered however short he made Hamlet's stay.

With Belleforest as a primary source there would have been much greater difficulty in seeing the wood for the trees. Not only does Belleforest follow Saxo; he manages to spin out the yarn about Hamlet's one-year stay in England to nearly three times its length in Saxo's chronicle. He is not content to tell the straightforward story of how Hamlet rejected food and drink at the English King's banquet because of their unpalatable origin (which nobody else knew of), how he was able to reveal the King's and the Queen's low birth (which was unknown to themselves), and how this so filled the King with admiration of Hamlet's wisdom that he gave him his daughter in marriage. Belleforest goes out of his way to give a discourse on Hamlet's powers of divination.[64]

Of the rest of the marginalia in (S), the second and fifth give the beginning and the end: the fratricide and the revenge. The fact that they stand out as headings may have branded "Vltio" on the reader's brain in such a way that it could resound so vigorously in the ghost scene in *Hamlet*.[65] The first marginal note is interesting as referring to "Fengo Rex" in the same way as the sixth talks about "Vuicletus Rex." This is in fact only a consequence of regarding Horwendillus as a king (see above, p. 188), though there is no such reference in Krantz. Again, if the status of Horwendillus and Fengo was uncertain to scholars and professional historians, it shows no radical initiative on the part of a dramatist if he set the scene in the royal Danish court.[66]

There is another point to be added here. As Dover Wilson rightly points out, contemporary near-at-hand material was used to fill in the details of the picture at this time when the historic sense, as we see it, had not yet awakened.[67] If now, as we have reason to believe, some first-hand knowledge of things Danish was used for *Hamlet,* any conclusion drawn from the contemporary state of affairs would rather have increased than decreased the confusion. Sønderjylland (South Jutland), as it was still named in Saxo's days, after 1386 called Slesvig, was from 1460 united with Holsten, a fief of the Germano-Roman Empire, in which year the Danish king, Christian I, became Duke of Slesvig and Count of Holsten. In 1490 it was divided between King John (Hans) and his younger brother, Frederick, but in 1523, when Duke Frederick became King Frederick I, it became sole possession of the Danish King. His son, later Christian III, succeeded him, but from 1544 shared Slesvig-Holsten with his two younger brothers, Hans and Adolph. After Christian III came Frederick II (1559-1588) and Hans died in 1580, after which the number of princes was only two. Adolph died in 1586, to be succeeded in turn by his three sons Frederick (†1587), Philip (†1590) and John Adolph (†1616). To summarize, these were the stages:

King John	+Duke Frederick	
	(later King Frederick I)	
King Frederick I		
King Christian III		
King Christian III	+Duke Hans	+Duke Adolph
King Frederick II	+Duke Hans	+Duke Adolph
King Frederick II	+	Duke Adolph and his sons.

With Danish kings as "Dukes of Jutland" and brothers, uncles and nephews of kings as co-dukes, one of whom became a king, it must have been very easy, especially for an outsider, to get mixed up, and it must have seemed to make little difference if "Iutiæ præfecti" with their exalted rank, were made directly associated with the throne.

To make matters even more complicated, the Danish kings made repeated attempts to incorporate the adjoining territory of Ditmarsh along the North Sea between the rivers Eider and Elbe. On its final pages the Danish section of Krantz's chronicle describes King John's unsuccessful campaign in the year 1500. In 1559, however, Frederick II and his two brothers, Dukes Hans and Adolph, won a victory and divided the territory between them. The long time it took before the Ditmarsh question was finally settled must account for the fact that to Belleforest Ditmarsh is the same as Jutland, surprising as it may seem.[68] However, this very confusion may be taken as a sign that it was as natural to associate Jutland with Sønderjylland/ Slesvig as it was to associate Jutish dukes with Danish kings.

The Hamlet story, as Krantz tells it, obviously does not give a great many details, but still has some interesting features. With all the rich material at his disposal he manages to organize it in the fashion of a good narrator: by grouping it round an episode which is told more fully than the rest. The episode he chooses is the equivalent of the closet scene, to which he devotes about half of Chapter xix (ll. 12-30). Moreover, this passage has, at its climax, been given the only remaining marginal note of the chapter, the appreciative "Insanię Ambleti felix exitus": after Hamlet's brilliant performance in the closet, the revenge itself seems to have been merely a matter of routine.

It is in this central passage that we can expect the most interesting details. The eavesdropper, who is not mentioned by name, is in Fengo's entourage (ll. 12-13) and later referred to as his friend (l. 27), all in agreement with Saxo (and Belleforest). His plan is put into practice during Fengo's absence, and again Saxo and Belleforest agree, but there is a difference in the description of the hiding-place. In Saxo, Hamlet lies down in the straw (Liber Tertius VI: 13: "Submissusque stramento delituit").[69] In Krantz, he is lying under the bed when Hamlet kills him (l. 23): his feet were showing in spite of the fact that he had made an effort to conceal himself: he had "pulled down the counterpane over himself where he lay hidden" (ll. 16-17). In Belleforest, before the event, when the friend puts his plan to the King, he suggests that Hamlet should be shut up alone with his mother in a chamber "dans laquelle soit cache quelqu'un au desseu de l'un et de l'autre" ("in which someone should be hidden unbeknownst to them both").[70] The post-*Hamlet* English translation of 1608 expands this into "wherein some other should secretly be hidden *behind the hangings,* unknowne either to him or his mother."[71] This, so far, is only the friend's suggestion and not a description of what actually happened. When we reach the stage in Belleforest, he says that the man entered the Queen's chamber "se cachant souz quelque loudier," which the 1608 translation renders "and there hid himselfe *behind the arras.*"[72] The disputable point is *behind* for *souz*. The word *loudier* means "couverture," "matelas,"[73] or, as Godefroy paraphrases it, "couvre-pied, courte-point de lit "[74] —in other words "bedspread," or "counterpane"—and *souz* is definitely "under."

But before drawing any conclusions let us look at the following, where the same point reoccurs. Saxo, with the friend of Fengo hidden in the straw makes Hamlet jump about, feel a lump under his feet, and pierce the eavesdropper with his sword (Liber Tertius VI:13).[75] Krantz makes him jump on to the bed, flapping his arms as if they were wings and crowing like a cock—obviously to show the "sleeper" that it was time to get up, whereupon he suddenly drives his sword into the side of the man hiding under the bed (ll. 21-23). Belleforest writes that Hamlet "sauta sur ce loudier[76], ou sentant qu'il y avoit dessous quelque cas caché, ne faillit aussi tost d'y donner dedans à tout son glaive," ("jumped *on to the bedspread,* where, feeling that something was hidden underneath, he did not tarry to pierce it with his sword"). This is the well-known point where the English translation of 1608 adds the "rat" line from Shakespeare's play. It runs: "[Hamblet] began to come like a cocke beating with his armes, (in such manner as cockes use to strike with their wings) *upon the hangings* of the chamber: whereby, feeling something *stirring* under them, he cried, A rat, a rat! and presently drawing his sword thrust it *into the hangings.*"[77] Even if there is nothing in Belleforest about Hamlet discovering the feet under the bed, there is nothing either to contradict that the eavesdropper should be in the same position as in Krantz. Belleforest's reference to "underneath" could mean either under the counterpane or under the bed (I have checked this with French speakers). If the man had been lying under the counterpane *on* the bed, there would have been no need for Hamlet to jump "sur ce loudier" to *feel* that there was something hidden "dessous": he would have seen it. And, after all, it is hardly likely that the man would have chosen such an exposed hiding-place without even having somebody to arrange the counterpane on top of him so as to divert suspicions. If, on the other

204

hand, he was hiding *under* the bed, jumping on the bed would be the right method to discover if there was a lump underneath, the support for the mattress being "a trellis of leather straps nailed to the bed frame."[78]

The "hangings" *behind* which the eavesdropper concealed himself are consequently the invention of the English translator. Since he took the "rat" line from Shakespeare's play, it may be that he had seen a production with Polonius behind hangings and adopted that as well. There is nothing in the stage directions of either the Quartos or the Folios to indicate where Polonius hid,[79] and so no way of ascertaining what the stage business was originally meant to be. It would of course be easier and also more dignified for Polonius to hide behind the hangings in an upright position. It is true that in Shakespeare (IV.i.9-12) the Queen reporting her son's deed to the King says that Hamlet "*Behind the arras* hearing something stir,/Whips out his rapier, cries 'A rat, a rat!'/And in his brainish apprehension kills/The unseen good old man," but it would still go well with Krantz's version, since arras does not necessarily stand for wall hanging but also for coverlet.[80]

Though it would be difficult to reach certainty on this point, there are two things in favour of Polonius hiding under the bed: one is, that Hamlet's "How now! a rat?" (III.iv.23) would be more natural if referring to Polonius's helpless squeaks from under the bed, as would the immediate thrust of Hamlet's sword to kill the rat; the second is, that if Polonius were killed under the bed, his dead body would not have to topple over and then remain prostrate on the floor as a distraction during the rest of this scene; it would be more naturally out of the way until it was dragged out by Hamlet.

Stage business that followed Krantz would also fit into the dramatic context. Hamlet comes to his mother's closet fresh from his frustration at not being able to exact a full revenge from the King in prayer. His most ardent wish is to find him "When he is drunk asleep; or in his rage,/Or in th' incestuous pleasure of his bed" (III.iii.89-90). It is psychologically correct that on hearing the squeaks he should jump to the conclusion that they are coming from the King, as he himself confesses after the event (III.iv.32: "I took thee for thy better"). And what could have better confirmed his suspicions than the presence of somebody in the classical position of a man surprised in a lady's bedroom?

However the scene may have been done on the stage, and whichever may have been the dramatist's direct source, the fact that there is such close agreement between Krantz and Belleforest shows that the one could very well have been the source of the other. There is nothing in the chronology to prevent this, as can be seen from the following Belleforest complement to the Saxo/Krantz list given above on page 193:

1576	Lyon
1582	Paris
1583	Lyon
1601	Lyon
1604	Rouen
1608	London (English translation).

The dates have been given according to Evans, *op.cit.*, p.73.

After Krantz has dwelt on Hamlet's ability of quick action in a dangerous situation, he gives an example of his verbal wit. This is the only occurrence of direct speech in the chapter and the only time, apart from the criticism of Saxo, that the author makes a personal comment (ll. 29-30). There are parallels in *Saxo* (and Belleforest), but they are purely descriptive, more wordy, and do not make the point so neatly. Saxo's version runs as follows: "[Amlethus] in cloacam illum ivisse retulit perque eius ima collapsum ac nimia cæni mole obrutum a subeuntibus passim porcis esse consumptum. Quod dictum, tametsi veri confessionem exprimeret, quia specie stolidum videbatur, autoribus ludibrio fuit." (Liber Tertius VI:15), or, in Oliver Elton's translation of 1894: "[Amleth] replied that the man had gone to the sewer, but had fallen through its bottom and been stifled by the floods of filth, and that he had been devoured by the swine that came up all about that place. This speech was flouted by those who heard; for it seemed senseless, though really it expressly avowed the truth."[81] Belleforest's version has been well rendered by his first English translator of 1608: "[Hamlet] answered and sayd, that the counsellor he sought for was gone downe through the privie, where being choaked by the filthynesse of the place, the hogs meeting him had filled their bellyes."[82]

In neither of these two versions is Hamlet's utterance so emphatic as in Krantz: "Sues illum ederunt." In this form, with the author's subsequent rather pedantic remark (derived from Saxo), it must have stuck better in a reader's mind, and may have been the seed of the dialogue in *Hamlet*, IV.iii.17-20:

> *King.* Now, Hamlet, where's Polonius?
> *Hamlet.* At supper.
> *King.* At supper! Where?
> *Hamlet.* Not where he eats, but where 'a is eaten.

It may be noted that Hamlet's utterance in Krantz appealed to Hans Sachs's ear for drama so much that he adopted it, preceded by a cheerful Bavarian interjection ("Hoha jn haben die Sew gfressen"; fol. CLII^r).

Apart from its central episode, Krantz's narrative is rather bare of detail, but all the time it bears the author's stamp of clarity and simplicity. Horwendillus figures in ll. 1-4, where nothing is added to Saxo; his wife is not mentioned by name: she is either "Regis germana" (l. 4) or "mater Ambleti" (l.16). His brother, called Fengo as in Saxo, deceitfully killed him. Krantz goes on to say, "uxore eius sibi deuincta" (ll. 6-7). The past participle would make it natural to take the phrase to mean "after he had tied his wife to himself (after he had won the love of his wife)." This may be euphemistically vague, coming from a man of the Church, and really indicate the adultery that Belleforest openly alleges.[83] But it may simply mean "after he had made his wife infatuated with him" or, with the loose use of the past participle, "and won her love," which may perhaps even simply imply "and married her." The rather drastic marginal note in (F), "Fengo fartris à se cæsi coniugem & regnum inuadit" would seem to indicate that Fengo took first his brother's wife and then his kingdom (*sic*), but the order may be editorial (human before non-human), rather than real.

The best rendering of the "deuincta" passage is probably the Ghost's own words in *Hamlet* (I.v.43 ff.): "With witchcraft of his wits . . . won [to his shameful lust / The will of my most seeming virtuous queen.]" This passage in Shakespeare "is not necessarily evidence of infidelity by Gertrude *before* her husband's death."[84] It is not only that the word *adulterate* "was used of almost any sexual immorality."[85] If it was a crime to marry a brother's wife after his death, the Ghost's outburst "Ay, that incestuous, that adulterate beast" (l.42) is sufficiently warranted where it comes. In the Ghost's well-planned speech we have just had his story about how he was stung by the serpent that now wears his crown (ll. 34-39), and what we are just going to hear might well be interpreted as the Queen's "falling off" from being faithful to the memory of her dead husband to incest with his much inferior brother. The Ghost's words in l. 42 could refer to the present state of things ("that beast who now lives in incest and adultery [because he has married my wife]") instead of to the past ("that beast who before my death committed adultery with my wife" — with "adultery" used in the modern sense of the word). When, after interrupting himself at the scent of the morning air (l. 58), the Ghost has given the horrible details about his murder, he sums up: "Thus was I, sleeping, by a brother's hand / Of life, of crown, of queen, at once dispatch'd" (ll. 74-75). Perhaps the order life — crown — queen is significant.

Even in Belleforest the context in which Geruthe's adultery is mentioned should be carefully considered before too much importance is attached to it. It is not presented as one of the main links in the chain of events. The narrator is concerned with Fengo's road to power: his envy, his plans, and his success, reached when he slays his brother at a banquet (a scene without equivalent in Saxo). But then he discusses how Fengo could carry out his plans so effectively "that no man once so much as suspected him" and how he cunningly "purged himselfe of so detestable a murther to his subjects."[86] He had sullied with incest his brother's bed and abused the wife of a man whose honour he ought to have aspired to attain ("il avoit incestueusement souillé la couche fraternelle, abusant de la femme de celuy, duquel il devoit . . . pourchasser l'honneur")[87] in order to win over Geruthe so that he could get away with the murder: she was after all the daughter of the King with great power to intervene. Before the common people and the nobility he then plays the hero: he pretends to have defended the lady from being innocently killed by his brother, which he has confirmed by false witnesses. This wins him the admiration of the court, and although it means incest, he even dares to marry her. It is obvious that this is no romance but cold-blooded calculation: Fengo's aim is a checkmate, and the queen has to be taken in the course of the game. In Geruthe's case it is the marriage that is the crowning wickedness. As opposed to his English translator, Belleforest shows compassion with her because she has had a rough deal. She is "celle qu'il [Fengo] entretenoit execrablement, durant la vie du bon Horvvendille" when the English translation for "treated execrably" says "used as his concubine"; she is "celle mal-hereuse" and "souffrit de s'abaisser," which in the English rendering is extended to "the unfortunate and wicked woman" whereas "souffrit" is left out; and the chapter in Belleforest does not end with a condemnation of the women for their faithlessness, as might have been expected, but with a probing question for the men: "If now woman is such an imperfect creature as they say, and they find this beast so impossible to tame as they complain of, why are they such fools as to run after them and so feeble and brutish as to entrust themselves to their caresses?", where the English translator tendentiously embroiders: "their deceitfull and wanton imbraceings," whereupon he adds for good measure, "But let us leave her in this extreamitie of laciviousnesse, and proceed to shewe you in what sort the yong prince Hamblet behaved himselfe, to escape the tyranny of his uncle."[88] The strict puritanism of the English translation must not be allowed to conceal Belleforest's true attitude to Geruthe. What is even more important to note is that Belleforest is stronger in his condemnation of the incestuous marriage with the murderer than in his judgement of what she "abased herself to" when her husband was alive: "celle mal-hereuse ... souffrit de s'abaisser jusques à telle villenie, que de luy faucer la foy (to be unfaithful to him): et qui pis est, espouser encor celuy, lequel estoit le meutrier tiran de son espoux legitime (*and what is worse even marry* the tyrant who murdered her legitimate husband).[89] Finally, not even Belleforest has any reference to adultery before the murder, when Geruthe's crime is brought up again in the equivalent of the closet scene.

To sum up, even if it is indisputable that adultery before the murder is mentioned in Belleforest, it is not certain that there is any evidence of it in Shakespeare's *Hamlet*. The point should not be pressed, since even in Belleforest it seems to be only of indirect relevance.

The rest of the Fengo story in Krantz's text is stripped of many of the details we find in Saxo and Belleforest. The most important of them is that which Evans has already noted (see above, p.189): Krantz has no equivalent of that episode in the story which may have contained the germ of the nunnery scene, with Ophelia as the bait for Hamlet to give himself away. The dramatist's source might have been either Saxo or Belleforest.

How did Fengo come to be called Claudius? Of course Latin chronicles gave all the kings latinized names, whatever their nationality, and one name is as good as another. But in Krantz there occurs a rather strange coincidence. There is one more place in his chronicle in which Ambletus appears. It is a much later chapter in the Norwegian section, which however must have been of a certain interest to British readers since it shows how before the Romans the Danes often took the chance to ravage Britain and Ireland.[90] It gives a rapid sweep over the centuries, and after dealing with Froto (the First) of Denmark it goes on: "Inde post aliquot secula Fridleuus Daniae Rex, post uastatam Hyberniam, oppidumque eius Duflinam euersum: Britanniam populatur. Et ante illum Ambletus Iutiae Praefectus: cum apud eundem Britanniae Regem exularet, in quas uoluit conditiones perpulit."[91] (After several centuries the Danish king, Fridleuus, then ravaged Britain, after laying Ireland waste and destroying its town, Dublin. And before him Hamlet, Governor of Jutland, forced his terms upon the same British king with whom he was staying as an exile.) Immediately after this a sentence each is awarded to Froto, the aged King who subdued Britain at the time when Christ was born, Caius Caesar, who "came to Britain without glory before he occupied the Kingdom, *Claudius,* who then made Britain into a province, and Seuerus, who quenched a rebellion there."[92] The Claudius mentioned is of course the Claudius of the Roman invasion of A.D. 43, but it is not difficult to imagine how easily an eye glancing over the page for information about Hamlet could have swept over the names in the next few sentences and how quite fortuitously an associative connection could have been established which at a later moment came in handy.

In the rest of his first Hamlet chapter Krantz does not add anything to what is already in Saxo (or was to appear in Belleforest), but his concentration and the repetition that goes with his simple language serve to stress certain points. Thus Krantz does not leave any doubt about Hamlet's youth, nor about his intelligence and good judgement: "adolescens" is used three times (ll. 7/8, 10, 15); there are references to his "ingenium mirabile" (headline), "ingenium acre" (ll. 8, 12), and "mirum ingenium" (l. 31), as well as to his "prudentia" (ll. 14 ff., 40). Hamlet feels insecure (headline, ll. 8, 26), and so feigns madness (headline, ll. 8/9, 9/10, 26, 29-30, 31-32), which helps him to elude his stepfather (ll. 9-10, 29-30), to surprise the eavesdropper (ll. 21-23), and to turn their own weapon against those who had orders to have him killed (ll. 31-32). His mother, however, is taken into his confidence (ll. 25-26), and there is nothing to say that she betrays it. This may seem remarkable with regard to what has gone before: not only has Hamlet killed a man in her room and dispensed with the body in a most macabre way, as it seems, under her very eyes, but, what is more, there has been a violent altercation in which no words have been minced (ll. 19-21); it is however in keeping with Saxo, Belleforest—and Shakespeare's play.

Krantz is here commendably concise, whereas Saxo takes the opportunity to compose a long speech for Hamlet, which Belleforest seems to have enjoyed so much that he extends it to a "harangue" about four times its length. Although, for all his brevity, Krantz gives the gist of Hamlet's speech, there is of course nothing to have prevented the English dramatist who may have used him from looking also at the fuller version in Saxo. In fact, there seems to be an indication that Saxo has been used. Hamlet's last words to his mother after he has revealed his secret and he has told her how superfluous it is for her to cry over his foolishness ("desipientia") instead of her own disgrace, are: "Cetera silere memineris" (Liber Tertius VI: 14).[93] They are generally taken to mean: "Remember to keep quiet about the rest,"[94] but there is nothing grammatically against "Remember the rest is silence" (with *cetera* as the accusative of the "accusative-with-infinitive" instead of the object of *silere)*[95]. The position of the sentence at the end of a long speech, its brevity, and the juxtaposition "Cetera silere" certainly make it look more than a coincidence that we should find it in an even more memorable form in the play as the dying Hamlet's last words, (V.ii.350), rounding off not merely an episode, but a life.

Krantz's chapter on Hamlet's revenge ends with a scene (ll. 39-43) that does not occur in Shakespeare's *Hamlet,* but which is well known from another of his plays, one that must have been in his mind at about the same time: *Julius Caesar.*[96] Saxo (as later Belleforest) gives the fuller story (Liber Quartus I:1-7) with Hamlet's great oration to the people. Hamlet's situation here is reminiscent both of Brutus's and of Mark Antony's. He has to answer to the people for a killing, like Brutus, but like Antony he also has to sway the people from a possible allegiance to Fengo to loyalty to himself, and like Antony he appeals to their feelings by using as his main argument the glorious memory of an assassinated man—his father. It would have been tempting to follow up this excursus more fully, but attention may just be drawn to a few places in Saxo, quoted here in Elton's translation. [Hamlet was first "in hiding till he had learnt what way the mob of the uncouth populace was tending." In the morning they found the ashes of the palace.] "Also they saw the body of Feng lying pierced by the sword, amid his blood-stained raiment. Some were seized with open anger, others with grief, and some with secret delight." [Hamlet came out, "finding the people so quiet" and began his speech:] "Behold the corpse, not of a prince, but of a fratricide. Indeed, it was a sorrier sight when ye saw our prince lying lamentably butchered by a most infamous fratricide—brother, let me not call him. With your own compassionating eyes ye have beheld the mangled limbs of Horwendil; they have seen his body done to death with many wounds. ... The hand that slew him made you slaves. Who then so mad as to choose Feng the cruel before Horwendil the righteous? Remember how benignantly Horwendil fostered you, how justly he dealt with you, how kindly he loved you. Remember how you lost the mildest of princes and the justest of fathers, while in his place was put a tyrant and an assassin set up . . . . "[97] In connection with this Antony part of Hamlet's speech there then follows a Brutus part, describing the evils that struck the country during Fengo's reign. Hamlet goes on: "And now all this is over; for ye see the criminal stifled in his own crimes, the slayer of his kin punished for his misdoings. What man of but ordinary wit, beholding it, would account this kindness a wrong? What sane man could be sorry that the crime has recoiled upon the culprit? Who could lament the killing of a most savage executioner? or bewail the righteous death of a most cruel despot? Ye behold the doer of the deed; he is before you. Yea, I own that I have taken vengeance for my country and my father. Your hands were equally bound to the task which mine fulfilled. What it would have beseemed you to accomplish with me, I achieved alone. ... Now haste up speedily, heap the pyre, burn up the wicked ... These must be the tyrant's obsequies, this the funeral procession of the fratricide."[98] Hamlet then goes on to stir their compassion for his own fate as well as for *his mother's* ("Pity also my stricken mother, and rejoice with me that the infamy of her who was once your queen is quenched. For this weak woman had to bear a twofold weight of ignominy, embracing one who was her husband's brother and murderer"), whereupon he does his summing up on the theme "Acknowledge my service, honour my wit, give me the throne if I have earned it."[99] "Every heart," Saxo resumes his narration, "had been moved while the young man thus spoke; he affected some to compassion, and some even to tears. When the lamentation ceased, he was appointed king (*sic*) by prompt and general acclaim."[100]

The last part of the speech has some bearing upon Shakespeare's *Hamlet* in that it shows the son's ambivalent attitude to his mother, condemning her for her inexplicable sinfulness, but allowing for human weakness (I.ii.146: "Frailty, thy name

210

is woman!") and, stepping "between her and her fighting soul" on the assumption that "Conceit in weakest bodies strongest works," sowing the seeds out of which repentance and forgiveness can grow![101]

This tolerant attitude is also found in Belleforest, which is only what could be expected from him after the way in which he regarded Geruthe's adultery. He largely follows Saxo, and though he makes Hamlet's oration at least twice as long as Saxo does, Hamlet's reference to his mother is of much the same length and content, with the note struck in the opening words: "Ayez pitié de la Royne jadis vostre Dame, et ma treshonoree mere."[102] If the frailty-thy-name-is-woman motif is not Shakespeare's own invention, it cannot be attributed to one source to the exclusion of any of the others.

In Krantz's second chapter on Hamlet (ll.44 ff.) we only get a glimpse of Hamlet's mother. The relationships it mainly deals with (like the corresponding sections in Saxo and Belleforest) are that between the new king and Hamlet and that between Hamlet and his wife. On the whole we now meet a different Hamlet — and here Saxo and Belleforest agree: he is no longer the ruthless man of action, quick to seize an opportunity, but rather a paragon of moderation and consideration for others, and a victim of circumstances. He has calmed down, much in the same way as Hamlet in the last act of Shakespeare's play, in which some critics find the Prince not so much youthful as rather middle-aged. But at the same time the change in him adds to his tragic stature and prepares for the grandiloquent epitaph he gets in Saxo, Krantz — and Shakespeare.

The two new relationships in this chapter, however, are not more individualized than that they could be fused with two very similar ones in the pre-revenge story into two main themes: the King versus Hamlet, who is now definitely not King of Denmark either in Krantz or in Saxo (Belleforest differs occasionally; see Gollancz, pp.302 and 306), and Hamlet versus the women, or woman.

The new king's attitude to Hamlet is much the same as Fengo's: meanness and envy (=Saxo and Belleforest), but — and this is true of Krantz only — even more than that suspicion and fear for his life. He is Hamlet's inferior, and his epitaph, following upon Hamlet's as it does in Krantz, forms an effective anticlimax, where Belleforest stoops to verbosity and sermonizing. In this connection we also have a reference to Hamlet's popularity as the reason for the King's fear (Krantz only; l. [53]); cf. *Shakespeare's Hamlet* IV.iii.4: "He's lov'd of the distracted multitude" and IV.vii.18: "the great love the general gender bear him."

But there is another side to the Wicletus/Hamlet story. Hamlet, who has no grievance against his king, is patient, compliant and conciliatory in much the same way as Shakespeare's Hamlet is with Laertes in the graveyard scene and at the beginning of the fencing scene (V.i.283-285 and V.ii.232-236). Both the Hamlets are forced into combat by the irreconcilability of their opponents: although they would rather have had things settled in a peaceful way, their honour makes it impossible for them to withdraw. In both cases fate ironically sends them to their death.

As far as this goes, Saxo, Krantz and Belleforest agree. But there are differences. In Krantz, it is obvious that Hamlet's conciliatoriness is genuine. In Saxo, his concessions to the King and his gifts are only a feint in order to *seem* to "return kindness for slander" (Liber Quartus II.1: "ut ... calumniam beneficio rependere *videretur*"):[103] afterwards he seizes a chance to take revenge by attacking Wicletus and defeating him, and from being a secret enemy comes out into the open (*ibid.*: "atque ex occulto hoste manifestus evasit"). This may be in keeping with the Hamlet who has feigned madness in order to revenge his father's death and his mother's ignominy, but definitely smacks of a more primitive moral code. Krantz, on the other hand, agrees well with what we find clearly expressed in Shakespeare as Hamlet's leading principle: *non videri sed esse* (I.ii.76).

Both Saxo and Krantz, however, let history repeat itself on another score: the faithlessness of women. Especially after Hamlet's own solicitude for his wife (ll. 63-64), in Saxo (Liber Quartus II:2), he is even casting about for a second husband for her before what was to be his last battle—one would not have expected her to be blamed for preferring life and a live man to death and a dead one. But she is judged as severely as Hamlet's mother who married Fengo after her first husband had been killed. Saxo, after admitting that her promise to share her husband's death on the battlefield was an unusual one, gets eloquent in his condemnation: "Thus all vows of women are loosed by change of fortune and melted by the shifting of time; the faith of their soul rests on a slippery foothold, and is weakened by casual chances; glib in promises, and as sluggish in performance, all manner of lustful promptings enslave it, and it bounds away with panting and precipitate desire, forgetful of old things, in the ever hot pursuit of something fresh."[104] Surely these words lifted out of their context could just as well have been put into Hamlet's mouth in the closet scene. Krantz lashes Hamlet's wife with his irony (l. 68: "coniunx magnificè pollicita"; ll. 69-70: "Egregia coniunx, oblita promissi, foemina fide," "uolitabat"). This misogynist attitude is understandable in two authors who were both of the clergy. It agrees with the description of Hamlet and his mother in the previous chapter. In Shakespeare it was to break through both in Hamlet's relationship with his mother in the closet scene and with Ophelia in the scene when she has been prevailed upon to expose her beloved, and to culminate in the misanthropy of II.ii.308-309: "man delights not me; no, nor woman neither."

Krantz, as little as in the previous chapter, deigns to mention the woman's name. It is uncertain which of the two wives Saxo attributes to Hamlet that he means. It is probably the Scottish Queen, who figures in the corresponding place in Saxo: Herminthruda, and it is worth noticing that the Queen's name in *Hamlet* contains both the first part of the name of Horwendillus' wife: Gerutha, and the second part of the name of Hamlet's wife: Hermin*thruda*. A contamination, conscious or unconscious, could easily have been made. So the occurrence of the name *Gerthrude* in Shakespeare could be explained simply from one of the printed sources of the Hamlet story: Saxo.

Perhaps there is an even more striking similarity between the scene of Hamlet and his wife before the battle on one hand and the dialogue of the Player King and the Player Queen on the other (*Hamlet*, III.ii): the Player King feeling he must soon leave his Queen and in magnanimous thoughtfulness sketching for her a life after

212

his death with "one as kind," and the Player Queen rejecting such thoughts as treason and protesting a love too great for a second marriage. What happened in Saxo/Krantz shows the truth of the Player King's worldly wise words (III.ii.208-210):

> Our thoughts are ours, their ends none of our own.
> So think thou wilt no second husband wed
> But die thy thoughts, when thy first Lord is dead.

What has been said of Gertrude's name in Saxo, as opposed to Krantz, applies just as much to Belleforest (*Geruthe: Hermentrude*). But his story of Hamlet's last battle, though substantially the same as Saxo's and Krantz's, presents a different pattern of relationships. His Danish King, called Vviglere, is *satisfied* with Hamlet's gifts ("si beaux et riches presens") and *withdraws* from Hamlet's territories, but then changes his mind, not only because of his greed for land, but because Hamlet's wife has "intelligence with him" ("avoit intelligence avec luy") and promises him marriage, provided he can take her away from her husband ("pourveu qu'il l'ostast des mains de celuy qui la detenoit").[105] As in his treatment of the Horvvendille ---Fengon--- Geruthe triangle Belleforest seems to insist on making the woman an accessory before the fact, with the same predilection for recurrent patterns as when he makes Horvvendille's murder take place at a banquet (for which he had not Saxo's authority), like Fengon's own (for which he had).[106] This, of course, gives Belleforest all the more reason to preach again on the disloyalty and inconstancy of women (cf. Saxo and Krantz and Shakespeare's *Hamlet*), so much so that he interrupts himself in his discourse, "vomissant choses indignes de ce sexe," with the excuse that he has let himself be carried away by Hermentrude's vices and "l'autheur d'où j'ay pris ceste histoire," who, a marginal note explains, is "Saxon Grammarien."[107] But it gives an unfavourable reflection on Belleforest's Hamlet (which is totally different from the flaw in Hamlet's character that Saxo attributes to him but which Belleforest agrees with Krantz in not including): he is "affole de sa femme . . . qu'il idolatroit," and with his too great confidence in her has lost "celle grande prudence, qui le rendoit admirable, par les pays voisins de l'Ocean Septentrional, et en toutes les Allemaignes."[108] Nor is he as unselfish as the Hamlet of Saxo and Krantz, or the Player King in Shakespeare: he is actually thinking — and this alternative is mentioned first — of her joining him in death and not only of her future happiness with a second husband ("[il] eust voulu, ou que elle luy eust tenu compaignie à la mort, ou luy trouver mary qui l'aimast . . .").[109] This explains the fact that Belleforest's epitaph of Hamlet reads as if he grieved not a hero but a fool — even if he admits that the same weakness afflicted Solomo ("le plus sage d' entre les hommes") and "la pluspart des grans, sages, vaillants, et discrets par apparence, de nostre temps."[110] In fact, Belleforest reaches a point when he finds he has to address to his reader a warning not to feed upon the corruption in the Hamlet story but to follow "la modestie, continence, et courtoysie, qui recommande Amleth en ce discours," who was sober at other people's banquets and who preferred "un amas de vertus" to the accumulation of riches, and who could thus, though of a barbarous nation which had not yet received the light of the gospel, set an example to be followed and surpassed by an age "plus purgé, subtil et gaillard."[111] It is difficult to see how this ending could better than Saxo's and Krantz's have contributed to creating the atmosphere of the last scene in *Hamlet*, in which the hero of the past is honoured by the inaugurator of a new age of Dano-Norwegian unity under a strong dynasty.

Of the two details in Belleforest which are missing in Saxo but which have been found to be in agreement with Shakespeare's *Hamlet*, one has already been dealt with: the adultery before the murder.[112] It has been shown (above, pp.206-207) that Belleforest is explicit about the matter, though in a context in which it could hardly be said to be of prime importance to the narrative, whereas both Krantz's and Shakespeare's texts admit, but do not enforce, an interpretation implying the

woman's guilt. The second detail, Belleforest's use of the word "melancholy" in connection with Hamlet, seems definitely to be of less importance. Melancholy, which has been called "the Elizabethan malady,"[113] occurs so often in Shakespeare that an incidental reference in a text would not have been necessary to put him on the track. Further, the word does not occur in a very prominent place: (a) it appears in the section which deals with Hamlet on his first visit to the English court and which has no equivalent in Shakespeare (or Krantz); (b) it is not part of the story but of the rather involved commentary on Hamlet's powers of divination. After stating the fact that Hamlet was in possession of such powers—though with the later reservation that they only implied revealing the past and not predicting the future, which is a divine prerogative—Belleforest attributes them to Hamlet's upbringing in a Scandinavia of long ago, "souz l'obeissance de Sathan," when there was "une infinité d'enchanteurs" and every young gentleman knew enough black magic for his needs,[114] but, he continues, he is not going to discuss what gives man

214

such astounding knowledge of things past. However, he cannot resist the temptation to touch upon a few possibilities, of which the first is whether Hamlet's intuitions were due to the "vehemence of melancholy" ("si ce Prince, pour la vehemence de la melancholie, avoit receu ces impressions") which is then described as if it were a kind of *furor poeticus*, the second is whether the knowledge is imparted by devils who take possession of the soul, and the third whether the machinations of magicians are involved.[115] As is seen, the question of melancholy is not brought up in any connection with the tragedies in Hamlet's family in Denmark; the focus of interest is on magic. It has much the same kind of indirect relevance as the question of the adultery.

If it is accepted that Belleforest has not got a very strong case—there still remains the question whether there was an early enough translation into English or the author of *Hamlet* could understand written French, if possible better than the English translator of 1608 (which would have been desirable), then it would not be impossible to argue that the Hamlet story as it appears in Saxo and Krantz would have been adequate material for the man who wrote the Hamlet play. If it is not accepted, then the facts presented here may have shown that besides Saxo, who is normally mentioned in this connection, other versions of the Hamlet story should be considered, in the first place Krantz. In Krantz the author of *Hamlet* would have found a concise story of the revenge plot (stripped of the "fables" in Saxo and Belleforest which are not in Shakespeare's *Hamlet*) and yet a few striking details (with parallels in Shakespeare), all in a language that should not have presented any difficulties even to a person with "small Latine," and besides a reference to Saxo that could be used for a study of the fuller story with details like Fengo's testing of Hamlet's insanity and Hamlet's speech to his mother in her closet. Krantz might finally have put a few seeds into a fertile mind in a way that will never be possible to prove conclusively—by triggering off associations.[116] Examples have already been given, and a final one may be added: the initial W of Krantz's chapters xx and xxi. Yorick's skull?[117] (See above, p.214.)

Notes:

(1)   *The Works of Thomas Nashe,* ed. Ronald B. McKerrow (London, 1910), III, 315, or the reprint, ed. F. P. Wilson (Oxford, 1958).

(2)   G. C. Moore Smith, *Gabriel Harvey's Marginalia* (Stratford-upon-Avon, 1913), p.xi. For the note itself, written in *The Workes of our Antient and lerned English Poet, Geffrey Chaucer, newly Printed* (London, 1598), see p. 232.

(3)   Peter Alexander, *Alexander's Introductions to Shakespeare* (London and Glasgow, 1964), p. 162.

(4)   The most common view.—Kenneth Muir, *Shakespeare's Sources* (London 1957), I, 110, states that "*Shakespeare's Hamlet* was based on a lost play of the same title, perhaps by Shakespeare himself, perhaps by an unknown dramatist," but in *Shakespeare: Hamlet* (London, 1963), p. 9, he thinks that the earliest version of *Hamlet* was "probably not by Shakespeare."

(5)   E. K. Chambers, *William Shakespeare,* (Oxford 1930), I, 411ff.

(6)   H. G. Wright, "The Elizabethans and the North" in his *Studies in Anglo-Scandinavian Literary Relations* (Bangor, 1919), p. 1.

(7)   A different opinion is expressed in Marshall Blakemore Evans, *Der bestrafte Brudermord.* Theatergeschichtliche Forschungen, herausgegeben von Berthold Litzmann (Hamburg and Leipzig, 1910), XIX, 19.

(8)   *Amleth,* or *Amlet,* is also the form used in the first translation of Saxo into Danish: Anders Søffrinssøn Vedel, *Den Danske Krønicke som Saxo Grammaticus screff / halfffjerde hundrede Aar forleden . . .* (The Danish Chronicle that S. G. wrote 350 years ago) (Copenhagen, 1575). There is an edition published by Samfundet til den danske literaturs Fremme (Copenhagen, 1851).

(9)   Charles Wareing Bardsley, *A Dictionary of English and Welsh Surnames* (London, 1901), p. 352. See also E. G. Withycombe, *The Oxford Dictionary of English Christian Names* (Oxford, 1945, 2nd ed. 1950), s.v. *Hamo(n),* and, for the Scandinavian forms, Sir Israel Gollancz, *The Sources of Hamlet* (London, 1926).

(10)   For this and the immediately following references to Chambers, see E. K. Chambers, *The Elizabethan Stage* (Oxford, 1923), II, 265ff.

(11)   Chambers, pp. 271-273.

(12)   Chambers, p. 266.

(13)   W. W. Greg, first page of introduction to *Hamlet, First Quarto, 1603.* Shakespeare Quarto Facsimiles No. 7 (London, 1951).

(14)   F. P. Wilson, *The Plague in Shakespeare's London* (Oxford, 1927), pp. 88 and 90.

(15)   Wilson, pp. 92 f.

(16)   Wilson, p. 93.

(17)   John Tucker Murray, *English Dramatic Companies 1558-1642* (London, 1910), p. 148.

(18)   A. W. Pollard & G. R. Redgrave, and others, *A Short-Title Catalogue of Books Printed in England, Scotland, & Ireland* (London, 1926), s.v. Almanacks and Kalendars.

(19)   Wilson, pp. 87, 90, 93, 105-106, 215; 110-111.

(20)   *Works,* III, 315.

(21)   Moore Smith, *Gabriel Harvey's Marginalia,* p. 232.

(22)   See, for example, Muir, *Shakespeare's Sources, I,* 110-112.

(23)   The edition of 1576, *Le cinqviesme livre des Histoires Tragiques . . .* par François Belleforest Comingeois, has been published in an appendix (pp. 71-145) of Evans, *Der bestrafte Brudermord* (see above, note 7), but if nothing else is indicated, quotations will be made from the second edition (Paris, 1582) in Gollancz, *op. cit.,* as more easily available.—See also p. 205.

(24)   *The Rape of Lucrece, Romeo and Juliet, Much Ado about Nothing,* and *Twelfth Night.*

(25)   *Allgemeine deutsche Biographie* (Leipzig, 1873), VIII, 396 f.

(26)   This figure has been taken from Saxo (1514), who has probably supplied the material.

(27)   Paris ed., fol. Aaii^v and diii^r (=fol. XXVII^r).

(28)   The date for when Horwendillus was slain is now different, however. Probably because Huitfeldt used a different edition of Gassarus, the year is given as 246 B.C. and anno mundi 3717 (p. 11).

(29)   "Saxonis Gesta Danorum ab incerto autore in compendium redacta et continuata" in his *Scriptores Minores Historiae Daniae Medii Aevi* (Copenhagen, 1917-18), I, 195-470 (editor's introduction, pp. 197-215).

216

(30) Gertz, pp. 197 f. and 217.

(31) From his preface (Gertz, p. 217). He also continued Saxo's work by adding what is now called the Jutish Chronicle (Chronica Jutensis), thus bringing his history up to 1340/42 (Gertz, pp. 201 and 440-458).

(32) Gertz, p. 201. Details of the Low German translation, published in 1502, to be found in J. Olrik & H. Raeder (eds.), Saxonis Gesta Danorum, Copenhagen, 1931), I. 561, and Conrad Borchling & Bruno Claussen, Niederdutsche Bibliographie, (Neumünster, 1931), I, No. 172 and 172a.

(33) Both in Suomalaisen Tiedeakatemian Toimituksia / Annales Academiae Scientiarum Fennicae, Sarja/Ser. B, Nid./Tom. 29,3 (294 pp.) and 35, 2 (260 pp.), respectively.

(34) Evans, p. 9.

(35) Evans, pp. 17-19.

(36) Hans Sachs's versified story is to be found in his work Das ander Buch Sehr Herrliche Schone Artliche und gebundene Gedicht mancherley art (Nürnberg, 1560), Der dritt theil, fol. CLI^v.— CLII^v. Evans refers to Hans Sachs, Herausgegeben von Adelbert von Keller, [Bibliothek des Litterarischen Vereins in Stuttgart CXXI] (Tubingen, 1874), VIII, 591-594.
"Fongo" is the form of the name used in Sachs's text. The index has Fengo as well as Horwendillum.
The lines referred to in (b) run: "Hielt auff jn in eim Holtz hernach / Am jaid hinterruck jn erstach / Das er im blut gewaltzet lag" (fol. CLII^r).

(37) Nordman, Die Wandalia, pp. 13-22.

(38) Nordman, Die Wandalia, p. 23.

(39) Nordman, Die Chronica, pp. 28-30.

(40) In his dedicatory epistle Eppendorff himself describes how he came across the manuscript, why he dedicated the book to the Danish King, and why he had translated it into German (fol. Aij).

(41) Nordman has noted the fact (Die Chronica, p. 14).

(42) Nordman, Die Chronica, p. 15.

(43) The final relationship between copies dated one year or the other cannot of course be established until they have all been inspected.

(44) The British Museum possesses copies of the German edition of 1545 (see above) and of the Latin editions of 1562, 1575, and 1583.

(45) Cf. Gollancz's categorical "Saxo's story of Amlethus reached England through the medium of Belleforest's Histoires Tragiques" (p. 35).

(46) Nordman, Die Chronica, pp. 240 f.

(47) "Ex catalogo Regum Angliae, Autor Normannorum Regiam dignitatem probat. Caput 1.," pp. 708 ff. On Krantz and Western and Southern Europe, see Nordman, Die Chronica, pp. 184-186.

(48) Translation by James Westfall Thompson in his The Frankfort Book Fair, The Francofordiense Emporium of Henri Estienne, edited with historical introduction, original Latin text with English translation on opposite pages and notes (Chicago, 1911), p. 171. The original, p. 25, runs, with abbreviations dissolved: "Nec verò philosophos tantùm celebres illae Academiae, Viennensis, VVitebergensis, Lipsiensis, Heidelbergensis, Argentoratensis, et inter peregrinas, Louaniensis, Patauina, Oxoniensis atque Cantabrigiensis: hae inquam, aliaeque quas longum enumerare esset, non philosophos tantùm illuc mittunt: sed et quosdam poetices, quosdam artis oratoriae,

quosdam historiae, quosdam mathematicarum scientiarum, nonnullos etiam earum simul omnium peritos."

(49)   I have had the privilege of discussing the Latin text with Professor Erik Wistrand and Dr. Ake Fridh, Gothenburg, as well as Dr. Michael Coffey, University College, London, who has also been kind enough to see that my translation does not offend too much against English usage. I make my acknowledgements with the greatest gratitude.

(50)   References to points that differ from one version to the other will be marked (S) for Strasburg and (F) for Frankfurt.

(51)   Cf., for our extract, the famous section in Saxo numbered Liber Tertius VI:1-Liber Quartus II:4 in Olrik & Raeder's edition of 1931, pp. 76-92. References to Saxo will be made to this edition.

(52)   Nordman, *Die Chronica*, pp. 72-94, especially pp. 74 and 91.

(53)   Krantz's only contribution to this passage is "tandem" in l.74, the stylistic value of which could be discussed.

(54)   *Allgemeine deutsche Biographie* (Leipzig, 1883), XVII, 44, draws attention to the fact that there is no knowing what Krantz himself would have sent to the press.

(55)   References to Shakespeare's *Hamlet* apply to Peter Alexander, *William Shakespeare: The Complete Works* (London/Glasgow, 1951). The possible link with Saxo has been noted by Edward Dowden in *The Arden Shakespeare: The Tragedy of Hamlet*, 8th edition revised (London, 1938), p. 22.

(56)   "Seems, madam! Nay, it is; I know not seems" (I.ii.76).

(57)   Quoted from the translation of 1608 (also in Gollancz), which here adequately renders the original. Gollancz, p. 307. Italics added.

(58)   Gollancz, pp. 308 and 309.

(59)   *Ibid.*

(60)   Nordman has observed this: *Die Chronica*, p. 214.

(61)   Saxo, Liber Tertius, VI: 17-21. Belleforest follows Saxo. (Gollancz, pp. 232-251).

(62)   Saxo, Liber Quartus, I:9-20. Belleforest follows Saxo. (Gollancz, pp. 262-311).

(63)   *Sakses Danasaga, Oldtid og Ældste Middelalder*, oversat af Jørgen Olrik (2nd ed., Copenhagen, 1925), I-II, 163 f. Olrik suspects the influence of one Lucas the Englishman, whose name Saxo mentions in another place as a good teller of tales.

(64)   We shall come back to this theme later (p. 214).

(65)   Cf. the often quoted passage in Thomas Lodge's *Wits Miserie* (1596), referred to, for instance, in Horace Howard Furness, *A New Variorum Edition of Shakespeare: Hamlet*, (Philadelphia and London, 1877), II, 9, and Chambers I, 411.

(66)   Cf. John Dover Wilson (ed.), *The Works of Shakespeare: Hamlet* (Cambridge 1936), p. lv.

(67)   John Dover Wilson, *What happens in Hamlet* (Cambridge, reprint of 1964), pp. 26ff.

(68)   Gollancz, pp. 180 and 181.

(69)   Gollancz, pp. 112 and 113.

(70)   Gollancz, p. 204.

(71)   Gollancz, p. 205. Italics added.

(72) Gollancz, pp. 206 and 207. Italics added.

(73) Edmond Huguet, *Dictionnaire de la langue française du seizième siècle*, Vol. 5 (Paris, 1961).

(74) Frédéric Godefroy, *Dictionnaire de l'ancienne language française . . . du IXe au XVe siècle*, Vol. 5 (Paris, 1888).

(75) Gollancz, pp. 112 and 113.

(76) This is the spelling of the 1st edition. Gollancz (p. 206), following the 2nd edition, has "lourdier," an obvious misprint.

(77) Gollancz, p. 207. Italics added.

(78) J. F. H. in *Encyclopaedia Britannica*, Vol. 3 (London, etc., 1963), s.v. *Bed*, p. 359.

(79) Furness, I, 285-287.

(80) *O.E.D.*, s.v. *Arras*, gives a citation from *Unton Inventories 7* (1596): "One olde coverlett of Ariste." See also the citations from 1790 Cowper *Odyss.* x. 14 and, s.v. *Arrased*, from 1600 Chapman *Iliad* v. 199.

(81) Gollancz, pp. 116 and 117.

(82) Gollancz, p. 229.

(83) Gollancz, pp. 186/188/190 and 187/189/191.

(84) R. R. Young, *The South Bank Shakespeare: Hamlet* (London, 1965), p. 67.

(85) *Ibid.*

(86) Gollancz, pp. 185 and 187.

(87) Gollancz, p. 186.

(88) Gollancz, pp. 188/190 and 189/191.

(89) Gollancz, p. 188.

(90) (S), pp. 618 f: "Danos ante Romanos, Britanniam, & Hyberniam depopulatos esse, per occasionem probat. Caput xxviij."

(91) (S), p. 619.

(92) (S), p. 619: "Froto deinde longaeuus Rex, per cuius tempora in terris natus est Christus Dominus, Britanniam expugnauit. Circa quae tempora primus ex Romanis Caius Caesar, ante occupatam Monarchiam, Britanniam inglorius attigit. Claudius in Prouinciam deinde redegit. Seuerus edomuit rebellantem & alij deinde Imperatores: quorum opportuno tempore mentionem ingeremus."

(93) Gollancz, pp. 114 and 115.

(94) Elton (Gollancz, p. 117): "On the rest see thou keep silence."

(95) I have had this point confirmed by Professor Otto Skutsch, University College London. It may also be pointed out that this is the only occurrence in Saxo of a transitive *sileo*, the other four being intransitive.

(96) Cf. Horatio's description of the omens at Caesar's death which occurs in the Quartos but not in the Folios (*Hamlet*, I.i.113-125).

(97) Gollancz, pp. 131 and 133.

(98) Gollancz, pp. 135 and 137.

(99)   Gollancz, pp. 137 and 139.

(100) Gollancz, p. 141.

(101) *Hamlet,* III.iv.113-114.

(102) Gollancz, p. 276.

(103) Gollancz, pp. 158 and 159, from which Elton's translation has been quoted.

(104) Elton's translation. Gollancz, pp. 161 and 163.

(105) Gollancz, p. 300.

(106) Gollancz, pp. 186 and 187.

(107) Gollancz, p. 306.

(108) Gollancz, p. 302. For the difference between Saxo and Belleforest, cf. also Peter Alexander, *Hamlet: Father and Son* (Oxford, 1955), pp. 165 ff.

(109) Ibid.

(110) Gollancz, p. 308. Cf. above pp. 200-202.

(111) Gollancz, p. 310.

(112) Muir, *Shakespeare's Sources, I*, 111 "The version of the story given in the *Histoires Tragiques* is much the same [as in Saxo]; but in that Gertrude and Fengon had committed adultery before the murder of Amleth's father and Belleforest speaks of Amleth's over-great melancholy'." There is another reference on his page 112.

(113) Lawrence Babb, *The Elizabethan Malady* (East Lansing, Mich., 1951).

(114) Gollancz, p. 236.

(115) Gollancz, p. 236 ff. Note that "over great melancholy" is the expression used in the English translation of 1608, which, by the way, in this non-narrative section could have been made with greater care.

(116) Cf. an example from *The Merchant of Venice* quoted in *Shakespeare Studies, II (1966)*, which has been kindly pointed out to me by the Editor.

(117) The present article would not even have reached its present stage without the encouragement and assistance of several people: Professor Harold Jenkins, whose constructive criticism was most helpful, and Professor Randolph Quirk, who helped me with some knotty problems of formulation, are only the two that first spring to mind. I would also like to express my gratitude to my old friend Dr. Harald Berg, Landskrona, Sweden, who with his historical expertise has always been stimulating and instructive.

The Danish Background in Hamlet

by Gunnar Sjögren

The Elizabethan dramatists paid little attention to local color in plays with a foreign setting. When such color is used it is often rather crudely applied or takes the form of a thinly disguised England. However, it has often been recognized[1] that Shakespeare's use of local color in creating an Italian atmosphere, for example, in *Romeo and Juliet*, *The Merchant of Venice* or *Othello* is unusually subtle. A few light touches, deftly applied, set the imagination of the spectator working in the right direction.

The local color in *Hamlet* has similar subtlety. It is generally agreed that a fair number of Danish characteristics are found in this play and most commentators acknowledge that at least some of them are introduced deliberately in order to create a suitable background for the Danish prince. But Shakespeare's achievement in this domain has not attracted the attention I believe it deserves.[2]

An attempt to evaluate his performance in this field must take into account not only the actual conditions in Denmark at the time, but also the Elizabethan conception—or misconception—of these conditions. And, in order to assess the originality of Shakespeare's achievement, we must first consider earlier attempts to introduce Danish local color into English works of fiction. To my knowledge only three such pieces survive; they are not of very high standard and can be summarized quite briefly.

Sir Clyomon and Sir Clamydes[3] is an anonymous play printed in 1599 but believed to have been written in the 1570's or 80's. It is a romance concerning two knights-errant, Clyomon, son of the king of Denmark, and Clamydes, son of the king of Sweden, set on a collision course. The plot is fantastic, distances are ignored, the scene shifting incessantly from Denmark to Sweden, Macedonia, "the Isle of the Strange Marches," Norway, and back to Denmark. There are no recognizable Danish features, geographical or otherwise, in the play. (Only once are we faintly reminded of *Hamlet* when Clyomon unmasks himself: "I am the Prince of Denmark's son, and heir unto the crown." One thinks of the churchyard scene: "This is I, Hamlet the Dane.")

The romantic comedy of *Faire Em, the Miller's Daughter*[4] is also anonymous and is believed to have been written about 1590. It was probably printed about 1593. This comedy tells, *inter alia*, of an apocryphal voyage of William the Conqueror to Denmark and of his dealings with the Danish king Zweno (Sven). Again Danish geography is ignored, although the curious fact that William lands in Liverpool on returning from Denmark may not be without interest. A Danish ambassador is called the Marquis of Lübeck indicating, perhaps, that the author believed that the important Hansa city of Lübeck belonged to Denmark.

My third instance is not a play but a romance, entitled *Euordanus*.[5] It was printed in London 1605 but was probably written earlier, and in this context it is more interesting. In the opening chapter the author tells how the Danish king Frederick married Alisonne, Countess of Flanders, to the extreme grief of Griffony, Duke of Holland, "as you may more at large read of in the Chronicle, written by our Cleonido, a Dane." (The chronicle is fictitious.) After the wedding the king and queen return to the Danish capital which—curiously enough—is Maience (Mainz). While walking in the woods near the city they are set upon by French outlaws. The king is taken prisoner and sold to Griffony, who throws him into prison. The queen runs into the forest and makes the acquaintance of a friendly lion who escorts her to his den, brings her bread and waits upon her; here she gives birth to a son, whom she calls Euordanus.

In the capital the nobles are greatly distressed by the king's disappearance, and various expeditions are sent in search of him. Many arrive at Griffony's castle, where they are promptly incarcerated.

Meanwhile the Duke of Saxony "passing ye Seas from England towards his own country" is stranded in a storm not far from the forest (near Maience) where the queen lives in the lion's den. He finds the boy Euordanus alone in the wood and takes him home to Saxony as a playmate for his own son Iago. When the boys grow up they join in the search for the Danish king, roving all over Europe. Eventually Euordanus comes to Griffony's castle and rescues Frederick and his Danish fellow-prisoners, by now numbering over a hundred.

The rescue comes in the nick of time. As the king has been away for so long, a party headed by the archbishop has offered the crown to the king of Scotland who "harkning unto this iolly proffer" loses no time in accepting it. Anticipating opposition from the people of Denmark, he sends an army headed by "his Cosen, the Lord Douglasse." The people rise as one man against the invaders and against the archbishop's army, but are on the point of being routed when King Frederick, his former fellow-prisoners and Euordanus arrive on the field and turn defeat into a resounding victory.

This story has of course no foundation in reality, but the identifiable titles of many of the nobles give some idea of the geography of this Denmark. The Dukes of Louenborge (Lauenburg), Newminster (Neumünster) and Litzenburge (Lütgenburg), the Bishop of Odelstoe (Oldesloe), the Counts of Mildorpe (Meldorf) and Opencade (Apenrade), the Lords of Londen (Lunden), Itzenho (Itzehoe), Newstadt (Neustadt) and Rensborge (Rendsburg), all appear in the story. These places are not in Denmark proper; they are all situated in the dukedoms of Schleswig and Holstein, which were held by the Danish kings in vassalage to the German emperor. Oddly enough, only the capital, Maience, is outside this region.

The action, however, gravitates towards the area round the towns of Lunden and Meldorf, in the territory known as Ditmarsse, which was also the setting for Belleforest's story of Amleth. Saxo records that the father and uncle of Amleth were made governors of Jutland by the King of Denmark, but Belleforest embroiders this, equating Ditmarsse with Jutland; "il donna le gouvernement de Jutie (qui s'appelle vulgairement à present Diethmarsen, et est assise sur le Chersonnese des Cimbres. . .)."[6] Later, when Saxo tells how Amleth, after killing his uncle, was elected king, Belleforest now equates Jutland with Denmark: "le declairent Roy de Jutie, et Chersonne, ce qui est à present le propre pays qu'on nomme Dannemarch."[7]

Against the background of this geographical muddle Shakespeare's placing the action of the play in Elsinore is a striking innovation. To shift the scene from a remote Jutland to a contemporary Elsinore, and to make Hamlet a royal Prince, the King of Denmark's son, and not the son of a governor and future usurper was a master stroke. For in Elizabethan England, where Jutland was hardly even a name, Denmark and Elsinore were well known.

In the 1590's a yearly average of 2800 ships of all nations passed through the Sound of Denmark in each direction, all having to pay duty to the Danish crown at Elsinore. Of these ships some 80 or 90 were English; they called at Elsinore twice a year—once in the spring on their way into the Baltic, to Lübeck, Elbing, Riga or Narve, and once later in the year on their homeward run.[8] Often they had to wait in the roads for a considerable time. The town itself was crammed with foreigners, and quite a few Englishmen had settled down here.[9]

It was Elsinore, not Copenhagen, that the Elizabethans naturally thought of as the principal city of Denmark. Thomas Dekker called it one of "the Capitall Citties, that beautifies the greatest Kingdomes of Europe."[10] Elsinore was the usual port of arrival and departure of English ambassadors. The town and the Sound were dominated by the castle of Kronborg, which was strongly fortified and armed with over a hundred heavy guns.[11] A skipper who failed to strike his topsails when passing the castle was liable to summary punishment. Shots were even fired at the ship carrying an English ambassador because it failed to acknowledge the Danish flag, and two men were killed.[12]

Ostensibly the Sound Toll, which had been levied since 1429, was a compensation enjoyed by Denmark for keeping the Baltic free from pirates. In fact a very small part of the huge receipts was used for this purpose, although now and then a crew of "dantzker Fribyttere" (pirates from Danzig) were taken to Elsinore to be hanged, to demonstrate to the foreigner the use to which their money allegedly was put.[13] But as often as not the Danes failed to keep the Baltic free from pirates and it may have been from the numerous tales of encounters with pirates in the Danish seas that Shakespeare got his idea of Hamlet's escape. There is even a record of "thieves of mercy" who "knew what they did."[14]

The Danish king, Christian IV, who came to the throne in 1596, often stayed at Kronborg during the trading season, personally supervising, in a high-handed manner, the collection of the duty. English traders had a special grudge, they complained that they were always discriminated against, indeed it is recorded that when Christian encountered English ships fishing off the coast of Norway, he gave the skippers a good thrashing with his own hands.[15] Such grievances, real and imagined, would color the minds of many English playgoers.[16] The Danish king was not popular in England.

The question of the accession to the Danish throne plays an important part in the plot of *Hamlet*. Professor Dover Wilson has expressed the opinion that Hamlet's Denmark was a mirror of England under Queen Elizabeth.[17] This is not altogether true. Had Hamlet been an English prince he would have been the lawful heir to the throne, and if his place had been usurped the whole country would have been in a turmoil. It would have been strange indeed to find him moving about freely at the court of the usurper and chatting in a friendly manner with his uncle's bodyguard. There is no hint in the play that Claudius's accession to the throne is not formally correct. Claudius's benevolently condescending attitude towards Hamlet is not that of a usurper but of the successful competitor towards his defeated rival.

It is not generally realized that such a situation could well have arisen in sixteenth-century Denmark, which both in theory and practice was an elective kingdom. Time and again an uncle or a second son had "popped in between the election and the hopes" of the deceased king's eldest son. It was to avoid such a situation that Frederik II, at the birth of his first son, set out to cajole the nobles in naming this son, Christian, as his successor. His pleas were eventually conceded grudgingly. Despite this agreement, a tricky situation arose when Frederick died in 1588, for Christian was still a minor. The Council immediately appointed regents, excluding both the dowager queen and Frederik's brother, Duke John, from any part in the government of the country. Both of them strongly resented this loss of potential power. The English ambassador, Daniel Rogers, in reporting to Lord Burghley, evidently believed that Duke John might have made an attempt on the throne but for the authority and skill of the old chancellor, Niels Kaas.[18] Indeed had Kaas come down on the side of Duke John a situation not unlike that found in *Hamlet* could have arisen.[19]

Questions of royal succession were of absorbing interest to the Elizabethans. Politically informed people in England would have no difficulty in recognizing the close resemblance between the constitution of the Denmark of Hamlet and that of Christian the Fourth. Such a resemblance can hardly be coincidental.

Shakespeare took good care that his audience should not forget that *Hamlet* is set in Denmark, the name of the country being mentioned no fewer than twenty-two times. Similarly, while Claudius's name is never mentioned, his queen's Danish name Gertrude appears fourteen times. Shakespeare also makes a great display of the very Danish names Rosencrantz and Guildenstern. No names could have been more fit for the companions of a Danish prince; at the coronation of Christian IV in 1596 no fewer than nine Guildensterns and seven Rosencrantzes were among the attendant noblemen.[20] Shakespeare did not commit the blunder of providing them with titles—like the "Marquis of Lubeck" in *Faire Em*—for there were no marquises (nor even barons or earls) in sixteenth-century Denmark. Although most of the other names are not Danish they compare favourably with the absurd names in Henry Burnell's *Landgartha,* also based on a tale by Saxo, where the Norwegian heroine's sister is called Scania, her aunt Elsinora, and her cousin—Fatima.

It is often argued that the portraits of the kings in the closet scene: "Look here, upon this picture and on this, / The counterfeit presentment of two brothers"

(III.iv.54-55) was meant to call to mind the suite of tapestries showing portraits of a hundred Danish kings, historic and legendary, which adorned the Great Chamber of Kronborg.[21] This may or may not be so. The tapestries enjoyed a certain fame and are mentioned in John Stow's *Annals*. On the other hand painted portraits of kings were common enough, and there is nothing to suggest that Shakespeare was thinking of tapestries here.

The word *Danskers* unobtrusively slipped in by Polonius in his interview with Reynaldo: "Inquire me first what Danskers are in Paris" is evidently meant as a touch of Danish local color. It is, however, based on a misconception, which Shakespeare shared—and still shares—with many literary Englishmen. In Danish *Danskers* did not at this time mean *Danes* but *Danzigers*. The fact that Danzig was known as *Dansk* in Polish caused much confusion. Seamen and merchants knew perfectly well that *Dansk* was just another name for Danzig, but many Englishmen who were not so well-informed believed that Dansk was just another name for Denmark, comparable to Moscovie (for Russia) or Almaine (for Germany). On the other hand this *Dansk* was known to be situated on the borders of Poland; indeed, most of the English trade with Poland passed through *Dansk*. It would not be difficult, therefore, to draw the false conclusion that Poland had a common border with Denmark. If Shakespeare thought that *Danskers* were Danes, as he evidently did, he probably also believed that Poland bordered on Denmark. This may explain how Hamlet's father came to fight "the sledded Polacks on the ice."

It is also possible that Shakespeare, and other Englishmen, shared Fynes Moryson's delusion that it was Norwegian territory one saw across the Sound from Elsinore.[22] This would explain the invasion scare in the first act—at any moment a Norwegian commando expedition might try to take the castle by surprise. It also supplies an answer to the question of how Hamlet, on his way to the ship that was to carry him to England, could encounter Fortinbras and his army. Most commentators have accepted the idea that this encounter took place in another part of Denmark, but Hamlet surely is supposed to sail from Elsinore, as Laertes did when he went to France. (There were virtually no other ports in Denmark than Copenhagen and Elsinore.) If Norway was believed to extend as far south as opposite Elsinore, this is where Fortinbras would cross with his army. It is on his way from the castle to the harbor that Hamlet encounters Fortinbras's men. The same geographical solecism may explain Fortinbras's presence in Elsinore in the last scene. He simply returns from Poland the same way as he came. The geographical implications of the Fortinbras sub-plot were certainly meant to add to the realistic Danish background of the drama, for Shakespeare's geographical misconceptions would probably have been shared by many of the spectators.[23]

The Danish word *crants* at Ophelia's burial is certainly used as was *Danskers* to lend color to the Danish background. Garlands or wreaths carried before, or placed on, the hearse at the burial of young girls was a custom well known in England, but the words *crants* was not used in this connection and was not familiar in England. In *Hamlet* it only appears in the Q2 text, whereas in the Folio *virgin crants* has been altered to *virgin rites*—which does not mean anything. It seems likely that somebody, the compositor perhaps, ignorant of the word believed it to be a printer's error. Shakespeare presumably used it because it has a foreign flavor and would serve as a piece of Danish local color — although the custom at the time was more German than Danish.

Other slightly foreign expressions may yet be recognized in the play. A Danish historian, for example, suggested that Horatio's intriguing "A piece of him" in answer to Bernardo's "Say, is Horatio here?" in the very first scene of the play might reflect one of the shibboleth's of the craft guilds.[24] A wandering journeyman had to use a certain vocabulary and on entering a workshop looking for work was supposed to stay by the door until asked by the master, for example, "Fremder Nagelschmied?" to which he should answer "Ein Stück davon" (a piece of one). This particular formula seems to have been known from Denmark to Switzerland[25] and may be the point of Horatio's otherwise rather feeble joke. Craftsmen in the audience at the Globe could well have relished such a catch-phrase.

"You false Danish dogs" seems a strange expression in the mouth of a Danish queen. It strongly suggests that she is not Danish born herself. Most Danish queens were in fact German princesses. The high-tempered and strong-willed Queen Dowager, Christian's mother, Sophia of Mecklenburg, intensely resented the treatment meted out to her by the Danish regents and was not averse to using invectives against them.

Claudius's guard of "Switzers" might well have served to maintain the impression of a foreign background. Only the Pope and the French king had a real Swiss guard, employed not for use in war but for peace-time duty. An authentic Swiss guard was a very expensive status symbol which few princes could afford.[26] The Danish kings had a guard of "dravantere" who, although not Swiss, were dressed in the red and yellow of Oldenburg, not unlike the Swiss guard of the French king, which wore the same colors, or the Pope's which wore red, yellow and blue. It is perhaps significant that at a pageant in Copenhagen during the coronation festivities in 1596, Christian's guard of "dravantere" was dressed up as a *real* Swiss guard in imitation of the Pope's. The Sackville company of players took part in the activities at the coronation and Shakespeare may have got the idea of the Switzers from one of them.[27]

Such words and expressions which convey a more or less authentic Danish local color are unobtrusive but fulfill a useful function in sustaining the foreign atmosphere of the play. The same applies to the bits of Danish lore taken from the spheres of customs and manners.

Hamlet's "intent in going back to school in Wittenberg" has long been recognized as an obvious instance of Danish local color. The University of Wittenberg was much favored by the Danish nobles. Even a Danish king, Christian III, had studied there as a boy.

The extravagant drinking habits of the Danes were often commented on by ambassadors and travellers, indeed Frederick II died from drinking too much. As the Italians were popularly regarded as poisoners, so the drunkenness of the Danes became a well-worn cliche in England;[28] Shakespeare, indeed, would have found a

226

mention of it in Belleforest.[29] But he uses this trait with moderation and great artistry in Hamlet's lines on "the stamp of one defect."[30]

Another trait of Danish royalty was the lavish expenditure of gunpowder at revels. At the castle of Kronborg large cannon, placed on the top of the great square tower could be used for this purpose. A letter of 1582 survives in which Frederick II ordered them to be made ready so that they could be fired when Lord Willoughby presented him with the insignia of the Garter. Lord Willoughby reports that a whole volley of shot was fired after the king's "affectionate and loving speeches to her Majesty and all of the order."[31] This custom is turned to very good account in Hamlet.[32]

It is also of some interest to establish what common conceptions of Denmark were rejected by Shakespeare. The prevalence of sorcerers and witches in the Northern countries was a well-established fact; everybody knew that they could raise storms, and that winds were bought and sold like any other commodity. Belleforest, of course, cannot resist this. Trying to explain how it was possible for Amleth to find out the truth about the food and drink offered to him by the King of England, Belleforest is not content with Saxo's explanation that Amleth was very intelligent and acute; he must needs find a more sensational explanation: "for that in those dayes, the north parts of the worlde, living then under Sathan's lawes, were full of inchanters, so that there was not any yong gentleman whatsoever that knew not something therein sufficient to serve his turne, if need required . . . and so Amleth, while his father lived, had bin instructed in the devilish art, whereby the wicked spirite abuseth mankind, and advertiseth him (as he can) of things past."[33]

But luckily Shakespeare was not tempted by Belleforest into making Hamlet a sorcerer. Nor did he adopt the prevalent notion among literary men of the severe cold prevailing in the Northern countries. Even if it was not quite so cold in Denmark as in Iceland, where people were said not to need bottles but to carry the congealed beer loose in their pockets,[34] it was a popular belief that even in Denmark the cold was difficult to endure. Hamlet's remark "The air bites shrewdly, it is very cold" as he comes out on the battlements in the middle of the night is surely just a comment on the weather and nothing more. Similarly the expressions "yon high eastward hill" (I.i.167) and "the cliff that beetles o'er his base into the sea" (I.iv.70-1) are chosen for poetical and dramatical reasons and are surely not meant to convey topographical information, in which case they would not be very apt.[35]

There must have been thousands of people in Elizabethan London with a more or less superficial personal knowledge of Denmark and the Danes—sailors and merchants engaged in the Baltic trade, as well as scriveners, gentlemen and servants belonging to the train of ambassadors to the Danish court. Such people would be on the look-out for Danish characteristics in a play ostensibly set in Denmark. Shakespeare did not let them down.

He had himself had many opportunities to gather information about this country. A succession of English entertainers had gone to Denmark and some had stayed there for some time. From 1579 several English musicians were regularly attached to the Danish court. Four of them accompanied the Danish ambassador Henrik Ramel on a short journey to London in 1586.[36] The same year saw the well-known visits to Elsinore of William Kempe and his boy, who stayed there two months, and of a troupe of five English entertainers, two of whom later became members of Shakespeare's company. They stayed three months. In 1596 the Sackville troupe performed in Copenhagen.

The lutenist Daniel Norcome was engaged in 1599 by Christian IV, but left after less than two years service without leave and managed to get back to England, to the great resentment of the Danish king. The most renowned of English artists active at his court was the lutenist and composer John Dowland, who stayed there for eight years from 1598. His second book of *Songs and Ayres for the Lute* is dated "Helsingoure 1 June 1600." He visited England in 1601 to buy instruments for the Danish court musicians. Even if Shakespeare did not write the sonnet in *The Passionate Pilgrim* beginning "If music and sweet poetry agree" which contains a fine compliment to Dowland, it is fairly certain that those two successful contemporaries, working as they did in related fields, knew each other.

Shakespeare seems to be the only Elizabethan author who tries to create a consistent Danish background to a play. He makes no serious blunders and he manages to stear clear of popular prejudices and crude generalizations. Many inconspicuous touches culled from different spheres of knowledge are deftly applied and serve to locate the action of the play in Denmark. Even if some of the alleged touches of local color are not strictly Danish, they serve their purpose well enough. Shakespeare uses his limited knowledge in a discriminating fashion, and, on the whole, turns it to good account.

Notes:

(1) E.g. by Mario Praz in "Shakespeare's Italy," *Shakespeare Survey, 7* (1954), 95-106.

(2) I have discussed several aspects of this subject in a popular book of essays in Swedish called *Strovtag i Shakespeares varld* [Rambles in the world of Shakespeare] (Stockholm, 1962). Some of my suggestions were adopted by Mr. Martin Holmes in his book *The Guns of Elsinore*, (London, 1964).

(3) Malone Society Reprints, 1913.

(4) Malone Society Reprints, 1927.

(5) *The First and Second Part of the History of the famous Euordanus, Prince of Denmark, with the strange Aduentures of Iago, Prince of Saxonie: and of both theyr seuerall fortunes in Loue* (London, 1605). The only known complete copy is in the John Ryland's Library, Manchester.

(6) I. Gollancz, *The Sources of HAMLET* (London, 1926), p. 180.

(7) *Ibid.*, p. 282.

(8) Nina Bang, *Tabeller over Skibsfart og Varetransport gennem Oresund 1497—1660* (Copenhagen, 1906), I.

(9) Laurits Pedersen, *Helsingor i Sundstoldstiden* (Copenhagen, 1926), Part II, pp. 32, 248.

(10) *Worke for Armorours*, 1609. *The Non-Dramatic Works of Thomas Dekker*, ed. Alexendor Grosart (London, 1885), IV, 106.

(11) "Ante castellum bombardae maximae, optime dispositae et sedulo curatae; amplius centenis," Josias Mercer's Journal. He accompanied the English ambassador Daniel Rogers to Denmark in 1588. *Danske Magazin*, 1913, p. 340.

(12) *Ibid.*, p. 342. Martin Holmes, wishing to illustrate his book *The Guns of Elsinore* with a picture of the very guns on the ramparts of the castle, unfortunately chose a detail from one of the Kronborg tapestries showing Christian III besieging his rebellious capital. The guns are siege guns pointed at Copenhagen.

(13) Lauritz Pedersen, *op. cit.* Part I, pp. 47-9.

(14) In 1570 Willian Burrough, commanding a fleet of 13 English ships, was set upon by "Danske Freeboters" (pirates from Danzig). He captured 83 of them and turned all of them over to the Russians except one, who had done great service to some English sailors when they had been taken prisoners, saving their lives "with great favour besides." Hakluyt's *Voyages* (Glasgow, 1903), III, 168.

(15) "His brother and he [the king] with their own hands beat and misused our men very unprincely, giving proud and contumelious words against our whole nation." Letter from John Chamberlain to Dudley Carleton, 1 Aug. 1599. Chamberlain, *The Letters* (Philadelphia, 1939), I, 79.

(16) The situation changed after James' accession, his queen being a sister of Christian IV. The amity between Denmark and England is duly stressed in V.ii.40-44 (Cambr. Ed.), a passage which is not found in Q1 and may have been a later interpolation.

(17) In *What happens in HAMLET* (Cambridge, 1935). Cf. E.A.J. Honigmann, "The politics in HAMLET and 'The World of the Play'" *Stratford-upon-Avon Studies*, 5 (1963).

(18) Henry Ellis, *Original Letters*, Ser. II, Vol. 3, letter 233.

(19) See my paper "HAMLET and the Coronation of Christian IV" in *Shakespeare Quarterly*, XVI (1965), 155-60.

(20) Martin Holmes, *op. cit.* p. 43, believes that Guildenstern (Gyldenstjerne) was not a Danish but a Swedish name, which he considers "near enough for our purposes." Actually there were both Danish and Swedish branches of the family, both belonging to the most prominent nobility of the respective countries.

(21) Martin Holmes, *op. cit.* pp 46-47, 53, who strongly advocates this view, makes a very natural mistake in supposing that Hamlet would have had his place among the legendary Danish kings. He is indeed included in certain manuscript tables of Danish kings, but his portrait was not found in the suite of tapestries. This followed Saxo's chronicle, in which Hamlet was a rebel and would-be usurper, defeated and slain by the rightful king, Viglet.

(22) "In this village [Elsinore] a strong castle called Croneburg lyeth upon the mouth of the Straight, to which the other side of the Narrow sea, in the Kingdome of Norway, another castle is opposite . . ." *Itineraries* (Glasgow, 1907-8), Part I, p. 124.

(23) For a fuller treatment of this subject see my paper "A contribution to the Geography of HAMLET," *Shakespeare Jahrbuch*, Band 100/101 (Weimar, 1965).

(24) Laurits Pedersen, *Kronborg Have* (Copenhagen, 1920), p. 83.

(25) Laurits Pedersen, *Helsingørske Lav* (Helsingør, 1918), p. 179; Werner Krebs, *Alte Handwerksgebrauche mit besonderer Berucksichtigung der Schweiz* (Basel, 1933), p. 88.

(26) A Danish traveller visiting Florence in 1626 tersely noted in his diary: "The Grand Duke has 100 German guardsmen dressed up as *Schwidzer* but they are not." *Christen Skeels Resedagbok 1619-1627* (Malmö, 1962), p. 96.

(27) "HAMLET and the Coronation of Christian IV," *Shakespeare Quarterly*, XVI (1965), 155-60.

(28) Cf. the extravagant piece of invective in Nashe's *Pierce Pennilesse:* "The Danes are bursten-bellied sots, that are to be confuted with nothing but Tankards or quart pots, and *Ouid* might as well haue read his verses to the *Getes* that understood him not, as a man talk reason to them that haue no eares but their mouths, nor sense but that which they swallowe down their throates." McKerrow, *Works*, I, 177.

(29) A note in the margin: "Yvrognerie vice commun aux peuples ou septentrion," Gollancz, *op. cit.*, p. 254. The Danes were well aware of this vice. The first Danish drama which was not a school-play, from 1609, ostensibly about Anthony and Cleopatra, was a tract against drunkenness.

(30) Cf. my note "The Stamp of one Defect' in *ZAA*, 2 (1962). The idea underlying this speech was taken from Belleforest, who in summing up Amleth's character cannot refrain from moralizing. He writes—in the words of the English translation of 1608—that Amleth "would have been worthy of perpetual memorie if one onely spotte had not blemished and darkened a good part of his prayses." Here Belleforest is giving vent to his disapproval of Amleth's inordinate interest in women, which saddles him with two wives. Shakespeare cannot use this, so he deftly applies the idea of the "one onely spotte" to the notorious drinking habits of Danish royalty.

(31) Both letters are reproduced in V. Wanscher, *Kronborgs Historie* (Copenhagen, 1939).

(32) Martin Holmes, *op. cit.* p. 174, points out how Shakespeare makes this practice an integral part of the plot. In the first act the custom is established and explained. During the fencing match in the fifth act the ritual is repeated: the king takes a drink from a cup, and, with utmost publicity, drops the poison (disguised as a pearl) into the wine before the eyes of everybody. It is done to the sound of drum, trumpet and cannon, and the king then sends the cup to Hamlet—a piece of almost breathtaking audacity. The spectator cannot but echo Horatio's words: "Why, what a king is this."

(33) Gollancz, *op. cit.*, p. 237.

(34) Thomas Nashe, "The Terrors of the Night," *Works*, I, 360.

(35) Martin Holmes, *op. cit.*, pp 47-48, 75, hazards the conjecture that Shakespeare got these topographical notions from a view of the castle in Braun and Hogenberg, *Civitatis Orbis Terrarum*, in which the curtain wall would have suggested the cliff and the promontory on the other side of the Sound the high eastern hill.

(36) Laurits Pedersen, *Kronborg Have*, p. 74.

Measure For Measure: Quid Pro Quo?

by A. D. Nuttall

Some people seem to have little difficulty in understanding *Measure for Measure;* for example, Professor Wilson Knight. His summary of the play's theme is at once lucid and deeply attractive: "'justice' is a mockery: man, himself a sinner, cannot presume to judge. That is the lesson driven home in *Measure for Measure.*"[1] It is difficult not to respond gratefully to this thesis, which exalts the loving prostitute above the censorious prig, charity of heart above Olympian pride of intellect. If mankind is frail, then we, as part of mankind, are frail, and the proper response to our situation is not judgement, but love. Further, Professor Knight's thesis is not only *inherently* attractive; it also accords well with the main movement of the plot, which is from judicial retaliation to forgiveness and harmony. Again, it attaches itself closely to certain passages in the play—passages which derive their beauty from their enormous moral power:

> How would you be
> If He, which is the top of judgement, should
> But judge you as you are? O, think on that,
> And mercy then will breathe within your lips,
> Like man new made.   *(II.ii.75-79)*

> But man, proud man,
> Dress'd in a little brief authority,
> Most ignorant of what he's most assur'd—
> His glassy essence—like an angry ape
> Plays such fantastic tricks before high heaven
> As makes the angles weep....[2]   *(II.ii.118-123)*

Within the world of *Measure for Measure* Professor Knight's thesis exalts, say, the forgiving Duke high above the frigid Angelo, which would seem to be very good sense, since the Duke is obviously the hero and Angelo the villain.

Unobviously, however, the situation is quite otherwise. If we allow ourselves to look at all hard at the play, a shadowy structure of a disturbingly alien shape becomes visible under the comedy surface. One thing we can learn quite quickly is, for example, the fact that Angelo is, on a modest computation (as Swift would say) worth about six Dukes. One begins to suspect that the whole trouble with Professor Knight's account is its very smoothness. It is occasionally salutary to ask oneself "If I had never read or seen *Measure for Measure*, but knew it only from Professor Knight's essay, what sort of idea of the work would I have? What surprises would I get when I turned to the play itself? In what ways would the real experience of *Measure for Measure* differ from the experience Professor Knight had led me to expect?" I think it is fair to say (and this goes not just for Professor Knight's account but also for the varying interpretations of Roy Battenhouse, Nevill Coghill and even F. R. Leavis)[4] that Shakespeare would give such a reader a much *rougher ride* than he had looked for. The first thing he would learn from a virgin text is that *Measure for Measure* is a jagged play.

It is also a highly dialectical play, perhaps the most audaciously metaphysical of all Shakespeare's dramas. In *Measure for Measure* Shakespeare (who had after all trained himself on such stories as that of *The Comedy of Errors*) wove a plot of astonishing ingenuity. As long as this play is treated as a work of abstract art, it will be found as smooth as your mistress's glass. So considered, its primary characteristics are intricacy and celerity. The principal idea (of vicarious action) is worked out in a very pretty sequence of variations meeting in a final resolution. For example, one may hear the theme in brilliant *accelerando* if one traces that strand of the plot which brings Lucio into contact with the Duke. In III.ii. Lucio slanders the Duke to the Friar, not knowing that the Duke and the Friar are one and the same person (though he seems to know that the Duke has disguised himself). Then, at V.i.130f., he slanders the Friar to the Duke, not knowing — again — that they are the same person. Thus Lucio's fertility in slander is frustrated by the Duke's fertility in subterfuge. The variety of the Duke's appearances cancels out the variety of Lucio's mendacity, leaving a single net offence — the slander of a prince.

So one pole of the play is, we may say, *technical* neatness. The other is, of course, *metaphysical* disorder. Thus the effect of the play may be expressed by describing it as having the tempo and intervals of a minuet worked out in a sequence of violent discords. For example: it is likely that the substitution of Mariana for Isabel in Angelo's bed is one of the elements in the plot which we owe to Shakespeare alone. The episode illustrates very clearly the double character of ingenuity and discordancy which I impute to the play as a whole. On the one hand it is expert comedy-plotting, a dramatic structure in itself intricate and mirroring other elements in the play, as for example the Friar-Duke-Lucio relationship I have just described. Isabel is a lady who has dedicated her virginity to God. She expresses herself as willing to give anything to save her brother's life. Angelo then turns the tables on her by asking for the one thing she feels she cannot give. In effect, the Duke's delegate strives to usurp the place of God in Isabel's life (for she is betrothed to God). But Angelo is (or was) betrothed to Mariana. Thus Isabel is able, by breaking faith with Angelo, to keep her faith with God. The venial sin of Mariana in sleeping with her betrothed formally echoes the venial sin of Claudio who slept with *his* and so began the whole chain of events. The stratagem of Isabel and the Duke mathematically cancels out the stratagem of Angelo, who is brought to commit the very crime for which he had sentenced Claudio. Angelo's attempt at usurpation is countered by another usurpation (Mariana's); and the double falsehood issues in a strange propriety. Thus we have a *peripeteia* within a *peripeteia*. What could be more elegant?

And yet, as we watch it happen, what could be more appalling? How can Isabel who so imperiously denounced her brother's action — "There is a vice that most I do abhor, / And most desire should meet the blow of justice . . ." (II.ii.29-30) — assent with such sprightly readiness to the suggestion that Mariana perform the selfsame action — "The image of it gives me content already . . ." (III.i.260). Note that Shakespeare could, had he wished, have made this much more comfortable for us. He could easily have caused Isabel to argue from the first that Claudio in effect committed no sin with Juliet.[5] This would have had the further consequence of making Isabel's duet with Lucio (in which they together try to divert the harsh purpose of Angelo) altogether more harmonious. But Shakespeare preferred to show us an Isabel forced by vicissitude into strange company, into what is almost an unholy alliance. Theoretically, she is really (as Mary Lascelles saw[6]) much closer to Angelo than to Lucio. Both are ethical precisionists. Both abhor the confusion of charity with indulgence, of licence with true mercy. Yet Isabel must plead against an insinuating counterpoint from Lucio which almost amounts to a parody of her argument. Certainly, the episode comes off more smoothly in Whetstone. But who prefers Whetstone's scene to Shakespeare's?[7]

That the play is full of ethical collisions, not to say inconsistencies, needs little labour to show. Isabel not only turns, in the words of Sir Arthur Quiller Couch,[8] from a saint into a bare procuress; she also lets down the Christian historicist critic. Thus in her early clash with Angelo we are told that anyone who thinks Isabel *ought* to submit to Angelo is the victim of a modern prejudice; that it could never have occurred to an Elizabethan that there could be anything vicious in fidelity to a vow of chastity. What's supernatural is supernatural. What's natural is only natural. And then, when all our learning has been lavished in defence of her supernatural dedication, she marries the Duke. Of course, such a defence of the automatically over-riding status of Isabel's vows was always bad history of ideas. Raymond Southall has shown[9] how the distinction between social and spiritual grace formed the material of open controversy in the sixteenth century — that is, if I have correctly understood the opening sections of his essay. J. W. Lever has[10] an interesting quotation from Tyndale on the pride of Lucrece, "which pryde god more abhorreth than the whordome of any whor." More could be added from Erasmus.[11] Indeed Lever has observed[12] that the affirmation of specifically "natural" values is a commonplace of humanism. To bring the argument nearer home we might observe that in the source-stories both of Cinthio and Whetstone the Isabel-figure actually does the inconceivable thing; she yields, and yet remains the heroine. If a Shakespearean voice is wanted to show that people *could* think unfavourably of chastity, there is Parolles — "virginity is peevish, proud, idle, made of self-love . . ." (*AWW*, I.i.149). Or, if Parolles disgraces the witness box, it must be granted that the Duke, in the present play, distinguishes plainly enough between an introverted preoccupation with one's own virtue and an outward-turned beneficence in his words to Angelo at I.i.29:

> Thyself and thy belongings
> Are not thine own so proper as to waste
> Thyself upon thy virtues, they on thee.[13]

These are dangerous sentiments to leave lying about in the neighbourhood of Isabel.

Of course I am aware that answers can be made to all these points; and, in particular, that Isabel can readily be cleared of the charge of simple egoism. I can even agree with E. M. Pope that the dominant feeling of the time would endorse Isabel's refusal to yield to Angelo.[14] I only submit that for a play as dense in texture as *Measure for Measure* to register a "dominant feeling" is not enough. We must be receptive to the presence of varying undermeanings. To assimilate the present scene to the basic tenets of the Elizabethan World Picture (which I begin to think was as real an entity as the Twentieth Century World Picture—imagine a critic three hundred years hence operating on, say, Muriel Spark, with *that*) is to empty the scene of stress. As it stands, the collision of values is immense. A crack runs rapidly across the scorched earth; the direct love of God is split from the love of neighbour. The two basic commands of the Gospels of which George Herbert wrote: "O dark instructions; ev'n as dark as day!"[15] prove, after all, not wholly perspicuous. There once appeared an ecclesiastical cartoon which showed a little monk praying fervently while his superior angrily shouted "Are you going over my head?" *Fabula docet.* As soon as we learn how to enter into a direct relationship with God, our relationship with the world can be viewed as a distraction. As long as one's love of God is naturally discharged by love of one's neighbour, Isabel's dilemma is impossible. Only with the birth of the monastic ideal and of the notion that I can love God best if I withdraw from my neighbour's society, does it become possible. Only then can God and my neighbour become rivals. In *Measure for Measure* God has two rivals for the love of Isabel, one loved and one detested but who working together are almost dangerous—namely Claudio and Angelo. Certainly Isabel's situation is ill described as egoism under attack. She cannot forget her own honour for the sake of Claudio since she has pledged that honour to God. If the reader feels something preposterous in this high piled metaphysical structure—something reminiscent of, say, Graham Greene, I am inclined to agree with him. I fancy Shakespeare felt it too; after all, he created the ironic witness Lucio and even Isabel cannot keep it up. But the metaphysical terror, though wafer-thin, is real.

Isabel's marriage, then, is as inconsistent as her attitude to sexual intercourse between engaged persons. But this is of small importance compared with the Grand Inconsistency of the whole play—namely the inconsistency between the ethic of government and the ethic of refraining from judgement. But having named this conflict I propose to postpone its discussion. It may profitably be left to germinate for a while in the reader's consciousness.

I have suggested a discrepancy between the "technical" smartness of this play and its ideological discordancy. The application of this distinction to, say, the character of Angelo is straightforward. Its effect is greatly to weaken the force of the plain man's argument against him, already cited: "Angelo is the technical villain; therefore it makes good sense to hold that he is contemptible." Isabel is the technical heroine, but she is not permitted to survive unmarked. Perhaps a correlative dispensation is extended to Angelo.

To begin from what is generally accepted: we all know better than Hazlitt now. Angelo is not a common hypocrite.[16] Isabel is at her very best when she says of him

> I partly think
> A due sincerity govern'd his deeds
> Till he did look on me.   *(V.i.443-445)*

The tone of this is subtle. It represents an effort of objectivity. It also expresses a kind of bewilderment. Isabel is finding that she has not really understood what happened, does not really understand Angelo. And indeed it is a question whether he is intelligible at all. His loneliness is so nearly complete.

His first words in the play—

> Always obedient to your Grace's will,
> I come to know your pleasure   *(I.i.25-26)*

—are perhaps faintly ridiculous. But the speech should be so delivered as to defeat an incipient risibility in the audience by its sheerly factual character. It is a part which should be played with a complete insensitivity to social overtones, and a complete attention to radical meaning. As the figure of Angelo moves before us we find a certain note struck again and again. It is the fundamental idea of the play—vicariousness—but in Angelo it finds its most intricate and powerful expression.

Angelo is, in the inherited story of the play, a deputy, the Duke's Vicar. But Shakespeare has extended this notion to color the very essence of Angelo. He is in himself a sort of surrogate human being. The Duke, gazing at Angelo on his first appearance, observes that the virtue of so excellent a man requires and merits public exercise. The sentiment is ordinary enough. But also present in the speech is the merest hint of a much more radical—indeed, a philosophical—idea, namely that virtue is essentially a matter of behaviour, that the man whose virtue is invisible cannot meaningfully be said to be virtuous at all. It is a speech I have already touched on:

> Thyself and thy belongings
> Are not thine own so proper as to waste
> Thyself upon thy virtues, they on thee.
> Heaven doth with us as we with torches do,
> Not light them for themselves; for if our virtues
> Did not go forth of us, 'twere all alike
> As if we had them not.   *(I.i.29-35)*

The Arden editor notes that this passage echoes language used elsewhere by Shakespeare of procreation. It also recalls Ulysses' philosophical exhortation of Achilles (though the similarity is in thought and style rather than in vocabulary):

> ...no man is the lord of anything...
> Till he communicate his parts to others;
> Nor doth he of himself know them for ought
> Till he behold them form'd in the applause
> Where they're extended; who, like an arch reverberates
> The voice again, or like a gate of steel
> Fronting the sun, receives and renders back
> His figure and his heat. *(Troilus and Cressida, III.iii.115-123)*

Angelo is the man suggested by the philosophizing of Ulysses; in himself nothing, pure function (at ll.ii.39 he actually uses the word "function" of himself). The Duke forthwith appropriates his identity: "be thou at full ourself" (I.i.43). The purely instrumental status of Angelo is repeatedly brought to our notice:

> Whether the tyranny be in his place,
> Or in his eminence that fills it up,
> I stagger in. *(I.ii.152-154)*

> I have on Angelo impos'd the office. *(I.iii.40)*

> How will you do to content this substitute...? *(III.i.186-187)*

> Lord Angelo dukes it well in his absence. *(III.ii.91)*

Through all the proliferating substitutions of the play, Angelo remains (so to speak) the supreme vicar. Yet he has his own kind of solidity (and it is a moral kind). Professor Coghill makes much[17] of his refusal personally to sift the evidence in the case of Froth and Bum—

> This will last out a night in Russia
> When nights are longest there. I'll take my leave,
> And leave you to the hearing of the cause;
> Hoping you'll find good cause to whip them all. *(II.i.133-136)*

It is, however, doubtful whether there is anything discreditable in the delegation of this tedious business to Escalus. Physical chastisement has acquired in modern times an added character of traumatic outrage and thus Angelo's parting words may shock a present-day audience where they would earn a sympathetic laugh in a Jacobean theatre. Nevertheless, the line retains a distinctly unpleasant force, which is principally located in the word "hoping." A certain relish of anticipation is implied. Perhaps we might say that this is the first faint sign in Angelo of the lust which will destroy him. But the real tenor of the speech is missed if we stop here. There is a further phrase in the line which, coming from the lips of Angelo, has the power to check and channel the suggestion of "hoping": I mean the phrase "good cause." At the very moment when Angelo's blood quickens, his grip tightens on the law. Although the tension of this speech is so gently hinted and so soon over, it is really present and foreshadows the later development of Angelo. Our dominant impression is still that of a hollow man, a sort of lay-figure. But as the play progresses we see that there persists in Angelo, even through the usurpation of his own soul by lust fully revealed and irresistible, a kind of integrity.

Which is more than can be said for the Duke. The Duke is a ruler who has let things slide. In order to restore good order in Vienna he appoints a substitute who will bear on his shoulders all the odium of renewed severity. This is the Grand Substitution of the play at the purely political level.

For this play is profoundly political. Roy Battenhouse described it (but without any consciousness of paradox) as "a Mirror for Magistrates founded on Christian love."[18] We can now look a little more closely at the conflict I have already alluded to—the conflict between the ethic of government and the ethic of refraining from judgement.

Anyone who has read through Cinthio's tale and Whetstone's two-part play can watch for himself the growth of a serious and rebarbative preoccupation with legal utility in the transplantation of this story from Italy to England. Mary Lascelles has noted[19] how the law in Cinthio has the status of a purblind dotard guarding an orchard from children among whom it is a point of honour to rob the trees; whereas in Whetstone we find a Tudor reverence for law itself with criticism reserved for defects in its administration. It seems doubtful whether Whetstone realized what a formidably un-Christian ethical force he had released by honouring human law in such a context. Indeed, to men who were seriously concerned with the ordering of institutions, the revolutionary morality of *Matthew*, vii, *Mark*, iv, and *Luke*, vi (the Scriptural sources for the title of this play) presented grave difficulties. Elizabeth Marie Pope has brilliantly shown what sort of effect these passages had on the magisterial mind. For example she quotes[20] Calvin and William Perkins to the effect that such Biblical texts should not lead a man to condone open and serious wrong. Attempts were made to resolve the difficulty by distinguishing between the actions of a private individual and the actions of the state. Private citizens may—indeed, should—be as Christian as possible, but judicial clemency is "limited in practice to considerations of ordinary common sense."[21]

But what then of the Prince, who, in his own person, *is* the State? Presumably he should *not* indulge a promiscuous clemency. Of course the Prince who condemns does so not in his own name but as the minister and vicar of God.[22] This in a way reproduces the dual morality of those Scriptural passages which lie behind the title "Measure for Measure." For example, in the verses from *Matthew*, vii we are told to refrain from judgement, not because judgement must be transcended by love, but "that ye be not judged." In *Mark*, iv[23] the over-riding context of divine retribution is even clearer. So the Prince *qua* man has no duty save to love and forgive his fellow creatures, but as God's substitute he must hunt out and punish the malefactor.

If we press hard on the argument, the ruler might appear to be metaphysically in a cleft stick. As the bloodless instrument of God's will he must perform actions which in a human creature count as sins; his office is eschatologically a millstone round his neck, for the obligation it confers is an obligation to sin.

There is, of course, a short way to resolve this difficulty. The only disquieting thing about it is that if we adopt it we come near to absolving Angelo of guilt in his treatment of Claudio. Thus we may point out that to say X does such and such a thing in the name of Y means that Y, not X, bears the responsibility for the action. Thus God, not the Prince, bears the responsibility for official executions. Now Angelo certainly condemns Claudio in the Duke's name. So whose is the responsibility now? It may be replied that this is sheer sophistry since the Duke never authorised Angelo to do *that*. But is it? The Duke was fully aware of Angelo's character. Hence, indeed, his appointment as substitute. The Duke wants Angelo for the job just because he will condemn people like Claudio. And to condemn the Claudios of Vienna is not just politically imprudent; it is too dirty a job for the Duke's squeamish conscience. Would not this reformation of justice seem more dreadful in yourself than in a deputy? Asks Friar Thomas:

> I do fear, too dreadful.
> Sith 'twas my fault to give the people scope,
> 'Twould be my tyranny to strike and gall them
> For what I bid them do: for we bid this be done,
> When evil deeds have their permissive pass,
> And not the punishment. Therefore indeed, my father,
> I have on Angelo impos'd the office;
> Who may in th'ambush of my name strike home,
> And yet my nature never in the fight
> To do in slander   *(I.iii.34-43)*

There are two arguments here: the first is straight Machiavelli: delegate unpopular actions. We need not look far in *The Prince* for an analogue to the Duke of Vienna:

> the province was a prey to robbery, assaults, and every kind
> of disorder. He [Cesare Borgia], therefore, judged it necessary
> to give them a good government in order to make them peaceful
> and obedient to his rule. For this purpose he appointed Messer
> Remirro de Orco, a cruel and able man, to whom he gave the
> fullest authority. This man, in a short time, was highly success-
> ful in rendering the country orderly and united, whereupon the
> duke, not deeming such excessive authority expedient, lest it
> should become hateful, appointed a civil court of justice in the
> centre of the province under an excellent president, to which
> each city appointed its own advocate. And as he knew that the
> harshness of the past had engendered some amount of hatred,
> in order to purge the minds of the people and to win them over
> completely, he resolved to show that if any cruelty had taken
> place it was not by his orders, but though the harsh disposition
> of his minister. And having found the opportunity he had him
> cut in half and placed one morning in the public square at

238

Cesena with a piece of wood and bloodstained knife at his side.
The ferocity of this spectacle caused the people both satisfaction and amazement.[24]

But to be sure, the Duke of Vienna pardoned Angelo.

Of course, to show that a character is Machiavellian is not *ipso facto* to prove
him a villain. The idea that a ruler should delegate odious offices is Aristotelian[25]
and was referred to with approval by Erasmus[26] before it was adopted by Machiavelli. Mario Praz has shown[27] how Machiavellian principles were implicitly
approved by Thomas More, Montaigne and Spenser. Mary Lascelles notes[28] that
the ideal governor in Elyot's *The Image of Governaunce* (1541) is allowed to use
subterfuge to ensure a just outcome. There is a whole essay to be written round
what might be called the "White Machiavel" in Shakespeare. Such an essay might
begin from Sonnet 94 ("They that have power to hurt") and end in a discussion
of the supreme White Machiavel, Prince Hal. W. H. Auden has already pointed
out[29] that one style is common to the soliloquies of Iago and Hal. Plainly, any
writer with as strong an interest as Shakespeare's in government could not long
escape seeing the bitter duties of a prince whose care for his people was more
than sentimental. But have we a White Machiavel in *Measure for Measure*? I
think perhaps we have, but the Duke is not he.

The good Machiavellian ruler, if we allow him to be saveable at all, is saved
by his resolute dedication to a good end. No such powerful direction is discernible
in the tergiversations of the Duke. Certainly, he preserves the luxury of a technically uncorrupted conscience; certainly he ensures that the laws are reinforced,
even if he proceeds by his orgy of clemency at the close to undo all the good
achieved. Note that we can approve his behaviour at the end of the play only at
the cost of condemning his behaviour at its outset. A man can play football or
cricket; but he cannot score goals with a cricket bat. At whichever end of the
ethical spectrum you begin, you will never make a satisfactory hero of the Duke.
I suspect that the essential frivolity of his nature really shows itself in the speech
with which he ends I.iii —

> Lord Angelo is precise;
> Stands at a guard with Envy; scarce confesses
> That his blood flows; or that his appetite
> Is more to bread than stone. Hence shall we see
> If power change purpose, what our seemers be.

Is it too curious to detect in this speech a certain relish of anticipation? Is there
not a slight shifting of ground from the opening scene in which the Duke professes
his trust in, and grave respect for, the ascetic probity of Angelo? Is there not the
merest shadow of a Lucio-like sneer at the chastity of Angelo? It is Lucio who
echoes the Duke's language at I.iv.57-58 — "a man whose blood / Is very snow-
broth." Again it is a matter of exclusive alternatives. If we welcome the mocking
tone of these lines, then we must surely reject as priggish the grave eulogy at

I.i.26-40. As Clifford Leech has observed,[30] the Duke cannot *both* be testing a suspected nature *and* tightening up the administration of Vienna by the most reliable means to hand. But perhaps this is too dubious an instance to hang an entire interpretation on. A surer index is the Duke's unblushing readiness to hear confessions (and talk about them afterwards). The priestly disguise holds no embarrassment for him: "I have confess'd her, and I know her virtue" (V.i.524). The Duke in *Measure for Measure* is, at the political level, at best an off-white Machiavel, incongruously elevated to the position of Presiding Genius. At the metaphysical level he is, perhaps, mere Machiavel.

The bare mention of Machiavelli, however, raises the ethical question of ends and means. Ought we to perform an action in itself wicked in order that a greater good may come of it? This question is fundamental in *Measure for Measure,* and I fancy that in raising it I have reached the point at which I can no longer even hope for unanimity in the responses of readers. Christian opinion is itself divided on the point. On the one hand there is the tender-minded view, as expressed by the Thomist Jacques Maritain (writing on Machiavelli); moral conscience, he says "is never allowed to do evil for any good whatsoever."[31] On the other hand Hilaire Belloc took up the tough-minded position when he defined sentimentality as the inability to see that the end justifies the means. I suppose most modern Englishmen implicitly assent to the proposition that the end justifies the means. Any clergyman, for example, who allows the possible existence of a just war thereby ranges himself with Belloc and against Maritain.[32] The Elizabethans, with their fear of anarchy, were, I think, a little quicker to see this than we. Having assembled my apparatus I must set it to work. According to the terms elaborated we may find in *Measure for Measure* two fundamental ethical views, tender and tough, of which the first must be subdivided into two further sections. Let us label them *Ia, Ib* and *II.*

Ia may be expressed as follows: No man who is not himself perfect has the right to judge a fellow creature. Man can only forgive and exercise charity. For example:

> *Isabel*
>
>   Go to your bosom,
> Knock there, and ask your heart what it doth know
> That's like my brother's fault. If it confess
> A natural guiltiness, such as is his,
> Let it not sound a thought upon your tongue
> Against my brother's life.
>
>   *(II.ii.137-142)*

Compare also II.ii.75f., IV.ii.81-83. Persons who hold to this opinion tend in practice to believe that the end cannot justify the means. The connection between these two notions is not immediately obvious. My own guess is that both stem from a powerful awareness of the supernatural authority of God and a correspondingly low estimate of man. To such a mind ethics tends to consist of a series of God-given imperatives. These imperatives cannot be appraised or placed in order of value by merely human intelligence. Ours not to reason why. This granted, man's right to ethical judgement is no greater than the child's right to judge the proficiency of his schoolfellow in, say, French prose composition. And to form projects involving the considered subjection of means to ends involves a similar assumption of Olympian authority. View *Ia* almost certainly lies behind the repulsion Escalus feels at Angelo's account of the law as a scarecrow, which if left unchanged will become the object of contempt (II.i.1f). Note that if we side with Escalus here we place ourselves in opposition to the Duke whose loving state-craft is very fairly represented by Angelo's words. But we are growing accustomed to these uncomfortable choices. Such then is ethic *Ia*; the high Christian variant of the tender view.

Ib is on the contrary, low and non-Christian, though still, of course, tender. It goes something like this: anybody without a bit of generous vice in him isn't properly human. The sexual appetite is in itself good; it is of the heart, and heart is more than head. This has a very twentieth-century flavour but is certainly present in *Measure for Measure*—most obviously in the "low" dialogue of the play, though the implied collision of values is never so clearly expressed as by Escalus in his rueful comment on Angelo's austere judicial conduct:

> Well, heaven forgive him; and forgive us all.
> Some rise by sin, and some by virtue fall.   *(II.i.37-38)*

The same ethical collision is asserted "from below," as the Arden editor noticed, in the comic misplacings of Elbow:

> But precise villains they are, that I am sure of, and void of all
> profanation in the world, that good Christians ought to have. *(II.i.54-56)*

To hammer the point home Escalus is here given a "Here's a wise fool" response. Isabel, after she has been battered down from her high Christian position, has recourse to the low-tender view: "'Tis set down so in heav'n, but not in earth" (II.iv.50).

Ethic *II*, the tough-minded one, has much less power (it will be noticed at once) to give us warm feelings. To begin with, it is white Machiavellianism. Ends (in this fallen world) justify means; to resist this is to lapse into sentimentalism; *of course* none of us is perfect but *of course* we must judge; the man who is willing to abolish the police force in order to luxuriate in a private orgy of conscience is less merciful than the magistrate who administers the law in the interests of the community. This ethic is impersonalist, pragmatic and anti-sentimental. Above all it is the ethic of Angelo. Ethic *II* yields no passages of moving poetry, as e.g. *Ib* does, in Lucio's "blossoming time" speech at I.iv.40f. That, I suspect, may be part of the point. Its ugliness and inaccessibility are correlative with the ugliness and inaccessibility of Angelo himself. It is supported "from below" by the dramatist, but in a manner appropriate to its nature. All the scenes in which the corruption of Vienna is conveyed work on its behalf. For, observe, human sexuality in *Measure for Measure* has two faces, one fair and one (from which Professor Wilson Knight appears to have averted his eyes) very foul indeed. Anyone who thinks of this play as a simple celebration of the procreative processes should read through, say, III.ii.

Now concerning these rival ethics I should like to put what might well be thought an indecorous question. Which of them, *as argument,* cuts deepest? Wood cuts butter; so Isabel cuts through the simple monster of ferocity she takes Angelo to be. Steel resists wood, so the real Angelo meets and parries every ethical thrust Isabel can produce from all the warmth of her heart and her understanding. In order to obtain a fair hearing for Angelo I must ask the reader to consider the moral questions before him not as if they were in a romance (where we should all applaud indiscriminate clemency without a moment's compunction) but as if they were a part of real life. *Measure for Measure* deserves no less. Now, do we really think that because none of us is perfect so no one should judge—that is, in hard terms, there should be no law-courts, no penal system, no juries, no police? Certainly judges are imperfect, but equally certainly it is a job that someone has to do. Men of tender conscience may preserve their charity intact, but only so long as others are willing to tarnish theirs a little.

Angelo grants at once that those who judge are not themselves free from sin. This may mean that they lack, at the metaphysical level, a "right" to judge, but it certainly does not mean that they cannot, at the practical level, do it:

> I not deny
> The Jury passing on the prisoner's life
> May in the sworn twelve have a thief, or two,
> Guiltier than him they try.... *(II.i.18-21)*

The naked intelligence of this transfixes the naive casuistry of the Duke's evasion of guilt at I.iii.36-40.

Of course Angelo is only half a man. He is, until invaded by terrible desire, pure intellect. But it may be salutary to remember how much less human beings can be, even than that. Angelo's lust is moved, strangely, and terrifyingly, by Isabel's virtue (II.ii.162, 168-70, 174-75, 180-84). It is as if he discovered that he was a pervert who could be stimulated only by manifest goodness in another person (note, once more, the conceptual audacity of *Measure for Measure*: those lines dispose finely of that slovenly abstractness of mind which defines love as a passion directed at the soul and lust as a passion directed at the body).

So Angelo falls. But notice how, as a dialectician, he is still in a manner secure. Nothing has happened to overthrow his original position. He had always been enough of a realist to know that among the jurors there might be one guiltier than the defendant. The conclusion is clear, and Angelo never shirks it. He is now himself properly the victim of the superhuman law.

For Angelo's view of the law is naturally impersonalist:

> It is the law, not I, condemn your brother;
> Were he my kinsman, brother, or my son,
> It should be thus with him. *(II.ii.80-83)*

242

This must always have been coldly shocking but perhaps a Jacobean audience would be quicker than we to think of Junius Brutus who condemned his own sons —to connect Christian sin with Roman virtue. Certainly the notion of an heroic suppression of humanity would be alien even then, but not perhaps entirely inaccessible.

The most invidious action of Angelo's is perhaps his going back on the promise to release Claudio. At this point in the play Angelo has descended into hell and it would plainly be absurd to defend its morality, yet a sort of consistency may persist even here. Consider it for a moment from the point of view of a white Machiavel. Remember that you are committed to the thesis that a strict administration of the law is in the best interests of the people, and that these interests have an overriding claim upon the conscience of the administrator. Suppose, then, the administrator finds himself drawn by a purely personal entanglement to remit the normal course of law —what ought he to do? Clearly, on such principles, he should disregard his personal commitment in deference to the general. He should pull himself together and exercise strict authority according to the law.

In fact however, the reason Angelo gives in his soliloquy is much less creditable than this. He says that he is afraid that Claudio, if allowed to live, may take vengeance on the ravisher of his sister. That at least is the most natural way (and, let us confess, the *right* way) to take this speech. Yet there is an awkwardness in the expression which seems to betray the presence of a contrary idea, struggling for admission. The line are these:

> He should have liv'd;
> Save that his riotous youth, with dangerous sense,
> Might in the times to come have ta'en revenge
> By so receiving a dishonoured life
> With ransom of such shame.   *(IV.iv.26-30)*

The crucial word is "By." Read without any awareness of context, that "By" would most naturally be taken as following closely on "have ta'en revenge." The meaning of the whole sentence would then be: "He should have been allowed to live, except that, if he had, his youthfully riotous nature might subsequently have taken a kind of revenge on him, by accepting a life of dishonourable vice, since that life had been bought in so shameful a way." The sentiment would then be parallel to that of Angelo's earlier speech at II.ii. 101-105. It might be objected that such a reading places an odd interpretation on "receiving," but the objection could not be sustained for long. Compare for example, *Twelfth Night,* III.iv. 199-200, "I know his youth will most aptly receive it,—into a most hideous opinion" or *Henry VIII,* II.iv. 168, "My conscience first receiv'd a tenderness." No, the real difficulty is that there is a much more probable interpretation—the one I have already stated—available. The only problem facing the orthodox interpreter is the word "By." *This* difficulty is not dispelled by citing instrumental uses of *by* such as "By this Lord Angelo perceives he's safe" (V.i.492). What is rather needed is a *causative* use of *by.* This, though very rare, appears to be possible Shakespearean English; for example:

243

> ...the remembrance of my former love
> Is by a newer object quite forgotten.   *(Two Gentlemen of Verona, II.iv.196-197)*

To show that a causative use of *by* is possible is, I think, to clinch the orthodox case. But to prove that an expression is possible is not to prove it normal. One can still legitimately feel that the sentence is oddly put together, that the thought is subject to a certain strain. It may be significant that by a trifling change of perspective a different, yet in one respect a *consistent* picture of Angelo's motivation emerges.

Whichever view is uppermost in Angelo's mind, his grip on it is uncertain. His next words betray unhappiness and bewilderment:

> Would yet he had liv'd.
> Alack, when once our grace we have forgot,
> Nothing goes right; we would and we would not.   *(IV.iv.30-33)*

Where, then, does this leave us? The judgement of the law must be imposed (all agree to that, except perhaps Lucio and his associates). To the question: Who shall impose the law since none of us is perfect? Angelo and the Duke return different answers. Angelo's answer is that men must sink their individuality in the law; that men must judge according to the law, and, when they err, submit to the same law; if it seems grotesque that a man should sit in judgement on other men, one should remember that the judge also is subject to the same rules. The Duke's answer is: Get someone else to do it.

This brings us back to the Duke's speech of explanation at I.iii.34f. I said that there were two arguments in this speech, the first being the Machiavellian thesis that unpopular actions should be delegated, according to the example of Cesare Borgia. The second argument I have yet to discuss. At first sight it looks more respectable.

> Sith 'twas my fault to give the people scope.
> 'Twould be my tyranny to strike and gall them
> For what I bid them do.

That is to say, it is not only imprudent for me to enforce the law personally, it would also be immoral; I should be a tyrant in so switching from indulgence to rigour. That this argument is slightly more poisonous than the other appears on a very little reflection. For the Duke *is* switching from indulgence to rigour. Such a process is hard on the more sentimental sort of conscience, and the Duke is struggling to keep his untroubled by wrapping it in a tissue of evasions. Angelo would say at once that if rigour is really what is required then no tyranny but rather benevolence is involved in its exercise (as he argues to Isabel at II.ii.101-105 that there is a more genuine mercy in the enforcement of the law than in its neglect). But the Duke's intelligence, unlike Angelo's, is cunning rather than comprehensive. Morals to him are not contextual. Every action is intrinsically good or bad. To release a prisoner is to be charitable. Actually to prosecute a prisoner is uncharitable. Such an atomistic view of morals rapidly breeds what might be called meta-ethical situations. Thus, it is uncharitable suddenly to change course and enforce the law (that is basic ethics) but somehow it seems as if that is what *ought* to be done (meta-ethics!). The contextual view of an Angelo, whereby ends justify means, instantly resolves this dilemma, of course. But which view does God incline to, the atomistic or the contextual? The thunderingly simple commands in the Gospels, urged with such power by Isabel, suggest that God is more than half an atomist, and, by implication, that the eschatological structure of the universe will reflect an atomistic ethic. In plain terms they suggest that a man who does not perform charitable actions (like releasing criminals)—for whatever reason—is a sinner, and may go to Hell.

It is, of course, a primitive ethic, but it is deeply embedded in the ritual comedy-story of the play. To perceive its presence is to learn that the Duke is not merely a political Machiavel; he is also (so to speak) a metaphysical one. The device which saves his reputation also preserves his soul. Certain kinds of practical virtue (being technical sins) are beneath the saintly charity of the Duke, so someone else must be found as a surrogate. This situation is exactly paralleled by Isabel's adoption of Mariana as her substitute.

The idea of substitution is paramount. One might map it with reference to two poles, Machiavelli in the south and Christ in the north. For, as Roy Battenhouse saw, the Grand Deception of the Atonement moves beneath the surface of the drama just as certainly as does the bloody subterfuge of Cesare Borgia. It is explicitly conveyed in some of the most moving words of the play:

> Why, all the souls that were, were forfeit once,
> And he that might the vantage best have took
> Found out the remedy.   *(II.ii.73-75)*

If we contemplate the structure of the Atonement for a while, we may be willing to draw the last, and most terrifying, lesson from this play. Mankind lay groaning under a burden of sin, of which the wages are death. The Son of God took these sins away from us, bore them on his own shoulders, and by his death on the Cross, discharged our debt. Thus Christ, by taking our sins, was the supreme substitute.

Battenhouse, with some difficulty, sought to identify the God of the Atonement with the Duke. This can be done as long as we restrict our attention to God the Father—as long, that is, as we ignore the cardinal fact of substitution, which above all else connects *Measure for Measure* with the Atonement. Suppose we ask, who, in this play, most obviously corresponds to the figure of Christ? It is not surprising that this question has been avoided. The answer is both unthinkable and only too plain.

There is a story[33] by Jorge Luis Borges about a certain theologian of the city of Lund who began by suggesting that Judas played the noblest part in the drama of the Crucifixion in that it was he who shouldered the necessary burden of sin — and ended by arguing that Judas was the real Christ. Readers who find this story just silly will probably be unwilling to follow me further. For I wish to suggest that the Doctrine of Atonement which underlies *Measure for Measure* is closer to that of Nils Runeberg of Lund than it is to that of Irenaeus or Anselm; that it is, in short, a critical version. After all, Shakespeare borrowed nothing which he did not change.

One element in the traditional doctrine which is obstinately unclear is the phrase "took upon his shoulders our sins." How could this be, since Christ was without sin? Of course one can deal with the phrase by saying that it simply means that Christ took upon his shoulders the *consequences* of our sins. But as soon as one substitutes this account one gets the feeling that something has been lost — that the central mystery of Christ's incarnation has been removed. If God really became man, if the crucifixion really involved the voluntary self-humiliation of God, then — we feel — "took upon his shoulders our sins" must bear a slightly stronger sense. But then we are confronted once more by the first difficulty. The good Christian cannot say that Christ *became a sinner* just like the rest of us. It is too much to require of God that he should deny his nature.[34]

Yet that is what is required of Angelo. In the atonement of *Measure for Measure* the implications of vicarious guilt are followed out to the very end. Angelo takes on his shoulders the necessary sins of human judgement. But in the morality of this comedy there is no such area of uncertainty as we found in the Christian doctrine of the Atonement. Angelo, unlike Christ, really sins. His hands do not remain clean.

Under the pressure of Shakespeare's genius the figure of the atoning sufferer begins to take on the lineaments of his anthropological ancestor, the scapegoat. Thus, while I must plead guilty to introducing the *bete noire* of present day criticism, the Christ-figure, yet Angelo is certainly a Christ-figure with a difference. For he is also a Devil-figure. We are now in a position to account for the strange resonance of Isabel's cry in the last scene — "You bid me seek redemption of the devil" (V.i.30). Angelo is at once a Redeemer and the polluted. Earlier in this essay I was forced to acknowledge (for what it was worth) that Angelo at the close of the play is forgiven by the Duke. At the civil level this must be seen as a mitigation of the Duke's Machiavellianism. But the Duke is also, as we have seen, a metaphysical Machiavel. And I am not sure that, at this level, his forgiveness of Angelo is not his finest stratagem. It had always been a necessary consequence of Angelo's view of law that that administrator should desire for himself, if found guilty, the same punishment he would impose on others:

> When I that censure him do so offend,
> Let mine own judgement pattern out my death,
> And nothing come in partial.
>
> (II.i.29-31)

Angelo (how different, here, from Hazlitt's arch-hypocrite!) is absolutely consistent on this point when the crisis comes:

> No longer session hold upon my shame
> But let my trial be mine own confession.

> Immediate sentence, then, and sequent death
> Is all the grace I beg.   *(V.i.369-372)*

Angelo's plea to cut short his own inquisition is no sort of evasion, for he knows that he is unmasked. In such circumstances he can scarcely hope that the knowledge of his crimes will be kept from the populace. His proposal is not a trial *in camera* but a full confession from the guilty party. Further, the paradoxical description of punishment as "grace" is not just a verbal flourish. It expresses a paradox *in rebus.*

> I crave death more willingly than mercy;
> 'Tis my deserving, and I do entreat it.   *(V.i.474-475)*

Again, the word "deserving" is not mere rhetoric. Angelo is pleading for justice. The ending of *Measure for Measure* is really not very like the ending of *The Winter's Tale* or *Cymbeline.* For Angelo the Duke's indulgent benevolence does not confer felicity; rather, it perpetuates his anguish. Any producer who has Angelo leave the stage at the close of the play in a state of happy tranquillity simply does not know his business. The fact that Angelo's eye quickens when Claudio is produced alive will bear another construction than that which the Duke places on it ("By this Lord Angelo perceives he's safe," line 492). If Angelo were preoccupied with his own safety he would have responded differently to Isabel's pleas on his behalf (441-75). The play leaves him in a state of torture, mitigated only by the fact that Claudio is not, after all, dead. The lines I quoted are the last Angelo is given. He longs to discharge his debt, to rest his burden. The Duke makes sure that he carries it to the end.

What, then, of the Duke? Just as Angelo is both Christ and Devil, so the Duke is both the Heavenly Father and supremely contemptible. Critics have joyously pounced on the lines which deify him:

> . . . your Grace, like power divine,
> Hath looked upon my passes.   *(V.i.367-368)*

and have forthwith become enmeshed in the difficulties which ensue. It is no part of my case that Angelo does nothing vile. On the contrary it is essential to it that he does. But I do want to say that the play gives him immense moral stature. Similarly with the Duke; I will not trouble to argue that he is not the hero, the presiding genius, the Prospero of the play. According to the Atonement structure I discern in it, he occupies the position of the Father. But I do want to say that he is utterly wanting in moral stature. Why else does Shakespeare repeatedly subject him to a kind of minor humiliation at the hands of the low persons of the play (see II.ii.89-92 and V.i.520-21)? Why else is he so utterly transcended (it is the only word) by *Barnardine*? Johnson's religious instinct was sure when he recoiled[35] from that awful Ciceronian consolation which the Friar-Duke churns out over the head of the suffering Claudio. According to the Runebergian heresy God the Father *is* a very odd character.

The whole of this argument concerning Angelo has, of course, a limited scope. I have tried, in a manner, to "account for" the mysterious resonance of Angelo's character by showing that the evil he does has its place in a necessary scheme of redemption. But not all the evil Angelo does can be accounted for in this way. The theory is readily applicable to Angelo's sin of harsh and presumptuous judgement (in Professor Knight's view the cardinal sin of the play). It does not apply at all to Angelo's sin against Isabel. It was no necessary part of his duties as redeeming scapegoat to fall victim to lust (though certain psychologists might see it as one of the hazards of the job). That is why I have been unable to claim for my scheme any higher status than that of a "substructure." If I am asked what is the relation between substructure and superstructure in this play, my reply must be "ragged and uncertain."

I certainly do not wish to suggest that Angelo and I are of one mind on questions of morals. He is (forsooth!) too illiberal for me. Yet I prefer his belief in the essential benevolence of the law to such liberalism as the Duke purveys.

At the beginning of this essay I expressed dissatisfaction with those critics who make *Measure for Measure* sound like a naive morality play. I now find myself concerned lest, in my reaction, I have fallen into the far grosser error of making it sound like something by Bernard Shaw.[36] Curiously, the charge of making it sound like Graham Greene frightens me far less. The ingenious structure of Machiavellian redemption, of substitution and atonement which I discern in this play is only an element in a larger whole. There is an exploratory reverence, a diffidence before the indefinitely recessive humanity of the persons of the play, which excludes all Shavian facility. Yet if the play has a fault it is perhaps a Shavian one. The vertiginous paradoxes with which the dramatist assaults his audience are achieved at some cost to reality. For example, we are led to suppose that the duties of government place man in a simple dilemma; either he must punish all, or he must forgive all. Some glimmerings of a third, less dramatic course appear in the person of Escalus but that is all. A great part of the tension of the play consists in the clash of theoretic absolutes.

Yet no play of Shakespeare is so moving in its assertion of concrete fact. The imminent death of Claudio and his fear entirely transcend the theoretic extravagance of Isabel. I am aware that in saying this I may offend some historicist critics who will tell me that to the Jacobean mind death was unreal compared with becoming a nun. I can only ask such readers to listen to the verse. The poetry given to Isabel works as hard for Claudio as it does for her:

> The sense of death is most in apprehension;
> And the poor beetle that we tread upon
> In corporal sufferance finds a pang as great
> As when a giant dies.   *(III.i.77-80)*

Let the historicist have his say: "Taken in their context, the lines clearly mean that even a giant feels at death no more pain than a beetle does." Of course. But is it pure accident that the common reader has always taken it to mean just the opposite?

248

Notes:

(1) "*Measure for Measure* and the Gospels," in his *The Wheel of Fire*, the 1964 reprint of the 4th edition of 1949, p. 76.

(2) All references to *Measure for Measure* are to the Arden Edition of J. W. Lever, 1965. All other Shakespearean references are to W. J. Craig's three volume Oxford Edition of 1911-12.

(3) W.M.T. Dodds noticed this twenty years ago in an admirable, if one-sided, article, "The Character of Angelo in *Measure for Measure*," *MLR*, XLI (1946), 246-255.

(4) Roy W. Battenhouse, "*Measure for Measure* and Christian Doctrine of the Atonement," *PMLA*, LXI (1946), 1029-1059; Nevill Coghill, "Comic Form in *Measure for Measure*," *Shakespeare Survey*, VIII (1955), 14-27; F.R. Leavis, "*Measure for Measure*," in his *The Common Pursuit* (London, 1962), pp. 160-172.

(5) So plead the Isabel-figures Epitia and Cassandra in the sources. See Geoffrey Bullough, *Narrative and Dramatic Sources of Shakespeare* (London, 1958), II, 422, 452-453.

(6) See her *Shakespeare's Measure for Measure*, 1953, p. 65.

(7) One is tempted to answer here, "Professor Coghill does." At least, the part of Lucio was pruned away from II.ii. when he helped to produce the play for the BBC in 1955. See J. W. Lever's Arden Edition of *Measure for Measure* (London, 1965), p. lvii.

(8) The New Cambridge Shakespeare *Measure for Measure* (London, 1961), p.xxx.

(9) "*Measure for Measure* and the Protestant Ethic," *Essays in Criticism*, XI (1961), 10-33.

(10) In his Arden Edition, pp. lxxx-lxxxi; J.C. Maxwell has argued that this quotation is irrelevant because Lucretia's situation is quite unlike Isabel's; see his "*Measure for Measure*, 'Vain Pity' and 'Compelled Sins,'" *Essays in Criticism*, XVI (1966), 253-255. Nevertheless, Tyndale's observation remains perfectly good evidence for the modest claim that chastity could, at this period, be regarded as springing from pride.

(11) See for example "Courtship," "The Girl with no Interest in Marriage" and "The Repentant Girl" in *The Colloquies of Erasmus*, trans. C.R. Thompson (Chicago, 1965), pp. 86-98, 99-111, 111-14.

(12) Arden Edition, p. lxxiii.

(13) Again, noted by Lever, *ibid.*, p. lxxiii.

(14) See her "The Renaissance Background of *Measure for Measure*," *Shakespeare Survey*, II (1949), 66-82.

(15) From "Divinitie," in *The Works of George Herbert*, ed. F. E. Hutchinson (Oxford, 1941), pp. 134-135.

(16) See Hazlitt's *Characters of Shakespeare's Plays*, first published in 1817, in *The Complete Works of William Hazlitt*, ed. P. P. Howe after the edition of A. R. Waller and Arnold Glover (London, 1930), VI, 346.

(17) *Op. cit.*, p. 19.

(18) Battenhouse, *op. cit.*, p. 1059.

(19) Lascelles, *op. cit.*, p. 59.

(20) Pope, *op. cit.*, pp. 68, 69.

(21) *Ibid.*, p. 75.

(22) *Ibid.*, p. 69.

(23) The strong context of unmasking villainy together with the presence of the injunction not to hide one's light under a bushel (possibly echoed in the Duke's speech to Angelo at I.i. 26f.) suggest that of the four Scriptural *loci* it may be *Mark* that was dominant in Shakespeare's mind at the time of writing *Measure for Measure*.

(24) Machiavelli, *The Prince*, the translation by Luigi Ricci revised by E. R. P. Vincent (London, 1935), pp. 31-32.

(25) Aristotle, *Politics*, v.11 (1315a).

(26) Erasmus, *The Education of a Christian Prince* (first published 1516), trans. L.K. Born (New York, 1936), p. 210.

(27) Mario Praz, "Machiavelli and the Elizabethans," Annual Italian Lecture of the British Academy, 1928, p. 10. The essay is reprinted in *Proc. Brit. Acad.*, vol. XIII.

(28) Lascelles, *op cit.*, p. 100.

(29) W. H. Auden, *The Dyer's Hand* (London, 1963), pp. 205-206.

(30) "The Meaning of *Measure for Measure*," *Shakespeare Survey*, III (1950), 66-73.

(31) Jacques Maritain, "*The End of Machiavellianism*" [first published in *The Review of Politics*, IV (1942)] in *Machiavelli: Cynic Patriot or Political Scientist?*, ed. De Lamar Jensen (Boston, 1960), p. 93.

(32) It may be objected that my account reduces Maritain's position to absurdity; that fighting Hitler would not count as doing evil for the sake of good since fighting Hitler is itself good. Of course it is perfectly possible to give an ethical description of an action with reference to its purposive context, but to do so is to reject any open consideration of the question of ends and means. As soon as we re-admit the distinction we shall see that such an objector (just *because* his ethical assessment of actions is conditioned by their ends) belongs with the tough-minded faction. And, naturally, to the tough-minded, Maritain's position *is* absurd.

(33) "Three Versions of Judas," in his *Ficciones* (Buenos Aires, 1962), pp. 151-157. My attention was drawn to this story by my colleague Gabriel Josipovici.

(34) The relevant passages in the New Testament do not make the matter any simpler: "Himself took our infirmities, and bare our sicknesses," *Matthew*, viii.17; "Who his own self bare our sins in his own body on the tree . . . ," *1 Peter*, ii.24; "For he hath made him to be sin for us, who knew no sin," *2 Corinthians*, v.21. Augustine (*Enchiridion*, chap. XLI, in Migne's *Patrologia Latina*, vol. XL) raises the question whether there is adequate textual authority for the view that Christ sinned, and rejects it. Writing against the Manichaeans who shrank from the notion that Christ really died on the cross, Augustine stresses the element of curse, says that a curse is the fruit of sin but nowhere concedes that Christ actually sinned (*Contra Faustum Manichaeum*, XIV.4, in Migne, vol. XLIII). It was left to the more extravagant theologians of the Reformation to draw the most disturbing conclusions from this language; Luther, in his 1535 Lectures on Galatians, strenuously affirmed that Christ on the cross was the accursed of God, and guilty of all sins (III.13; in *Luther's Works*, ed. J. Pelikan and W. A. Hauser [Saint Louis, Mo., 1963], XXVI, 287-290; in *D. Martin Luthers Werke*, [Weimar, 1883-1921], XL, 448-452). Calvin, likewise, is not content to say that Christ accepted our punishment, but wishes to add that, in a manner, he accepted our guilt: "This is our absolution, that the guilt, which made us obnoxious to punishment, is transferred to the person of the son of God," *Institutes of the Christian Religion*, II.xvi, in John Allen's translation (Philadelphia, 1935), I,460. See also J. S. Whale, *The Protestant Tradition* (Cambridge, 1955), pp. 76-80. John Donne speaks as a good Anglican when he describes the Redemption as Christ's humiliation (*The Sermons of John Donne*, ed. E. M. Simpson and G. R. Potter [Berkeley, Cal., 1953], VI, 341.)

250

(35) See Johnson's note on the lines; in the Augustan Reprint Society's *Johnson's Notes to Shakespeare,* ed. A. Sherbo, (Berkeley, Cal., 1956), p. 35.

(36) Shaw's comments on the Atonement are, in fact, not wholly irrelevant. He held that Christ may have bewitched Judas into betraying him. See the Preface to *Androcles and the Lion,* in *Prefaces by Bernard Shaw* (London, 1934), p. 545.

Shakespeare and Dürer's Apocalypse

by Helen Morris

A remarkably small proportion of the great bulk of writing about Shakespeare's sources is concerned with the pictures which he may have seen, and which may have inspired some of his images. But Dr. Dover Wilson has suggested that an image in *Henry V* may come from a woodcut in Holinshed's *Historie of England*,[1] and Dr. T. R. Henn has pointed out that Holbein's Emperor ("Keyser") [Fig. 1] in his *Dance of Death* is most particularly described in *Richard II*.[2] In this woodcut Death as a skeleton is clearly seen perching "within the hollow crown / That rounds the mortal temples" of the Emperor, while "with a little pin" he "bores through his castle wall."[3] I should like to suggest that in another series of woodcuts we may find a possible source of inspiration for various passages in *Antony and Cleopatra.*

It is obvious that what is found during any study of Shakespeare's images depends on the predilections of the searcher. Dr. Caroline Spurgeon, in the final

Der Keyser.

Figure 1: Holbein's *Keyser* (1526)
Figure 2: Dürer: *Die Verteilung der weissen Gewander und der Sternenfall.*

252

tables of her seminal book, *Shakespeare's Imagery*, classified only some forty images as "Biblical." The Rev. E. A. Armstrong, on the other hand, finds as many Biblical images and references in *As You Like It* alone.[4] Clearly, the ascription of images to any particular category must be a matter of taste and judgement. But most authors who discuss Shakespeare's Biblical knowledge agree in virtually omitting reference to the *Book of the Revelation of St. John*, or make only the most tenuous and far-fetched connections.[5]

Richmond Noble remarked of *Antony and Cleopatra* that "its scriptural interest is small,"[6] nevertheless Miss Ethel Seaton has conclusively shown that when Shakespeare was writing this play he made, consciously or unconsciously, frequent reference to the Apocalypse.[7] She gives many examples of close parallels between the language, thought and imagery of the play, particularly in Acts IV and V, and of the *Apocalypse*. And surely, in addition to these particular instances, the whole apocalyptic theme of the end of the world and the destruction of Babylon finds echoes in the destruction of Egypt. The New Testament references to a "great whore" surrounded by "the kynges of the earth," to "chiefe capitaines," to an "olde serpent," to the "woman arayed in purple and scarlet colour and decked with golde," to "scorpions with stings in their tails," have obvious parallels in the play.[8]

Praising Miss Seaton's discovery, Jack Lindsay noted that W. W. Tarn has shown how "the Sibylline verses were composed during the war between Rome and Cleopatra, and how Cleopatra sought to dramatise herself and Antony, with their children, in terms of the millenary hopes agitating the peoples of the Near East," a most striking coincidence.[9]

Shakespeare's familiarity with *Revelation* cannot have arisen from hearing it read in church; in the ordinary course of the lessons read daily in the Anglican service, all other books of the New Testament were read through three times every year; but there was no provision for reading the relevant parts of the *Book of Revelation*.[10] We must presume that Shakespeare read these for himself.

There is no general agreement about the version of the Bible used by Shakespeare. Certainly there was choice enough. Every parish church had, by law, to possess a Bible, and every M.A. a copy of the New Testament.[11] There was the "Great Bible" of 1539, the Genevan Bible of 1560 (which ran to 160 editions before the Civil War) and the Bishops' Bible of 1568, which appeared in its 19th and last edition in 1606.[12] There were also many editions of the New Testament alone.[13]

Many of these Bibles and Testaments contain illustrations, and the *Book of Revelation* in particular is often profusely illustrated by a series of 18 to 21 woodcuts, varying greatly in quality of execution, but with traditional choice of subject and traditional iconography. Very similar, sometimes identical, series are found in Latin, German and Dutch Bibles.[14]

The Book of Revelation has always appealed to illustrators. No fewer than ninety-three illustrated MSS of the Apocalypse survive from the 13th, 14th and 15th centuries.[15] When printing came in the Quentell Bible of about 1479, and its derivatives the Koberger Bible (1483) and the Grüniger Bible (1485) provided illustrations which were imitated widely,[16] and which Panofsky believes were "carefully consulted" by Albrecht Dürer himself.[17] Dürer's own magnificent *Apocalypse,* published in 1498 and 1511, influenced almost every later illustrator.[18] Dürer's prints "had an enormous circulation, and not only in Germany," and though his *Apocalypse* was issued as a volume, the cuts were also sold singly. His compositions "were copied not only in Germany but also in Italy, in France and in Russia."[19] Their indirect influence was transmitted "by a master like Holbein, as well as by such modest craftsmen as the illustrators of the Luther Bibles."[20] We can also see free copies of Dürer's designs in books of iconography such as Jost Amman's *Neuwe Biblische Figuren* (1569) and his *Bibliorum Utriusque Testamenti Icones* (1571).

Dürer published sixteen designs; those which illustrated more than one episode were frequently copied as two or more separate pictures. He used, but transformed, the traditional iconography of earlier illustrators, and few indeed of Dürer's imitators have conveyed any part of the majesty and power of his designs. Among the larger and livelier of the imitative series is that which is found in the *Newe Testament* (?1566) (*STC* 2873) and reproduced again, this time elaborately framed, in the *Bishops' Bible* of 1568 (*STC* 2099). This series consists of twenty pictures, each inserted at the correct place in the text.[21]

It is noticeable that the passages in *Revelation* for which Miss Seaton has found parallels in *Antony and Cleopatra* are very often those which are vividly illustrated. Antony declares that his

> good stars, that were my former guides
> Have empty left their orbs and shot their *fires*
> Into th'abysm of hell. *(III.xiii.145-47)*

Falling stars are a constant symbol in the Apocalypse, and one most frequently illustrated; *der Sternenfall,* showing falling stars with flaming tails like *fireballs,* is the lower half of Dürer's sixth cut [Fig. 2].

When Antony has unsuccessfully attempted to kill himself, he is found by the guards:

2nd Guard:	The star is fall'n.
1st Guard:	And time is at his period.
All:	Alas, and woe!
Antony:	Let him that loves me strike me dead.
1st Guard:	Not I.
2nd Guard:	Nor I.
3rd Guard:	Nor any one.
Dercetus:	Thy death and fortunes bid thy followers fly. *(IV.xiv.106-113)*

This passage, as Miss Seaton shows, echoes lines from *Revelation,* viii.10 ("there fell a great starre from heaven") to ix.6. This great star invariably calls forth an illustration, and is sometimes pictured with a man's face [Figs. 3 & 4]. In Dürer's *Die sieben Engel mit den Posaunen* (The seven Angels with the Trumpets), amid scenes of horrific destruction by land and sea, a single great star falls into a well in the left foreground, while an eagle above cries "Vae, vae. vae"—"Alas and woe!"[22]

B. Ioannis Apoftoli.   130

datæ funt illis feptem tubæ. Et alius angelus venit,& ftetit ante altare,ha bens thuribulum aureū:& data funt illi incenfa multa,vt daret de orationibus fanctorum omnium fupra altare aureum quod eft ante thronum dei. Et afcendit fumus incenforum de orationibus fanctorum de manu angeli coram de . Et accepit ange **B** lus thuribulum aureum,& impleuit illud de igne altaris,'& mifit in terram,& facta unt tonitrua,& voces, & fulgura,& terræmotus magnus:& feptem angeli qui habebant feptem tubas,præparauerunt fe vt tuba canerent. Et primus angelus tuba cecinit. Et facta eft grando & ignis,mixta in fanguine,& miffum eft in terram. Et tertia pars terræ combufta eft : & tertia pars arborum concremata eft,& omne fœnum viride com **C** buftum eft. Et fecundus angelus tuba cecinit:& tanquam mons magnus igne ardens miffus eft in mare. Et facta eft tertia pars maris fanguis, & mortua eft tertia pars creaturæ eorum quæ habebant animas in mari, & tertia pars nauium interiit. Et tertius angelus tuba cecinit: & cecidit de cœlo ftella magna ardens tanquã facula,& cecidit in tertiam partem fluminum, & in fontes aquarum, & nomen ftellæ dicitur abfinthium. Et facta eft tertia pars aquarum in abfinthium:& multi hominum mortui funt de aquis,quia amaræ factæ funt. **D** Et quartus angelus cecinit : & percuffa eft tertia pars folis, & tertia pars luuæ,& tertia pars ftellarum, ita vt obfcuraretur tertia pars corū, & diei non luceret pars tertia,& no ctis fimiliter. Et vidi & audiui vocem vnius aquilæ volantis per medium cœli,dicentis voce magna,Vę, vę,vę,habitantibus in terra:de cæteris vocibus tubæ trium angeloru, qui erant tuba canituri.

Cantum quinti angeli lapfus ?el læ à cœlo,locuftorū pernicies, & ma ledictiones fequuntur:at fexti angeli cãtu,angeli in Euphrate 'gati fol uuntur.   I X.

A ET quintus angelus tuba cecinit : & vidi ftellam de cœlo cecidiffe in terrã:& data eft ei clauis putei abyf

fi:& aperuit puteum abyffi:& afcen dit fumus putei ficut fumus fornacis magnæ : & obfcuratus eft fol & aer de fumo putei.Et de fumo putei exie **Infr.14.c.** runt locuftæ in terram:& data eft il **19.a.** lis poteftas ficut habent poteftatem **Supr.7.a.** fcorpiones terræ. Et præceptum eft illis ne læderent fœnum terræ, neqȝ omne viride, neqȝ omnem arborem: **Ezec.9.b** nifi tantum homines qui non habēt **Sup. 6.d.** fignum dei in frontibus fuis. Et di **Ifa.2.d.** ctum eft eis ne occiderent eos:fed vt **Ofce.10.c** cruciarent mēfibus quinqȝ.Et crucia **Luc.23.c.** tus eorū,vt cruciatus fcorpii cũ per **Sap. 16.b.** cutit hominē.Et in diebus illis quæ **B** rent homines mortem, & non inuenient eam: & defiderabunt mori, & fugiet mors ab eis. Et fimilitudines locuftarum fimiles equis paratis ad prælium:& fuper capita earū tanquȝ coronæ fimiles auro:& facies earum, tanquam facies hominū.Et habebãt capillos ficut capillos mulierū:& dē tes earum,ficut dentes leonum erãt. Et habebant loricas ficut loricas fer reas : & vox alarum earum, ficut vox currum equorum multorum currentium in bellum. Et habebant caudas fimiles fcorpionum,& aculei erant in caudis earum: & pote
R R ii

Figure 3: *Kitto Bible*, LXIX, 10940.

Even the scattered references and echoes which pervade the play recall various woodcuts. Antony declares that their love must "needs find out new heaven, new earth" (I.i.17). St. John "sawe a newe heaven & a newe earth: . . . the holy citie . . . prepared as a bride garnisshed" [or, in the Genevan Bible, "trimmed"] "for her husbande" (xxi. 1-2), reminding us also of Cleopatra's death scene—"Husband, I come" (V.ii.286)—while, at the last, Charmian was "trimming up the diadem"

Figure 4: *Bishops' Bible* (1568), p. cxlviii.

(V.ii.341) of the queen. The final picture of each series is invariably of the new Jerusalem—and Dürer's vision is of a most stately and beautiful city, memory of which may have strengthened Shakespeare's memory of the words of *Revelation* also. Again, Miss K. M. Lea suggests that Antony's

> Yea, very force entangles
> Itself with strength: seal then, and all is done. *(IV.xiv.48-49)*

might recall the seven seals of the book and the sealing of the servants of God in their foreheads[23] (*Revelation*, vii.3-8); this is illustrated in Dürer's seventh cut, *Die vier Engel, die Winde aufhaltend, und die Besiegelung der Auserwahlten* (The four Angels holding the Winds and the sealing of the Elect).

Professor Leeds Barroll, in his very detailed study of "Enobarbus' Description of Cleopatra"[24] points out that "the allegorical picture of Cleopatra as Venus, the goddess of lechery, enthroned on the water, . . . may have reminded the audience of a Biblical theme which had appeared in drama at about the same time. . . . The 'great whoore' who also 'sytteth vpon many waters,' and 'with whome haue committed fornicacion the kynges of the earth' is the subject of Dekker's play, *The Whore of Babylon* (1607)." She, like Cleopatra, "glorified her selfe & lyved wantonly," and the resemblance is emphasised when Caesar declares bitterly that Antony

Figure 5: Dürer: *Die babylonische Buhlerin.*

Figure 6: Dürer: *Johannes das Buch verschlingend.*

<blockquote>
hath given his empire
Up to a whore, who now are levying
The kings o'th'earth for war: *(III.vi.66-68)*
</blockquote>

and Antony in his rage describes Cleopatra as "Triple-turned whore!" (IV.xii.13). Dürer's *Die babylonische Buhlerin* (Whore of Babylon) [Fig. 5] used as model a sketch of a "Lady in Venetian Dress" (1495) which in his notebook is contrasted with another of a sober Nuremberg Hausfrau.[25] With a crown holding her elegant ringlets she perches sideways on her ferocious seven-headed beast, her embroidered, low-necked dress exposing shoulders and half-concealing her breast, while she holds up an elaborately-wrought "cup of golde" towards "the kynges of the earth." Is this also Cleopatra's cup, which Antony suggests that Caesar will fill "to the brim / With principalities" (III.xiii.18-19)? The richness of Dürer's black and white almost implies the "purple and scarlet colour and decked with golde" (*Revelation,* xvii.4) with which Enobarbus endows Cleopatra (II.ii.191-193).

Miss Seaton's most remarkable parallels occur between Cleopatra's dream of Antony and St. John's Angel with the Book.

<blockquote>
His face was as the heavens, and therein stuck
A sun and moon, which kept their course and lighted
The little O, the earth. . . .
His legs bestrid the ocean, his reared arm
Crested the world: his voice was propertied
As all the tuned spheres, and that to friends;
But when he meant to quail, and shake the orb,
He was as rattling thunder.   *(V.ii.79-86)*
</blockquote>

<blockquote>
And I sawe another myghtie Angel come down frō heavē, clothed with a cloude, and ye raynbowe upon his head, and his face as it were the sunne, and his feete as it were pillers of fyre. . . . and he put his ryght foote upon the sea, and his left foote on the earth: And cryed with a loude voyce, as whē a Lion roreth: And when he had cryed, seven thunders uttered their voyces. . . . And the Angel which I sawe stande upon the sea and upon the earth, lyft up his hande to heaven.   *(Revelation x.1-6)*
</blockquote>

The astounding image of Antony's eyes as a sun and a moon, both at once in the heavens, is clarified by a glance at Dürer's *Die Verteilung der weissen Gewander und der Sternenfall* (The distribution of white robes and the fall of the stars) [Fig. 2]. The sun on the left and the moon on the right glare like two great eyes on either side of the dark, nose-like triangle of falling stars. Though the two descriptions above tally very closely indeed, there is little verbal reminiscence or echo — "his legs bestrid the ocean"; "he put his ryght foote upon the sea, and his left foote on the earth." But each very precisely describes both Dürer's Angel in *Johannes das Buch verschlingend* (John devouring the Book) [Fig. 6] and the Angel in the corresponding picture in the 1568 Bishops' Bible [Fig. 7]. The face

Figure 7: *Bishops' Bible* (1568), p. cxlix.

Figure 8: *Bishops' Bible* (1568), p. cli.

of each is "as the heavens"—surrounded by brilliant rays, exactly as the sun is portrayed throughout the series. The "reared arm" of each does indeed crest the world. Panofsky considers that Dürer's Angel is one of the latest of the series, because it is so simplified, strong and uncrowded;[26] surely, therefore, it is particularly memorable.

Cleopatra continues:

> For his bounty,
> There was no winter in't; an antonie (?autumn) 'twas
> That grew the more by reaping. *(V.ii.86-88)*

Can it be a mere coincidence that in Dürer's *Das Tier aus dem Meere and das Tier aus dem Festlande* (The Beast from the Sea and the Beast from the Land) God is holding a sickle, and an angel with a sickle is setting forth to reap? (In many of the Biblical series of woodcuts, angels are actually reaping corn [Fig. 8].)

Cleopatra then describes Antony's "delights" as "dolphin-like" (V.ii.88,89). There is no mention of a dolphin in *Revelation*, nor in the woodcuts in the *Bishops' Bible*. But in the sea at the feet of Dürer's great angel, among ships and swans, there swims an unmistakeable dolphin.[27]

Notes:

(1) *Henry V* (Cambridge, 1947), note on 2 Prologue 9-10, p. 132.

(2) T. R. Henn, *The Lonely Tower* (London, 1950), p. 225n.

(3) *Richard II*, III.ii.160,169. Citations from Shakespeare are taken from the New Cambridge edition of each play.

(4) *Shakespeare's Imagination* (Lincoln, Neb., 1963), pp. 125-128.

(5) E.g.: Richmond Noble, *Shakespeare's Biblical Knowledge* (London, 1935); Charles Wordsworth, *Shakespeare's Knowledge and Use of the Bible* (3rd ed., London, 1880); Thomas Carter, *Shakespeare and Holy Scripture* (London, 1905).

(6) Noble, p. 238.

(7) Ethel Seaton, "*Antony and Cleopatra* and the *Book of Revelation*," *Review of English Studies*, xxii (1946), 219-224.

(8) *Book of Revelation*: "whore" xvii.1.16; xix.2: "kynges" vi. 15; xvii.2,18; xvii.3; xix. 19; xxi.24; "chiefe capitaines" vi.15; "serpent" xii.9; xx.2: "woman" xvii.4: "scorpions" ix.10. Citations are from the *Bishops' Bible* (1568).

(9) *Review of English Studies*, xxiii (1947), 66, quoting Tarn, *Journal of Roman Studies*, xxii (1932).

(10) Noble, p. 14.

(11) Noble, p. 9.

(12) Carter, p. 2.

(13) See T. H. Darlow and H. F. Moule, *Historical Catalogue of Printed Editions of Holy Scripture*, 2 vols.(London, 1903).

(14) E.g. in Holbein's "*Icones Historiarum Veteris Testamenti*" ed. H. Green (London, 1869) there is a list of fourteen vernacular Bibles illustrated by plates, dated 1498 to 1545, p. 8.

(15) A. G. and W. O. Hassall, *The Douce Apocalypse* (London, 1961), p. 10.

(16) David Bland. *A History of Book Illustration* (Cleveland and New York, 1958), p. 108.

(17) Erwin Panofsky, *Life and Art of Albrecht Dürer* (Princeton, 1955), pp. 53-54, and *Albrecht Dürer* (Princeton, 1943), II, 36.

(18) Panofsky, *Life and Art,* pp. 51, 59; James Strachan, *Early Bible Illustrations* (Cambridge, 1957), p. 42; Ph. Schmidt, *Die Illustration der Lutherbibel 1522-1700* (Basel, 1962), p. 181.

(19) Bland, pp. 113, 114; Panofsky, *Life and Art.* p. 59.

(20) Panofsky, *Life and Art,* p. 59.

(21) Many other examples of such series, illustrating *Revelation,* related to Durer and to each other, appear in Bibles and Testaments, e.g.:

1537 *The Byble* (Matthew's Bible, Antwerp). 21 crude cuts with borders of conventional leaves all round, 8.8 cm. by 6.1 cm.

1542-3 *Den Bibel* (Dutch, Antwerp) contains the same cuts, but with side borders only.

1540 *Die gantze Bibel* (Froschauer, Zurich). 20 cuts, 8.5 by 8.5.

1545 *Biblia das ist Die Gantze Heilige Schrift* (Lufft, Wittenberg). 26 free and lively cuts, 11 by 15.

1549 *Newe Testament* (no place or printer) (STC 2856). 21 cuts, 6.7 by 4.3.

1549 *The Byble* (Day and Seres) (STC 2077). 21 cuts, 5 by 3.6.

1562 *Great Bible* (STC 2096), the same cuts.

1553 *The Newe Testament* (STC 2869). 21 cuts, 8.2 by 5.4.

1572 *The holie bible* (Bishops') (STC 2107). 18 cuts, 4.2 by 6.4, all printed together in correct order on one sheet.

1574 *The holy byble* (Bishops') (STC 2109). The same.

1575 *The holy byble* (Bishops') (STC 2111). 17 tiny cuts, 3.2 by 4.7, very similar to those of *STC* 2109 but inserted separately and carelessly, the same block repeated twice.

(22) In *Revelation,* viii. 13, the English version has an angel, the Vulgate an eagle.

(23) *Review of English Studies,* xxii (1946), 223n.

(24) *Texas Studies in English,* xxxvii (1958), 61-78.

(25) Panofsky, *Dürer,* II, plate 59; Rudolph Chadraba, *Duerer's Apokalypse* (Prag, 1964), plate 85.

(26) Panofsky, *Life and Art,* pp. 58-59.

(27) In the equivalent illustration in *Die gantze Bibel* (Froschauer, Zurich, 1540) there is no creature in the sea, but strange sea monsters in the clouds. These do not seem relevant to this enquiry. The only angels accompanied by dolphins which I have seen are in (1) a direct copy of Dürer, acknowledged, in an early Dutch Bible, date unknown (Huntington Library, *Kitto Bible,* Vol. 69, p. 10940), and (2) "Apocalypsis X," one of a series in Jost Amman's *Neuwe Biblische Figuren* (Frankfort, 1569). There is a very large fish, *possibly* a dolphin. I am most grateful to the Director and Librarian of the Huntington Library, San Marino, California, for giving me permission to use photographs from materials in their collection, numbers 2 to 8 inclusive.

262

Coriolanus: A Study in Political Dislocation

by Clifford Davidson

It is generally recognized that Shakespeare's *Coriolanus* confronts the modern critic with special problems. For E. K. Chambers, of course, this play is evidence of a "Shakespeare . . . become tedious"; it would seem that this tediousness is due to the "slackening of [his] creative energies" at the close of "the great tragic cycle."[1] And Theodore Spencer finds *Coriolanus* "an excellent piece of dramatic craftsmanship," but simultaneously complains that "though we admire it, we admire it in cold blood."[2] In his well known analysis of the play, Oscar James Campbell claims that the drama makes sense only if it is regarded as "tragical satire."[3] But A. P. Rossiter writes: "*Coriolanus* is the last and greatest of the Histories. It is Shakespeare's only great political play; and it is slightly depressing, and hard to come to terms with, because it is political tragedy."[4] Obviously, *Coriolanus* is not a play with which the critic may easily feel comfortable.

The greatest difficulty presented by *Coriolanus* would seem to arise from the fact that Shakespeare's art fails to conform to certain assumptions about dramaturgy which are believed to be universally valid. As a renaissance dramatist who wrote for the popular stage, Shakespeare neither submits to the rules of Aristotle, nor does he always present characters which fulfill the expectations of many contemporary critics or audiences. Too many of us still prefer our tragedies to be somewhat tinged with melodrama, for thus we may more easily recognize the "hero" for whom we are to feel empathy. We must, however, avoid the temptation to apprehend plays as we view sporting events — in which our sympathies are engaged on one side against the other. With the exception of *Titus Andronicus*, Shakespeare's tragedies deserve a far more complex response on the part of his audience, for he is quite liable to present us with situations which are so ambiguous that we are unable to throw our emotions behind any single figure or group. In a play that is tragedy simply because it presents the story of a man who falls from a high place, easy alternatives are often eschewed. In *Antony and Cleopatra*, for example, neither Caesar nor Cleopatra represent choices with which we may ultimately have sympathy. Mark Antony is poised between the instruments of the world and of the flesh;[5] we feel the attraction of the flesh as bodied forth in Cleopatra, but must recognize its essential falsity just as we recognize the teleological emptiness of Caesar's world. Similarly, *Coriolanus* gives a situation which is thoroughly ambiguous; neither the "hero" Coriolanus nor the common people he opposes can truly deserve our good will. If we fail to respond to the ambiguous situation, however, the fault may lie in our own sensibility. It is not possible that Shakespeare's contemporaries responded coldly to the issues raised in *Coriolanus*.

263

Coriolanus is not merely a dramatization of a piece of dead history or an entertaining story out of the past. Shakespeare, like most Englishmen of his time, was interested in history mainly for its practical application—i.e., for the light which it was believed to throw on contemporary events and problems. Thus the authors of the poems in *The Mirror for Magistrates* had been interested in England's past because the past might hold the mirror up to living magistrates; the result was to be better leadership in England. We have sufficient evidence to prove that, for Shakespeare, history might be read in terms of an instructive pattern.[6] In *Macbeth*, the Porter's reference to equivocation is an astounding anachronism, but it reminds us that Shakespeare conceived of the play not as a drama merely about conditions in eleventh-century Scotland. Shakespeare was fascinated by the past because of its relation to and illumination of the present happenings of 1605-1606 when England was convulsed with hysteria after the discovery of the Gunpowder Plot. Likewise, *Coriolanus*, while based upon North's translation of Plutarch, is presented in a manner which brings it into line with Shakespeare's own political concerns and the political problems of the England of 1607-1608. The material of the play is ordered about a central question: what is the proper relation between an individual and his state? The question is not positively answered in *Coriolanus*, of course; nevertheless, the implications of what happens in the play would not have been lost upon those who attended its earliest performances.

Stated quite simply, *Coriolanus* depicts a national disaster—a national tragedy which is due to the fact that the main character and the patricians associated with him do not properly perform their part in the Roman state. The leaders of kingless Rome abdicate their responsibilities toward the order of the commonwealth. The role of Coriolanus is especially ambiguous. He is a cause of dissention in the state, but is nevertheless a defender of Rome in war: he has "deserved nobly of [his] country, and [he has] not deserved nobly," as one of the citizens aptly comments (II.iii.94-95).[7] The equivocal nature of Coriolanus' service to Rome in the first three acts results in his banishment, and from that point his pride and vengeance drive him to the worst sort of treason.

The central question in Shakespeare's mind—what is the proper relationship between an individual and his state?—finds illustration in the analogy of the state and the human body. This analogy is introduced in the well-known speech by Menenius Agrippa to the rebellious populace:

> There was a time when all the body's members
> Rebell'd against the belly. . . .   *(I.i.99-100)*

The members—the rebellious people—are demonstrating because they are hungry; the belly—the patricians and the wealthy—has not been distributing the essentials of life properly to the members. In Plutarch, the rebellion had been against usurers, but Shakespeare has altered the situation so that it would relate organically to the parable about the belly and the members. Furthermore, Shakespeare sees to it that Menenius' genial defense of the belly meets but inadequately the pleas of the rebellious populace. Of course, it is unnatural for the members

264

to rise up against another part of the body; Tudor and Stuart political doctrine utterly condemns all rebellion against the government.[8] Yet for the belly to be "idle and unactive, / Still cupboarding the viand" is to be irresponsible in its treatment of the members. Menenius's statement of the ideal could hardly be found genuinely satisfying to the starving citizens who hear him:

> Your most grave belly was deliberate,
> Not rash like his accusers, and thus answered:
> "True is it, my incorporate friends," quoth he,
> "That I receive the general food at first
> Which you do live upon; and fit it is,
> Because I am the store-house and the shop
> Of the whole body. But, if you do remember,
> I send it through the rivers of your blood,
> Even to the court, the heart, to th'seat o'th'brain;
> And, through the cranks and offices of man,
> The strongest nerves and small inferior veins
> From me receive that natural competency
> Whereby they live.   *(I.i.132-144)*

When Caius Marcius enters and harangues the people, the ambiguous nature of the situation is now completely spelled out: he—a highly favored patrician— is much more rash and violent in his speech than are the citizens. We see at once that the belly is in actuality the unnatural enemy of the members.

Shakespeare's handling of the parable of the belly and the members sharply delineates the character of the class war between plebians and patricians. The belly, whose job it is to convert food to the use of the members,[9] is in *Coriolanus* associated with appetite and gluttony.[10] Previously, in *Antony and Cleopatra*, Shakespeare had used imagery of food to represent lust: Cleopatra is "a morsel cold upon / Dead Caesar's trencher"; bewitched by her, Mark Antony surfeits in Egypt where he is held by chains of idleness. In *Coriolanus*, the "idle and unactive" stomach is emblematic of other kinds of gluttony and greed in the social structure. The Roman patricians' lust will not allow them to treat the lower classes as they should be treated, and rash Coriolanus, while not himself affected by any great desire for wealth, passionately defends those who set their minds on economic gain. It should be remembered that the book of *Homilies* is sharply critical of those who, like the inhabitants of Sodom and Gomorrah, wickedly spend their time in "proud banqueting and continual idleness, which caused them to be so lewd of life, and so unmerciful toward the poor."[11] Instead of being temperate, the highly placed Romans who represent the belly in the body of the state are gluttonous or rash. The belly in *Coriolanus* has become a symbol of intemperance.[12]

Elizabethan and Jacobean writers did not ordinarily, however, represent the leader (or leaders) in a state as being like the belly in the human body. Ultimately they appear to have followed John of Salisbury, who appears to have introduced the state-body analogy in the twelfth century. For John of Salisbury, the prince is like the head of the body and the senate is like the heart, while the soul, which rules over the whole body, is analogous to the hierarchy of the Church. The belly finds its analogue in the officers of finance (*Policraticus*, V. ii). Edward Forset, whose book *A Comparative Discourse of the Bodies Natural and Politique*[13] deals at length with the analogy between the commonwealth and the human body, mentions Menenius' handling of a *"tale of this proportionable respectiveness of the parts in mans body"* in his introductory remarks "To the reader." But throughout Forset's treatise there is no further treatment of the belly as analogous to nobles or magistrates. Furthermore, the notice given to Menenius' parable in the introductory remarks may well have been an afterthought.[14] Forset fails to dwell long on Menenius' speech and passes quickly on to the following statement:

> *The like comparison is most divinely enlarged by a much better Orator, and in a much more important poynt of the unseparable union of the members of Christ with their head, and of the necessary communion of their distinct gifts and works amongst themselves. . . .*

In the body of this discourse, Forset compares the king or leader of the civil state to the soul of the body, to the heart—the seat of the soul—and to the head—"the first wheele and s[p]ring of motion, giving force and order to the whole frame."[15]

Forset, like Shakespeare, assumes that a single leader or king is the natural direction from which power must flow in a state. Perfect order in a commonwealth comes when those who are beneath the king submit themselves to his authority as the body submits itself to the authority of the soul. The commons thus are like "affections" which, "so long as they be obedient unto reason, standeth the soule in great steede; but if they become violent and unrulie, then (of their disordering, and disturbing of the minds tranquillitie) they be rightly tearmed perturbations."[16] When they become mutinous or cause civil tumult, citizens must once again be brought under the control of the rational soul. The "beast / With many heads" (IV.i.2) is representative of a lower level of understanding and therefore ought to submit itself to the higher powers. The class war in *Coriolanus*, however, is the natural outcome of the lack of proper order in the state. Lacking "The kingly crowned head" (I.i.119), republican Rome is more subject to civil tensions than it would be with a firm monarch at its head. The patricians, who should give order to the state, are instead more concerned with their own unruly passions and appetites. On the contrary, as Forset points out, "just governours" will strive not "to do what they lust" but to support law and justice in the realm; they will not attempt to act "to the hurt, but to the good of subjects."[17] The leaders of the state should indeed care for the common people "like fathers" (I.i.79).

The head of state is to govern, not to tyrannize, his subjects. So far from arguing in favor of kingly oppression, King James warns Prince Henry that "the over-common use of it in this nation, as if it were a vertue, especially by the greatest ranke of subjects in the land, requireth the King to be a sharpe censurer thereof."[18] The king continues:

266

Be diligent therefore to trie, and awfull to beate downe the hornes of proud oppressours: embrace the quarrell of the poore and distressed, as your owne particular, thinking it your greatest honour to represse the oppressours: care for the pleasure of none, neither spare ye anie paines in your owne person, to see their wrongs redressed: and remember of the honourable stile given to my grand-father of worthie memorie, in being called *the poore mans King*.[19]

Also James scores the nobles' "arrogant conceit of their greatnes and power" which leads them to oppress citizens, to favor their own friends and servants against the cause of justice, and to take arms against their neighbor.[20]

Dislocation in the civil state was most often seen in renaissance England as deriving from irresponsibility and injustice at the top, though some difficulties with the unruly commons were always expected. According to William Baldwin, "if the officers be good, the people can not be yll. Thus the goodnes or badnes of any realme lyeth in the goodnes or badnes of the rulers."[21] Rulers who treat the commons as Coriolanus does surely are bound to have their abuse turned back upon themselves. Such treatment invariably produces disobedience and rebellions. Any wise leader will recognize that his rule is with the consent of the governed.[22] At the same time, of course, the commons in *Coriolanus* are not without guilt for their lack of patience in enduring injustices. Guilt is divided between the callous and grasping patricians and the plebians who rebel against their leaders.

E. C. Pettet has suggested that the peasant uprisings in the midlands during the spring of 1607 may have been in Shakespeare's mind as he wrote *Coriolanus*.[23] While Shakespeare was undoubtedly appalled at the actions of Warwickshire peasants who broke down the boundaries of enclosed lands, he might also have understood quite well some of the sociological and economic grounds for their insurrection. In *Coriolanus*, the plebians are characterized as generally kind and fair-minded, though utterly lacking in direction or purpose. Beneath the surface of *Coriolanus* perhaps lies a fear that England too might be torn by class war, provided that demagogues have some grievances of the people with which to work. Shakespeare's abhorrence of class conflict and of the division of the realm into two parties—the party of the rich and the party of the poor—is everywhere apparent. Menenius' statement that he has been of Coriolanus' faction (V.ii.30-31) must have sounded harshly on the ears of Shakespeare's contemporaries. Party feeling was thought to be the antithesis of the right feeling which one ought to have for the civil state.

The bond which binds together the hierarchal order of the state is not dissention but *love*. Sir John Cheke's *The Hurt of Sedition* (1549) had asserted: "Love is not the knot only of the Commonwealth, whereby divers parts be perfectly joined together in one politique body, but also the strength and might of the same, gathering together into a small room with order, which, scattered, would else breed confusion and debate."[24] Class war militates against "degree, priority, and place" (*Troilus and Cressida,* I.iii.86) and is symptomatic of deep disorder in the structure of the realm. Love—or, to use Erasmus's term, *pietas*—binds the servant to his master, the son to his father, the citizen to his king so that the whole body of the state functions smoothly. Aristotle had stressed the necessity of the civil order for human beings, who must of necessity depend on others if their needs are to be met. Inevitably, "the whole is before the part: for if the whole perish, there will remaine neither foote nor hand, saving in name onely: as for example, if one should call that a hand which is made of stone, because a dead hand would be like unto it."[25] The translator of the 1598 edition of the *Politiques* glosses the above:

> when the whole perisheth, the partes perish and loose their use, and so consequently their right name: As for example, when a man is dead, there remaineth no longer in him neither eye, foote, nor hand. . . . I meane, the eye wherwith we see, and wherein lyeth the power of seeing; the foote wherwith we walk, and wherin lieth the power of walking; the hand wherewith we handle, and wherin lyeth the power of handling: which members when they cease to be such.[26]

The need for all the parts of the body politic to work together for the common good led to the medieval and renaissance emphasis upon the idea of the state as an organism which ought at once to be orderly and fortunate.[27] If the various parts of the body politic neglect a proper understanding of order and degree, the civil state will then fall into discord and chaos.

> Then everything includes itself in power,
> Power into will, will into appetite;
> And appetite, an universal wolf
> So doubly seconded with will and power,
> Must make perforce an universal prey,
> And last eat up himself.   (*Troilus and Cressida,* I.iii.119-124)

Thus the Rome of *Coriolanus,* lacking the love which should unite the social fabric, fragments into parts which consume each other.

From the first, Coriolanus seems to be alienated from his state. His prowess in war is said not to result from his love of *patria* but from his pride and his desire "to please his mother" (I.i.37-40). He shows no concern for the poor, nor does he have any desire to promote the unity of the body of the commonwealth. His heroic acts in war grow not from his love of the whole fabric of the civil organization, but they derive from his abstract sense of honor and have their end in himself. Honor has become an entity separated from the common good. The military deed and its reward—"the oaken garland"—mean that Coriolanus will be nominated for consul, a position that he clearly believes he deserves. Yet, in order to be a good ruler, one must accept one's identity as a member of the community of men. King James points out that the leader of state should "Foster trew Humilitie, in bannishing pride . . . toward God (considering yee differ not in stuffe, but in use, and that onely by his ordinance, from the basest of your people). . . ."[28] In contrast, Coriolanus wears the garment of humility as if he is an actor playing a part — and not even playing it very well. The tribune Brutus comments: "With a proud heart he wore his humble weeds" (II.iii.161). He even refuses to show his wounds to the people, but will, since there is no other way, "make much of [their] voices, and so trouble [them] no further" (II.iii.116-117). To Coriolanus, the commons are merely to be repressed. Surely no man who sees the political order in terms of struggle against the commons would make an adequate ruler. He would rend the unity of the body of the state from his position at the top.

It is actually only a short step from Coriolanus's attitude toward the people in the opening portion of the play to the complete alienation which he represents after his banishment. His rejoinder to the people—"I banish you!"—is his final word to the human society which has nurtured him. This is his declaration of independence from the holy ties of his country and family.[29] From this point onward, he will attempt to play God, wrecking vengeance upon his native city. He will join his enemy Aufidius, and with the Volscian hosts he will attempt to pour war even into the bowels of Rome. Appropriately, he leaves his city alone, "Like to a lonely dragon" (IV.i.30). The dragon, that fabulous but demonic creature, is a fit emblem for Coriolanus from this point onward in the play. Medieval iconography had associated the dragon with the devil whose ways are directly opposed to the order of civil society. The demonic nature of Coriolanus' work is also pointed out in his first conversation with Aufidius in IV. v when he offers his "revengeful services," indicating that he "will fight/ Against my cank'red country with the spleen/ Of all the under fiends." Thus Coriolanus' relation to his society becomes that of an antagonist who wishes to destroy whatever stands opposed to him. His alienation from his society is utterly complete.

Earlier, Menenius had defended Coriolanus' bad manners to Brutus and Sicinius:

> Consider this: he has been bred i'th'wars
> Since 'a could draw a sword, and is ill school'd
> In bolted language.
> (III.i.320-322)

Such an upbringing is criticized in a passage from Aristotle cited by F. N. Lees, who also quotes his 1598 translator's comments on the faults of educators in dealing with their pupils: "they make them beastlike and cruell, by directing their whole training to one martiall vertue alone."[30] An education in war does not produce good manners; however, good manners, despite Touchstone's witty remark to Corin, are necessary to the civilized life. Good manners are indicative of good order within the soul, achieved by the process of education which helps to some extent to repair the damages inherent in the human race since Adam's fall. An education in good manners helps to restrain the passions and appetites by giving strength to the rational soul.[31]

Like King Lear and Hotspur, Coriolanus is a choleric man—a type Shakespeare apparently considered dangerous to the state. He obviously regarded the choleric nobleman or leader with considerable suspicion, for anger more than anything else causes divisions which disturb the peace and order of the commonwealth. Coriolanus' lack of temperance helps to pour the sweet milk of concord into hell so that the unity of the Roman state will be confounded. His "soaring insolence/ . . . will be his fire / To kindle [the people's] dry stubble," the tribunes predict (II.i.270-274). Coriolanus' choler, once exploded, will set the city ablaze against him. Fire is a traditional symbol of anger in iconography.[32] In an engraving which illustrates anger, Peter Brueghel uses the imagery of fire with terrifying effectiveness. *Ira* herself carries a sword in one hand and a torch in the other. In a shed at the left of the engraving, a fire is burning and over it a demon is roasting a human body. Above the pavilion of *Ira*, two humans are being stewed alive in a large cauldron set over a fire, and in the background an army is attacking a flaming citadel. In the play, Coriolanus shows his nature time after time by flaming out in fiery anger. Touched off by the tribunes, he lashes out: "The fires i'th'lowest hell fold in the people!" (III.iii.68). Later, in V.ii.26-28, he is quoted as saying that he is prepared to burn his native home in his fury.

But the worthy political leader must first of all possess control over himself. King James opens his *Basilicon Doron* with the following words: "As he cannot be thought worthy to rule and command others, that cannot rule and dantone his owne proper affections and unreasonable appetites, so can hee not be thought worthie to governe a Christian people, knowing and fearing God, that in his owne person and heart, feareth not and loveth not the Divine Majestie."[33]

Shakespeare's King Henry V, speaking to the French ambassadors, similarly announces that he is "no tyrant, but a Christian king,/ Unto whose grace [his] passion is . . . subject" (*Henry V*, I.ii.241-243). Likewise, we hear of Cordelia that she is "queen/ Over her passion" even in a moment of great stress (*King Lear*, IV.iii.15-16). Coriolanus, however, demonstrates an impious nature which is ruled by his irascible passions: he is unable to be temperate.

In iconography, temperance has been portrayed in various ways. An illumination in the ninth century Cambrai Gospels shows an anonymous ruler surrounded by the four cardinal virtues; *Temperantia* stands in the lower left-hand corner with a torch in one hand, while pouring from a jug of water with the other.[34] Passion is not to be stamped out, but in order for its heat to be moderated, the good ruler draws upon the water of grace. Coriolanus, unequipped except with a torch, is unable to cool the heats which his choleric moods generate. His ability to lead is clearly very limited. He is a man of war but he is neither a good man nor a good nobleman; he would, therefore, have been a worse consul.

Coriolanus is also lacking in the other cardinal virtues. As we see in battle, he is not a prudent but a rash commander. To enter the gates of Corioli alone—or even with a small force—would indeed be foolhardiness, as the First Soldier suggests (I.iv.46).[35] Next, Coriolanus does not possess sufficient fortitude to suffer the vicissitudes of his public life with a steady and patient mind. North's Plutarch comments specifically on his lack of fortitude when he is banished from the city; he shows no passion only because "he was so carried away with the vehemency of

270

anger, and desire of revenge, that he had no sense nor feeling of the hard state he was in . . . ."[36] Shakespeare dramatizes the scene and makes some basic changes: he has Coriolanus explode with anger in public, thus showing his extreme lack of fortitude in the situation. Finally, Coriolanus, possessed by his revenge, offends against the cardinal virtue of justice. Always swayed by his emotions against the common people, Coriolanus as consul would have poured his hatred into the balance against them.[37] In his campaign of revenge against Rome, he thinks of himself as an avenger working out a kind of doomsday against the Roman people. Cominius and Menenius are shocked that Coriolanus would not even stoop to pick his friends from the "noisome musty chaff" which he is determined to incinerate.

> He said 'twas folly,
> For one poor grain or two, to leave unburnt
> And still to nose th'offense.   *(V.i.26-28)*

In the great judgment, however, God *will* separate the wheat from the chaff; to do otherwise is to wish destruction upon all, good and bad alike, in an orgy of demonic destruction. In attempting to revenge his wrongs, Coriolanus wishes to usurp the place of God; as a human being pretending to super-human vengeance, he perverts justice and violates the natural order. Menenius exclaims:

> For one poor grain or two!
> I am one of those; his mother, wife, his child,
> And this brave fellow too, we are the grains.   *(V.i.28-30)*

Coriolanus is breaking all natural ties in order to carry out his devilish task against his own city of Rome.

Yet, despite his determination, he finds that natural feeling does well up within him during the meeting with his mother in V.iii. His maternal ties force him to forget the traitor's part that he is acting. He begs:

> Do not bid me
> Dismiss my soldiers, or capitulate
> Again with Rome's mechanics; tell me not
> Wherein I seem unnatural; desire not
> To allay my rages and revenges with
> Your colder reasons.   *(IV.iii.81-86)*

His mother "most dangerously" prevails upon him to save the city of Rome. Ironically, this last deed—a deed of moderation—will provide envious Aufidius with his excuse: he will level charges against Coriolanus. The drama of Act III is acted out once more: Coriolanus responds to Aufidius' charges of treason with unrestrained anger.

Coriolanus represents not virtue but *virtus* and, like Hotspur, he illustrates its failure as an ethic. The Roman warrior also is so sensitive about his honor that he is willing to betray his country for the sake of his own pride. Of course, Coriolanus is in a sense valiant, and herein Aufidius may close the play with his ambiguous words about the "noble memory" which he will have. Haughty valor, however, is not to be praised in a leader of men. The good magistrate will take a quite different attitude toward the citizens who are placed under him.

Proper response to the tragedy of *Coriolanus* demands that the audience should not pick sides between the plebians and the patricians. Identification of a hero is neither necessary nor possible in this play, for no one emerges as satisfactory according to the standards which are implicit in the play itself. Political unity is needed in Rome, but no one seems interested in promoting it. No sheriff or U.S. marshal out of the American West rides up to set things straight in the last act. *Coriolanus* is a drama full of characters with confused political values, but this does not mean that Shakespeare himself was unclear about what would be the ideal commonwealth. Like *Troilus and Cressida* and *Timon of Athens*, *Coriolanus* is set in a state of political and moral chaos. As a study in political and moral dislocation, *Coriolanus* is not alone among the dramas of Shakespeare. Any short view of tragedy which excludes or distorts *Coriolanus, Troilus and Cressida,* and *Timon of Athens* must be subjected to revision to bring it into line with Shakespeare's dramatic method in these plays.

Notes:

(1) E. K. Chambers, *Shakespeare: A Survey* (New York, 1925), p. 258.

(2) Theodore Spencer, *Shakespeare and the Nature of Man*, 2nd ed. (New York, 1961), p. 177.

(3) Oscar James Campbell, *Shakespeare's Satire* (New York, 1943), pp. 198-216.

(4) A. P. Rossiter, *Angel with Horns*, ed. Graham Storey (New York, 1961), p. 251.

(5) See the interpretation advanced in John F. Danby, *Elizabethan and Jacobean Poets* (London, 1965), pp. 128-151.

(6) This point is adequately demonstrated, I believe, by E. M. W. Tillyard, *Shakespeare's History Plays* (London, 1944), *passim.*

(7) Quotations from *Coriolanus* and other Shakespearean plays are from *The Complete Plays and Poems of William Shakespeare*, ed. William Allan Neilson and Charles Jarvis Hill (Boston, 1942).

(8) The classic Tudor statement against civil disobedience is to be found in "An Homily Against Disobedience and Wilful Rebellion," which appears in *Sermons or Homilies Appointed to be Read in Churches in the Time of Queen Elizabeth*, 4th ed. (Oxford, 1816), pp. 468-516.

(9) See *Bartas His Devine Weekes and Works*, trans. Joshua Sylvester (Gainesville, Fla., 1965; reprint of 1605 edition), sig. P$_8$, p. 215.

(10) The Second Citizen charges that "the cormorant belly" which "is the sink o'th'body" usurps leadership in the body (I.i.119-126). Significantly, Pliny associates the belly with greed and gluttony; he concludes: "when all is done, no man ever thinketh how base and abject this part of the body is, considering that filthy odour and excrement which passeth from it in the end."— *The Natural History*, trans. Philemon Holland, selected and introd. by Paul Turner (Carbondale, Ill., 1962), p. 244.

(11) *Homilies*, p. 252.

(12) See D. A. Traversi, *An Approach to Shakespeare*, 2nd ed. (Anchor ed., Garden City, N. Y., 1956), pp. 221-222.

272

(13) London, 1606.

(14) The printing of the text of the book was begun with signature B, and apparently only when it had been completed were the table of contents and the prefatory matter set up in type. In order to accommodate unexpectedly lengthy preliminaries, three leaves were inserted into the beginning of the book to make room for the seven page introduction. Thus we may perhaps assume that the printer did not have the prefatory matter in hand when his compositor began work on the book. It therefore appears most likely that the prefatory remarks were written as the book was in the process of going through the press.

(15) Forset, p. 27.

(16) Forset, pp. 17-18.

(17) Forset, p. 21.

(18) *The Political Works of James I*, ed. Charles Howard McIlwain (New York, 1965; reprint of 1946 edition), p. 21.

(19) *Political Works*, pp. 21-22.

(20) *Political Works*, pp. 24-25.

(21) *The Mirror for Magistrates*, ed. Lily B. Campbell (New York, 1960; reprint of 1938 edition), p. 64.

(22) See Russell A. Fraser, *Shakespeare's Poetics in Relation to King Lear* (London, 1962) p. 82.

(23) E. C. Pettet, "*Coriolanus* and the Midlands Insurrection of 1607," *Shakespeare Survey*, III (1950), 34-42.

(24) Quoted in J. W. Allen, *A History of Political Thought in the Sixteenth Century* (London, 1957), p.141. Allen also cites *A Dialogue between Cardinal Pole and Thomas Lupset* by Thomas Starkey, which was not published until the nineteenth century; Cardinal Pole asserts that the true commonwealth exists where "al the partys, as membrys of one body, be knyt togyddur in perfayt love *and* unyte; every one dowyng hys offyce *and* duty, aftur such maner that, what so ever state, offyce, or degre, any man be of, the duty therto perteynyng wyth al dylygence he besyly fulfyl, *and* wythout envy or malyce to other accomplysch the same" — *England in the Reign of King Henry the Eighth*, EETS, E. S. XII (London, 1878), p. 55.

(25) *Aristotles Politiques, or Discourses of Government*, trans. [from French] by I.D. (London, 1598), p. 15, as quoted in F. N. Lees, "*Coriolanus*, Aristotle, and Bacon," *RES*, I (1950), 119.

(26) *Aristotles Politiques*, p. 16, as quoted in Lees, p. 120.

(27) See Forset, p. 48: "It is not therefore called a Commonwealth, that all the wealth should bee common; but because the whole wealth, wit, power, and goodnesse whatsoever, of every particular person, must be conferred and reduced to the common good: and that in the same sort and semblance, as the distinct members of the bodie, being ordained to different uses, do yet concurre in this consonance of intention, as to impart and referre all their helps and indevours (to the uttermost reach of their abilities) for the procuring and preserving of the comfort and continuance of this one bodie."

(28) *Political Works*, p. 41.

(29) See the brief but excellent discussion of "autonomous man" in R. M. Frye, *Shakespeare and Christian Doctrine* (Princeton, 1963), pp. 122-125.

(30) *Aristotles Politiques*, p. 162, as quoted in Lees, p. 121.

(31) See *Shakespeare's Plutarch*, ed. C. F. Tucker Brooke . . . Brooke (New York, 1909), II, 139.

(32) Fire imagery is, of course, already present in North's Plutarch. See *Shakespeare's Plutarch*, II, 174-175. See also E. M. W. Tillyard, *The Elizabethan World Picture* (Vintage ed., New York, n.d.), p. 69.

(33) *Political Works*, p. 12.

(34) Adolf Katzenellenbogen, *Allegories of the Virtues and Vices in Medieval Art* (New York, 1964), Plate XVII.

(35) A similar situation of rash conduct is described in Caesar, *The Gallic War*, VII, 47-51. During the siege of Gergovia, a group of over-zealous soldiers make their way into the city. The soldiers' rashness causes the death of almost 700 and brings forth a harangue from their commander-in-chief. See also Paul A. Jorgenson, "Divided Command in Shakespeare," *PMLA*, LXX (1955), 750-761.

(36) *Shakespeare's Plutarch*, II, 174.

(37) *Justitia* is always pictured with a pair of scales. See Katzenellenbogen, Plate XVII and *passim*.

Pericles' "Downright Violence"

by John P. Cutts

F. D. Hoeniger, in the introduction to his edition[1] of *Pericles*, asserts that G. Wilson Knight[2] is wrong in his argument that Pericles is somehow infected by the evil of Antiochus' daughter whom he tried to woo, and that Kenneth Muir's[3] suggestion that Thaisa upon suddenly marrying Pericles broke a vow to Diana is equally misleading, and that to seek for a moral cause of Pericles' troubles is to assume·the role of Job's comforters. On the contrary I think that to take Hoeniger's own position that Pericles is the plaything of Fortune and the gods, that he is "an impeccably good man, man without defect," is to make of Pericles an unnecessary Job. From the totality of the play's structure one must be very uncomfortable with Pericles as a Job as I hope to be able to show by modifying, elaborating upon and adding to both Wilson Knight's and Muir's arguments.

The play's opening, couched in medieval terminology, would surely have us consider "man's infirmities" (I.ch.3) to teach "frail mortality to know itself" (I.i.43) as a restorative. Any estimate of the play's total impact will certainly have to allow for the striking effect of the reincarnation of the medieval poet, but he is surely there not simply as a makeshift device for holding the play's sprawling action together, nor is he explainable by the colorful garb he wears suggestive of the quaintness of an archaic world. Gower's presence makes certain that the audience be made aware of mortality and man's infirmities. One would be hard pressed to find an exemplum in medieval drama that treated of its main figure as an "impeccably good man, a man without defect."[4]

It is too easy to suggest that Pericles *accidentally* finds himself imbroiled in the discovery of Antiochus' incest, that he was innocent of any thought of wrongdoing when he approached Antiochus' court in the first place. It was hardly naïveté which led him to believe that he would be successful where many had failed before, that he would solve the riddle, Oedipus-like, win the daughter and become "son to great Antiochus" (I.i.27). He is in such a hurry[5] to interrupt Antiochus, who is about to unfold all the dangers and difficulties, that when Antiochus merely addresses him as "Prince Pericles" Pericles rushes in with "That would be son to great Antiochus." But even if we were to allow him genuine innocence *before* he reaches Antiochus' court there can surely be no doubt of his impetuousness, his rashness, and his infatuation with moral danger once he is there. All the visible signs around him cannot be mistaken for anything but what they are, powerful indications of death on an insidious scale. Thinking "death no hazard in this enterprise" (I.i.5) he is little removed from Hamlet's "I'll speak to it, though hell itself should gape / And bid me hold my peace" because his "fate cries out," or from Faustus' "Ile conjure though I die therefore" or from Hotspur's "Albeit I make a hazard of my head" in his drunk-with-choler mood. "Thus ready for the way of life or death" (I.i.55) Pericles awaits the "sharpest blow" (I.i.56). Antiochus, like Mephistopheles with Faustus, does not equivocate on the mortal dangers inherent in Pericles' presumption. He points out the skulls of "sometimes famous princes" (I.i.35) which advise Pericles to desist "for going on death's net, whom none resist" (I.i.41). Pericles is in a House of Death and cannot but be sensitive of this fact. It is instructive, I think, to see how at the end of the play, where there are so many cross-references to Antiochus' court, Lysimachus will try to excuse his presence in a brothel house by claiming that he had not brought "[t]hither a corrupted mind" (IV.vi.103), but he protests too much his innocence for us to be convinced; "For me, be you thoughten / That I came with no ill intent : for to me / The very doors and windows savour vilely" (IV.vi.108-110). The same criterion he used in judging Marina—"Why, the house you dwell in proclaims you to be a creature of sale" (IV.vi. 76-77)—must surely be exercised against himself. The house he has stepped into proclaims him to be a creature *buying*, and the Bawd, Pander and Boult evince no surprise at his seeking such a commodity.

Pericles' own terminology in the House of Death gives him away. To greet Antiochus' daughter, presented by the father as fit for "the embracements even of Jove himself" (I.i.8), as

> See, where she comes apparell'd like the spring
> Graces her subjects, and her thoughts the king
> Of every virtue gives renown to men! *(I.i.13-15)*

is to mistake the House of Death for the House of Life, and to invite consideration of Jove's immoral ventures rather than chaste behavior. Strangely enough Pericles himself sums up this confrontation with Antiochus' daughter by presuming "To taste the fruit of yon celestial tree" (I.i.22), thereby putting the whole situation in the context of Eden's tree of life or tree of death. Nor is this merely random rhetoric, for Antiochus' very next words place Pericles' quest in the context of Hercules' twelfth labor:

> Before thee stands this fair Hesperides,
> With golden fruit, but dangerous to be touch'd:
> For death-like dragons here affright thee hard.
> Her face, like heaven, enticeth thee to view. *(I.i.28-31)*

Jacobeans would hardly miss the Biblical implications of the fruit of that forbidden tree. *Comes' Mythologiae* (1567),[6] in which the meaning of the golden apples is explained as symbols of wealth which is given to men almost as a touchstone by which to test their souls,[7]

> quare praeclare dictum est a sapientibus diuitias tanquam
> lapidem indicem animi cuiusquam esse datas hominibus, quae
> viris bonis & prudentibus facultates essent

276

makes the message doubly clear. Pericles is entering into very great temptations. Like Guyon in Mammon's cave confronted with "a woman gorgeous gay, / And richly clad in robes of royaltye, / That neuer earthly Prince in such aray / His glory did enhaunce, and pompous pride display,"[8] and tempted to taste of the golden apples of this Proserpina's garden and to sit in her silver stool, Pericles is tempted by the magnificence, the wealth, and the power of Antiochus' daughter, but, unlike Guyon, he commits himself and asks for the passport, staking his whole "riches" (I.i.53) on the issue of the die. His easy couplet

> For death remember'd should be like a mirror
> Who tells us life's but breath, to trust it error   *(I.i.46-47)*

could well be interpreted as a good man's recognition that he is dust and to dust shall return. But the mirror rhetoric is picked up again only a few lines later, after the anticlimax of the riddle, and heaven's countless eyes viewing man's acts are bidden not to peep through the blanket of the dark, but to hide their fires, to cloud their sights perpetually, not just because the *revelation* of the riddle causes Pericles to consider "There's nothing serious in mortality" as a consequence of Antiochus' action, but much more significantly if ironically because the "Fair glass of light" (I.i.77), Antiochus' daughter, in which he saw mirrored forth his conquest of magnificence, wealth and power, has now been shattered. Instead of that glorious image of himself he is now forced to acknowledge that like Pandora he has opened "this glorious casket stor'd with ill" (I.i.78), the gift of all the gods to his way of thinking, and let loose in the world that which will work no peace, no rest, no comfort, until his sea voyage of life returns him a belief again in that innocence which his action in the court of Antiochus lost—his Marina, a symbol of his own personality (not just a symbol of the fruition of his marriage with Thaisa),[9] and returns him a link again with human affairs, his purpose in life, his Thaisa—a symbol of his own personality, his link not just with his marriage partner but with his hold on life.

Surely when Pericles exclaims immediately after his mention of the casket that "[his] thoughts revolt; / For he's no man on whom perfections wait / That, knowing sin within, will touch the gate" (I.i.79-81), this can hardly refer only to his post-riddle revulsion against accepting Antiochus' daughter as a bride. It is true that Antiochus' anxious answer "touch not upon thy life" (I.i.88) interprets Pericles' response to the daughter in this light, but Antiochus must keep *drawing attention* to his own boldness, must have his deeds in the limelight. Like Aaron or much more subtly Iago, he must feel that he has been so clever in flouting all conventional morality. Getting away with it is not enough: he must have praise. This, I feel certain, is the deep significance of a riddle that is no riddle. As others have pointed out, there are far more potent examples throughout the play that deserve seriously to be considered as enigmatic conundrums. Pericles face to face with Marina at the end of the play describes her in terms that deliberately contrast with Antiochus' daughter:

Who starves the ears she feeds, and makes them hungry
The more she gives them speech.   *(V.i.112-113)*

His "no man on whom perfections wait / That, knowing sin within, will touch the gate" is very powerfully suggestive of his own motives in succumbing to the temptation in the first place. That he should in any way either before or after temptation think of himself as a man on whom perfections wait is open to criticism. The remarkable imagery he uses for finally describing Antiochus' daughter:

> You are a fair viol, and your sense the strings
> Who, finger'd to make man his lawful music,
> Would draw heaven down and all the gods to hearken;
> But being play'd upon before your time,
> Hell only danceth at so harsh a chime   *(I.i.82-86)*

operates on more than one level. Of course it functions as an encomium of chastity, as Prospero similarly suggests in his talk with Ferdinand over Miranda—"but / If thou dost break her virgin-knot before / All sanctimonious ceremonies may / With full and holy rite be administer'd, / No sweet aspersions shall the heavens let fall / To make this contract grow" (V.i.14-19). But much more significantly it represents, too, Pericles' own destruction of musical harmony. Everything from now on will be discord to varying degrees until the music of Marina makes it possible for him again to hear the music of the spheres, for him again to be tuned in to the normal thoroughfare of kingly responsibilities. The play abounds with musical references and terminology. Although I consider Hoeniger's claim "Though Shakespeare was fond of music, nowhere else did he use it as often and as widely except in the great play which *Pericles* so clearly anticipates, *The Tempest*" (p.lxxix) to be a little exaggerative especially when one considers *Twelfth Night*, yet his attempt to draw attention to the emphasis on music in *Pericles* is very sound. After mastering the riddle of Antiochus' court Pericles goes on to master the riddle of Simonides.

Pericles is described by Simonides as "music's master" (II.v.30) on the basis of his "sweet music this last night" (II.v.26), his "delightful pleasing harmony" (II.v.28). Hoeniger and others are led by Simonides' remarks to suggest that "Pericles should make a brief appearance on the stage with a musical instrument, no words spoken, somewhere between the end of this scene [i.e.,II.ii] and the opening of II.v." This is being too literal, and adds quite unnecessarily to the "textual corruption" theory which editors have for so long been at pains to "prove." Simonides immediately asks Pericles what he thinks of Thaisa and states that Pericles "must be her master" (II.v.38), and she his scholar. It seems clear to me that the musical entertainment of the previous evening which had so delighted Simonides' ears was the dance in which Pericles chose Thaisa as his partner at Simonides' request. Professor Long cleverly suggested as long ago as 1956[10] that this second dance in contradistinction to the dance of the Knights "Even in [their] armours, as [they] are address'd" (II.iii.94) is a duet involving Pericles and Thaisa

278

only, and this is, I believe, right. Hoeniger's objection that Long in making much of the absence of "Ladies" in the scene's opening stage direction in the 1609 Quarto fails to take into account that "such omission means little in a play where so many stage directions are either missing or incomplete"[11] is well taken, but the argument does not stop there. It may well be as Long suggests that Pericles, having demonstrated his skills in tilting and in the artful sword-dance, is now examined for his fitness in the art of love, the last part of his "threefold chivalric test," despite Hoeniger's claim that there is little in the play to suggest such a test in stages. Structurally such a testing could well be paralleled with other testings Pericles undergoes. But I think that what is being appealed to is the distinction between antimasque and masque. The vanquished five knights dance in their armor; they are characterized by the "loud music" (II.iii.97) of the clashing of their armor, "too harsh for ladies' heads." That Pericles *may* be included in this armor dance is conceivable, of course, though I think it very unlikely. In the first place he has always drawn attention to himself by being on one side, not of the group, and secondly, Simonides specifically calls for the knights' dance in an effort to awake Pericles from his melancholy, as if it were an entertainment *for* Pericles. Immediately after the knights' dance Simonides approaches Pericles separately to offer Thaisa as his dancing partner. It is of course, possible, as Hoeniger suggests, that this corresponds to the revels[12] part of the masque in which the "courtier-masquers, after the 'Main,' danced with chosen members of their audience," though this would be awakward since it would be relegating Thaisa to the least elevated part of the masque. Much more likely is the probability that the vanquished knights are made by Simonides to dance as a foil to the main dance of Pericles and Thaisa, an antimasque to the main. By this procedure, antimasque to main masque. Pericles is afforded great dignity. It seems to me that Simonides is fixing this procedure himself, that it is part of his shoddy treatment of the knights. Since Pericles has been successful in the tourney, there is really no need to have to apologize to the disappointed knights by cooked up excuses "That for this twelvemonth she'll not undertake / A married life" (II.v.3-4), and that "One twelve moons more she'll wear Diana's livery: / This by the eye of Cynthia hath she vow'd, / And on her virgin honour will not break it" (II.v.10-12). Ironically Thaisa will wear Diana's livery for fourteen years! Simonides is inventing an excuse for ridding himself of the other knights, but making vows to the gods as his excuse is bound to bring such repercussions. Professor Muir has suggested that Thaisa's misfortunes are brought about by Diana, the play's presiding deity, who is incensed by Thaisa's breaking of her vow. This is not strictly true, as Hoeniger points out[13] by comparing Apollo's role in *The Winter's Tale,* which is a clear case of an incensed god actively interfering in human affairs. The problem with Thaisa is best tackled from Thaisa's own motivation and from her father's. The court of Simonides has its own riddle. "[P]rinces and Knights come / from all parts of the world to joust and tourney" (II.i.107-108) for the love of the King's daughter, only to be told that she will wear Diana's livery. Thaisa and Simonides seize on Pericles: Antiochus' daughter apparently approved of Pericles:

> Of all, 'say'd yet, may'st thou prove prosperous!
> Of all, 'say'd yet, I wish thee happiness   *(I.i.60-61)*

and though it is possible to conclude that she has said this to every suitor before, it does not diminish its effectiveness on a Pericles who imagines himself different from all the other applicants. If we concentrate on the dramatic structure of Antiochus' court and Simonides' court, likened as they are by Pericles joining in the lists and tourneying for the princess, then I think it becomes obvious that they represent two sides of one coin. At Antiochus' court Pericles is the brash, dashing, impetuous, ambitious, proud knight: at Simonides' the melancholy, retired, subdued, "mean knight." The "gentler gamester is the soonest/winner" *(Henry V*, III.vi.117-118).

Pericles can take no real credit for reading Antiochus' open book. His "blind mole—poor worm" (I.i.101,103) description of himself hardly fits the facts. He would like to hide behind his need to tell the world of Antiochus' incest, to warn others of oppressors, and to hide behind his fear for his own death at the hands of the tyrant, but the mole's activity is the result largely of ambition and pride, as is clearly evidenced by Shakespeare's use of the molehill in *3 Henry VI* where both Richard Plantagenet and Henry VI find themselves on molehills largely of their own making, Richard actively tunneling in the dark and casting "copp'd hills towards heaven" (*Per.*I.i.102), daring the force of the Lord's anointed, and Henry VI much more passively but no less inexcusably allowing Margaret and Suffolk to undermine England's power at home and abroad. Pericles' ambition to become "son to great Antiochus" and to solve the world's riddle has "cast / Copp'd hills towards heaven" and he will suffer for it by a kind of spiritual death. Antiochus, in toying with him, allowing him "[f]orty days" (I.i.117) longer, emphasizes his wilderness existence. Henceforth Pericles will "shun the danger" (I.i.143) of Antiochus, will flee from the symbol of his own destruction of peace of mind. Not an hour can "breed [him] quiet" (I.ii.6). His subjects for whom he professes kingly care sense his mental anxiety—"keep your mind, till you return to us, / Peaceful and comfortable" (I.ii.36-37), and, though they are sharply rebuked by Helicanus for "flattery" because "reproof, obedient and in order, / Fits kings, as they are men, for they may err" (I.ii.43-44), Helicanus himself "knows" ("but thou know'st this" [I.ii.78]), without being told, what Pericles has gone through at Antiochus' court as Pericles well realizes, because guilt is written all over his face.

Pericles tries to turn his anger against Helicanus' boldness in speaking disrespectfully about a king, but the anger Helicanus sees in Pericles' looks does not derive from Helicanus' breach of feudal etiquette. Pericles has "ground the axe [him]self" (I.ii.58) as much as Helicanus has, but the nearest he comes to recognizing this is to suggest that Antiochus will make pretence of wrong that Pericles has done him and all must feel war's blow "for mine *if* I may call offence" (I.ii.92; italics mine). His whole speech, I.ii.79-91, prior to this half-admission is full of fears and doubts acknowledging fears for his own safety but attributing doubts to Antiochus, when in point of fact it is he himself who is full of doubts too. When he delegates the responsibilities of government to Helicanus "whose wisdom's strength can bear it" (I.ii.119) and pleads that, although in exile himself and Helicanus at the head of the state, nevertheless "in our orbs we'll live so round and safe" (I.ii.122), it is not difficult to see in this a parallel with the musical imagery which opened the play on the appearance of Antiochus' daughter—"The senate-house of planets all did sit / To knit in her their best perfections." Both are stressing harmony and order and both represent anything but that. There is a neat parallel, too, in the way Pericles' and Thaisa's *dance* is stopped by Simonides with "Unclasp, unclasp" (II.iii.106) and in the very next scene Helicanus is described as knit in harmony with the rest of the peers of Pericles' kingdom—"we'll clasp hands: / When peers thus knit, a kingdom ever stands" (II.iv. 57-58)- after he has successfully argued that they should wait a twelvemonth longer for Pericles and not force him to take their present wish to make him king and thus cause him to "leap into the seas, / Where's hourly trouble for a minute's ease" (II.iv.43-44).

For the rest of the play Pericles will be a figure of varying degrees of disorder and discord. Delegating his responsibilities to Helicanus is *not* conducive to good government, as the play very well points out when the lords of Tyre understandably pester Helicanus with their overflowing griefs and desire to know whether Pericles "lives to govern [them]" (II.iv.31).

Before Pericles once again enters the lists to tourney for a princess he is put through an instructive performance at Tharsus, which is complaining about man's infirmities and asserting that to relate tales of others' griefs hoping to learn thereby how to forget its own is like blowing at fire in hope to quench it:

> For who digs hills because they do aspire
> Throws down one mountain to cast up higher.   *(I.iv.5-6)*

This recalls the blind mole imagery of Pericles, and there are other correspondences. Tharsus, described as having towers which bore their "heads so high they kiss'd the clouds" (I.iv.24), "men and dames so jetted and adorn'd, / Like one another's glass to trim them by" (I.iv.26-27)—examples of pride similar to Pericles' —is a clear indication that a parallel with Tyre is intended. When Pericles enters Tharsus and plays savior to it by giving it "life whom hunger starv'd half dead" (I.iv.96), his cautionary remark that his gift horse should not be construed as another Trojan horse psychologically betrays him. He has opened up one casket of mischief at Antiochus' court and is trying to make amends now by opening up a casket of good. The citizens of Tharsus help to restore his former image for him by building "his statue to make him glorious" (II.ch.14), thinking that everything he utters is gospel truth. The whole process is not so much different from Bolingbroke's wish to keep his presence "like a robe pontifical" (III.ii.56) in his purpose to "lead out many to the Holy Land" to prevent people looking "[t]oo near unto [his] state" (*2 Hen.IV.*, IV.v.212) or his son's preoccupation with religious scruples whereby he can condemn the last of the Mortimer faction, the French, and the remnants of the Eastcheap world in a hardly understood effort to show penitence, though before Agincourt's immense odds Hal does verbalize his realization that:

> More will I do;
> Though all that I can do is nothing worth,
> Since that my penitence comes after all,
> Imploring pardon. *(Henry V, IV.ii.308-311)*

For Pericles the sojourn at Tharsus must necessarily be brief. The play's use of a Dumb Show to indicate Helicanus' warning to Pericles that "in Tharsus was not best / Longer for him to make his rest" aptly suggests that no matter how hard Pericles tries to give expression to his "savior" needs the real cause of his distress will not be dumb. Thoughts of what he did at Antiochus' court mount in virulence against him, tempests toss him, and symbolically strip him naked on the shores of life like Lear and Macbeth upon the blasted heath of their own making, but unlike them refusing to acknowledge *openly* any sinning but only being sinned against. His observation that "earthly man / Is but a substance that must yield" (II.i.2-3) to the elements and that he as "fits [his] nature" (II.i.4) does obey recalls Lear's similar submission to the elements and is another example of frail mortality being made to know itself. It looks like passiveness, putting up with bad fortune because that is all man can do, but the fishermen commenting on the situation draw attention to man's dual nature, half beast, half flesh, almost in terms of Lear's recognition:

> Down from the waist they are Centaurs,
> Though women all above:
> But to the girdle do the Gods inherit,
> Beneath is all the fiend's. *(IV.vi.126-129)*

The fishermen keep such a "jangling of the bells" (II.i.41) in the belly of the rich miser of a whale that the causer of the oppression cannot possibly forget how he has behaved. Pericles is moved to comment how "[t]hese fishers tell the infirmities of men" (II.i.49), thus affording us a link with the play's opening chorus, and yet he does not realize that in praising them for exposing men's wrongdoings, for they "recollect/All that may men approve or men detect" (II.i.50-51), he is ironically commenting upon himself. He the huge whale in his "wat'ry empire" has devoured all the "poor fry before him" in his determination to prove the only survivor of the Antiochus riddle, and at one mouthful too, one rapid stroke. One may indeed search the calendar in vain for an honest man as the fisherman suggests, and the sea was certainly a drunken knave casting Pericles in their way when they are discussing what honesty is. *Lear*'s "to-and-fro-conflicting wind and rain" (III.i.11)—"the tempest in [Lear's] mind" (III.iv.12)—becomes in *Pericles* a "vast tennis-court" (II.i.60), in which the waters and the wind have made Pericles "the ball/For them to play upon" (II.i.60-61). The tennis metaphor aptly fits Pericles, who must suffer many more setbacks before he realizes there is something wrong with his tennis-playing. The tennis metaphor tends to rob its user of the dignity he is striving for. Henry V is no more successful in trying to turn the Dauphin's tennis-balls to gun-stones because he claims he will "play a set/Shall strike his father's crown into the hazard" (I.ii.262-263), when in point of fact as the play shows and as Henry VI goes on to emphasize with his revealing

> I'll leave my son my virtuous deeds behind;
> And would my father had left me no more! *(3 Henry VI, II.ii.49-50)*

things "evil got had ever bad success" (*3 Henry VI*, II.ii.46). The end result of Henry V's tennis is to strike Bolingbroke's crown into the hazard.

Pericles reborn from the sea has not yet learned that he has "suffer'd like a girl" not like a man "[e]xtremity out of act" (V.i.137;139). His determination to enter the lists for good Simonides' daughter is basically to try to convince himself that his first entering of the lists in the play was equally as honest. The savior episode at Tharsus stilled his conscience for a while: the shipwreck episode makes him think of starting afresh all over again; but the episode with the fishermen ironically comments on the situation with "what a man cannot get, he may lawfully deal for with his wife's/soul" (II.i.113-114). The fishermen obviously refer first to a man's willingness to rent out his wife to another man in order to prosper in the world. When this is seen as a reflection on Pericles one is faced with the conclusion that Pericles is out to get something unlawfully at the expense of his "wife" to be. The last words of Pericles at this juncture, "This day I'll rise, or else add ill to ill" (II.i.165), surely emphasize the ironical overtones of what the fishermen have been saying. The rusty armor which they provide for him from the seas, this "garment" which they make for him "through the rough seams of/the water" (II.i.148-149), should remind him of his common humanity, his link with the ebb and flow of human suffering, but he turns it to his proud advantage in several ways. Identifying it as the armor of his father it becomes the symbol of his discovery of an identity, a father image, his evolution from a "wat'ry grave" (II.i.10) to a new life, which will soon find its expression in his attitude toward Simonides. Disastrously he treats it as an indication that his "shipwreck now's no ill, / Since [he has] here [his] father gave in his will" (II.i.132-133), and he clothes himself in steel despite "all the rapture of the sea" (II.i.154) and once more becomes in his own mind the knight-errant "looking for adventures in the world" (II.iii.83), mounting himself upon "a courser, whose delightful steps / Shall make the gazer joy to see him tread" (II.i.157-158), which powerfully recalls the concentration on outward magnificence contrasted with inward worth which the play emphasizes throughout. When Pericles has to admit that his equipment is yet "unprovided of a pair of / bases" (II.i.159-160) and has to accept a pair from one of the fishermen who brings him to the court himself this should be another reminder of his "human infirmity," instead of which "What [he has] been [he has] forgot to know" (II.i.71), and he behaves like the rich miser driving the poor fry of the fishermen before him and at last devouring their use at a mouthful.

When next we see Pericles he is playing the "mean Knight," the psychological opposite of his role in Antiochus' court. Now everything is humility. He counts on discerning people noticing how

> Opinion's but a fool, that makes us scan
> The outward habit by the inward man   *(II.ii.55-56)*

and once again attempts to show up all the other "princes and Knights come / from all parts of the world to joust and tourney" (II.i.107-108) for a princess's love, but this time by excessive modesty, humility, and an appeal to inner worth. His reticence and non-participation make Simonides think that his "court / Ha[s] not a show might countervail [Pericles'] worth" (II.iii.55-56). He even goes so far as to tell Simonides that he "never aim'd so high to love [his] daughter" (II.v.47), which is almost in flat contradiction of his statement to the fishermen.

The tournament of Knights is a masterpiece of set organization. To consider this, however, as merely another piece of colorful pageantry as so often unfortunately is the prevailing approach,[14] as for instance is the case with the tournament in *Richard II,* is to miss the careful symbolism of the whole. The five Knights in the city of Pentapolis obviously call for careful scrutiny, and for us as well as Thaisa "to entertain / The labour of each Knight in his device" (II.ii.14-15). Thaisa is described at this point as "Beauty's child, whom Nature gat / For men to see, and seeing wonder at" (II.ii.6-7), which is a clear enough parallel with the description of Antiochus' daughter:

> Nature this dowry gave: to glad her presence,
> The senat-house of planets all did sit
> To knit in her their best perfections.   *(I.i.10-12)*

The general description of the princely Knights as a "model which heaven makes like to itself; / As jewels lose their glory if neglected, / So princes their renowns if not respected" (II.ii.11-13) takes on particular significance in Pericles' case, for in the immediately preceding scene Pericles, girding himself with a *rusty* armor, refers to his new-found equipment as a "jewel hold[ing] his building on [his] arm" (II.i.155). Pericles has certainly lost his glory by neglecting matters that truly concern princes as models of heaven. His own actions have set him on a course not unlike that of an unruly meteor that cannot be brought back into obedient orb until its motion is linked again with the harmony of the spheres.

To compare the dramatist's description of the five Knights and their devices with the various descriptions and mottoes in Wilkins' *Painfull Adventures,* and then to suggest strongly that "Q provides an imperfect report with some lines missing and others replaced"[15] is surely to miss the point. Nor is the difference between the *full* description of the Knights in Wilkins and the less full description in the play to be explained away as "deliberate, in the interest of brevity."[16] The deliberate alteration of what passes for source material is usually attributable to *dramatic* necessity in a constructional sense. The alteration of Hotspur's age is effected not simply to telescope history and battles, but to afford a dramatic comparison and contrast between Hal and Hotspur of the same age and to make it

284

possible for Bolingbroke to see in Hotspur an image of his own youthful ambition. I suggest that the play's alteration of the description of the Knights and their mottoes is deliberately calculated to take it out of *categorical* pointing, mere automatic listing, and to point the emphasis elsewhere. In one sense the description is obviously satirical. The elaborate outward show of the Knights contrasts immediately with the "rusty outside" of Pericles' outward show, but does it more accurately reflect the inward man of Pericles' inward show in five stages eventually summed up by the sixth? The technique is not all that different from the tedious brief show in *A Midsummer-Night's Dream* where the lovers are looking on at Pyramus and Thisbe without recognizing how much they are looking in a mirror.

The first, a Knight of Sparta with the black Ethiop reaching at the sun, and his motto of *Lux tua vita mihi* is interpreted by Simonides very simply as "He loves you well that holds his life of you" because Simonides considers it only from Thaisa's angle. More accurately surely this would mean Spartan courage of a stranger presuming to reach at the "Fair glass of light"—Pericles in Antiochus' court. If so, then "He loves you well that holds his life of you" ironically parallels Pericles' last summation of his love for Antiochus' daughter before the riddle is given to him: "But my unspotted fire of love to you, / Thus ready for the way of life or death, / I wait the sharpest blow" (I.i.54-56). The black Ethiop reaching for the sun figures the darkness and ignorance of the stranger seeking the light, and this again points rather to Pericles than to any other Knight, and to Pericles' own estimation of how he had no idea what he was getting himself into. Some of the Lords commenting later on Pericles make much of his being a stranger and of his appearance befitting one who has "practis'd more the whipstock than the lance" (II.ii.50).

The second contender, an armed Knight from Macedon "that's conquer'd by a lady," bearing his motto *Pue Per doleera kee per forsa*,[17] is not commented on by Simonides. That the motto is described by Thaisa as Spanish is perhaps best interpreted as Thaisa's mistake rather than the Quarto's. Macedon is surely meant to recall Alexander the Great; certainly Fluellen makes a great fuss over Macedon and Alexander "for / there is figures in all things" (*Henry V*, IV.vii.34-35), and it seems clear to me that the dramatist has deliberately cut down on the derivations of the five Knights so that Macedon and Sparta are the only two Greek ones remaining, Corinth and Athens having been dropped. Sparta and Macedon have immediate application in Spartan courage and Alexandrian cutting of the Gordian knot. "More by gentleness than by force" is surely more applicable to Pericles than to any of the five Knights, as he plays the gentler game. That he should be conquered by a lady might be interpreted also as an early indication that the overtures to love are made by Thaisa helped by her father, both of them intrigued by Pericles' obvious appeal to the inward rather than the outward man.

The third Knight, uncommented on by Simonides, and described as coming from Antioch, "his device, a wreath of chivalry" and his motto "*Me Pompey*[18] *provexit apex*" is surely a clear reflection of Pericles himself, who has come from his chivalric "adventure" at Antiochus' court where he hoped to reach the crown of triumph in solving the riddle.

Simonides' comments on the fourth Knight's device of a burning torch turned upside down and the motto *Qui me alit, me extinguit* that this shows "beauty hath his power and will,/Which can as well inflame as it can kill" (II.ii.34-35) indicate how Simonides is interpreting it as he did the first Knight's, that is, from Thaisa's point of view. However, if we look at it as another description of Pericles it is not difficult to see how appropriate it is that Pericles should be extinguished by the self-same wax which was the cause of his light. In Antiochus' court he carried his torch aloft: in Simonides' he is turning it upside down—his elevated pride is turned to submissive humility.

The fifth and last of the Knights, uncommented on by Simonides, and described as a "hand environed with clouds,/Holding out gold that's by the touchstone tried" with a motto *Sic spectanda fides* is surely a neat summation of the need for Pericles to be tested not by words and aspirations only but by actual deeds also. Pericles has borne his head so high to kiss the clouds, hoping to seize the golden apples of Hesperides at Antiochus': now he must be put to the test of deeds not riddles at Simonides' court.

The derivations, where given, and the emblems and devices of all five Knights suggest ironical comments on Pericles' own condition. When he himself is introduced as a stranger with the device of a "wither'd branch, that's only green at top" and the motto *In hac spe vivo*, Simonides' interpretation of this pretty moral as "[f]rom the dejected state wherein he is,/He hopes by you his fortunes yet may flourish" (II.ii.45-46) makes the parallel with Antiochus' court—"That would be son to great Antiochus"—very effective. The black Ethiop reaching at the sun, the armed Knight that's conquered by a lady, the Knight drawn to this enterprise by the crown of the triumph, the burning torch upside down, the hand from the clouds holding gold to be tried—all reach their conclusion in the branch that's withered but yet maintaining a little life at top. Pericles on "set purpose" (II.ii.53) is trying to dissociate all the Antiochus experiences from himself and to revert to the significance of his father's rusty armor for confidence, and his emblem and motto represent the wish that he has not completely ruined his life but left a small vestige of hope.

I think it is entirely possible that the five Knights may represent the five senses. The first with his concentration on light (sun, *lux*) representing sight; the second with his emphasis on gentleness of a lady suggesting either touch or smell, but since the fifth clearly stands for touch, the second could presumably be smell. The third concentrates on drawing people from afar to this chivalric enterprise, and thus may be hearing. The fourth's concentration on feeding and extinguishing is obviously taste, and the fifth with its references to hand and touchstone clearly could stand for touch. If this allegorization is possible then it would certainly afford a very smooth yet subtle transition into the next scene—a banquet at which Thaisa is described as "queen o' th' feast" (II.iii.17).

Simonides and Thaisa have not made comments on each of the contenders, and I think the explanation of this lies in quite a different quarter than is represented by Hoeniger's asseveration that "It is a good guess that the King explained the motto in similar words [to those in Wilkins] in the uncorrupted text."[19] The dramatist is surely deliberately having Simonides and Thaisa *impatient* with all the Knights except Pericles, and Simonides' final statement of how foolish it is to "scan/The outward habit by the inward man" is a careful enough indication where he is prepared to exercise patience. Before long the play reveals how Simonides has had suspicions that the stranger "for aught [he] know[s], /May be (nor can [he] think the contrary)/As great in blood as [he] [him] self" (II.v. 77-79), and it is presumably on this intuition that he has been acting in promoting his daughter's advances to Pericles, and in commending her choice and decision to "wed the stranger knight." The whole business is not unlike Prospero's machinations whereby Ferdinand is secured for his daughter Miranda, though it is not so easy to see the initial stages of the process with Simonides. By the time he bids his daughter make advances to Pericles by taking the "standing-bowl of wine to him" (II.iii.65) even against her outward expression that this is unbecoming to a lady and even impudent:

> if befits not me
> Unto a stranger knight to be so bold;
> He may my proffer take for an offence,
> Since men take women's gifts for impudence   *(II.iii.66-69)*

though, of course, her aside shows that she is secretly delighted at the opportunity to make advances to Pericles (II.iii.72), Simonides' interference is being clarified. Its real extent is not revealed, however, until Simonides palms off the other contenders for Thaisa's hand in marriage with spurious excuses. Thus he plainly shows his hand in securing this stranger, not a "wheeling and extravagant stranger" as in *Othello* where Brabantio hardly recognizes how he is "fixing" his daughter's marriage despite his "dream" of such a likely accident (I.i.142), but a Knight-errant who "only by misfortune of the seas/Bereft of ships and men, cast on this shore" (II.iii.89), according to Pericles' *own* report. The strength of the Quarto's use of "only" is obvious in this interpretation. One need not resort to suggestions that "*only* may well be corrupt,"[20] or to emend it to "newly" as Elze[21] conjectured.

Pericles hides behind his father figure, Simonides, and allows himself to be manipulated, deliberately keeping in the background and letting Simonides and Thaisa manage things the way they wish. He describes himself as a "glow-worm in the night,/The which hath fire in darkness, none in light" (II.iii.43-44). It is the *radiance* of Simonides' court which recalls his own father's splendor who "[h]ad princes sit like stars about his throne,/And he the sun" (II.iii.39-40) and contrasts with his own poor light. By this means he tries to eradicate from his mind his own self searching for a wife on *his* terms—the disastrous Antiochus affair—and tries to convince himself that the wife he is now gaining comes with his father's blessing and approval. Thaisa represents in this sense his tie and bind, his attempt to convince himself that he is part of normality, of normal human affairs. It is yet another attempt to combat his sense of guilt over his Antiochus experience.

When at the beginning of Act III the dumb show and chorus report "Antiochus and his daughter dead" and Pericles urgently summoned back to Tyre to prevent the men of Tyre from mutinying and placing the crown on Helicanus' head, it is highly significant that Pericles' attempts to comply immediately run him into a violent storm off Tharsus. The death of Antiochus and his daughter frees Pericles from the fear of death at Antiochus' hands, but does not free him from the conscience effects of that association. Try as hard as he can to get back to Tyre successfully with his bride, as if the whole Antiochus affair had never taken place, as if Thaisa were the bride he set out for in the first place and was bringing home to be his consort, the microcosmic storm belies his attempt to think all is as it had never been. How eloquently he calls upon the god of the great vast to rebuke the surges, to bind the winds in brass, to still the deafening, dreadful thunders, and to quench the storm's sulphurous flashes, but all this is "as a whisper in the ears of death/Unheard" (III.i.9-10). The storm that is within him will not subside. That which he gained so easily[22] Thaisa, is just as rapidly snatched away, and his sea-sorrow is given visible embodiment in Marina. His grief has lingered long in the chambers of the sea, but now it is given birth, a local habitation and a name, and he must cast for ever from him the comforting thought that Thaisa made up for Antiochus' daughter, that his credit ledger with the gods cancels out his debit. All is suffering till ripeness be all. His "priestly farewell" (III.i.69) to Thaisa with Nestor (the cup) and Nicander (man's victory) as priestly assistants, attended by Lychorida (unbinding and loosing), is full of ceremonial implications that he must sacrifice (cup) his victory, his gaining of Thaisa, and give it to the gods. Temporarily his heart is in the coffin there with Thaisa, or already in the sea:

> Ay me whilst thee the sounding seas and shores
> Wash far away wherere thy bones are hurled....
> Where thou perhaps under the whelming tide
> Visit'st the bottom of the monstrous world   *(Lycidas)*

with the "belching whale." In some sense he has "ravin[ed] up/[His] own life's means" (*Macbeth*, II.iv.28-29), has devoured the poor fry before him, has engulfed others in his own tempestuous seas. His short-lived victory had been wrested out of his first sea-wrecking; the sea symbolically claims it back. And he finds himself willingly going back to Tharsus, ostensibly to leave his babe at "careful nursing" (III.ii.80) there, but subconsciously to take refuge in a place which still thinks of him as a savior, a place that had erected a statue to his glory. What irony it is that the next time he visits Tharsus, fourteen years later, he is presented with a monument with epitaphs in "glitt'ring golden characters" (IV.iii.44) expressing general praise of Marina. Since the audience knows Marina is alive Pericles' confrontation with a glorious statue monument is powerfully suggestive of mirror techniques. Pericles is made to see his life's statue, his savior role, turned into his death's monument, the destruction of his attempts to hide behind good deeds and to blame all his difficulties on the "wayward seas" (IV.iv.10). Deprived of Thaisa and Marina, he is back again in mind at Antiochus. He "bears/A tempest, which his mortal vessel tears" (IV.iv.29-30).

The concentration on Diana at this part of the play deliberately contrasts the unchaste atmosphere of the Antiochus affair, which will soon be set in very sharp relief by the brothel. Pericles is careful in his instructions to Cleon and Dioniza to look after Marina till she be married and to swear

> By bright Diana, whom we honour, all
> Unscissor'd shall this hair of mine remain,
> Though I show will[23] in't.
>
> *(III.iii.28-30)*

His wife Thaisa through the connivance of her father had put off his rivals by making a vow "on her virgin honour" to wear Diana's livery for twelve more months, and promptly married Pericles. There should be no wonder that when Thaisa is revived by Cerimon her first expression should be "O dear Diana" (III.ii.106), and her resolved intention to take a vestal livery in Diana's temple. Thaisa has offended against Diana and in her own mind will go on making reparation to Diana until Pericles come to Diana's temple and claim her in all proper religious propriety. Like Leontes in *The Winter's Tale* Pericles will "[n]ew woo [his] queen" (III.ii.156), but this time under the auspices of Diana.

The vision of Diana that comes to Pericles is surely prompted by his hope that by propitiating her deity for his part in the transgression—wedding a votaress of her order *before* the twelvemonth was up—he might somehow have Thaisa as miraculously restored to him as Marina was. Psychologically, too, it is obvious that he would make for Ephesus near whose coast Thaisa had been cast overboard. His mind is functioning not just along the lines of recovering a wife, however, but of a bridegroom meeting a bride as his very ready response to Lysimachus' hint that when they come ashore Lysimachus has a suit to prefer to Pericles indicates. Lysimachus "shall prevail,/Were it to woo [his] daughter" (V.i.259-260). That Pericles' explanation to Diana for his journeying in the past is little better than his explanation to Thaisa in her father's court should not disturb us. Pericles' awakening, recognition, restoration to harmony is worked out almost totally symbolically. He does not have glimpses of his real self, of his real wrongdoing as Lear does, but then he has the vision of Diana. The nearest he is made to come to an admission of disturbance is his expression that he was "frighted from [his] country" (V.iii.3) and then went on to wed Thaisa. At Simonides' court he had hidden behind the chivalric statement that he was trained in "arts and arms" (II.iii.82) and had been "looking for adventures in the world" when he was washed up on Simonides' shore. "Frighted" is *nearer* the truth, but a long way from it. His Antiochus affair in the House of Death, his Simonides' court affair in the House of "the gentler gamester is the soonest winner," his abandonment of Marina to the place where his image is made glorious—all these are nearer to the truth. He "puts on sackcloth" (IV.iv.29), swears never to wash his face, nor cut his hair—and these are "but the trappings and the suits of woe" (*Hamlet*, I.ii.86). They are indeed "actions that a man might play" (I.ii.84). Hamlet's indictment against the "inky cloak" as one of these actions could well be paralleled with the "banners sable" of Pericles' ship which is "trimm'd with rich expense" (V.Ch.19). He plays the man of grief in excessively rich *outer* show.

What his inner self should have been like is revealed by the play's concentration on Marina's "lasting storm," and how she endured it (IV.i.19). The fourth act is almost entirely devoted to her sea-changes, which she later claims "might equal" the stranger King's "if both were justly weigh'd" (V.i.88), and even Pericles is moved to believe that a comparison between her sufferings and his is possible, though, of course, his must be the greater or else she has suffered like a man and he like a girl.

When Marina, faced with her murderer-to-be, stresses her innocence in that she did never hurt Dioniza's daughter in all her life, never spoke a bad word, "nor did ill turn/To any living creature" (IV.i.75-76), never killed a mouse, hurt a fly or "trod upon a worm" (IV.i.78) against her will, she pleads from an innocence that is never in doubt, and contrasts sharply with her father's position in which he claims that like the poor worm he must die for telling the earth it is wronged with man's oppression. Marina's confrontation with Boult's court, the Mytilene brothel, is also in sharp distinction with her father's in Antiochus' court. The "sore terms" the brothel "stand[s] upon with the gods" (IV.ii.32) are known to the proprietors and customers of the establishment, whose one redeeming feature is that they acknowledge they would not do thus if they could "pick up some pretty/estate" (IV.ii.30-31), and thus keep their doors closed, because theirs is neither profession, trade, or calling. And indeed Boult is very willing to speak for himself and for the Pander and the Bawd in finding gold "tractable enough" (IV.vi.198).

What irony it is that the gold Marina thus buys herself out of the brothel with and with which the brothel people can begin to restore some kind of respect to themselves came from Lysimachus! Marina has indeed been brought to the brothel by "wayward fortune" that did "malign [her] state" (V.i.89), but has not lost faith in the gods whom she does not accuse but calls on their defence and commends her chastity into Diana's keeping (IV.iii.147). Her beauty is promulgated abroad through the market of the world as was Antiochus' daughter's, and prospective clients have been lured to "joust" for her, Monsieur Verolles, the pox, to try to "cut a caper at the proclamation" (IV.ii.105-106), a Spaniard to mouth-water "to bed to/her very description" (IV.ii.98-99), and "of every nation a traveller" (IV.ii.112) to scatter his crowns in the shadow of the brothel's sun. Each knows precisely why he is visiting a brothel and each is presented with some kind of riddle to try to excuse his presence there. The first two gentlemen clients visit what they took to be a bawd and hear "vestals sing" (IV.v.7), but could they not be said to be feeding on "mother's flesh which did [them] breed" (I.i.66), especially with regard to Monsieur Verolles who "brought his disease/[T]hither: here he does but repair it" (IV.ii.108-109). Lord Lysimachus (end of the battle for Marina and Pericles!) comes "disguis'd" to "do the deeds of darkness" (IV.vi.29) with some "wholesome iniquity" that a man "may deal withal, and/defy the surgeon" (IV.vi.24-25), as if "after a long voyage at sea" (IV.vi.42), and is faced with the riddle of how Marina could have been at the same trade "[e]'er since [she] can remember" (IV.vi.72), and tries to argue his way out of his embarrassing presence in a brothel by pleading an incorrupt mind, but the gold he gives her is another way of scattering his crowns. His very presence is his indictment.

The brothel episodes thus function as a foil for Pericles' behavior particularly in Antiochus' court. The riddle that man goes to solve is basically the riddle of his own going. It would be better not to let one's feet travel in that direction in the first place, but if one does fall then it is better to be able to buy oneself out by pleading

> best men are moulded out of faults,
> And, for the most, become much more the better
> For being a little bad.   *(Measure for Measure, V.i.437-439)*

The clients visiting the brothel exhibit "man's infirmities" on a far smaller scale than Pericles visiting Antiochus' court. A little gold washes them clean, but Pericles' hands that opened Pandora's box "will rather/The multitudinous seas incarnadine/Making the green one red" (*Macbeth*, II.ii.60-62) wherever he travels. Coming back to reclaim his daughter after fourteen years of absence he does "[s]ail seas in cockles"24 (IV.iv.2) trying to thwart the "wayward seas" (IV.iv.10) rather than admit his own waywardness, piloting his ship to Tharsus as modern emendators of the text will have us read whereas the original Quarto quite clearly suggests in its spelling and capitalization of "Pilat" ("this Pilat thought," IV.iv.18) a pun on the state of mind in which he is going to Tharsus, trying to wash his hands clean of any thought of not having done the right thing. And he symbolically finds his glorious image is dead, reads his own epitaph in Marina's monument—"wither'd in her spring of year" (IV.iv.25) recalling the withered branch again-and retreats into his scallop shell of unquiet while his lost innocence, Marina, will "never stint,/Mak[ing] raging battery upon shores of flint" (IV.iv.42-43), making "a batt'ry through his deafen'd ports,/Which now are midway stopp'd" (V.i.46-47).

It is fitting that it should be a Lysimachus who must persist in bringing the maid of Mytilene to the dumb statue of Pericles to try to breathe life into it once more. Like the fishermen earlier Lysimachus makes up this garment for Pericles through the rough seams of Mytilene's waters. The fishermen presented Pericles with the rusty armor of his father and equipped him with a pair of bases: Lysimachus presents him with a jewel of a maid who reminds him of his wife and daughter (V.i.106-108) and furnishes him with "her sweet harmony" (V.i.44). They both "tell the infirmities of men" (II.i.49) and the need for condolements, and both hope if Pericles thrives that he will "remember/from whence [he] had them" (II.i.150-151).

Marina's song certainly begins to soften the shores of Pericles' flint. The statue comes alive, and it is as if it has all been a dream. A sea of joys rushes in upon Pericles "[o]'erbear[ing] the shores of [his] mortality" (V.i.193). The recognition of another's griefs, his daughter's caused by his own misdeeds, makes him no longer boast that nothing could prove even the "thousandth part/Of [his] endurance" (V.i.135-136), but acknowledges of Marina, "[She] that beget'st him that did [her] beget" (V.i.195), the true answer to the riddle "[on] mother's flesh which did [him] breed," the recognition that man himself destroys the music of his life, and forgets the source from whence it came. When he hears the music of the spheres he is mentally back again in tune with the world and with the gods, and from there it is an easy transition to his vision of Diana.

The end of the play is full of echoes of its beginning. The Antiochus affair looms very large. That Pericles should be in conference with Marina shortly after the drama has shown her visited by the two Gentlemen and Lysimachus might vaguely suggest that Pericles is in their line, too. Indeed were he really tempted to do her violence as his initial pushing her back made her suspect, and her asking him "Whither will you have me" (V.i.176) echoing as it does the same question to Boult about to ravish her (IV.vi.153) shortly after she has related to him the story of the plot on her life and of the pirates bringing her to Mytilene, then the play's initial theme of incest would be rounded out in an extraordinary way. The kind of wife Pericles was looking for in Antiochus' court was a daughter image rather than a peer, a co-equal partner. As far as he himself was aware his pursuit of Antiochus' daughter was a means to Antiochus' wealth, a strong enough impediment to a marriage of true minds. When Marina's sea-sorrow fuses daughter and wife in one image for him it makes possible the beginning of the search for a real wife for herself alone. The return of his daughter could never be a sufficient substitute. In the temple of Diana all impurities of excessive material impediments in a plus sense as represented by the Antiochus' court affair, and of excessive material impediments in a minus sense as represented by the Simonides' court affair, are purged away, but man is still left with his infirmities that glorify the blessed gods. His mortal weakness is the gods' immortal strength.

Notes:

(1)   See F.D. Hoeniger, ed., *Pericles* (New Arden Shakespeare, Cambridge, Mass. 1963; rev. ed. 1966), Introduction, p. lxxxi.

(2)   See G. Wilson Knight, *The Crown of Life* (London, 1958), pp.32-75.

(3)   See Kenneth Muir, *Shakespeare as Collaborator* (New York, 1960), pp.80-81.

(4)   Hoeniger, Introduction, pp.lxxx-lxxxi.

(5)   Thelma N. Greenfield, "A Re-Examination of the "Patient" Pericles," *Shakespeare Studies*, III (1967), 51-61, rightly takes exception to the prevalent view of Pericles as a type of the patient man, and less convincingly substitutes a view of Pericles as "the Renaissance descendant of the wily Greek traveler, a solver of riddles, a master of escape and incognito, skilled in the arts, and in his accomplishments and understanding a born ruler of men." Pericles is by no means a Ulysses, nor is he an Oedipus, but a prince of dark corners, avoiding, and retreating from princely responsibilities. I am grateful to Professor J. Leeds Barroll for allowing me to see Professor Greenfield's paper in galleys.

(6)   See Natalis Comitis, *Mythologiae* (Venetiis, 1568; foreword dated 1567 — B.M. copy 704.d7), *Liber Septimus, Cap.* VII, 38-40, Sig. Iiiv. The version in the 1581 edition is the same.

(7)   See Douglas Bush, *Mythology & the Renaissance Tradition in English Poetry* (New York, 1963, new rev.ed.), p.94 for the general importance of the *Mythologiae* for the Renaissance, and p.98 for this allegorical interpretation of the golden apples.

(8)   See J.C. Smith and E.de Selincourt, eds., *The Poetical Works of Edmund Spenser* (London, rep.1963), II, Canto VII,44, p.104.

(9)   See Hoeniger, Introduction, p. lxxxvi.

(10) See S.H. Long, "Laying the Ghosts in *Pericles*," *SQ*, VII (1956), 39-42.

(11) See Hoeniger, p.64 fn.

(12) "Measures" line 103 but "revels" line 93. See Hoeniger, p.65 fn. carry over.

(13) Hoeniger, p.70 fn.

(14) Hoeniger lists Kyd's *Spanish Tragedy* and *Soliman and Perseda* together with Middleton's *Your Five Gallants*. His only Shakespearean analogy is *Troilus and Cressida*, I.ii, which is quite different in technique. Most critics tend to ignore this part of the play, or concentrate only on Pericles' own emblem, and that in a rather perfunctory manner. See Derek Traversi, *Shakespeare: The Last Phase* (Stanford, Cal., 1955), p.24.

(15) Hoeniger, pp.51-52, footnote to beginning of II.ii.

(16) Hoeniger, p.182.

(17) This has caused quite unnecessary confusion (See Hoeniger, p.54). Critics have emended it to Spanish and to correct Italian. Hoeniger suggests that "the reporter or anyone else" may be responsible for these corruptions. In point of fact the Q spells the Italian words as they sound, as for instance is the case later in this scene where Q has "Pompey" for Pompae" and in IV.vi where the Q has "Caualereea" for "cavalleria." The only "corruption" is the first "e" of "doleera" which should be emeded to "c"; "e" for "c" is an Elizabethan common error.

(18) I suggest "Pompey" may well indicate how the word was to be pronounced. See previous note.

(19) Hoeniger, p.55 fn.30.

(20) Hoeniger, p.63 fn.88-89.

(21) See *Englische Studien*, IX (1885), 282.

(22) See Frank Kermode, ed., *The Tempest* (New Arden Shakespeare, Cambridge, Mass., 1958, 6th ed.), III.i.n.1-2 for the relevance of a passage in St. Augustine's *Confessions*: "Yea, the very pleasures of human life men acquire by difficulties. . . . It is . . . ordered, that the affianced bride should not at once be given, lest as a husband he should hold cheap whom, as betrothed, he sighed not after" (Book VIII.7-8).

(23) Hoeniger accepts Theobald's and Malone's conjecture "show ill" and finds support in Wilkins, *The Painful Adventures*: "himselfe in all vncomely," but I think this is quite unnecessary emendation. Pericles does show "will" in many ways, and showing "will" is showing "ill." If we emend do we not lose the possibility of the double meaning?

(24) Not just the fairy tale atmosphere of the play as Hoeniger's note to line 2, p.121, suggests.

The Use of Scripture in Cymbeline

by Naseeb Shaheen

Part of the difficulty in dealing with Shakespeare's last plays, the so-called "romances," arises from the fact that these plays contain so many diverse elements. All four plays from *Pericles* to *The Tempest* give increased prominence to music, and this is used not only for entertainment, but as a functional part of the drama at critical moments in the action. All four plays have more myth than do most of Shakespeare's plays, and the myth haunts the reader with the suggestion that there is a hidden meaning to be found. All four plays employ such romance devices as wanderings, disguises, narrow escapes, and surprise reunions with long-lost relatives. Finally, all four plays emphasize such themes as the father-daughter relationship, appearance versus reality, country life versus city life, foregiveness, and reconciliation.

With such diversity of themes and elements, it is no wonder that the interpretations of the romances are legion. Most critics favor the view that the plays have veiled religious meanings. They describe the plays with such expressions as "myths of immortality," or myths of "reconciliation and regeneration." Some critics interpret the plays as paralleling Christian doctrine, as versions of the fortunate fall involving sin, repentance, penance, and ultimate redemption. The guilty renounce their misdeeds, are forgiven, and brought to a new life.

Since a religious interpretation of the plays is a favorite one, it should be worthwhile to reconsider Shakespeare's use of Scripture in these plays. This may prove to be the most direct way of ascertaining if and to what extent Shakespeare was expounding Christian doctrine in his final phase. Shakespeare made use of Scripture in all his plays, sometimes quoting directly, sometimes referring to Biblical characters or events, at other times borrowing phrases and ideas. As a playwright, he was ever alert to find new words, images, and ideas that he could use in his plays, and in a religious age it was only natural that references to religion and Scripture should find their way into his works. In the romances these references are more numerous than we might suspect, for whereas Biblical references are usually easy to detect in the early plays, in the later plays the Biblical source is often subtly woven into the text. Of the four romances, Scripture is used most freely in *Cymbeline*. Throughout the play the reader is confronted with references to and borrowings from the Bible. As will be shown, however, this does not imply religious didacticism on Shakespeare's part, but wholesale use of Biblical source material as the suitable vehicle to convey themes that parallel Christian belief. Always the dramatic end is foremost.

The extent of Scriptural allusion in *Cymbeline*, however, seems to have escaped the notice of most commentators, including those who favor a religious interpretation. Even works which compile lists of the number of Biblical references in each of Shakespeare's plays fail to present *Cymbeline* as one of those plays in which Shakespeare makes extensive use of Scripture. Richmond Noble[1] makes the comment, "The play's Scriptural interest is not large," and then lists fourteen Biblical references for *Cymbeline*. Even Thomas Carter,[2] who tends to find more allusions to Scripture in Shakespeare than is warranted, lists only twenty-three. The fact is, however, that there are upwards of forty allusions to the Bible in *Cymbeline*, besides a large number of religious terms and images. An examination of these seems to indicate not only conscious use of Biblical sources, but also that these Biblical references are subservient to the action of the play.

First, however, the problem comes up of what degree of certainty can be attached to the Bible's being the source for some of the passages to be cited. In the case of some quotations we can be fairly certain of a Biblical origin. A case in point is V.iv.138, "When as a lion's whelp. . . ." It seems safe to say that this is a direct reference to *Genesis*, xlix.9. Every English translation of the Bible available to Shakespeare reads "lion's whelp" at this verse. Another case is I.vii. 176-178: "The love I bear him / Made me fan you thus, but the gods made you / (Unlike all others) chaffless." This seems to be a clear echo of *Luke*, iii.17 in thought, imagery and wording. If the modern reader is skeptical, it should be kept in mind that the Bible was the best-known book in Shakespeare's time and Christian doctrine was everyday knowledge. Church attendance was compulsory, and in the course of a year the Elizabethan became familiar with an impressive corpus of Scripture that was either read or commented upon in sermons, and often both.

Less certain of a Biblical origin, but quite probable, would be the case at V.iii.3-4: "For all was lost, / But that the heavens fought," and that of V.v.351-352: "The benediction of these covering heavens / Fall on their heads like dew." These seem to be drawn from *Judges*, v.20 and *Psalms*, cxxxiii.2,3 respectively. Of course, no one who refuses to accept these cases as being drawn, at least ultimately, from Scripture can be proven wrong. But the ideas and the phraseology bear a noticeable resemblance to the Scriptures cited, and the fact that in both cases religious imagery is used would make a religious source most likely. In the absence of evidence that reference was made to a source other than the Bible, and in view of the availability of a close Biblical passage, the conclusion that such cases allude to Scripture seems sound.

A third category would be those instances where a Biblical origin for a passage in Shakespeare is possible but where we are dangerously close to having nothing more than a parallel idea, a mere resemblance rather than a reference. These are the most troublesome to deal with, and *Cymbeline* is no exception in having its share of parallels. Without Shakespeare himself to consult we are left in a quandary whether to include or exclude such items from our list. To exclude them when the possibility exists that their origin is Biblical, would be to withhold evidence that should be considered in weighing the case. It would seem better, therefore, to list them and let the reader be the final judge, yet taking care not to include items that are obviously too remote.

It should be borne in mind that the reader's familiarity with the Bible affects his reaction as to the probability of a passage's being based on Scripture. If the reader's familiarity with the contents and the spirit of the Bible is great, so also the Biblical overtones suggested by a passage in Shakespeare will be many. On the other hand, the person with only a passing knowledge of Scripture might be inclined to doubt dependence on Scripture except in the most obvious cases. It should also be remembered that it is not just a matter of borrowing words or ideas that is involved, but also the borrowing of cadences and balance of thought and utterance. Perhaps the classic example of this occurs in *Hamlet*. Do Hamlet's words, "O shame! where is thy blush?" echo St. Paul's words at I *Corinthians*, xv.55: "O death, where is thy sting?" If so, then the borrowing is clearly not one of ideas but of apt utterance, and the seeker of Biblical allusions in Shakespeare must search for these also. But the important point is that in applying a uniform standard of locating allusions to Scripture in Shakespeare's plays we are confronted with the fact that certain plays, including the romances, contain a conspicuously greater density of both direct references and of parallelisms than other plays. This seems to indicate consciously increased use of Biblical sources by Shakespeare in certain plays. In using *Cymbeline* as an example of this, we shall first list its Biblical references in the order in which they occur in the play and then see what patterns emerge, what aspects of the play were developed most by this extensive use of scripture.

Of the forty-three items in the list, several may not seem to belong to the Biblical references assigned to them. At first sight they seem to be little more than doubtful parallelisms, perhaps nothing more than accidental analogies. The very first item is one of these. But as explained in the notes or elsewhere in this article, in view of their context and/or the pattern of which they are a part, their inclusion becomes more tenable. The first citation, for example, should be considered in view of the second and third, which immediately follow it in the play. Finally, the overall pattern that evolves should be kept in mind.

I have put in parentheses those items of which I myself am doubtful yet which bear a resemblance to Scripture and have been included for the sake of completeness. The reader can accept or reject as many of these as he wishes. However, even when all doubtful references are removed to each one's satisfaction, an impressive number of allusions remains. Moreover, in the appendix are listed some thirty-five religious terms and images in the play which are not based directly on Scripture. The combined evidence, therefore, seems to point to extensive use of religious sources. Quotations are made from the New Arden edition of *Cymbeline* and the Geneva Bible as printed in 1594, unless otherwise stated.

(I.i.38-40: He quit being; and his gentle lady,
> Big of this gentleman (our theme) deceas'd
> As he was born.
> *Hebrews*, vi.20-vii.3: Euen Jesus that is made an hie Priest for euer after the order of Melchi-sedec. For this Melchi-sedec . . . without father, without mother, without kinred, . . . but is likened vnto the Sonne of God.)

296

I.i.40-44: The king he takes the babe
      To his protection, calls him Posthumus Leonatus,
      Breeds him, and makes him of his bed-chamber,
      Puts to him all the learnings that his time
      Could make him the receiver of.

      Acts, vii.21-22: And when he was cast out, Pharaos daughter tooke him vp, and nourished him for her owne sonne. And Moses was learned in all the wisedome of the Egyptians, and was mightie in wordes and in deedes.

I.i.47-50: Most prais'd, most lov'd;
      A sample to the youngest, to th' more mature
      A glass that feated them, and to the graver
      A child that guided dotards.

      Luke, ii.40-47: And the childe grewe, and waxed strong in spirite, and was filled with wisedome, and the grace of God was with him. . . . And when he was twelue yeeres old, . . . they found him in the Temple, sitting in the middes of the doctours, both hearing them, and asking them questions. And all that heard him, were astonished at his vnderstanding, and answers.[3]

(I.i.59-60: I' th' swathing-clothes the other, from their nursery
      Were stol'n.

      Luke, ii.12, Bishops' Bible: Ye shal finde the childe wrapped in swadling clothes.[4])

I.ii.59-60: The gods protect you,
      And bless the good remainders of the court!

      Romans,xii.14: Blesse them which persecute you: blesse, I say, and curse not.

      Matthew, v.44: Loue your enemies: blesse them that curse you: doe good to them that hate you.

      [See also I *Corinthians*, iv.12; *Proverbs*, xxv.21; I *Peter*, iii.9.[5]]

I.vi.64-66: Nay, I prithee take it;
      It is an earnest of a farther good
      That I mean to thee.

      Ephesians, i.13-14: The holy spirit of promise, which is the earnest of our inheritance.

      II *Corinthians*, i.22: Who hath also sealed vs, and hath giuen the earnest of the Spirit in our hearts.

      [Also see II *Corinthians*, v.5.]

I.vii.7-9: Bless'd be those,
       How mean soe'er, that have their honest wills,
       Which seasons comfort.

Matthew, v.3-4: Blessed are the poore in spirite: for theirs is the kingdome of heauen. Blessed are they that mourne: for they shall be comforted.

I.vii.32-36: Hath nature given them eyes
       To see this vaulted arch, and the rich crop
       Of sea and land, which can distinguish 'twixt
       The fiery orbs above, and the twinn'd stones
       Upon the number'd beach?

Genesis, xv.5: Looke vp nowe vnto heauen, and tell the starres, if thou be able to number them.

Genesis, xxii.17: And will greatly multiply thy seede, as the starres of the heauen, and as the sande which is vpon the sea shore.

Hebrews, xi.12: So many as the starres of the skie in multitude, and as the sand of the sea shore which is innumerable.

I.vii.176-178: The love I bear him
       Made me fan you thus, but the gods made you
       (Unlike all others) chaffless.

Luke, iii.17: Whose fanne is in his hand, . . . and will gather the wheate into his garner, but the chaffe will he burne vp with fire.

(II.iii.98-99: One of your great knowing
       Should learn (being taught) forbearance.

Colossians, iii.13: Forbearing one another, and forgiuing one another.

Ephesians, iv.2, Bishops' Version: Forbearying one another.[6])

II.iii.112-113: You sin against
       Obedience, which you owe your father.

[Compare also *I.ii.17-19.*]

Ephesians, vi.1-2: Children, obey your parents in the Lord;
for this right. Honour thy father and mother.

[See also *Exodus,* xx.12, the fifth commandment, and *Deuteronomy,* v.16.]

III.iii.60-61: Then was I as a tree
       Whose boughs did bend with fruit.

Psalm, i.3: He shalbe like a tree planted by the riuers of waters, that will bring foorth her fruit in due season.

Jeremiah, xvii.8: He shall be as a tree that is planted by the water, . . . neither shall cease from yeelding fruit.

(III.iii.74-76: He that strikes
        The venison first shall be lord o' th' feast,
        To him the other two shall minister.

Luke, xii.37: Blessed are those seruants, whome the Lord when he commeth, shal finde waking: . . . hee will gird himselfe about, and make them to sit downe at table, and will come forth, and serue them.[7])

III.iii.91-92: Thus mine enemy fell,
        And thus I set my foot on's neck.

Joshua, x.24: Joshua . . . saide vnto the chiefs of the men of warre, which went with him, Come neere, set your feete vpon the necks of these kings: and they came neere and set their feete vpon their neckes.

III.iv.36-37: Rides on the posting winds, and doth belie
        All corners of the world.

Revelation, vii.1: I sawe foure Angels stand on the foure corners of the earth, holding the foure windes of the earth.

[See also *Isaiah*, xi.12.]

III.iv.81-85: The scriptures of the loyal Leonatus,
        All turn'd to heresy? Away, away,
        Corrupters of my faith! . . .
        . . . thus may poor fools
        Believe false teachers.

II *Peter*, ii.1: But there were false prophets also among the people, euen as there shall be false teachers among you: which priuily shall bring in damnable heresies.

III.iv.85-87: Though those that are betray'd
        Do feel the treason sharply, yet the traitor
        Stands in worse case of woe.

Matthew, xxvi.24: But woe be to that man, by whome the Sonne of man is betrayed: it had bene good for that man, if he had neuer bene borne.

[See also *Mark*, xiv.21; *John*, xiii.21.]

III.iv.119: [See note 8.]

III.iv.125-126: I'll give but notice you are dead, and send him
　　　　　　Some bloody sign of it.

　　Genesis, xxxvii.31-32: They tooke Josephs coate, and killed a kid of the
　　goates, and dipped the coate in the blood. So they sent the particoloured
　　coate, . . . vnto their father.

III.vi.1: I see a man's life is a tedious one.

　　Wisdom, ii.1: Our life is short and tedious.[9]

(III.vi.2-3: I have tir'd myself: and for two nights together
　　　　　　Have made the ground my bed.

　　Hebrews, xi.37-38: They wandred vp and downe in sheepes skinnes, and
　　in goates skinnes, being destitute, afflicted, and tormented: Whom the
　　worlde was not worthie of: they wandred in wildernesses, and mountaines,
　　and dennes, and caues of the earth.)

III.vi.26-28: All gold and silver rather turn to dirt,
　　　　　　As 'tis no better reckon'd, but of those
　　　　　　Who worship dirty gods.

　　Isaiah, ii.20: At that day shall man cast away his siluer idoles, and his golden
　　idoles (which they had made themselves to worshippe them).[10]

IV.ii.4-5: But clay and clay differs in dignity,
　　　　　　Whose dust is both alike.

　　Romans, ix.21: Hath not the potter power of the clay to make of the same
　　lumpe one vessell to honour, and another vnto dishonour?

　　Ecclesiastes, iii.20: All was of the dust, and all shall returne to the dust.

(IV.ii.156-159: Would I had done't:
　　　　　　So the revenge alone pursued me! Polydore,
　　　　　　I love thee brotherly, but envy much
　　　　　　Thou hast robb'd me of this deed.

　　Judges, viii.1: The men of Ephraim sayde vnto him, Why hast thou serued
　　vs thus that thou calledst vs not, when thou wentest to fight with the
　　Midianites? And they chode with him sharply.[11])

(IV.ii.244,250-251: He was a queen's son. . . .
　　　　　　And though you took his life, as being our foe,
　　　　　　Yet bury him, as a prince.

300

II *Kings*, ix.34: Visit nowe yonder cursed woman, and burie her: for shee is a kings daughter.)

IV.ii.258-259: Fear no more the heat o' th' sun.
　　　　　　Nor the furious winter's rages.

Revelation, vii.16-17: They shall hunger no more, neither thirst any more. neither shall the sunne light on them, neither any heate.

Isaiah, xlix.10: They shal not be hungry, neither shal they be thirstie, neither shall the heate smite them, nor the sunne.

Psalm, cxxi.6: The sunne shal not smite thee by day, nor the moone by night.

IV.ii.260-261: Thou thy worldly task hast done.
　　　　　　Home art gone and ta'en thy wages.

Revelation, xiv.13: Blessed are the dead, which hereafter die in the Lorde. Euen so sayth the spirit: for they rest from their labours, and their workes follow them.

I *Corinthians*, iii.8: Euery man shall receiue his wages, according to his labour.[12]

IV.ii.262-263: Golden lads and girls all must.
　　　　　　As chimney-sweepers, come to dust.

IV.ii.246-247: Though mean and mighty, rotting
　　　　　　Together, have one dust. . . .

Genesis, iii.19: Thou art dust, and to dust shalt thou returne.

Ecclesiastes, iii.20: All was of the dust, and all shall returne to the dust.

IV.ii.264-265: Fear no more the frown o' th' great,
　　　　　　Thou art past the tyrant's stroke.

Job, iii.17-19: The wicked haue there ceased from their tyranny, and there they that laboured valiantly are at rest. The prisoners rest together, and heare not the voyce of the oppressour. There are small and great, and the seruant is free from his master.

IV.ii.289-290: The ground that gave them first has them again:
　　　　　　Their pleasures here are past, so is their pain.

Genesis, iii.19: Till thou returne to the earth: [*ground*, Bishops'] for out of it wast thou taken.

(IV.ii.377-379: If I do lie, and do
No harm by it, though the gods hear, I hope
They'll pardon it.

II *Kings,* v.18: Herein the Lorde be mercifull vnto thy seruant, that when . . . I bowe my selfe in the house of Rimmon: . . . The Lord bee mercifull vnto thy seruant in this point.[13])

V.i.25-26: So I'll die
For thee, O Imogen.

V.iv.22-23: For Imogen's dear life take mine, and though
'Tis not so dear, yet 'tis a life; you coin'd it.

V.iv.26-27: And so, great powers.
If you will take this audit, take this life.

Matthew, xx.28: Euen as the sonne of man came not to be serued, but to serue, and to giue his life for the ransome.

John, x.15: I lay downe my life for my sheepe.

I *Timothy,* ii.5-6: The man Christ Jesus, who gaue himselfe a ransome.

John, xv.13: Greater loue then this hath no man, when any man bestoweth his life for his friends.

Deuteronomy, xix.21: Life for life, eie for eie, tooth for tooth, hand for hand, foot for foot.[14]

V.iii.3,4: For all was lost,
But that the heavens fought.

Judges, v.20: They fought from heauen, euen the starres in their courses fought against Sisera.

V.iv.101: Whom best I love I cross.

Hebrews, xii.6: For whom the Lord loueth, he chasteneth: and he scourgeth euery sonne that hee receiueth.

Hebrews, v.8: Though he were the Sonne, yet learned he obedience, by the thinges which he suffered.

Proverbs, iii.12: For the Lord correcteth him, whom he loueth, euen as the father doeth the childe in whome he delighteth.

V.iv.103: Your low-laid son our godhead will uplift.

302

Philippians, ii.8-9: Hee humbled himselfe, and became obedient vnto the death. . . . Wherefore God hath also highly exalted him.

V.iv.105: Our Jovial star reign'd at his birth.

Matthew, ii.2-9: Where is ⌈he⌉ that is borne? for wee haue seene his starre in the East. . . . And loe, the starre which they had seene in the East, went before them, till it came, and stoode ouer the place where the babe was.

V.iv.138: When as a lion's whelp . . . .

Genesis, xlix.9: Judah, as a Lyons whelpe . . .

Revelation, v.5: The Lion which is of the tribe of Juda, the roote of David.

V.iv.140-141: When from a stately cedar shall be lopp'd branches.

V.v.454-455: The lofty cedar, royal Cymbeline,
           Personates thee.

Ezekiel, xvii.3-4: The great egle . . . came vnto Lebanon, and tooke the hiest branch of the cedar, and brake off the toppe of his twigge.

Ezekiel, xxxi.3-12: Asshur was like a cedar in Lebanon with faire branches, and with thicke shadowing boughes, and shot vp very hie, . . . his branches are fallen, and his boughs are broken.

Daniel, iv.17-19 (iv.20,22 Authorized Version): The tree that thou sawest. . . . it is thou, O king.

[Shakespeare seems to have had in mind the parallel accounts of *Ezekiel* and *Daniel,* details of which he combined to suit his needs.]

V.iv.141-143: Which, being dead many years, shall after revive,
           be jointed to the old stock, and freshly grow.

Job, xiv.7-9: For there is hope of a tree, if it bee cut downe, that it wil yet sproute, . . . though the roote of it waxe old in the earth, and the stocke thereof be dead in the ground, yet by the sent of water it will bud, and bring forth boughs like a plant.

Daniel, iv.20 (iv.23 Authorized Version): Hewe downe the tree, and destroy it, yet leaue the stumpe of the rootes thereof in the earth, . . . till seuen times passe ouer him.

V.iv.174: I am merrier to die than thou art to live.

Hebrews, xii.2: Looking vnto Jesus . . . who for the ioy that was set before him, endured the crosse, and despised the shame.

V.iv.178-181,190-191: First Gaol. . . . For, look you, sir, you
know not which way you shall go.

Post. Yes, indeed do I, fellow. . . I tell thee, fellow, there
are none want eyes to direct them the way I am going.

John, xiii.36: Simon Peter sayd vnto him, Lorde, whither goest thou? Jesus
answered him, Whither I goe, thou canst not follow mee now: buut thou shalt
follow me afterwards.

John, xiv.4: And whither I goe, ye know, and the way ye know.

V.iv.187-189: And how you shall speed in your journey's end, I
think you'll never return to tell on.

Job, xvi.22: I shall go the way, whence I shal not returne.[15]

V.v.222: Spit, and throw stones, cast mire upon me.

II *Samuel,* xvi.13: And cursed as he went, and threw stones against him, and
cast dust.

V.v.351,352: The benediction of these covering heavens
Fall on their heads like dew.

Psalm, cxxxiii.2-3: It is like the precious ointment vpon the head, . . . as
the dewe of Hermon, which falleth vpon the mountaines.

Song of Solomon, v.2: For mine head is full of dewe.

Daniel, iv.22 (iv.25 Authorized Version): They shall wet thee with the dewe
of heauen.

The foregoing array of Biblical allusions could easily lead one to think that the
import of the play is religious. Why, then, did we say that Shakespeare's purpose
in *Cymbeline* was primarily dramatic? Because of the inconsistencies that arise
in regard to the hero and heroine.

Twelve of the above allusions relating to Posthumus portray him as a Bible hero.
More specifically, eleven of them relate him to Christ and one to Moses. Thus
Shakespeare seems to have had especially the person of Christ in mind as a model
when developing Posthumus. Moreover, four additional allusions to Scripture
develop Imogen, betrothed to Posthumus, as the "bride" of Christ, that is, the
Christian saints. Thus a total of sixteen of the forty-three Biblical allusions in the
play center around Christ and his bride as types for Posthumus and Imogen. However, whenever this apparent Biblical precedent did not lend itself to Shakespeare's
purpose in the play, then Shakespeare had no qualms about abandoning it and
developing his plot independently of and even contrary to the Biblical precedent.
Thus it is obvious that the interests of the play came first and not the Biblical

analogy, which would have been the case had any theological purpose been intended. We can only conclude, therefore, that the Biblical allusions were subservient to the interests of the play and that Shakespeare used these Biblical sources dispassionately and in the same spirit in which he used classical allusions in plays where classical allusions predominate.

To appreciate this, we will now list the twelve Biblical allusions that liken Posthumus mainly with Christ. Both the passage from the play and the Scripture which seems to have inspired it will again be listed for comparison, but this time our list will be arranged to follow the events in Posthumus' life chronologically from birth onward, rather than the order in which the passages appear in the play.

V.iv.105: Our Jovial star reign'd at his birth.

> *Matthew*, ii.2-9: Where is [he] that is borne? for wee haue seene his starre in the East. . . . And loe, the starre which they had seene in the East, went before them, till it came, and stoode ouer the place where the babe was.

I.i.38-40: He quite being; and his gentle lady,
　　Big of this gentleman (our theme) deceas'd
　　As he was born.

> *Hebrews*, vi.20-vii.3: Euen Jesus that is made an hie Priest for euer after the order of Melchi-sedec. For this Melchi-sedec . . . without father, without mother, without kinred, . . . but is likened vnto the Sonne of God.

> [Strictly speaking, this Scripture is about Melchizedek. It is the writer of *Hebrews*, presumably St. Paul, who likens Melchizedek to Christ. The point that concerns us is that in saying Melchizedek (and Christ according to *Hebrews*) was fatherless and motherless, we have a birth similar to Posthumus' birth, whose very name is based on this fact.]

I.i.40-44: The king he takes the babe
　　To his protection, calls him Posthumus Leonatus,
　　Breeds him, and makes him of his bed-chamber,
　　Puts to him all the learnings that his time
　　Could make him the receiver of.

> *Acts*, vii.21-22: And when he was cast out, Pharaos daughter tooke him vp, and nourished him for her owne sonne. And Moses was learned in all the wisedome of the Egyptians, and was mightie in wordes and in deedes.

> [This is the one allusion where a Biblical source is used that likens Posthumus to Moses, rather than Christ. However, as in the case of Melchizedek, the writer of *Hebrews* also likens Christ to Moses in *Hebrews*, iii.1-5 and in the entire ninth chapter. Whether Shakespeare had this in mind is impossible to say. In any case, reference to the Scripture quoted seems likely.]

I.i.47-50: Most prais'd, most lov'd;
> A sample to the youngest, to th' more mature
> A glass that feated them, and to the graver
> A child that guided dotards.

Luke, ii.40-47: And the childe grewe, and waxed strong in spirite, and was filled with wisedome, and the grace of God was with him. . . . And when he was twelue yeeres old, . . . they found him in the Temple, sitting in the middes of the doctours, both hearing them, and asking them questions. And all that heard him, were astonished at his vnderstanding, and answers.

V.iv.101: Whom best I love I cross.

Hebrews, xii.6: For whom the Lord loueth, he chasteneth: and he scourgeth euery sonne that hee receiueth.

[See also *Hebrews*, v.8 and *Proverbs*, iii.12, quoted earlier.]

V.i.25-26: So I'll die
> For thee, O Imogen.

V.iv.22-23: For Imogen's dear life take mine, and though
> 'Tis not so dear, yet 'tis a life; you coin'd it.

V.iv.26-27: And so, great powers.
> If you will take this audit, take this life.

Matthew, xx.28: Euen as the sonne of man came not to be serued, but to serue, and to giue his life for the ransome.

John, xv.13: Greater loue then this hath no man, when any man bestoweth his life for his friends.

[See also *John*, x.15; I *Timothy*, ii.5-6; *Deuteronomy*, xix.21.]

V.iv.174: I am merrier to die than thou art to live.

Hebrews, xii.2: Looking vnto Jesus . . . who for the ioy that was set before him, endured the crosse, and despised the shame.

V.iv.178-181,190-191: First Gaol. . . . For, look you, sir, you
> know not which way you shall go.

> Post. Yes, indeed do I, fellow. . . I tell thee, fellow, there
> are none want eyes to direct them the way I am going.

John, xiii.36: Simon Peter sayd vnto him, Lorde, whither goest thou? Jesus answered him, Whither I goe, thou canst not follow mee now: but thou shalt follow me afterwards.

306

John, xiv.4: And whither I goe, ye know, and the way ye know.

V.iv.30-151. [This is the comforting vision that Posthumus had
while in prison awaiting death. It can be seen as corresponding
to the comfort and divine intervention Jesus received in Geth-
semane just prior to his crucifixion.]

Luke, xxii.43: And there appeared an Angell vnto him from heauen, comforting him.

V.iv.103: Your low-laid son our godhead will uplift.

Philippians, ii.8-9: Hee humbled himselfe, and became obedient vnto the
death. . . . Wherefore God hath also highly exalted him.

[This item and the two following are all associated with Posthumus' vision
as he lay in jail.]

V.iv.138: When as a lion's whelp . . . .

Genesis, xlix.9: Judah, as a Lyons whelpe . . . .

Revelation, v.5: The Lion which is of the tribe of Juda, the roote of David.

[*Genesis*, xlix.9 is considered a clear Old Testament prophecy of Jesus in
Biblical exegesis. *Revelation*, v.5 confirms the fulfillment. Marginal comments in both the Geneva and Bishops' versions of the Bible so explained
these texts.[16]]

V.iv.139-140: Be embraced by a piece of tender air.

[Inasmuch as this clause follows hard on the heels of "lion's
whelp," a definite reference to Christ, it might very well be that
the idea of being embraced by air was suggested by baptism
with Holy Spirit, as of Jesus at Jordan, *John*, iii.5-8; *Acts*, ii.1-4 and
other Scriptures compare the wind or air to the Holy Spirit.
It should be noted that this item and the one at V.iv.30-151
were not listed as such in the previous list of Biblical references
since it was felt that sufficient groundwork had not been laid for
them, and since this item does not correspond to any one Scripture while that of V.iv.30-151 involves a vision of over 100 lines.
However, although the vision at V.iv.30-151 did not appear as a
unit in our original list, six of the forty-three items in that list
were taken from it.]

We now turn to the Biblical allusions in *Cymbeline* that link Imogen with Christ's
followers, or with the bride of Christ. There are only four of these. But if it is true
that Shakespeare consciously followed Biblical events surrounding Christ's life

as he developed the character of Posthumus, then it is reasonable to assume that the following four parallels of Imogen with the Christian saints were also conscious on Shakespeare's part. However, our case is admittedly not as strong as in the case of Posthumus.

III.vi.2-3: I have tir'd myself: and for two nights together
      Have made the ground my bed.

> *Hebrews,* xi.37-38: They wandred vp and downe in sheepes skinnes, and in goates skinnes, being destitute, afflicted, and tormented: Whom the worlde was not worthie of: they wandred in wildernesses, and mountaines, and dennes, and caues of the earth.[17]

I.vii.7-9: Bless'd be those,
      How mean soe'er, that have their honest wills,
      Which seasons comfort.

> *Matthew,* v.3-4: Blessed are the poore in spirite: for theirs is the kingdome of heauen. Blessed are they that mourne: for they shall be comforted.

IV.ii.258-259: Fear no more the heat o' th' sun,
      Nor the furious winter's rages.

> *Revelation,* vii.16-17: They shall hunger no more, neither thirst any more, neither shall the sunne light on them, neither any heate.

> *Isaiah,* xlix.10: They shal not be hungry, neither shal they be thirstie, neither shall the heate smite them, nor the sunne.

> *Psalm,* cxxi.6: The sunne shal not smite thee by day, nor the moone by night.

> [The latter two texts are considered Old Testament prophecies of the Christian saints.[18]]

IV.ii.260-261: Thou thy worldly task hast done,
      Home art gone and ta'en thy wages.

> *Revelation,* xiv.13: Blessed are the dead, which hereafter die in the Lorde. Euen so sayth the spirit: for they rest from their labours, and their workes follow them.

> I *Corinthians,* iii.8: Euery man shall receiue his wages, according to his labour.

While it is true that the Biblical allusions that portray Imogen as Christ's bride are few, there is a compensating factor. This is the part that Imogen plays in the drama, the events that befall her which strongly suggest the experiences that befall Christ's followers.

To begin with, the very fact that she is betrothed to one who seems to be patterned after the figure of Christ, casts her in the role of the bride of Christ. But she is subsequently separated from her bridegroom. So it is that Christ's followers are separated from their Lord and likewise yearn intensely to be united with him. Imogen is a virgin and this fits St. Paul's description of Christ's followers at II *Corinthians*, xi.2: "I am jealous over you with godly jealousy; for I have espoused you to one husband, that I may present you as a chaste virgin to Christ" (Authorized Version). Although such texts are not referred to in the play, the role Imogen plays could have been suggested by them.

Both Christ's followers and Imogen suffer as they seek to remain chaste to their lord. Imogen is first tempted with promises of an earthly kingdom and with other attractions if she will only forget Posthumus. Next she encounters physical hardships almost to the limit of her endurance. These are exactly the experiences Christ's followers have to undergo. They must resist the attractions and endure the persecutions of a hostile world. This is the tenor of much of the New Testament. "We must through much tribulation enter into the kingdom of God," is typical.[19]

Finally, Christ's followers must undergo death and resurrection to be united with Christ in heaven. Imogen acts out this part of the parallelism very closely. She undergoes a "death" from which she rises to be reunited with her rightful husband. Her death is only a seeming death. This corresponds with the Christian scheme of things wherein death is only an outward appearance, but in reality, there is an afterlife.

Yet all this is not without its problems, and it is from the serious discrepancies that arise between the play and the Biblical pattern that we can see where Shakespeare's real interests lay. Had the relationship between Posthumus and Imogen as outlined above continued, then it could very well be argued that the intent of the play was theological, that a religious allegory was being enacted by the hero and heroine. This, however, is hardly the case. Instead, events in the play lead Posthumus and Imogen to distrust and rail against each other. So much so, that Posthumus lays careful plans to have Imogen slain and thus avenge himself on her. Imogen escapes this fate, but is later deceived into believing that Posthumus had been beheaded by outlaws under circumstances that do not at all correspond to Christ's crucifixion. It would take a great deal of tenuous argument to try and make these events fit the Biblical relationship of Christ and his bride. A reading of such scenes as II.iv; III.iv; IV.ii.1-332 should convince the reader that play and Scripture have parted company. Had Shakespeare intended a Biblical allegory to be primary, he could easily have avoided these glaring discrepancies.

A consideration of the sources used for *Cymbeline* will indicate what Shakespeare's primary intentions were, as well as explain why the action of the play seems to undercut the Biblical suggestions about Posthumus and Imogen. Shakespeare relied mainly on Holinshed for the historical setting, and on Boccaccio and related tales for the wager plot. His use of Holinshed is revealing. According to Holinshed, Cymbeline became king of Britain in 33 B. C. and reigned for thirty-five years. Either Cymbeline or a successor refused to pay tribute to Rome and so came into conflict with Caesar. Shakespeare uses this pseudo-history concerning Cymbeline at III.i, but the account of the battle at V.iii comes not from Holinshed's account of early Britain, but from his account of how a Scottish farmer named Hay, together with his two sons, helped defeat the Danish invaders at the Battle of Luncarty in A. D. 976.[20] Shakespeare did not hesitate to fuse two accounts widely separated in time and place when it was to the play's advantage to do so.

The same principle applies to Imogen's rejection by Posthumus, based on a wager story which enjoyed great popularity in Shakespeare's day. Shakespeare followed the details of this story so closely that it is clear he gave it precedence over the Biblical suggestions in the play. In Boccaccio's version of the tale, Ambrogiuolo made a wager with Bernabo that Bernabo's wife Zinerva would be unfaithful to him. Ambrogiuolo then managed to enter Zinerva's bedroom in a chest and, as she slept, noted the details of the room including a mole on her breast. He also stole a few items before re-entering the chest, which was conveyed from the room. In this way Bernabo was deceived into thinking that his wife had been unfaithful to him, and he sent a servant to slay his wife.

This is the plot that Shakespeare was primarily concerned with and he enriched it with Biblical material. He gave depth to the protagonist's character by patterning him after the outstanding Biblical hero, Christ. Although Imogen's rejection by Posthumus ran counter to this Biblical pattern, yet the rejection was in accord with the wager plot, which came first. It was no more inconsistent for Shakespeare to fuse such seemingly disparate elements than it was for him to be historically inaccurate in his borrowings from Holinshed.

If *Cymbeline* is an indication of Shakespeare's general practice as regards his usage of Scripture, then the conclusion of the matter suggests that even in plays where Shakespeare makes extensive use of Scripture, his interests were primarily dramatic. Whether increased use of Biblical materials be explained in terms of a new type of theater and audience, in terms of a change of attitudes and outlook on Shakespeare's part, or in terms of other factors, it seems clear that there is no basis in *Cymbeline* for arguing for overt theological intent on Shakespeare's part. Shakespeare's greatness is partly due to the fact that his plays are primarily artistic and not didactic. And his artistic methods, varying as they do throughout his career, deserve careful analysis.

Appendix:

This is a list of religious images and terms in *Cymbeline* other than the specific Biblical references already presented. The list is selective rather than comprehensive, only the more important items being chosen. General references to the gods, as in an oath, have been omitted. Also omitted are such words as *heaven(s)*, *Devil*, *faith*, *pray you*, *prithee*, etc., especially when used merely for emphasis.

I.ii.67-68: Cym. Past grace? obedience?
      Imo. Past hope, and in despair, that way past grace.

310

I.iii.26-27: If it be a sin to make a true election, she is damn'd.

I.iv.27,31-33: How I would think on him at certain hours, . . .
             At the sixth hour of morn, at noon, at midnight,
             T' encounter me with orisons, for then
             I am in heaven for him.

I.v.87-90: Post. . . . The other is not a thing for sale, and only
             the gift of the gods.

      Iach. Which the gods have given you?

      Post. Which by their graces I will keep.

I.v.141-142: But I see you have some religion in you.

I.vi.62-63: It is a thing I made, which hath the king
             Five times redeem'd from death.

I.vii.lll: That all the plagues of hell. . . .

I.vii.133: Live like Diana's priest, ...

I.vii.166: Such a holy witch. . . .

I.vii.169-171: He sits 'mongst men like a descended god;
             He hath a kind of honour sets him off,
             More than a mortal seeming.

II.iii.20: Hark, hark, the lark at heaven's gate sings.

II.iii.23: On chalic'd flowers . . . .

II.iii.49-51: Make denials
             Increase your services: so seem, as if
             You were inspir'd to do those duties.

II.iii.125-126: Profane fellow.
             Wert thou the son of Jupiter, ...

II.iv.185-186: In a true hate, to pray they have their will:
             The very devils cannot plague them better.

III.ii.36-37: Lovers
             And men in dangerous bonds pray not alike.

III.iii.1-10: Stoop, boys: this gate
        Instructs you how t' adore the heavens; and bows you
        To a morning's holy office. . . .
        Hail, thou fair heaven!

III.iii.99-100: O Cymbeline, heaven and my conscience knows
        Thou didst unjustly banish me.

III.iv.76-77: Against self-slaughter
        There is a prohibition so divine.[21]

III.iv.110: Th' elected deer before thee.

III.iv.180-181: Thou art all the comfort
        The gods will diet me with.

III.vii.15-17: By Jupiter, an angel! or, if not,
        An earthly paragon! Behold divineness
        No elder than a boy!

IV.ii.48: How angel-like he sings!

IV.ii.54-55: The smile mocking the sigh, that it would fly
        From so divine a temple.

IV.ii.169-171: O thou goddess,
        Thou divine Nature; thou thyself thou blazon'st
        In these two princely boys.

IV.ii.302-305: Good faith,
        I tremble still with fear: but if there be
        Yet left in heaven as small a drop of pity
        As a wren's eye, fear'd gods, a part of it!

IV.ii.310-312: His foot Mercurial: his Martial thigh:
        The brawns of Hercules: but his Jovial face—
        Murder in heaven!

IV.ii.379-381: Luc. Thy name?

    Imo. Fidele, sir.
    Luc. Thou dost approve thyself the very same:
    Thy name well fits thy faith; thy faith thy name.

IV.ii.391: And on it said a century of prayers.

V.i.7-33: [This is a prayer by Posthumus to the gods.]

V.iii.84-85: Great Jupiter be prais'd, Lucius is taken:
           'Tis thought the old man, and his sons, were angels.

V.iv.9-29: [This is another prayer by Posthumus, while in jail,
           to the gods.]

V.v.220-221: A sacrilegious thief, to do't. The temple
           Of Virtue was she.

V.v.268-269: My tears that fall
           Prove holy water on thee.

V.v.398-399: Let's quit this ground,
           And smoke the temple with our sacrifices.

V.v.477-484: Laud we the gods,
           And let our crooked smokes climb to their nostrils
           From our blest altars. . . .
           And in the temple of great Jupiter
           Our peace we'll ratify.

NOTES:

(1)   Richmond Noble, *Shakespeare's Biblical Knowledge* (London: Society for Promoting Christian Knowledge, 1935), p. 244.

(2)   Thomas Carter, *Shakespeare and Holy Scripture* (London: Hodder & Stoughton, 1905).

(3)   This is the well-known account of the twelve-year-old Jesus among the elders. It clearly seems to be the inspiration for the passage at I.i.47-50, where Posthumus is described as "a child that guided dotards." If so, this could lend support to the Scriptural basis of the first two citations at I.i.38-40 and I.i.40-44, which occur within the space of a few lines. The first of these, however, is admittedly the most likely of the three to be more of a resemblance than the actual borrowing of a Biblical idea.

(4)   The relationship of I.i.59,60 with *Luke,* ii.12 is obviously one of terminology. Most of the English versions of the Bible available to Shakespeare read "swadled" or some variation of it at this verse. Shakespeare may have borrowed the words used for the birth of Jesus to describe the nursery of Guiderius and Arviragus. It bears noting that Shakespeare's phrase "swathing-clothes" is considerably closer to the Bishops' Bible, 1568 edition. The Geneva Bible reads: "Yee shall finde the childe swadled, and layde in a cratch."

(5)   This is not just a blessing in general, but a blessing of one's enemies. Cymbeline banishes Posthumus from the court and from Imogen and at the same time reviles him with such words as "Thou basest thing, . . . thou'rt poison to my blood." Posthumus replies with the quoted blessing. The most likely source for this blessing of one's enemies is Scripture, as this is the tenor of much

313

of the New Testament, and was frequently the subject of Elizabethan sermons. That these Christ-like words are especially appropriate for Posthumus, we shall see later.

(6) I hesitate to include this passage on the basis of merely one word, but follow Noble, who begins his list of Biblical allusions in *Cymbeline* with this passage. Here, again, if *Ephesians*, iv.2 is a valid source for Shakespeare, this would be according to the Bishops' Bible, 1568. The Geneva Version reads, "Supporting one another" at this text. However, both versions read "forbearing" ("forbearyng," Bishops') at *Colossians*, iii.13.

(7) This is a good example of a case where the resemblance between play and Scripture may be just a coincidence, where we might have a parallel idea, and not at all a reference. Whatever the relationship, the matter is presented for the reader's consideration.

(8) Of the fourteen Biblical references in *Cymbeline* listed by Noble, I have excluded that at III.iv.121 (III.iv.119, New Arden edition). Noble sees Pisanio's words, "But if I were as wise as honest," as referring to the parable of the Unjust Steward at *Luke*, xvi.8.

(9) *Wisdom* was one of Shakespeare's favorite Bible books. Quotations from the Apocrypha are also from the Geneva Bible.

(10) Even if the text at *Isaiah* is not as close to the passage from *Cymbeline* as we would like, yet it should be remembered that exhortations against idolatry occur frequently in the Bible. In England, these texts were emphasized anew after the break with Rome. Thus III.vii.26-28 may not have been based on *Isaiah*, ii.20, but on the general religious climate which derived ultimately from Scripture.

(11) Here, again, it is impossible to state whether Shakespeare had the *Judges* account in mind, although the context is the same. It should be mentioned, however, that at V.iii.3,4 we have another reference to *Judges* with which we can be considerably more comfortable, and the two accounts are only two chapters apart. Thus Shakespeare could be reflecting *Judges* in both cases.

(12) I believe that *Revelation*, xiv.13 is much closer in substance to these lines of the funeral dirge than is *Matthew*, xx.1-16, which Noble cites as Shakespeare's source. The *Matthew* account is the parable of the workers in the vineyard and has nothing to do with death. *Revelation*, xiv.13, on the other hand, is said concerning the saints who died for the "faith of Jesus," and is used in the Burial Service.

(13) Compare this use of II *Kings* with that at IV.ii.244,250-251, already quoted. Neither case is a certain reference to Scripture by any means. But does a second similarity to incidents in II *Kings* add to the likelihood of these cases being *bona fide* references?

(14) The play's stress on Posthumus' giving up his life in behalf of Imogen, stated in terminology reminiscent of the Christian doctrine of the ransom, is too strong to be ignored. Compare, for example, the word "audit" at V.iv.26-27 with *Deuteronomy*, xix.21. This point will be developed further later on.

(15) Like *Wisdom*, *Job* was another of Shakespeare's favorite Bible books.

(16) The gloss supplied by the translators of the Geneva Bible at *Genesis*, xlix.8 reads: "As was verified in Dauid and Christ." At *Genesis*, xlix.10 the gloss on "Shiloh" reads: "Which is Christ the Messiah, the giuer of all prosperitie."

At *Revelation*, v.5 the cross-reference for "Lion" refers the reader back to "Gen 49.9." The gloss on *Revelation*, v.6, identifying the "Lion which is of the tribe of Juda," reads: "This vision confirmeth the power of our Lord Iesus, which is the Lambe of God."

The 1594 edition of the Geneva Bible was used in this paper. Marginal comments in most editions of the Geneva version are essentially the same. See Richmond Noble's discussion of Tudor printed versions of the Bible, *op. cit.*, pp. 6-9.

314

(17) Strictly speaking, this text is about the pre-Christian men of faith whom St. Paul likens to the Christian saints.

(18) The Geneva gloss on *Isaiah*, xlix.9 reads: "Being in Christes protection, they shall be safe against all dangers." Those on *Psalm*, cxxi.3 and 6 state: "He sheweth that Gods prouidence not onely watcheth ouer his Church in generall, but also ouer euery member thereof." "Neither heate nor colde, nor any incommoditie shall be able to destroy Gods Church: albeit for a time they may molest it." The cross-reference on *Revelation*, vii.16 is "Isa 49.10."

(19) *Acts*, xiv.22.

(20) See the introduction to the New Arden edition of *Cymbeline*, pp. xvii-xxviii.

(21) This is one of Noble's fourteen Biblical allusions for *Cymbeline*. I include it only in the appendix inasmuch as there is no specific Scripture forbidding suicide.

I am indebted to Professor Robert Dent for his careful reading of this article.

Prospero and the Drama of the Soul

by Herbert R. Coursen, Jr.

The final plays of Shakespeare, *Pericles*, *Cymbeline*, *The Winter's Tale* and *The Tempest*, move from initial discord and alienation to ultimate harmony and reconciliation. If chaos is represented, whether a husband's conviction of a wife's infidelity or a storm at sea, it gradually dissipates during the play; it does not develop into the violent darkness of Scotland under Macbeth or culminate in the murder of a Desdemona or a Cordelia. Instead, *The Tempest* imitates the comic action described by Northrop Frye, which parallels "the central myth of Christianity.... The framework of the Christian myth is the comic framework of the Bible, where man loses a peaceable kingdom, staggers through the long nightmare of tyranny and injustice which is human history, and eventually regains his original vision. Within this myth is the corresponding comedy of the Christian life. We first encounter the law in its harsh tyrannical form of an external barrier to action, a series of negative commands, and we are eventually set free of this law, not by breaking it, but by internalizing it: it becomes an inner condition of behavior, not an external antagonist as it is to the criminal."[1] With mild qualifications, this description applies to Ferdinand, Alonso, and particularly, to Prospero.

Prospero attempts to put Alonso and the other conspirators through a penitential experience, to evoke within each a "heart's sorrow" leading towards redemption—"a clear life ensuing" (III.iii.81-82).[2] The banquet spread before the sinners disappears, a Communion Feast deferred "until," in the words of the 1559 version of *The Book of Common Prayer*, "[the sinner] has openly declared himself to have truly repented and amended his former naughty life."[3]

Immediately after the table is removed, Alonso repents:

> O, it is monstrous, monstrous!
> Methought the billows spoke and told me of it;
> The winds did sing it to me, and the thunder,
> That deep and dreadful organ-pipe, pronounc'd
> The name of Prosper; it did bass my trespass.
> Therefore my son i' th' ooze is bedded, and
> I'll seek him deeper than e'er plummet sounded
> And with him there lie mudded. *(III.iii.95-102)*

Here "heart's sorrow" is not a precondition for salvation but for suicde. Alonso's reason *will* be obliterated (it will, in Prospero's metaphor, lie "foul and muddy": V.i.82). But Alonso, like Lear, will awaken on the far side of annihilation. The repentance speech contradicts the impulse towards suicide by implying the essential

316

rhythm of *The Tempest*—the transition from storm ("billows," "wind," "thunder") to harmony ("sing," "organ-pipe," "bass").[4]

Prospero's manipulation of the ship-wreck victims is an admittedly imperfect device; it suffers from the shortcomings of those it would redeem. Not all can achieve the "inner condition" Frye describes. Prospero's effort is partial; the marriage at the play's end, idyllic as it seems, occurs within a world from which the negation of the tragedies can never be wholly dispelled. But if the limitations of man and his world have been exposed in the tragedies, the *significance* of man has deepened. In the early comedies, the manipulation of Biron and his mates, of Beatrice and Benedick, and of Orlando aimed at exposure of foolish attitudes and the reformation of their possessors. Religious terms were *metaphors* for change. These plays usually ended with good-natured laughter all around. Prospero's play exposes not folly but sin, and aims at repentance. In *The Tempest*, religious terms are *symbolic* of change; manipulations have deepened from the rituals which awakened Biron, Beatrice and Benedick, and Orlando to the sacrament which moves Alonso. Manipulation does not merely educate the self in *The Tempest*, it redeems the soul. The play ends solemnly; its experience has been too deep for laughter.

The Tempest is largely, as D. G. James says, "a story issuing from the commanding magic of Prospero."[5] This discussion will center, as the play does, on Prospero, on his awareness of what he is attempting, and on his control of the production which brings harmony out of discord. Prospero's initial approach to his production is primarily intellectual; the results of his play, however, force his human feelings to catch up with his understanding. The *feeling* of charity at last coincides with the concept of charity, and the fusion occurs, appropriately, at the moment when Prospero discards his role as God and submits to the limitations of mankind.[6]

While Prospero's play brings himself as well as Alonso to harmony, it is not true, as James suggests, that "nothing can resist the power of Prospero."[7] The play surrounding Prospero's manipulation reveals clearly the limitations of his effort at redemption. No amount of external manipulation can alter a hardened heart; some men, like Antonio, choose not to be redeemed. As Auden suggests, Prospero's "all is partial"; Antonio remains "by choice myself alone."[8] If the comic vision is exposed by the shallowness of a Claudio on whom it cannot function, it is questioned more profoundly by the defiance of an Antonio who refuses to permit it to function. At the same time, however, those who have been moved by Prospero's play have reached awarenesses more significant than that of a courtly lover stripped of his affectations. *The Tempest*, then, is about the extent and limits of man's control over the inner lives of other men.

Even more basically, perhaps, *The Tempest* explores the nature of freedom, and concludes that freedom and responsibility are linked, that freedom without responsibility is license and, ultimately, bondage.[9] Prospero's Epilogue imposes on the spectator the test to which the characters have been subjected, asking the spectator to make the experience of the play *his* experience and to decide whether

317

he stands with Alonso and Prospero inside the circle of reconciliation, or with Antonio willfully beyond it. Appropriately, at the end of his comedy, Prospero asks the spectator to consider the play on a level deeper than that of entertainment. The play occurs, as James Russell Lowell says, "in the soul of man, that still vexed island hung between the upper and the nether world, and liable to incursions from both."[10] Unless the spectator experiences it this way, the play means nothing. As Jan Kott says, "the island is a stage on which the history of the world is being acted and repeated,"[11] and the spectator is invited through the medium of Prospero's play to participate in that reenactment.

I

Act I is *The Tempest* in microcosm. Its dominant figure is Prospero, presiding over its stormy opening and prompting its harmonious close, pointing to Miranda as a product of his education, but acknowledging the limits of education personified by Caliban, who has learned language only to curse. The sojourn on the island has educated Prospero himself; he has learned something more basic than meteorological control. While his problem is similar to Hamlet's—to revenge or not to revenge—he has had the crucial advantage of viewing it from the objective stance of time and distance.

Prospero raises a tempest to recreate for those aboard the ship his own sea experience, which began with the treachery of Antonio, who cast them adrift "To cry to the sea, that roar'd to us" (I.i.149). The sea did them "but loving wrong," (151) however, and their "sea sorrow" (170) terminated in proof of "Providence divine" (159). The sea brought them to the island where Prospero has had time to come to terms with the wrong done him, to achieve calmness where anger had been, to harmonize an experience which began discordantly. In losing himself, he has found himself. The crucial thing he has learned, as Margaret Webster says, is "that freedom often turns out to be different from what we had imagined, involving responsibility and not merely license, and that each of us must find his own way to the resolution of the conflict within himself."[12] Although they can't know it yet, some of the passengers bound back from Tunis to Naples will reenact Prospero's voyage, the archetypal voyage of Jonah, Odysseus, the Ancient Mariner, Ishmael, and the *Narcissus* into zones having no geography or chronology, into the tempestuous darkness of the self, and from thence to rebirth.

The opening tempest symbolizes the spiritual storm of its victims. Their turmoil is greater, in fact, than that around them, as the boatswain suggests:

> A plague upon this howling! They are louder
> than the weather or our office. *(I.i.39-40)*[13]

Ferdinand's cry as he leaps from the sinking ship applies both to the fury of the storm and to the guilty passengers:

> Hell is empty,
> And all the devils are here. *(I.ii.214-215)*

That his words apply to some of the passengers is confirmed later by Prospero, who says, "some of you here . . . are worse than devils" (III.ii.35-36). Prospero parallels inner and outer weather again in explaining to Miranda:

> I have with such provision in mine art
> So safely ordered that there is no soul—
> No, not so much perdition as an hair
> Betid to any creature in the vessel
> Which thou heard'st cry, which thou saw'st sink.   *(I.ii.28-32)*

With the interlocking construction he employs occasionally,[14] Shakespeare makes "cry" the verb of "creature" and "sink" the verb of "vessel." The ship in the storm symbolizes souls in torment. Three times in the first thirty lines of scene ii, the people on the ship are called "souls," an emphasis suggesting the area with which Prospero is most concerned. Although admittedly Shakespeare often uses "souls" without religious overtones, here the religious sense is enforced by the word "perdition."

If the storm is for the passengers the first movement in a reenactment of the sea sorrow of Prospero, the first act provides several further comments on the storm and anticipations of its ultimate result. The stories of Ariel, Caliban, and Ferdinand and Miranda reflect the themes of freedom and bondage, of losing oneself to find oneself.

Ariel's career parallels what Prospero hopes will be the experience of those arriving on the island; it begins in confinement and pain, but ends in freedom:

> Thou best know'st
> What torment I did find thee in; thy groans
> Did make the wolves howl and penetrate the breasts
> Of ever-angry bears. It was a torment
> To lay upon the damn'd, which Sycorax
> Could not again undo. It was mine art,
> When I arriv'd and heard thee, that made gape
> The pine, and let thee out.   *(I.ii.286-293)*

Those who roared while caught in the power of the storm have been brought safely to land. The storm represents the torment of the damned ("All the devils are here"), which Prospero will attempt to subdue as he did the spell of Sycorax (who also had an intimate connection with the devil).[15] The tree in which Ariel was imprisoned (a "cloven pine": I.ii.277) suggests the world, the flesh, and the devil which have trapped the guilty passengers. Only a higher power can triumph over these forces, as Prospero did over Sycorax and her god, Setebos.

When Ariel proves moody, agitating for freedom, Prospero threatens to "rend an oak / And peg thee in his knotty entrails till / Thou hast howl'd away twelve winters" (294-296). Ariel immediately begs for "pardon," (297) and his submission brings a prompt promise of freedom. Not only in the account of Ariel's previous history but in the scene itself, we observe a movement from pain (or the threat of it) to freedom. The threat is followed by a successful plea for pardon. The episode anticipates the pattern Prospero hopes to impose on those now scattered about the island—the movement from torment to a recognition of the need for pardon, the need to submit to a power greater than that of their own wills, the submission which becomes freedom.

A contrast to this scene and a comment on it is the ensuing one with Caliban, who represents the willful refusal to be free. Although he knows Prospero to be stronger than his "dam's god, Setebos," (I.ii.373) he curses Prospero in the name of his mother:

> All the charms
> Of Sycorax—toads, beetles, bats, light on you!   *(I.ii.339-340)*

He receives not a promise of freedom, but threat of more pain:

> I'll rack thee with old cramps,
> Fill all thy bones with aches, make thee roar
> That beasts shall tremble at thy din.   *(I.ii.369-371)*

Like those howling in the storm, Caliban is captive not of external agents but of his inward refusal to yield to powers greater than that of his own will or that of his discredited god. Prospero defines this condition when he calls Caliban "slave," as he does five times in the scene.

Walter C. Curry's description of Macbeth applies equally to Caliban: "Irrational acts have established habits tending to further irrationality and one of the penalties exacted is dire impairment of the liberty of free choice."[16] That Caliban is a self-made slave accounts for Prospero's otherwise excessive anger at Ariel in the previous scene. His anger does not necessarily prove that Prospero is a "crusty and irascible old pedant";[17] this is to define a symptom and ignore the cause. Prospero does not wish Ariel to become a slave to self-will, particularly since Ariel is so crucial an instrument in Prospero's project to free others from self-will. Caliban's disordered nature demands the retribution with which Prospero threatens Ariel. Even though Caliban knows that Prospero's "spirits hear [him]." he "needs must curse" (I.ii.3-4). Caliban represents the limits of Prospero's efforts at education, a warning built into the play that we must not expect too much of Prospero's redemptive drama. Caliban is

> A devil, a born devil, on whose nature
> Nurture can never stick! on whom my pains,
> Humanely taken, all, all lost, quite lost!
> And as with age his body uglier grows,
> So his mind cankers. I will plague them all,
> Even to roaring.   *(IV.i.188-193)*

Prospero can produce the roar of torment induced by the spirits pinching Caliban. He can thwart the several plots hatching malignantly on his island. He cannot change the nature of the plotters. At the end, however, Caliban seems to have begun a positive education, leaving Antonio more profoundly alone in his self-chosen isolation.

While Ariel and Caliban comment on the ultimate hopes and limitations of Prospero's project, the most complete exemplification provided by Act I of Prospero's purpose is the relationship of Ferdinand and Miranda. It is an idyllic and allegorical version of what is to happen to Alonso, idyllic and allegorical because the lovers represent a pre-lapsarian perfection not to be found in their world-stained elders. The love story begins stormily, involves a test (largely external, but not without significance) and ends in harmony and fair weather. The story illustrates explicitly one of the themes of *The Tempest* and *the* theme of Prospero's manipulation—that one must lose himself to find himself.

Having leaped in frenzy from the sinking ship, Ferdinand enters, drawn by Ariel's song suggesting reconciliation:

> Come unto these yellow sands
> And then take hands. *(I.ii.376-377)*

The music soothes Ferdinand as later it will soothe Alonso. Ferdinand reiterates the equation between inner and outer weather:

> Sitting on a bank
> Weeping again the King my father's wrack,
> This music crept by me upon the waters,
> Allaying both their fury and my passion
> With its sweet air. *(I.ii.389-393)*

Here the storm is not analogous to souls gripped by damnation but to Ferdinand's grief. His concern for another is, in *The Tempest*, an essential precondition for his *own* redemption. His grief for his father wins him a vision of "the goddess / On whom these airs attend" (I.ii.421-422). Later, his father's grief for him will precede Alonso's beatific "vision of the island" (V.i.176). In her concern for those aboard the sinking ship, Miranda has already fulfilled this condition. The storm makes her suffer "with those that [she] saw suffer," (I.ii.6) and has "touch'd / The very virtue of compassion in [her]" (27).

Although Prospero's soul prompts their love (419), he devises a harsh playlet designed to educate Ferdinand somewhat as Biron and Orlando were educated, but more deeply. As with Ariel, Prospero imposes bondage on Ferdinand. The Prince responds not with the self-punishing defiance of a Caliban but with submission and expressions of freedom:

> My father's loss, the weakness which I feel,
> The wrack of all my friends, nor this man's threats
> To whom I am subdu'd are but light to me,
> Might I but through my prison once a day,
> Behold this maid. All corners else o' th' earth
> Let liberty make use of. Space enough
> Have I in such a prison. *(I.ii.487-493)*

Prospero's harsh control of Ferdinand as of Ariel is a way to freedom. His irascibility is that of a man with a master plan in mind which others cannot understand until they have *experienced* it. While it could be explained it would then have no meaning except in the mind, and it is not with the mind that Prospero hopes to work. His anger also derives from the fact that it is primarily in *his* mind that Prospero understands his production. His emotions have yet to coincide with his intellectual conception.

We see the positive results of Prospero's test of Ferdinand in the first scene of Act III. Ferdinand enters "bearing a log" (s.d.) but not complaining because "sweet thoughts" of Miranda "refresh [his] labours" (III.i.14). Miranda enters, her compassion aroused by Ferdinand's exertions. She bids him rest and offers to assume his task. He refuses, with a metaphor suggesting how much his inner weather has changed since his arrival on the island:

> No, noble mistress. 'Tis fresh morning with me
> When you are by at night. *(III.i.33-34)*

They exchange vows, each pledging service to the other: "The very instant that I saw you," says Ferdinand, "did / My heart fly to your service; there resides, / To make me slave to it; and for your sake / Am I this patient log-man" (64-67). "To be your fellow / You may deny me," Miranda replies, "but I'll be your servant, / Whether you will or no" (84-86). Ferdinand accepts her as his wife, "with a heart as willing / As bondage e'er of freedom" (88-89). The reiteration of the freedom-bondage theme suggests again that voluntary service for another constitutes freedom, that while the lovers have lost their individual selves, they have found themselves in each other. Prospero's blessing on the exchange makes yet another meteorological reference:

> Fair encounter
> Of two most rare affections! Heavens rain grace
> On that which breeds between 'em. *(III.i.74-76)*

The gentle and nourishing rain is reminiscent of the tears Ferdinand shed for his father, and which Miranda dropped at the sight of the ship-wreck and of her lover's labors. Later, speaking directly to Ferdinand, Prospero repeats the suggestion of a blessed rain, but in a negative context:

> If thou dost break her virgin-knot before
> All sanctimonious ceremonies may
> With full and holy rite be minist'red,
> No sweet aspersion shall the heavens let fall
> To make this contract grow; but barren hate,
> Sour-eyed disdain, and discord shall bestrew
> The union of your bed with weeds so loathly
> That you shall hate it both. *(IV.i.15-20)*

The words prove not that Prospero is an "irritable old man,"[18] but assert his belief that responsibility is the concomitant of freedom, that value emerges from sub-mission to control, in this case, self-control. As Frye suggests, "The chastity of Miranda is a controlled energy that must develop from virginity to marriage by observing the proper rhythms of time and of ritual, otherwise the whole order of nature will go out of alignment."[19] The formal rites of marriage will have mean-ing only if the partners accept a law higher than that of their individual wills, only if their spiritual reality coincides with the words of the ceremony coupling them. Else would the world be peopled all with Calibans.

Prospero's talk of beneficent rains from heaven anticipates the "fellowly drops" (V.i.64) which finally will fall from his own eyes. When this occurs, *The Tempest* will have reached its climax, for it will show that while he may have thought the concept of forgiveness all along, his heart has at last consented. The education of Prospero comprises the central drama of *The Tempest*.

II

While Prospero clings to his original conception without intruding to destroy it, he is not at peace with himself. While his anger at Ariel can be described as the impatience of a master-planner with the quibblings of a subordinate, the vehe-mence of it and the tone of his words to Caliban and Ferdinand suggest a source deeper than mere impatience—the struggle, perhaps, of the man who is "with their high wrongs . . . struck to the quick" (V.i.25) against the God attempting to abstract himself from the human desire for vengeance; or, more basically, the conflict between his godlike hopes for his manipulation and his human awareness that it may fail. The conflict is clearest as he breaks up the masque; the harmony is achieved soon after, as Ariel reports the pitiable condition of Prospero's enemies. Prospero's godlike conception of his manipulation surrenders to his human experi-ence of it. He is freed of the necessity of playing God, and as he releases the role, he finds his humanity again. His manipulation succeeds most profoundly within himself, and its success there, of course, is essential to his permitting it to have its way with the others.

Prospero's masque is, for Ferdinand, such a "majestical vision" (IV.i.118) that he thinks himself in "Paradise" (125). This is precisely where he is not; "Caliban and his confederates" (140) are approaching to murder Prospero. In the midst of his masque, Prospero remembers the imminent incursion of the real world and interrupts the performers, who "to a strange, hollow, and confused noise . . . heavily vanish" (s.d.). Here, discord supplants harmony. The discord emerges from Prospero's inner state; he is "distemper'd" (145), "vex'd" (158), "troubled" (159). Caliban's pathetic conspiracy alone could not evoke such distress. But Caliban represents the uneducable element, the factor which casts doubt on the potential success of Prospero's project. Perhaps the plot "reminds him of the trials of the past twelve years, which are now being rapidly reenacted;"[20] if so, the petty incur-sion reminds him of the reiterated perfidy of Antonio, of the world's inherent dis-order, of the dark zones which must remain ever unilluminated. Caliban represents unredeemable anarchy, the "born devil." When Prospero warns Ariel that they "must prepare to meet with Caliban" (166), he means not merely with an entity but with a principle—of unregeneracy and compulsive rebellion. Prospero is disturbed also that he "forgot the foul conspiracy" (134) in presenting his masque. The prospective father-in-law produces a trifle at the potential expense of the grand design of the god. He has ignored his own injunctions about control, demonstrating the lack of awareness he has admonished in Ariel, chastised in Caliban, and refined away in Ferdinand. At this point, he not only despairs at those his project may never touch, he is also angry at himself. As Van Doren says, "Prospero to his own confusion forgets for a moment when he loses himself in a certain 'vanity' of his art. . . ."[21] His negligence has almost permitted a repetition of the original crime against him (after he became "transported / And rapt in secret studies": I.ii.76-77). He has already averted another version of that crime by dispatching Ariel to rouse the slumbering Alonso and Gonzalo (II.i.).

Prospero's magnificent speech ("Our revels . . .") must be read in the context of his disturbed state. The speech is perhaps the most important in the play; Brower has shown that it expresses almost all of the play's key metaphors, and when we hear it we feel that it is Prospero's mature pronouncement on life. (Some productions place it at the end of the play, making it refer to *The Tempest* itself).[22]

The speech seems to say several conflicting things at once. Harbage interprets it as saying that "our lives are not the final reality, anymore than stage representations are our lives."[23] This view would make the speech an affirmation of immortality. Halliday, however, sees it as referring to "the oblivion that lies beyond life's dream."[24] The thrust of this discussion would make the speech mean that recognition of the world's transience is the beginning of freedom. To be free one must recognize that the things of this world are nothing. As Auden has Prospero say, "I am glad I did not recover my dukedom till / I do not want it."[25] Prospero himself says at the end, "Every third thought shall be my grave" (V.i.311).

Life, then, is no more than a dream; but what lies beyond that dream? Prospero could be suggesting that "our revels"—the masque we have witnessed—are meaningless compared to the redemptive drama he is producing, and that *that* play, in turn, fades to insignificance before the goal of that redemption. Our little lives, then, are the stuff of eternity. What dreams come *then* must give us pause, for they will be the sweet dream of salvation or the eternal nightmare of damnation. Our lives decide what our souls will be once all material things have dissolved. Prospero could be suggesting, however, that *all* man's efforts fade finally to insignificance. As Walter Kaufmann says, the speech can mean "that man is thrown into the world, abandoned to a life that ends in death, with nothing after that."[26] The speech does not hint strongly of an after-life, particularly if we remember the equation between sleep and death employed by such seventeenth-century figures as Lady Macbeth, John Donne, and Octavius Caesar. James suggests that "there is no need to assume that 'rounded' means 'finished off'; it may equally well be taken to mean 'encompassed by' and therefore 'occurring within' a 'sleep' —'we are such stuff as dreams are made on.'"[27] Life becomes, then, a dream within a dream, a moment of partial wakefulness within oblivion. "We are such stuff as dreams are made on"—we are no more substantial than dreams and are doomed to be flicked out as quickly as the masque, or, we are the basis of dreams, of greater realities beyond this insubstantial life.[28]

Which is the correct reading? Probably neither. The speech emerges from two Prosperos, hence carries traces of each. He is the god carrying on a project which the man, thinking of Caliban, knows may fail. He is the god, calling down blessings on the marriage of Ferdinand and Miranda and the man who knows well that the world poses deep threats to such beginnings. In context, the speech is bound to convey contradiction; it is a product of a divided man, expressing pessimism and affirmation, encompassing Caliban and Ferdinand, unredeemed darkness and potential illumination. Majestic and impressive as the speech is, Prospero's vision as he utters it is not clear—nor can it be, for he is not God, as he is coming to admit. But his speech is profoundly Shakespearean; it can be read in two ways; it throws back an image not of its creator but of its interpreter.

III

The climax of Prospero's redemptive drama and of *The Tempest* comes once each of his enemies "Lies at [his] mercy" (IV.i.264). It may be, as Kenneth Muir suggests, that "when he has his enemies in his power Prospero has to overcome again the natural desire towards vengeance."[29] It is tempting to believe that Prospero has struggled all along with his inclination to revenge, that his outbursts have been signs of inner conflict. In the absence of much solid evidence for this view, however, it is safer to suggest that Prospero finally experiences the truth of what until now has been an intellectual conception. His decision is better described as between the alternatives of judging and not judging. On returning from where Prospero's enemies stand spellbound, Ariel poses a crucial question:

> Ariel   The good old Lord Gonzalo['s]
> . . . tears run down his beard like winter's drops
> From eaves of reeds. Your charm so strongly works 'em,
> That if you beheld them, your affections
> Would become tender.
> Prospero Dost thou think so, spirit?
> Ariel   Mine would, sir, were I human.   *(V.i.15-20)*

Ariel askes, "Are you human, Prospero? Or have your removed yourself so far into your godlike role that you have lost the ability for compassion?" Ariel hints that thus far Prospero's affections have *not* been tender. Ariel's is another of the analogues of compassion presented to Prospero—Miranda's for those on the ship and later for Ferdinand, Ferdinand's for his father, Alonso's for Ferdinand, Gonzalo's for his companions, and now Ariel's.

Compassion, in *The Tempest*, relates directly to the theme of control and freedom. Compassion, in fact, is a kind of *self*-control. It represents the suspension

325

of self-will. Self-will, of course, is the *opposite* of self-control (a contradiction resolved by the freedom-service equation of the New Testament). Compassion represents an alignment of the individual exhibiting it with the supernature presiding over him.[30] If dormant traces of the supernature reside within the conspirators, Prospero's production will activate them.

Now, his manipulation brings his own humanity out from behind the godlike facade:

> Hast thou, which art but air, a touch, a feeling
> Of their afflictions, and shall not myself,
> One of their kind, that relish all as sharply
> Passion as they, be kindlier mov'd than thou art?   (V.i.21-24)

Prospero, in the words of David Horowitz, "is moved to mercy by the image of himself, suffering in their agony."[31] Having himself achieved compassion, he reasserts the concomitant—control, applying the principle appropriately to himself as he had earlier applied it to Miranda, Ferdinand, Ariel, and, more harshly, to Caliban:

> with my nobler reason 'gainst my fury
> Do I take part. The rarer action is
> In virtue than in vengeance. They being penitent,
> The sole drift of my purpose doth extend
> Not a frown further. Go, release them, Ariel.
> My charms I'll break, their senses I'll restore,
> And they shall be themselves.

In breaking his charms, he becomes himself. Prospero the god has accomplished all he can and the need for the role is over. He frees himself, achieving the harmony he hopes to have encouraged in his enemies. He throws over the magic which "'twixt the green sea and the azur'd vault / Set roaring war" (43-4) in favor of "heavenly music" (52), the last outward manifestation of his potent art. He had been like the Christ who stilled the "great tempest in the sea, so that the ship was covered with waves" (*Matthew*, viii.24); and when he said, "not so much perdition as an hair / Betid to any creature in the vessel" he echoed the Apostle Paul who had said "there shall not an haire fall from the head of any of you" to a group of frightened men on a tempest-tossed boat (*Acts*, xvii. 34).[32] Prospero is most Christlike, however, as he descends from the remote reaches of godhead to rejoin humanity as healer and man of compassion:

> A solemn air, and the best comforter
> To an unsettled fancy, cure thy brains,
> Now useless, boil'd within thy skull! . . .
> Holy Gonzalo, honourable man,
> Mine eyes, ev'n sociable to the show of thine,
> Fall fellowly drops.   (V.i.58-64)

As Theodore Spencer says, "Prospero is purged, but his purgation is exactly oppo-site to the purgation of Alonso: Alonso sinks *below* reason before returning to it; before Prospero returns to the rational human level he has lived for a time *above* it. The important thing to notice is his return."[33] The "fellowly drops" shed by Pros-pero for "Holy Gonzalo" are reminiscent of Cordelia's tears, "holy water" (IV.iii.32), which she hopes will restore Lear:

> All blest secrets,
> All you unpublish'd virtues of the earth,
> Spring with my tears! Be aidant and remediant
> In the good man's distress. (IV.iv.15-18)

While the situations are similar, the primary restoration occurring with Prospero's tears is his own.

Significantly, Prospero does not provide the rationale behind his production until Act V. (Ariel, of course, has done so earlier: "Heart's sorrow / And a clear life ensuing": III.iii.81-82.) Prospero's explanation coincides with his return to humanity from the remote and lofty plane he had inhabited. Appropriately, we are invited to identify with him at this "sociable" moment; as he finally takes us into his confidence, we experience his return to humanity. The moment represents a perfect coalescence of a character's awareness of himself and the spectator's awareness of the character.

Prospero recognizes that the quality of redemption is not strained. Were he to continue playing god he might destroy whatever his production may have accom-plished *within* its participants. Instead, he surrenders his role and frees himself from the bondage of his will, becoming a humble exemplification of the theme of his play, of *The Tempest*, and of The Sermon on the Mount, forgiving others as a precondition to his own suit for grace. He recognizes the potential irony of his position (Ariel points it out clearly), and in surrendering one of his roles, he elimi-nates the ironic possibilities inherent in the dichotomy between man and god. He recognizes that the injunction about judging applies to him; instead of judging, he forgives and submits to the judgment of the God whose role he had temporarily assumed, becoming, like Christ, a man who exemplifies the doctrines of that God.

Gonzalo's "all of us [found] ourselves / When no man was his own" (212-213) is obviously optimistic—but typical of the old man's tendency towards over-generalization. The success of Prospero's drama is measured by its effect on those who have acted in it. Alonso obviously has been deeply affected; Antonio watches the ending with a sneer. Alonso expresses his guilt in a speech which, like Prospero's abjuration speech, moves from storm to music (III.iii.95-102). His reunion with Ferdinand is obviously reminiscent of Lear's with Cordelia:

> But, O, how oddly will it sound that I
> Must ask my child forgiveness. (V.i.197-198)

Unlike Lear's, Alonso's redemption is not a prelude to deeper anguish. Those most profoundly affected by the production, Prospero and Alonso, are rewarded for their reunion with mankind by the union of Ferdinand and Miranda.

Some see Caliban as unregenerate. "What . . . does Prospero's art finally accomplish?" asks Rose A. Zimbardo; "it had never been able to fix form on Caliban."[34] The ending, however, suggests that Caliban is not "the begged question" Auden makes of him,[35] but has begun to free himself of his compulsive and self-punishing defiance. While Prospero calls him a "Demi-devil" (271) and a "thing of darkness" (275), Caliban calls himself a "thrice-double ass . . . to take this drunkard for a a god / And worship this dull fool!" (291-297). While Caliban never exhibits the compassion so often the beginning of freedom in *The Tempest,* he begins to respond to Prospero at the end. "How fine my master is!" (262) he exclaims on seeing him in his ducal robes. His only previous use of "master" for Prospero had been "Farewell, master" (II.ii.182). He uses the word for Stephano, of course, along with "lord" and "king." Ariel uses "master" some nine times, once, significantly, after Prospero's promise of freedom. Perhaps Caliban glimpses the equation between service and freedom; when Prospero promises Caliban "pardon" for the trimming of his cell, Caliban leaps off with the alacrity of an Ariel:

> Ay, that I will! and I'll be wise hereafter,
> And seek for grace. (V.i.294-295)

That he can say "grace" suggests that he now grasps concepts unphrasable in his former vocabulary.

Antonio remains. He has not felt "This deity [conscience] in [his] bosom" (II.i. 277-278), and has apparently felt none since, in spite of Prospero's effort. He stands forgiven but not accepting that forgiveness, his only response to the "high miracle" (V.i.177) of the ending a sneering comment on Caliban:

> one of them
> Is a plain fish, and, no doubt, marketable. (V.i.265-266)

His comment places him squarely in the company of Shakespeare's other calculator-villains—Richard III, Don John, Iago, Edmund, Iachimo, *et al.* Antonio remains unredeemable, refusing to participate in the symbolic taking of hands of the ending ("Come unto these yellow sands / And then take hands"), preferring like Milton's Satan to know God only as pain. His "inward pinches therefore are most strong" (V.i.77). As Robert Hunter says, "More than any other of Shakespeare's plays, *The Tempest* insists strongly upon indestructibility of evil . . . Antonio, in some form, will always exist and can only be forgiven for existing."[36] As Frank Kermode suggests, however, "A world without Antonio is a world without freedom."[37] In choosing the freedom of self-will, Antonio chooses slavery, of course, but helps emphasize the freedom the others have won by submitting to a mastery more encompassing than that of their own wills. Ariel's final mission before he merges with the Mediterranean sky is to provide weather symbolic of the inner harmony achieved by most of the characters in Prospero's production, weather leading back towards mankind. "[I] promise you," says Prospero to Alonso, "calm seas, auspicious gales, / And sail so expeditious that shall catch / Your royal fleet far off" (314-16). For this final service, Ariel is enlarged at last.

Prospero can be said to continue Hamlet's play from the point at which the Prince interrupted it. As Francis Fergusson says, "[Prospero] has a ripeness and a clarity and a power which Hamlet lacks, but for that very reason he helps one to see what Hamlet, with his play, was trying to do."[38] The ripeness is all. Prospero comes to recognize during his long exile that revenge is worse than meaningless — it reduces the revenger to the level of the criminal's corruption. Unlike Hamlet, Prospero allows his production to find its meaning in the characters manipulated. His magic is primarily external; it can achieve no inward changes unless its participants have the capacity for change. It is this magic, this method of reaching the spirit, which Hamlet gets hold of and fails to recognize. Hamlet defines himself as modern man,[39] oppressed and isolated, seeing the sacraments as a convention irrelevant to the soul of man. He is wrong about their power as Claudius's efforts at prayer prove. Prospero recognizes that a reenactment of guilt may evoke a penitential response from guilty creatures and that it is the only method worth trying. He defines himself as medieval man, servant finally of forces larger than himself. He experiences at the end what he has known all along — that he is subject to those forces. Hamlet could not retain the conception of his play which he himself had expressed — that "guilty creatures" can be "struck so to the soul" that they will "proclaim their malefactions." Hamlet destroys his play before it can explore this possibility. Prospero does not. "The rarer action is in virtue than in vengeance" because it can achieve a restoration to self and humanity not only for the guilty participant in a penitential drama, but for the dramatist as well.[40]

IV

If the themes of *The Tempest* are captured anywhere they are found in Prospero's often neglected, often maligned Epilogue. It is more than the conventional Plautine request for applause, and while "It is conventional," as Spencer says, "for an actor to step half out of character in an epilogue," it is not true, as he goes on to suggest, that "that is what Prospero is doing here."[41] Prospero is stepping further *into* character; as he has met his enemies not as a controlling god but as mere man, so now he faces his audience.[42] He poses to the spectator the question he has already answered for himself. Would you be free? — then you must free others. Or, to put it in his terms,

> my ending is despair
> Unless I be reliev'd by prayer,
> Which pierces so that it assualts
> Mercy itself and frees all faults.
> As you from crimes would pardon'd be.
> Let your indulgence set me free.   *(Epilogue, 15-20)*

This is as close a paraphrase of Christ's injunction on prayer in The Sermon on the Mount or of the words on forgiveness in His prayer as could be found.

Prospero knows that his production has worked only if it changes the characters inwardly. Now, he asks a group of guilty creatures sitting at a play whether the play has changed *them*. If not, while his manipulation may have worked on the stage, it has not reached beyond it. As Northrop Frye says, "We are told that the characters, as usual, will adjourn to hear more about themselves, but we need not follow them, for it is our own identity that we are interested in now."[43] Are you willing to do for me, Prospero asks, what I have done for my enemies? Have you undergone a penitential experience like Alonso's, or do you leave the theater like Antonio, with a shrug? The Epilogue asks the same question of the spectator as *The Tempest* has of its characters. The answer determines the meaning of "the great globe itself," and the meaning of the play which has filled an afternoon in a microscopic globe.[44] Theater and world reflect each other, yet the meaning of each will be found only in the individual responses of individual spectators. The Epilogue, then, leaves the meaning of Prospero's great "revels" speech with the spectator, and leaves with the spectator the meaning of the play, the meaning of the mysteries within it and beyond it. The meaning of Prospero's play could not be clear until he experienced its relevance within his own emotions. The Epilogue asks the spectator to do the same for *The Tempest*—for if he cannot, it has had no meaning, and the world becomes an insubstantial pageant signifying nothing.[45]

Notes:

(1) *A Natural Perspective* (New York, 1965), p. 133. I take mild exception to Professor Frye's description of man's regaining "his original vision." C. S. Lewis's description of the movement of *Paradise Lost* is, to my thinking, more accurate on this point: "*Paradise Lost* records a real, irreversible, unrepeatable process in the history of the universe; and even for those who do not believe this, it embodies . . . the great change in every individual soul from happy dependence to miserable self-assertion and thence either, as in Satan, to final isolation, or as in Adam, to reconcilement and a different happiness" (*A Preface to Paradise Lost* [New York, 1961], p. 133).

(2) Quotations accord with *The Complete Plays and Poems*, ed. William A. Neilson and Charles J. Hill (Cambridge, Mass., 1942).

(3) On the Communion aspects of Ariel's feast, see Robert G. Hunter, *Shakespeare and the Comedy of Forgiveness* (New York, 1965), pp. 227-241. Another banquet—Macbeth's—is not deferred but destroyed. Macbeth has cut himself off permanently from the healing powers of Communion. He has "Put rancours in the vessel of [his] peace" (III.i.67). See J. P. Dyson, "The Structural Function of the Banquet Scene in *Macbeth*," *SQ*, XIV (1963), 369-378, and my "In Deepest Consequence: *Macbeth*," *SQ*, XVIII (1967), 375-388.

(4) On the poetry of *The Tempest*, see Reuben Brower's superb essay in *The Fields of Light* (New York, 1951), pp. 95-122.

(5) *Scepticism and Poetry* (London, 1937), p. 238.

(6) This interpretation of Prospero places him closer to Marston's Altofronto than to the self-deposed Vincentio. Vincentio insists on controlling his manipulation to the very end and produces not a redemptive drama but a self-vindication. He is finally exposed by his production. As D. R. C. Marsh suggests, "The shifting vision of the play, which has exposed the pretensions of all the characters in turn, is turned in the final scene back on the Duke, showing how even his justice is rooted in the concerns of the self" ("The Mood of *Measure for Measure*," *SQ*, XIV [1963], 37) For another negative view of Vincentio, see Rebecca West, *The Court and the Castle* (New Haven,

Conn., 1961), pp. 44-48. Most critics, of course, equate Vincentio and Prospero. See Harold S. Wilson, "Action and Symbol in *Measure for Measure* and *The Tempest*," *SQ*, IV (1953), 375-384, G. Wilson, *The Wheel of Fire* (New York, 1957), pp. 76 and 79, and Francis Fergusson, Introduction to *The Tempest* (New York, 1961), p. 14. For a contrast between Vincentio and Prospero as dramatic devices, see Bertrand Evans, *Shakespeare's Comedies* (Oxford, 1960), p. 332.

(7) *Scepticism and Poetry*, p. 239.

(8) "The Sea and the Mirror," *Collected Poetry* (New York, 1945), p. 361.

(9) Cf. Dowden: "A thought that runs through the whole of *The Tempest* . . . is the thought that the true freedom of man consists in service" (*Shakspere: His Mind and Art* [New York, 1962], p. 419), and Fergusson: "'Freedom' in many different ways is the main motive of the play" (Introduction to *The Tempest*, p. 9).

(10) Quoted in *Shakespeare's Critics* (Ann Arbor, 1964), p. 305.

(11) *Shakespeare: Our Contemporary* (New York, 1964), p. 180.

(12) *Shakespeare Without Tears* (New York, 1961), p. 215.

(13) The opening scene, with its emphasis on the equation between controlling a ship and controlling oneself and on the contrast between the rules of the sea and the land, is remarkably Conradian. Cf. *The Nigger of the Narcissis*, *Typhoon*, *Youth*, *The End of the Tether*, *Lord Jim*, *Shadowline*, and *The Secret Sharer*.

(14) Cf. *Macbeth*: "Speak then to me, who neither beg nor fear/Your favours nor your hate" (I.iv.60-61).

(15) Prospero is, in the Old Testament sense, a "type of Christ." His defeat of Setebos is analogous to Samson's of Dagon (in *Judges*)—a contest, in Miltonic terms, to determine "whose god is God"—and to Elijah's victory over Baal *(I Kings)*. In Milton, Christ chases away the pagan gods in "On the Morning of Christ's Nativity," defeats the rebel angels in *Paradise Lost* and Satan in *Paradise Regained*.

(16) *Shakespeare's Philosophical Patterns* (Baton Rouge, La., 1937), p. 134.

(17) Rose A. Zimbardo, "Form and Disorder in *The Tempest*," *SQ*, XIV (1963), 55.

(18) Bernard Knox, "*The Tempest* and the Ancient Comic Tradition," *English Institute Essays, 1954* (New York, 1955).

(19) *A Natural Perspective*, p. 136.

(20) Frank Kermode, ed., *The Tempest* (Cambridge, Mass., 1958), p. 104, n. 159.

(21) *Shakespeare* (Garden City, N.Y., 1939), p. 285.

(22) See, for example, *Shakespeare Without Tears*, p. 214.

(23) *William Shakespeare: A Reader's Guide* (New York, 1963), p. 478.

(24) *The Poetry of Shakespeare's Plays* (New York, 1964), p. 52.

(25) "The Sea and the Mirror," p. 352.

(26) *From Shakespeare to Existentialism* (Garden City, N.Y., 1960), p. 3.

(27) *Scepticism and Poetry*, p. 241.

(28) Cf. Leslie Fielder, "The Defense of the Illusion and the Creation of Myth," *English Institute Essays, 1948* (New York, 1949), p. 82: "The world *does* decay, and only the individual, in his moment of discovery or passion or tragic insight, is forever. In this sense the apparent contradic-

tion between our being immune to death ('Not a hair perished') and yet 'such stuff as dreams are made on' is reconciled."

(29) *Last Periods of Shakespeare, Racine, and Ibsen* (Detroit, 1961), p. 52.

(30) The most cogent description of the relationship between nature and supernature that I have seen is Ralph Baldwin, "The Unity of *The Canterbury Tales*," *Chaucer Criticism*, ed. Schoeck and Taylor (Notre Dame, Ind., 1960), II, 14-51. Professor Frye's recent books, *A Natural Perspective* and *Fools of Time* are very helpful in defining the relationship of time to supernature.

(31) *Shakespeare: An Existential View* (New York, 1965), p. 87. For a contrasting version of Prospero's control over his inclination towards revenge, see Bertrand Evans, *Shakespeare's Comedies*, pp. 333-337. For criticism which tends from other points of view to support the present analysis, see Frye, *A Natural Perspective*, pp. 118-159, and David William, "*The Tempest* on the Stage," *Jacobean Theater, Stratford-Upon-Avon Studies, I (1960), 133-157.*

(32) Paul's ship, like Alonso's is bound to Italy from Asia Minor, when it is "tossed with an exceeding tempest." An angel appears before Paul, telling him that the ship's passengers "must be cast into a certaine Iland." Paul promises the passengers that "there shall not an haire fall from the head of any of you." The voyage ends as "some on boardes, and some on certaine pieces of the shippe . . . they came all safe to land" (*Acts*, xxxvii, Geneva Version). For an illuminating demonstration of how Shakespeare expanded his sources into *The Tempest*, see Phillip Brockbank, "*The Tempest*: Conventions of Art and Empire," *Stratford-Upon-Avon Studies*, VIII (1967), 183-201.

(33) *Shakespeare and the Nature of Man* (New York, 1961), p. 198. See also Henri Fluchere, *Shakespeare and the Elizabethans* (New York, 1956), pp. 248-249.

(34) "Form and Disorder in *The Tempest*," p. 55.

(35) "The Sea and the Mirror," p. 374.

(36) *Shakespeare and the Comedy of Forgiveness*, pp. 240-241.

(37) Kermode, *The Tempest*, p. lxii.

(38) "*Hamlet*: The Analogy of Action," *The Idea of a Theater* (Garden City, N.Y., 1953), p. 52.

(39) Very much as D. G. James describes him in *The Dream of Learning*. The paralyzed Hamlet James describes is *not* the Hamlet who plans the play for Claudius. Before and after the play, however, James's thesis pertains.

(40) For the elaboration of this argument about Hamlet and *Hamlet*, see my forthcoming monograph, "The Rarer Action: Hamlet's Mousetrap," University of Wisconsin Literary Monographs.

(41) *Shakespeare and the Nature of Man*, p. 198.

(42) A similar use of an epilogue as an *extension* of a play's meaning is that of Pandarus at the end of *Troilus and Cressida*. That he should have the last word suggests the degradation into which the world of that play has fallen. Thersites has fled the battle, suggesting that "If the son of a whore fight for a whore, he tempts judgement" (V.vii.21-22). Hector has killed a pocky coward in sumptuous armor. Achilles has treacherously slain Hector. Pandarus's last word, appropriately is "diseases" (V.x.57). The rottenness of the Trojan world is extended by Pandarus to London ("Some galled goose of Winchester": 55), just as the hope for grace encompassed within *The Tempest* is extended by Prospero to his seventeenth-century audience. Perhaps the most conventional pleas for applause in Shakespeare are the King's at the end of *All's Well that Ends Well* ("The king's a beggar, now the play is done . . .": V.iii.337), and Puck's ("Give me your hands, if we be friends . . .": V.i.444). In anticipation of Prospero, Puck promises to "restore

amends" if the audience will grant "pardon." Obviously, the spiritual emphasis does not pertain to Puck's "pardon."

(43) *A Natural Perspective*, p. 159.

(44) *The Tempest* may, of course, have been performed at Blackfriars. See Bernard Beckerman, *Shakespeare at the Globe: 1599-1609* (New York, 1962), Gerald E. Bentley, *The Jacobean and Caroline Stage* (Oxford, 1941), and "Shakespeare at the Blackfriars Theater," *Shakespeare Survey,* I (1948), and E. K. Chambers, *The Elizabethan Stage* (Oxford, 1923), II.

(45) This essay was prepared with the help of the Bowdoin College Faculty Research Fund. I am grateful for this assistance.

Shakespeare's Henry VIII:
Romance Redeemed by History
by H. M. Richmond

One of the more paradoxical statements in Hardin Craig's *Complete Works of Shakespeare* appears in his preface to *Henry VIII*, where he writes: "There seems no very close correlation in Shakespeare's plays between literary excellence and stage success. Indeed, *Henry VIII*, comparatively speaking is not a great play . . . *Henry VIII* has, nevertheless, a rather illustrious stage history."[1] This sharp discrepancy between aesthetic theory and theatrical fact is no mere invention of Craig's; in 1957 R. A. Foakes made similar observations in his introduction to the New Arden edition of the play. After noting the success of past productions like Henry Irving's, which "was immensely popular,"[2] he went on (p.lxvii) to predict that, though the play "has long been subjected to a barrage of hostile criticism, it will probably continue to tempt actors by the fine parts it offers, and producers by its colour and pageantry."

How have so many modern critics and scholars come to lose touch with the enduring theatrical appeal of *Henry VIII*? The play was not always denounced by critics in such savage terms as W. A. Wright's in the Clarendon edition, where he describes *Henry VIII* as a play "without plot, without development, without any character on which interest can be concentrated throughout."[3] A century earlier Dr. Johnson could rate one of its scenes (IV.ii) "above any other part of Shakespeare's tragedies, and perhaps above any scene of any other poet."[4] And as late as 1840, Charles Knight could still write: "there is no play of Shakespeare's which has a more decided character of unity—no one from which any passages could less easily be struck out."[5] The date of this appreciation is not insignificant, because the turning point in the play's academic reputation came just ten years later, after Tennyson "told his friend James Spedding that the metre of much of *Henry VIII* was like that of Fletcher" (Craig, *Works*, p.1272). As a result of this inspiration Spedding published a close verbal analysis in *The Gentleman's Magazine* under the title "Who Wrote Shakespeare's *Henry VIII*?"[6]—a *non sequitur* typical of the coherence of some of the subsequent discussion. In the paper, his "main argument was from his feeling that two very different styles representing two writers could explain what he saw as an incoherence of design" (Foakes' edn., p.xviii). It says much for the arbitrariness of educated critical taste that once the play's authorship became contested, the tradition of its excellence became intolerable to most scholars. For there is no doubt of the rightness of Frank Kermode's judgment that "this assumption of Spedding's underlies the dearth of critical comment on the play itself; it is assumed to be of interest only in that it was a collaboration of such a kind that no unity of conception and design ought to be expected of it."[7] Certainly the arguments for the play's inferiority only became generally accepted after the "assumption" of its divided authorship: "it is significant that support for Fletcher has always been associated with condemnation of *Henry VIII* as bad, or lacking in unity" (Foakes' edn., p.xxii).

The trouble with the whole case for Fletcher's participation is that the evidence is all internal. Unlike the other cases of known collaboration with Shakespeare, such as *Pericles* and *The Two Noble Kinsmen*, there were no contemporary suggestions of divided authorship: "*Henry VIII* was printed as Shakespeare's by the editors of the Folio, and its authorship remained unquestioned until the middle of the nineteenth century" (Foakes' edn., p.xvii). The idea that "contrasting" styles or mannerisms prove divergent authorship and not just varying transmission or artistic virtuosity is an old weapon of the "disintegrationists," which no discriminating scholar would risk using unaided elsewhere in the Shakespearean canon, even where there might be some slight objective justification for it, as in *Henry VI*. The technical points about the style of *Henry VIII* are inconclusive on the question of divided authorship because in matters of minor verbal conventions like the use of "ye" and "'em" we can never confidently reject the possibility that such forms may well have been affected by scribal or compositorial interference of which the play's stage directions display clear examples. The assumption that there are uniquely individual styles is equally debatable "on a wider examination of texts, words and phrases said to be characteristic of Fletcher turn out to be fairly common in the period"(Foakes' edn., p.xx)[8] A cautious sense of literary history may therefore tend to confirm Craig's earlier judgment that "the only plausible solution of the difficulty is that of Peter Alexander, who gives reasons for thinking that the entire play is by Shakespeare. It is a well known fact that Shakespeare's later style, with its superabundance of feminine endings, became more and more like that of Fletcher" (Craig, *Works*, p.1272)—just as W. B. Yeats changed his style in old age to compete with his younger Imagist contemporaries.

However, Foakes does concede that "perhaps the argument for Fletcher's part-authorship that is most difficult to answer is the most intangible one, based on the feeling that some scenes are un-Shakespearean" (Foakes' edn., p.xxii), and on this point his defence of the play seems to falter a little, for he asserts later that "it is worth noting that it cannot be fitted into the scheme of the earlier histories" (p.xlii). Still, he does recognize a "similarity in compassionate tone and outlook between *Henry VIII* and the other late plays" (p.xxv). And G. Wilson Knight is even more forthright: "The arguments for spuriousness are quite untenable; for though the suspected scenes may contain some minor phrase-reminiscences from Fletcher's work, they offer many reminders, of far greater force and importance from Shakespeare's."[9] Wilson Knight's study finally brings us to the heart of the whole debate by pointing out that the crux of authorship is largely irrelevant, "even were *Henry VIII* proved to have been composed by two, three, or any number of separate authors writing independently . . . no less . . . than if the play were incontrovertibly known to be the child of Shakespeare's undivided and unprompted invention" (pp.271-272). One has only to think of the irrelevance of the same issue of individual initiative to our admiration of Chartres or any other major medieval cathedral in order to see how tangential the Romantic mystique of unique authorship must be to our immediate aesthetic responses.

The ultimate question for the critic about *Henry VIII* must surely therefore not be "Who wrote it?" It should be "Is this a good play, and if so, why?" Shakespeare's authorship is no guarantee of distinction (witness *All's Well*); nor is the partial absence of his hand an omen of disaster. In view of the debated authorship, the most currently interesting variant of the question of the play's worth might be "How well does *Henry VIII* compare with Shakespeare's major achievements?" In other words: what standard of praise can it sustain? My answer to this touchstone trial corresponds to traditional audience reaction by suggesting that the play not only meets the highest tests afforded by comparisons with Shakespeare's earlier works, but also carries on their line of development into territory hitherto unexplored by Shakespeare. Either we have here the culmination of Shakespeare's career, or a dramatist who understood Shakespeare's evolution of interest so well that he managed to complete the sequence by an insight denied to the master himself. Recognition of the play's worth thus becomes essential to our understanding of Shakespeare's political ideas, and a vindication of the evolution of his art.

The most obvious starting point is to note the bearing of *Henry VIII* on Shakespeare's last plays, and particularly the one popularly considered to be his "last": *The Tempest*. To most students of Shakespeare's political thought Prospero proves to be a happier version of the masterful yet apparently hypocritical personality which Shakespeare favored so paradoxically in Sonnet 94, and illustrated uneasily in Prince Hal and Octavius Caesar. Nevertheless, as a romance, *The Tempest* seems no more likely than *Pericles* or *The Winter's Tale* to provide any acceptable resolution of the political problems raised in the earlier history plays—even if elements in it are borrowed from English accounts of actual voyages to the Bermudas. While the play does theoretically complete the cycle of thought about the evolution of the ideal ruler initiated in Shakespeare's earlier history plays, *The Tempest* also seems to stand at a distance from any other Shakespearean histories that deal with this subject: it appeared about half a dozen years after his last Roman play, in which the calculating Octavius triumphed so coldly. It is precisely because of this divergence between the English and Roman history plays and the worlds of the last romances that Shakespeare's probable involvement in *Henry VIII* becomes so critically exciting. For it alone seems to illustrate in plausible historical terms the application of the spirit in which *The Tempest* was written to the actual events of the English sixteenth century.

It has been well observed that in Shakespeare's last plays "Time is compressed, movement expanded, and events are organized in a range of coincidences rather than in an ordered succession. A machinery of the supernatural . . . is needed to bring this about. Human fallible justice is overridden by accident, by the interference of the gods, or by the improbable survival of a Belarius or a Hermione. The nature of *Henry VIII* becomes clearer in the light of these contrivances, as an attempt to create a similar total effect within the ordinary terms of causality and succession, terms which the material of history helped to impose" (Foakes' edn., p.xliv). This opinion is corroborated by Craig's comment that most of the play "follows with surprising fidelity Holinshed's *Chronicles* . . . not only in text, which often seems a paraphrase of prose in verse, but in event and in conception of characters" (Craig, *Works*, p.1271). This practice is emminently Shakespearean and totally uncharacteristic of Fletcher, and it lends probability to the alternative title to the play (noted in Wotton's account of the burning of the Globe during its performance): *All is True*.[10] Such a title strengthens the calculated counterpoint with Shakespeare's romances resulting from the play's close adherence to its sources. It establishes a personal dialectic unlikely to arise except in a mind directly involved in both phases of the discussion.

This is not to say that the dramatist is narrowly bound to his historical sources for all his scenes, or for his attitudes and interpretations. These are highly individual to the point of a calculated distortion of emphasis and sequence to make them fit an ideological pattern appropriate to Shakespeare's last phase.[11] Inevitably (if he were Shakespeare) the writer sees the Tudor dynasty with nostalgia and regret, though never falsifying the harshness that inevitably went with that family's genius for rule. This nostalgic mood colors such scenes as Cranmer's christening of the future Queen Elizabeth (here and later I quote from Foakes' edition):

> This royal infant (heaven still move about her)
> Though in her cradle, yet now promises
> Upon this land a thousand thousand blessings,
> Which time shall bring to ripeness: she shall be
> (But few now living can behold that goodness)
> A pattern to all princes living with her,
> And all that shall succeed: . . .   *(V.iv.17-23)*

The play has many such prophetic passages, and much of that high rhetoric and formality characteristic of Shakespeare's last plays: as in the Masque of Ceres in *The Tempest* and the prophetic dream of Posthumus in *Cymbeline*. Such effects recur in *Henry VIII* with the ritual tableaux of the trial, coronation, and christening of the various Tudor queens. These scenes have confirmed the contemptuous judgment of the play by scholarly readers (unchallenged by most critics, who scarcely bother with the play). Thus G. B. Harrison sees *Henry VIII*[12] as a clumsy series of excuses for pageantry, loosely tied together by a random selection of events from Holinshed's ambivalent chronicle of the king's reign (a chronicle which was itself based on the awkwardly conflicting accounts of the Italian Catholic Polydore Virgil and an English biographer favorable to Wolsey).

The very quality which excites orderly-minded, scholarly readers like E. K. Chambers[13] against the play is probably its greatest strength: the author's Shakespearean sense of the paradoxical nature of human performance, which may shift abruptly in motivation and moral significance as the observer's perspective changes. The rigidity and reflexive nature of the critics favoring Fletcher's intervention appears in their response to this supple and subtle evolution of plot and character:

"the play has been condemned as failing in its general design through the influence of Fletcher, who is said to have 'sentimentalized' each major character in turn, so that each in his or her final appearance is shown behaving in a manner quite different from what might have been expected. In consequence, it is said, interest is not maintained" (Foakes' edn., pp.xlv-xlvi). Ironically this criticism would destroy the "interest" of many of Shakespeare's best plays, which depend on the shocking effect of a planned but unpredictable discontinuity: be it the collapse of the poised Othello into hysteria, or the villainy to which the heroic Macbeth can sink, or the grotesque farce produced by Lear's tragic removal from his customary social setting. Indeed, the fascination of even *Henry VI*, with which Shakespeare began his career, lay in its utter indifference to the narrow, selective unity of Aristotelian aesthetics, an indifference which substituted the rich complexity and discontinuities of multiple narrative for the implausible coherence of neoclassical art. The virtue of Holinshed as a historian also lies in just those characteristics which complicate the perspective of his account of the reign of Henry VIII among others: an eclectic allusion to various, and often conflicting authorities, which in turn gives to Shakespeare's recensions that rich ambiguity for which he has been so much admired. Neither Shakespeare's *King John* nor his *Henry V* evoke a simple response in the way invited by Polydore Virgil's account of the former, or by Drayton's poem about Agincourt. Scholars like L. L. Schucking[14] have even attacked Shakespeare's portrait of Cleopatra for a similar paradoxical inconsistency in her blend of shrewish wit and sensual verve on the one hand and her regal dignity and idealism on the other. One of the best reasons for accepting Shakespeare's authorship of *Henry VIII* lies in its comparably calculated oscillation of values, and the frequent reversal of our formal judgments and expectations of the principal characters. On the evidence of earlier writings, only a Shakespeare would dare to juxtapose the pathetic divorce of Queen Katharine with the intimations of the splendor of Elizabeth's reign which this earlier tragedy made possible. Among his contemporaries the lack of such convincing reversals suggests that only Shakespeare could modulate the almost Marlovian harshness of the portrait of Cardinal Wolsey's ambition into the moving, Christian conclusion of his downfall. The contrast with the grim consistency of the end of *Dr. Faustus*, or with the merely frivolous fluctuations in *The Maid's Tragedy* illustrates the uniquely Shakespearean character of this change of heart.

However, there is a larger unity in the play than such paradoxes and reversals might suggest. It is surely not accidental that the action of the play involves what amounts to four successive "trials" of intimates of the king: the Duke of Buckingham, Queen Katharine, Cardinal Wolsey and Archbishop Cranmer. The first three result in the fall, and at least imply the death, of the accused—but significantly the king's intervention preserves the fourth figure, Cranmer, from the fate of the others, and this climactic departure from the norm suggests that we may perhaps seek a systematic progression in the other trials, confirming that the play is a moralized history concerned once more with what had been Shakespeare's profoundest preoccupation earlier, the nature of human justice. The cyclic rhythm of the action may also remind us of that of *Richard III*, where a similar schematic series of Falls of

Princes is presented. As in Chaucer's *Monk's Tale*, there is a certain relentlessness and studied gloom in the latest play, which has little relief of the kind afforded by Richard III's wit, as the Prologue recognizes in its opening lines:

> I come no more to make you laugh; things now
> That bear a weighty and a serious brow,
> Sad, high, and working, full of state and woe;
> Such noble scenes as draw the eye to flow
> We now present.
> (Prologue, 1-5)

The opulent opening movement of the play sustains this tone with its evocation of the meeting of Henry VIII and Francis I at the Field of the Cloth of Gold. Norfolk's account of it rivals that by Enobarbus of the meeting of Cleopatra and Antony at Cydnus; but Norfolk modulates rapidly into an analysis of national political forces, when he hears Buckingham's censure of Cardinal Wolsey's "fierce vanities" as organizer of the meeting.

Buckingham's censure of Wolsey is both savage and circumstantial—identifying the calculated malice of the Cardinal in compelling the English aristocracy to ruin itself with the expenses of the diplomatic festival, and also noting the secret diplomacy which he carries on behind the king's back. Yet Buckingham's choleric nature echoes the folly of Hotspur's irascibility (1 *HIV*, I.iii.125-136):

> I'll to the king,
> And from a mouth of honour quite cry down
> This Ipswich fellow's insolence.
> (I.i.136-138)

Norfolk by contrast plays the counsellor of outward moderation, like the elder Percys in *Henry IV*:

> Be advis'd;
> I say again there is no English soul
> More stronger to direct you than yourself,
> If with the sap of reason you would quench,
> Or but allay the fire of passion.
> (I.i.145-149)

At the very moment of accepting this admonition, Buckingham decides that he will still denounce Wolsey to the king as "corrupt and treasonous." However, he has barely expounded the substantial grounds for his charges when he is himself arrested on similar ones. The close analogy to the fatal reversal which follows Hastings' hubristic plans to be revenged on his enemies in *Richard III* (III.ii.50-70) is unmistakable, but the function of the later episode is very different. With Hastings we recognize primarily the irony of fate; with Buckingham the issue is more significant, as his case provides the basis for the subsequent discussion and illustration of the forces at play in the government of England.

The king unquestioningly accepts the validity of the charges against Buckingham in the very next scene, confidently awaiting the demonstration of their truth in the "trial" which Wolsey is to stage. Buckingham has already warned the audience that, in a charge of high treason:

> It will help me nothing
> To plead mine innocence, for that dye is on me
> Which makes my whit'st part black. The will of heav'n
> Be done in this and all things: I obey. *(I.i.207-210)*

Wolsey's asserted powers of duplicity are fully demonstrated by an interruption in the discussion of Buckingham's guilt, which results from the unexpected entrance of Queen Katharine. She pleads with the king on his subjects' behalf against the savage taxation levied with Wolsey's connivance. Wolsey first evades responsibility for the taxes, then secretly arranges to claim the merit of interceding himself for their revocation. Obviously the prosecution of Buckingham in self-defence is well within the scope of so wily a prelate, and the king's acceptance of the charges reflects a hasty and extreme judgment. Henry VIII echoes Henry V's pompous reaction to Scroop's conspiracy (*HV*, II.ii.94ff) in his explanation of Buckingham's case to Queen Katharine:

> This man so complete,
> Who was enroll'd 'mongst wonders (and when we,
> Almost with ravish'd list'ning, could not find
> His hour of speech a minute) he, my lady,
> Hath into monstrous habits put the graces
> That once were his, and is become as black
> As if besmear'd in hell. Sit by us; you shall hear
> (This was his gentleman in trust) of him
> Things to strike honour sad. Bid him recount
> The fore-recited practices, whereof
> We cannot feel too little, hear too much. *(I.ii.118-128)*

Not only does the imagery, and dependence on hearsay in this passage also parallel Othello's misjudgment of Desdemona, but we must set this excessive susceptibility to alienating ideas alongside the similar tendencies shown by Cymbeline, and Leontes in *The Winter's Tale*. The author of *Henry VIII* has found immediate historical occasions to realize the bizarre patterns on which the plots of Shakespeare's late romances are founded.

Queen Katharine manages to complicate the proceedings by her womanly intuition, rather as the wholly fictional Isabella had done more stridently in Angelo's judgment against Claudio in *Measure for Measure*. When Wolsey fans the king's wrath by emphasizing Buckingham's personal hostility to the king: "Not friended by his wish to your high person;/His will is most malignant" (I.ii.140-141), the Queen intervenes to remind "the learn'd lord cardinal" that (as a truly Christian prelate) he should "Deliver all with charity." The implicit admonition to the king is reinforced by her challenge to the principal witness against Buckingham:

> If I know you well,
> You were the duke's surveyor, and lost your office
> On the complaint o' th' tenants; take good heed

340

You charge not in your spleen a noble person
And spoil your nobler soul: I say, take heed;
Yes, heartily beseech you. *(I.ii.171-176)*

But the king is completely insensitive to the warning, eagerly brushing it aside
with the exclamation "Let him on," and capping the revelations with enthusiastic
cries: "A giant traitor!" (I.ii.199). The scene ends with a speech of the king's in
marked contrast to the merciful tenor of the queen's interventions:

Call him to present trial; if he may
Find mercy in the law, 'tis his; if none,
Let him not seek't of us. By day and night,
He's traitor to th' height. *(I.ii.211-214)*

There can be no doubt of the naive inadequacy of his response, and the next two
scenes further associate the king with idealistic and overprompt emotional reactions such as betray many of Shakespeare's tragic heroes. The king proclaims a
total reformation of English manners, corrupted by French influence, in a puritanical spirit comparable to Angelo's attempted purge of Viennese license in *Measure for Measure*. Yet the following scene shows the king himself not only succumbing
to Wolsey's carefully planned revelry, but entering his adulterous liaison with Anne
Bullen in the courtly mood that usually figures so ominously in Shakespeare's
presentation of sexual love. It might be Romeo, not a prince married twenty years,
who salutes a young lady thus:

The fairest hand I ever touch'd: O beauty,
Till now I never knew thee. *(I.iv.75-76)*

and proceeds:

Sweet heart
I were unmannerly, to take you out
And not to kiss you. *(I.iv.94-96)*

And even in the midst of this too mannerly indulgence, the king still finds it possible to take a censorious tone to Wolsey for his extravagance:

You hold a fair assembly; you do well lord:
You are a churchman, or I'll tell you cardinal,
I should judge you now unhappily. *(I.iv.87-89)*

The first act of the play thus establishes Henry VIII in the line of those potentially
good but frequently misguided Shakespearean figures like Angelo, Othello, Lear and
Antony: prone by their very enthusiasm and promptness of response to fall into
false courses. However, it is also true to the subtle balance of judgment characteristically struck by Shakespeare that the next act should start with a statement
of the substantial corroboration of Buckingham's guilt offered by several witnesses
at his formal trial, and his total failure to shake the evidence, as well as the fact that

341

his nerve snaps, so that he "something spoke in choler, ill and hasty" (II.i.34). In contrast, his demeanor on the way to death is noble and he accurately perceives the failures in the king which have brought him to death:

> The law I bear no malice for my death,
> 'T has done, upon the premisses but justice:
> But those that sought it I could wish more Christians:
> Be what they will, I heartily forgive 'em:
> Yet let 'em look they glory not in mischief,
> Nor build their evils on the graves of great men,
> For then my guiltless blood must cry against 'em,
> For further life in this world I ne'er hope,
> Nor will I sue, although the king have mercies
> More than I dare make faults.   *(II.i.62-71)*

Buckingham's own frame of mind is the best commentary on that of his accusers, for even as he is led to execution he is able to say "I forgive all" (II.i.83) — a far more salutary statement in this bitterly realistic historical context than Prospero's comparable statements (*The Tempest*, V.i.17-32, 130-134), or Cymbeline's (V.v.422), when each condescendingly forgives his defeated enemies.

It is clear that the conjunction of a susceptible personality like the king's with a manipulative mastery like Wolsey's must lead to a series of royal misjudgments of a progressively more grotesque kind. The central one of these, of course, motivates the divorce proceedings launched against the queen. The circumstances surrounding their initiation are as deliberately complex and ambiguous as the issues behind the duel that dominates the opening scenes of *Richard II*. Public conjecture blames Wolsey:

>   Either the cardinal,
> Or some about him near, have, out of malice
> To the good queen, possess'd him with a scruple
> That will undo her.   *(II.i.156-159)*

However, Suffolk drily rejects this "scruple" of the king's:

>   No, his conscience
> Has crept too near another lady.   *(II.ii.17-18)*

To this Norfolk assents, yet blames Wolsey somewhat unfairly for this also:

>   'Tis so;
> This is the cardinal's doing: the king-cardinal,
> That blind priest, like the eldest son of fortune,
> Turns what he list. The king will know him one day.   *(II.ii.18-21)*

Suffolk's reply epitomizes the central concern of the play: "Pray God he do! he'll never know himself else" (II.ii.22). For the king's self-awareness has been utterly obscured hitherto by Wolsey's subtle interventions, which have results scarcely less drastic than Iago's:

He dives into the king's soul, and there scatters
Dangers, doubts, wringing of the conscience,
Fears, and despairs, and all these for his marriage:
And out of these, to restore the king,
He counsels a divorce, a loss of her
That like a jewel has hung twenty years
About his neck, yet never lost her lustre;
Of her that loves him with that excellence
That angels love good men with; even of her
That when the greatest stroke of fortune falls,
Will bless the king.   *(II.ii.26-36)*

It is startling to see how history is here made to throw up examples resembling even such gross conduct as Leontes' repudiation of his queen—so that the exotic patterns of the late romances are domesticated and intensified by circumstantial fact. And, of course, in this realistic variant, not only is the noble queen destroyed by the conjunction of Wolsey's policy and the king's romantic attachment, but Anne Bullen is more plausibly betrayed into a liaison as tasteless and perilous as that into which Shakespeare had allowed Richard III to lead an earlier Anne, after similar protestations that such a match could not be entertained.

Henry VIII is never shown as a Richard III, but his erratic self-defence at the queen's trial suggests a man like Lear, who "hath ever but slenderly known himself." He clears the cardinal of all responsibility for his decision to launch divorce proceedings, thus revealing an ignorance of the dependence of his own initiatives on the cardinal's suggestions; and yet his own guilty awareness of his dishonorable motives is continually reflected in this imagery in his speech at the "trial":

                    Thus hulling in
The wild sea of my conscience, I did steer
Toward this remedy.   *(II.iv.197-199)*

His potent testimony confirming the queen's memorable and passionate assertion of her wifely integrity only compounds the appalling moral and political confusion into which he has betrayed himself —for, by his match with Anne, he has also falsified Wolsey's sole motivation in forwarding the divorce: to facilitate a further diplomatic marriage for purely dynastic and political motives.

The queen's behavior throughout these trials is evoked with a memorableness worthy of its historical subject, and providing powerful literary parallels to the heroic stature of Webster's two historical heroines: the long-suffering Duchess of Malfi, and the more legitimately accused Vittoria Corombona. The queen is both passionate and firmly dignified, yet she also remains modest and even, ultimately, humble:

Do what ye will, my lords; and pray forgive me;
If I have us'd myself unmannerly,
You know I am a woman, lacking wit

To make a seemly answer to such persons.
Pray do my service to his majesty:
He has my heart yet, and shall have my prayers
While I shall have my life. Come reverend fathers,
Bestow your counsels on me; she now begs
That little thought when she set footing here
She should have bought her dignities so dear.   *(III.i.175-184)*

Clearly Katharine's character represents the norm against which we must measure
the other characters: charitable yet just and tenacious, knowing her own status
yet able gracefully to surrender in the face of relentless pressure. However, it is
interesting to see that not only does the irascible Buckingham meet his death in
a similar frame of mind, but also that even Katharine is not left implausibly without
any malice such as Buckingham displayed against Wolsey. She greets the news of
the death of her enemy, the cardinal, with mixed feelings, and permits herself a
strong and unequivocal censure of Wolsey's faults (IV.ii.33ff.) — only to be answered
boldly by one of her attendants who firmly catalogues the late cardinal's virtues:
his generosity and love of learning, his eloquence and his ultimate humility.

For such is the rhythm of the play that even the high and mighty Cardinal Wolsey
learns modesty and wins grace when he is brought low. Like the queen he meets
his challengers boldly, plausibly denying many of their charges, so that we are less
confident in our censure of him than earlier appearances allowed. Yet once his
downfall is assured, he wisely accepts his fate and turns it to good account, assuring
Cromwell that before he was:

Never so truly happy, my good Cromwell;
I know myself now, and I feel within me
A peace above all earthly dignities,
A still and quiet conscience. The king has cur'd me,
I humbly thank his grace; and from these shoulders,
These ruin'd pillars, out of pity taken
A load would sink a navy, too much honour.   *(III.ii.377-383)*

The author is careful to establish the new scrupulousness of Wolsey as something
more than a rhetorical gesture by showing him dismissing Cromwell from his service
so that he may not lack advancement —though in doing so he gives advice which
shows that virtue may be identical with refined policy, like the generous peace
made by the victorious Cymbeline with his defeated Romam enemies:

Love thyself last, cherish those hearts that hate thee;
Corruption wins not more than honesty.
Still in thy right hand carry gentle peace
To silence envious tongues.   *(III.ii.443-446)*

If the fall of Wolsey illuminates, in this play (as it did in real life), the nobler sides
of his character and of political policy in general, the question remains of the con-

dition in which it leaves the king. We have already seen that the divorce proceedings were conducted with a greater show of generosity and consideration than the trial of Buckingham. The fall of Wolsey unexpectedly displays an even greater mercifulness on the part of all concerned. Formally speaking, Wolsey is only deprived of his improperly accumulated property and his political offices, and even his faults are urged against him temperately: the Lord Chamberlain reproaches Surrey for his increasing severity:

> O my Lord,
> Press not a falling man too far; 'tis virtue:
> His faults lie open to the laws, let them,
> Not you, correct him. My heart weeps to see him
> So little of his great self.   *(III.ii.332-336)*

The fall of Wolsey, like that of Antony, is thus associated with a series of ennobling touches —not least of which is the cosmic image in which he reflects the character of his life, one worthy of *Paradise Lost* (indeed, perhaps alluded to in the fall of Mulciber, I.740-751):

> Nay then, farewell:
> I have touch'd the highest point of all my greatness,
> And from that full meridian of my glory
> I haste now to my setting. I shall fall
> Like a bright exhalation in the evening,
> And no man shall see me more.   *(III.ii.222-227)*

If there is a sense here of Wolsey as a sun god dispensing light and glory (as on the Field of the Cloth of Gold), there is also the sense of the cyclical movement of the Wheel of Fortune, and more ominously still of the fall of Lucifer and the other rebel angels from heaven. In all these roles Wolsey's fall has a bearing on the king's character. With the death of Katharine, Henry has indeed lost the noblest wife a man could wish for —but her virtues were always neutralized by the masterful policies of Wolsey. The marriage to Anne Bullen is a repudiation of this high policy in all its phases, both good and bad —an act of spontaneous affection, however injudicious— and the last act or so of the play is devoted to vindicating the personality of the king now that it has liberated itself from the manipulations of Wolsey's well-meant but amoral subtleties. The king's ultimate role defies the adequacy as well as the need for Machiavellian policies, which Shakespeare had seemed to assume in his portrayal of figures like Henry IV and Octavius Caesar. An aura of grace for the moment surrounds even the ill-fated Anne Bullen:

> Sir, as I have a soul, she is an angel;
> Our king has all the Indies in his arms,
> And more, and richer, when he strains that lady;
> I cannot blame his conscience.   *(IV.i.44-47)*

Like Antony's, Henry's adultery is somehow vindicated in the event; but unlike

Antony, Henry is able to defy the revolutions of the Wheel of Fortune, and out of this inauspicious marriage is born the princess who is to be England's glory and Shakespeare's patron. Nemesis is finally defeated, by the intervention of Christian Providence.

It is no accident that Archbishop Cranmer pronounces the eulogy of the infant Elizabeth. His survival in the play with all his dignities reflects the sustained improvement in the atmosphere of the court and the heightened political awareness of the newly emancipated monarch. For Cranmer is the victim of a similar persecution to Buckingham's, but one of whose probable nature the king is at last aware:

> Know you not
> How your state stands i'th' world, with the whole world?
> Your enemies are many, and not small; their practices
> Must bear the same proportion, and not ever
> The justice and the truth o'th' question carries
> The due o'th' verdict with it: at what ease
> Might corrupt minds procure knaves as corrupt
> To swear against you? Such things have been done.   *(V.i.127-134)*

The king is thinking of Christ's trial, but it is obvious that his words would also apply to Buckingham's. His present awareness of the perils of judgment marks a vast step forward towards that goal of mercy above the law which Buckingham identified as the true attribute of greatness (along with such earlier characters as Portia and Isabella). Moved by the humility of Cranmer, the king gives him a ring which will serve to temper the hatred of Cranmer's enemies on the Council by showing that he still retains the king's favor.

The Council meeting follows the familiar pattern, of public slights to the proposed victim, followed by relentless accusations—but with several divergencies from the earlier norm. The king indignantly observes the cruelty with which Cranmer, an Archbishop, is kept waiting at the door of the Council in which he himself rightly should be seated. The king recognizes finally that he must preserve his own initiative in evaluating those around him:

> Is this the honour they do one another?
> 'Tis well there's one above 'em yet; I had thought
> They had parted so much honesty among 'em,
> At least good manners, as not thus to suffer
> A man of his place, and so near our favour
> To dance attendance on their lordships' pleasures.   *(V.ii.25-30)*

In the council itself the examination of Cranmer is conducted with the usual indifference to common law, despite Cranmer's pleas:

> I do beseech your lordships
> That in this case, of justice, my accusers,
> Be what they will, may stand forth face to face,
> And freely urge against me.   *(V.ii.79-82)*

The Bishop of Winchester pursues Cranmer with such fury that Cromwell intervenes in the same spirit that the Lord Chamberlain has checked attacks on the ruined Wolsey:

> My Lord of Winchester, y'are a little,
> By your good favour, too sharp; men so noble,
> However faulty, yet should find respect
> For what they have been: 'tis a cruelty
> To load a falling man. *(V.ii.107-111)*

One recalls Antony's rather surprising censure of Caesar's comparable mean-spiritedness:

> He seems
> Proud and disdainful, harping on what I am,
> Not what he knew I was. *(Ant., III.xiii.141-143)*

Both Antony and Cromwell deplore a purely local judgment of a man's stature, with this difference, that Cromwell's intervention comes before the fatal point that would assure Cranmer's ruin has been passed. Cromwell's speech is one of a series of checks to the relentless apparatus of persecution—it is to be followed by Cranmer's production of the king's ring, and finally by the direct intervention of the king himself, who brings the whole sadistic procedure to a halt. It is clear that in the course of the earlier proceedings the king has learnt the dangers of politically motivated "justice":

> Why, what a shame was this? Did my commission
> Bid you so far forget yourselves? I gave ye
> Power as he was councillor to try him,
> Not as a groom: there's some of ye, I see,
> More out of malice than integrity,
> Would try him to the utmost, had ye mean,
> Which ye shall never have while I live. *(V.ii.175-181)*

The sense of the need for temperance in the administration of all justice which is implicit in this admonition perfectly corresponds with the mood of the other late plays of Shakespeare. The hasty temperament of Henry VIII is shown to evolve historically through a series of mistakes that are perhaps analogous to Prospero's initial, fabled one, of naively neglecting politics, in his case for learning (*The Tempest*, I.ii.66-151). Henry ultimately attains to an awareness of the nature of his role as chief magistrate comparable to that attained by the omniscient Duke in *Measure for Measure*. The crucial difference is that the Duke's wisdom is merely assumed to exist from the start, while Henry's is shown to evolve through a plausible series of historical errors of judgment. The conjunction of moral and historical evolution is plausibly suggested, and it is fitting that, at this supposed high point of wisdom in Henry's career, the birth of Elizabeth and the implicit dawn of a new, even nobler age should be celebrated.

Of course, the actual historical role of the king has been sweetened, in the last phase of the play particularly. His earlier injudicious harshness to Buckingham, and the misguided treatment of Katharine are shown with fair historical truth, as also is the tempered censure of Wolsey. But the climactic last episode with Cranmer has been deliberately elevated in significance for moral and artistic purposes. Henry here becomes a model "magistrate," a status to which he had all too little claim in history. However, there is a kind of symbolic truth in that for an instant Henry should acquire vicariously that aura of distinction with which his new-born daughter certainly was haloed in the eyes of Shakespeare and many of her subjects—even if she also was capable of the egotistical malice and political ruthlessness of all her family. In this context one recalls the repeated failures of Cymbeline and Posthumus, even after they acquire wisdom: in the last scene of *Cymbeline* the newly aware king still manages to sentence his own son to death, and the humbled and repentant Posthumus physically assaults Imogen, the wife whose loss he regrets so deeply. There is no reason to assume the author of *Henry VIII* was unaware of the comparable capacity of his more historical king to relapse from his momentary wisdom into that sadism which disfigured much of his later career. After all, the very figure of Anne Bullen perpetually evokes a sense of ominous potentiality in the last scenes of *Henry VIII*. Nevertheless, out of the sinister and shifting events of Henry's reign an author with the insight of the mature Shakespeare has plausibly woven a sequence of scenes which both illustrate and confirm the political potency of that high dignity and mercifulness with which his last romances were concerned. By transposing these values to an overtly historical cycle he has worthily vindicated their substantiality and done much to mitigate the sour dichotomy between moral and political distinction which has made Shakespeare's earlier history plays such ominous prefigurations of his great tragedies. The unregenerate spirit of Richard III is finally exorcised from the genre of the history play. In the presentation of a reign rather more horrifying in fact than Richard's was supposed to have been in legend, an author with all the authority of Shakespeare convincingly displays to us the universal power of Divine Providence: as Cymbeline finally says, "Pardon's the word to all." The systematic fusion of this high sentiment with a substantially historical plot is an achievement worthy of Shakespeare's maturity. It is hard to believe its detailed realization is not entirely his.[15]

Notes:

(1) *The Complete Works of Shakespeare*, ed. Hardin Craig (New York, 1951), p. 1273.

(2) *King Henry VIII*, ed. R. A. Foakes (London, 1957), p. lxiv. I am much indebted to this edition, whose sympathetic approach to the play is my best precedent for the present essay. My quotations are keyed to this third edition of the play in the Arden series.

(3) *Henry VIII*, Clarendon ed. (Oxford, 1891), p.xxii.

(4) *Johnson on Shakespeare*, ed. W. Raleigh (Oxford, 1915), p. 150.

(5) *Shakespeare's Works*, ed. C. Knight (London, 1840), *Histories*, II, 398.

(6) clxxviii (August-October, 1850), 115-124 and 381-382; see also his similar title in *Notes and Queries* for 24 August, 1850, p.198.

(7) Frank Kermode, "What is Shakespeare's *Henry VIII* about?" *Shakespeare: the Histories*, ed. E. M. Waith (Englewood Cliffs, N.J., 1965), p. 169.

(8) The opposite view had been fully presented by A. C. Partridge, *The Problem of "Henry VIII" Re-opened* (Cambridge, 1949); but after the publication of Foakes' edition the counter arguments to its dismissal of stylistic clues to authorship were re-affirmed strongly: see R. A. Law, "The Double Authorship of *Henry VIII*," *SP*, LVI (1959), 471-488; M. Mincoff, "*Henry VIII* and Fletcher," *SQ*, XII (1961), 239-260; M. P. Jackson, "Affirmative Particles in *Henry VIII*," *N&Q*, n.s. IX (1962), 372-374; also J. C. Maxwell's edition of 1961. In his revised edition of 1964, Foakes answers some of these challenges and others (pp. xxvi-xxviii), moving towards the critical position taken in this paper.

(9) G. Wilson Knight, *The Crown of Life* (New York, 1966), p. 270.

(10) Sir Henry Wotton, *Reliquiae Wottonianae* (London, 1872), p. 425.

(11) This aspect of the play is fully discussed by H. Felperin, "Shakespeare's *Henry VIII*: History as Myth," *SEL*, VI (1966), 225-246. He also concludes that the work displays a Shakespearean unity.

(12) W. Shakespeare, *The Complete Works*, ed. G. B. Harrison (New York, 1948), p. 1505.

(13) E. K. Chambers, *Shakespeare, a Survey* (New York, n.d.), pp. 316-324.

(14) L. L. Schucking, *Character Problems in Shakespeare's Plays* (London, 1922), pp. 119ff.

(15) This essay may be read as an epilogue to my study of the history plays: *Shakespeare's Political Plays* (New York, 1967).

Internal Evidence and Elizabethan Dramatic Authorship: An Essay in Literary History and Method: *Review Article*

by *Thomas Clayton*

The "Literary . . . Method" of the subtitle is a casual inaccuracy that hardly affects the accomplishment of this book,[1] which provides a thorough and sobering *caveat scholasticus* that begins with a history of frequently abortive attributional endeavors and concludes with an exposition of eight cautionary principles for modern students of attributional problems. Schoenbaum's record of attempts to fix the authorship of anonymous or doubtful plays is one chiefly of errors, and he is "conscious of having more than once passed severe judgment on my predecessors"; but he has thought it "essential to maintain an austere standard for a species of inquiry which has in the past so often tolerated rationalized impressionism masquerading as impartial science" (pp. viii, ix). Certainly he was right to find fault when it lay in his way, and almost certainly a more widespread "refreshing interest in general principles" (p. 30), as he implies and states here and there throughout, would have *oftener* insured appropriate caution in the definition and treatment of evidence than was usually the case. At times, of course, erroneous speculation was the inevitable concomitant of inadequate evidence, and attempts to force a quantity from a nullity were necessarily misguided from the start. And some errors were, it is clear, acts of all-too-human obliviousness and will that no commitment to the abstract principles of truth or probability could have avoided. Some manifestations of folly and wisdom were (and are) as much temperamental as intellectual—and, it may be added, "truth" is sometimes a function of consensus or convenience rather than of certainty or high probability. Finally, perhaps there is even something to be said for checkered shades and chiaroscuro: if the history of scholarship, as of other human activities, had only monuments for the marking, it might well come a noonday churchyard.

The favorable reception *Internal Evidence* is likely to have retained when all the reviewing returns are in had been heralded, at the time of the present writing, in four reviews and a summary notice,[2] and I concur in the unanimous view that it is important and could be ignored only at their peril by students of Renaissance drama, especially of plays of which the authorship is entirely or in part uncertain —a very considerable number, as Schoenbaum shows. Precisely because this is an important and wide-ranging book, it seems to me to merit detailed consideration and to warrant a concluding examination of something of a test case—Cyrus Hoy's study of the authorship of *Henry VIII*—for one of the currently favored attributional methods, the "linguistic." And, having recorded my general approval, I hope it will be understood that some of the virtues of Schoenbaum's book are allowed to speak for themselves here. It should be added, by the way, that *Internal*

Evidence was companioned into print by another book of major importance on the same subject, which no students of attribution can afford to be without; namely, David V. Erdman and Ephim G. Fogel, ed. *Evidence for Authorship: Essays on Problems of Attribution* (Ithaca, New York, 1966; noticed in Schoenbaum's "Postscript," p. 258).

I.

Internal Evidence purposes to fill the need "for a historical perspective and impartial methodology" that "the present state—and status—of attribution study makes evident" (p. xvi), and it is generally structured as the statement implies, though methodological observations are naturally incorporated throughout. The major portion of the book is divided between the two well-established modern scholarly genres of the critical survey (Parts I and II) and the table of the laws (Part III). The title of Part I, "Mischief on Gower Street," refers to the "vast outpouring of imaginative speculation inspired by intuition, fortified by learning, and sustained by industry" (p. 4) of the New Shakspere Society, which first met at University College, London, on "Friday the thirteenth of March, 1874" (p. 3). Its eight chapters (pp. 3-62) carry the critical and historical survey of the investigation —and sometimes licentious generation—of problems of Renaissance dramatic authorship from the seventeenth-century cataloguers, Rogers and Ley, Archer, and Kirkman, to about the end of the nineteenth century. The twelve chapters of Part II, "The Golden Age and After" (pp. 65-143), bring the history as nearly up to date as possible (*ca.* 1965). "The Golden Age" flourished approximately from 1900 to 1930, when "The Conservative Counterthrust" (p. 119) had already well begun to deliver the *coup de grace* to the late practice of "rationalized impressionism" (the running-head of Chapter IX is "Conservatism Ascendant"). Part III (pp. 147-219), "Avoiding Disaster," sets out the laws, commenting on various kinds of external evidence and articulating Schoenbaum's eight principles; it is a revised version of the author's 1960 English Institute paper, "Internal Evidence and the Attribution of Elizabethan Plays" (see *BNYPL*, LXV [1961], 102-124). Chapter VII of this section discusses in detail the problem of *The Revenger's Tragedy*, to which Schoenbaum devoted the first chapter of his earlier book on *Middleton's Tragedies* (1955), and which, as "the most important Elizabethan play of seriously disputed authorship," serves as his chief "object lesson in the perplexities and frustrations of canonical research" (pp. 199, 200).

Supplementing the three major sections are "A Note on Dramatic Collaboration" (Appendix, pp. 223-230), a bibliography of "Works Cited," a Postscript, and a generally excellent index. "A Note" conveys how complex the problem of collaboration must be in the face of so little factual knowledge of its practice, which apparently varied considerably in the nature of division and the times and means of accomplishment; for example, Dekker described his parts in *Keep the Widow Waking* as Act I and "a speech in the last Act of the Boy who killed his mother" (see p. 229). The Postscript, written after the book had already gone to press, conscientiously and helpfully takes account of important contributions to attributional study made after Schoenbaum's original writing—and sets in relief the melancholy fact that, in an age of massive scholarly activity, tangible printed results and obsolescence are virtually simultaneous (is Marshall McLuhan right about the printed book?)

One or two peripheral observations might be added on the printed presentation of *Internal Evidence.* "Because a great many journals are cited in the footnotes," Schoenbaum has "so far consulted the reader's convenience as to supply readily understandable abbreviations in preference to the symbols prescribed by current convention; thus I refer"—I substitute a different example, which I find rather jarring—"to [*Rev. of Eng. Stud.*] rather than to [*RES*]" (p. x). I can't see this: the scholar or graduate student to whom this book is addressed either will or should know the conventional abbreviations given in *"Pub. Mod. Lang. Soc."* (an abbreviation Schoenbaum of course doesn't use). At the opposite extreme, precisely four types are saved in *"Jour. of the Hist. of Ideas."* Surely a list of abbreviations used, if thought necessary, would be sufficient consultation of convenience. On the other hand, Schoenbaum seems to me absolutely right to have the notes "placed at the foot of the page rather than gathered together at the back, where they are more easily ignored" (p. viii). This kind of book demands reference to the notes, and the more accessible they are the better; I for one should gladly pay a proportional surcharge in preference to having my purse consulted at the expense of my convenience, not least because it is exasperating to claw for an *"Ibid."*

All the major figures are here, in their habit as they attributed and, as the narrative exposes them, very often erred. In the seventeenth and eighteenth centuries, Langbaine, Ravenscroft (who probably first attacked the authenticity of a First Folio play), Rowe, Pope, Bentley, Theobald, Hanmer, Warburton, Dr. Johnson, Capell, and Malone: only three fare very well as attributionists, Dr. Johnson, Capell, and Pope's "slashing Bentley," who rightly put asunder the *Epistles* from *Phalaris* and joined them with a better prospect, "with overwhelmimg erudition and remorseless logic" (pp. 12-13)—timeless methodological resources of intelligent scholars, be it noted, though "his instrument is internal evidence."

The disintegration of the Shakespeare canon that reached its zenith in the late nineteenth and early twentieth centuries arose in the seventeenth century and was well in the ascendant in the eighteenth. Edward Ravenscroft (1687) had "been told by some anciently conversant with the Stage" that *Titus Andronicus* was not "originally" Shakespeare's; Rowe doubted *Pericles*—rightly, it is now generally agreed; but Pope launched "a large-scale attack on the integrity of the First Folio," doubting the authenticity of numerous passages and adding *Love's Labor's Lost* and *The Winter's Tale* to the growing list of "doubtful" plays. Theobald cast doubt upon the *Henry VI* trilogy; Hanmer rejected *The Two Gentlemen of Verona* and Warburton *The Taming of the Shrew* and *The Comedy of Errors* (as well as *1-3H6* and *Tit.*); and by this time "the judgments, based upon stylistic impressionism, of the earlier commentators, especially Pope, were already showing signs of hardening into an orthodoxy" (p. 16). But Dr. Johnson, "noteworthy for his statements of principle, which are conspicuously absent from previous discussion"

(p. 16), provided respite in restoring the *Henry VI* plays; and "Capell's *Shakespeare* was a precedent-shattering achievement" (p. 17): he returned to the early quartos and the Folio, challenged "on all fronts the disintegrators of his day," and "recognized—as others had not—the relevance of chronological succession to questions of authenticity," and his "hypothesis that Shakespeare participated in the composition of *Edward III* has had reputable advocates to this day" (pp. 17, 18, 20). The end of this line was Malone (pp. 21-26), at once "the last and greatest of eighteenth-century Shakespeareans," "the Ptolemy of attributional study," and "our first great cautionary case": with his investigation, *Titus Andronicus* and *Henry VI, Part I* once more fell from the canon, but he "anticipates the modern approach by his application of knowledge and reason—rather than mere impressionism—to problems of authorship, and by his consistent willingness to set forth the evidence on which his conclusions rest" (p. 24). He was hailed by the New Shakspere Society as the inventor of the "Ryme-Test" later exploited wholesale by Fleay, as E. H. Seymour was, in 1805, of the "double-ending test," both "tests" easily subject—and duly subjected—to distortion and abuse. Not surprisingly, perhaps, "Coleridge's reflections on problems of the Shakespeare canon are laconic, fragmentary, or random" (p. 27).

And then there came, in 1833 and after, Spalding, Hickson, and Spedding, whose work on *The Two Noble Kinsmen* and *Henry VIII*—though from 1850 "for a quarter of a century these documents gathered dust" (p. 29)—inaugurated the great flurry of attributional study of the late nineteenth and early twentieth centuries and posed—and schematically gave one of the answers to—two of the major and still much-vexed questions of the Shakespeare canon. Their distribution of portions of these plays between Shakespeare and Fletcher is still far from universally accepted, but the influence of their studies upon later research can scarcely be overestimated; they deserve the extended treatment they are given (pp. 29-38; they are recurred to in this review).

"Spedding's essay on *Henry VIII* provided an authentic model for subsequent investigators," and "the modern movement in authorship study... properly begins with the establishment of the New Shakspere Society" (p. 38), a "movement" so constituted by the reliance of its founding director, F. J. Furnivall, "on cooperative effort to achieve scholarly goals" (p. 39). "Scientism" in this field began in earnest with F. G. Fleay, "the first of the great fantastics of attribution study" (p. 40), who rose like a sun, shone for a time, and set like a meteorite, leaving in his wake a prodigious amount of attributional work begotten of heat and generating little enough light, though, as Schoenbaum concedes, "he is sometimes right" (p. 49); he was perhaps never far from justifying the title visited upon him by his fellow Cambridge undergraduates, "the industrious flea." Fleay's distinctive attributional weapon was the metrical test, yielding quantitative data based on counts of rhymes, double endings, Alexandrines, and broken lines; he was also, of course, a theoretician and methodologist, and himself offered to the Society "ten 'canons of method' for the guidance of investigators using the tests" (p. 42). Schoenbaum—appropriately, it would seem—gives Fleay the detailed due of his majority and deficiency on pages 40-48 and a measure of reputational resurrection on pages 49-50: Fleay first apportioned the parts of *The Changeling* almost unanimously accepted by modern scholars, and he frequently pointed the way and "provided a stimulus to the succeeding generation" (p. 50). The plants of most of his great labors, in short, in others' orchards grew.

Brief attention to other members of the Society, Richard Simpson, Jane Lee, and Harold Littledale, is followed by a chapter (VII) on Robert Boyle, an almost lawless disintegrator, who gave most of his attention to "what he took to be the Beaumont, Fletcher, and Massinger plays" but found time to give Shakespeare's previously acknowledged parts in *Henry VIII* and *The Two Noble Kinsmen* to Massinger (p. 55). Part I concludes with a brief chapter (running-head, "Editions and Journals") on editorial work and "the advent of learned journals in the modern languages" that made possible the new emphasis of which Boyle's own work was symptomatic.

II.

Substantial sections of Part II (twentieth century), like the last chapter of Part I, consist in annotated bibliography presented in narrative form, to some advantage, though no such translation can compensate for the virtual unassimilability of the volume of material to be accommodated. This part also attempts to give historical perspective to the progress of attributional study, but closeness in time as well as the burgeoning labors of scholars give the plotted progress something of an air of rationalized wish-fulfillment rather than of sequential fact. "The New Wave" (W. S. Gaud, T. M. Parrott), with some attention to internal evidence as such, gives way to "1900-1910" (II), which epitomizes a considerable amount of work. Chapter III is devoted to "the incomparable Greg"—a just epithet somewhat debased by its titular association with a popular singer of the 1940's—who is himself used as a cautionary example: "If the greatest Elizabethan scholar of his generation could wander down so strange and deviously winding a path, what, one may ask, is reasonably to be expected of lesser mortals?" (p. 84). This single example, in which Greg's enormous contribution to modern scholarship is largely taken for granted, dramatizes the primarily cautionary purpose of Schoenbaum's entire history.

E. H. C. Oliphant (IV) and H. Dugdale Sykes (V), who "qualifies as leader of what Greg called 'the parallelographic school'" (p. 89), are followed by "1911-1930" (VI), during which "other players swelled the scene"; this chapter is devoted to discursive bibliography and to "new or comparatively untried tests" of authorship, of which "the first and most important" is "the 'em-them test" devised by A. H. Thorndike and applied by Willard Farnham to Beaumont, Fletcher, Massinger, and Shakespeare (p. 97). It is also noted that "comprehensive studies of individual dramatists became more numerous during this period" (p. 100). The establishment of "The *More* Fragment" (VII, pp. 104-107) as probably Shakespearean in hand and authorship is one of the few major successes recorded in *Internal Evidence,* and perhaps it, too, like Greg's work, is well enough known to demand no more than the few pages Schoenbaum gives it; certainly he accords just praise to the contributors to *Shakespeare's Hand in the Play of Sir Thomas More* (1923), which A. W. Pollard edited. The pontifically wrong-headed and prolific J. M. Robertson, "prince of disintegrators," and "the baseless fabric of his vision" are anatomized in Chapter VIII: "The primary significance of the Robertson affair to this inquiry lies in the fact that it served to call into question the whole endeavor to establish authorship on the basis of style. In Abercrombie and other commentators the very word 'internal' became a compromising epithet. The Golden Age was over" (p. 119).

The record of "Conservatism Ascendant" begins most notably with the work of Baldwin Maxwell, Peter Alexander, and E. K. Chambers (IX). Chapters X and XI summarize the attributional work of the years 1931-1965, "The Major Studies" (X) concerning itself prominently with the work and influence of Caroline Spurgeon and Alfred Hart, and the important individual studies of A. C. Partridge on *Henry VIII* and Cyrus Hoy on the Beaumont and Fletcher canon. "Miscellaneous Articles, &c." (XI) epitomizes in narrative-bibliographical form the matter of the title, and Chapter XII concludes Part II with a "Retrospect," which ends with a certain ambiguity: "the follies which show so baldly in the work of Feuillerat and Pitcher"[3]—as examples of recent abuses they are discussed in some detail—"appear in less blatant form in a host of attribution studies, early and late. If learning has so often gone fearfully astray, it must be owing in large measure to the investigator's ignorance or abuse of *just* method" (p. 143; italics mine). Or to the frequent willfulness of scholarly human nature, or to differences of evaluation of "just" method, or to all three. "To believe in the inevitability of scholarly progress is to cherish an illusion" (p. 140), and Schoenbaum is broadly skeptical; but there is, perhaps, a wistful Manicheism in his horror of the darkness of "rationalized impressionism" alleviated by his implicit hope for the ultimate triumph of the light through "just method."

III.

Parts I and II deal chronologically with individual scholars and the metamorphoses of attributional fashion, through which plays have been shifted back as well as forth from hand to hand as method and information, *tempora* and *mores*, dictated. "Who wrote *x*?" has been asked and answered recurrently—perhaps most often of *Henry VIII*, *The Revenger's Tragedy*, and *The Two Noble Kinsmen*— because "we want to know; something there is that doesn't love an anonymous play" (p. 218), implying the extent to which historical and critical questions of fact and value seem inevitably to interdepend. As his chief object lesson, *The Revenger's Tragedy* receives detailed discussion in a single place, but Schoenbaum also has much to say here and there about *Henry VIII*, which is nearer the center of Shakespearean interest and may usefully serve as an index of attributional fluctuation and of Schoenbaum's own narrative and interpretative method, especially since there is recent detailed work on the subject. In their annotated bibliography, Erdman and Fogel give pages 457-478 of *Evidence for Authorship* to *Henry VIII*, and, in *Shakespeare and The Two Noble Kinsmen* (New Brunswick, N. J., 1965), Paul Bertram covers much of the same ground as Schoenbaum in his chapter supporting Shakespeare's sole authorship (III, pp. 124-179).

Schoenbaum's first substantive mention of *Henry VIII* quotes the proud announcement of the New Shakspere Society, in its First Report (1875), that "it has made known to this generation the genuine and spurious parts of *Henry VIII*" (p. 4); the survey of work preceding the Society's—the "Movement that is the subject" of Part I—then follows. Dr. Johnson regarded the prologue and epilogue as doubtful (p. 16); Malone assigned the play to 1601 "and, after Johnson and Farmer, postulated later revisions, possibly by Jonson" (p. 22). The history of the first real "disintegration" begins with James Spedding's "Who Wrote Shakespeare's *Henry VIII*?" which, published in *The Gentleman's Magazine* for August 1850, "prompted the publication, in *Notes and Queries* for the same month, of Hickson's independent findings with regard to the same problem" (p. 29). So far as I know, Paul Bertram is the only critic who has emphasized that, on the evidence, Hickson's "independent findings" consisted only in dubious assertions; as Hickson wrote, he had been "anticipated in at least the publication of a discovery I made three or four years ago," and his "present object is to strengthen the argument of the writer [Spedding] . . . by recording the fact that I, having no communication with him, or knowledge of him, . . . arrived at exactly the same conclusion as his own" (quoted from Bertram, p. 133).[4] According to Schoenbaum, "Spedding in turn responded with a letter in the October issue of *The Gentleman's Magazine*" (p. 29), which—remarks Bertram—"one suspects was designed to undercut Hickson after he had been so forward" (p. 135). And where Schoenbaum writes that, "in conversation with Spedding several years before the essay was written, Tennyson had expressed the view that the style in some portions of *Henry VIII* resembled Fletcher's" (p. 34), Bertram quotes Spedding (p. 134), who would appear to be mustering the support of a Higher Authority, and notes that "Tennyson's only *recorded* comment . . . [was] made in 1883 after Shakespeare's presence in the play had evidently been questioned" and sounds "defensive of Shakespeare" (p. 136n; italics mine). Schoenbaum is scarcely less scornful of Spedding's impressions and methods of proof than Bertram; the point of the comparison here is that Bertram has read signs that Schoenbaum has ignored, and the implications of the signs are surely of interest in a critical survey of the *faux pas* of earlier scholarship. Schoenbaum himself is, however, duly skeptical about the Higher Authority: "The critic who is himself a poet has often been regarded as speaking with special authority on the identity of the poet's [i.e., Shakespeare's] voice. Yet, as Pope's example shows, even a poet of genius may go sadly astray. Browning and Eliot were to prove no less vulnerable in their pronouncements on authorship" (p. 11); and "the versification [of *Henry VIII*],' Browning solemnly asserted," in "uncritical endorsement" of Boyle's division, "'is nowhere Shakespeare's'" (pp. 179, 180).

Schoenbaum goes on to recount the support of Spedding's metrical data and conclusions—which "fail to satisfy the requirements of sound statistical procedure, for Spedding ignores the possibility of an alternative explanation" (p. 37)—in Fleay's "rhyme test" and Furnivall's "stopped-line test." He concludes his account of the early history by justly remarking that Spedding's "essay must be credited with providing an impetus for all subsequent investigation," and he had just previously remarked that Spedding's original "hypothesis of Fletcher-Shakespeare collaboration" has received "powerful new support in the form of linguistic data" in the twentieth century (pp. 37-38). Robert Boyle's award of Shakespeare's part to Massinger is discussed in an account centered on Boyle's scholarship in general (pp. 54-59; esp. pp. 54, 55, 56); as Schoenbaum notes, Boyle's "'evidence' is, of course, all internal," and "the authenticity of the First Folio is thus rejected outright" (p. 55). H. Dugdale Sykes's "reviving the justly neglected theories of Boyle" (p. 90) is discussed in another thumbnail sketch of a fallen star of scholarship, and references to "disintegrative" discussions of the play by Marjorie Nicolson and Willard Farnham are incorporated (pp. 96, 97) in a survey of the period 1911-1930.

Peter Alexander's 1930 defense of "the homogeneity of *Henry VIII* against mortar fire from the joint-authorship partisans" is cited as an example of "The Conservative Counterthrust" (pp. 119-120); Caroline Spurgeon's 1931 suggestion that figurative language "is a factor which should be taken into account in any investigation of the [attributional] problem" is quoted (p. 124); and what may reasonably be described as Schoenbaum's summary comments on the present scholarly position of *Henry VIII* are given on pages 128-130.[5]

Schoenbaum's concluding case for Fletcher's part is about evenly divided between A. C. Partridge (1949, revised 1964) and Cyrus Hoy (1962). "Partridge's evidence is satisfyingly concrete" but it is "not so statistically impressive as to sweep all before it," as R. A. Foakes had summoned details to demonstrate in his New Arden edition (pp. 128, 129). "Hoy introduces no fresh evidence of his own, but he makes shrewd use of Charlton Hinman's discovery that the play was set in part by compositor B. That compositor tended to alter *ye* to *you,* and so Hoy is able to discount the relative infrequency of the former in the Fletcherian scenes of *Henry VIII*. Foakes's point thus loses some of its sting, but it is not rendered irrelevant; the play remains a great puzzle. Hoy may be justified, however, in feeling that the burden of proof has shifted to the proponents of single authorship" (p. 130). "The play remains a great puzzle" is a temperate, indeed almost noncommital but just, conclusion, and "Hoy *may* be justified" is a reservation, I think, of greater than its intended force. It can be demonstrated that, despite Compositor B's tendency to alter *ye* to *you* elsewhere, almost none of the *you*'s in any part of *Henry VIII* can safely be attributed to him, and that, whoever wrote the passages in which they occur, *ye* and *you* are deliberately if variously differential; Hoy's conclusions, therefore, are not justified by his evidence.[6]

Schoenbaum's conclusion probably would not have been much different if he had taken account of the many other articles written on *Henry VIII* in the past twenty years, but, in the interests of balance, some should certainly have been included that are not, notably the arguments for the play's overall unity (and for Shakespeare's sole authorship by the first two) by G. Wilson Knight, Hardin Craig, and Frank Kermode; and at least one should perhaps have been given greater prominence than citation in a footnote and the bibliography: Marco Mincoff's "*Henry VIII* and Fletcher," which attempts to sweep the field for Fletcher's traditional part through a comprehensive discussion of earlier arguments and evidence.[7] "The extensive bibliography should serve as a useful finding list for those wishing to pursue the subject [of attribution] further" (Preface, p. viii), but it is not up to the pursuit of such individual—and major—problems as the authorship of *Henry VIII*, which as a both major and methodologically typical case has strong claims to a more extensive bibliography. It must be noted here, without prejudice to the less specialized purposes of Schoenbaum's book, that *Evidence for Authorship* is distinctly superior in its provision of a more inclusive "finding list" that categorizes subjects (from the general to the particular, including individual works), lists contributions in chronological order, and provides more than adequate annotation in the form of objective summary quotations and comment. And it is worth quoting the editors' summary comment on *Henry VIII*: "When one takes into account all the metrical, rhetorical, and linguistic discriminators that have been brought forward in more than a century of controversy about *Henry VIII*, 'the overall picture seems certainly more consistent with the theory of collaboration than with that of single authorship.'[8] That the result has been achieved almost entirely by the use of internal evidence, both literary and statistical, should give heart to those who wish to support their intuitions about authorship by patient and responsible argument" (p. 478).

"Who wrote Shakespeare's *Henry VIII*?" has yet to be definitively answered, especially since (as neither Schoenbaum nor the editors of *Evidence for Authorship* point out, but Foakes does) Cyrus Hoy reduced "Fletcher's share . . . from the usual ascription of ten and a half scenes to six, or, in terms of lines, by rather more than half."[9] Paul Bertram has argued strongly for an entirely Shakespearean *Henry VIII*, first in 1962 but authorship has not been much at issue in recent writing on the play. In three of the four other discussions that treat or prominently touch on *Henry VIII* published in 1962-66, the problem of authorship is ignored, dismissed, or regarded (inaccurately) as solved.[10] Three mainly critical articles cannot adequately sustain generalizations about the current attributional status of *Henry VIII*, but they are provocatively suggestive, and they imply an aspect of the problem that could bear further emphasis (no one, I think, now ignores it); namely, the tension between the "critical" and "scholarly" status of the play, which has always been, though often covertly, at issue. Not only in earlier perspectives, disunity + divided authorship and unity + single authorship tend to be concomitant views of *Henry VIII*. In the absence of incontrovertible external evidence (certainly the most comforting kind, however its importance might be exaggerated), the general cause of doubt and confusion seems to be that the internal evidence is of kinds unlikely to be equally well received by the same person: the evidence of linguistic, prosodic, and bibliographical minutiae and that of the semantic aspects of the work. Those interested in the "problem" of authorship tend to treat the play as play perfunctorily, and those interested in the play as play have little interest in the authorship problem. The division of spirits here is not, I think, between the wise and foolish virgins; it rather takes the "form in which A says a certain object is blue and B says no, it is not blue, it is anthropomorphic,"[11] or "good" versus "not good, but collaborate." Expressed in these terms, as the dispute often is, it is bootless. As is clear in Kermode's discussion, and in Irving Ribner's willingness to assign what he regards as a disunified play to Shakespeare's sole authorship,[12] the positions of students of the play need not and indeed should not be so exclusive. In a different context, Hoy proffers a reconciliatory view that may stand as a (temporary) last word: "*Henry VIII* has its place—and it remains secure when the disintegrators of Shakespeare have done their worst—in a greater canon than the Beaumont and Fletcher one" (*SB*, XV, 76). And would it but set the barrel new abroach to add that *Henry VIII* is a play by Shakespeare in which Fletcher possibly had a collaborator's hand of uncertain extent and touch? Probably.

IV.

Whether the problem is *Henry VIII* or any other, "Avoiding Disaster" in attribution is possible through appropriate local applications of circumspectness, temperance, and judgment. In the opening chapter of Part III, Schoenbaum assesses "The Fatal Flaw" of unsuccessful attributional studies as an "astonishing indifference to method," resulting in failure to establish "basic principles of procedure" and "to define the nature of evidence" (p. 148). "The investigator's task," as he sees it, then, "is to isolate and describe the special character of a literary work of unknown or doubtful authorship, to show the extent to which a known writer's work partakes of that special character, and from this evidence to arrive at an appropriate conclusion" (p. 149). That might well be a statement of final uncertainty; and it should be added that an hypothetical work by an absolutely unknown author could only by "probability" or degree of resemblance—and falsely—be given to the most eligible "known" candidate for its authorship. It is here that Schoenbaum rejects "Arthur Sherbo's 'basic premise' that, in questions of authorship, 'internal evidence deals with essentials while external evidence deals with accidentals,' and that 'short of an unequivocal acknowledgment by the author himself, the value of internal evidence outweighs any other.'"[13] Schoenbaum insists that "external evidence may and often does provide incontestable proof; internal evidence can only support hypotheses or corroborate external evidence" (p. 150), the second part of which is logically irrefutable, though "only" underemphasizes the conviction extensive internal evidence can communicate by establishing high probability. In his review Sherbo takes Schoenbaum especially to task over "incontestable," pointing out that, as Schoenbaum "quite honestly and necessarily shows," every kind of external evidence "can be and has been untrustworthy." He suggests—twice—that Schoenbaum "has made out a strong case for the greater value of internal evidence" despite his reservations, quoting against him his observations that, "despite the prevailing skepticism, a number of attributions dependent upon internal evidence have gained general acceptance, even in such rigorously conservative summations as Bentley's" (p. xix), and that the isolation of Shakespeare's hand in *Sir Thomas More* "serves as a stunning vindication of the role of internal evidence in attribution study" (p. 107).

Some of these differences strongly insisted upon seem to me to be more apparent, theoretical, and semantic than strictly substantive and practical, as *Proof* "evidence sufficient (or contributing) to establish a fact *or* produce belief" (*SOED) acts* as something of a common denominator to suggest. "Evidence" may establish as mathematical fact the validity of a geometrical theorem, but neither external nor internal evidence alone can, in the strictest sense, establish as historical fact the validity of an assertion, whenever made: Sherbo's "unequivocal acknowledgment by the author himself" begs the question, however venially, of the "true" relationship between speaker and work, though, as he implies, *this* "accidental" species of external evidence would outweigh the "essentials" of internal evidence. We do not accept everything asserted as "established fact"; but we do accord belief where we acknowledge various probability. "The poet nothing affirmeth" in the fictional world of his work, but his work, as fact, is evidence potentially "sufficient (or contributing)" to "produce belief" in the validity of one or more hypotheses that may come to be regarded as facts according to their degree of probability (or, frankly, sometimes simply a broad "appeal" that commands a general assent catalyzed by indifference or exhaustion).

Schoenbaum and Sherbo would probably agree that it is right to treat external evidence—as commonly—as itself an hypothesis subject to corroboration by other external *and* internal evidence. Where external evidence is wanting, internal evidence alone (though often assisted by analogy) can suggest and support hypotheses, and not infrequently it evenly supports alternative ones. Since the text and its particulars are the subject of explanation, one can scarcely ignore the internal evidence, because they are it (hence Sherbo's "essentials"); on the other hand, one would scarcely ignore external evidence when available: even if it does not constitute proof, it may suggest hypotheses not suggested by the text itself. Two major sources of difference seem to me insistence upon generalized principles at the expense of the individual case, which ever demands modification of them; and disagreement over what constitutes sufficient proof, often itself a matter of the individual case. *Are* a title similar to *The Atheist's Tragedy* and Archer's fifty-years-later ascription "evidence" of Tourneur's authorship of *The Revenger's Tragedy*? (See Schoenbaum, pp. 200-201, 216, and Sherbo, p. 129.) If so, they are contributing rather than sufficient proof. Is the distribution of *'em-them* in *Henry VIII* evidence of the respective hands of Fletcher and Shakespeare? Perhaps, but in itself insufficient, especially without attention to context: the degree of "delicacy" to be admitted or demanded in the treatment of quantitative "linguistic evidence" is not, I think, a matter of universal agreement. The nature and acceptability of evidence are not matters simply of paying one's money and taking one's choice, but there are enough inherent unknowns and fluctuations in the market to make the evaluation of a stock a difficult and variable matter. We do well to have as a marginal nth the "N3CAC principle": "No code can cover all contingencies."

His case for external evidence stated in the opening chapter, Schoenbaum discusses the kinds in detail with helpful examples: title-pages, the Stationers'

Register, the Revels Office-Book, booksellers' catalogues, and miscellaneous allusions and citations; as Dent notes in his review, Henslowe's Diary (though frequently cited elsewhere) is inexplicably missing here. Chapter III takes up the "particularly complex problems [that] arise when the external evidence is contradictory" (p. 159), and Chapter IV sets out Schoenbaum's eight "First Principles." Schoenbaum cannot "really apologize for the elementary character of the procedures" because "they do need stating," as "the illustrations (as well as some of the cautionary tales in Parts One and Two of this study) will, I trust, demonstrate" (p. 163). "All eight reflect my dissatisfaction with the casual methodlessness of stylistic impressionism" (p. 183), and most have already been adumbrated. Dent is surely right to describe all eight as "fundamentally unquestionable," but he adds the reservation that "at least half of them are to some degree obscured by imprecise formulation or inadequate development" and very helpfully discusses principles 2, 3, 5, and 6 (*RN*, XIX, 397). Even if the principles somewhat arbitrarily constitute an *oct*alogue of *these* sometimes loosely formulated principles, it must be observed that the number and constitution of the Decalogue have not gone unquestioned (or disobeyed), and that the statement of each principle *is* accompanied by detailed and useful discussion.

There are, however, one or two further reservations to be expressed. Principles 4—"Textual analysis logically precedes stylistic analysis"—and 8—"Wherever possible, stylistic evidence should be supplemented by bibliographical evidence" —are sufficient corollaries of each other scarcely to warrant separate entry. Principles 2,

> If stylistic criteria are to have any meaning,
> the play must be written in a style,

4, and 8 refer to "style," but as No. 2 suggests Schoenbaum's conception of style is not made very clear. Of "a style" in No. 2 Dent asks, "What happens to collaborated plays containing a variety of styles?" On page 70 Schoenbaum remarked that "internal evidence consists of the small details of style—particular words, phrases, images—and also larger literary correspondences: thought, characterization, incident"; but "even hacks like Chettle and Munday . . . may have *occasional strange quirks of individuality*" (p. 169; italics mine) implies mannerism and manifest idiosyncrasy as a prominent characteristic of style. No doubt it is, to the potential imitator as well as to the disinterested beholder, but has it much legitimate differential value for purposes of attribution? Considerably less, as Schoenbaum would probably agree, than minute and ostensibly "neutral" grammatical preferences, favored syntactical constructions, and the like, as is now widely recognized by literary scholars as it has been for some time by specialists in linguistics.[14] A *style*, I suppose, ought to be specially defined for attributional purposes in some such terms as "a distinctive compound unity in a body of writing demonstrable from the presence of a statistically and distributionally significant number of occurrences of a differential practice or coincidentally related practices, in which 'sub-literary' phenomena are allowed greater prominence than 'literary'"—practices of a kind, one might add, appropriate to the perspective, which might be orthographical, bibliographical, paleographical, and so on, rather than "stylistic" in the linguistic and rhetorical senses.

"Stylistic analysis" is, implicitly, defined by Schoenbaum as something like the sum of abstractive procedures and "tests" referred to here and there throughout the book. Chapter V deals with "The Major Tests" helpfully, but I cannot see why, in a cautionary book on attribution, "it is *not* possible here to deal with all of the tests by means of which investigators in their wisdom or folly have sought to prove authorship by style. Some of the criteria that have been employed are, in any case, too feeble even to require citation; a few minor tests have already been discussed briefly in previous parts" (pp. 183-184). If not here, where? Schoenbaum's own testimony belies the superfluity of mention on grounds of feebleness. And it would have been useful for him at least to list and briefly describe the "minor tests" in this section. The "Major Tests" are "Verse Tests" (pp. 184-186), "Imagistic Tests" (pp. 186-189), "Parallel Passages" (pp. 189-193), and "Literary Correspondences" (pp. 193-195). Certainly all these are commonly used in making comparisons between works, are in varying degrees valid, and are subject to abuse by the willful or unwary, as Schoenbaum shows in his examples.

In his discussion of "Parallel Passages," Schoenbaum quotes, from an article written by Miss M. St. Clare Byrne in 1932 and generously neglected since, "five Golden Rules, as she reasonably described them, for the improvement of parallel-hunting" (p. 191; Rules, pp. 191-192).[15] These Rules alone are worth the price of admission to this section of the book, and they have a self-subsistent economy, concreteness, and clarity that is rather less conspicuous in Schoenbaum's own principles, though he deserves much credit for bringing them once more to general attention. Take the first two, for example: "(1) Parallels may be susceptible of at least three explanations: (*a*) unsuspected identity of authorship, (*b*) plagiarism, either deliberate or unconscious, (*c*) coincidence; (2) *Quality* is all-important, and parallels demand very careful grading—e.g. mere verbal parallelism is of almost no value in comparison with parallelism of thought coupled with some verbal parallelism" (p. 191).

Chapters VI-VIII conclude the book proper, the first by assessing the present and future in "Promise and Limitations," the second by an extended example in *"The Revenger's Tragedy,"* and the third by an economical advocacy of prudence epitomized in the suggestion that "the scholar no less than the poet must have his own kind of negative capability" (p. 219). The crucial point about the investigation of evidence of any kind is made in Chapter VI: "The ultimate effect sought is a cumulative one, in which all the internal evidence—stylistic, bibliographical, and linguistic—converges inexorably upon a single possible author-identification, an identification compatible with the known external information" (p. 195); where no such convergence results, identification must be made tentatively or uncertainty admitted. A reserved but cheerful annunciation is made of "the trend away from simple impressionism to a more analytical criticism" and the computer is cautiously heralded as a serviceable tool that "may in future be expected to play an essential role, although we must discount the more fantastic claims made" in its behalf (pp. 197, 198). The claims of the computer to employment by the attributional scholar will not be gainsaid and increase in no petty pace from day to day, as witness the proliferation of such journals as *Computers and the Humanities* and the series of conferences jointly sponsored by the IBM Corporation and various universities.[16]

Though far from a zealot of scientism, Schoenbaum inveighs with striking frequency against the "rationalized impressionism" that is linked with the "intuitions, convictions, and subjective judgments" that "carry no weight as evidence" (principle 7). Scholarship implies a commitment to objectivity that is inescapable in principle, but commitments to literature based on long, wide, and thoughtful reading entail exercise of judgment impossible—and almost certainly undesirable— of suppression. Compare Schoenbaum:

> Poor Fleay! His "scientific" method, like some computer gone berserk, was forever playing tricks on him. Deliberate and bookish Webster is the least plausible claimant for the intensely immediate *Revenger's Tragedy*, although, given his well-known assimilative tendencies, he may well have been influenced by it. (p. 203)

This seems to me stark impressionism, but in principle I applaud rather than deplore it as partaking of some of the essence of literary study: tests and statistics may prove or disprove assertions, as hypotheses, but it is the apprehensions and the assertions, right or wrong, that matter in the beginning and the end. In many respects, "rationalized impressionism" is precisely what literary study is.

V.

Not least because *Internal Evidence* is prominently concerned with the scholarly fashions and limitations of different periods, several aspects of the style of this book are of particular historical and professional interest in their own right. I was repeatedly struck by three: a discursive style that, though it is enlivened by a humor that belies Schoenbaum's apology that "the reader may find [it] dry and inelegant" (p. ix), unfortunately lapses occasionally into the near-sarcastic and apparently uncharitable, especially at the expense of our damned and erring scholarly predecessors; and the casual, though perhaps deliberate as contemporaneously vivid, uses of the terms of contemporary academic-administrative conditions and of political ideology. Defects of tone (at least as I see them) are venial, and I comment on these only because they seem innocently and mildly to reflect a contemporary scholarly temper that at its worst combines an arrogant sense of imminent ascension with a canny awareness of the main chances and mischances of a profession compressed to something like a running, familial conventionalism by logarithmic expansion, darting mobility, and instant grape-vinery.

"*Notes and Queries*, that last playground for the amateur, has effected an admissions policy" is an inoffensive piece of parochial drollery, but from a lesser scholar, at least, it might seem of questionable propriety as possibly self-interested to add "under the firm editorial hand" of the present editor (p. 140). And it is to me discomforting to find, in place of such "neutral" terms as "prolific" and its kindred, the apparent enthronement of industrial values in such phrases as "[Sykes's] *productivity* tapered off" (p. 91), "Wells *produced* several articles" (p. 95), "[J. M. Robertson's] *productivity* astonishes and disheartens" (p. 107), and "despite a general expansion—spectacular in recent years—of scholarly *production,* the sheer volume of attribution work has shrunk somewhat" (p. 122)—with shades of the rise and fall of the attributional empire. Tactics and fashion have an undercurrent ring in "[Chambers's strictures,] of concern only to an audience of specialist scholars, . . . were *unstrategically* presented in a popular edition" (p. 116); "never again were Robertson's views to be regarded as intellectually *respectable*" (p. 117); and "a novel and especially interesting imagistic test has recently attracted notice as a result of its employment . . . in a *sympathetically received* study" (p. 187; cf. p. vii). What seems unfortunate here is the emphasis.

Schoenbaum's use of the language of ideological politics has been indicated above in the quotation of his tag and running-head, "The Conservative Counterthrust" and "Conservatism Ascendant" (II. ix), with which compare the ironical confusion resulting from "*revolutions,* alas, rarely have entirely beneficient results" (p. 81) and "they [the 'enthusiasts' of the Golden Age] failed to grasp the significance of the bibliographical *revolution* taking place under their noses" (p. 148). There are numerous occurrences scattered throughout the book, in "extremist position" (p. 20; cf. p. 118), "the grandest achievements of this period . . . sum up the conservative position" (p. 121), "enlightened conservatism" (p. 122), a "stand . . . less strenuously anticollaboration" (p. 129, n. 120), "the triumph of the fundamentalists" (p. 137), and "doubters, disintegrators, and revisionists" (p. 166), for example. But the most gratuitous obtrusion is to be found in Schoenbaum's chapter on J. M. Robertson (II. viii), who "began his career as a radical journalist," and whose "fantastical extremism" was wisely rejected at last (pp. 107, 118): "one suspects that Robertson's political radicalism, maintained to the end, informs and directs at least in part his animus against conservative scholarship, an impression that is reinforced by his uncivil treatment of Lord Balfour" (p. 110)! I personally find an "historical perspective and impartial methodology" more than *stylistically* vitiated by a strong ideological coloration of any kind, though one can easily understand how the partisan temper and polemic expression of our time can all too readily creep into scholarship itself, despite its definitional commitment not to an age but to all time.

That Schoenbaum's ideological phrases may not be mere rhetorical infelicities seems to me suggested by, for example, "the modern *movement* in authorship study" (p. 38), and far more in his persistent advocacy of "general principles" (p. 30): "It is, I believe, this astonishing indifference to method that is the fatal weakness of the conjecturists of the Golden Age and the source of the anarchy still prevalent in attribution work" (p. 148). And, of course, he may be right. What seems evident, however, is that Schoenbaum's faith and expression are very much reflections of our own time, and future scholars, like Schoenbaum himself, will no doubt take interested cognizance of the design and texture of the glass.

Of ideology and scholarship, principles and practice, it is perhaps not inappropriate to observe that Brutus, an honorable man, has impeccable if often equivocal because abstract principles, but the bookish theoric falls repeatedly, finally not to rise, before the rookish empiric. Scholarship is not politics, but there is even here ample latitude for slips betwixt the manual and the match. Still, if men are men, the odds are better on the match if one knows a parry from a thrust.

VI
The "Ye/You Test" and the Authorship and Composition of Henry VIII

Schoenbaum gives the last word on the authorship of *Henry VIII* to Cyrus Hoy, who is uniquely qualified, by his exhaustive work on the Beaumont and Fletcher canon, to speak with authority for Fletcher's claims—which he supports in a substantial reduction of Fletcher's traditional share.[17] The importance of Hoy's general contribution to the problem of authorship is not to be disputed, his insistence that "*Henry VIII* has its place—and it remains secure when the disintegrators of Shakespeare have done their worst—in a greater canon than the Beaumont and Fletcher one" (p. 76) is eminently sane, and even such summary critical observations as "anyone who is familiar with Fletcher's rhetorical cascades cannot fail to recognize his manner" in speeches by Katherine, Henry, and Cranmer (p. 84) cannot be dismissed as unfounded casual impressions. But, as Hoy notes, "the case for Fletcher's presence in *Henry VIII* is, in large part, based on the widespread use of *ye* in the text of the 1623 Shakespeare folio" (p. 71), and it is doubtful whether he has contributed "powerful new support in the form of linguistic data" (Schoenbaum, p. 38) to his attribution of even a nearly-halved share in *Henry VIII* to Fletcher. And it is demonstrable from his study that the evidence of authors' and compositors' known or inferential linguistic "preferences," especially when it is employed in an analysis of frequency and distribution that largely ignores considerations of literary and dramatic context as a possible determinant of the exercise of preference, can seriously mislead.

Citing with approval the late Philip Williams's study of the occurrences of *ye* and *you* in *Henry VIII* and commenting that the distribution approximately coincides with the Folio pages set by Compositors B and C (the latter earlier identified as X),[18] Hoy goes on to question the foundation for R. A. Foakes's expression of uncertainty—and some skepticism—about the extent of Fletcher's hand in *Henry VIII* (see the New Arden edition, ed. Foakes, 1957 and, with corrections and a "Postscript, 1962," 1964). "Mr. Foakes is aware . . . that Compositor B altered *ye* to *you* in *Troilus and Cressida*; he does not seem to be aware of the extent to which Compositor B did so in *Henry VIII*, for he can say . . . 'that the peculiarities assigned to different authors existed in the copy on which the Folio text is based': 'However, we do not know how far, or in what differing degrees these compositors altered their copy for this particular play, or who was responsible for that copy.' In view of Williams's statistics, I would suggest that only the last part of this statement is entirely true" (p. 79). But Williams's statistics do nothing to discount the substantial validity of the first part of Foakes's assertion, because they are distributed only according to compositorial division. A certain un-benign circularity appears here in the fact that the distribution of *ye* and *you* attributed to Compositors B and C is simply a different distribution of the linguistic evidence that otherwise seems to support divided authorship.

Williams found that Compositor B's pages contained "a ratio of 208 *you*'s to 25 *ye*'s, or eight to one, while on the pages set by Compositor X (B's partner [and Hinman's C]) he found a ratio of 191 *you*'s to 48 *ye*'s, or four to one" (Hoy, p. 78; Williams, p. 10). Since Compositor B also set proportionally more "Shakespearean" work (about six of his thirteen pages) than did Compositor C (about five-and-one-half of fifteen pages), it is clear that, "given Compositor B's known habit regarding *ye*, one can hardly expect the chief feature of Fletcherian linguistic usage to appear in undiminished abundance in the printed text of any play on which he worked" (p. 79); or, put another way, the same statistics cannot, without elaborate hypotheses and commentary, simultaneously support divided authorship and a divided composition that obscures it. In short, Foakes's expression of uncertainty is not entirely without foundation. The overlapping of this linguistic evidence for both authorship and composition is most easily seen in tabular form ("Fletcher" is the traditional attribution, "*Fletcher*" is the portion of the traditional attribution accepted by Hoy):

PORTION OF PLAY	ATTRIBUTION	COMPOSITOR	FOLIO SIGNA- TURES	FOLIO PAGES
I. i. 1-137	Shakespeare	B	$t3^{r+v}$	205-6
I. i. 138-I. ii	Shakespeare	C	t4-5	207-9
I.iii-iv	*Fletcher*	C	t5-6	209-11
II. i-ii	Fletcher	C	$t6-v1^{v}$	211-14
II.iii-iv (*SD*)	Shakespeare	C	$v1^{v}$ -2	214-15
II. iv. 1-119a (*SD*)	Shakespeare	B	$v2^{v}$	216
II. iv. 119b-239 (*end*)	Shakespeare	C	v3	217
III. i. 1-108	*Fletcher*	C	$v3^{v}$	218
III. i. 109-184 (*end*)	*Fletcher*	B	v4	219
III. ii. 1-203	Shakespeare	B	v4-5	219-21
III. ii. 204-459 (*end*)	Fletcher	B	v5-6	221-23
IV. i-ii	Fletcher	B	$v6-x1^{v}$	223-26
V. i	Shakespeare	B	$x2^{r+v}$	227-28
V. ii. 1-19	*Fletcher*	B	$x2^{v}$	228
V. ii. 20-V. iv	*Fletcher*	C	$x3-4^{v}$	229-32

In a number of scenes traditionally ascribed to Fletcher (notably II. i-ii and IV. i-ii) Hoy is "convinced that Fletcher has done nothing more than touch up a

Shakespearean passage, or insert a passage of his own in a Shakespearean context" (p. 79). Accepting the traditional assignment of I. iv to Fletcher, he solves the admitted problem of accounting "for the low proportion of ye's to you's [4/23]" by explaining that "because they are distributed throughout the scene (at lines 2, 50, 63, and 86 of Alexander's edition) they provide better evidence for regarding that scene as wholly Fletcher's than do the 4 ye's of the following II, 1 found at lines 1, 130, 131, and 132" (p. 80)—on the assumption (or inference) that "the occurrence of ye in single isolated clusters within a scene, and its periodic occurrence throughout the whole of a scene, is . . . of considerable importance for the authorial evidence that attaches to the form" (p. 81): clusters tend to support Fletcherian interpolations rather than his authorship of an entire scene (the latter a forced inference of a kind common in early attributional studies of distributional evidence). This kind of principle need not be stigmatized as the "distributional fallacy," but it is open to question; and it is not unreasonable to suggest that analysis should include investigation of the literary context of the passages in which the forms occur. Distribution aside, the ratio in I. iv militates against Fletcher's authorship, and Compositor B, who did not set this scene (as Hoy notes), cannot be held responsible for inferential alterations of Fletcherian ye's. The ye's occur in the following contexts, which, though brief, are perhaps sufficient to suggest that the form is used deliberately (though not necessarily for the same reasons) in each case (*Henry VIII*, ed. Foakes):

> *Sir Henry Guilford.* Ladies, a general welcome from his grace
> Salutes *ye* all; this night he dedicates
> To fair content, and *you*: none here he hopes . . . . *(1-3; cf. 63)*

> *Lord Chamberlain.* Look out there, some of *ye.*
> *Cardinal Wolsey.*   What warlike voice,
> And to what end is this? Nay ladies, fear not . . . .
> I shower a welcome on *ye*: welcome all.   *(50-51, 63; cf. 1-3)*

> *Cardinal Wolsey.*   Let me see then,
> By all your good leaves, gentlemen; here I'll make
> My royal choice.
> *King* [*unmasking*].   *Ye* have found him Cardinal;
> *You* hold a fair assembly; *you* do well lord:
> *You* are a churchman, or I'll tell *you* cardinal,
> I should judge now unhappily. . . .   *(84-89)*

The crux of ambiguity is to be found in such an assertion as Hoy's "III, 1 provides the strongest linguistic evidence of Fletcher's presence to this point in the play. It also provides a striking example of differences in the practice of two compositors. The scene in the Folio occupies sigs. v3ᵛ and v4ʳ. Sig. v3ᵛ was set by Compositor X [C]. It contains 13 ye's, 14 you's. Sig. v4ʳ was set by Compositor B. It contains 7 ye's, 16 you's" (p. 80). It is of interest that the ratio on these pages, 1(B)/2(C), is the lowest common denominator of exactly the same ratio attributed by Williams and Hoy to Compositors B and C in the play as a whole, and it is not without significance that the distribution of "raw" statistics here is seriously misleading.

It must also be noted of the distribution that Katherine uses a majority of the *ye*'s in the scene, a consideration that seems to me to override the compositorial (and authorial) implications of the statistics, or at the least to compete with them in affording another explanation of the distribution. Sig. v3^v contains lines 1-108, in which 12 of 13 *ye*'s, but only 4 of 14 *you*'s, are Katherine's; sig. v4^r (composed by B, who is said to change *ye*'s to *you*'s in *Troilus and Cressida*) contains lines 109-184, in which all 7 *ye*'s, but only 3 of 16 *you*'s, are Katherine's. The hypotheses that would account for this kind of distribution would be that (1) the *speeches* with high and low *you/ye* ratios were composed by Compositors B and C, respectively, which is very doubtful indeed; (2) Fletcher wrote Katherine's speeches, Shakespeare the rest, which is not impossible; and (3) the scene was written by a single author who was deliberately making distinctive use of *ye* and *you*, which seems the least strained explanation. There seems little ground for doubt that Katherine's use of *ye* was not less intended to be, than in effect it is, dramatically differential; and that kind of consideration ought surely to be taken into account in formulating hypotheses to explain the nature and distribution of linguistic evidence. Here, the evidence of compositorial interference with copy is scant and extremely equivocal, and the evidence for Fletcher's authorship—based on the use of *ye*, at any rate— very doubtful. Other evidence must be allowed proportionally greater weight, since this linguistic evidence seems only to support conscious dramatic purpose, in whomever that is to be otherwise found.

Where he comments that the usages of *ye* and *'em* in *Henry VIII* "are not Fletcherian enough," Foakes notes that the 1647 Folio text of *Bonduca* "has 349 instances of *ye*, while *you* appears very rarely indeed" (pp. xx-xxi).[19] And one of my students, Mrs. Colleen Davidson, in an excellent paper on *"Henry VIII* and A. C. Partridge: A Study Presented in the Spirit of a Counter-Example,"[20] remarks that "in *Bonduca ye* is used without regard for the dramatic situation," an observation confirmed by Hoy's description of "the Fletcherian pattern" as "marked above all by the constant use of *ye*" (*SB*, VIII [1956], 144). Almost everywhere it is used in *Henry VIII, ye* seems to have an emotional or a dialectal force, or both, and to be expressive of character in general or of character in a particular situation.[21] In III. i, for example, Katherine becomes overwrought and is from the first insistent upon her fully converted nationality (ll. 42-50):

> O good my lord [Wolsey], no latin;
> I am not such a truant since my coming
> As not to know the language I have liv'd in;
> A strange tongue makes my cause more strange, suspicious:
> Pray speak in English; here are some will thank *you*,
> If *you* speak truth, for their poor mistress' sake;
> Believe me she has had much wrong. Lord cardinal,
> The willing'st sin I ever yet committed
> May be absolv'd in English.

Katherine's *you*'s here give way to a preponderance of *ye*'s beginning in line 69. at which point such reginal dignity and composure as she is able to command in the speech just quoted also gives way to more emotional expressions of bitterness and fear.[22] The uses of *ye/you* in III. i do not seem to me to warrant Hoy's confidence in either the "evidence of Fletcher's presence" or "a striking example of differences in the practice of two compositors."

Hoy is—as many would agree, rightly—"not at all sure that one is justified in attributing to Fletcher the superb speeches made by Wolsey after his fall [III. ii. *post* 203]," but it is doubtful here, as in III. i, whether "what we are dealing with is, once again, Fletcherian interpolations [notably of *ye*'s] in a scene that is essentially Shakespeare's" (p. 80). Hoy entertains the possibility that Compositor B here altered a number of Fletcher's *ye*'s to *you*'s, but concludes for Fletcherian interpolations, partly because he finds "the distribution of such occurrences of *ye* as are present suspicious" owing to their clustering. The *ye*'s in Fletcher's traditional part of the scene occur in lines 239, 240, 241, 242, 278, and 365; and where the clustering occurs, it should be noted that in Wolsey's at-bay response to Suffolk (ll. 236-250), who bears the king's oral command to Wolsey "to render up the great seal Into our hands," there are differences in the dramatic and verbal context in which the four *ye*'s of lines 239-242, and the *you*'s of lines 244 (with an 'em) and 246, occur. Here then, it would seem, Fletcher clearly exercised differential dramatic propriety rather than—fitfully—a customary preference in supplying *ye*'s, or Compositor B wisely or fortuitously left a few *ye*'s in appropriate places, or both. And it should be noted that the uses of *ye/you* by Katherine in III. i and Wolsey in III. ii are broadly comparable, as the scenes themselves are as visitations of the fallen by the potent.

Hoy finds Act IV, set entirely by Compositor B, doubtfully of Fletcher's (traditional) sole authorship, but probably touched up by him, on very much the same grounds that led him so to conclude of III. ii. *post* 203: only 8 *ye*'s against 13 *you*'s, for which Compositor B could be held responsible except that here, too, the *ye*'s tend to be clustered (pp. 80-81). And again an examination of the context of the *ye*'s shows that they have local dramatic or other kinds of rhetorical significance. The three *ye*'s of IV. i. 114, 115, and 117 are used by the Third Gentleman in a jovial imperative speech of modest condescension (with which compare Henry's somewhat similar use of four *ye*'s at the end of the play in V. iv. 69-74); the other two Gentlemen answer, *"You* must command us, sir" (l. 117). In IV. ii, the first *ye* (l. 22) is almost certainly of dramatic significance: Griffith is quoting the fallen Wolsey, who in III. ii had used four *ye*'s in a passage significantly beginning "Now I feel" (238-242, cited above).

In her paper mentioned above, Mrs. Davidson plotted the use of *ye/you* by individual characters in different scenes as a means of checking the apparent significance of scene-by-scene ratios of occurrences as inferred without regard to the speaker. She found, as a suggestive example, that the Lord Chamberlain uses *ye/you* 20 times (5/15) in six scenes (four traditionally ascribed to Fletcher, two to Shakespeare), as follows: I. iii. 0/2 (*Fl.*; C); I. iv, 1/4 (*Fl.*; C); II. ii, 0/1 (*Fl.*; C);

II. iii, 0/5 (*Sh.*; C); III. ii, 1-203, 0/3 (*Sh.*; B); V. iii, 4/0 (*Fl.*; C).[23] Since Compositor C set all the passages but one, the Lord Chamberlain's use of *ye/you* may be said almost certainly to represent the form used in the printer's copy, where, presumably, it represented the author's intention; and his use of *you* almost everywhere — in passages written (traditionally) by both Shakespeare and Fletcher — may be said to reflect his character as it is expressed in different situations.

Because of the "violence" of the contrast, the Lord Chamberlain's use of 4 *ye*'s and no *you*'s in V. iii is indeed striking, and it should be born in mind in considering Hoy's concluding remarks on Acts III and IV: "Perhaps we can best appreciate this distinction" — between "isolated clusters" and "periodic occurrence" — "when we move from Act IV of *Henry VIII,* where I am convinced the traces of Fletcher that are discernible are mere interpolations, to the last three scenes of Act V, of which I am equally convinced he is the sole author. These, together with III, 1, constitute his strongest claim to a share in the play. With V, 2-4 we are back in the presence of Compositor X[C] once more, and the traces of *ye* become much stronger: 12 in V. 2 (as against 42 *you*'s), 7 in V. 3 (13 *you*'s), 6 in V. 4 (3 *you*'s)" (p. 81). I don't propose to comment in detail on the 54 *ye/you*'s in V. ii, but it ought to be noted that the scene is formal and ceremonial, for the most part, and the *ye*'s are here, as elsewhere, clustered — in emotional utterances: Cranmer uses 3 (of the 12) in line 147, and Henry uses 5 in lines 176-181, for example. The linguistic evidence of *ye/you* is, according to Hoy's principles, stronger for interpolation than for Fletcher's sole authorship here as it is in Acts III and IV, and so it is in V. iii-iv. In scene iii, the Porter uses 3 *ye*'s (and 5 *you*'s) in nine lines (1-3, 5-10), and the Lord Chamberlain uses the other 4 in lines 77-85, where, in a state of great excitement, he is condemning the Porter and his man for not being better able to control the people clamoring to see the christening of Elizabeth. In Scene iv, Cranmer uses a *ye* in line 8 and Henry the other 5 *ye*'s in lines 13 and 69-73. It is surely clear here why Foakes says that the usage of *ye* in the play is "not Fletcherian enough" (p. xx); indeed it is not. And if the use of *ye per se* is not very strong evidence of Fletcher's hand in the play, since he seems to have a general preference for the form, the clustering of *ye*'s is not much stronger evidence of interpolation, especially when there seem to be contextual reasons for the use. At any rate, the same clustering in scenes whose sole Fletcherian authorship Hoy doubts is equally in evidence in V. ii-iv, of which Hoy is "convinced he is the sole author."

Aside from considerations of linguistic evidence, I must say that the attribution of the "Porter Scene" (V. iii) to Fletcher has always mystified me. Strictures on "parallelography" notwithstanding, and "impressionism" conceded, this scene seems distinctly Shakespearean — more pervasively and directly than even the *Shakespearean* use of *ye* would suggest. That there is, or might be, a Shakespearean use of *ye* — however infrequent it might be — is hardly to be seen in either Hoy's discussion of *Henry VIII* or his "Linguistic Tables for Unaided Plays by Shakespeare" (p. 88), which include only nine plays, none of them a History play.[24] The Porter scene in *Macbeth* may be taken for granted as an obvious parallel and potential model (as Schoenbaum might remind us, though it was first printed in 1623), but in *Henry IV, Part 1* there are equally striking—and less obvious— parallels with parts of the Porter scene in *Henry VIII,* and also, for example, in one scene alone—II. ii (106 lines)—13 *ye*'s against 7 *you*'s, both widely, *and* significantly, distributed. Compare the opening lines of *Henry VIII,* V. iii (with passing note taken of the "ale and cakes" of line 9), especially the intermixture of *ye* and *you* and "Belong to th' gallows and be hang'd *ye* rogue" (ll. 5-6), with Falstaff's "Whew! A plague upon *you* all, give me my horse, *you* rogues, give me my horse and be hanged! . . . What a plague mean *ye* to colt me thus? . . . Hang thyself in thine own heir-apparent garters!" (*1H4* II. ii. 28-30, 36-37, 42; New Arden edition, ed. A. R. Humphreys, 1965).

The most telling Shakespeareanism of *Henry VIII,* V. iii, however, is to be seen in the varied and vivid "characterization" of the nose of "a fellow somewhat near the door" (ll. 38-49), which, though it uses few of the same terms, is intimately akin to Falstaff's imprecatory paean on Bardolph's nose (*1H4,* III. iii. 22-49), a "parallel" that seems something more which I do not recall seeing noted:[25]

> *Falstaff.*   Do thou amend thy face, and I'll amend my life: thou
>   art our admiral, thou bearest the lantern in the poop, but 'tis
>   in the nose of thee: thou art the Knight of the Burning Lamp.
> *Bardolph.* Why, Sir John, my face does you no harm.
> *Falstaff.*   No, I'll be sworn, I make as good use of it as many a
>   man doth of a death's-head, or a *memento mori.* I never see
>   thy face but I think upon hell-fire, and Dives that lived in
>   purple: for there he is in his robes, burning, burning. If thou
>   wert any way given to virtue, I would swear by thy face: my
>   oath should be "By this fire, that's God's angel!" But thou art
>   altogether given over; and wert indeed, but for the light in thy
>   face, the son of utter darkness. When thou ran'st up Gad's Hill
>   in the night to catch my horse, if I did not think thou hadst
>   been an *ignis fatuus,* or a ball of wildfire, there's no purchase
>   in money. O, thou art a perpetual triumph, an everlasting
>   bonfire-light! Thou hast saved me a thousand marks in links
>   and torches, walking with thee in the night betwixt tavern
>   and tavern: but the sack that thou hast drunk me would have
>   bought me lights as good cheap at the dearest chandler's in
>   Europe. I have maintained that salamander of yours with fire
>   any time this two and thirty years, God reward me for it!
> *Bardolph.* 'Sblood, I would my face were in your belly!
> *Falstaff.*   God-a-mercy! so should I be sure to be heartburnt.
>   *(1H4, III. iii. 23-49)*
> *Man.* The spoons will be the bigger sir: there is a fellow some-
>   what near the door, he should be a brazier by his face, for o'
>   my conscience twenty of the dog-days now reign in's nose; all
>   that stand about him are under the line, they need no other

> penance: that fire-drake did I hit three times on the head, and
> three times was his nose discharg'd against me; he stands
> there like a mortar-piece to blow us. There was a haber-
> dasher's wife of small wit near him, that rail'd upon me till
> her pink'd porringer fell off her head, for kindling such a
> combustion in the state. I miss'd the meteor once, and hit
> that woman . . . .   *(H8, V. iii. 38-49)*

If we admit Shakespeare's tendency to paraphrase but not much to quote himself, the very differences, combined with what may be called a Shakespearean way with the "plurisignative dramatic conceit," suggest Shakespeare's strong hand in V. iii of *Henry VIII*; certainly the imaginativeness and complexity of the series of linked metaphors are not characteristic of Fletcher's work. The case for Shakespeare's authorship of V. iii certainly seems to me strong enough to impose a considerable onus of disproof upon advocates of Fletcher's authorship.

Hoy's general conclusions on the authorship of *Henry VIII* rest partly on linguistic and partly on non-linguistic "evidence." He deprives Fletcher of his traditional authorship of some scenes (II. i-ii, III. ii. *post* 203, IV. i-ii) because "there are no convincing traces of Fletcher's syntactic or rhetorical practices in the[se] scenes[,] in which the linguistic evidence suggests mere Fletcherian interpolation" (p. 82). I have tried to show that the linguistic evidence does not strongly suggest even Fletcherian *interpolation*. Immediately before the passage just quoted, Hoy asserts that, "finally, the best non-linguistic evidence for Fletcher's presence in *Henry VIII* (evidence which makes it possible, I think, to view the *ye*'s of the Folio text as valid signs of his presence) is all contained in the six scenes (I, 3-4; III, 1; V, 2-4) which, as the linguistic evidence implies, are wholly his." Here it is to be noted that the implications of the "linguistic evidence" are only as sound, apparently, as the Fletcherianism they acquire by association with the "non-linguistic evidence" of "syntactic or rhetorical practices," of which Hoy cites examples. But Hoy's first two examples of Fletcherian style in *Henry VIII*—"This night he makes a supper, and a great one" (I. iii. 52) and "O, very mad, exceeding mad, in love too" (I. iv. 28)—do not seem to me very strikingly differential, despite his explanatory assertions about "Fletcherian structure" and "the repetition with different modifiers, and the use of 'too,' [which] is typically Fletcherian" (p. 82). Compare, for example, "I heard a humming, And that a strange one too" (*Tmp.* II. i. 318), which *may* be an imitation of a Fletcherian stylistic mannerism but has never been thought non-Shakespearean. Hoy goes on to cite other—stronger—examples of the Fletcherian style, and these are not so easily discounted. But neither, without the support they seem to have in other kinds of evidence, are they very convincing. But they ought to be noted.

Of the third line of (III. i. 50-53)

> Noble lady,
> I am sorry my integrity should breed,
> And service to his majesty and you,
> So deep suspicion, where all faith was meant,

Hoy comments, "I would submit that there is no stronger evidence for Fletcher's presence in *Henry VIII* than the occurrence in the play of this particular syntactic arrangement"—that is, separation of the elements of a compound subject by an intervening verb phrase;[26] and he cites parallels from six plays by Fletcher to substantiate the assertion. One cannot, and for the present purpose need not, dismiss this kind of parallel as of questionable authorial significance, but *general* rhetorical parallels in Shakespeare—in which the expected syntactical progression is dramatically interrupted and then resumed—spring to mind readily enough, as, for example, in *Othello, IV.* i. 251-256, where Othello punctuates syntactical fragments of address to Lodovico with laconic asides to Desdemona. This is admittedly not quite the same thing as Hoy has in mind, but if "there is no stronger evidence for Fletcher's presence in *Henry VIII*" than this, then it would seem that this had better be stronger than it is.

When Hoy finally concludes that "the syntactic and rhetorical practices" that the six scenes "display, taken together with the linguistic evidence of the Folio text, establish his claim to a share in the play's authorship" (p. 85), one is bound to reply that the claim rests on unstable foundations. And when he adds, "this will never be granted by those who are bent on viewing *Henry VIII* as entirely Shakespeare's, but the burden of proof is on those who would deny Fletcher's presence there," one may reasonably reply that "bent" carries a burden of manifestly excessive weight whichever way it inclines, that if leverage is applied without bias the case remains open, and that they also serve who only stand and wait. R. A. Foakes's formidable case for the artistic unity of *Henry VIII* (ed. 1964, pp. xxxix-lxiv) does not "prove" single authorship, but its authorial implications cannot be lightly brushed aside. And even if they could be, the critical case would remain well made and worth the making.

Perhaps a summary comment is in order. I have tried to demonstrate that the linguistic "evidence" of *ye/you* in several of the scenes Hoy allows to Fletcher neither supports the non-linguistic evidence, as it cannot if it is not itself evidence, nor can be viewed as constituting "valid signs of his presence," because of its occurrence in the same scenes where ratios with a high enough proportion of *ye*'s to seem to support Fletcher can be explained as due to the same dramatic considerations that inferentially determine the use of *ye* in Shakespeare's scenes—including one in *Henry IV, Part 1*. In the first article in his series on the Beaumont and Fletcher canon,[27] Hoy wrote:

> Of the linguistic forms cited in the tables below, *ye* is much the
> most important for purposes of authorial evidence. Since Flet-
> cher employs the form as both subject and object, direct or
> indirect, in either singular or plural number, the rate of its
> occurrence in his unaided plays is very high. In the fifteen
> unaided plays of Massinger, the form occurs but twice [p. 142].
> . . . To summarize the chief features of the linguistic patterns
> of Fletcher and Massinger: *the Fletcherian pattern is one which*

> is marked above all by the constant use of ye [p. 144; italics mine].

The "average occurrence per play" of ye is 322—versus 71 occurrences in *Henry VIII*, which is, however, far higher than the average occurrence of ye in any Shakespearean play investigated by Hoy. It is easy to see why Hoy (reasonably) ignores the potential rhetorical uses of ye/you in Fletcher and Massinger, since, apparently, Fletcher almost invariably used ye and Massinger practically never used it; the niceties of rhetoric here would appear to be irrelevant, for Hoy's purposes.

But rhetorical considerations are not irrelevant in a study of *Henry VIII*, and I think it is not excessive to suggest that the proper use of any order of literary evidence ought to include, at least experimentally, a closer scrutiny of context than is directly or necessarily involved in assignment to such easily quantifiable categories as usually underlie analyses of distribution and frequency: a nullity is no more, raised to an exponential power, and a "linguistic preference" is something else if its expression is prominently a function of context and it sometimes gives way to formal variation apparently on the same account. One need not be persuaded that Hoy is entirely wrong about the authorship of *Henry VIII* in order not to be convinced that he is right. The evidence remains. And so, I think, does much of the problem, so far as the Fletcherian solution is concerned.

The University of Minnesota

NOTES:

(1) Samuel Schoenbaum, *Internal Evidence and Elizabethan Dramatic Authorship: An Essay in Literary History and Method* (Northwestern University Press, 1966), pp. xx + 281. $7.50.

(2) R. W. Dent, *RN*, XIX (1966), 396-399; W. T. Jewkes, *SCN*, XXIV (1966), 60-61; Arthur Sherbo, *JEGP*, LXVI (1967), 127-129; anonymous, *TLS*, August 25, 1966, p. 761; and M. A. Shaaber, "Recent Studies in Elizabethan and Jacobean Drama," *SEL*, VII (1967), 351-352. The thoughtful reviews by Dent and Sherbo, especially, are well worth consultation.

(3) *The Composition of Shakespeare's Plays* (1953) and *The Case for Shakespeare's Authorship of the Famous Victories* (1961), respectively.

(4) Cf. Bertram: "many editorial references to the same letter down to the present day speak solemnly of its 'independent' confirmation of Spedding's thesis. Perhaps the present writer is blinded by prejudice, but he fails to see why Hickson's collection of ditto-marks should have been allowed to pass as scholarly evidence for so many years" (p. 145n).

(5) Later, s.v. "Imagistic Tests," he cites Edward A. Armstrong's employment of image-clusters as a criterion of authorship, remarking that Armstrong "got down to cases only to the extent of suggesting that Shakespeare's share was small in *Henry VIII*," pp. 187-188; Armstrong's *Shakespeare's Imagination* was published in 1946.

(6) See Hoy, "The Shares of Fletcher and his Collaborators in the Beaumont and Fletcher Canon (VII)," *SB*, XV (1962), 71-90, and the discussion in section VI below. Hoy's study of *Henry VIII* is sane and intelligent, and despite the fact that "the case for Fletcher's presence . . . based on the widespread use of ye in the text of the 1623 folio" (p. 71) is decidedly faulty as presented. I am not persuaded that his conclusions about division are absolutely wrong; indeed, the inci-

dental reasons he gives, though perhaps more "impressionistic" in Schoenbaum's terms, seem more convincing than the statistical "linguistic evidence."

(7) Knight, *The Crown of Life* (1948); Craig, *An Interpretation of Shakespeare* (1948); Kermode, "What is Shakespeare's *Henry VIII* About?", *DUJ*, n.s. IX (1948), 48-55; Mincoff, *SQ*, XII (1961), 239-260.

(8) Internal quotation from MacD. P. Jackson, "Affirmative Particles in *Henry VIII*," *N&Q*, n.s., IX (1962), 372-374.

(9) Foakes, ed. *King Henry VIII* (1964), p. xxvii; Hoy, *SB*, XV (1962), 71-88, esp. 79.

(10) Bertram's earlier essay, "*Henry VIII*: The Conscience of the King," is in *In Defense of Reading*, ed. Reuben A. Brower and Richard Poirier (New York, 1962). The other articles referred to are: John Wasson, "In Defense of *King Henry VIII*," *RS*, XXXII (1964), 261-276; C. H. Hobday, "Why the Sweets Melted: A Study in Shakespeare's Imagery," *SQ*, XVI (1965), 3-17, esp. 14-15; Howard Felperin, "Shakespeare's *Henry VIII*: History as Myth," *SEL*, VI (1966), 225-246; and—which I have not been able to see—Horst Oppel, "Shakespeare oder Fletcher? Die Bankett-Szene in *Henry VIII* als Kriterium der Verfasserschaft," in *Abhandlungen der Akad. der Wissenschaften und der Literatur, usw.* (Jhg. 1965, No. 7), pp. 475-508.

(11) Graham Hough, *An Essay on Criticism* (1966), p. 163.

(12) See *The English History Play in the Age of Shakespeare* (1957), pp. 289ff.

(13) Sherbo, "The Uses and Abuses of Internal Evidence," *BNYPL*, LXIII (1959), 5-22; Sherbo reiterates his views in his review of *Internal Evidence* (see n. 2).

(14) See, for example, Alvar Ellegard, *A Statistical Method for Determining Authorship: The Junius Letters, 1769-1772* (Goeteborg, 1962), and, in Jacob Leed, ed. *The Computer and Literary Style* (Kent, Ohio, 1966), Sally Yeates Sedelow and Walter A. Sedelow, Jr., "A Preface to Computational Stylistics" [1964]; Ivor S. Francis, "An Exposition of a Statistical Approach to the *Federalist* Dispute"; and Louis T. Milic, "Unconscious Ordering in the Prose of Swift" (and see the review in *CHum*, I [May 1967], 252-260). For a disciplined, subtle, and searching empirical approach to critical stylistics, see Ralph Cohen, "The Augustan Mode in English Poetry," *ECS*, I (1967), 3-32.

(15) See "Bibliographical Clues in Collaborate Plays," *The Library*, 4th ser., XIII (1932), 21-48.

(16) See Edmund A. Bowles, ed. *Computers in Humanistic Research: Readings and Perspectives* (Englewood Cliffs, N. J., 1967), "the direct result of a series of six regional conferences throughout the country, which were devoted to the role of the computer in humanistic research."

(17) See p. 358 and ref. cit. in n. 6 above.

(18) See Williams, "New Approaches to Textual Problems in Shakespeare," *SB*, VIII (1956), 10. On Compositor C's work on *Henry VIII*, see Charlton Hinman, *The Printing and Proof-Reading of the First Folio of Shakespeare*, 2 vols. (Oxford, 1963), esp. II, 212-252.

(19) Hoy's count of 352 occurrences is not significantly different; it is of some interest that, as he notes, "the percentage of *ye*'s to *you*'s" in the 1647 Folio "is the highest to be found in any play of Fletcher's unaided authorship," whereas in Edward Knight's scribal transcript "the play would present the lowest percentage of *ye*'s to *you*'s in all Fletcher" (*SB*, VIII [1956], 139).

(20) Written for a course in Advanced Shakespeare given at the University of Minnesota in the Summer of 1967. I quote Mrs. Davidson with her permission, and I have occasion to refer to her paper again below.

(21) The alternative use of *ye* and *you* also seems sometimes to be phonetically determined; and, in I.iv.86 (quoted above) and III.i.145, *ye* is certainly intended to be elided with the following

"[h]ave," as "y'" (used, for example, in V.iii.69 and 79, also composed by Compositor C) would more clearly indicate. At some points, e.g., III.ii.244, a case for Compositor B's interference could perhaps be made on the grounds that one would expect to find "Y'" or "Ye" in place of the "You," which must be elided with the following "have."

(22) The general parallel between this scene and "The Arraignment of Vittoria" (III. ii) in Webster's *The White Devil* (1612) is not less interesting and striking than the following individual parallel with the lines of Katherine quoted above, and Wolsey's antecedent *"Tanta est erga te mentis integritas Regina serenissima—"* (ll. 40-41), would suggest:

> Lawyer.   *Domine judex converte oculos in hanc pestem mulierum*
> *corruptissimam.*
> Vittoria.   What's he?
> Francisco.   A lawyer, that pleads against you.
> Vittoria.   Pray my lord, let him speak his usual tongue—
> I'll make no answer else.
> Francisco.   Why you understand Latin.
> Vittoria.   I do sir, but amongst this auditory
> Which come to hear my cause, the half or more
> May be ignorant in't.
> Monticelso.   Go on sir:—
> Vittoria.   By your favour,
> I will not have my accusation clouded
> In a strange tongue: all this assembly
> Shall hear what you can charge me with.

See the Revels edition, ed. John Russell Brown, 2nd ed. (1966), III. ii. 10-20; Brown notes that Katherine, in *Henry VIII*, "also insists on English for proceedings with her judges" (p. 65, l. 13n).

(23) Since *A Complete and Systematic Concordance to the Works of Shakespeare*, ed. Marvin Spevack (Am Dammtor, Germany: George Olms, 1967-69), contains "a concordance to each character," scholars and critics are happily being spared this kind of drudgery—where archaic forms have not been lost through modernization; the Clarendon Press concordances to the plays of the First Folio, edited by Trevor Howard-Hill, of course retain the archaic forms.

(24) The plays—evidently selected as representative more-or-less "late" plays—are (in Hoy's order) *Tmp., WT, Cym., Tim., Cor., Ant., Tro., MM,* and *AWW*. The Tables do not include counts for *you*, and the plays listed have decidedly low counts for *ye*; not an intentionally "loaded" list, I'm sure, but a misleading one, all the same.

(25) For an important and perceptive study of Shakespeare's way in different dramatic contexts with essentially the same figurative matter, see the article by C. H. Hobday cited in n. 10 above.

(26) Hoy's description; the syntax in rhetorical terms is perhaps a combination of mesozeugma and synchysis, in which we have one element of a compound subject, then the verb, then the second element of the subject, and last the direct object. As Hoy notes, Foakes comments on the apparent "dramatic intention" and manifest dramatic effects of the phrasing, which troubled Singer enough to make him transpose lines 52-53 (see ed. *Henry VIII*, p. 93, n. on III. i. 52-53).

(27) "The Shares of Fletcher and His Collaborators in the Beaumont and Fletcher Canon (I)," *SB*, VIII (1956), 129-146.

Measure For Measure as Royal Entertainment by Josephine Waters Bennett. Columbia University Press, 1966. Pp. x + 208. $6.00. Reviewer: Roy Battenhouse.

Measure for Measure was the play selected to open the Christmastide festivities at White-hall in 1604. Professor Bennett believes it was planned and written especially for this occasion, and that Shakespeare himself acted the leading role of the Duke. She reviews, as others have done, various of the play's motifs which echo ideas King James had set forth in his Basilikon Doron. The playwright, she argues, assumed the posture of pupil to his monarch and entertained him with "the image which King James instructed his subjects to see in him." Through the role of Duke, moreover, Shakespeare was displaying his own skills as actor-playwright by producing, in Act V, a miniature five-act play within the play. Here, as the King's puppet, he was amusing his royal auditor with a witty and clever manipulation of puppet-characters and at the same time epitomizing, within the theatre's make-believe world, the King's concept of himself as God-ruler within the real world. Politely Shakespeare reduced his own role's title to duke instead of king, Mrs. Bennett explains, and furthermore he heightened the artificiality of his story in order to encourage James to feel superior to the humorous tour de force of the comedy. "King James must, surely, have been delighted with this stage Duke."

This approach offers a rather attractive way of rehabilitating the play for present-day esteem. Yet it may be questioned in a few respects. Can we quite accept, for instance, Mrs. Bennett's contention that the play, from beginning to end, is "based on absurdity, like The Mikado"? Can a play be basically absurd and yet be, as she elsewhere comments, "a nativity play, but a highly sophisticated one"? I would fully agree as to its high sophistication, but would correlate this with a "mystery" in Christmas which has an underlying order of divine reasonableness. Mrs. Bennett has rightly recognized in the play various "echoes" of the pattern of man's fall and redemption, and the fact that this "archetype," as one appropriate to the seasonal celebration of Christ's coming, was being intentionally used by Shakespeare to provide a "serious core of meaning for the wiser sort's after-meditation." But how thoroughly is the archetype influencing the shape of Shakespeare's literal plot? Not enough is said on this point. Perhaps out of fear of being labelled an allegorist, Mrs. Bennett remarks that Shakespeare's method is "at the opposite pole from allegory." If all allegory must be of Spenser's kind, her dictum is defensible. Yet can there not be another kind—allegory as a dimension of parabolic implication within a fully human and literal story? This more sophisticated sense of the play—developed by critics such as Coghill, Bryant, and myself—is drawn on in part by Mrs. Bennett but without integrating it carefully with the total shape of Shakespeare's plot. The theme of the play in her view is simply the testing of Angelo and Isabella, for which the Duke uses a Friar's disguise as "a comic device," and then as an afterthought brings in Mariana as a "clever ruse" for manipulating a happy ending. Omitted from this reading is any comment on the archetypal significance of the "monstrous ransom" proposed by Angelo, or on the mythic implications of the bed-trick by which the Friar meets that ransom with holy craft. Unmentioned also is the Duke's announced intent to "Visit both prince and people" (the motif which is most basic to Christmas) and the "grave and unwrinkled" quality of the Duke's love.

Furthermore, can we be sure that Shakespeare "did not attempt to advise or instruct" King James but, on the contrary, "took instruction from him" as his puppeteer? Did James approve of Friars? Is a Friar's way of preparing for a merciful denouement the way which James had been advocating? We find Mrs. Bennett saying that the Duke "embodies the

Divine mercy which watches over man" (which must certainly mean that he is allegorical in *some* sense); and she supposes that Shakespeare found warrant for the Duke's Friar-role in James' advice that a king should be the "naturall father" to his subjects and a "loving nourish-Father to the Church." But let us note how Shakespeare construes this. Does not his Friar act as a *super*natural father—one who undertakes to nourish the church only after taking instruction first from Friar Thomas, and who mentions later the Holy See as sanction for his role? How might James have reacted to such a re-construction of his ideas in the *Basilikon Doron*? Does it not imply some playful recasting of his Divine right theory— perhaps in the direction of improving on it? Even in a fiction, Shakespeare's portrait may have seemed to James too enigmatic to be wholly to his taste. He never asked later, so far as we know, for a repeat-performance of *Measure for Measure*. Whose measure, actually, was being offered—or taken?

Indiana University

The Jacobean and Caroline Stage by Gerald Eades Bentley. The Clarendon Press, 1968. Vol. VI, pp. xii + 310; Vol. VII, pp. vi + 391. $9.25 each. *Reviewer: James G. McManaway.*

The long awaited sixth and seventh volumes bring to completion *The Jacobean and Caroline Stage,* to which Gerald Eades Bentley has given some forty years of his life. The first volume was published in 1940, but Bentley had begun in London at least a decade earlier on this continuation of Chambers' *The Elizabethan Stage*. Comparison of the two works is inevitable, but it will not lead to the verdict that one author is a better scholar than the other. The conditions under which the two men worked were entirely different. Chambers seems to have done much of his reading and planning as he traveled about the country in the performance of his educational duties. His intention was to collect all that had been published and then to evaluate it, order it, and reinterpret it. In the nature of the case, he worked largely with secondary materials. If an earlier scholar had used a document or literary manuscript and quoted from it, it seems likely that Chambers was ordinarily restricted to what had been quoted or summarized, for he would have lacked the opportunity to hunt out all the originals and, perchance, recognize significances not hitherto perceived. He must have had enormous industry, extraordinary patience and pertinacity, and remarkable judiciousness to organize the mass of data with which he grappled. *The Elizabethan Stage* deserves all the acclaim it received upon publication, and it is still indispensable.

Bentley worked under conditions never possible for his predecessor. Between 1923 and 1940, a new world of scholarship had come into being. There were new and more numerous learned journals than before; annual bibliographies; and analytical card catalogues in university and other libraries, which had become more numerous and far richer in primary and secondary materials than in Chambers' heyday. The tools of scholarship had been increased by the development of photostat and microfilm cameras. There were foundations to aid scholars by the award of fellowships. And great new concentrations of manuscripts and books became available in such endowed libraries as the Morgan, the Newberry, the Huntington, and the Folger. There were also new standards of scholarship. *The Jacobean and Caroline Stage* speaks with magisterial authority, because its author has worked from primary materials, supplemented on occasion by secondary books of scholarly excellence. I do not claim for him that he personally examined every document that is cited; in fact, he tells us that

378

The Annals of Jacobean and Caroline Theatrical affairs in volume vii and the discussions of the Court theatres in volume vi repeatedly make use of the Declared Accounts of the Treasury of the Chamber. In 1957 Professor F. P. Wilson very kindly loaned me his transcripts of dramatic entries in these accounts, and all the extracts I use were taken originally from his copy. When the Malone Society published these transcripts four or five years later in volume vi of the Collections, *I simply checked the quotations I had used in the Public Record Office and changed the citations to the Malone Society Collections.* [Preface, VI, vii. I supply the italics.]

The quoted sentences are typical of Bentley's forthrightness and a measure of his standards of accuracy. (It may be remarked parenthetically that some scholar of ambition, intelligence, and industry equal to Bentley's should be starting a new *Elizabethan Stage.*)

Volume VI gives a history of the theaters, public and private, Court, and projected, and summarizes what is known of their location, size and shape, capacity, and methods of staging. The text was complete late in 1962; so it cannot take into account more recent books, such as Irwin Smith's important *Shakespeare's Blackfriars Theatre* (1964) or Sidney Fisher's lecture, *An Engineer Looks at Shakespeare* (1967). The latter challenges the genuineness of a manuscript from which Bentley quotes for the demolition of the Second Blackfriars (VI, 42), Salisbury Court (VI, 114), Fortune (VI, 177), Second Globe (VI, 200), and Hope (VI, 213-14). The theatrical section of this anonymous piece, formerly Phillipps MS. 11613 and now Folger Shakespeare Library V.b.275, was published by F. J. Furnivall in *The Academy*, XXII (28 October 1882), 315, and again in The Shakespeare Library, *Shakespeare's England. Harrison's Description of England in Shakespeare's Youth* . . . Part IV. The Supplement, §2 (London: Chatto and Windus, 1909), pp. 197-214 (the text relating to the theaters is on p. 212). When Professor Lucyle Hook used the portion of the manuscript relating to the Curtain (*SQ*, XIII, 131, 138), she echoed the cautionary warning in the Folger card catalogue that the document may be a Collier forgery. Mr. Fisher is more positive. He states (p. 21) that Collier published the document in 1844 [it appears in note 6 on pp. ccxli-ccxlii of Collier's Life of Shakespeare in *The Works*, vol. I (1844)] and adds: "This account [of the destruction of the Globe in 1644] has long been suspect, and is now found to be surely false. In one of his views of London after the Great Fire of 1666, Wenceslas Hollar . . . shows the Globe standing. . . ." Fisher reproduces a portion of the Hollar view and then cites Mrs. Piozzi's statement of 1819 that she saw the ruins of the Globe in 1767 and also Chalmers' report in 1797 that the manager of the Barclay and Perkins brewery (formerly Thrale's) had seen the ruins. If the MS is indeed a Collier forgery, he was extraordinarily lucky, for no detail cited by Bentley about any of the five theaters named contravenes the details of the manuscript.

Fisher's lecture rejects Hotson's identification as the Theatre and the Curtain of two buildings depicted in the University of Utrecht Library's unique print of London and argues persuasively that what Hotson calls the Curtain is the Theatre and that a third building is the Curtain (pp. 17-20). He is convinced that the Globe stood on a site about 280 feet to the east of the location generally accepted today (pp. 21-23).

In Volume VII, two appendices discuss Lenten performances and Sunday performances in London theaters and at Court. Appendix C, compiled at the suggestion of Sir Walter Greg, gives "Annals of Jacobean and Caroline Theatrical Affairs" (pp. 16-128). These three sections are invaluable, but their utility is as nothing in comparison with the "General Index for Volumes I to VII" which fills pp. 129-390. This is printed in double columns of 59 lines.

Under the heading, Players, there are 50 specific subject headings. The list of characters in plays occupies 13½ columns; Theatres, 7¾ columns; and London, 6 columns. The Index is a gold mine.

For the sake of making the second printing even more accurate than the first—and only for this purpose—I list a few errors and typographical mistakes. On VI, 135, in line 11 from the bottom, read "Peter Heylin" instead of "Barton Holyday"; VI, 142, read "w^{ch}" instead of "wth" at the end of line 19; VI, 207, line 10 from bottom, not "forest" but "∫orest"; VI, 47, next to last line, not "that" but "than"; VI, 74, line 21, not "say" but "says"; VI, 117, the point is omitted at the end of note 1; VII, 130b, s.v. "Affezionati," not "Comedia" but "Commedia." In VI, 220, line 3, one would expect "message" instead of "messuage," but the word is spelled "messuage" in *M.S.C.*

The Folger Shakespeare Library

Bibliography and Textual Criticism by Fredson Bowers. The Lyell Lectures, Oxford, Trinity term, 1959. The Clarendon Press, 1964. Pp. xii + 207. 35s.

On Editing Shakespeare by Fredson Bowers. University Press of Virginia, 1966. Pp. ix + 210. $2.45. *Reviewer: T. H. Howard-Hill.*

If textual bibliography is experiencing "a fresh upward movement of surprising dimensions," as Professor Bowers remarked during his recent lecture to the Bibliographical Society, London, there can be little doubt that much of the impetus of recent years must be credited to Professor Bowers himself. By precept and example he has done more than any living scholar to stimulate the deep analysis of bibliographical problems and fruitful discussions of principles and practice which have made modern bibliography at once so demanding and so rewarding. Professor Bowers' own direct contributions to the advance of Shakespearian bibliographical scholarship have been small, and rarely definitive, but his influence upon the development of bibliography (in its major forms) could scarcely have been greater. That the textual criticism of Shakespeare has not made the great leap forward that might have been expected (for which Professor Bowers has sometimes been held personally responsible) lies not so much in the nature of the claims he has made for bibliographical method as in the reluctance of scholars to practice, under the guidance of his writings, a discipline in which effort, results, and prospects of certainty are all too often disproportionate. To the layman Professor Bowers is perceived most clearly in his role as advocate of the proper application of bibliographical method and as a rigorous, vigorous, upholder of the appropriate analytical standards. Greg, Pollard, and McKerrow had earlier largely determined the materials of bibliographical analysis and delimited the areas of their application, but the rationalisation of their use, and the high standards which should govern the deployment of bibliographical tools and argument owe most to Professor Bowers. The Rosenbach lectures, *On Editing Shakespeare and the Elizabethan Dramatists* (1955), the Sandars lectures, *Textual and Literary Criticism* (1959), the Lyell lectures, *Bibliography and Textual Criticism* (1964) and numerous articles and monographs testify to his preoccupation with the nature of his discipline and to his pre-eminence as the populariser of bibliographical method. This is not merely to be pejorative for many of his writings have been properly directed as much to the bibliographically-naive as to the initiated.

Professor Bowers' pre-occupation with the relationship of bibliographical method to textual criticism, and with the principles and practice of editing is exemplified by each of the works under review. To a large extent he has occupied ground of his own seizing and so has fallen under fire from both flanks, being assailed both by literary critics for the seemingly-restrictive bibliographical base of his textual criticism, and by bibliographers for the literary or textual orientation of his descriptive or analytical researches. The dominant impression from *Bibliography and Textual Criticism*, however, is that Professor Bowers is rather more concerned with the nature of bibliography as a discipline than with the problems to which bibliographical method may be applied. In pressing his often justified claims for bibliographical analysis he appears to neglect the possibilities of attaining various ends by different means: there are many ways to skin a cat. Not all textual problems are bibliographical problems: if the scholar's objective is to resolve a crux rather than merely to perform a disciplinary rite, he will need to pass beyond bibliography (and the sphere of Professor Bowers's interest and influence) to historical, literary and philological considerations. In rebuttal one should in fairness add that Professor Bowers' manifest concern is *only* with those problems for which bibliographical analysis has, or pretends to have, some relevance. But very often in *Bibliography and Textual Criticism* one finds him deploring not so much the outcome but the way in which the game has been played. His frequent admonishment of Dover Wilson for failing to apply techniques and knowledge which often only the work of later bibliographers has developed leads one to reflect to what extent the New Cambridge edition would have won Professor Bowers' favour for its critical emendations had its editor not so often attempted to justify his emendations on bibliographical grounds. On another subject Professor Bowers comments, "It is small wonder that the discipline has sometimes got a bad name when guesses from false evidence masquerade...as scholarship" (p.127). The real point here is not whether bibliography is highly regarded or not but whether the "guess," bibliographical evidence being ambiguous, is a good one: good guesses, alas, can arise from false evidence without depending on it. Until everything is known of the bibliographical determinants of literary texts—a condition unlikely to be realised—informed eclecticism, as Professor Bowers recognises, is the last refuge and the supreme test of an editor.

The definition of analytical bibliography and its relationship both to descriptive bibliography and textual criticism which is set out in the first chapter of *Bibliography and Textual Criticism* are sufficiently familiar from his earlier writings to need no summary here. The substance of the book is concerned with "the nature of the evidence on which textual bibliography operates, the logical forms of its reasoning, the techniques it uses, and the results it can achieve" (p.7), most extensively, with the degrees of confidence with which the bibliographer can come to conclusions from different types of bibliographical evidence, in varying situations. Undoubtedly, when the lectures were delivered, Professor Bowers' reflections were fresh and novel to many of his hearers. Five years passed to publication, during which time the volume of Professor Bowers' writings on these themes, and the consequent repetition, has been so extensive as to dull the reader's perception of what is new here. His comments on a host of particular bibliographical problems in many cases are neither made here for the first time nor arise from the author's own researches. Particularly, I find difficulty in deciding whether a simple text-book of logic would not better have served the novice in these studies, for although Professor Bowers writes of "bibliographical logic," reflection assures us that there is nothing peculiar to bibliographical evidence which demands a logical treatment different from that of other disciplines in order to obtain valid conclusions, whereas knowledge and understanding of bibliographical history and processes is yet so incomplete that the correctness of bibliographical conclusions is not assured, regardless of the validity of the arguments. In a sense, *Bibliography and Textual Criticism* is already dated and its simplistic discussion of method is unlikely to command these essays a permanent position in a literature already threatened by advances in the factual bases of bibliography. Nevertheless, the style is vigorous, the general position challenging, and the book will serve until Professor Bowers writes an extensive treatment of bibliographical and textual criticism. For that, unlikely to come in our lifetimes from as competent a source, posterity would be truly indebted.

Professor Bowers is not always observed following his own dicta: the evidence that Ralph Crane transcribed the copy for the various groups of Folio comedies mentioned in different combinations from time to time has not been examined with the rigor that his standards demand, and he should not—unless he has private evidence—state Crane's transcription as a fact, as he does on p.146 of *On Editing Shakespeare* in an argument of extreme dubiety. Indeed his ascription of the copy for F *Wiv.* to Crane's pen is held so strongly that it has blinded him to the inconsistency of his position where he states that F *Wiv.* derives from "a manuscript copied out . . . by . . . Crane" (p.108) and "this good text was type-set directly from the manuscript that the company furnished . . . this line of transmission gives us our best texts" (p.120). If Professor Bowers seriously maintains that a scribal transcript of a playhouse manuscript of as yet unknown character and provenance gives us our best texts, he were best to say so explicitly so less perceptive scholars can re-evaluate their positions. But, as he says in *Bibliography and Textual Criticism* (p.30) "bibliographical method has been abused . . . sometimes in cynicism when it is treated merely as one of the arts of persuasion." This comment might well apply to the skirmishes around the subject of F *R3* with J. K. Walton whose thesis, published in 1955, of a Q3 copytext for F *R3* was accepted by Sir Walter Greg—as Professor Bowers mentions—and by Bowers himself—as he does not. Since the retraction of his endorsement of Walton's view in *Shakespeare Quarterly*, Professor Bowers has seldom refused an opportunity to take up cudgels with Walton who has reciprocated in reviews in *Shakespeare Survey* and *Notes and Queries*. When two able bibliographers can neither agree on the facts of the case nor persuade the other to see the light, is it not clear that evidence sufficient to resolve the conflict is not available, and that to persist in unedifying debate is an abuse of "bibliographical method."

On Editing Shakespeare promises more humane studies and is familiar under the title *On Editing Shakespeare and the Elizabethan Dramatists*, first published in 1955. To the present reprint has been added "What Shakespeare wrote" from *Shakespeare Jahrbuch*, 1962, and "Today's Shakespeare Texts, and Tomorrow," from *Studies in Bibliography*, 1966, as "the simplest means of attempting an updating" (p.viii). Reviewing the first edition in *Shakespeare Quarterly*, Sir Walter Greg made strong comment both on infelicities and ambiguities of expression and various misrepresentations and misinterpretations, none of which has been corrected in the present edition. (Nor is it indexed.) It is a pity that Professor Bowers could not have undertaken a revision, or at least reprinted Greg's review in place of a popular and substantively repetitive article and another which is widely available in its original publication.

There is no need to go over the familiar ground of the earlier articles; there is some interest however in the article on Shakespearian editions, a subject which Professor Bowers has discussed earlier in "Principle and practice in the editing of early dramatic texts" in *Textual and Literary Criticism* (1959) and occasionally since in passing. After considering and dismissing the Cambridge edition of 1863-66, the Globe edition which still enjoys a regrettable vogue amongst the bibliographical illiterati, and more recent editions, faulty in conception, execution, or both, Professor Bowers passes to the contemplation of the editions of the future. He finds ready answer: "any reader who is concerned with the most accurate and intimate approach to Shakespeare will require a critically edited old-spelling text, not a modernized version that constantly draws a veil between him and the subtleties of the original" (p.164). Few reasonable readers would disagree, for who would suggest that Shakespearian scholars, unlike the students of Gawain, Chaucer, Dante and Goethe, should seek their primary inspiration in a modern rendition. That serious scholars must work from an edition which presents a text as close as possible in every significant aspect to that which Shakespeare wrote is so widely accepted that one must wonder why Professor Bowers has felt impelled to assert a view so widely disseminated both by himself and other scholars in other places. Although there is some interest in Professor Bowers's discussion of the form in which an old-spelling edition should be presented, the most pertinent considerations pertaining to the old/modern spelling question are essentially educational—when it is conceded that there should be an old-spelling edition at least for scholarly use—and these he touches on but briefly. It is not necessary for me to repeat the criticism of Professor Bowers' limited conception of what an edition is, so cogently expressed by Professor D. F. McKenzie in *The Library*, 1959, save to remark that on the evidence of Professor Bowers' recent writings it remains pertinent. (However, readers should refer again to Professor Bowers' letter concerning his Dekker edition, in *The Library*, December, 1955.) Professor Bowers takes little account of the literary and linguistic aspects of the editorial process: to him text and edition remain equivalent. The form of an old-spelling text is fairly clear, largely determined by the existing bibliographical materials and their proper deployment. The urgent questions are, at what level students can best be introduced to old-spelling texts (I believe with Professor Bowers that no undergraduate should find a properly edited old-spelling text too intimidating), what editorial apparatus in the form of textual discussion, glosses, and commentary is suitable for the various categories of reader, and how the modernising editors—for such there must be—can best deal with ambiguities in what from year to year becomes increasingly a process of translation. The rather special requirements of editions for the American market might also warrant closer examination. But these, though important pedagogically, are not bibliographical questions, and receive scant attention from Professor Bowers.

Finally, readers who are directly concerned with the type of editorial problem which Professor Bowers discusses may find some instruction in this salutary passage from *Bibliography and Textual Criticism* (p.67)—I quote exactly—"This is a distinction that needs repeating and repeating, Common experience shows the frequency of human error within the confines of a routine operation when the full intention was to carry out the routine." Perhaps it might usefully be used to replace as appropriate in Professor Bowers' future writings one of the examples of bibliographical solecisms and cases at point which, as for example *The Wild Gallant*, contribute to one's sense of dèjá vu on first looking into Professor Bowers' recent writings.

The University of Oxford

Education in Renaissance England by Kenneth Charlton. Routledge & Kegan Paul, 1965. Pp. xv + 317. $8.25.

Education and Society in Tudor England by Joan Simon. Cambridge University Press, 1966. Pp. xi + 452. $13.50. *Reviewer: Margaret Aston.*

The sixteenth century was a period in which education was as topical a subject as it has become in our own. An enormous amount of thought, writing and activity were devoted to educational theory and practice. More people, and many classes of people, were being educated in more ways. It was a time of educational boom and contemporaries, themselves well aware of this explosive expansion, saw and discussed it in its social context. There were justifications as well as fears of poor men's sons rising through learning to positions of influence; there was alarm at one moment of the gentry usurping the educational places intended for the poor, at another of their subverting the traditional position of the nobility. The generation which coined the term *upstart* and over-used the word *gentleman* was hyper-sensitive about the role of education in the commonwealth.

These two books, after introductory sections, both concentrate upon English educational developments in the sixteenth century, and there is therefore a certain amount of inevitable overlapping. Both necessarily start with treatments of humanist innovations; both describe the course of studies in schools, universities and inns of court; both consider the aim and content of the education of the gentleman, which became such a major preoccupation of sixteenth-century England. Yet despite their common ground there is such a fundamental difference of outlook, treatment and conclusion between the two works that they are more complementary than repetitive, and may well be read in conjunction.

Mr. Charlton's primary concern, as his title indicates, is to examine English education from the point of view of its assimilation of Italian humanist ideals. The first section of his book on "Origins," after sketching in the medieval background, succeeds in giving a fresh and stimulating survey of the "Renaissance Debate" and its translation into English society, particularly in the changed pattern of nobility to be found in Sir Thomas Elyot's *The Governour* and the works which followed. "The humanists' ideas of an educated gentleman engaging himself in affairs of State, having survived the transition from civic to princely Italy, moved on to England there to be translated into a monarchical milieu by Elyot and others." The next part of the book, concerned to see how far these ideas were realized in educational practice, takes the reader in turn into grammar schools, universities and inns of court (the examination of the last being fuller than Mrs. Simon's, and corrects her rather misleading statement, p. 19, that "English [came] into its own in pleadings at law"—as opposed to arguments in court—et the turn of the fourteenth century). In his description of the institutions of formal learning Mr. Charlton has much illuminating illustration from both precept and practice, but the center of his argument and probably the most informative (if rather over-burdened) part of his book lies in its third section, on "Informal Education." Here he treats of education in the family, the education of women, private tutors, foreign travel, and London lectureships, but above all devotes much attention to the flood of vernacular books on different subjects—music, foreign languages, classical translations, history, accounting, navigation, discovery, logarithms, farming, surveying. For Mr. Charlton it was through books, English books on this great variety of subjects, that English education was transformed in the sixteenth century, and that England absorbed the classical tradition. It was essentially a vocational, self-educative process, which largely took place outside the curricula of schools and formal ways of learning. Books, especially books in English, covered more ground and taught more people more subjects than could be approached in institutions. "The problem of communication and its solution by use of the vernacular and the printing press constitute, perhaps, the most important aspect of the history of education in Renaissance England." And in the author's thesis it was pre-eminently through the spate of printed classical translations that Renaissance learning penetrated into England. "It was through translations . . . that the classical heritage, which the Italian humanists had resuscitated, was gradually assimilated into the general culture of the educated classes of Renaissance England. Without them the widespread acquaintance with classical literature could hardly have been possible."

For Mr. Charlton, then, "education had become 'modern'" in this age in the sense that "knowledge should be shared." And more significant than institutional learning was the "self-educative process" of books, associated with the "undoubtedly . . . extensive reading of the upper classes." It was the "non-traditional means of education," the private teacher and the printed manual, which were becoming "a crucial part of the total educational provision in England." Stress is laid upon the limitations of formal learning. Though there were changes of curriculum in school and university, both fell short of the essentials of humanist training. Neither the universities nor the inns of court were geared to the special needs of sons of the nobility and gentry, who went to both in increasing numbers, and Mr. Charlton (with an emphasis unlike Mrs. Simon's) considers that the importance of both in the education of gentlemen has been exaggerated. Only in exceptional cases were members of the upper classes able to supplement the predominantly traditional university teaching with the help of enlightened tutors, and the inns of court made little practical contribution to the legal training which humanist writers emphasized for gentlemanly service to the state. So the inns have been given "an exaggerated place in the history of what we call a liberal education," and "a gentleman of Renaissance England fitted himself for his future rôle of governor more often than not *after* he left university." There was, in fact, in both schools and universities a setback after the promising early years of the century. In neither was it until later centuries that humanist studies were realized, and the explanation must be sought in political and religious events, particularly governmental policy of using education to enforce uniformity. "Instead of acting as breeding grounds for humanist ideas, a distinct possibility at the beginning of the period, the grammar schools became instruments of national policy, a means of strengthening the State against religious innovation"; and in the universities by the later sixteenth century "there was nothing to compare with the wide range of interest of the humanists of the early part of the century." The Reformation stands responsible for failure.

Mrs. Simon's work contrasts sharply with these conclusions. Hers is a chronological rather than an analytical account, which concentrates upon institutions and formal procedures of learning. Her treatment of "Humanists, the new learning and educational change" has less to say of Italy than Mr. Charlton, though she delays longer over Erasmus and Vives. And though here, too, we read of printing as having "heralded a revolution in education and self-education," this topic receives no concentrated attention. Mrs. Simon's avowed purpose is to describe educational programs and practice in relation to "wider social movements since it is in large part failure to do this that invalidates former assessments." Although there are many suggestive passages dealing with social questions in the book, it may be objected that the title is misleading, and that its contents would more justly have been indicated under the heading of one of the author's own articles, "The Reformation and English Education." The book in fact stems from and sets in a broader context Mrs. Simon's revisions of A. F. Leach's conclusions about the damaging effects of the Reformation upon English education. "It was the original intention of this study to outline the actual course of events at the Reformation in order to correct the view that many schools were destroyed and education suffered a setback for many years." And that is the main thing the book does. Its prime contention is that "it was at the Reformation—not, as is still universally [?] taught, in the nineteenth century—that state intervention in English education began" and that "to recognise this is to see all subsequent developments in a new light." Between the reigns of Henry VIII and Elizabeth the educational system was remodelled to "ensure unity in religion and consolidation of the social order" and there can be seen developing "a system of schools administered locally by lay governing bodies under the general supervision of the state. This was the major change initiated at the Reformation." What was new and important was not the increase of secularism, for "ecclesiastical control had ceased to be a reality in the later middle ages." It was the arrival of central state controls which came with the Reformation. "The school system was essentially a product of the Reformation." We are given, in effect, a history of education in the Reformation, set in a conventional narrative of religious change, with attention focused—as it must focus—upon the dissolution of monasteries, and chantries, and the resulting alterations in the educational system. This was something which needed doing, and Mrs. Simon's careful and comprehensive account (with helpful bibliography) is a valuable addition to the subject.

At the center of the argument and book is the reign of Edward VI. Mrs. Simon's "saintly young scholar king" replaces Leach's "poor, rickety, over-educated boy,"[1] and here her work provides an answer to the question indicated as "not yet settled" by A. F. Pollard over sixty years ago (four years after the appearance of Leach's book on the subject): the question, that is, of the effect of the chantry dissolution upon educational endowment. Without denying his contributions to the history of education, it is clear that a revision of Leach's sometimes intemperate and loosely argued work was needed. Writers on the subject (including Mr. Charlton) have already benefited from Mrs. Simon's criticisms of the conclusions embodied in *English Schools at the Reformation, 1546-8* (1896) and *The Schools of Medieval England* (1915), so that the thesis presented here is not new. Her main revision has already become familiar: namely the denial of the long-standing idea (derived from Leach) that the Chantries Act of 1547 resulted in the destruction of many schools. She argues that Leach's idea of the disruptive effects of Edward VI's reign was based upon misapprehensions, arising particularly from his indiscriminate treatment of the different kinds of teaching mentioned in the chantry certificates. He both overestimated the amount of schooling provided by collegiate churches and chantry colleges, and underestimated the development of lay-sponsored education before the Reformation. He also misinterpreted the evidence for the continuation of schools. One must agree with Mrs. Simon's strictures about Leach's use of the chantry commissioners' certificates, and his lax readiness to take references to schools or schoolmasters from different dates as evidence for the continuous existence of a school. She provides convincing evidence, county by county, of the widespread re-foundation of schools in the years 1548-1553. We emerge, therefore, with something nearer to the original picture of Edward VI's reign as a time of educational development. At the end of it, though much still remained to be done, there had been formed "a nucleus of well-organised grammar schools, independent of any ecclesiastical institution and administered by lay bodies of governors," and "there had been effective steps towards establishing a school system to serve the needs of a protestant nation." In place of Leach's "doleful record of . . .

havoc,"[2] we have a remarkably planned "new departure . . . following on what had been virtually a national survey of school provision, they [the schools] were conceived of as units in an educational system serving a protestant nation."

While the main lines of this account stand firm, and while it is abundantly clear how— through controls of schools, teachers and books—governmental influence upon education vastly increased with the Reformation, Mrs. Simon may seem at times to have overstated her case. In her emphasis upon the degree of systematic organization which lay behind the foundations and re-foundations under Edward VI, she seems to advance beyond the evidence she quotes. There certainly were individuals with ideas about the overall availability of schools, such as Hugh Latimer and (earlier) Thomas Starkey, for example, or Martin Bucer who in 1551 suggested a homily on the provision of grammar schools. But when it came to practice—as Mrs. Simon herself shows—a great deal depended upon local or individual initiative in promoting or refloating schools. The whole argument, running through the book, of the emergence of central controls over education, needed to be placed more clearly in the context of Reformation propaganda as well as Reformation thought, setting the attention to schools and universities beside the increased governmental manipulation of all means of opinion-making—proclamation, pulpit and press. And one cannot help wishing, since this forms so much the core of the work, that the chantry certificates had been subjected to closer analysis.

It must also be noted that we are still far from being able to reach any final assessment of the effect of the Reformation upon the number of schools. Perhaps, in any case, this is not the most realistic or important of criteria. While, however, it is clear that there were plenty of new foundations, as well as continuations of old schools, in the sixteenth century, effective comparison with the school provision of the fifteenth century must await the completion of further research. Final revision of this part of Leach's work cannot therefore yet be attempted, though it is beginning to appear what a large amount of teaching may have been available (perhaps considerably higher, at least to judge by Yorkshire, than Professor Jordan's meagre estimate). Yet even when the collection of this information has gone further, the picture may still remain far from clear, in view of the great diversity of schools and schoolmasters, and the mortality of both.

In addition to this stress upon the institutional aspect of education, Mrs. Simon diverges from Mr. Charlton in her interpretation of the continuum of humanist teaching. Far from seeing religious change as having damped the promise of the earlier years of the century, she considers that it carried on and merely directed into different patterns nascent English humanism. Humanist ideas were developed in the cause of reform by the growing body of reformers, and it is mistaken to suggest that after flourishing in the early decades of the century they were "overwhelmed," "thrust from the scene" or "abruptly cut off at the Reformation." Through the courses of studies in universities and schools (university lectures on Greek and Latin, stipulations about the teaching of ancient languages in schools) humanist ideas were adopted and promoted. "The schools . . . had their faults but there is a clear line of development to be traced. It was here that humanist educational precepts found their most detailed application," though this was through the vernacular as well as teaching of the classics. Further, "Puritanism did not wither the humanist heritage, even though schools became progressively more godly, but rather developed this tradition." At this point the two authors most clearly reach an impasse, and one which can scarcely be readily unlocked, when so much hangs upon that large and most evasive of concepts, Renaissance —not to mention the ambiguities of "humanist" and "puritan."

It is certainly true, as Mrs. Simon says that the reformers (for their own reasons) continued and stimulated the study of ancient languages. Yet the fact that classical studies were carried on by individuals and institutions by no means indicates that humanist ideals of education were being inculcated; a schoolmaster's use of classical texts might reveal the separation, rather than the unity between humanist and reformer, between style and content. Understanding might be sought at the expense of literature when it was believed, as Professor Baldwin put it, that "one must first save his soul, elegantly if possible, but inelegantly if he must."[3] The upheaval and confusion of religious controversy—whatever the outcome for the schools—did for a critical phase produce a narrowing of horizons. Leading Englishmen for a generation after 1529 were caught up in the turmoil of Reformation politics, religious polemics and doctrinal change. The intellectual climate was greatly altered, and it seems hard to deny that some forces in England were redirected, or pushed aside, by the impact of those years. Meanwhile the Reformation made its own contribution to the development of the vernacular and to English literacy. It is here that Mr. Charlton's book may seem to carry more conviction, chiming in as he does with current ways of thinking about the importance of books and readers, emphasizing the role of the vernacular and of informal beside formal ways of learning. England undoubtedly made notable advances in Latin and Greek (and Hebrew) studies in the sixteenth century, yet after the generation of Colet and More, a large part of the absorption of classical learning in England has to be traced through the vernacular. And since, as C. S. Lewis pointed out, it is the "Golden Age" of Elizabethan literature which is responsible for so many of the "emotional overtones of the word *Renaissance*" in England,[4] the small Latin and less Greek aspect must be allowed consideration in any attempt to evaluate English humanism. We cannot dismiss the schools, but we cannot consider them alone.

It is disappointing that neither book contains any sustained discussion of the question of literacy. Granted, this is an under-studied subject awaiting more research. Yet both authors assume and allude to the spread of literacy in ways which merit further treatment, and the gap is the more significant in that both draw attention to reading as a process of self-education. Nor has either anything significant to add to our knowledge of the frequency—or infrequency, if we are to accept A. M. Stowe's conclusions about the reign of Elizabeth[5] —of printed books actually available for use in schools, and their influence upon teaching methods. There are many aspects of literacy which call for consideration, various of them touched on by Mrs. Simon. If more books produced more readers, one would like to see more exploration of the role of particular books. Already among the Lollards, from the late fourteenth century, it is possible to find examples of individuals who learnt to read in order to study the Bible, and if some existing readers made Protestants, Protestantism undoubtedly helped to make more Bible readers. From the time of the arrival of the Great Bible in parish churches, religious instruction and exhortations to read went hand in hand —as is evident from the Injunctions of 1538, 1547 and 1559. The setback of 1543, when Henry VIII restricted Bible reading to the upper classes, might be taken as some sort of indication of the demonstrated literary interests of humbler persons, and the succession of books which were enjoined for parochial reading in the course of the English Reformation, turned parish churches into potential places of study, as well as worship. The long-standing idea of every parish clerk as a teacher, came nearer reality. At the end of the century, literacy had made gains among many classes besides the gentry (of whose literacy at its beginning Professor Stone holds such a low estimate),[6] but was a matter still challenging to Puritan endeavours. The Puritan movement may here (as Knappen suggested) have made a noticeable impression, with its emphasis upon the duties of parents and pastors to teach reading and writing to children and adults. The Dedham classis took steps to have children taught to read, and the example of the Puritan minister who is said to have taught forty people over forty to read, makes the movement sound like a form of adult education. Perhaps there was always some ingredient of this in radical religious reform, and for certain adults first direct encounters with books may contain an element of spiritual regeneration, quite apart from fresh encounters with doctrine. Mr. Charlton's book, with its focus upon the growth of vocational reading and the increasing need for books among men of affairs, shows how England (following Italy) extended literacy among apprentices. That the demands for literacy among such learners may have reached far beyond the provisions of formal schooling, is suggested by both teachers and books. From London comes the example of William Swetnam, fishmonger, licensed by Archbishop Whitgift in 1599 to teach children reading, writing and accounting, in any parish in the city, and John Brinsley in 1612 refers to the scriveners who taught writing as they went round the country. The very large editions of ABC's printed (and the booksellers' interest in the patents over these books) indicate their wide circulation, which is unlikely to have been restricted to childish learners. Edmund Coote's *English Schoolmaster* of 1596, which aimed to teach "the most easie, short, and perfect order of distinct Reading, and true Writing our English-tongue," was avowedly made "not only for Children,"[7] and received its twenty-fifth printing in 1636.

Mrs. Simon's over-exclusive concern with the institutional aspects of learning means that various subjects upon which one might fairly look for guidance in a book with her title, are more fully treated by Mr. Charlton. This is the case, for instance, with education in the family (a particularly notable lack in the context of the Reformation) and the education of women, both barely mentioned by Mrs. Simon but to which Mr. Charlton devotes illuminating pages. On the question of household education (as distinct from the family) and private tutoring, she has a lot to say which is unfortunately scattered through the book, showing how much may be lost by a too chronological approach. This is an important subject upon which both authors are informative, and yet to which perhaps neither does full justice, lying as it does halfway between formal and informal learning. A great deal of the history of the changing patterns of sixteenth-century education could be written from the point of view of changes in household instruction.

In the late fifteenth and early sixteenth centuries the medieval system of sending children away to be educated in the great household was still in practice. This ancient form of education could serve for the introduction of humanist teaching (witness the households of George Neville, Archbishop of York, or of Cardinal Wolsey), as well as the newer style circle of Thomas More. The great household could to some extent do for England what the ducal court did for Italy. At the end of the period, in the later sixteenth century, household education was still greatly in vogue but now instead of taking children in, it rather sends its pedagogic nucleus out. The private tutor was ubiquitous, teaching boys of the nobility and gentry in family circles until they were of an age to go to the university or inns of court, accompanying charges to Oxford and Cambridge, and going further afield on the foreign tours which were coming to be the fashionable finishing school for young men. The fact that "it was now widely accepted among gentlemen that education was a worthwhile investment" (Simon, p. 357) meant that the gentry increasingly utilized all forms of educational opportunity, and household teaching and private tutoring should be set alongside the influx of gentlemen's sons into schools, universities and inns of court.

It seems possible, indeed, that several reasons may have combined to reactivate or extend the home tutoring system among the gentry during the reign of Elizabeth. One factor, surely not to be left out of account, is social snobbery. "Some gentlemen aped their betters, as it now seemed, by providing tutoring at home." Mrs. Simon, without going into details (pp. 367-8) suggests that by the end of the century the majority of country gentlemen were sending their sons to school, and that by this scholastic mixing "mutual understanding was fostered between gentlemen and the ranks immediately below them." Certainly, as Mr. Charlton shows (p. 97) in a passage which would properly have appeared in Mrs. Simon's book, gentry such as Philip Sidney did brush shoulders with sons of yeomen and humbler persons in some of the greater schools. There are also known cases in lesser ones, such as Sir William Faunt's son in the village school at Wigston Magna near Leicester. But the evidence is lacking which would enable one to draw firm general conclusions about the amount of social interchange which resulted. One might suppose that the choice of schooling, then as now, was influenced by the quality of local education available, as well as the extent of a father's means, in which case perhaps there was more social mixture, as well as better teaching, in such schools as Shrewsbury or Merchant Taylors'.

In the meantime many of the gentry in the later sixteenth century might have had other good reasons for thinking in terms of a tutor before they thought of a school. In the first place, as Mr. Charlton shows very clearly, because of the curriculum. The teaching of grammar school and university alike was not adapted to the education of the gentleman, about which people had written and were still writing so much. French and Italian as well as Latin and Greek, music, dancing and drawing, physical training (riding the great horse, wrestling, fencing) were all elements of this upbringing, a range of studies obviously quite out of line with the statutory courses of institutions. More specialized subjects like geometry and history, cosmography and geography, depended largely on the employment of tutors, as did modern languages which were quite "outside the range of the grammar school curriculum" (Charlton, p. 234), though provision might in some schools be made for them. Mrs. Simon gives the example of Bedford, where a son of Sir John Wynn was able to learn French, Italian and music, as well as Latin, Greek and Hebrew. And Richard Mulcaster (headmaster of Merchant Taylors' for twenty-five years and of St. Paul's for half as long) who was rare in fulfilling his own ideal of a schoolmaster who could teach Hebrew, Greek and Latin, was also remembered by Sir James Whitelocke, his pupil, for the instruction in singing and instrumental playing he had provided.

Besides such matters of manners and studies, religious considerations may also have turned the gentry towards private tutors and away from schools. Reformation influences might here join forces with humanist aspirations, for the fact that schools were made part of Anglican uniformity meant that Roman Catholics and Puritans alike had incentives to keep their children out of school. The Catholic missionaries frequently found niches as tutors in private households, and teaching of this kind was also a feature of Puritanism. These practices did not escape attention. In 1563 schoolmasters had to swear the oath of supremacy (under penalties of life imprisonment and death) and that year some bishops ordered detailed enquiries into the damaging activities of tutors in gentlemen's houses. Controls upon tutors and schoolmasters were stepped up in the 1570's and 80's, including the insistence in 1571 that both should receive episcopal license, and from that time bishops' injunctions generally dealt with tutors alongside schoolmasters.[8] This concern may be taken in conjunction with Richard Mulcaster's question in 1581 as to why private teaching was so much favoured, and his warnings about the dangers of such education, as giving too much freedom to the parent to "serve his owne humour, be it never so distempered: by the secrecie of his owne house, not to be discovered."[9]

Finally one might connect this apparent vogue for private tutoring with the educational boom itself, which provided so many potential employees, young men fresh from the educational mint, successors to the Wolseys, Tyndales and Cranmers of an earlier generation, for whom services of this kind had proved an important stepping-stone on the path of religious objectives.

This last consideration prompts other questions, relevant to both authors' themes, raised by both, but not fully faced by either. To what extent did the reorientation of sixteenth-century education—whether one views it from the angle of increasing secular interest, the institution of the gentleman, or the changes in schools—reflect or effect a changing balance of professional vocation in society as a whole? Can it be argued that already in this century the expansion of education was leading to over-education in the sense that too many people were being educated for too few of the same things? It seems highly probable that this was so, and that there was a conspicuous imbalance of professional recruitment in the third quarter of the century. Both authors point to the cry of reformers, especially in the middle years of the century when the universities were at a low ebb, for better educated clergy, a cry which was old but which became louder and more insistent as educational standards improved at large, and with the growing emphasis upon preaching. This reiterated call was combined, however, with a significant change. Whereas before the Reformation individuals such as More and Colet were suggesting that an improvement in clerical standards could be achieved by a reduction in the number of clergy, in the mid-sixteenth century the lament of Jewel and Grindal ran quite the other way. The need was not for higher selection but for more recruits. Ordination figures from the diocese of Durham between 1531 and 1559 indicate a drastic reduction in the numbers of men joining the ministry during the critical years of the Reformation. Not only had the religious orders been removed from the scene but—as both Mrs. Simon and Mr. Charlton indicate—the economic rewards of a career in the church had also been winnowed away.[10] One might, however, also connect this clerical reduction with wider changes in the balance of social forces and ideals, expounded (though not in this connexion) in both books. If the prizes of an ecclesiastical career (even after the worst years of ecclesiastical dislocation and uncertainty were over) were insufficient to attract many gentry, the rewards of a secular career, lesser or greater, may have seemed more honourable. The decline in the social standing of the clergy perhaps owed something to the humanistic as well as financial aspirations of the gentry, whose whole training was framed for public office and secular service—hence the concentration upon knowledge of the law. The church did not belong to this scheme of things, and it was open to discussion whether a man could enter the church and retain his nobility. Lyly rebuked those gentlemen who "thinke it a blemmish to their auncestours, and blot to their owne gentrie, to read or practize Divinitie," and Mulcaster asked why gentlemen did not "of choice [become] both divines, and physicianes" instead of all turning to the law and the court.[11] New educational ideals—economic motives apart—might reinforce as well as shift old social prejudices. Some gentlemen proudly disdained deep learning, said Sir Thomas Elyot, deeming that "to a great gentleman it is a notable reproach to be well learned and to be called a great clerk."[12] While, in Professor Hexter's words, the sixteenth century dedicated "a spate of words...to the proposition that all gentlemen worthy of the name must be clerks,"[13] the very idea of their gentry, their institution as gentlemen, indisposed them from turning their new clerkliness towards service in the church.

If the gentry had to be persuaded into the church against other persuasions, one of the telling arguments might have been the shortage of professional opportunities open to the large number of those who, with their social graces and smattering or more than smattering of the law, looked expectantly to court, office and parliament. Too many similarly qualified individuals competing for a limited number of positions formed a potential threat to society, and one which had already reflected back upon educational theory before the sixteenth century turned into the seventeenth. It had come to be seen that the commonwealth might be endangered by an excess of learning, an over-production of professional men. "If anything about the gentry 'rose' it was their standard of education" writes Mr. Charlton at the conclusion of his book. By the end of the sixteenth century contemporaries, who had so interminably sifted and weighed the contribution of learning to the body politic, were facing the latest worry—too much education.

The Folger Shakespeare Library

Notes:

(1) A. F. Leach, *English Schools at the Reformation, 1546-8* (London, 1896), Part I, p. 5.

(2) *Ibid.*, Part I, p. 122.

(3) T. W. Baldwin, *William Shakspere's Petty School* (Urbana, 1943), p. 119.

(4) C. S. Lewis, *English Literature in the Sixteenth Century excluding Drama* (Oxford, 1954), p. 64.

(5) A. M. Stowe, *English Grammar Schools in the Reign of Queen Elizabeth* (New York, 1908), pp. 119, 139-40.

(6) L. Stone, *The Crisis of the Aristocracy, 1558-1641* (Oxford, 1965), pp. 675-676.

(7) Baldwin, *op. cit.*, p. 25.

(8) A. C. F. Beales, *Education under Penalty* (London, 1963), pp. 56, 74.

(9) Richard Mulcaster, *Positions*, ed. R. H. Quick (London, 1888), p. 186.

(10) P. Hughes, *The Reformation in England*, III (London, 1954), p. 53, n. 1; C. Hill, *Economic Problems of the Church from Archbishop Whitgift to the Long Parliament* (Oxford, 1956), pp. 199-223; M. H. Curtis. "The Alienated Intellectuals of Early Stuart England," *Past and Present*, No. 23 (1962). pp. 25-43.

(11) R. Kelso, *The Doctrine of the English Gentleman in the Sixteenth Century* (Urbana, 1929), p. 55; Mulcaster, *op. cit.*, p. 218.

(12) Sir Thomas Elyot, *The Book named The Governor*, ed. S. E. Lehmberg (London and New York, 1962), pp. 40-41.

(13) J. H. Hexter, *Reappraisals in History* (London, 1962), p. 49.

Records of Plays and Players in Kent. 1450-1642 edited and collected by Giles E. Dawson. Malone Society Collections, VII, 1965. Pp. xxi + 211. *Reviewer: Stanley J. Kahrl.*

In his review of the Malone Society's plays for 1963, Robert K. Turner once again questioned the wisdom of continuing to use type in preparing the Malone Society reprints.[1] At the same time that techniques of photographic reproduction make it increasingly possible for individual scholars to consult early printed texts in their original form, human error continues to persist in preventing any printed book from being an absolutely accurate reprint of its original. Thus even Giles Dawson, an editor whose standards are a model of painstaking accuracy, includes on page xxi of the introduction to *Collections VII* the following sentence: "After 1487 there a gradual decline in this kind of hospitality is observable." If gold ruste, what shal iren do?

Yet the effort to produce as accurate a text as possible must always be made; because it has been made continually, and most strenuously by editors of Renaissance dramatic texts following the principles established by Pollard, McKerrow, and Greg, scholars studying these texts are far better off than their colleagues working in other fields. Anyone who has tried to work with medieval dramatic texts is only too painfully aware of the difference. And where a misplaced word or comma is not as crucial to the sense of the material being edited as it is in the case of a play, then the rigorous procedures developed for old spelling editions come most fully into their own. The Malone Society has always had as its second object "the printing of documents relating to the English drama."[2] For example, the very first volume published by the Society included "The Remembrancia," a collection of letters sent to the Court of Aldermen of the City of London from the Sovereign, and answers, running from 1579-1640, and 1660-1664; the Lansdowne Manuscripts, also known as the Burghley Papers; royal patents for players; and dramatic records from the Privy Council Register, 1603-1642. These records were edited by Chambers and Greg. There is no need to list the contents of the other early *Collections*; a full account can be found in the list of the Society's publications, pp. 17-25 of *Collections IV* (1956). What is worth remarking here, however, is that the Society's initial appetite for such fare seems to have quickly been sated. Volumes of *Collections* appeared in 1907, 1908, 1909, 1911, 1913, then there was a ten year gap until 1923, an eight year gap until 1931, after which none appeared until the publication of "A Calendar of Dramatic Records in the Books of the Livery Companies of London" in 1954, published as *Collections III.*

This failure to pursue the Society's second goal was a pity. Anyone who has seen the use to which the *Collections* have been put by Alfred Harbage, in *Shakespeare's Audience,* or Glynne Wickham, in *Early English Stages, 1300 to 1660,* to name but two examples, will realize that such records have great value to the scholarly community. And none of the dramatic records lend themselves to photographic reproduction. Relevant entries in account or minute books are buried amidst countless other entries of no interest to students of the early drama. Furthermore no other society has the same interest in publishing such records. Fortunately F. P. Wilson, and his successor as General Editor, Arthur Brown, both have recognized the unique role the Society can play in increasing our knowledge of the conditions under which the early plays were produced, and we may expect regular appearances of *Collections* in the future.

There is no dearth of material. Giles Dawson's collected "Records of Plays and Players in Kent, 1450-1642" provides both an example of what direction future *Collections* might take, and a model of the principles to be followed. I would like to take these two points in order. Dawson states at the beginning of his introduction that his purpose has been to reexamine in one county the records used by J. O. Halliwell-Phillips and J. T. Murray in preparing their two studies of English dramatic companies. Halliwell-Phillips confined his researches to the visits of Shakespeare's company to the provinces; he did obtain his information from the local archives. Murray, on the other hand, extended the range to include information about all the companies between 1558 and 1642. As Dawson remarks, "Murray lacked experience with old records and relied wherever he could upon secondary sources, and his *English Dramatic Companies, 1558-1642* (1910) therefore falls short of complete success" (p. vii). Dawson might have remarked further that another authority whom we have all consulted for years also "relied wherever he could upon secondary sources." In my own research in the archives of Lincolnshire for medieval and sixteenth century dramatic records I have had frequent occasion to consult E. K. Chambers' standard study of *The Mediaeval Stage*. I have found no case where he consulted provincial archives. I presume this to be the case with *The Elizabethan Stage* as well.

Obviously the study of early drama would not be in the state that it is today were it not for the work Chambers did. But I am not at all certain he himself recognized the dangers inherent in using secondary sources when one is developing an hypothesis from the information derived from local archives. At the head of Appendix W of *The Mediaeval Stage*, a list of "Representations of Mediaeval Plays," Chambers allowed that "Probably the number [of local plays] could be increased by systematic search of local histories and transactions of learned societies" (II, 329). My experience with "local histories and transactions of learned societies" in one county leads me to the conclusion that they are notoriously unreliable. Some transcripts will be excellent, and complete; others will be selective and impressionistic, the latter particularly when the local historian is not too proficient in deciphering early handwriting. The selectivity built into these published accounts can ultimately lead to a distortion of the evidence, which in turn leads to critical misinterpretations. For example, in his chapter discussing "Guild Plays and Parish Plays," Chambers stated that "Parochial plays, whether in town or country, appear to have been in most cases occasional, rather than annual" (*Mediaeval Stage*, II, 122). My own research,[3] and Dawson's Appendix A.III, an alphabetical list of the towns which sent performers to other towns in Kent, and the years for which there are recorded visits, suggests that the case was quite otherwise.

The example is not adduced to castigate Chambers. He, after all, was one of the editors of *Collections I*. It is rather a plea for more research of this kind. One need only read through Dawson's introduction to realize the kinds of questions that can be answered, at least in part, by even a study of one county. For example, Dawson's carefully documented assertion that minstrels, *mimi*, and *histriones* are one kind of performer, and that players, *lusores*, *ludatores*, and *homines ludatores* are another seems to be borne out by a reading of the entries. If the same distinction holds true elsewhere, as it most probably will, it certainly seems worth determining when the troupes ceased to be musicians and became players. Dawson suggests that the change occured around 1475. What, one wonders, is the relation of this change to the dates of the early interludes?

Or, to take another instance, much more evidence about banncriers than we have had available before appears in these accounts. Chambers had suggested (*Mediaeval Stage* II, 114) that the towns with cycles "sent round their officers to read the proclamation or 'banns' of the play" annually. The entertainment laid on and the size of payments made to banncriers, as, for example, on the occasion of the visit of the banncriers from Lydd to Hythe in 1508-09, suggests that a performance of some kind took place. Banncriers, as in this case, often received a mark, apparently a common reward of players until the last quarter of the sixteenth century. The gradual shift from marks, to crowns, to pounds in the accounts is also an interesting development whose significance I am not qualified to judge. It is clear that by the end of the sixteenth century the troupes were often receiving two pounds for a mayor's show. When this is compared to ten pounds for a court appearance, or eight for a good day's house in London, one may surmise that the reluctance of the troupes to play the counties had a financial origin.

It is a measure of the value of this book that the more one becomes familiar with its contents, the more one wishes he knew. Dawson rightly asserts, in discussing the "Incompleteness of the Record" in his introduction (pp. xxvi-xxvii), that the records we have represent only a small proportion of the actual dramatic activity of the period in question. What we do have is admirably presented, which brings me back to the matter of Dawson's, and the Society's, editorial principles. Each town's archives are described with great care, both as to location and condition. The entries from each town are arranged chronologically, using the accounting year of the town in question. The individual entries are reproduced in accordance with the Society's general rule for manuscripts, that "the text should be as far as possible literally reproduced, including all contractions, and that the general arrangement should as a rule be preserved. Beyond this it would be useless to lay down any general rules."[4] Procedures have been worked out for handling the standard contractions, however; prospective editors should be careful to consult the list of contractions set out in *Collections III* (1954), x, as well as the principles followed by Dawson, explained on pp. xxx-xxxi of his introduction.

The result is a readable, attractive text, where every item of importance is included, and where the reasons for gaps in the accounts are clearly identified. I have only one suggestion for future editors of such material as to how such volumes might be improved. Dawson threw his net far wider than did his predecessors, covering a far greater chronological period than either Halliwell-Phillips or Murray. Furthermore, in Appendix B he included a quantity of information not about traveling players, but about stationary productions of town plays. As a result, his book is of interest not only to those interested exclusively in the drama of the Elizabethan and Jacobean periods, but also to those concerned with establishing the continuity of medieval and Renaissance drama.

For this second group of readers Dawson's decision to establish 1450 as his *terminus a quo* will be a disappointment, particularly in the case of the records for New Romney, which apparently go back considerably earlier. As the focus of his interest, and thus the impetus for the collection, is the visits of traveling players, the limit of 1450 is perfectly understandable. However, it is unlikely that such a study will be done again, and it would have been a great help to have had the relevant material from the medieval period included as well. Certainly one must establish some limits to the work, or it will not get done. However, if it is true, as it seems to be, that the kind of drama produced in the latter half of the sixteenth century more often than not followed patterns established in the fourteenth century, it would seem of value to all readers of the Malone Society's *Collections* to include early dramatic records where they exist. But we must be grateful to the Malone Society and Giles Dawson for bringing this wealth of material to our attention. May many more such volumes follow.

The University of Rochester

Notes:

(1) See his review of *A Knack to Know a Knave* and *The Miseries of Enforced Marriage, Shakespeare Studies*, I (1965), 359-362.

(2) See F. P. Wilson's account of "The Malone Society, The First Fifty Years: 1906-56" in *Collections IV* (1956), 14.

(3) See, for example, "Medieval Drama in Louth," *Research Opportunities in Renaissance Drama, Medieval Supplement*, X (1967), 129-133.

(4)   Rule 11 of the "Rules for the Guidance of Editors of the Society's Reprints," first printed in *Collections I.ii* (1908-09), revised and reprinted in *Collections IV* (1956), 69.

Jonson's Romish Plot: A Study of "Catiline" and its Historical Context by B. N. De Luna. The Clarendon Press, 1967. Pp. x + 415; pl. 1. $10.40. *Reviewer: Maurice Charney.*

It is surprising, in 1967, to find a book so conscientiously and so enthusiastically devoted to topical allusionism. One would have thought that Lilian Winstanley's *Hamlet and the Scottish Succession* (1921), *Macbeth, King Lear, and Contemporary History* (1922), and *Othello as the Tragedy of Italy* (1924) had killed off any possibility of a respectable "parallelograph," as Mrs. De Luna calls it. But *Jonson's Romish Plot* offers a massive and meticulously documented demonstration

> that—far from being merely the most dismally "Roman" drama in English— *Catiline* was, in addition, consciously intended and in some circles understood as a classical parallelograph designed to "shadow forth" the most sensational "Romish" conspiracy of that or any other century: the still-controversial Gunpowder Plot of 1605. This is of particular interest and importance because Jonson, who in 1610 had rather noisily recanted his Catholicism of twelve years' standing, had played some obscure, though perhaps definable, role in that strange affair.

Jonson's "obscure" role is explored in Chapter IV, where we are invited to speculate on a teasing question: What was Jonson doing at a private supper party given by Robert Catesby, the arch conspirator of the Gunpowder Plot, on October 9, 1605, less than a month before the Houses of Parliament were to be blown up?

That the Gunpowder Plot was frequently compared to the Conspiracy of Catiline should come as no surprise, since the Conspiracy of Catiline, like that of Brutus and Cassius, was among the best known plots of classical antiquity. Every schoolboy would have read Cicero's insinuating orations on Catiline, some of which are reproduced with tedious exactness in Jonson's play. The analogy probably also works, with less force, the other way around, and spectators of *Catiline* might have been expected to recall those lurid disclosures of some six years earlier about the Catholic plot to put England under papal subjection. Mrs. De Luna begins with the general assent and good will of the reader, but she quickly loses it by her strenuous insistence that no example is too trivial to be included. Her unwillingness to lose a trick in the game of parallels finally convinces us that it is all only a game, in which ingenuity is the only virtue.

Let us look at the eleven parallels that are so crucial to Chapter VI. These tend to fall into two categories: the excessively specific and the excessively general. How many members of Jonson's audience, or even learned readers, could possibly have recognized the following similarities between the Catilinarian Conspiracy and the Gunpowder Plot? 1) Both would be immediately followed "by a rising in the provincial region *northwest* of the capital"; 2) "some men were taken into the plot principally because of their ability to supply horses"; 3) "The Catilinarians sought aid from Spain and Gaul, the Powder Plotters from Spain, France and the Low Countries"; 4) "Matching the complicity of the Allobrogian ambassadors from Gaul in the Catilinarian Conspiracy was the suspected complicity of the

French ambassador in the Powder Plot"; 5) "Both conspiracies included plans for the kidnapping of certain children who were then to be held as hostages to better the conspirators' bargaining position after the coup."

Besides these research scholar's parallels, there are some so broad as to apply to almost any conspiracy in the history of mankind. What is exclusive and distinctive about the following? 1) "Both conspiracies were to come to fruition with a sudden catastrophic 'blow' struck in the capital city"; 2) "Both conspiracies arose 'out of the dead ashes of former Treasons'"; 3) "Both groups were made up principally of indebted gentry and disgruntled, unemployed 'swordsmen'"; 4) "Both groups of conspirators partook of a 'sacrament' together to seal their oath of secrecy"; 5) "Both conspiracies resulted in the governments' immediate exaction of loyalty oaths from their citizens."

These examples are only a selection from Mrs. De Luna's set of parallels, all argued with a fullness of detail that cannot be reproduced here. But eleven examples are not necessarily eleven times more convincing, and excessive demonstration seems to stimulate a protective skepticism in the human spirit. Faced with such a formidable argument, I have the same irrational malaise as someone who receives a note of apology that reads: "I regret that I cannot accept your kind invitation, but I have two previous engagements."

The parallels in Chapter VI also include a pairing of the characters in the two conspiracies. Catiline is Robert Catesby, Cicero is Sir Robert Cecil, Cethegus is Thomas Percy, Gabinius Cimber is Guy Fawkes, Quintus Curius is Jonson, Cato is Sir Edward Coke, the Ghost of Sylla is the Ghost of Essex, etc. No loose characters are left untied, but the reasoning is sometimes as tenuous as the following: "Both conspirators were, at the time of their attempted coups, comparatively young men (Catesby was thirty-two, Catiline forty-six) of slender and supple build. . . ." Readers who themselves happen to fall between these two ages are not likely to be persuaded by the closeness of the parallel.

In the later discussion of the imagery of *Catiline*, there are much wilder and more Jungian thrusts. The predominance of winter imagery in the play is explained by three points: 1) For Elizabethan Protestants, winter would symbolize that harsh period of Mary's Catholic reign (1553-1558); 2) "ten of the thirteen Powder Plotters were either themselves Winters (Thomas and Robert) or were related to the numerous and well-connected Catholic family of Winter"; and 3) "the supposed etymological connection between the Latin adjective meaning 'wintry', *hibernus*, and the commonest Latin name for Ireland, regarded by Protestants as the one 'Papist cancer' within the English body-politic."

When these notions are applied to a specific passage in *Catiline*, Mrs. De Luna arrives at what can only be considered a divinely inspired, delphic vaticination. The passage is:

> Meane while, all rest
> Seal'd vp, and silent, as when rigid frosts
> Haue bound up brookes, and riuers . . . .   (I. 518-520)

Her comment is:

> How completely Jonson had mastered the art of parallelography can be seen in his perfectly natural working-in of the "brookes, and rivers" bound up by rigid frosts, which surely do not just happen to be also the cipher-names of the two best known of the many English Jesuits most effectively "bound up" (i.e., prevented from revealing the Plot) by means of a clever stratagem of Catesby's when the Winter-alliance took over the leadership of this latter-day "Enterprise of England." For Father John Gerard, the Jesuit who, according to the Government,

administered the Oath of Secrecy and the Sacrament to the conspirators, was also widely known by the *alias* "Brooke" and Garnet himself by the *alias* "Rivers", as was derisively noted at the Powder Plot trials.

This is the most fascinating nonsense I have ever read, and Mrs. De Luna succeeds in endearing herself to us by her confidences, but I cannot see how the interpretation is a "perfectly natural working-in" of anything, or how it has any relation at all to the passage in Jonson's play.

I am willing cheerfully to concede that I may be a square, but it seems to me that Mrs. De Luna has some strange notions of what literature is, and particularly, what a play is. She is constantly speaking of the mystery that needs to be unlocked, the covert allusions that need to be made overt, and the "dark conceit" that must be "unriddled." The "dramatists writing in the age of Elizabeth and James were a sly lot, and they were writing for a sly lot," and Mrs. De Luna offers herself to us as a learned cicerone who can guide the uninitiate through the maze of this "labyrinthine art." I reject completely the foppish assumption here that the critic exercises a priestly function.

I also object to Mrs. De Luna's constant assertion that her parallelograph redeems Jonson's *Catiline* and makes it a lively and exciting play. The fullest statement of this point of view is at the end of Chapter IX:

> Fortunately for Jonson's reputation as an artist, it is at long last possible to unmask *Catiline*, to understand it almost as well as 'the Judicious part of that Auditory' understood it in 1611, and, finally, to understand why Jonson himself regarded the play with especial affection. We may possibly, as a result, like Jonson less as a personality, but we will surely like him more as an artist when we cease thinking of him as the author of a Latinate monstrosity which long has seemed to be nothing more than a vehicle for his pedantry.

By a trick in logic, we must either agree with Mrs. De Luna or continue thinking of Catiline as a "Latinate monstrosity." But this makes a mockery out of criticism. Nothing in *Jonson's Romish Plot* can account for the extraordinarily sophisticated confrontation of Fulvia and Sempronia in Act II—these are the best drawn women in any of his plays—as well as the failure of Jonson's adulatory classicism in the character of Cicero (which is echoed, through Cicero's orations, in the negative portrait of Catiline). In all fairness to Mrs. De Luna, she does not claim to be writing a critique of *Catiline*, but there is something disturbing in the fact that a book of more than four hundred pages has so little to do with the play that is its ostensible subject.

Mrs. De Luna's hint that she is already at work on a sequel to *Jonson's Romish Plot* dealing with *Sejanus* fills me with alarm, and the sample parallelographs for *Bartholomew Fair* suggest an even more alarming series of volumes to cover Jonson's complete works. I would read Mrs. De Luna with unbounded interest if she decided to abandon Jonson, since she is an erudite commentator on the social and intellectual history of England in the early seventeenth century. Her presentation of the Gunpowder Plot makes for fascinating reading, and her researches into the minor satirical literature of the period are full of intelligent surmises. She has done significant work in the primary materials of her topic, as evidenced by her 827 footnotes and her extensive bibliography.

It is only when she is speaking about Jonson as a playwright and *Catiline* as a play that she seems so irrelevant. To use one of her favorite words (after "apodictic"), why "skew" it all onto Jonson? Jonson himself might protest, as in *The Poetaster*, against the "sinister application" of a malicious interpreter:

who will distort, and straine
The generall scope and purpose of an authour,
To his particular, and priuate spleene.   (V.iii.142-144)

Rutgers University

James Shirley, *The Cardinal* edited by Charles R. Forker. Indiana University Press, 1964. Pp. lxxii + 142. $6.00. *Reviewer: R. G. Howarth.*

As the outcome of a doctoral dissertation this edition evinces the utmost textual and bibliographical thoroughness. Six copies of the play have been collated and the text so constructed has been treated in accordance with the best current principles. The design of the book, too, makes for pleasant reading and easy study. Since as yet there is no modern *Collected Works* of Shirley this scholarly presentation of his masterpiece in tragedy will provide a model for the future general editor, thus enabling him to do justice to a dramatist whose publicationary fortune was not always happy, who fell posthumously into the wrong editorial hands (to be only partially rescued by Alexander Dyce) and in consequence has not received his due. *The Cardinal,* first printed in 1652 and collected into *Six New Plays* the following year, enjoyed, like the other five, the benefit of Shirley's own revision and overseeing, so that an editor could feel some confidence at the outset of his task. Even so, as has now been done, the techniques and standards of today remained to be applied.

It is permissible to wonder at the exclusion from the collation of the play of copies in British and other libraries (not to speak of those in private hands). For what this is worth, my notes on the holdings by the British Museum and the Bodleian agree with Professor Forker's descriptions. Perhaps he could well have turned up my own article on "A Manuscript of James Shirley's *Court Secret"* in *The Review of English Studies* for July 1931, with its pendant in the issue of April 1932, wherein the publication history of the *Six New Plays* is partly discussed. It seemed to me that on this occasion a significant difference, involving a distinction between acting and printing rights, occurred between the author and the publisher. This directly concerned *The Court Secret* but must have affected *The Cardinal* and the other plays included as well. But who, except the most thorough-going Shirleian, would necessarily have looked under my title for bearing on another of the dramatist's pieces?

The list of "Major Works Cited" by the editor reveals that only F. L. Lucas's *Complete Works* of John Webster, issued in 1927 (not also his revised editions of *The White Devil* and *The Duchess of Malfi,* 1958), was consulted. Considering the great value of Forker's demonstration of Webster's influence on Shirley, particularly in *The Cardinal,* this cavil may be made. Of less relevance is surprise at the presence in the list of the Braybrooke *Pepys* instead of the Wheatley.

A sheet of "Errata and Addenda" accompanies the volume and should be fully noted. It does not, however, include correction of the Latin inscription under the portrait of Shirley reproduced in the *Plays* from his *Poems* of 1646 and here prefixed: on page xviii of the introduction for "*six*" read "*sic*" and for "*devilis*" read "*debilis*" (a classic case of intrusion by the printer's devil!).

Possibly of greatest interest to the student of Shirley and of Caroline drama is the section in the introduction on the topical significance of the play. Forker argues persuasively that the Cardinal's fate alludes to the fall of Archbishop Laud, who is credited by tradition with having deterred Shirley from taking holy orders. Although the poet was not of a vindictive nature, perhaps he left the way open to such a contemporary interpretation as is here expounded, with the added subtlety that the editor discerns in it—what he styles the "delicious irony" of the Catholic dramatist's appeal to anti-Catholic sentiment. Even so, this may still contain an element of deference to theatrical convention.

The critical examination of the play by Forker well repays attention, whether or no one may differ over the degree of moral candour shown by the Duchess in her love-complications. The final estimate of the tragedy remains high.

University of Cape Town

A Companion to Arber: Being a Calendar of Documents in Edward Arber's Transcript of the Company of Stationers of London, 1554-1640 edited by W. W. Greg. The Clarendon Press, 1967. Pp. x + 451. $13.40 *Reviewer: Akihiro Yamada.*

To the late Sir Walter Greg scholars of bibliography and literature in the sixteenth and seventeenth centuries are again indebted. The presentation of this volume, however, is entirely to the credit of Mr. I. G. Philip and the late Mr. C. C. Blagden, who undertook admirably the difficult task of revising and preparing Sir Walter's original material for publication.

This volume comprises the Calendar, the Supplementary Documents, and an Index. The Calendar is a chronological compilation of all the documents, "a large mass of illustrative matter" as Arber put it himself, which he has interpolated into his transcript of the registers. Sir Walter's own note to the Calendar offers an explanation of his object: "The summaries, of course, cannot, and are not intended to, take the place of the full texts of the documents, but it is hoped that they may prove of assistance to, and even up to a point satisfy the needs of, those who have not got Arber constantly at their elbow." An excellent embodiment of this aim is exemplified, for instance, in no. 296, where he skilfully summarizes in about five hundred words those nineteen articles of agreement in 1635 between the journeymen and master printers for their mutual benefit, for which Arber had to sacrifice nearly four pages. The Calendar covers the period 1357-1683, which occupies a quarter of the volume, and the total number of documents summarized is 346. About 200 out of these cover the period between the coronation of James I and the closing of the theatres. To some extent, the Calendar resembles Professor G. B. Harrison's work in his *Elizabethan Journals* and *Jacobean Journals*. But Sir Walter Greg quite naturally restricted himself to documents relating to the book-trade only, thus providing his reader with a historical sense of its important aspects.

The value of the Calendar itself is greatly enhanced by the second section of the book— descriptions with Sir Walter's own annotations of other documents relating to the same subject: documents drawn from the same sources, particularly the Burghley papers among the Landsdowne manuscripts in the British Museum and the State Papers Domestic in the Public Record Office. But some relevant documents have been excluded: as Mr. Philip notes in the Preface to this book, the few scattered entries Arber printed (II, 880-883) from the Court-Book section of Register had already found their place in W. W. Greg and E. Boswell's *Records of the Court of the Stationers' Company, 1576-1602*, 1930, and the documents for the following period 1602-1640 were edited by the late Professor W. A. Jackson in his *Records of the Court of the Stationers' Company, 1602-1640*, 1957, pp. 340-437. The nature of the second section of Sir Walter's new book—the Supplementary Documents—, therefore, is basically the same as that of these two books of *Records* published by the Biblio-graphical Society. These Documents are arranged in chronological order and are classified by subjects. Every item in the Calendar and the Documents is provided with a cross-refer-ence where available. The period the Documents cover ranges from 1563 to 1640, and the documents relating to the reign of Elizabeth (Doc. 1-16) occupy only forty pages while those relating to the years 1603-1640 (Doc. 17-92) cover over two hundred pages. This proportion seems to suggest the editor's interest in, and emphasis on, a documentary history of the book-trade in the reigns of James I and Charles I, which are periods of great significance and interest from both a political and a literary points of view. The recent completion of Professor G. E. Bentley's monumental *The Jacobean and Caroline Stage* in seven volumes will certainly facilitate scholarly activities in the field of the seventeenth-century drama, but this work does not contain the sort of documents scholars have been grateful to have in E. K. Chambers' *The Elizabethan Stage*. This defect of Professor Bentley's work is, to some extent, compensated for by Sir Walter Greg's extensive collection of the Supplemen-tary Documents in *A Companion to Arber*. And it is clear that only in a combined use of both Professor Bentley's work and Sir Walter's can one more clearly realise that what Sir Walter wrote in 1930 about Elizabethan literature can also be applied to the Jacobean and Caroline literature: "it is never safe to forget that it was in some important respects a con-trolled output" (Greg and Boswell, *Records*, p. lxi).

The arrangement of the Documents, particularly in the classification and the cross-refer-ences, is of great convenience to a student who wishes to deal with such particular topics as the Boislore-Wood-Symcock patent (Doc. 28), the controversy about the printing and licensing of Prynne's *Histriomastix* (Doc. 64), etc. The Documents as a whole naturally offer material for the discussion of many other subjects which are of great interest to scholars of this period: master printers, apprentices, journeymen printers, and their mutual relations, Master and Wardens of the Stationers' Company, its organization, its relations with the Government, patents and privileges, copyrights, licenses, offences and seizure, etc. As these topics, most of which still remain open to serious discussions in the detail which they deserve, suggest, students not only of literature and bibliography but also of history and politics may well find opportunities of obtaining some kind of raw material for research from the Documents. For instance, Doc. 40 is a transcription, with Sir Walter's annotations and cross-references to the Calendar, of a series of documents relating to a 1624 proclamation of James I, who refused to sign the proclamation against seditious popish books until it was amended to include Puritanical works as well; Doc. 79 similarly presents a few documents concerning a proposal to establish an office for enforcing censorship—probably in 1635, when copies must frequently have been radically changed between licensing and printing "to the great dangerous disquietinge of both the state and church."

A world of topics of a more specific nature, which are as interesting and as significant, is to be found in an elaborate Index occupying nearly a hundred pages. It is extremely informative, and the reading of it will turn out to be almost as profitable as the reading of the text itself. The indication in each entry of the date of the document, in which the sub-ject indexed has originated, is an admirable system for an index to a book of this kind. Now that we have a massive collection of the documents edited in the useful trio of Greg and Boswell's *Records, 1576-1602*, Jackson's *Records, 1602-1640*, and Greg's *A Companion to Arber*, it may be reasonably sensible to extend a welcome to anyone who wishes to devote himself to a compilation of an index to all these three books, hopefully following in general the admirable system of Greg's last work.

Shinshu University

The Early Shakespeare by A. C. Hamilton. The Henry E. Huntington Library, 1967. Pp. ix + 237. $6.50. *Reviewer: Marco Mincoff.*

With each new book of Shakespeare criticism, the suspicion seems to justify itself more and more that, for the time being at least, the vein has been exhausted and there is nothing left to say. Professor Hamilton treats a relatively little exploited section of the canon, yet it is only with a more than Alexandrian ingenuity that he seems able to treat it at all. His approach is fairly varied, at least it is not tied down to any very definite method, except in as far as portraiture and plot-construction seem taboo; but then total meaning is also left out of the account, and style too. What in fact remains? one may ask, and it is not very easy to give an answer. The central preoccupation is perhaps the search for patterns— of every kind: the relations between the plays tend to be expressed as patterns, and the discussion of each separate play largely follows the same sort of line. But there is some-thing very forced and arbitrary about most of these patterns: "The comic form that is achieved through plot in *The Comedy of Errors,* and through theme and character in *The Two Gentlemen of Verona* is gained through spectacle in *Love's Labour's Lost,"* while the fairy world of *A Midsummer Night's Dream,* it is said, "resolves the four comedies as a group" (whatever "resolves" may mean in this context). How many people, I wonder, could give off-hand the details of the plot of *Errors?* Situation one might perhaps accept (and the distinction is not mere hair-splitting), but though the situations are in fact beautifully hinged together, one is scarcely aware of just how this is achieved. And the comedy is after all a good deal more than just a sequence of intricately connected situations: Adriana is more of a character (and so, in the other play, are Berowne and the Princess) than anyone in *The Two Gentlemen,* except perhaps Launce, who is on a very different level; while the theme of marital relations, and especially the final grouping of the three couples, is surely much more weighty than the very conventional treatment of love and friendship in *The Two Gentlemen.* Nor is *Love's Labour's Lost* lacking in pungent situations either, or in themes. None of these questions is so much as touched on in Professor Hamilton's very fragmentary discussions, still less is it shown in what way the fairy world "resolves" them. In fact the formula simply will not bear inspection. That suggested for a general pattern of comedy is even less convincing: "Strictly speaking nothing happens in a comedy: the comic form frustrates whatever the characters intend. In *The Comedy of Errors,* the husband intends to punish the wife, she intends [?] to make the brother her husband, and he intends to flee; in *The Two Gentlemen of Verona,* the Duke intends Thurio to have Silvia, Proteus intends to rape her, and Valentine intends to offer her to his friend [?]." What the brother intends in the first place is to discover his twin, and in that he is not frustrated; and what Valentine intends throughout most of the play, and what Julia and Silvia intend through all of it, may apparently be left out of the account. On this system *Macbeth* or *Antony and Cleopatra* would seem to be essentially comic, for they too end in frustration.

Within the separate plays the patterning scarcely works any better. It is supposed to be significant that in *1 Henry VI* Joan is hailed as a star, that she brandishes a torch when she is at the height of her powers, and is snuffed out by a torch at the end. Ever since Spur-geon's work the chasing of running images has been a favourite sport of critics, but it is doubtful whether all but a very few attempts to go beyond Spurgeon will bear scrutiny, and not even all of hers are equally convincing. Basically I believe there are only two types of running images that are of any real significance: those like the clothes images in *Macbeth* that reflect a certain bias on the author's part and so help to document his intentions, and those like the images of disease in *Hamlet,* the ravening beasts of *Lear,* or, one might add,

402

the cosmic images of *Tamburlaine,* which create a definite emotional atmosphere. Beyond that, a theory that seems to see in any grouping of images—with an average of a couple of hundred images to a play groups are inevitable—not only something significant in itself but often enough a sort of proof of excellence, is scarcely satisfactory. It would, for instance, make of *Locrine* not merely a great play, but one of the very greatest, because of the unique concentration of river imagery it presents, on which (Heaven forfend!) a whole treatise might be written. It is not enough simply to point to an image group or to a thematic pattern; the question is what it does, and my heart does not beat the faster for realizing that Joan is thrice connected with fire. Moreover, does a reference to the planet Venus really combine with the torches in any sort of meaningful relation? In a rather similar way it is maintained that the scene between Talbot and the Countess is paralleled by Joan's enticing of Burgundy and by the effeminate peace of the end, and that this is its justification. Even if one can bring oneself to feel the parallels, which is more than I can, it will not necessarily make the scene a good scene, or a pattern which one feels to have been achieved through an excrescence a good pattern.

There are points—keeping to the same play—with which one may agree. The objections to interpretations in the light of a providential view of history, or as an object lesson against dissension, are cogent enough. But there is very little to put in their place. The play is never brought into focus as a play, or even as a totality, something that works as a whole and produces some sort of total effect to which the parts contribute. Yet the play has a certain rugged force as a whole; probably, as I believe it was originally planned, it worked even more strongly than it does now, and its epic sweep would have been worth bringing out. As it is we have merely an ingenious juggling with fragments that remain fragments, as though the author were adding chance gleaning as a postscript to someone else's basic interpretation. And that is characteristic of the approach throughout the book, even with much better integrated works than *Henry VI.*

The University of Sofia

Conceptions of Shakespeare by Alfred Harbage. Harvard University Press, 1966. Pp. viii + 164. $4.95. *Reviewer: Leonard Nathanson.*

Professor Harbage's performances on the lecture platform during the 1964 quadricentenary, along with some related essays, are gathered together in his most recent book on Shakespeare. His subject is the "Shakespearean afterimage"—how men in aftertimes have seen the life and character, the art and mind of the dramatist. The author's concern in these lectures, delivered before general academic audiences, is not to engage questions at the frontiers of critical inquiry but to take stock of past and present illusions and misconstructions, chiefly of biographers, actors, and directors, and to put things in a sensible state of order. The history of Shakespeare biography—external and spiritual—and of theatrical interpretation and production does not lend itself to temperateness of expression, for there is much indeed to be vehement about. Professor Harbage, however, manages to be unfailingly urbane and charitable, even as he dissects the most freakish aberrations.

We are reminded first that during Shakespeare's own time, and for a good many decades thereafter, "his standing was that of the popular entertainer rather than the literary artist" (p. 5), and that his contemporaries thought him a man and a dramatist of affable sweetness, altogether central to normal human kind; certainly not the dark genius or secret sinner imagined by posterity. Professor Harbage considers in turn three afterimages that have persisted with especial tenacity: "Shakespeare the enshrined, Shakespeare the socialite, and Shakespeare the penitent pilgrim" (p. 7). The first has given rise to that veneration of Stratford and of any object associated with the poet that is the least harmful form of idolatry. As the biographical research of the eighteenth century "placed [Shakespeare] more and more firmly within a bourgeois setting" (p. 10), dispelling his image as an example of pre-eminent genius born among the peasantry, a countermovement grew to establish him as a familiar friend of the most glittering and talented members of the Elizabethan aristocracy. Anything but a son of the lower middle class, motivated by desire for material success and content with the company of his fellow actors. Since it could not be shown that Shakespeare himself was an aristocrat, and mere association was inadequate, perhaps it could be shown that some aristocrat was the author of the works so absurdly attributed to a man of common-place background and life style. What sprang from all this scarcely requires comment here and certainly not rehearsal. What is interesting are the consequences of this biographical deformation for the interpretation of Shakespeare's plays by actors, editors, and critics.

As Shakespeare "assumed superhuman proportions," his inconsistencies of fact and "lapses" of taste, as eighteenth-century editors regarded his verbal quibbles and indecencies, were readily attributed to the barbarousness of the players and the ignorance of the printers. The habit of editorial sophistication that grew from this assumption was soon to be attacked, but the "myth of perfection" was not abandoned. "Idolatry was not falling into decay; it was rebuilding on higher ground" (p. 30)—as in Malone's rationalization of a numerical slip (the "nineteen-fourteen" years discrepancy in *Measure For Measure*) into a deliberate and subtle beauty. But hindsight about the excesses of the past is safe and easy enough. Professor Harbage goes over this familiar and no longer embattled ground in order to place in perspective some current aberrations that spring also from the super-stition of a total perfection that is not critical praise, but only nonsensical absurdity, to attribute to works of human art. This can take the form of refusing to recognize obvious flaws in construction and in all matter of detail, or, still worse, of dismissing the observable data of character and action in order to reconstruct every detail into a perfectly meshed composition that bodies forth some great idea, "unmistakable, and yet hitherto mistaken, perfectly expressed, yet in need of 'interpretation'" (p. 37). While tampering with the text to satisfy critical presuppositions may no longer be tolerated, is not, Harbage asks, our "idolatrous transformation" of the dramas into embodiments of beautiful thoughts about humanity as naive and as groundless a critical activity as earlier programs for fitting Shakespeare to other myths of perfection? The danger is "that we shall trade our birthright of great artistry for a mess of third-rate philosophy" (p. 37).

Two succeeding chapters are devoted to the Shakespearean theater of the eighteenth and nineteenth centuries ("These Our Actors") and to the latest currents in our own theater ("Weighing Delight and Dole"). Harbage insists upon the essential rightness, the truthfulness to their spirit of conception, of the older actors in their portrayals of the tragic protagonists, despite acting conventions that are now outworn. The difference must be recognized between an obsolete style—the overemphasis of gesture and tone—and inter-pretation that is "wrong" because it distorts the fundamental nature of a character, as in criticism and productions which portray Hamlet as "weak, and even sinister." "The great actors never portrayed Hamlet as anything but admirable, the noble, aspiring, cruelly afflicted Prince" (p. 49). The actors were on the whole good in that they were faithful to the dramatist's conception of his characters; but their productions were radically bad from the standpoint of fidelity to Shakespeare's larger dramatic design and effect. The nineteenth century failed not only because of external theatrical conditions but because it was determined to make Shakespeare popular to audiences in terms of its own theater. "Art may be 'universal' without being universally appealing . . ." (p. 54). "Shakespeare the popular artist became Shakespeare the popularized artist" (p. 55).

In the next lecture, Harbage considers the fortunes of the plays as the directorial theater of our own time replaced the actors' theater of the previous century. The older actors assimilated Shakespeare to their sense of theatrical effectiveness, to melodrama; the modern director has increasingly assimilated Shakespeare to philosophic trends currently favored. The result of this up-dating is a falsification more serious, because more fundamental, than the popularization of last century. Shakespeare's balanced human centrality. his unfailing capacity to confront good and evil without collapsing into either a sentimental optimism or into an equally sentimental categorical pessimism, has been discarded in favor of a sour-minded nihilism, a heavy-handed self-congratulatory knowingness, that matches the mood of much current serious drama. Harbage offers particular strictures on Peter Brook's recent production of *King Lear* which reinforce the censure that Maynard Mack aimed from a somewhat different standpoint in his recent study, *King Lear in Our Time.* The cuttings and the innovations of business of actors and directors alike are scarcely new, representing each generation's attempt to bring Shakespeare's truth most forcibly to bear upon its own audience. But Brook's deletion, for example, of the choric lines of Cornwall's servants after the putting out of Gloucester's eyes involves something more than an altered emphasis. For in this production a piece of business was added in which "one of the servants gave the blinded man a hostile push as he groped his way from the stage" (p. 74), an act which deliberately rejects and reverses what Shakespeare explicitly insists upon here. As such it "betray[s] a lack of belief in the work itself" (p. 74). Harbage cites a "revolution in sentiment, and to an undetermined degree in private morality, so that an estrangement from Shakespeare exists in some areas not unlike that which existed among the literati of the Restoration," (p. 70) as the motivating impulse for directors to superimpose upon the plays editorial ideas that will bring them up-to-date and convey a vision more like that of dramatists writing today. Nothing is allowed to hinder this interest: "Speeches in conflict with the chosen *idea* of the play may be thrown away or rendered self-satirizing. Business can be contrived to reverse the bearing of a whole dialogue or even an action" (p. 71).

The resemblance between Harbage's notion of a "commentary," "some editorial idea, original or borrowed" (p. 71) and what Maynard Mack has called "sub-texts" is certainly significant, as each is an independent recognition of the same phenomenon, and one that applies, of course, to literary criticism as well as to Shakespeare in the theater. I would add that a play like Tom Stoppard's *Rosencrantz and Guildenstern are Dead* is an inevitable and altogether legitimate result of the inability of many to accept Shakespeare's central meanings. This hyperverbally brilliant exercise in corrosive anti-tragedy functions both as a successful, if all too single-dimensioned, theater piece in its own right, and also as an embodiment in dramatic form of what must be acknowledged to be a widely received response to *Hamlet,* as witnessed even in a good deal of recent academic criticism of the play and its protagonist. If these *are* the only terms in which Shakespeare's plays can speak to audiences for whom only the vision of a Genêt or a Beckett is viable, then by all means let us have more *original* plays based on Shakespeare's plots and characters but shaped to meanings that are felt to be relevant. But for a director surreptitiously to work the values of these modern writers into Shakespeare's text is neither to create something new nor to renew something old, but only to engage in a dishonest tampering with something he does not value intrinsically but whose prestige he wishes to exploit. To illustrate by reference to another art, a musical conductor, if one can conceive of such, who finds the very lucidity and order of Mozart a dreary and predictable bore, might properly ignore him and program twentieth-century composers for whose technique and idiom he has greater sympathy, or he might, like Prokofiev, write a classical symphony that exaggerates and spoofs Mozart, thus wittily answering the conservative taste that cannot see beyond Mozart to the value of modern music. But to offer as a serious performance of Mozart a reading that attempts to make him sound like a Hindemith or a Stockhausen would do justice neither to any of these composers nor to the concert audience.

A chapter devoted to the rationale and history of the "philosophical impact" of *King Lear* ("The Fierce Dispute") seeks to account for the problem of interpretation by setting the Elizabethan notion of tragedy—"not psychological and aesthetic, but religious and didactic" (p. 78)—with its roots in the medieval attitude of *contemptus mundi,* in the lesson of *de casibus,* and in the view of "tragedy as commemorative of heroic self-sacrifice" (p. 79) against the expectations and assumptions of later periods. The chapter is a useful and illuminating guide to the background of current critical controversy about *Lear,* but its own conclusions, posited in sharply abbreviated compass rather than demonstrated do not provide anything more than a restatement of such generally accepted views as "It seems to say that everything depends upon what men do, and yet to say that men cannot do all" (p. 97).

A section titled "Related Essays" rounds out this volume. Harbage considers "Shakespeare as Culture Hero" and accounts for the anti-Stratfordianism of James Wilmot, Delia Bacon, Mark Twain, and Sigmund Freud, by reference to their mythmaking propensities which spring from "family romance fantasy." From this psychologizing of the psychologizers of Shakespeare the author turns to the defining in one brief chapter of "Shakespeare's Ideal Man." While in no sense controversial, this chapter strikes me as the most dubious in the book—dubious for the same reasons as the author's fuller exposition of Shakespeare's ethical preferences in *As They Liked It* and elsewhere. It is one thing to assert in the face of romantic psychologizing that Shakespeare in his dealings with his fellows was a man of unexceptionable normality and sweet-natured decency, but quite another to limit the perception and statement of the plays to what can be fitted within the range of the temper and outlook of such a man as man. No such limits necessarily apply to the artist. The fact that Shakespeare was a popular dramatist may well mean that he could not have succeeded had his primary intent appeared to be the reshaping of his audience's basic beliefs, rather than appealing to beliefs already held and assuming them as guides to his audience's judgments about character and action. But surely this does not rule out effects and meanings larger than (if not actually at variance with) the kind of complacent bourgeois vision that Harbage seems almost to revel in. The kinds of ramifications that the author of this book points to in *Lear* themselves break the confines of ethical loyalties and interests that are induced for Shakespeare the composite. To say that Shakespeare lacks interest in or admiration for the man shaped by ideology seems to me perfectly true (I am not aware that anyone taken seriously has argued otherwise). But this does not mean, as Harbage's argument might imply, that the world of thought is not relevant to the values that Shakespeare's admired characters do hold or to the actions they perform. The main difficulty here is the level at which we can agree with Harbage's easy-going generalizations about the Shakespearean ethic: This scants the plays as unique works for which Shakespeare-the-man's ethical attitudes are idly, if not misleadingly, asserted, since it is only within the separate coherency of each play that ethical meanings take definite shape and not the other way around.

Vanderbilt University

Validity in Interpretation by E. D. Hirsch, Jr. Yale University Press, 1967. Pp. xiv + 287. $6.50. *Reviewer: Joseph Margolis.*

Professor E. D. Hirsch has written, in *Validity in Interpretation*, a book that is at once learned and extremely naive. In a sentence, his thesis is that "the only compelling normative principle that has ever been brought forward [for the valid interpretation of literary texts] is the old-fashioned ideal of rightly understanding what the author meant" (p. 26). Put more circumspectly, Hirsch belongs in the tradition of hermaneutics focussed principally by Schleiermacher, August Boeckh, and most recently by Emilio Betti. He traces his reliance on the notion of "intrinsic genres" to Schleiermacher—which notion, as we shall see, is essential to his thesis about valid interpretation; and he acknowledges an open debt to Betti's distinction of types of interpretation (corresponding to the nature of the texts involved, e.g., literary, dramatic, sacred) and favors, in Betti's terms, "viewing interpretation [of literary texts] as a re-cognition of the author's meaning" (p. 26). The issue is undoubtedly one of the master questions facing professional literary criticism: it is extremely helpful—without prejudice to the force of Hirsch's own thesis—to have it canvassed by a partisan of the most conservative and venerable position possible. For, *if* it is genuinely possible to determine "what the author meant" in his text and *if* to determine this is to exhaust the work of interpretation, a great many of the ingenious and inventive efforts of literary commentators are simply irrelevant to an *understanding* of the text itself, however suggestive they may be in the context of a *criticism* of it.

Hirsch himself is quite explicit about his "rigid separation of meaning and significance with respect to textual commentary" (p. 142): by "understanding," he means "a perception or construction of the author's verbal meaning, nothing more, nothing less"; and by "judgment" ("commentary," "criticism," "evaluation" serve limited clarificatory functions), he means the judging or assessing of the significance of a work whose meaning is already correctly construed. As Hirsch says, "In the first instance [understanding or re-cognitive interpretation] one submits to another [the author]—literally, one stands under him. In the second, one acts independently—by one's own authority—like a judge" (pp. 142-143). He offers, usefully, some remarks on Hamlet criticism, in order to fix our picture of his program:

> We have posited [this is purely hypothetical, for the sake of an illustration] that Shakespeare did not mean that Hamlet wished to sleep with his mother. We confront an interpretation which states that Hamlet did wish to sleep with his mother. If we assert, as I have done, that only a re-cognitive interpretation is a valid interpretation, then we must, on the basis of our assumed premise about the play, say that the Freudian interpretation is invalid. It does not correspond to the author's meaning; it is an implication that cannot be subsumed under the type of meaning that Shakespeare (under our arbitrary supposition) willed. It is irrelevant that the play permits such an interpretation. The variability of possible implications is the very fact that requires a theory of interpretation and validity. (Pp. 122-123)

It is, I think, clear that we need to know what Hirsch means by "the author's verbal meaning," what the "author willed," and how he proposes that we determine his meaning, how we are to separate correct or valid interpretations of texts from merely plausible interpretations. More broadly construed, Hirsch's account may be taken to explore the ontology of a work of art, the nature of interpretation and criticism in the arts, and the intentionality of language and art. I confess I am not in the least attracted to his position; but I also believe that, although the book provides us with a strong sense of the complexity and scope of the relevant issues, there are quite simple and fundamental difficulties that Hirsch has failed to resolve and that, to my mind, are incapable of being resolved in any way favorable to his thesis.

Consider, then, that Hirsch does not actually deny that "the Freudian argument [respecting *Hamlet*] *could* be valid" (p. 125). In fact, he holds explicitly that "for some genres of texts [literature and law, for instance] the author submits to the convention that his willed implications must go far beyond what he explicitly knows" (p. 123); a valid interpretation might well be "strange and foreign to the original author" (p. 126). One might reasonably be tempted to say that Hirsch is holding fast to the fiction of the author's will in order, precisely, to assimilate to his model historically emergent and compelling interpretations that, on more normal grounds, would be construed as exceeding the author's intentions — whatever they may be supposed to be. He himself is aware of the reasonableness of such a challenge and he has an answer ready: "the human author's willed meaning can always go beyond what he consciously intended so long as it remains within his willed type" (p. 126n). But, of course, his reply attenuates the force of his original thesis; for, it is not merely that we are to interpret a given work in accord with "what the author meant" but rather that the author may be said to have meant his work to be understood in ways in which, by hypothesis, *he could not* (in an obvious sense of "meant") *have meant* his work to be taken. We may accept Hirsch's adjustment, for the sake of the argument, but we must see that the quarrel between Hirsch and theorists who reject the "author's meaning" as the sole defensible norm of valid interpretation is completely altered and even, perhaps, made quite pointless. If, for instance, an interpretation admitted to be plausible on the strength of an examination of the text, without regard to the author's intentions but in accord with linguistic usage, may, retroactively so to say, be validly attributed to the author's "will," then, surely, Hirsch's standard is a pure fiction and could never serve to disqualify any proposed interpretation at all (which is not to say all interpretations are equally admissible). It must, however, in fairness to his argument, be admitted that our objection is a conditional one and depends on the defensibility of Hirsch's notion of what he calls the author's "willed type."

Interestingly enough, Hirsch supports his thesis by drawing parallels between the interpretation of literary texts and the law. It is quite true, as he points out, that "the conventions of law-making and law interpreting must include the notion of analogy," that the "idea of a law contains the idea of mutatis mutandis" (p. 125). But it is very difficult to see how this entirely legitimate observation can be made to confirm his own doctrine. There is, in fact, an absolutely fundamental equivocation in Hirsch's use of "author's will" and "author's intention." For, on one reading, the interpreter is expected to unearth or discover the author's meaning, which is, in some sense, to be found in the work once and for all; and on another reading, the interpreter is entitled to ascribe meanings to the work, that might well exceed the author's (conscious) intent (or even likely extensions in terms of culturally prevalent usage and belief), drawing on all sorts of novel considerations arising with cultural changes, provided only that the added meanings may be shown to accord with certain criteria of admissible analogy and extension. It is unreasonable to hold that, for both readings, one may speak of the author's intention univocally. Furthermore, Hirsch's parallel between literary and legal texts obliges us, contrary to his own claim, to consider the possible irrelevance of the author's intention. For, who reflecting on the American Constitution (Hirsch's own instance) could possibly suppose that the extension of interpretations of positive law into our own day is, in some distinct sense relevantly bearing on validity, grounded only on the original authors' intention or meaning and not on the continuous liberalizing (within changing boundaries of coherence) of the sense of the Constitution (cf. pp. 121-125)? It is closer to the truth to concede that we christen the law extended by interpretation as "constitutional" and thus in accord with the original intent than that we find whether or not it does accord with that intent—safely formulated (or formulable) once and for all in an independent way. Analogical argument doubtless has its own distinctive logic, but its clarification will surely not permit—what Hirsch requires—a clear demarcation line between justified *decisions* respecting extending the sense of the law (through interpretation) or extending the sense of literary texts (through interpretation) and confirmed *discoveries* of the sense of the law and of literary texts. Hirsch speaks, as we have noted, of "a sharp separation" between interpretation and criticism, but he nowhere demonstrates that it can be sustained.

The argument goes deeper. For one thing, Hirsch holds that "a verbal meaning is determinate . . . [that is] that it is an entity that is self-identical . . . an entity which always remains the same from one moment to the next—that it is changeless" (p. 46). The entire effort to oppose historicism, therefore, is altogether futile if Hirsch cannot (and he neither can nor does) specify a procedure by which to fix once and for all the author's meaning by which to test all candidate interpretations. Also, it is not at all necessary to adopt an extreme historicism (contrary to Hirsch's expectation) if one rejects the notion of an eternal and changeless "verbal meaning" proper to each and every literary text: it is entirely possible to introduce canons of plausibility among competing interpretations without supposing either that all defensible interpretations are compatible or that defensible interpretations accord with the author's intent—however generously (and not vacuously) that may be construed. For another thing, Hirsch nowhere demonstrates that the work of literary interpretation *is* solely to unearth the author's intention or intended meaning. He says, very plainly, that interpretation's "exclusive object is verbal meaning," which itself provides "the only proper foundation of criticism" (p. 57). Nevertheless, critics very often suppose that, in the face of puzzling texts, that is, texts whose internal order and coherence is not obvious, they may be called on to *propose* or to *invent* interpretations that the text may be said plausibly to *support* or to *admit*. And if this is so—which seems eminently reasonable in the light of actual professional practice as well as of the conceptual difficulties of Hirsch's alternative—then we see once again that the division of interpretation and criticism cannot be sustained and the likelihood of generating defensible interpretations that are incompatible with one another is very much increased. What is most important, however, is that the conception of interpretation itself is fundamentally affected by the acceptance or rejection of the normative role of the author's meaning. Here, it is sufficient to observe that Hirsch's own account of the work of interpretation allows, as we have seen, for the validation of interpretations that cannot be said to have been "willed" by the author, in any narrow sense confined to his original conscious intentions or even to usage or belief prevalent in his contemporary culture. Consequently, there is no clear line of demarcation that can, consistently with his view, be set to divide what is found somehow hidden *in* a given work and what may be defensibly ascribed *to* it. But this is precisely how Hirsch had supposed interpretation and criticism to be distinguished (pp. 62-63). The paradox of Hirsch's view is simply that, on his thesis, novel interpretations of a literary text may be said to disclose meanings "in the work itself" in spite of the fact that they could not be said to be in it in the sense of being part of what the author clearly and determinately "willed" — which, paradigmatically, determines what is in the work.

Hirsch, of course, must be tracked through further subtleties. He is aware of the paradox and attempts to resolve it by reference to his theories of implication and of intrinsic genres. "The logic of implication," he says, "is always . . . a genre logic, as common sense tells every interpreter. Whether an implication is present depends upon the kind of meaning that is being interpreted" (p. 91). The point of these remarks is that disputes about interpretations usually concern a "disagreement about genre" (p. 98), that is, that "understanding can occur only if the interpreter proceeds under the same system of expectations [as the speaker or writer], and this shared generic conception, constitutive both of meaning and of understanding, is the intrinsic genre of the utterance" (pp. 80-81). So it appears that a grasp of the "intrinsic genre" of any utterance (read, "literary text" — for Hirsch quite without debate assimilates literary works of art to speech utterances, which may well explain his emphasis on the speaker's or author's will — but see pp. 246, 248) is a necessary condition to understanding both what an author is saying and what, in the generous sense already explored, he may be said to "imply." The difficulty, of course, is simply that the metaphor of language games (here, Hirsch borrows rather misleadingly from Wittgenstein's picture of language, p. 93) obviates rather than supports the need to rely on the primacy of the author's will. For, in the Wittgensteinian sense of language games, interpretations *both* based on the author's alleged intention and plausibly supported by the text (but not independently linked to the author's intention) could be construed as falling within the same language game.

Alternatively put, it is inconceivable that the Wittgensteinian theory of language (or, in fact, any comparable view — Saussure's distinction between *langue* and *parole* for instance, pp. 69-70) could supply the necessary criteria for determining so-called intrinsic genres by which valid and invalid interpretations may be identified. What Hirsch confuses — and I cannot soften the charge that he is guilty of a confusion — is the analysis of the phenomenon of language in intentional terms and the specification of a speaker's intention in using language. Language as a system of verbal activity cannot be satisfactorily analyzed without attention to what for instance C. S. Peirce marks as the triadic relationship of communicating by symbols — baldly put, that, minimally, something means something to someone. Applied to Hirsch's account, one may say that merely in speaking a language one's meaning can be construed by reference to the rough rules and regularities of the language. Reference to a speaker's intention can never be more fundamental; on the contrary, a speaker's intention is itself formulable in terms of such rules. Anything else would lead to an intentional or solipsistic theory of language: that what is said is what a speaker means in issuing an utterance, in terms prior to all public language conventions. Similarly, then, for the tracing of "implications": they may be marked out, if they may be marked out at all, by reference to the rules of language. But this means that, given the intentionality of language, the meaning of what is said may be determined without any reliance at all on Hirsch's central thesis: that "valid interpretation" depends on "the old-fashioned ideal of rightly understanding what the author meant." Hirsch himself, it must be noted, concedes that "linguistic norms at the very least always impose limitations on verbal meaning" (p. 29), that is, on "what the author meant." But here too, as indeed everywhere in his text, Hirsch conflates the intentionality of speech and language and the determinate intentions of particular speakers on particular occasions (cf. pp. 31, 46, 47, 51, 52; also, Appendix I). To offer one instance of the inherent equivocation, consider the following: "That discriminating force [which causes the meaning to be *this* instead of *that* or *that* or *that*] must involve an act of will, since unless one particular complex of meaning is *willed* (no matter how 'rich' and 'various' it may be), there would be no distinction between what an author does mean by a word sequence and what he could mean by it. Determinacy of verbal meaning requires an act of will" (p. 47). But of course as long as a determinate speech act has occurred, we may construe its meaning in accord with the rules of language, even if we are attending to the additional complication of determining what the author intended by *what he said*; otherwise, the reference to "will" is nothing more than a nod in the direction of the intentionality of the very phenomenon, language—which has nothing whatsoever to do with the special problems of valid interpretation (applying as it does to invalid interpretation just as well, not to mention alternative interpretations now according with the author's intention, now not).

There is, it may also be observed, a strong inclination, in Hirsch's account, to favor Dilthey's use of the concept of *Verstehen* (cf. p. 242n). This of course suggests a strongly voluntaristic reading of his own hermaneutic principles. But even his detailed remarks regarding "implications" may readily be construed without serious regard to this reading. The irony is that Hirsch's initially strong emphasis on the author's will pretty well peters out by the end of the book and "will" falls nearly completely into the role of merely registering the intentional nature of language. Thus, in various locations, Hirsch holds that "a verbal meaning is a willed type" (p. 51)—here, "type" refers to the type-token distinction, that "an implication belongs within a verbal meaning as a part belongs to a whole" (p. 64), and that "implications are derived from a shared type that has been learned, and therefore the generation of implications depends on the interpreter's previous experience of the shared type" (p. 66). Clearly, if to identify the "implications" of an utterance or text depends on experience with the public regularities of a language, reference to the author's will and intent is pointedly irrelevant to understanding the meaning of his text and all linguistically appropriate interpretations will meet Hirsch's criteria, whether or not they may be squared with the author's intention and whether or not they may be jointly compatible. One may almost say that Hirsch's conception may be taken to justify precisely the greatest freedom in proposing *plausible* as distinct from *valid* interpretations—though always, of course, against his own objective.

The equivocation already noted may be traced as well through Hirsch's linking of the concepts of "implication" and "intrinsic genres." He holds "that the implications of an utterance are determined by its intrinsic genre" (p. 89). But he also holds, in attempting to clarify this thesis, both that "a genre conception is constitutive of speaking as well as of interpreting" (p. 78) (which diminishes the role of the author's will in favor of public rules of linguistic usage) and that "the purpose of a genre is the communicable purpose of a particular speaker, nothing more nor less" (p. 101n) (which tends rather to favor the author's deliberate will and intention). It is also true that he dabbles with the notion, following Boeckh, that "*Zweck* must be an entelechy, a goal-seeking force that animates a particular kind of utterance" (p. 101), which suggests the inescapable equivocation of even seemingly straightforward explanations. Also, he regularly hedges on the reality of so-called intrinsic genres (pp. 108-126), employs Wittgenstein's notion of family resemblances to avoid (properly) holding to strict classes (pp. 114-115), but is ultimately reduced merely to insisting in a question-begging way that "there emphatically is such a thing as the intrinsic interpretation of a text" (p. 115), that is, interpretation in terms of intrinsic genres. Thus, it is not in the least clear whether we should assimilate interpretations to what is "embraced by the author's will," by appeal to our antecedent genres (whose mode of determination is an utter mystery), or whether we should assess our interpretations in accord with heuristically proposed genres by attention to "what the author meant" (*really* meant— which is another mystery) (pp. 123-124).

Hirsch himself raises the most serious methodological difficulty facing his own thesis or any similar thesis that holds to there being in principle *a correct interpretation* of a given text, namely, the self-confirming nature of interpretations (p. 165), the "inevitable circularity" of every interpreter's effort, that "all his internal evidence tends to support his hypothesis because much of it was constituted by his hypothesis" (p. 166). Indeed, he goes so far as to say that the "tendency of interpretations to be self-contained and incommensurable is . . . the principal handicap that will always plague the discipline of interpretations" (p. 167). In the light of these concessions, difficulties already noted, and his remarks about the probabilism of interpretation, it is difficult to see how he could or why he would hold that, with respect to a given text, "two disparate interpretations cannot both be correct" (pp. 173, 230).

There are essentially two strategies by which Hirsch attempts to support his thesis. By one, he construes his entire claim in probabilistic terms (p. 180). This is a curious move, since it is by rights an irrelevancy: the probabilistic nature of interpretive hypotheses has nothing whatsoever to do with the defense of the thesis respecting the primacy of the author's will. Actually, Hirsch is driven to admissions of the indecisiveness of evidence, primarily because of the so-called "hermaneutic circle" (p. 76) mentioned just above— which would lead us to a range of alternative interpretations comparable in plausibility and supported by a given text but not necessarily compatible with one another ("disparate," in Hirsch's terms). But he manages to construe this sort of indecisiveness somehow as strengthening his own theory. He turns the trick by breaking out of the circle, denying the sufficiency of "internal evidence" with respect to any text and insisting on "a consideration of all the known relevant data" (p. 192)—which is to say, he recommends appraising interpretations in terms of external evidence as well ("date, authorship, milieu, and so on," p. 198). The trouble is that the appeal to external evidence certainly leads us in the direction of coherence and plausibility rather than in the direction of fidelity to the author's intention *in a particular work* and of uniquely correct interpretations; also, it can only be seen as ironic that the internal evidence of any given text produces the hermaneutic circle. Hirsch nowhere considers the problem that an author may well have *intended* to produce a work of a sort quite different from what he may have intended in other of his efforts (even without psychologizing 'intention'—cf. Appendix I). Consequently, he cannot really effectively defend his critical program—that holds that "genuinely intrinsic judgment is founded entirely on the author's aims and norms" (p. 151)—and he cannot defend a clear demarcation line between internal and external criticism (pp. 152-154). And if he cannot, he cannot show that interpretations can, in principle, be more than plausible or that "disparate" interpretations cannot jointly be confirmed ("validated") and not merely allowed to stand for want of deciding evidence (p. 172). The appeal to a Keynsian view of probability (pp. 173-180) is further spoiled by Hirsch's confusion between the concept that what is probable is probable-relative-to-the-evidence-given and the concept of what may be known, with certainty or as probable. In any case, he speaks rather casually, in the context of Keynes' views, of the author's meaning as a "reality" that may "never be known with certainty" (pp. 175, 240). Probabilism, of course, may be adopted by Hirsch's opponents as well as by Hirsch; and skepticism with respect to the author's purpose can hardly be counted on to vindicate Hirsch's thesis against those, precisely, who refuse to construe the author's intent as normative. It is worth adding that Hirsch's paradigmatic cases of interpretation are characteristically occupied with fixing the sense of particular words and phrases (pp. 184-190; 199-202)—which surely bypasses his principal thesis; and that when he considers full-fledged interpretation (as with Wordsworth and Blake), he sees the constant threat of the hermaneutic circle (pp. 190-196).

The book concludes with three Appendices. The first is rather marred by an altogether inapt appropriation of Frege's distinction between *Sinn* and *Bedeutung* to clarify Hirsch's own distinction between meaning and significance (interpretation and criticism). It offers an early version of the principal thesis and employs the strong term "verification" in place of the somewhat skeptical and probabilized term "validation"; but in its exploration of Husserl, Dilthey, and Saussure, it fails, as far as I can see, to discuss clearly the critical relevance of a psychologized notion of the author's intention and a non-psychologized notion of what Hirsch calls " the author's subjective stance" (p. 238). The psychologized alternative leads to the Intentional Fallacy and solipsism; but the non-psychologized alternative does not satisfactorily yield Hirsch's required contrast between intentional and non-intentional criticism—as for instance even against Wimsatt and Beardsley's view "that the text, being public, means what the speech community takes it to mean" (p. 233), or against Eliot's view that the changing meaning of a literary work depends on the "changing literary tradition" (p. 215). In a word, there is absolutely nothing that Hirsch offers to support the feasibility of achieving the *Verstehen* theorist's goal of interpretation: "a deliberate reconstruction of the author's subjective stance to the extent that this stance is relevant to the text at hand" (p. 238). But without such support, Hirsch cannot distinguish, as he wishes, the "two horizons of textual criticism," interpretation and criticism (p. 224).

The second Appendix contains a critical review of Hans-Georg Gadamer's *Wahrheit und Methode* (Tubingen, 1960), which construes hermaneutic theory along historicist lines influenced by Heidegger. I am entirely prepared to agree with the charge of incoherence against historicism—and along broader lines than Hirsch himself pursues. But it would be a mistake to suppose that a rejection of Hirsch's own theories leads one to either psychologism or historicism, that Hirsch is at pains to defeat (Ch. 1); and the truth is that Gadamer (whose work I am not familiar with) is concerned to attack "the premise that textual meaning is the same as the author's meaning" (p. 247), apart from advancing his own positive theories. Hirsch regularly supposes that it is impossible to construe interpretation as an objective venture if the norm of the author's meaning is rejected. But, as I have argued, Hirsch nowhere shows this to be so (he conflates the issues with that of historicism); and, furthermore, it appears to be genuinely difficult to demonstrate that his own proposals do actually permit us to mark out the division between the "re-cognition of the author's meaning" and the inventive ascription of meanings on grounds of plausibility. The final Appendix provides an excursus on types. But here I find myself rather at a loss. The obvious purpose of the account is to demonstrate "the indispensable heuristic function of type ideas" as well as their "inescapable constitutive function" (pp. 271-272) and to sympathize with *verstehende* views of idiographic knowledge (p. 271). But if the argument were granted (and it is altogether too casual and vague to be discussed—"type" seems to change its sense for Hirsch from context to context: now it is used in terms of the type-token distinction, now it refers to logical puzzles regarding the theory of types, now it refers to the Wittgensteinian problem of classes and family resemblances, now it refers to determinate and closed intentions and the subsumption of particulars under open-ended categories, now it refers to the problem of Lockeian abstractionism, now it refers to ideographic vs. nomethetic knowledge—), it would inevitably turn out, as most of what Hirsch has to say, to be altogether neutral to the dispute respecting his central thesis.

I cannot, in a word, see that Hirsch either establishes or could establish his thesis.

Temple University

The Life and Times of Sir Thomas Elyot, Englishman by Pearl Hogrefe. The Iowa State University Press, 1967. Pp. x + 410; pl. 7. $6.50. *Reviewer: Leland Miles.*

I

Professor Hogrefe's admirably fulfilled purpose in this volume is to relate the writings of Tudor humanist Elyot to the political events of Henry VIII's reign. On returning from his embassy to Charles V in June, 1532, Elyot remonstrated with the king concerning the Anne Boleyn issue; sent a report (in cipher) on the king's reaction to Charles V's chaplain De-Puebla; then proceeded openly to consult with Chapuys, Charles' ambassador in London. Miss Hogrefe correctly emphasizes that such tactics required courage. It was a time when most men were carefully avoiding Chapuys lest they offend the king. In April, 1531, for example, Sir Thomas More had begged Chapuys to keep his distance.

Elyot's discreetly aggressive efforts on behalf of Catherine and conservative religion are shown by Hogrefe to be reflected in four successive works. In the first of these, *The Book Named the Governor* (1531), Elyot sought to influence the king's character by stressing the danger of carnal appetite and by placing limitations on the king's power. Elyot (like Bacon later) contended that such power must be used solely for the welfare of the people. Running through the *Governor* is a strong plea for the freedom of subjects, especially counselors, to speak frankly to their masters. This theme is reiterated in *Pasquil the Plain* (1533). *Of the Knowledge Which Maketh a Wise Man* (also 1533) treats the banishment of Plato by the tyrant Dionysus. Three questions are raised: How does a true king differ from a tyrant? How do we reconcile adversity with a good God? Why especially does God permit good men to suffer?

We should reflect seriously on Hogrefe's conjecture (inspired by Edwin J. Howard's suggestion in 1946) that Dionysus and Plato are here intended as allegorical screens for Henry VIII and More. In 1532 More had resigned his Lord Chancellorship, ostensibly because of ill health. The actual reason was More's agitation over the course of events which soon led to the break with Rome. Given the political background, we must also accept as reasonable Hogrefe's contention that Elyot, in discussing the suffering of good men, had More in mind. During the months following More's resignation in May, 1532, he was reduced to relative poverty, became increasingly ill, and was falsely charged with taking bribes. Incidentally, Elyot's discussion of adversity in the *Knowledge* treatise closely parallels More's argument a year later in *A Dialogue of Comfort against Tribulation* (1534). In both cases the list of adversities or tribulations includes loss of high office, authority, riches, and material possessions. In both cases, God's permitting good men to suffer is justified on the grounds that such adversity cures men of pride, ambition, and other vices. (Note

414

this reviewer's edition of More's *Dialogue,* Bloomington: Indiana University Press, 1965, Part I, Chapter 7-10; Part III, Chapters 4-15. Also Intro., pp. xxxix-xl.)

In the three works just analyzed, Hogrefe shrewdly notes Elyot's growing disillusionment with Henry VIII. In the *Governor,* there is every indication that Elyot had hopes of swaying the king on the issue of private morality. In *Pasquil,* there is a disappointed recognition that vicious affections are poisoning the "master's" mind. In the *Knowledge* piece, Elyot finds the ruler hopeless and has shifted his concern to his long-time friend, the "banished philosopher" More.

In April, 1534 Sir Thomas More was sent to the Tower for refusing to swear the oath of supremacy. To strengthen More's resolution was possibly one motivation for Elyot's fourth volume (July, 1534), a combined translation of St. Cyprian's sermon *On the Mortality of Man* and Pico della Mirandola's *Rules of a Christian Life.* This reviewer has suggested elsewhere (*Dialogue of Comfort,* Intro., p. lxx) that Margaret Roper, knowing More's fondness for Pico, might well have taken this volume to More in prison at the time (summer, 1534) he was composing the *Comfort* treatise. In any event, Cyprian was much on More's mind as he wrote the *Dialogue* and as he prepared for the scaffold on the morning of his execution (*Ibid.,* Intro., pp. xxx, lxix). In his preface to Cyprian's sermon, Elyot had stressed its appropriateness for persons facing persecution and death. More no doubt had read Cyprian earlier (Erasmus' edition was published in 1519-20); but More's attention might well have been refocused on Cyprian by the publication of Elyot's little book coincidentally with More's own imprisonment.

It is altogether possible, as Hogrefe appealingly suggests, that the Cyprian-Pico volume was Elyot's own *Dialogue of Comfort,* through which he sought, as did More in the parallel work, to strengthen himself for disaster and death. Elyot might well have fancied himself refusing the oath of supremacy. Yet eventually he took the oath. Flesh won out over spirit.

II

If we were to consider Elyot's writings only through the year 1534, we would need to characterize him as a skillful and bold defender of Queen Catherine and orthodox religion. Indeed, as late as 1534, Elyot was playing a dangerous game: namely, trying to persuade the Emperor Charles to take action on behalf of Catherine. Yet a short year later, according to evidence supplied by Hogrefe, Elyot had beaten a startling retreat. In a letter to More's archenemy Cromwell (late 1535 or 1536), Elyot plaintively stresses his friendship for that now powerful figure, and asserts (much to the reader's amazement) that he has never favored those who advanced "the pompous authority of the Bishop of Rome." He meekly agrees to turn in the one or two "seditious" volumes in his possession. Apparently alluding to More, he now claims that his desire for religious reform had led him into contention with certain people, resulting in the breach of old friendships. In a later letter to Cromwell (February, 1537), Elyot specifically mentions More and implores Cromwell to forget that Elyot and More were ever friends. The *Castle of Health* (1536?) is dedicated to Cromwell; its avowed purpose is to aid Cromwell in his illness. Simultaneous with these developments, we find Elyot coming back into favor and being named to government commissions.

Despite Professor Hogrefe's tactful attempts to minimize this turnabout, it is obvious that we have here a pathetic change of position. How do we explain it? In this reviewer's judgment, we explain it through two closely related events occurring respectively in May and July, 1535. In the first instance, Father Reynolds of Syon House was disemboweled along with three anti-oath Carthusian monks. In the second instance, Sir Thomas More was beheaded. Both events shocked Elyot to the core—the first, because he had three step-sisters at Syon; the second, because it was hard to comprehend the legal murder of a friend whose prestige had seemed to make him impervious to harm.

There is no evidence that Elyot dreaded physical pain to the extent that More did. But Elyot (as he demonstrates in the *Governor* and elsewhere) venerated material possessions to a degree which did not allow for losing them if it could be avoided. By contrast, More (like his old friend John Colet) was contemptuous of physical ownership (see *Comfort*, Intro., p. xlv, and Part III, Chapter 6. Also Roper's *Life*, pp. 82-84). To be sure, Elyot had once made a statement startlingly similar to More's on the scaffold. "I am all the king's except my soul," Elyot had written to the Duke of Norfolk (March, 1532). But in the last analysis, the soul ranked lower than material well-being in Elyot's scale of values. Miss Hogrefe concedes that "Elyot was not the man to become a martyr." Despite this concession, the author plaintively insists in her summary chapter that Elyot's life was characterized by "integrity" and a veneration for friendship. On the basis of evidence supplied by the author herself, this reviewer is reluctant to come to such a conclusion.

As implied by the foregoing, there emerges from *The Life and Times of Sir Thomas Elyot, Englishman* a comparative study of Elyot and More. Both refused bribes and sympathized with the poor. But the contrasts are more striking than the similarities. Elyot lacked More's most appealing qualities—zest, warmth, humor, imagination. Also, the early Elyot naively thought Henry reformable, whereas More from the start perceived the ruthlessness lying just beneath the regal affability. Thus early in the game More commented to Roper: "If my head could win him [Henry] a castle in France . . . , it should not fail to go" (Roper, p. 21).

III

Professor Hogrefe's biography has many merits. Her stature in the field of creative writing is confirmed by her sometimes vivid characterization and her frequently memorable turns of phrase. There is a useful detailed analysis of the *Governor*—its contents, classical sources, and especially its direct relation to English life in Elyot's treatment of archery, dancing, and music. There is a cogent, comprehensive, and unusually fair-minded analysis of religious conservatives and reformers in the Tudor Age. There are examples of careful historical research for the purpose of eliminating prior misconceptions. For example, Hogrefe assembles ample evidence to repudiate the view that the shortness (nine months) of Elyot's ambassadorship to the Emperor Charles (1531-2) was an indictment of his abilities. Although the bibliography is sketchy, Appendix II ("Alleged Influences of Elyot on Other Writers") supplies helpful summaries of a number of appropriate articles.

Most important, Miss Hogrefe avoids the typical biographer's sin: she sturdily resists the temptation to puff up her subject. She concedes that Elyot had little political influence, and that much of his literary work was minor. She nonetheless has the courage to argue a point which will irritate many More devotees: namely, that as a strictly 16th century *English* writer, Elyot was more significant than More (for a similar argument, see the Introduction to the Indiana University Press edition of the *Dialogue of Comfort*, pp. xxxvi-xxxviii). When all is said and done, however, Elyot wrote no classic like *Utopia*. We must agree with Miss Hogrefe that Sir Thomas Elyot, Englishman, was for an age only, not for all time.

Alfred University

Lear's Self-Discovery by Paul A. Jorgensen. University of California Press, 1967. Pp. viii + 154. $4.50. *Reviewer: Terence Hawkes.*

Nosce *teipsum* commonly looms through the confusion of much Elizabethan and Jacobean tragedy as an ostensible yet oddly indeterminate principle barrenly confronting the protagonists. Professor Jorgensen's attempt to breathe new life into the concept of self-knowledge, both as a maxim of morality and as a stratagem for the organization of a dramatic structure, proves bracing in the circumstances; the more so because it handles interestingly and intelligently a subject which, it is admitted, has become riddled with cliché, petrified by stereotype.

As a result, the account this book gives of *King Lear* as "perhaps the greatest drama of self-discovery in all literature," adds a valuable dimension to our understanding of that play's construction. For as Professor Jorgensen rightly points out, its dynamic quality subtly mimics the heuristic process by whose means the self is gradually revealed to the seeker. If what Lear attains at the end is self-knowledge, self-*discovery* proves to be the dramatic as well as the intellectual means whereby it is attained.

After a shrewd survey and account of the various critical approaches to the theme of self-knowledge in the play, in the course of which the major stereotype is uncovered, that "self-discovery means acknowledging that one has erred," Professor Jorgensen turns to a detailed consideration of what the concept of self-knowledge actually meant for the Renaissance. His examination reveals that, far from the simple recognition of an error in judgement, the tradition of self-knowledge which Shakespeare inherited demanded a rigorous and shattering analysis, of the body as well as of the mind, in pursuit of what one contemporary writer terms "the chefyst poynt of wysdome and direccyon of a mannes lyfe." Self-knowledge of that sort involves nothing less than a total anatomizing whose intimacy has a distinctly modern ring. It necessitates, in the words of Charron,

> a true, long and daily study of himselfe, a serious and attentive examination not only of his words, and actions, but of his most secret thoughts (their birth, progresse, continuance, repetition) and whatsoever is in him, even in his nightly dreames, prying and pinching him even to the quicke.

Naturally enough, a thinker such as Calvin, whose *Institutes of the Christian Religion* contains two substantial sections on the subject of *nosce teipsum*, will seize the opportunity such investigation affords

> to call to mind our miserable condition after Adam's fall; the awareness of which, when all our boasting and self-assurance are laid low, should truly humble us and overwhelm us with shame.

Certainly, this catches more of the "universal" scale on which *King Lear* seems to have been conceived, than does the notion of the discovery on Lear's part of single (albeit disastrous) "mistake" made by himself. In Professor Jorgensen's terms, the play accordingly becomes one "showing the grim progress of an old man, through the agony of learning how wretched he and mankind are, towards redemption."

That grim progress links itself symbolically with Lear's grotesque royal "progress" across England to the extremity of Dover, and towards the "self" that awaits him there: the play seems centrally concerned with charting this painful process. In fact, Professor Jorgensen considers Lear's "emergence" as a thinker, gradually learning more and more about himself as he gropes his way towards the truth, as the climax of a discernible series of earlier experiments in the same vein. His chapter on Shakespeare's interest in and development of the tragic hero's role as thinker provides a provocative context for the subsequent examination of this play, since it juxtaposes Lear revealingly with other emergent thinkers and discoverers of the self such as Titus Andronicus, Richard III, Richard II, Brutus, Hamlet and Othello.

Nevertheless, the establishment of such a matrix is not without its dangers, and if anything mars Professor Jorgensen's sensitive account of *Lear,* it is his occasional determination to fit the King to this pattern of emergent thinkers at all costs. Thus, two instances where Lear indicates that he has given or will give thought to certain matters, "I will look further into't." (I. iv. 72-6) "No more of that; I have noted it well" (I. iv. 81) are made to bear the weight of a commentary whose enthusiasm simply flattens them;

> At this point in the play Lear has begun to think, and to think in a responsive way.
> But what is dramatically remarkable and almost new about it is that it has not
> been put into words. In one respect, then, Lear is the ultimately pensive hero,
> since he does not even feel the need to communicate his thought.

To offer these rare moments—perfectly acceptable as the grumpy social withdrawals of old age on any level—as a "striking way of depicting thought" seems superfluous.

Happily, Professor Jorgensen's argument proves more flexible for the most part, and his account of the gradual evolution of Lear's mind, from the static intransigence of the first act to the supple dynamism of the last, is of considerable sensitivity. Seen in this light, Lear's madness has the quality of a kind of intuitive thinking "closer to one's deepest nature than the controlled thinking of sanity": a manifestation, ultimately, of the *ratio superior* in action, reaching directly and immediately to the truth. So-called "sanity," here as in *Hamlet* presented as a set of rigorously rational restrictions on the mind, appears almost as a barrier between man and redeeming knowledge of himself.

The other characters in the play fare less well than Lear, failing, Professor Jorgensen argues, fully to take part in the journey of self-discovery. Cordelia's chief quality is assessed as adamancy, an unwillingness to change, to adapt, to seek the truth inside herself. Presented thus, she seems oddly closer to Edmund than might be thought appropriate, unless it is recognized that, after all, both these characters may be said to know their different selves pretty thoroughly from the first. Edgar on the other hand engages in a literal transformation of himself, and accompanies Lear at least part of the way towards total self-recognition.

Perhaps the most surprising judgement is that passed on Gloucester who, it is said, under circumstances not too different from Lear's "did not learn much about himself." But surely Gloucester may be said to have achieved in another key a degree of self-discovery that matches Lear's, even as his ordeal does? He learns to see where Lear learns to feel; both ultimately learn to love. Gloucester's "despair" can be simply isolated, it is true;

> He found, after a brief exposure to feeling and self-responsibility, that an old age
> spent on the rack of feeling is intolerable. And even though he has learned how
> to see 'feelingly', mere feeling of itself will avail little in this kind of world.

—but in the context of the play, "mere feeling" seems altogether too dismissive a way of referring to what, after all, proves to be the proper moral antidote to the kind of "blind" seeing that sparks the tragedy. Ultimately, in *King Lear,* feeling is believing.

Lear's journey finally enables him to confront the overwhelming question of personal identity that holds the key to self-discovery: "Who is it that can tell me who I am?" In Lear's case, such self-knowledge occurs in the comprehensive mode intimated by Calvin; he learns what it means to be a member of mankind. As Professor Jorgensen recognizes, Lear "never, in a single summary speech tries to put into words just what he has learned about himself" and the play perhaps gains its tremendous sense of "universal" applicability from the fact that it eschews a concern with the discovery of one man's "mistake" that would inevitably prove diminishing.

In fact, *King Lear* is of an exemplary character, and Lear discovers himself as *humanum genus*, albeit with an individual body subject to the grossest needs and corruptions. But even this, as Professor Jorgensen shows, can provide its own grim "universal" instruction. For the secret of the self must lie eventually within the body of man and of woman, and in that love to which the body yearns to give crude expression. At the end of the play, Lear finds himself confronted by love of a generic sort; an all-embracing, all-forgiving response to human weakness which replaces the "measuring" kind of love with which his journey began.

When Lear learns to recognize this love, he learns who and what he is, and what we all are; he plumbs that "art of our necessities" which "nature needs" to redeem unaccommodated man. Professor Jorgensen's account of this process proves to be an account of the play that is sensitive, subtle, and carefully argued within its own clearly defined limits. And without exceeding those limits it manages finally to probe to the play's heart.

University College
Cardiff

The Early Elizabethan Succession Question: 1558-1568 by Mortimer Levine. Stanford University Press, 1966. Pp. viii + 245. $6.95. *Reviewer: Alice Lyle Scoufos.*

The modern scholarship concerned with Elizabethan history would seem comprehensively contained within the broad range of studies from the abundant minutiae of J. A. Froude to the graceful ambage of A. L. Rowse, but this is not the actual case. Indeed, in spite of the excellent coverage of the Elizabethan succession problem in Sir John Neale's parliamentary works, the plethora of studies on Mary, Queen of Scots, and her aims at the throne, the detailed analyses of Henry VIII's will by A. F. Pollard and L. B. Smith, there has not been made available to the history student a detailed study of the complex problems of the claimants to the Tudor crown until the recent publication of Mortimer Levine's study. Mr. Levine, it is true, has limited his prospect to one brief decade, but the context of the work itself presents a broad sweeping view of the involved problem. The author has skillfully avoided the usual pitfalls of the narrowly focused study by tracing the complexities of the succession question beyond its dimensions as a legal problem into the areas of diplomacy and religion, of domestic politics and counterplots. The study is divided into what the author designates the three major aspects of the early development of the English problem: the initial question of no heir-apparent and the frustration of the Parliament of 1563; the spate of succession tracts which followed the *Tempestas Halesiana*; and the climax and transformation of the question in 1568 after the death of one contender and the flight of Mary Stuart from Scotland to England. Although the major emphasis of the work is placed upon the two strongest contenders, Lady Catherine Grey (who bore the Suffolk claim to the crown) and Mary, Queen of Scots (who sought a dual role, that of heir-apparent or that of actual claimant of Elizabeth's crown), space is allotted to a brief consideration of the succession claims of Lady Margaret Douglas, Countess of Lennox, of Lady Margaret Strange, and of Henry Hastings, Earl of Huntingdon, all of whom had some partisan support as claimants during these early years. The author has perhaps foreshortened his work by ignoring the murky business which was going on in England in the spring and summer of 1562 when De Quadra, Philip's ambassador to England, sent an important letter containing the names of certain dissident English Catholics (who were adherents of the Countess of Lennox) to the Duchess of Parma. De Quadra's Spanish courier was hijacked by Cecil's men, and the list of names fell into the hands of Elizabeth's Secretary. The whole affair was hushed, but Lady Margaret Lennox was put under constant surveillance from that point forward. Levine chooses to ignore the incident. Nor does he mention the publication by Gabriel de Saconay, the ecclesiastical censor at Lyons, of a French work asserting the claims of Mary Stuart to the English throne and defaming the characters of Henry VIII, Anne Boleyn, and the "illegitimate" Elizabeth. But these are minor points.

It is refreshing to observe the skill with which the author handles the problem of William Cecil's supposed involvement in the Catherine Grey-Lord Hertford affair. Mr. Levine is careful to preserve the rectified image which his respected mentor, Conyers Read, created for Cecil in the noteworthy study of Lord Burghley's early career (*Mr. Secretary Cecil and Queen Elizabeth*), but at the same time the author preserves his own integrity and presents his skeptical version of Cecil's "innocence" by the repeated use of rhetorical questions: Did Cecil have answers [to interrogatory forms] suppressed? Did Cecil wittingly allow Sir Nicholas Bacon, his brother-in-law, to shoulder the blame for the affair? Did Cecil deliberately shield Thomas Dannett in 1564? Was Cecil also trying to conceal as much as he could for John Hales's benefit? And so on. Asked within the context of Cecil's indebtedness to the former Duke of Suffolk, Cecil's distaste and hostility for the Queen of Scots, the questions imply unstated affirmative answers, in spite of the author's tactful summary-conclusion.

It is also refreshing to see emphasis placed upon the writing and production in 1562 of Sackville and Norton's tragedy, *Gorboduc*, a propagandistic Senecan drama which Mr. Levine rightly calls "a succession tract." As a general rule historians do not persevere in purely literary studies, but fortunately this author does; he considers the 1562 production of the gentlemen of the Inner Temple an important part of the succession debate, and he analyzes with some skill the vital fifth act as the earliest presentation of the arguments for Catherine Grey's succession claim.

The discussion of the rise of a new force of public opinion in England, which followed the publication of John Hales's *Declaration* and the remonstrances it occasioned, is pertinent. Mr. Levine declares that the readers of the sophisticated pamphlets were primarily laymen who were independent of the court influence of the day. In line with the general English respect for the common law, they were avidly interested in the issue of the applicability to the succession problem of the common-law rule against alien inheritance in England. The author traces the growth of the rule from its origin after the loss of Normandy when the English found it expedient to deprive Frenchmen of their lands in England. But did the rule apply to the succession of the crown? And above all, did it apply to the case of Mary Stuart? Levine's answer is that there were no precedents from which the Elizabethans could judiciously draw a conclusion; the analogies which the tract writers used, Stephen of Blois, Henry II, Arthur of Brittany and John Lackland, were unconvincing, and the problem was actually one which had never been faced before in England. In his final analysis of the question of Mary Stuart's claim to the succession, the author concludes that "Mary's Scottish birth probably made her ineligible according to English law to succeed to the English crown."

Perhaps more forthrightly the author answers the problems of Henry VIII's will. In that famous document the claims of the Stuarts were set aside and the Suffolk line of succession was appointed to follow that of Henry's own children and their issue. Mr. Levine contends that the will should be regarded as a valid document and that its succession provisions should have been deemed the law of the land. As a result of this conjecture, the author suggests that Lady Catherine Grey rather than Mary, Queen of Scots, had the best legal right to succeed Elizabeth on the throne of England. This conclusion is also based upon a step-by-step analysis of the legitimacy of the Suffolk line. As readers of Tudor history know, the legitimacy of the Suffolks was a complex problem involving three cases of marriage: that between Mary Tudor (daughter of Henry VII) and Charles Brandon, that between Frances Brandon and Henry Grey, and the third between Catherine Grey and Henry Herbert. All three cases of matrimony are judged valid contracts by the author, but the third marriage was legally annulled after the tragedy of the Northumberland conspiracy when the Earl of Pembroke realized the precariousness of the match he had made for his young son. All of this careful estimating of the private and public matches leads to Levine's important decision concerning the clandestine marriage of Catherine Grey and Lord Hertford. Elizabeth's Commission of Inquiry declared against the marriage (influenced possibly by the Queen's hostile attitude), but Levine's carefully documented analysis of the case, based upon the English law that a couple who exchanged consent *per verba de praesenti* before two witnesses were legally wedded, leads him to challenge the Commission's verdict and to insist that there were no irremovable obstacles to the succession claims of Catherine Grey or her sons.

With this strong assertion of the legality of the Suffolk claims to the succession the book ends. The final postulation is in the realm of fantasy, but it is interesting: What would it have meant for the English nation of the seventeenth century to have had a Suffolk monarchy? A Suffolk dynasty would not have been misled by notions of divine rights; "its title doubtless would have been basically a Parliamentary one. . . . The seventeenth-century development probably would not have been too different, but it might well have been more peaceful." And so we all build Utopias!

The book is adequately indexed, and it contains not only a useful bibliography but genealogical charts as well. Mr. Levine's writing style is clear and precise and his documentation is limited to essential details. The book is a good one and it fills a basic need. One is inclined to wish for the logical sequel covering the succession problem in the later Elizabethan period. Perhaps Mr. Levine would then abandon his position that "King James came easily to the English crown" and agree with a contemporary historian who witnessed the trauma of 1603: "The English crowne will not haply fall to the ground for lack of heads to wear it."

The California State College, Fullerton

The New Shakespeare. The Poems ed. J. C. Maxwell. Cambridge University Press, 1966. Pp. xxxvi + 258. $5.50.

The New Shakespeare. The Sonnets ed. J. Dover Wilson. Cambridge University Press, 1966. Pp. cxxvi + 267. $5.50. *Reviewer: Hallett Smith.*

The two final volumes of *The New Shakespeare* are *The Poems*, edited by J. C. Maxwell, and *The Sonnets*, edited by John Dover Wilson. Thus comes to completion a famous series of thirty-six small brown volumes, commissioned by The Syndics of the Cambridge University Press and inaugurated with *The Tempest* in 1921. The first fourteen plays were edited jointly by Sir Arthur Quiller-Couch and Dover Wilson. After Q's death in 1944, Wilson brought out fifteen plays under his single editorship, two with G. I. Duthie, two with Alice Walker, and four with J. C. Maxwell. By the time the series was finished Wilson was blind.

Maxwell's *Poems* is truly, as Wilson says in a prefatory note, an admirable edition. There are of course few textual problems in *Venus and Adonis* and *The Rape of Lucrece*, because the publication was authorized, based upon good copy and produced by the excellent printer Richard Field, Shakespeare's fellow townsman. Maxwell accepts W. S. Walker's emendation in line 466 of *Venus and Adonis*, "But blessed bankrupt that by loss so thriveth!" where the Quarto reads "by *love*," and the same critic's emendation of line 1662 in *Lucrece*, "With sad-set eyes and wreathed arms across" where the Quarto reads "*wretched.*" There are proof-corrections in some copies of *Lucrece* which do the text more harm than good, so Maxwell does not believe that Shakespeare saw these two poems through the press.

Besides the two major non-dramatic poems, the New Shakespeare edition contains *The Passionate Pilgrim, The Phoenix and the Turtle,* and *A Lover's Complaint.* The first of these contains nothing certainly by Shakespeare that is not found elsewhere, but the text of the first poem in it (Sonnet 138, "When my love swears that she is made of truth") is of great interest if, as Maxwell maintains," in spite of weighty opinion to the contrary, it does seem that Jaggard had access to an earlier version of the sonnet than appears in the 1609 collection, and not just an inaccurate transcript (as, for instance, with 2 [probably] 3, 5 and 16)."

In these three points Maxwell differs from F. T. Prince, whose New Arden edition (1960) is a friendly rival. Though the two editions serve different purposes and conform necessarily to the designs of their own series, comparison between them is inevitable. Prince is more conservative textually; he has a good deal more apparatus—appendices on the sources, and longer notes at the foot of the page, though Maxwell compensates, in part, by the customary and useful glossary at the end. In the critical introduction Maxwell is vastly superior. He understands the critical problems involved in reading the poems, he deals fairly and judiciously with the various critics who have interpreted them, and he gives the reader, as he does in his editions of *Pericles, Timon, Cymbeline* and *Henry VIII* the benefit of great learning and sound judgment.

The Phoenix and the Turtle is a case in point. Maxwell steers through the treacherous seas of Platonism, scholastic tradition, "pure poetry" and metaphysical poetry to carry us to safe harbor of recognition of what this poem, so unlike anything else Shakespeare wrote, really is. It is too bad that he could not have included in his concise and incisive review of scholarship and criticism the recent study of the poem by William H. Matchett.

A Lover's Complaint, which was published with the Sonnets in 1609, is included in the New Shakespeare *Poems,* though the New Arden is reserving it for the forthcoming edition of the Sonnets by Winifred Nowottny. Maxwell comments on Rollins' generalization that most writers base their views of the poem's value and date upon their notions about the authorship: "I feel myself an exception . . . since I believe it to be a poem of Shakespeare's maturity, but a poem of very little merit." There are more textual problems than in the other poems, but the errors are no more numerous than they would be, Maxwell thinks, in a reasonably good dramatic text.

The *Sonnets* volume presents a problem to the reviewer. It consists of 126 pages of Introduction, 76 pages of text, and 186 pages of notes. The Introduction was published separately, in 1963, to participate in the hullabaloo created by A. L. Rowse, so its contents are now well known. Wilson favors Pembroke as Mr. W. H. and the Fair Youth, Chapman as the Rival Poet. The Dark Lady is not identified but she is demoted to The Dark Woman. The sonnets are not earlier than 1597. Sonnet 107 refers to the Queen's death and 124 to the Gunpowder Plot. Wilson now rejects Thorpe's order and accepts Brents Stirling's proposals for the order of 127-154.

Wilson's text generally follows Malone, as do most editors'. His punctuation is sometimes surprising, since he reverts to Percy Simpson's principles, which he was forced to abandon in editing the plays. His commentary owes most to Beeching and Dowden, and there is nothing remarkable about it, unless one excepts such fancies as that Sonnet 20 "might have been occasioned by a bathe in the Thames" and that the guilt and absence sonnets refer to Shakespeare's absence in the provinces after the trouble about *The Isle of Dogs*. Wilson admits that there is not one tittle of evidence to connect Shakespeare with that play. But most of the discussion of the occasion, date, persons referred to and order of the sonnets, here and elsewhere, is based not upon evidence but upon the author's whim. Wilson says (p. lxxxv) that after publishing his first draft of a preface in 1963 he "came upon a matter not of theory but of fact which put a fresh complexion on the group [100-126] as a whole." This discovery is the linking of 104 to the absence-series 97-99; but 104 is not an absence sonnet—it is a spring, birthday sonnet celebrating the reunion of poet and fair friend after an absence, and on the fair friend's birthday. This makes the occasion April 8, 1600, Pembroke's twentieth birthday, and Sonnet 99, which has fifteen lines, was left unfinished in the haste of preparing the birthday offering. "This is of course surmise, as so much of one's interpretation of the sonnets must be." So says Dover Wilson.

California Institute of Technology

Two Concepts of Allegory: A Study of Shakespeare's The Tempest and the Logic of Allegorical Expression by A. D. Nuttall. Routledge and Kegan Paul, 1967. Pp. xiii + 175. $6.00. *Reviewer: Robert L. Montgomery, Jr.*

Judged by title and subtitle, this would be an important and timely book: the problems of locating and explaining the allegorical forms and of relating a reasonable concept of allegory to Shakespeare's work (often read allegorically and more often denied all allegorical status) are serious and real. Furthermore, recent years have seen increasing critical interest in the formal status of allegory as a literary mode. Yet Mr. Nuttall's effort tells us very little about Shakespeare that would either excite or alarm us, and its conclusions about allegory, while occasionally interesting, will make little difference in the way critics or readers will be disposed to use the term.

This is too bad, because at the beginning Mr. Nuttall's approach to his topic seems perfectly proper: "I shall be . . . asking not 'What does *The Tempest* signify allegorically?'

but rather 'What sort of thing are people doing when they talk of allegorical significations; what sort of reasons prompt them to do so in connexion with *The Tempest?*'" (p. 1). He then proceeds in his first chapter to review various Romantic and post-Romantic allegorical readings of *The Tempest*, noting the ontological assumptions behind them (reality is transcendent), and to provide a critique of the difficulties generated by C. S. Lewis's notorious polarization of allegory and symbolism (or sacramentalism) into two opposed concepts.

So far, so good. There have been more pertinent objections to Lewis's formula, notably those of Morton Bloomfield and Bertrand Bronson, but Mr. Nuttall's suggestion that personifications and sacramental symbols usually coexist in the same work is a point worth making. He uses an intelligent critique of Prudentius' *Psychomachia* (pp. 37-40) to illustrate the logical difficulties that arise when "pure" allegory is attempted, but his discussion of Dante (pp. 24-31), which concludes that *The Divine Comedy* is a species of "sacramentalism," is less forthright and it touches too briefly on too many issues which Mr. Nuttall fails to resolve. Assuming that most great allegories are not pure, he pursues the line that they are not so because general qualities (Man, Hope, Love, etc.) can be imagined as individual and that hence the way for the critic to examine allegory and its images is to explore psychology. From here through the next two chapters Mr. Nuttall chiefly concerns himself with surveying philosophical observations on the nature of mental images.

I find both these chapters distracting. Mr. Nuttall might have made his point that there is a connection between "concretely instantialized, self-predicable universals and mental imagery" (p. 50) more briefly and in more acceptable language. His excursions into philosophy are needlessly detailed and involve remarks which demonstrate his knowledge of such as Ryle and Sartre, but fail to offer more than the conclusion that it is possible for the mind to generate "unspecified" images. I am not convinced that a similarity between such images and what we find in certain literary works is the best clue to the nature of allegory, and the author's pursuit of psychology neglects the force of convention in governing the nature of allegorical fiction. Moreover, I am still left wondering if Mr. Nuttall sees anything distinctive about an allegorical image. His nearest approach seems to be his belief that allegory, or the near-sacramental form which he prefers, partakes of the metaphysical. This last issue is what his fifth chapter, "The Use of the Imagination in the Sixteenth and Seventeenth Centuries," is about. Here are two representative statements:

> It was important to establish the fact that the logically curious features which we find in sophisticated allegories may be found also at the most subliminal level of non-specific mental imagery. We thus provide allegory with a natural foundation. So far from being the last arbitrary construction of a tired tradition, it has its roots in the most primitive levels of our mental lives. (p.94)

It is really not necessary to defend allegory in this way at the present time. One wonders also what Freudian or Jungian psychology would make of Mr. Nuttall's grasp of the primitive levels of our mental life. Finally, what becomes of allegory as a deliberately constructed fiction if this statement is taken at face value?

> Sixteenth-century poetry is, among other things, an art if [sic] incarnating spiritual essences (p. 103).

Again, where and how do we isolate allegorical poetry? Isn't this close to Lewis's definition of allegory which Mr. Nuttall has previously objected to?

Mr. Nuttall's final two chapters deal with Shakespeare. Chapter V, "Shakespeare and the Idea of Love," is largely devoted to the Sonnets, though it gets there by way of G. E. Moore's struggles with the idea of the Good and the general Renaissance expectation that loving and valuing will be identical (Mr. Nuttall is here concerned to demonstrate that the Renaissance mind and the post-Romantic mind are different). If he has not already slipped his leash, he surely does it now, for in treating Shakespeare's expression of the Elizabethan fear that the ideal world may be subverted by earthly existence, he has ceased discussing a theory of allegory in favor of some of its thematic substance. Dealing with the Sonnets he even indulges in some quasi-biographical speculation, interesting enough by itself, but tangential at best to a discussion of allegorical form or Shakespeare's use of it.

The final chapter, *"The Tempest,"* is somewhat more comforting because Mr. Nuttall's evocation of its dreamlike quality, its peculiar combination of remoteness and familiarity, is sensitive and well-put. But this feature, which is indeed suggestive in thinking of the play as allegory, is not sufficiently exploited as a way of connecting *The Tempest* to general features of allegorical form. Rather Mr. Nuttall considers it the theme of the play, and concludes his book in puzzling fashion. He asks, "Is *The Tempest* allegorical? If I have done my work properly, the question should have shrunk in importance." In the next breath he says, "The principal object of this book has been to show that allegorical poetry is more curiously and intimately related to life than was allowed by the petrifying formula of C. S. Lewis" (p. 159). Some confusion of purpose is apparent here. A bit later he adds that the characters in *The Tempest* are not really allegorical, but may be seen as types. Such results are no alternative to Lewis, but they do raise the suspicion that Mr. Nuttall, almost in spite of himself, has tried to do away with "allegory" as a viable critical term.

In spite of all I have objected to, the reader will find moments where an ingenious and fresh critical mind is at work. It is a pity that these qualities are not more steadily realized, and it is also a pity that minor errors in printing and an inconsistent bibliographical form have not been corrected somewhere along the line. The bibliography is extensive, but nowhere does one find reference to Northrop Frye who has had a great deal to say about allegory, and some mention of the books on the subject by Rosemund Tuve, Edwin Honig, and Angus Fletcher would also be welcome.

The University of California
Irvine

Shakespeare and the Common Understanding by Norman Rabkin. The Free Press, 1967. Pp. viii + 267. $6.95. *Reviewer: William Rosen.*

J. Robert Oppenheimer's discussion of "complementarity" in *Science and the Common Understanding* gave Professor Rabkin the term and general outlook which inform his study of Shakespeare's vision and art. Oppenheimer defines "complementarity" (a principle of physics associated with the work of Niels Bohr) as the idea "that an electron must sometimes be considered as a wave, and sometimes as a particle. . . . There is this same duality for all matter and for light. In a little subtler form this complementarity means that there are situations in which the position of an atomic object can be measured and defined and thought about without contradiction; and other situations in which this is not so, but in which other qualities, such as the energy or the impulse of the system, are defined and meaningful. The more nearly appropriate the first way of thinking is to a situation, the more wholly inappropriate the second, so that there are in fact no atomic situations in which both impulse and position will be defined well enough to permit the sort of prediction with which Newtonian mechanics has familiarized us."

Commenting on the ways in which features of modern physics have "broadened and humanized our whole understanding of the natural world," Oppenheimer discourses on two ways of thinking, "the way of time and history and the way of eternity and timelessness," and how both are "part of man's effort to comprehend the world in which he lives. Neither is comprehended in the other nor reducible to it. They are, as we have learned to say in physics, complementary views, each supplementing the other, neither telling the whole story."

"Complementarity" points to a complex world in which contrarieties and paradoxes have no apparent resolutions; and such a world of irreconcilable conflicts is found, says Rabkin, in Shakespeare's work: every play "refuses to satisfy us with a simplistic statement about experience. Rather, it makes clear to us the ways in which an aspect of experience is problematic, and makes it impossible for us to resolve the problem" (p. 55). As soon as Rabkin commits himself to "complementarity" as a critical framework for Shakespeare's plays, he traps himself into reducing total dramatic experience to pairs of themes. There seems no way of avoiding this: since complementarity describes "duality for all matter and for light," the literary critic, in his attempt to imitate the scientific method, has to set up opposing elements in the plays so that he can show them as "complementary views, each supplementing the other, neither telling the whole story." There is little surprise, therefore, when we find the following principles in Rabkin's approach: (1) "the true constant" in Shakespeare's artistry "is the dialectical dramaturgy. It may be the most notable constant in Shakespeare's work" (p. 11); (2) "Shakespeare tends to structure his imitations in terms of a pair of polar opposites—reason and passion in Hamlet, for instance, or reason and faith, reason and love, reason and imagination; *Realpolitik* and the traditional political order, *Realpolitik* and political idealism; hedonism and responsibility, the world and the transcendent, life and death, justice and mercy" (p. 12).

"Dialectic" and "complementarity" serve as Rabkin's keys to Shakespeare's work. *Hamlet* presents the ideal of reason in such a way that we recognize its "absolute claim on our moral allegiance, and then entirely subverts that ideal by demonstrating that its polar opposite is the only possible basis for the action its protagonist is morally committed to perform" (p. 6). The vision of *Hamlet*, Rabkin argues, is typical of Shakespeare: we are asked to choose, yet no choice is right.

Troilus and Cressida presents value as a function of time; value exists neither in the subjective will of the valuer nor in the assessment of rationalists who think they see the real object, but "only in that object as time disposes of it" (p. 53). Rabkin's thematic development of the play leads to the conclusion that time is omnipotent: "the theme is the idea that a time which has its own purposes indifferent to ours determines the meaning and value of events without regard to our hopes or fears or even our actions" (p. 54). Such a resolution would violate the principle of complementarity; but Rabkin takes care of this by stating that "because of the complementary nature of the play, the theme is not identical with that total communication which we call the meaning of the piece" (p. 55). We are still able to suspend judgment, therefore, because the play may prove Troilus' protestations of faith to be foolish, but does not deny them; neither does it deny the rationalism of Hector and Ulysses nor Achilles' concern for glory. We experience "an unresolvable complex": "Whatever the intellectual judgment the play brings us to, we have no choice but to recognize the complementarity of the values it would seem by the end to have demolished" (p. 54).

So exclusively are "dialectic" and "complementarity" applied to each play that many readers will feel that a self-enclosed system has used the plays to work out its own highly predictable patterns. Is it not likely that if the critic designates at the beginning of a discussion the opposing elements of a play, without showing through analysis of action why these (and only these) themes are primary, the results will neatly bear out his expectations?

The oppositions set up in this book lead to the acceptance of everything; we are asked to affirm nothing and to deny nothing because, as Rabkin says, "Always the dramatic structure sets up the opposed elements as equally valid, equally desirable, and equally destructive, so that the choice that the play forces the reader to make becomes impossible" (p. 12). Othello, we are told, is best understood by recognizing "the love that defines and destroys him" (p. 62). The final assessment is not unexpected: "The paradox of the tragedy is that the faith which makes Othello great makes him helpless as well, and that that faith is superior to what subverts it. We find ourselves rejecting not the faith that Othello abandons, but the mental process that enables him to do so" (p. 73). "The tragedy of *Richard II*," we are informed, "is the complementarity of its protagonists' virtues" (p. 95); where one level of the play deals with political success and the ideal of the commonwealth, Bolingbroke is admirable; where, on another, it "is about what it is to be a fully sentient human being," Richard commands our respect (p. 92). *Measure for Measure* is studied for its "view of the tragic complementarity of human nature": Isabella is right, and so is Claudio, "who is right in his own terms" (p. 104). And so, presumably, is the critic; such total acceptance makes it impossible for him to be wrong.

Sometimes Professor Rabkin's conclusions seem to suit his theory more than the issues he most fully develops. Discussing in detail the logic of the revenge conventions in *Julius Caesar*, he argues that Shakespeare lets us "see and consider before the assassination the identity between Caesar and Brutus which is at the center of the play" (p. 119); and by "making us see the similarity between Brutus and Caesar, Shakespeare has made the assassination rather a criminal mistake . . . than an act of public virtue." His conclusion, however, involves a shift to Brutus as hero: "In his attractiveness is the true complementarity of the play" (p. 119-120).

Because the dramatist "makes us understand most fully the tragic complementarity of all solutions to the political world he sees" (p. 144), Rabkin considers *Coriolanus* to be the fitting conclusion to Shakespeare's career as a writer of history plays. Examining "idealism and grubby reality," the play comes to no answer. It offers alternative ideas of the state— "as unbending moral imperative and the idea of the state as a community organized for the benefit of its members" (p. 139). In dramatizing the ways in which the hero's virtue is also his vice, the play is ambivalent about the honor which Coriolanus stands for: we admire its strength in accomplishment "but fear it as inimical to civilization" (p. 143).

In line with the thesis and methodology of this book, the chapter entitled "Eros and Death," which discusses *Venus and Adonis, Romeo and Juliet,* and *Antony and Cleopatra,* has formulaic conclusions: "Shakespeare tells us that love, the most intense manifestation of the urge to life, is ineluctably linked with the self-destructive yearning for annihilation that we recognize as the death wish" (p. 151). And we are shown, in detail, that "Love must always be judged from contradictory points of view" (p. 157). Where there are no incompatible views to be found, where Shakespeare seems to assume a simple moral position and does not call into question the nature of being, we are simply told that we have a bad play: "the trouble with *Timon of Athens* is that it is not complementary" (p. 193). And "*Pericles* shares *Timon*'s weakness . . . in that the process of the protagonist's education fails to involve the audience in the tension generated by conflicting systems of value" (p. 195). (It does seem that there are more obvious structural reasons for the weakness of each play, reasons which may also involve the incomplete or corrupt state of the text we possess.) In *The Winter's Tale,* however, Shakespeare "fully expresses the complementary vision of the value of art" (p. 222), and *The Tempest* "carries to the point of final clarity his complementary vision, his ethical commitments, his interest in art and its meaning, and what he has been saying in his tragedies and his comedies" (p. 230).

Most readers will find Professor Rabkin's observations on specific points to be intelligent and well-informed; particularly interesting are the discussions of *Hamlet, Richard II, Coriolanus,* and the analysis of the tragic dilemmas which Shakespeare sees in politics. The least successful part of the book is the attempt to provide "a completely new conceptual framework for understanding Shakespeare's art." In spite of Rabkin's reminders that Shakespeare's plays refuse to satisfy us with "a simplistic statement about experience," his relentless and tiresome tracking down of oppositions tends to limit rather than expand our understanding of plays. When the bells ring out for complementarity at such regular intervals, and we are invited so repetitiously to view life's issues as insoluble, we feel—sometimes unfairly—that the critic has only compounded simplistic observations, not eschewed them.

The "new conceptual framework" of this book finally turns out to be quite similar to other systems—usually romantic in outlook—which explain dramatic craft in terms of dualities. In *The Birth of Tragedy,* where Nietzsche presents an essentially psychological reading of Greek tragedy, the formulation comes very close to the conclusions which Rabkin derives from complementarity: "And so the double-being of the Aeschylean Prometheus, his conjoint Dionysian and Apollonian nature, might be thus expressed in an abstract formula: 'Whatever exists is alike just and unjust, and equally justified in both.'" This acceptance of all experience is also the basis of Keats' doctrine of "Negative Capability," the ability of the poet to hold incompatible or apparently contradictory concepts "without any irritable reaching after fact and reason." And the results of complementarity are not significantly different from what A. P. Rossiter calls "Ambivalence" in his essay on "The Dialectic of the Histories" (*Angel with Horns*): "that two opposed value-judgments are subsumed, and that both are valid (i. e. for that work of art or the mind producing it). The whole is only fully experienced in a 'two-eyed' view; and all 'one-eyed' simplifications are not only falsifications; they amount to a denial of some part of the mystery of things."

Although Rabkin's theory of complementarity accords with Rossiter's "two-eyed view," its rigid application cuts out responses to the play which may violate the efficient operation of the system. Is it not one-eyed, for instance, to discuss characters as representations of polar oppositions and exclude considerations of plot and genre, components of drama which certainly work strongly upon the playgoer in forming his reactions? Believing that the "technique of presenting a pair of opposed ideals or groups of ideals and putting a double valuation on each is the basis of Shakespeare's comedy as well as his tragedy" (p. 12), Professor Rabkin reduces characters to what they represent in his system, and therefore slights motivation and moral response. Complementarity ought, surely, to be relevant to the theories of critics also, warning us not to look at all plays through a glass that may suit a play like *Hamlet* yet be inadequate elsewhere. Rabkin, with his dualities, sees more than the critic who insists on resolving conflicts in plays so as to provide philosophic or religious or cultural formulas. Complex issues are shown to be complex. But Rabkin traps himself in the single viewpoint he decries, and is prevented from seeing an organization of relationships more complex than the simple claims of polar opposites. A system which demands acceptance of everything should not require us to exclude so much.

The University of Connecticut

Editing Sixteenth Century Texts: Papers given at the Editorial Conference, University of Toronto, October, 1965 edited by R. J. Schoeck. University of Toronto Press, 1966. Pp. 138. $5.00. *Reviewer: Robert K. Turner Jr.*

Although certain editorial principles may be universal, there are natural chronological and territorial divisions between textual scholars according to the technical means available in various eras and countries for the propagation of written words. Unfortunately there does not seem to have been much sharing of editorial expertise across such boundaries, though the editor of Shakespeare, to choose but one example, probably has as much to learn from a Spanish scholar working on the text of Lope de Vega or Calderón as from an English scholar editing Swinburne or even Donne. Specialization, however, has drawn disciplinary lines all too firmly. Thus one can only applaud the establishment at the University of Toronto of "a continuing conference on editorial problems at which scholars actively at work upon editorial tasks could come together for a free discussion of their work, learning from each other's experience, pooling their common intellectual resources, and seeking out expert opinion and counsel" (p. 3). The volume under review contains, in addition to notes on the proceedings and a brief account of the Yale edition of St. Thomas More by Professor Schoeck, the six papers read at the first of these conferences. They are nothing if not international in scope.

The longest in the collection is an account by Natalie Z. Davis of the career of the learned Lyonnais merchant-publisher Guillaume Rouillé, who was remarkable not only for extensiveness of production (more than 830 editions) but the accuracy of his books and the beauty of their illustrations and typography. Professor Davis surveys the kinds of books Rouillé published and the reasons, both practical and personal, governing his publication policy. Unlike the humanist publishers who were noted for their interest in the classics, Reformation theology, and contemporary literature, Rouillé's main concerns were "Italian literature, emblem books, a small number of classical editions, humanist textbooks in civil law and medicine, botanical and surgical writings, and, out of an undistinguished miscellany of religious publications, a line of Bibles and Bible pictures" (p. 86). Such diversity was in part simply good business practice, but the demands of certain markets also had an effect: some emblem books and religious works were produced for Spanish readership; the Italian works were aimed at French buyers who had acquired the language as well as at cultured members of the Italian business community in Lyon; and the medical and legal works, often in "hand size," were intended for a growing number of student readers. Sometimes considerations of trade and Rouillé's personal tastes converged; his handsomely illustrated *Historia Generalis Plantarum*, for example, not only responded to a general need for an extensive botanical treatise but also reflected his own "highly developed taste for the visual arts" (p. 92). His life, his work, and his interests were richly diversified, and Professor Davis's survey succeeds in ordering this diversity in such a way as to make clear the important place Rouillé and men like him had in the intellectual life of their age.

Max Kortepeter contributes a review of "the most important events in the development of *zeitung* literature during the century of the Reformation" (p. 114), the period which saw the transformation, because of the spread of printing in Europe and the need for news, of "tidings" from oral and handwritten accounts to something approaching not only the modern newspaper and news-magazine but also the modern history. The influence of *Zeitungen* and *Flugschriften* on public opinion, the cities (particularly those in Germany) which became centers for the dissemination of news, the *Zeitungen* as sources for more formal histories, and the changes through which *zeitung* literature passed are all surveyed, and the usefulness of these ephemeral pamphlets and newssheets as historical sources is emphasized. Quite a different approach is taken by Victor E. Graham, the editor of Desportes, who speaks to beginners of the practical aspects of editing lyric poetry—the need to make oneself familiar with the poet's biography and bibliography, the unlikely sources of information about editions and manuscripts that may yield unexpected help, the management of a complicated apparatus, and the need for self-discipline in glossing and documentation.

The English Renaissance is represented by three essays. E. J. Devereux shows how some translations of Erasmus were used by reformers to reinforce their own arguments for the purification of the ecclesiastical polity, some by conservatives to support the established order, and some by scholars to advance the cause of humanism, all tending in the end to spread Erasmus' "ideas and attitudes into the ordinary homes in which renaissance and reformation were to be achieved" (p. 43). Abbé Germain Marc'hadour investigates the relationship between three early editions of St. Thomas More's *Dialogue of Comfort,* concluding, mainly on the evidence of the treatment of biblical quotations, that Tottell's edition of 1553, for all its defects, is the least sophisticated. S. Schoenbaum surveys recent activity in the editing of Elizabethan plays; deplores duplication of titles in the several series of plays now being published, the lack of new anthologies, and idiosyncratic introductions; and declares a preference for old rather than modern spelling. To Professor Schoenbaum's paper are appended remarks by Clifford Leech, who defends the practice of the Revels Plays, of which he is the general editor, against Schoenbaum's gentle strictures.

The aspirations of the organizers of the conference were high, and Professor Schoeck's remarks (p. 6) about the papers delivered are flattering. Schoenbaum's and Graham's essays "firmly stress dramatic and poetic editing . . . from the point of view of the modern editor, with many ideas and possibilities thrown out for the beginning scholar." Schoenbaum, however, was really talking about the present state of editions of the English drama rather than the art of editing, and he and others have often thrown out these ideas before. Graham, whose essay is said to provide neophytes with sound bearings and a firm "sense of *Methodenlehre"* does not mention the generic relationship of the basic editions of Desportes and advises the beginners that ultimately they must "decide intuitively" what the copy-texts of their editions are to be (p. 34), surely good advice for Satan's kingdom. Devereux and Marc'hadour chart some "problems of sixteenth-century translators and editors," but they do so with the kind of elaborately detailed documentation that only another expert, or at least a specifically interested reader, can love. In the papers of Davis and Kortepeter "newer ground is broken" and in fact both do deal with novel and significant subjects. Professor Davis is remotely concerned with editing in that the professional career of a publisher has relevance to the general matter of the transmission of literature, but Professor Kortepeter is chiefly attentive to *Zeitungen* as a "source for the social, economic, and political history of the sixteenth century" (p. 114), touching upon editorial problems only casually.

However good an idea the conference may be, its first session seems rather to have belied its announced theme. There is much erudition in some of the papers, perhaps too much for aural understanding; there is some superficiality in others, perhaps because subjects too large were handled in too little time. One wonders if the audience ever got the sense that the hunt is up, the excitement of the chase that ought to characterize good scholarship; and one wonders further if the representatives of the various areas of study really had much to say to each other when it came time to pool their common intellectual resources in free discussion. Perhaps here as elsewhere, however, the truly interesting part of the conference came after the formal proceedings ended.

The University of Wisconsin
Milwaukee

The Vocal Songs in the Plays of Shakespeare by Peter J. Seng. Harvard University Press, 1967. Pp. xiv + 314. $8.95. *Reviewer: John P. Cutts.*

Seng's book, bearing the mark of his 1966 Harvard Ph.D. dissertation, is primarily intended as a reference work to past studies on the vocal songs in Shakespeare. It contains no new information on texts and musical settings, and basically no new insights into dramatic function. Its chief merit is its clear format and systematic organization, each play being tackled separately and in a reasonable chronological order. Seng has assembled an enormous amount of information from widely scattered sources and has obviously benefitted immensely from reactions to other studies of this kind within the last ten years particularly. His apparent control of thousands of references is in itself no mean accomplishment. The less informed reader will be inclined to think the book definitive and to accept its claim to be bringing together "all of the relevant material on the vocal songs in Shakespeare's plays" and to "make available to the modern reader a chronological history of the textual and analytical criticism of the songs, information about the original or early musical settings when these exist, and a critical examination of the dramatic functions of the songs within the plays" (p.xiii). The more informed reader, however, will be disturbed by some very serious and startling omissions of matter, and by some unobjective opinions which distort the putative accuracy of the manner in which the *reference* material is presented.

The book does not present any of the music either in photographic reproduction of original manuscript and/or early printed version, or in edited form—thus bravely skirting one of the most thorny problems with regard to settings of Shakespearean songs, *how* to edit them, over which there are as many different opinions as writers. This in itself would not be a blemish on the book if Seng were purely objective in his reporting and analyses, but his frequent tendency to set himself up as an arbiter in musical matters totally undermines the effectiveness of his "Music" sections.

Without a first-hand knowledge of the problems involved in dealing with the relevant music manuscripts in which the settings have been discovered and located and information regarding the musicians painstakingly assembled, it is really impossible to be truly authoritative and scholarly. Seng has to report on the MSS and musicians second-hand, and this becomes very dangerous on his own admission when at times so much depends on the question of the authenticity of the manuscript setting (p.215). All the work that has been assiduously accomplished in the location, description, and bibliographical cataloguing of music MSS, and the findings with regard to Shakespeare musicians—made available in *Music & Letters*, 1953; *Musica Disciplina*, 1956, 1959, 1962, 1964; *Shakespeare Quarterly*, 1956; *Review of English Studies*, 1959, and *Notes & Queries*, 1962—is strangely lacking from Seng's bibliography. Seng's comments in particular on the important musicians Robert Johnson and John Wilson must stem from others' findings particularly in *Music & Letters*, 1955, 1960, and in *Notes & Queries*, 1962, but the uninformed reader will not notice the lack of the 1960 and 1962 acknowledgments in the bibliography. After the reader has plowed through pp.v-vii of meticulous acknowledgments to librarians, museums, presses etc. for permissions to reproduce extracts etc. he will expect the same kind of assiduity in the bibliography, but in vain.

At times it seems as if Seng is falling over backward not to acknowledge the first source of information by trying to credit a later one with it, as for instance is the case on p.217 where one scholar is credited with a suggestion (that a particular musical setting might well be Johnson's) which on Seng's own admission had actually been made several years earlier by another. Seng is guilty of allowing personal judgements to distort the scholarly framework of chronology which he laudably appointed himself. A similar observation must be made about his remark that in *Musique*, 1959, p.115 there is a statement that Wilson's setting of "Take oh take those lips away" was to be found in Wilson's *Cheerful Ayres*. A careful study of the table on p.114 where all the early printed musical versions are listed will show *no* entry for *Cheerful Ayres*, and the listing, fortunately, was not subject to the French press's mistranslation of a subjunctive "If Wilson *had* included" as "If Wilson *has* included." Seng was too willing to pounce on a discrepancy which was obviously unintentional.

The same goes for his willingness to draw attention to Thurston Dart's "apparently mistaking the orthography of the title in the Nottingham manuscript" and calling the tune "the goddess of love" instead of the accurate "goddes of love" (p.62). The comment would be perfectly valid if Seng himself were strict in reproducing exact manuscript orthography, but his introductory remark to the effect that he has normalized "manuscript abbreviations which would require special fonts or superscript letters for exact reproduction" (p.xix) shows that he is not, and he has had to rely on second-hand information regarding the spelling characteristics of the transcriber of Drexel MS.4041. Seng's version of the extra stanza for "Get you hence" from *The Winter's Tale* mistranscribes "wallking" as "walking" and silently omits the second "darke" in the penultimate line. His transcript gives no indication of the manuscript's indication of repetitions attributable to musical licence and chorus needs, whereas the version in *Shakespeare Survey* IX (1956), 88 and footnote 7 on on 89 carefully suggests the repetitions so that it is comparatively easy to fit the second stanza to the music of the first. Seng's claim that the version in *Shakespeare Survey* does not attempt to fit the second stanza to the music (p.244) is thus flagrantly wrong. While he was pointing out errors he ought, perhaps, to have drawn attention to the numerous errors in Pafford's (New Arden, 1963) edition of *The Winter's Tale*, p.174 where the following occur: never for neuer; Who for who; raced for rated (it is quite clear from the word "recant" which is near that it is "rated" and not "raced"); walking for wallking; and the omission of indications of repetitions and refrains at the end. Instead Seng commends Pafford's suggestion regarding the second stanza that "lyrics and stage songs were often expanded in broad sheets in the 17th century." While this is true of such popular songs as "Have you seen but a white lilly grow" (See *Musique*, pp.151-152) it is hardly likely to be the case with "Get you hence" which is by no means in the same category of popularity. First-hand acquaintance with the music of "Get you hence" would never allow Seng to describe it as a ballad (p.245). The song sung by Mopsa, Dorcas and Autolycus is a very sophisticated "art" setting, composed specifically for that set of words alone.

Seng's book does not concern itself with the latest modern scholarship on attribution of *Henry VIII*, *Pericles* and *The Two Noble Kinsmen* to Shakespeare—the first and last contributing lavishly to dramatic use of songs—thus conveniently begging out of some very difficult albeit very interesting and rewarding problems. "Orpheus with his lute" in *Henry VIII* has been the detailed subject of a very recent discussion in *Shakespeare Jahrbuch*,

1963, and the climate of scholarly opinion is moving toward accepting the songs in *The Two Noble Kinsmen* as Shakespeare's.

Seng is obviously unwilling to cast himself upon musicological and hitherto believed *extra*-canonical seas, and the less informed reader may well sympathize, but what is to be made of the exclusion of the witches' songs in *Macbeth* over which there has been so much lively and voluminous discussion? Robert E. Moore's scholarly work on the music of *Macbeth* in his "The Music to *Macbeth*," *Musical Quarterly*, XLVII (January, 1961), 22-40 and in his *Henry Purcell & the Restoration Theatre* (Harvard, 1961) make nonsense of the attempt to dismiss consideration of the witches' songs in the only Shakespearean version of *Macbeth* that we have. To dismiss them on the grounds that "no certain texts exist" (p.xix) is to beg out of scholarly responsibility. The texts *do* exist, and there is too much scholarship on them to conveniently dismiss them as from Middleton's *The Witch* and therefore having no relevance for *Macbeth*. Their dramatic function in *Macbeth* based only on their opening words as given in the 1623 Folio is of great importance. When one considers how remarkably well Seng himself has dealt with the dramatic function of Falstaff's small fragment "When Arthur first in court" in *2 Henry IV* one can only be puzzled at the arbitrary dismissal of the *Macbeth* fragments.

The omission of Falstaff's fragment "Haue I caught my heauenlie Iewel" from *The Merry Wives of Windsor* is startling, especially in view of its having been drawn to readers' attention as recently as *Shakespeare Quarterly*, 1960. It no less "relates to major and minor themes of the play as a whole" (Seng, p.46) than "When Arthur first in court."

Ignoring the blank songs in Shakespeare (that is, places where songs are specifically called for but no texts exist) may be covered by Seng's provision (p.xix) not to include songs "for which no certain texts exist," but it is somewhat arbitrary, especially in view of the significance of the dramatic function. Marina's "song" in *Pericles*, in an undisputed Shakespearean part of the play, is functionally integral, for instance, even though the text does not exist. It obviously prepares the way for Pericles' later hearing of the music of the spheres.

Seng is generally at his best when discussing the dramatic function of the songs, but he seems to be in haste to dismiss some of them. His dismissal of Noble's observations on "Who is Sylvia" with "Nothing in the song suggests that it is Shakespeare's composition or that it is not. Its diction, imagery, and metaphors are the hackneyed stuff of most lovers' poetry. In short, it is a song that 'will serve the turn'" is rather naive. "Who is Sylvia" is a delicious touchstone lyric and is deliberately enigmatical. Who is Sylvia? What is she? She is really Julia to Proteus, when, his protean journey over and unmasked in the green woods' episode, he apparently recognizes his true love, his "wish for ever." She is Sylvia when in his sea-change into something not rich but certainly strange Proteus is foresworn to Valentine, Thurio, the Duke, and more importantly to himself, in the wooing of her. The very popularity of the song belies Seng's arbitrary dismissal of it.

To dismiss the two songs "When Isacles hang by the wall" and "When Dasies pied, and Violets blew" in *Love's Labour's Lost* as probably having no other than the plain function of representing a "simple return to reality" (p.25) in sharp contrast with the tone and language of the rest of the play is likewise much too naive. The two songs with their postscript warning about the cuckoo mocking married men and the staring owl singing the "merry note" of "greasy Joan's" desolation are an ironical comment on the possible outcome of marriages "made in heat of blood." It is strange that Seng is willing to allow a mere snatch by Falstaff to be related "to major and minor themes of the play as a whole" and let whole songs go by with nods of approval to those critics who have suggested that some of Shakespeare's songs, particularly the *Love's Labour's Lost* ones "are largely extraneous" (p.25). The same criticism must be levelled at his comment on the companion songs "Under the greenwood tree" and "Blow, blow, thou winter wind" in *As You Like It* that they "find value in the seasons' extremes" (p.76). Both songs ironically represent the wishful thinking of those who believe they are escaping from usurpation and tyranny but become themselves usurpers and tyrants in the natural world. The "Arcadian existence" is postlapsarian; they corrupt the natural world with their gold and lasciviousness and become victims of a green woods' complex. The two songs are very integral to major and minor themes of the play as a whole.

Wayne State University

The British Broadside Ballad and its Music by Claude M. Simpson. Rutgers University Press, 1966. Pp. xxxiii + 922 [with 540 music examples]. $17.50. *Reviewer: F. W. Sternfeld.*

The student of English life and letters in the later sixteenth century, in particular, the student of Shakespeare, meets constant references to all kinds of tunes and ditties. The exploration of this Elizabethan treasure and the identification of its contemporary verbal tags — "Greensleeves," "Bonny Robin," "Callino" — has been a task to which music historians and antiquarians have addressed themselves for many generations. In the eighteenth century we have Hawkins, Percy and Ritson; and the towering figure in the nineteenth century is, of course, William Chappell, whose *Popular Music of the Olden Time* (2 vols., 1855-59, reprinted 1965) is a remarkably accurate and comprehensive collection, supplemented furthermore by many other of his publications, such as the *Roxburghe Ballads* (edited jointly with Ebsworth in 8 vols., 1871-99). Needless to say, Chappell's *Popular Music* is dated in many ways: harmonizations in a nineteenth century style were added to the original tunes; the concordances are incomplete; a few of the references are misleading (in Cambridge the "University Library" is termed the "Public Library"); and in a few instances the verbal texts have been cleared up for the sake of decorum (though that last eventuality happens rarely). Still, so excellent was Chappell's work that the history of Elizabethan song in the century since then has been largely an attempt to revise Chappell, to refine his terms of reference, and to provide information which conforms to modern bibliographical methods. To begin with, two great American scholars addressed themselves to two separate categories, Child to the ballad based on the oral tradition, and Rollins to ballads based on printed broadsides. Recently Professor Bertrand Bronson of Berkeley has published a detailed investigation of the Child tunes, and now Professor Simpson of Stanford has addressed himself to the problem of the broadside tunes.

In order to keep this volume within manageable size and, perhaps also for the sake of intellectual neatness, Simpson differs from Chappell in several important respects. For one thing, many tunes have been dropped because they are not related to broadsides, as in the case of "O death rock me asleep," which is referred to in *Henry IV* and is included in Chappell (and in Wooldridge in his revision of Chappell). The same is true of the love song "Western wind," frequently encountered in discussions of John Taverner and Thomas Campion. Both of these tunes are "Old English" and "Popular," but they are not "Broadside." Consequently, the student of Elizabethan music will have to supplement Simpson by other and sometimes older works of reference.

Secondly, Simpson, unlike Chappell (or Wooldridge) does not offer harmonizations. Of course, the absence of a Victorian accompaniment is to be applauded. But in many instances there are extant Elizabethan harmonizations for such accompanying instruments as the lute, virginals, cittern, or all three. But, on page 80 Simpson offers "Callino Casturame" (referred to in *Henry V*) and on page 60 "Bonny Sweet Robin" (referred to in *Hamlet*), in monophonic versions, ignoring the accompaniments offered by Elizabethan lute and other commonplace books. Again, it could be argued that a ballad requires merely a tune for singing and that harmonizations should be dealt with in other books.

Thirdly, Simpson differs from Chappell in that he prints the tunes without texts, whereas Chappell "underlays" the words, i.e., prints certain syllables under certain notes. Of course, the texts are usually to be found in some other volume such as the *Handful of Pleasant Delights*, the *Pills to Purge Melancholy*, or the modern edition of the *Roxburghe Ballads*, the *Pepys Ballads*, etc. Moreover, the underlaying of the syllables is tricky and difficult, and many church hymnals print the texts on a lower portion of the page, not directly under the music. But Simpson leaves the text out altogether. On pages 119-122 there is a discussion of "Come live with me and be my love" without Marlowe's poem from the *Passionate Pilgrim* or the reply, usually attributed to Ralegh, or the garbled version in the *Merry Wives of Windsor*. Certainly, the average student of literature and of Shakespeare would require a musician's help to find a workable underlay of the syllables (and would certainly find it more convenient if he did not have to consult another book for the text that goes with the tune).

On the whole, then, Chappell's work, in comprehensiveness and usefulness, is far from being superseded. It would be churlish, however, not to acknowledge Simpson's cardinal merits. It is simply that today's accepted standards of accuracy and neatness demand that the work of the giants of the nineteenth century be divided into several volumes and that modern notions of team-work have supplanted books by single authors in all aspects of "old" English music from the "Sumer Canon" to Restoration songs. Simpson has obviously laboured for many years over this task, his concordances of musical sources are models of comprehensiveness and lucidity, and he has covered about twice as many broadside tunes as Chappell. His references to ballad collections, unknown to Chappell, and to the relevant scholarly literature, published in the century since Chappell, are ample. This is an indispensable, reliable, and accurate work of reference. I advise all students who have Chappell's work on their shelves to supplement it with the present volume. But I would also advise them to hang on to old, dated, Chappell; at least for the time being.

The University of Oxford

Holbein and Henry VIII by Roy Strong. Routledge & Kegan Paul; Pantheon Books, 1967. Pp. x + 75. pl. 55 + frontispiece. 40 s. *Reviewer: John M. Steadman.*

"White-hall utterly burnt to the ground, nothing but the walls & ruines left." In a few terse words John Evelyn pronounced the epitaph of one of the most sumptuous of Tudor and Stuart palaces, destroyed—almost completely—early in 1698. Among the more notable sacrifices to Vulcan was the Privy Chamber, with its "fresco" by Hans Holbein the Younger. Painted in oils and bearing the date 1537, it had glorified the Tudor dynasty in the persons of its first monarchs and their wives—Henry VII and Elizabeth of York, Henry VIII and Jane Seymour.

Mr. Strong's lucid and well-argued book attempts to "re-create" the lost masterpiece and thereby "reinterpret the last decade" of Holbein's life. Stressing the crucial importance of the Reformation for the final phase of the artist's career, he sees Holbein's art as "one facet of a whole complex of literary and artistic forms used to bolster up the Crown into its new omnipotent position as arbiter of Church as well as State." Re-examining Holbein's late work against the background of a "sustained campaign of propaganda on behalf of the new concepts of Monarchy"—a claim to imperial status consciously evoking the example of Constantine; an assertion of supreme jurisdiction in church and state; an archetype of the reigning monarch as the disseminator of Gospel truth and protector of true religion— he emphasizes the different political climates, and different conditions of patronage, that the painter encountered on his first and second visits to England.

On his first visit, in 1527, Holbein had been closely associated with the "pious humanist circle of Sir Thomas More and his friends." His return to England, on the other hand, "coincides with the years of revolution and opens with the complete collapse of the circle" from which he had formerly received patronage. From 1537 until his death in 1543 he held the position of King's Painter and appears to have been associated with the circle of royal propagandists headed by Thomas Cromwell. "Three main groups of his works executed either during or just after his painting of the great fresco" link him, in fact, with Reformation propaganda. His frontispiece to the English Bible (1536) creates an "image of the King as purveyor to his people of the Word of God," an iconographical motif that "can be traced down through representations of Edward VI and Elizabeth I on into the Stuart period." A group of anti-clerical woodcuts, depicting the scribes and pharisees in monastic habit, were probably designed "in connexion with the attack on the monastic orders which reached its height in 1536." His portrait of the infant Prince of Wales (painted, of course, later than the fresco) contains Latin verses composed by Sir Richard Morison, "a key figure linking Holbein directly into the circle of those who, under the guidance of Thomas Cromwell, were paid apologists for the official policy of the Crown."

The Privy Council fresco not only embodies a characteristic Tudor *topos*—the Union of the Roses—and the humanist conception of history as a "pageant of heroes." It also reflects —more specifically—the "political mood" of 1537. Henry had "emerged triumphant from the greatest single crisis of his reign: the Pilgrimage of Grace." The Queen's pregnancy offered hopes for an heir to perpetuate the Tudor dynasty. "The theme of the wall painting is one of victory and fruition," and there are grounds for inferring that Henry himself commissioned it.

In endeavoring to "re-create" Holbein's painting, Mr. Strong attempts to reconstruct not only its biographical and historical context but also its architectural context. This is a difficult undertaking, inasmuch as reliable evidence is scanty. "Whitehall as it was in 1537 is not easy to reconstruct," and "no detailed description or drawing of the interior of the Privy Chamber . . . is known to exist." Moreover, for the appearance of the fresco itself the scholar must necessarily rely primarily on two mid-seventeenth-century copies by Remigius van Leemput (which disagree in important details) and on the fragmentary Chatsworth Cartoon. (The latter contains the original drawing for the full-length portraits of the two kings, but does not contain the two queens and the middle portion of the painting.)

On the whole, the author meets this challenge admirably. Through a judicious use of sixteenth- and seventeenth-century records he gives us a coherent picture of the general

436

plan of Whitehall Palace, "the staggering opulence" of its state rooms, the "lingering medievalism" of its wall decorations, and "the nodal point that the Privy Chamber occupied in palace etiquette forming a bridge between the public and private aspects of the King's life." He argues convincingly that Holbein must have organized his composition around an actual window (instead of the "stone altar" depicted in Leemput's copies) and that it must, therefore, have been located in the upper level of the room, above the panelling. He suggests plausibly that the "niches, pilasters and frieze Holbein depicts" may be "a continuation of the reality in plaster around the remainder of the upper part of the room." He proposes an ingenious solution to a problem in composition—the apparent lack of a "focal point." The real focal point, he suggests, was located outside and below the fresco; it was the living King himself rather than the painted image. The most logical position for the "dais, chair and cloth of estate" was "beneath the great wall painting itself, the King transforming into actuality the world of paint above him."

Comparing the iconography of the four royal figures with other portraits of the same persons, Mr. Strong finds in their arrangement a "compositional form" reminiscent not only of Holbein's earlier portrait *The Ambassadors* but also of "the classic high renaissance formula for a Madonna and Child enthroned within a room flanked by saints." Henry's own pose embodies a favorite Renaissance "formula for the heroic" that can be traced back to Donatello, Pollaiuolo, and Perugino. "With this image of Henry VIII, the use of royal portraiture in England as propaganda in the modern sense of the word begins"; its "effect on the iconography of his heir . . . was decisive." In Holbein's decorative motifs, and indeed in his whole "concept of wall painting," the author detects the influence of Mantegna.

The Privy Chamber fresco had no successors; the growing passion for mannerism made it seem dated "almost as soon as it was finished." Within a decade "the early Tudor court had managed at whirlwind speed to run through the final phase of late medieval narrative painting, on through the quintessence of high renaissance illusionism, arriving finally at a riot of ebullient mannerism." Holbein's painting is, therefore, unique, as "the sole manifestation of high renaissance illusionistic wall painting in England as it was known in renaissance Italy."

Mr. Strong's study contains a brief appendix outlining the history of the Chatsworth Cartoon and a short index of names. His illustrations have been well chosen, and both support and clarify his argument. Typographical errors are few: "Polliainolo's" (p. 42) and "Eylot" (p. 33). The transcription (p. 57) of the Latin verses that appear on Leemput's copy in the Royal Collection appears to be faithful. It is interesting to note, however, that Leemput's own version contains several inaccuracies (VIDESSE in line 1 and INDIGNOSI in line 8) and that the punctuation frequently obscures the syntax of certain passages (e.g., the periods after PATERNE in line 3 and VICIT in line 4 and the comma between CERTAE and VIRTUTI in line 9). It is equally interesting to observe that the engraving by George Vertue not only corrects the Latin (substituting VIDISSE and INDIGNOS) but omits all punctuation except the final period at the end of each distich. In view of Leemput's apparent carelessness (or faulty Latinity) in the previous verses, it seems not unlikely that the split couplet (in lines 9 and 10), which breaks the distich pattern, may be an error resulting from faulty punctuation. (Leemput inserts a comma after CESSIT in line 9 and omits a period after MANU in line 10; Vertue's emendation, which seems more convincing, omits the comma but inserts a period after MANU, thereby preserving the distich pattern.)

The translation of this passage is correct, though the final phrase IN HONORE SVO may be read "in *his* due honor" as well as "in *their* due honor." If we accept Vertue's emendation of Leemput's punctuation, the final distichs would read as follows: "When Henry VIII in his hand wielded the sceptre, the presumption of popes yielded to outstanding virtue. (True) religion was restored during his reign, and the precepts of God began. . . ."

On page 62, the author observes that "The cartouches supported by mermen and mermaid [sic] that appear over the heads of Henry and his Queen in the Cartoon bear their initials, H and J intertwined by true lovers knots, but according to the Leemput copy the cartouches finally carried the date: ANNO 1537." This statement may mislead an unwary reader. The initials *do* appear over Henry's head not only in the Cartoon, but also in Vertue's copy of Leemput's painting in the Royal Collection. Since we possess only half (or less than half) of the Cartoon, we have no way of ascertaining whether or not the cartouche above the queen also contained the intertwined monograms. In the Vertue engraving this cartouche bears the date "1537." We have no reason to assume that in the original painting (or in the original Cartoon) it bore an interlaced monogram instead of a date.

Finally, we should consider the possibility that the fresco may conceivably have been commissioned *after*, rather than before, the birth of a male heir to the throne and the death of his mother. Though the author apparently assumes that the queen herself was "one . . . of the sitters" (p. 62), we cannot take this for granted. As he himself observes, "All the portraits are initially based on ones already in existence. . . ." Though in Henry's case there seems to have been a "new sitting" (p. 37), there is no evidence, apparently, for a new sitting on the part of the queen. Though it is possible to interpret Holbein's glorification of the Tudor dynasty as an expression of the sense of "victory and fruition" felt after the collapse of the Pilgrimage of Grace and the news of the queen's pregnancy (pp. 62-4), there are equally valid grounds for reading it as the celebration of a royal birth and the memorial of a royal death—interlinked events that made the painted encomium of the dynasty more than a magnificent boast. Perhaps, in the mind of the artist and his patron, the real "focal point" of the picture was not the present king, the father, but his son, the future king. Perhaps the living figure beneath the fresco, for whom the whole genealogical tableau had been intended and who alone could complete its genealogical as well as its pictorial design, was not Henry VIII but the future Edward VI. Enthroned on his dais, under the cloth of estate, Henry's heir as the reigning Tudor monarch and living representative of his dynasty, would complete the family group, the pictorial representation of his royal lineage.

One would not be altogether unjustified, therefore, in regarding this picture as a king's more-than-royal birthday-gift to his new-born heir and ultimate successor. Or indeed as a posthumous coronation-present—for the composition would not be strictly complete until the young king himself ascended the dais under the fresco.

It is tempting to see in Holbein's painting a representation of the prince's line of descent, arranged tier below tier, generation below generation, from Henry VII and Elizabeth of York through Henry VIII and Jane Seymour to Edward himself—grandparents, parents, and grandson. If the composition demanded the presence of a monarch to complete its formal pictorial design, it required—specifically—the presence of Edward VI to complete its genealogical pattern. Possibly Remigius van Leemput thought so too. His copy of the painting (at Petworth House) portrays Edward on the level below his parents and two steps below his grandparents. (See Plate 26.) His composition (perhaps intentionally) arranges the five figures on levels corresponding to three generations.

This scholarly yet sensitive exploration of a highly significant aspect of the "Tudor myth" and its relation to iconographical tradition will be valuable to students of Renaissance history and literature as well as to specialists in art history.

The Henry E. Huntington Library

Allegorical Imagery: Some Mediaeval Books and Their Posterity by Rosemond Tuve. Princeton University Press, 1966. Pp. x + 461. $12.50. *Reviewer: Chauncey Wood.*

Professor Tuve's last work, published posthumously, is a fitting capstone to a distinguished scholarly career, and is an extremely valuable contribution to current discussions of the nature and function of mediaeval and Renaissance allegory. As Spenser said in "Ruines of Rome":

> But her brave writings, which her famous merite,
> In spight of Time, out of the dust doth reare,
> Doo make her idole through the world appeare.

While the present book is primarily oriented toward Spenser, the poet whose works Miss Tuve says she would most like to illuminate the reading of, there is also much here that is important for the study of other Renaissance poets, dramatic as well as non-dramatic. The materials on which the book is based were chosen primarily for their availability to Renaissance readers, and not merely to readers with *recherché* literary interests. Miss Tuve is concerned with the broadest, most basic problems of allegory, and addresses herself to determining both what sixteenth century writers *meant* by allegorical reading and what they *enjoyed* in it. Moreover, while some of the materials under discussion are so late as to be without significance for the student of English mediaeval literature, others are not. Miss Tuve's discussion of the system of the virtues employed by Chaucer's Parson, her study of Guillaume de Deguileville's *Pèlerinage,* and her brilliant analysis of the *Roman de la rose* constitute a contribution to mediaeval studies of considerable importance, as does her general discussion of literary allegory.

Perhaps Miss Tuve's most significant departure from the bulk of recent writings on mediaeval and Renaissance literary allegory is her concentration on mediaeval allegories themselves rather than on mediaeval, Renaissance, or modern theories about what an allegory is or is not. Setting aside all *post hoc* definitions of allegory—definitions that have unfortunately obscured some contemporary discussions of the subject—Miss Tuve also downgrades early theories about allegories in favor of an inductive approach *via* the allegories themselves. Her goal is, then, "to discover, instead of impose, a definition of allegory" (p. 3). The advantages of this approach are obvious, for even poets themselves sometimes expound theories that are not easy to reconcile with their practice. Whether we concern ourselves with Wordsworth's "language really used by men," or Dante's distinction between the allegory of poets and the allegory of theologians, whenever we attempt to relate poetic theory to poetic practice one can be sure that the effort will be attended by controversy. The possible disadvantage of the inductive method is a certain excessive rigorousness about what is and is not to be subsumed under a rubric so scientifically derived from data "discovered not devised," but Miss Tuve happily steers around this pitfall, and firmly states that "these are not rules for allegories—with cards to be presented at entrance, texts otherwise not admitted" (p. 27).

In the course of Miss Tuve's analyses of the allegories themselves she manages to remark upon many currently popular conceptions about allegory that in one way or another do not harmonize with actual practice. With reference to personification she notes that in the visual arts accompanying allegories the personifications indicate the presence of allegorical meaning, but do not themselves provide the meaning (p. 25), and she also observes very shrewdly that some personifications are more subtle than others (p. 177, n. 17). The often heard notion that allegorizations of the classics were made in order to overcome their "naughtiness" is laid to rest (p. 304), with the further observation that some kinds of allegory can actually offend piety (p. 236). The contemporary concern to judge the merit of allegories by their degree of relationship to modern psychological fiction is also noted by Miss Tuve, who does not argue about the assignations, but observes that the accolades awarded are bestowed on a *genre* that "has little use for such a strength" (p. 252). By far her most important contribution to our understanding of how to pursue the study of allegories is her insistence that "equation is simply not the character of the allegorical relation" (p. 404). Not seeing this, critics commonly assume that if a literary work has an episode symbolic of an event in the life of Christ, the literary work should then proceed to an episode symbolic of a sequential event in the life of Christ, a notion which makes the completely mistaken assumption that a poet's goal is to re-tell an Evangelist's story (p. 405, n. 43). Such are the ultimate perils of equation. As Miss Tuve nicely puts it, when literary characters do not equate with their meanings, "their stories need not echo each other, but merely meet where meanings touch" (p. 404).

Miss Tuve's specific treatment of allegory begins with a chapter on "Problems and Definitions," which is given over to a discussion of certain mediaeval allegories that were well-known in the Renaissance, such as the *Dialogues of Creatures Moralised* and Christine de Pisan's *Épitre d'Othéa,* and Miss Tuve observes that when the former was taken up by a very ordinary Renaissance figure like Lodge the typically mediaeval moralizations of the stories are of primary interest to him. Miss Tuve's insight is a useful counterbalance to the customary modern downgrading of moralization, typified by Seznec's remark that Petrarch leaves out the moralizations in adapting his source materials because he is a "humanist and man of taste."[1] Chapter II, "Allegory of Virtues and Vices," contains an important discussion of Spenser's idea of virtue as devised by Aristotle "and the rest," in which Miss Tuve notes that "the rest" are doubtless common Christian writings such as the *Somme le roi.* The exposition found in these writings of seven spiritual or evangelical virtues that are different alike from the Aristotelian virtues and the well-known Christian system of four moral and three theological virtues provides Miss Tuve with a firm basis for a reconsideration of the poetic function of these virtues. Chapter III, "Guillaume's Pilgrimage," returns to the method of the first chapter and analyzes how a seventeenth century redactor of Guillaume's *Pélerinage* abridged the work markedly, but did not cut or water-down its allegory, and tempered "no winds of outrageous imagery to seventeenth-century lambs" (p. 195). Chapter IV on "Imposed Allegory" discusses both allegories "imposed" on classical materials in the Middle Ages, with specific attention to Christine's *Othéa* and the various moralized Ovids, and allegories imposed in the early Renaissance on an already allegorical work, the *Roman de la rose.* Here, in a valuable piece of criticism, Miss Tuve shows us first how the allegories of Marot and Molinet that were imposed on the *Roman de la rose,* however interesting in themselves, run counter to the allegory already present in the *Roman,* and having declared this she demonstrates it with a very praiseworthy explication of the work. Finally, in Chapter V, "Romance," Miss Tuve shows how the romances, with their digressions and *entrelacement* supplied Spenser with the form of the *Faerie Queene* to the neglect of Aristotle's concern for unity of action. Throughout the work Miss Tuve elaborates various elements of her discussion with analyses of the illustrations of literary allegories found in both manuscripts and printed books, and the analyses are invariably enlightening. There are 110 pictures in the book, so in scope as well as quality we have here an important adjunct to current concerns over the relationship between iconography and literature.

No survey of such a multifaceted work can do justice either to its scope and complexity or to the problems it naturally raises. On the whole, however, one might venture the judgment that the book's major strength is in its *readings*—whether of Spenser, of the *Roman de la rose,* or, if we extend the term to iconographical analysis, of the many pictures in the mediaeval allegories examined. On the other hand, the *theorizing* is sometimes less well handled, and even when we are convinced of the correctness of the author's position her circuitous exposition of argument often makes subsidiary problems arise even as the basic issue is being resolved. Moreover, while Miss Tuve's avoidance of any lengthy recapitulation of various recent critical positions in regard to mediaeval and Renaissance allegory gives her freedom to concentrate on the texts themselves, nevertheless she might have profited from introducing in more detail some of the work already done on the vexing problem of the literal level. Miss Tuve's examination of primary sources permits her to educe the fact that a distinction was observed in practice, albeit tacitly, between "moral allegory," concerned with how we should act, and "strict" allegory, which has to do with our beliefs (p. 15), but her neat handling of *quid agas* and *quid credas* does not prevent her from encountering some difficulty with *littera.* For example, Miss Tuve strikes out at those who would characterize allegory by its "*substitution* of allegorical for literal senses, its disregard of historical, literal, or fictional reasonableness, or its schematized and devitalized paralleling of abstraction with concretion" (p. 48, n. 22). There is no quarrel with the objection to *substituting* allegorical for literal senses, but there is a problem here with "literal reasonableness," for as Miss Tuve herself elsewhere notes, most allegories are "superlatively fantastic" although "unselfconsciously so," yet are "presented with some care as to be credited" (p. 222, n. 1).

If Miss Tuve is to maintain simultaneously that allegory does not disregard literal reasonableness and yet can be fantastic, it is clear that we are in need for more definition of the problem than she subsequently provides us with. A very similar difficulty has occurred with regard to the understanding of the literal level in Dante, which Professor Singleton has maintained is a fiction, though taken as real in the act of reading.[2] Indeed, in a larger context the exact nature and importance of the literal level in mediaeval and Renaissance allegories has been one of the major bones of contention among the disputants. Because of this it is regrettable that Miss Tuve did not avail herself of the distinctions of Boccaccio, first pointed out by Professor Robertson.[3] Boccaccio distinguishes three kinds of poetic fables, each of which has a scriptural analogy. First there are fables that lack all appearance of truth, like beast fables, and this type appears in Judges. Second, there are those that mingle truth and fiction on the surface, like much of the Old Testament, and finally there are fables that are more like history than fiction, because they concern things that might well have happened, and this type is like the parables of Christ.

A difficulty of a somewhat different kind arises with Miss Tuve's objections to a certain kind of imposed allegory—specifically the imposition of Christian doctrinal interpretations (as opposed to merely moral interpretations) on classical figures and stories. Miss Tuve claims that this habit "produced page upon page of bad allegory" (p. 227), and yet we must admit that the fact that this kind of thing may be uncongenial to some or all of us today does not make it intrinsically "bad." Indeed, Miss Tuve herself elsewhere adopts a much more realistic view of the situation, as when she grudgingly admits that although Molinet's allegory is imposed on rather than educed from the *Roman de la rose,* "we have no right to hold this against him" (p. 245). The same sort of objection may be offered to Miss Tuve's repeated injunction that the success or failure of any kind of imposed allegory depended upon the "truth of the underlying similarity of import" (p. 295).

Now, this may be true enough for the success of these effects by our own standards of literary taste and discrimination, but their very existence argues that some people thought highly enough of them at the time to write them. Doubtless they were read and admired by some people, and we should not really condemn their taste any more than we should denigrate flamboyant Gothic for being "decadent." Miss Tuve grants that there may have existed "a little pocket of taste, a smallish public" (p. 313), that was interested in certain kinds of imposed allegories, and yet she does not let the matter go at that, but notes that the group in question was lax in poetic taste. She goes so far as to allow that we should grant some of these writers "hospitality" if they are indeed "serious" (p. 311), but it may be noted that they are in fact the hosts and we are the guests. Furthermore, this concern for the "truth of the underlying similarity of import" neglects the fact that the Biblical exegetes, on whose practice the secular allegorizers modelled their own work, were in the habit of ignoring this underlying similarity of import. Whether we consider St. Augustine interpreting the teeth of the beloved in *Canticles* as teeth of the church cutting men off from error, or whether we consider Pierre Bersuire's ingenious interpretations of the world about him *in bono* and *in malo*, we must grant that there was ample precedent for this facet of the work of the imposing allegorizers.

Whatever minor objections may be raised with regard to Miss Tuve's theorizing about allegory, her ability to read mediaeval and Renaissance allegories is so great that from her readings of specific passages we deduce valuable postures for the general interpretation of other allegories. For example, while interpreting a woodcut showing a mariner leaping into the sea in the general direction of a buxom mermaid, Miss Tuve notes that we do not need to be told that we should mistrust the mermaid or that the unfortunate sailor will be destroyed. By the same token, there can be unstated significance in verbal images too, and this is one of the major objections to current clichés about depending only on what is "in" a poem (pp. 19-20). Similarly, when discussing Book I of the *Faerie Queene* Miss Tuve asks why the first enemy of the Pride of Red Crosse is Error rather than Arrogance, his first victim Sans*foy* rather than Sans-humbleness, and why the basic strife in this book is between Truth and Duessa rather than Humility and Vainglory. Turning to the iconographic representation of Pride in the *Somme le roi* she notes that its representative is Ahaziah of IV Kings, who was not vainglorious, but in *error* sought out false gods to inquire about the future, since he lacked *faith* (p. 120). Thus at a stroke the problems posed are sorted out. As a final instance of her perception we may glance at some of her analyses of the method used to convey meaning in the *Roman de la rose.* At one point she observes that the author typically envelops his point "in some bland contradiction that no one on the scene recognizes as an outrage, though we are expected to" (p. 241). The Lover, she remarks, "is shown as falling for one after another insufficient or damaging definition of the Rose" (p. 242), and of Jean de Meun's encyclopedic details, which have often been seen as intrusive, she argues that they are rather "just such details . . . as will nail the speaker to a monstrous inadequacy" (p. 259).

On balance, then, this book's abundant insights far outweigh its occasional lack of clarity and its numerous stylistic peculiarities. In spite of the fact that the author did not live to see the book through the press, there are fewer typographical errors than one might expect. There are, however, a rather high number of inconsistencies of reference—e.g. we encounter Guillaume de St. Amour on pp. 248-249, and Guillaume d'Amour on p. 256. A few authors' names have become altered during the course of composition, too. Professor "Lain" in the last line of note 39, p. 294 should be Lavin, and "D. N. Fowler" of note 39, p. 395 should be D. C. Fowler. On p. 261, 1.3 and 1.10, La Vieille is wrongly spelled "Veille."

McMaster University

Notes:

(1) Jean Seznec, *The Survival of the Pagan Gods,* tr. Barbara F. Sessions, Bollingen Series, 38 (New York, 1953), p. 174.

(2) Charles S. Singleton, "The Irreducible Dove," *CL,* IX (1957), 129-135. This article is a rejoinder to an article by Professor Green, which in turn is partly concerned with rebutting Professor Singleton's position as stated in his book. See further, therefore, Richard Hamilton Green, "Dante's 'Allegory of Poets' and the Mediaeval Theory of Poetic Fiction," *CL,* IX (1957), 118-128, and Charles S. Singleton, *Dante Studies I* (Cambridge, Mass., 1954). Another useful contribution to this subject is Phillip Damon, "The Two Modes of Allegory in Dante's *Convivio,*" *PQ,* XL (1961), 144-149.

(3) D. W. Robertson, Jr., *A Preface to Chaucer* (Princeton 1962), p. 352. *Cf.* also the distinctions of Radulphus de Longo Campo (p. 346) and mediaeval ideas about the literal level in Boethius' *Consolation* (p. 359). Professor Robertson addresses himself to the problems raised by Dante's distinctions on pp. 348-349.